PLUNKETT'S SOLAR POWER, WIND POWER & RENEWABLE ENERGY INDUSTRY ALMANAC 2023

The only comprehensive guide to the alternative energy industry

Jack W. Plunkett

Published by:
Plunkett Research®, Ltd., Houston, Texas
www.plunkettresearch.com

PLUNKETT'S SOLAR POWER, WIND POWER & RENEWABLE ENERGY INDUSTRY ALMANAC 2023

Editor and Publisher:
Jack W. Plunkett

Executive Editor and Database Manager:
Martha Burgher Plunkett

Senior Editor and Researchers:
Isaac Snider

Editors, Researchers and Assistants:
Charles Bui
Bryant Huynh
Annie Paynter
Gina Sprenkel

Information Technology Manager:
Rebeca Tijiboy

Special Thanks to:
American Wind Energy Association
BP plc, *BP Statistical Reviews*
Global Wind Energy Council
International Energy Agency
International Geothermal Association
U.S. Department of Energy, and the editors and analysts at the *Energy Information Administration* and the *Alternative Fuels Data Center*
U.S. National Science Foundation

Plunkett Research®, Ltd.
P. O. Drawer 541737, Houston, Texas 77254 USA
Phone: 713.932.0000   Fax: 713.932.7080
www.plunkettresearch.com

Copyright © 2022, Plunkett Research®, Ltd. All rights reserved. Except as provided for below, you may not copy, resell, reproduce, distribute, republish, download, display, post, or transmit any portion of this book in any form or by any means, including, but not limited to, electronic, mechanical, photocopying, recording, or otherwise, without the express prior written permission of Plunkett Research, Ltd. Additional copyrights are held by other content providers, including, in certain cases, Morningstar, Inc. The information contained herein is proprietary to its owners and it is not warranted to be accurate, complete or timely. Neither Plunkett Research, Ltd. nor its content providers are responsible for any damages or losses arising from any use of this information. Market and industry statistics, company revenues, profits and other details may be estimates. Financial information, company plans or status, and other data can change quickly and may vary from those stated here. **Past performance is no guarantee of future results**.

Plunkett Research®, Ltd.
P. O. Drawer 541737
Houston, Texas 77254-1737
Phone: 713.932.0000, Fax: 713.932.7080 www.plunkettresearch.com

ISBN13 # 978-1-62831-665-0 (eBook Edition # 978-1-62831-990-3)

Limited Warranty and Terms of Use:

Users' publications in static electronic format containing any portion of the content of this book (and/or the content of any related Plunkett Research, Ltd. online service to which you are granted access, hereinafter collectively referred to as the "Data") or Derived Data (that is, a set of data that is a derivation made by a User from the Data, resulting from the applications of formulas, analytics or any other method) may be resold by the User only for the purpose of providing third-party analysis within an established research platform under the following conditions: (However, Users may not extract or integrate any portion of the Data or Derived Data for any other purpose.)

a) Users may utilize the Data only as described herein. b) User may not export more than an insubstantial portion of the Data or Derived Data, c) Any Data exported by the User may only be distributed if the following conditions are met:

   i) Data must be incorporated in added-value reports or presentations, either of which are part of the regular services offered by the User and not as stand-alone products.
   ii) Data may not be used as part of a general mailing or included in external websites or other mass communication vehicles or formats, including, but not limited to, advertisements.
   iii) Except as provided herein, Data may not be resold by User.

"Insubstantial Portions" shall mean an amount of the Data that (1) has no independent commercial value, (2) could not be used by User, its clients, Authorized Users and/or its agents as a substitute for the Data or any part of it, (3) is not separately marketed by the User, an affiliate of the User or any third-party source (either alone or with other data), and (4) is not retrieved by User, its clients, Authorized Users and/or its Agents via regularly scheduled, systematic batch jobs.

LIMITED WARRANTY; DISCLAIMER OF LIABILITY: **While Plunkett Research, Ltd. ("PRL") has made an effort to obtain the Data from sources deemed reliable, PRL makes no warranties, expressed or implied, regarding the Data contained herein. This book and its Data are provided to the End-User "AS IS" without warranty of any kind. No oral or written information or advice given by PRL, its employees, distributors or representatives will create a warranty or in any way increase the scope of this Limited Warranty, and the Customer or End-User may not rely on any such information or advice.** Customer Remedies: PRL's entire liability and your exclusive remedy shall be, at PRL's sole discretion, either (a) return of the price paid, if any, or (b) repair or replacement of a book that does not meet PRL's Limited Warranty and that is returned to PRL with sufficient evidence of or receipt for your original purchase.

NO OTHER WARRANTIES: TO THE MAXIMUM EXTENT PERMITTED BY APPLICABLE LAW, PRL AND ITS DISTRIBUTORS DISCLAIM ALL OTHER WARRANTIES AND CONDITIONS, EITHER EXPRESSED OR IMPLIED, INCLUDING, BUT NOT LIMITED TO, IMPLIED WARRANTIES OR CONDITIONS OF MERCHANTABILITY, FITNESS FOR A PARTICULAR PURPOSE, TITLE AND NON-INFRINGEMENT WITH REGARD TO THE BOOK AND ITS DATA, AND THE PROVISION OF OR FAILURE TO PROVIDE SUPPORT SERVICES. LIMITATION OF LIABILITY: TO THE MAXIMUM EXTENT PERMITTED BY APPLICABLE LAW, IN NO EVENT SHALL PRL BE LIABLE FOR ANY SPECIAL, INCIDENTAL OR CONSEQUENTIAL DAMAGES WHATSOEVER (INCLUDING, WITHOUT LIMITATION, DAMAGES FOR LOSS OF BUSINESS PROFITS, BUSINESS INTERRUPTION, ABILITY TO OBTAIN OR RETAIN EMPLOYMENT OR REMUNERATION, ABILITY TO PROFITABLY MAKE AN INVESTMENT, OR ANY OTHER PECUNIARY LOSS) ARISING OUT OF THE USE OF, OR RELIANCE UPON, THE BOOK OR DATA, OR THE INABILITY TO USE THIS DATA OR THE FAILURE OF PRL TO PROVIDE SUPPORT SERVICES, EVEN IF PRL HAS BEEN ADVISED OF THE POSSIBILITY OF SUCH DAMAGES. IN ANY CASE, PRL'S ENTIRE LIABILITY SHALL BE LIMITED TO THE AMOUNT ACTUALLY PAID BY YOU FOR THE BOOK.

PLUNKETT'S SOLAR POWER, WIND POWER & RENEWABLE ENERGY INDUSTRY ALMANAC 2023

CONTENTS

Introduction	1
How to Use This Book	3
Chapter 1: Major Trends Affecting the Solar Power, Wind Power & Renewable Energy Industry	7
1) Introduction	7
2) Solar Installations Soar While Solar Panel Costs Plummet	10
3) Photovoltaic Technologies, Thin Film Solar and Solar Panel Efficiency	12
4) Utility Scale Solar Plants	12
5) Wind Power	14
6) Hydroelectric Power	17
7) Geothermal Power	17
8) Biomass, Waste-to-Energy, Waste Methane and Biofuels from Algae	19
9) Ethanol Production Soared, But U.S. Federal Subsidy Expires	20
10) Cellulosic Ethanol Makes Slow Commercial Progress	21
11) Tidal Power	22
12) Fuel Cell and Hydrogen Power Research Continue/Fuel Cell Cars Enter Market	23
13) Electric Cars and Plug-in Hybrids (PHEVs) to See Massive New Investments by Auto Makers	25
14) Major Research and Advancements in Lithium Batteries/Tesla and Panasonic Operate the Gigafactory	27
15) Natural Gas-Powered Vehicles Gain in Popularity/Long Term Potential Is Bright Thanks to Low Shale Gas Prices	29
16) Homes and Commercial Buildings Seek Green Certification	29
17) Smart Electric Grid Technologies Are Adopted	32
18) The Energy Industry Invests in Storage Battery Technologies with an Eye on Distributed Power and Renewables	33
19) Nuclear Energy Moves Ahead in India, China and the Middle East	35
20) Nuclear Fusion Technologies Might Create Unlimited, Emission-Free Power	39
21) New Display Technologies with PLEDs	40
22) Electric Utilities Adopt Coal Emissions Scrubbers While the Industry Tests Carbon Capture and Clean Coal Technologies	41
23) Superconductivity Provides Advanced Electricity Distribution Technology	42
24) Lower Energy Intensity Is a Prime Focus in China/U.S. Achieves Dramatic Energy Intensity Reductions	43
Chapter 2: Solar Power, Wind Power & Renewable Energy Industry Statistics	45
Global Alternative Energy Industry Statistics and Market Size Overview	46
U.S. Alternative Energy Industry Statistics and Market Size Overview	47
Approximate Energy Unit Conversion Factors	48

Continued on next page

Continued from previous page

Biomass Energy Resource Hierarchy	49
Comparison of Alternative Fuels with Gasoline & Diesel	50
World Total Primary Energy Consumption by Region: 2017-2050	52
Share of Electricity Generation by Energy Source, U.S.: Projections, 2021-2050	53
Energy Consumption by Source & Sector, U.S.: 2021	54
Primary Energy Flow by Source & Sector, U.S.: 2021	55
Net Electrical Power Generation by Fuel Type, U.S.: 2021	56
Net Electrical Power Generation by Fuel Type, U.S.: 1990-July 2022	57
Energy Production by Renewable Energy, U.S.: Selected Years, 1955-2021	58
U.S. Renewable Energy Consumption by Energy Source, 2015 vs. 2021	59
Fuel Ethanol Production & Consumption, U.S.: 1981- July 2022	60
Biodiesel Production & Consumption, U.S.: 2001- July 2022	61
Top 10 Countries by Installed Wind Generating Capacity: 2021	62
Top 15 U.S. States by Installed Wind Generating Capacity: 2nd Quarter 2022	63
U.S. Department of Energy Funding for Science & Energy Programs: 2021-2023	64
Federal R&D & R&D Plant Funding for Energy, U.S.: Fiscal Years 2020-2022	65

Chapter 3: Important Solar Power, Wind Power & Renewable Energy Industry Contacts 67
(Addresses, Phone Numbers and Internet Sites)

Chapter 4: THE RENEWABLE ENERGY 250:

Who They Are and How They Were Chosen	**103**
Index of Companies Within Industry Groups	104
Alphabetical Index	112
Index of Headquarters Location by U.S. State	114
Index of Non-U.S. Headquarters Location by Country	116
Individual Data Profiles on Each of THE RENEWABLE ENERGY 250	119

Additional Indexes

Index of Hot Spots for Advancement for Women/Minorities	372
Index by Subsidiaries, Brand Names and Selected Affiliations	373

A Short Solar Power, Wind Power & Renewable Energy Industry Glossary   **381**

INTRODUCTION

PLUNKETT'S SOLAR POWER, WIND POWER & RENEWABLE ENERGY INDUSTRY ALMANAC is designed to be used as a general source for researchers of all types.

The data and areas of interest covered are intentionally broad, from the various types of businesses involved in alternative energy, to advances in renewable forms of power, to an in-depth look at the major for-profit firms (which we call "THE RENEWABLE ENERGY 250") within the many industry sectors that make up the renewable energy arena.

This reference book is designed to to assist with market research, strategic planning, employment searches, contact or prospect list creation and financial research, and as a data resource for executives and students of all types.

PLUNKETT'S SOLAR POWER, WIND POWER & RENEWABLE ENERGY INDUSTRY ALMANAC takes a rounded approach for the general reader. This book presents a complete overview of the entire renewable energy industry (see "How To Use This Book"). For example, advances in solar energy technologies are discussed, as well as those in wind, hydroelectric, biomass, ethanol and geothermal.

THE RENEWABLE ENERGY 250 is our unique grouping of the biggest, most successful corporations in all segments of the alternative energy industry. Tens of thousands of pieces of information, gathered from a wide variety of sources, have been researched and are presented in a unique form that can be easily understood. This section includes thorough indexes to THE RENEWABLE ENERGY 250, by geography, industry, sales, brand names, subsidiary names and many other topics. (See Chapter 4.)

Especially helpful is the way in which PLUNKETT'S SOLAR POWER, WIND POWER & RENEWABLE ENERGY INDUSTRY ALMANAC enables readers who have no business background to readily compare the financial records and growth plans of alternative energy companies and major industry groups. You'll see the mid-term financial record of each firm, along with the impact of earnings, sales and strategic plans on each company's potential to fuel growth, to serve new markets and to provide investment and employment opportunities.

No other source provides this book's easy-to-understand comparisons of growth, expenditures, technologies, corporations and many other items of great importance to people of all types who may be studying this, one of the fastest growing industries in the world today.

By scanning the data groups and the unique indexes, you can find the best information to fit your personal research needs. The major companies in the alternative and renewable energy are profiled and then ranked using several different groups of specific criteria. Which firms are the biggest employers? Which companies earn the most profits? These things and much more are easy to find.

In addition to individual company profiles, an overview of renewable energy markets and trends is provided. This book's job is to help you sort through easy-to-understand summaries of today's trends in a quick and effective manner.

Whatever your purpose for researching the alternative energy field, you'll find this book to be a valuable guide. Nonetheless, as is true with all resources, this volume has limitations that the reader should be aware of:

- Financial data and other corporate information can change quickly. A book of this type can be no more current than the data that was available as of the time of editing. Consequently, the financial picture, management and ownership of the firm(s) you are studying may have changed since the date of this book. For example, this almanac includes the most up-to-date sales figures and profits available to the editors as of late-2022. That means that we have typically used corporate financial data as of the end of 2021.

- Corporate mergers, acquisitions and downsizing are occurring at a very rapid rate. Such events may have created significant change, subsequent to the publishing of this book, within a company you are studying.

- Some of the companies in THE RENEWABLE ENERGY 250 are so large in scope and in variety of business endeavors conducted within a parent organization, that we have been unable to completely list all subsidiaries, affiliations, divisions and activities within a firm's corporate structure.

- This volume is intended to be a general guide to a vast industry. That means that researchers should look to this book for an overview and, when conducting in-depth research, should contact the specific corporations or industry associations in question for the very latest changes and data. Where possible, we have listed contact names, toll-free telephone numbers and internet site addresses for the companies, government agencies and industry associations involved so that the reader may get further details without unnecessary delay.

- Tables of industry data and statistics used in this book include the latest numbers available at the time of printing, generally through the end of 2021. In a few cases, the only complete data available was for earlier years.

- We have used exhaustive efforts to locate and fairly present accurate and complete data. However, when using this book or any other source for business and industry information, the reader should use caution and diligence by conducting further research where it seems appropriate. We wish you success in your endeavors, and we trust that your experience with this book will be both satisfactory and productive.

Jack W. Plunkett
Houston, Texas
December 2022

HOW TO USE THIS BOOK

The two primary sections of this book are devoted first to the energy industry as a whole and then to the "Individual Data Listings" for THE RENEWABLE ENERGY 250. If time permits, you should begin your research in the front chapters of this book. Also, you will find lengthy indexes in Chapter 4 and in the back of the book.

THE SOLAR POWER, WIND POWER & ALTERNATIVE ENERGY INDUSTRY

Chapter 1: Major Trends Affecting the Solar Power, Wind Power & Renewable Energy Industry.
This chapter presents an encapsulated view of the major trends that are creating rapid changes in the alternative energy industry today.

Chapter 2: Solar Power, Wind Power & Renewable Energy Industry Statistics.
This chapter presents in-depth statistics on consumption, output and more.

Chapter 3: Important Solar Power, Wind Power & Renewable Energy Industry Contacts – Addresses, Telephone Numbers and Internet Sites.
This chapter covers contacts for important government agencies, alternative energy organizations and trade groups. Included are numerous important Internet sites.

THE RENEWABLE ENERGY 250

Chapter 4: THE RENEWABLE ENERGY 250: Who They Are and How They Were Chosen.
The companies compared in this book were carefully selected from the alternative energy industry, largely in the United States. Many of the firms are based outside the U.S. For a complete description, see THE RENEWABLE ENERGY 250 indexes in this chapter.

Individual Data Listings:
Look at one of the companies in THE RENEWABLE ENERGY 250'S Individual Data Listings. You'll find the following information fields:

Company Name:
The company profiles are in alphabetical order by company name. If you don't find the company you are seeking, it may be a subsidiary or division of one of the firms covered in this book. Try looking it up in the Index by Subsidiaries, Brand Names and Selected Affiliations in the back of the book.

Industry Code:
Industry Group Code: An NAIC code used to group companies within like segments.

Types of Business:
A listing of the primary types of business specialties conducted by the firm.

Brands/Divisions/Affiliations:
Major brand names, operating divisions or subsidiaries of the firm, as well as major corporate affiliations—such as another firm that owns a significant portion of the company's stock. A complete Index by Subsidiaries, Brand Names and Selected Affiliations is in the back of the book.

Contacts:
The names and titles up to 27 top officers of the company are listed, including human resources contacts.

Growth Plans/ Special Features:
Listed here are observations regarding the firm's strategy, hiring plans, plans for growth and product development, along with general information regarding a company's business and prospects.

Financial Data:
Revenue (2021 or the latest fiscal year available to the editors, plus up to five previous years): This figure represents consolidated worldwide sales from all operations. These numbers may be estimates.

R&D Expense (2021 or the latest fiscal year available to the editors, plus up to five previous years): This figure represents expenses associated with the research and development of a company's goods or services. These numbers may be estimates.

Operating Income (2021 or the latest fiscal year available to the editors, plus up to five previous years): This figure represents the amount of profit realized from annual operations after deducting operating expenses including costs of goods sold, wages and depreciation. These numbers may be estimates.

Operating Margin % (2021 or the latest fiscal year available to the editors, plus up to five previous years): This figure is a ratio derived by dividing operating income by net revenues. It is a measurement of a firm's pricing strategy and operating efficiency. These numbers may be estimates.

SGA Expense (2021 or the latest fiscal year available to the editors, plus up to five previous years): This figure represents the sum of selling, general and administrative expenses of a company, including costs such as warranty, advertising, interest, personnel, utilities, office space rent, etc. These numbers may be estimates.

Net Income (2021 or the latest fiscal year available to the editors, plus up to five previous years): This figure represents consolidated, after-tax net profit from all operations. These numbers may be estimates.

Operating Cash Flow (2021 or the latest fiscal year available to the editors, plus up to five previous years): This figure is a measure of the amount of cash generated by a firm's normal business operations. It is calculated as net income before depreciation and after income taxes, adjusted for working capital. It is a prime indicator of a company's ability to generate enough cash to pay its bills. These numbers may be estimates.

Capital Expenditure (2021 or the latest fiscal year available to the editors, plus up to five previous years): This figure represents funds used for investment in or improvement of physical assets such as offices, equipment or factories and the purchase or creation of new facilities and/or equipment. These numbers may be estimates.

EBITDA (2021 or the latest fiscal year available to the editors, plus up to five previous years): This figure is an acronym for earnings before interest, taxes, depreciation and amortization. It represents a company's financial performance calculated as revenue minus expenses (excluding taxes, depreciation and interest), and is a prime indicator of profitability. These numbers may be estimates.

Return on Assets % (2021 or the latest fiscal year available to the editors, plus up to five previous years): This figure is an indicator of the profitability of a company relative to its total assets. It is calculated by dividing annual net earnings by total assets. These numbers may be estimates.

Return on Equity % (2021 or the latest fiscal year available to the editors, plus up to five previous years): This figure is a measurement of net income as a percentage of shareholders' equity. It is also called the rate of return on the ownership interest. It is a vital indicator of the quality of a company's operations. These numbers may be estimates.

Debt to Equity (2021 or the latest fiscal year available to the editors, plus up to five previous years): A ratio of the company's long-term debt to its shareholders' equity. This is an indicator of the overall financial leverage of the firm. These numbers may be estimates.

Address:
The firm's full headquarters address, the headquarters telephone, plus toll-free and fax numbers where available. Also provided is the internet address.

Stock Ticker, Exchange: When available, the unique stock market symbol used to identify this firm's common stock for trading and tracking purposes is indicated. Where appropriate, this field may contain "private" or "subsidiary" rather than a ticker symbol. If the firm is a publicly-held company headquartered outside of the U.S., its international ticker and exchange are given.

Total Number of Employees: The approximate total number of employees, worldwide, as of the end of 2021 (or the latest data available to the editors).

Parent Company: If the firm is a subsidiary, its parent company is listed.

Salaries/Bonuses:

(The following descriptions generally apply to U.S. employers only.)

Highest Executive Salary: The highest executive salary paid, typically a 2021 amount (or the latest year available to the editors) and typically paid to the Chief Executive Officer.

Highest Executive Bonus: The apparent bonus, if any, paid to the above person.

Second Highest Executive Salary: The next-highest executive salary paid, typically a 2021 amount (or the latest year available to the editors) and typically paid to the President or Chief Operating Officer.

Second Highest Executive Bonus: The apparent bonus, if any, paid to the above person.

Other Thoughts:

Estimated Female Officers or Directors: It is difficult to obtain this information on an exact basis, and employers generally do not disclose the data in a public way. However, we have indicated what our best efforts reveal to be the apparent number of women who either are in the posts of corporate officers or sit on the board of directors. There is a wide variance from company to company.

Hot Spot for Advancement for Women/Minorities: A "Y" in appropriate fields indicates "Yes." These are firms that appear either to have posted a substantial number of women and/or minorities to high posts or that appear to have a good record of going out of their way to recruit, train, promote and retain women or minorities. (See the Index of Hot Spots For Women and Minorities in the back of the book.) This information may change frequently and can be difficult to obtain and verify. Consequently, the reader should use caution and conduct further investigation where appropriate.

Glossary: A short list of solar power, wind power and renewable energy industry terms.

Chapter 1

MAJOR TRENDS AFFECTING THE SOLAR POWER, WIND POWER & RENEWABLE ENERGY INDUSTRY

Major Trends Affecting the Solar Power, Wind Power & Renewable Energy Industry:

1) Introduction
2) Solar Installations Soar While Solar Panel Costs Plummet
3) Photovoltaic Technologies, Thin Film Solar and Solar Panel Efficiency
4) Utility Scale Solar Plants
5) Wind Power
6) Hydroelectric Power
7) Geothermal Power
8) Biomass, Waste-to-Energy, Waste Methane and Biofuels from Algae
9) Ethanol Production Soared, But U.S. Federal Subsidy Expires
10) Cellulosic Ethanol Makes Slow Commercial Progress
11) Tidal Power
12) Fuel Cell and Hydrogen Power Research Continue/Fuel Cell Cars Enter Market
13) Electric Cars and Plug-in Hybrids (PHEVs) to See Massive New Investments by Auto Makers
14) Major Research and Advancements in Lithium Batteries/Tesla and Panasonic Operate the Gigafactory
15) Natural Gas-Powered Vehicles Gain in Popularity/Long Term Potential Is Bright Thanks to Low Shale Gas Prices
16) Homes and Commercial Buildings Seek Green Certification
17) Smart Electric Grid Technologies Are Adopted
18) The Energy Industry Invests in Storage Battery Technologies with an Eye on Distributed Power and Renewables
19) Nuclear Energy Moves Ahead in India, China and the Middle East
20) Nuclear Fusion Technologies Might Create Unlimited, Emission-Free Power
21) New Display Technologies with PLEDs
22) Electric Utilities Adopt Coal Emissions Scrubbers While the Industry Tests Carbon Capture and Clean Coal Technologies
23) Superconductivity Provides Advanced Electricity Distribution Technology
24) Lower Energy Intensity Is a Prime Focus in China/U.S. Achieves Dramatic Energy Intensity Reductions

1) Introduction

Renewable electricity has been generated with great success for many decades in the form of hydroelectricity—that is, water flowing over a turbine installed at a dam site, with that turbine powering an electric generator. Today, renewable energy comes from many other sources. The non-hydroelectric resources are growing at a stunning rate worldwide.

Despite the rapid growth in the renewables field, the traditional sources of coal and natural gas (and to a lesser extent, nuclear energy) remain the primary sources of electric generation in most of the world. There are some noteworthy exceptions to this statement. For example, Brazil, long a world leader in hydropower, gets about 60% of its total electricity generation from hydroelectricity.

The energy mix is slowly shifting towards renewables, but it will take years of development and vast investment before renewable generation of electricity dominates over fossil fuels and nuclear. In late 2021, the International Energy Agency (IEA) stated that, through 2026, renewables would account for nearly 95% of the increase in global electricity production capacity—mostly in the form of solar. The IEA further stated that, by 2026, global renewable electricity capacity will rise more than 60% from 2020 levels to over 4,800 gigawatts (GW)—equivalent to 2021's total worldwide capacity of nuclear and fossil fuel-powered electric plants combined. (However, it is important to note that the IEA is talking about capacity, not output. Nuclear and fossil fuel electric plants are generally available to generate electricity 24/7, while renewable capacity is not always producing. For example, solar plants cannot gather sunlight 24 hours per day.)

Meanwhile, some of the world's leading oil and gas companies, including Royal Dutch Shell, are increasing their investments in renewable energy sources and technologies. BP and ExxonMobil are also increasing investment in the industry.

U.S. electric production from all renewable sources was 20.0% of total electric power in 2022, up from only about 7.6% in 1970. In this case, "renewable" includes conventional hydroelectric and geothermal, along with solar, wind and biomass. (In 1970, such production was almost entirely from hydroelectric sources.)

Wind Power has seen rapid growth worldwide. Major technological advances in wind turbines (including much larger blades creating very high output per turbine, as well as blades that suffer very little downtime and are thus more efficient) have made wind power more economically feasible. At the same time, massive government incentives are encouraging investment in wind generation. Analysts at BP estimated total wind generation capacity worldwide at 824,874 megawatts in 2021. The Global Wind Energy Council forecasts it to climb to 908,000 megawatts in 2023. In 2021, U.S. wind capacity was only 132,738 megawatts. Wind projects, like other renewable power initiatives, benefit from tax credits and subsidies from government.

Solar Power is enjoying significant technological innovation. The important factors in solar are the percent of captured solar energy that is converted into electricity, and the cost per installed watt of potential output (which has been steadily declining).

Analysts at BP report that installed global solar photovoltaic (PV) capacity was only 4,245 megawatts at the end of 2005. By 2011, that number had soared to 71,251 megawatts, and in 2020 it surged ahead to 855,700 megawatts.

The Solar Energy Industries Association (SEIA) estimates that the American solar industry grew by 10,000% from 2006 through 2019, with much of that growth spurred by tax credits. (The fact that solar panel costs plummeted also fueled extreme growth.)

Biomass energy (including the generation of energy using waste, such as wood chips and landfills, and the production of bioethanol) has also grown rapidly over the long term, both in the U.S. and elsewhere.

Nuclear Power, both expensive to build and controversial as to its safety, is in a state of great change. The construction of new nuclear generating plants is continuing in China, where demand for electricity is booming and many new nuclear plants are planned. New plants were also recently contemplated or underway in the UAE, India and South Korea. In the UK, a controversial new plant has been under development at Hinkley Point, and in France, a new plant has been under development at Flamanville. However, a history of construction cost overruns and a vast regulatory burden make it virtually impossible to construct a nuclear plant today in the U.S. and many other nations. Nonetheless, nuclear provides an emission-free alternative to solar and wind, and it is generally reliable 24 hours-a-day. Today's advanced nuclear plant technologies are vastly improved and are thought by many to be virtually fail-safe.

Hydroelectric Power: World hydroelectric consumption increased by 5.5% during 2021. North American hydroelectric consumption decreased by 4.0%. Like geothermal power, hydropower is among the cleanest and most reliable renewable sources of all.

It should be noted that the use of renewable sources does not always mean clean power generation. For example, burning wood or trash for energy under the wrong conditions can create significant pollution. Also, the clearing of land, such as forests, for planting of biomass to be used in ethanol or biodiesel refining can be highly destructive to the environment while creating huge quantities of carbon emissions. In addition, many types of renewable energy production require vast quantities of water. These trade-offs continue to create significant debate and controversy.

A Brief History: In the U.S., emphasis on alternative energy and conservation has a varied history. The 1973 oil trade embargo staged by Persian Gulf oil producers greatly limited the supply of petroleum in America and created an instant interest in energy conservation. Thermostats were turned to more efficient levels, solar water heating systems sprouted on the rooftops of American homes (including a system that was used for a few years at the White House) and tax credits were launched by various government agencies to encourage investment in more efficient systems in buildings and factories that would utilize less oil, gasoline and electricity. Meanwhile, American motorists crawled through lengthy lines at filling stations, trying to top off their tanks during the horrid days of gasoline rationing.

While some consumers maintained a keen, long term interest in alternative energy from an environmentally friendly point of view, most Americans quickly forgot about energy conservation when the price of gasoline plummeted during the 1980s and 1990s, and again in 2014. Low gasoline prices were common for many years. As advancing technology made oil production and electricity generation much more efficient, a long-term, oil price trend kept market prices under control. (Although price spikes do occur from time-to-time.) As a result, Americans returned to ice-cold air-conditioned rooms and purchased giant, gas-guzzling SUVs, motor homes and motorboats. The median newly constructed American single-family home built in 1972 contained 1,520 square feet; by 2018 it contained 2,386 square feet. More square footage means more lights, air conditioning and heating systems to power. Meanwhile, federal and state regulators made efforts to force automobile engines and industrial plants to operate in clean-air mode, largely through the use of advanced technologies, while requiring gasoline refiners to adopt an ever-widening web of additives and standards that would create cleaner-burning fuels.

Fortunately, the first energy crisis in the early 1970s did lead to the widespread use of technology to create significant efficiencies in many areas. For example, prior to that time, as much as 40% of a typical household's natural gas consumption was for pilot lights burning idly in case a stove or furnace was needed. Today, electric pilots create spark ignition for gas burners on demand. Likewise, today's refrigerators use about 70% less electricity than models built in 1970. Many other appliances and electrical devices have become much more efficient, through better design and engineering, better insulation, more efficient motors, efficient lightning and smarter building controls. While the number of electricity-burning personal computers proliferated, computer equipment makers rapidly adopted energy-saving PC technologies.

Likewise, in transportation, today's jetliners burn up to 70% less fuel per passenger seat-mile than they did in 1970. Meanwhile, trucks, ships, buses and trains all have increased efficiency dramatically.

Renewable energy sources, cleaner-burning fuels, fuel-efficient automobiles, as well as homes and buildings that utilize energy-efficient materials and controls are of great appeal to the large number of consumers worldwide who have developed a true interest in sustainability or in protecting the environment. For example, surveys have shown that many consumers are willing to pay somewhat more for electricity if they know it is coming from non-polluting, renewable sources. Nonetheless, the vast, recent drops in the market prices of oil and natural gas pose a significant challenge to alternative and renewable energy sources on a purely economic basis.

Other Developments: Bioethanol and biodiesel, from an economic and environmental point of view, are questionable at the least, and extremely misdirected at the worst. Some production of bioethanol appears very efficient, particularly in Brazil where easily grown sugar cane is the feedstock. However, in the U.S., the diversion of corn and soy from the food chain to the energy chain for ethanol or biodiesel may be a very bad idea from a wide variety of measures.

Advanced technologies that capture carbon dioxide and utilize it to grow oil-producing algae appear to be a somewhat promising alternative source for oil, but much research and development remains to be done in this area, and costs remain high.

At least two geothermal energy projects, where deep holes are drilled to tap the high temperatures of the inner Earth, have recently been cancelled due to concerns that these activities cause earthquakes.

Tidal energy looks promising, but both installation costs and maintenance remain huge obstacles. Nonetheless, technologies are advancing in this field, and many prototype projects, as well as a few permanent installations, have been completed.

Smaller-scale, rooftop solar power installations have become extremely popular in sunny climates. The cost of solar cells has plummeted to the point that solar power produced at homes and commercial buildings is becoming economically viable after government incentives are factored in. While the solar cells themselves are now relatively cheap, installation remains costly. Meanwhile, solar cells require regular maintenance, and their efficiency degrades steadily as they age in place.

Massive, utility-scale solar has been a different story. Such plants required multi-billion-dollar investments in relatively unproven technologies. Many of the largest projects have been total disappointments.

The renewable energy sector will continue to evolve rapidly, as new technologies offer breakthroughs and greater efficiencies are reached. The biggest gains will occur when powerful new batteries are finally developed that make it cost-effective to store solar and wind power where they are produced, for release as needed even when wind or sunlight are not available.

2) Solar Installations Soar While Solar Panel Costs Plummet

What could be more appealing than generating electricity from sunshine? Ever since scientists at the famed Bell Laboratories first demonstrated a solar cell based on silicon in 1954, solar power has been seen as one of the most desirable, if technically challenging, means of creating electricity or heat.

Solar power accounted for about 1,501 trillion BTUs (British thermal units), or 3% of all renewable energy (of all types) consumed in the U.S. during 2021, up from 1,246 trillion BTUs during 2020, according to the U.S. Department of Energy. Installed solar power capacity on a global basis rose from only 0.39 gigawatts in 2010 to 843.1 gigawatts in 2021, according to BP.

Solar power capacity may skyrocket over the long term, according to the Solar Futures Study released by the U.S. Department of Energy (DOE) in 2021. The study forecasted that 37% of the nation's electricity could be produced from solar power by 2025 and 44% by 2050. To reach these goals, spending on new solar projects, both public and private, would have to increase by $562 billion between 2020 and 2050. Solar power was already experiencing rapid growth in 2020, when a fifth of America's solar power capacity was installed according to the DOE.

The U.S. government offered a 30% investment tax credit (ITC) for the installation of solar panels in homes and commercial installations during 2019 and earlier years. The credit declined to 26% in 2020 and will decline further to 22% in 2023. After 2023, the residential credit falls to zero and the commercial credit drops to a permanent 10%. Commercial and utility-scale projects which have commenced construction before December 31, 2023, may still qualify for the 26% or 22% ITC if they are placed in service before January 1, 2026. (However, it is always possible that Congress will create new credits.) In 2022, the U.S. Inflation Reduction Act established a tax credit of 30% of total investment in stand-alone energy storage projects regardless of the energy source. Previously, the credit applied to energy storage paired with solar only. The credit could expand to 50%, if the project is built with at least 40% U.S. manufactured components (which tacks on another 10% tax credit); and if the project is located in areas previously major employers in the fossil fuel sectors (the other 10% credit).

The Solar Energy Industries Association (SEIA) estimates that the American solar industry grew by 10,000 from 2006 through 2019, with much of that growth spurred by the tax credits. (The fact that solar panel costs plummeted also fueled extreme growth.) While firms in the U.S. and EU that install panels or finance their purchase have benefited from the solar boom, much of the demand for the solar panels themselves has been to the benefit of manufacturers based in China. Chinese manufacturers took vast amounts of global market share for solar panels away from makers based in the U.S., Germany and Japan.

China continues to dominate the world's solar panel industry, controlling more than 80% of the global solar panel supply chain. In addition to serving the export market, China is using large quantities of these solar panels domestically. The U.S. government-imposed tariffs on solar panel imports under both the Obama and Trump administrations, which spurred investment in domestic panel production. American manufacturer First Solar, Inc. (www.firstsolar.com) broke ground in 2021 on a $680 million panel factory in Ohio, gambling on the Biden administration's promise to make the U.S. electric grid carbon free by 2035. The plant would be First Solar's third solar panel plant in Ohio and have an annual capacity of 3.3 gigawatts (enough to power approximately 570,000 homes). The plant was scheduled to begin operations in 2023.

The Biden administration established, in 2022, tax credits for renewable power projects that use American-made equipment. U.S. solar equipment manufacturer First Solar, Inc. announced plans to increase its investment in U.S. manufacturing capacity by 75%, spending up to $1.2 billion. Hanwha Solutions Corp., a subsidiary of South Korea's Hanwha Group, plans to invest billions of dollars in creating a solar supply chain in the U.S. Qcells, another unit of Hanwha Solutions, has been scouting potential locations in Texas, Georgia and South Carolina for solar component manufacturing plants.

Other nations, particularly India, plan to reduce their reliance on China for both completed solar panels and the necessary raw ingredients for their manufacture. India plans very aggressive expansion in panel manufacturing. Meanwhile, India is imposing substantial tariffs on Chinese-made panels. It is likely that the EU will also increase domestic panel manufacturing substantially.

At one time, 40+ U.S. states offered a generous version of a credit system called net metering, which pays commercial and residential customers for unused renewable energy that consumers or businesses sell back to utilities. This is primarily for rooftop installations of solar panels, so the customer can be as small as a single-family home, or as large as a shopping mall. If the property owner doesn't need all of the solar power that is being generated on-site at any time, then that excess power can be sold back to the electric grid or electric utility. This has historically been at very generous prices, so net metering has been one of the key drivers of new solar installations.

However, many states are reining in their net metering allowances, as some observers believe these property owners are gaining unfair advantage, while many electric utilities claim that they are being forced to overpay for the power—thus driving up the total electric bill of all customers who do not happen to own solar panels. (That is, forcing all other electric customers to subsidize solar panel owners.) While net metering is often remaining in place, state legislatures are, in many cases, cutting the rates that utilities must pay to buy the excess power.

The average cost of residential solar installations in the U.S. (including hardware, permits and labor) dropped from $9.00 per watt in 2006 to an estimated $1.34 per watt in 2020, per the Solar Energy Industries Association (SEIA). In the utility-scale fixed-tilt sector, costs fell to about $1.00 per watt. In 2022, typical single-family home costs, including the panels, labor, etc., were generally in the $15,000 to $30,000 range, but could vary widely based on the total solar generation capacity.

Large solar finance companies enable homeowners to enjoy solar panels at no cash outlay to the homeowner. Companies such as SolarCity Corp. provide turnkey deals, with lease financing for the equipment and installation, and packaged services that apply for government grants and rebates, and then monitor the ongoing operations of the systems. This makes SolarCity and similar firms into *de facto* solar power generation companies. The homeowners benefit through net metering, the process by which solar power that is not used by the home goes into the grid. While this is happening, the home's electric usage meter literally goes backward, reducing the final monthly bill for the home. SolarCity calls its service SolarLease.

In May 2018, California became the first U.S. state to require solar panels on all new homes. Starting in 2020, residential buildings of up to three stories, including single family homes and condominiums, must be equipped with solar panels. By late 2020, solar power accounted for 15.43% of the state's electricity supply.

Europe has been quick to install rooftop systems due to generous government subsidies (however, some governments have cut those subsidies as part of recent austerity programs). Germany leads the world in rooftop installations. However, this renewable energy is driving total energy costs significantly higher. The German government's subsidies for wind and solar power were cut, resulting in skyrocketing electric power prices for consumers.

Germany has announced plans to wind down all of its nuclear power plants over the mid-term. However, traditional coal- and gas-fired power plants are still required in large numbers, particularly since neither wind nor solar can be counted on for full time output. Likewise, only traditional power plants can be called on to fill surges in need during peak periods of demand. The entire world is attempting to learn from Germany's grand experiment. Meanwhile, German consumers are suffering higher prices and Germany's carbon output has not decreased to the extent expected.

In the UK, solar capacity has skyrocketed. In 2010, capacity was under 100 megawatts. By late 2020, the UK had 13.44 gigawatts of capacity, according to the Department for Business, Energy and Industrial Strategy.

> ***Internet Research Tip: Solar Power***
> To find out more about solar power and the Solar America Initiative, visit the U.S. DOE, SunShot Initiative at www.energy.gov/eere/solar/sunshot-initiative.

3) Photovoltaic Technologies, Thin Film Solar and Solar Panel Efficiency

Traditionally, photovoltaic (PV) technology was based on layers of silicon assembled within panels that are engineered to attract the sun's rays and create a flow of electric current to electrodes (the "photoelectric effect"). However, new developments in this technology are emerging continually.

Immense amounts of effort and venture capital are being invested in solar technology, both in the U.S. and abroad. Significant progress is being made each year. The efficiency of solar cells is rising while costs per unit of electric output have plummeted. However, solar panels remain expensive to install, and they require continuing maintenance in order to keep them clean enough to operate at peak power. Current standard PV technology converts about 20% to 25% of available sunlight into electricity. However, breakthroughs in technology and efficiency are occurring in the laboratory at a rapid clip, thanks to intense new investments in research. High efficiency is important when you consider the fact that peak sunlight is available only a limited part of the day.

For many years, the Holy Grail of the PV industry was to be able to sell solar cells at less than $1.00 per watt of electricity produced (equal to five to six cents per kilowatt-hour), which would make PV relatively price competitive with traditional electric generation in sunny locations. (Watts are measured at mid-day peak output of the cell.) This $1.00 per watt barrier has not only been achieved but significantly surpassed, as it is possible to purchase certain types of solar equipment far below the $1.00 per watt range.

Traditional, crystalline solar cells are heavy and expensive to manufacture. However, their efficiency in converting sunlight has historically been superior to the lighter weight alternative known as thin film. Crystalline cells are constructed with silicon semiconducting materials. Thin film, also known as amorphous, can offer advantages in some installations. It is somewhat flexible. Also, thin film can be less expensive to manufacture.

The challenge for thin film companies has been to enhance the efficiency of the units. First Solar held a record 22.1% conversion efficiency for cadmium telluride as of late 2019 and was maintaining between 17.9% and 19.0% for its Series 6 modules in 2021. The firm has invested more than $1 billion since 1998 in research and development of a "cad-tel" spray, and has renovated its Toledo, Ohio manufacturing plant to be almost completely automated. The panels produced there are three times the size of the company's previous model, cost as little as 20 cents per watt and produce 244% more power.

A breakthrough in solar cell manufacturing is a hybrid in which solar cells made of crystalline silicon are topped with a thin layer of another form of silicon and a layer of a semiconductor oxide. SolarCity (which is part of Tesla) acquired a company that was a pioneer in the hybrid solar cells called Silevo. The cells are more efficient than standard silicon cells and cheaper to make. Tesla manufactures the cells at its massive Gigafactory 2 plant in Buffalo, New York.

Meanwhile, there are compounds with a crystal structure that have the potential to be used as semiconductors within solar cells, either as an alternative to, or in combination with, traditional silicone. Called perovskites, they allow semi-transparent solar cells to be easily and cheaply made in large rolls by mixing special chemical solutions and pouring the result onto a suitable backing. Silicone is believed to have reached its maximum efficiency in converting light to electricity, while perovskites could conceivably achieve much higher levels.

4) Utility Scale Solar Power Plants

Governments in many nations, including the U.S. and Spain, have provided massive financial aid to firms that constructed the world's largest (utility-scale) solar plants—those capable of powering thousands of homes at once. At various times, this aid has included loan guarantees, tax credits and research and development credits. These projects may utilize one of a few technologies, including photovoltaics (PV), concentrating solar power (CSP) or concentrating photovoltaics (CPV). Some of these projects also include methods that enable them to store a portion of their output for future use. The business model is based upon selling power at wholesale to utilities that, in turn, distribute the power to end users.

Many of these early, massive projects were based on CSP and CSV, and frequently turned out to be financially, operationally or environmentally unviable. Critics state that complicated and costly solar projects, such as the $2 billion Ivanpah, are not

cost-effective. Spain-based Abengoa, the lead developer of many major renewable projects in the U.S. and elsewhere, filed for bankruptcy in 2016. Tonopah Solar Energy, owner of a major solar plant in Nevada, filed for bankruptcy in August 2020.

However, falling prices for simple solar panels (similar to those installed on the rooftops of homes) have created a comeback for utility-scale, large-capacity solar projects. Solar panels are vastly easier to install and operate than complex systems such as concentrated solar power (CSP), even when a large project requires tens of thousands of such panels.

A new boom in large, utility-scale installations based on traditional solar panels is underway. This is due to multiple factors, including growing demand for renewable energy, readily available investment money, declining costs and generous government incentives. Major investors have backed or acquired immense new solar farms, based on solar panel technologies. These investors are encouraged by the fact that utility companies are forced by state legislation to provide a growing percent of their electricity from renewable means. Berkshire Hathaway Energy purchased the 550-megawatt Topaz Solar Farm in California from First Solar. The electricity will be sold under a 25-year contract with PG&E, a major utility firm that is facing a requirement that 33% of California's electricity come from renewables by 2020.

As of mid-2021, in excess of 800 utility-scale solar power plants were under planning or development, capable of generating as much as 70,000 total megawatts capacity. Some $25 billion in total guarantees have been approved in the U.S., covering projects, mostly in the Southwestern United States. However, the availability of a guaranteed approval did not mean that a project would be able to find all of the necessary funding, obtain environmental and construction approval and successfully negotiate a wholesale distribution contract with a buyer for the power. Also, in many cases, environmentalists are attempting to block these plants for various reasons.

A boon to operators of large-scale solar facilities is the use of robots to assist with installation and panel cleaning, which are both labor intensive. Alion Energy, a manufacturer in Richmond, California, installed its robotic machines in three projects in California, Saudi Arabia and China. Serbot, a Swiss firm, manufactures robots that clean solar arrays as well glass windows in skyscrapers.

SPOTLIGHT: Community Solar Power Installations
Local solar power sites of modest size are rapidly growing in popularity. In the U.S., this trend is referred to as community solar. Typically on tracts from 20 to 200 acres, community solar is designed to create enough power to provide much of the needs of a local neighborhood. Several types of ownership and financing are utilized, ranging from ownership by private investors to partnerships between electric utilities and local governments. In many cases, "shares" equal to the cost of one solar panel, are sold to homeowners in the neighborhood. While interest in this concept has been strong, it has historically been growing in the handful of U.S. states with the most supportive laws and incentives. These states include Florida, Massachusetts, New York and Minnesota. Investor interest could wane if generous tax credits become no longer available.

KPMG forecasted India's share of electricity generated by solar means to rise from less than 1% in 2016 to 12.5% in 2025. The $2.5 billion Pavagada Solar Park in Karnataka, which spreads over 20 square miles with millions of solar panels capable of generating two gigawatts of electricity (the equivalent of two large nuclear plants), was commissioned in April 2019. Two other solar parks, the five-gigawatt project in Gujarat and the 2.3-gigawatt project in Rajasthan are underway.

Solar Thermal (or "CSP," Concentrating Solar Power): This technology utilizes solar arrays of curved mirrors that focus sunlight onto solar cells, which concentrates sunlight 500 times. These cells' efficiency in sunlight conversion can be greater than 38%, compared to the 20% to 25% efficiency for standard solar cells. CSP can also be used to heat fluids to extreme temperatures (up to 750 degrees Fahrenheit), which produce steam that then drives a turbine.

A state-of-the-art CSP project, the Delingha 50-megawatt plant in the Qinghai province in China, went into operation in October 2018. The plant was built by China General Nuclear Power Corporation (http://en.cgnpc.com.cn/), and uses parabolic-trough CSP technology, supplemented by nine-hour molten salt heat storage.

A landmark project in the Mojave Desert in California called Ivanpah opened in early 2014. The $2.2 billion project, built by BrightSource Energy (www.brightsourceenergy.com) and initially owned by Google and NRG, is one of the largest solar thermal projects in the world, engineered to have a capacity between 370 megawatts and 392 megawatts, enough to power more than 140,000 homes during peak hours of the day. Ivanpah is comprised of three separate plants built in phases over several years. Unfortunately, Ivanpah has faced a vast number of challenges and problems. It was delayed and had cost overruns due to the need to protect the endangered Desert Tortoise. Later, heat from the plant's 170,000 mirrors was estimated to be killing 3,500 birds yearly. It also has turned out to be more time-consuming and costly to start up the plant each day (with natural gas used to produce steam at start up). BrightSource also supplied a 100-megawatt central tower plant to ACWA Power's 700-megawatt DEWA plant in Dubai.

In December 2015, an immense, 580-megawatt plant in Morocco, the Quarzazate CSP plant, saw its first unit go online. Nations in the Middle East and North Africa may be the best hope for future utility-scale development by solar firms.

CSP can be combined with unique power storage technologies. For example, a system of heat storage based on pressurized water or molten salt allows solar heat to be captured during daylight hours, and then used to turn turbines for electric generation during evening hours. CSP can also be combined with traditional natural gas generation at one location. This may be referred to as ISCC (integrated solar combined cycle).

The $2 billion, 280 megawatt "Solana" plant in Arizona can generate electricity up to six hours after the sun goes down. Heat is stored in giant tanks of molten salt. Solana began commercial production in October 2013. Its storage capabilities inspired the California Public Utilities Commission to approve a rule that requires its three investor-owned utilities and other electricity providers to install storage technology by 2024. It remains to be seen whether or not effective storage technologies can be implemented by that time. Due to exorbitant costs, construction of new CSP plants has tapered off worldwide.

Space Solar Power (SSP): First proposed in 1968 by then-president of the International Solar Energy Society Peter Glaser, this technology, based on collecting sunlight from a geostationary orbit high above the Earth would enable the gathering of constant light that is eight times as strong as that on the ground. A solar panel on the orbiting structure would convert the light to electric current, which would then be beamed to Earth by microwave to a specified antenna. Researchers estimate that satellites with solar panels would have to be more than one mile long. The catch is that the final output, which is only a few hundred watts per kilogram, is too low to justify the enormous costs related to such a project, initially estimated to be $305 billion (in 2000 dollars). Since then, costs may have fallen somewhat due to technological advances.

The University of Neuchatel in Switzerland developed a technique using a film created for use in space that yields power densities of 3,200 watts per kilogram. There is also interest in SSP in Japan, where the JAXA space agency has expressed interest in launching a satellite that would spread into a sizable solar array capable of beaming 100 kilowatts of microwave or laser power to Earth.

In late 2022, the European Space Agency approved Solaris, a research study on the cost effectiveness of building solar farms in outer space and transferring collected solar energy to electricity grids on Earth via microwave beams. In September 2022, engineers at Airbus successfully transmitted two kilowatts of power collected from solar cells to receptors more than 30 meters away in Munich. In a separate initiative, a UK government assessment of SSP found that a satellite capable of producing two gigawatts of electricity (about the same as a terrestrial power station) might be possible as early 2040. However, many technical and financial hurdles remain.

SPOTLIGHT: Floating Solar Farms

As large pieces of real estate suitable for solar panel arrays become scarce in certain smaller countries and densely populated areas, a small number of new installations are shifting to floating systems. In the Netherlands, for example, an island comprised of a circle of 180 floating solar panels called Proteus has a total installed capacity of 73 kilowatts of peak power. Proteus was built by SolarisFloat, a Portuguese company. Similar floating farms are in Brazil, Japan and Singapore. Global floating solar capacity reached 1,300-megawatt peak power in 2020, up from 70-megawatt peak power in 2015. Long-term, significant demand for floating solar systems could develop.

---

5) Wind Power

Mankind has utilized wind as a form of energy ever since the first sail was hoisted on a crudely built boat thousands of years ago. In the 12th century, it was used to power the first windmills. It is only natural that wind would eventually be viewed as an attractive means of generating electricity.

Today, wind turbine manufacturers have continually enhanced technology. As a result, wind turbines are much taller than before, with vastly wider blade spans. Modern wind turbines have extremely high output and are less costly to maintain for a given amount of generation than their recent predecessors. New models also have much less downtime due to breakdowns. As a result, wind turbine farm development has become more effective, both economically and in terms of total power created. Analysts at Lazard reported that the cost of generating one kilowatt-hour of wind power fell from 13.5 cents in 2009 to 3.3 cents in 2021 (before government tax credits).

In 2021, wind generated 16% of America's renewable energy consumption (or 3,332 trillion Btu), according to the U.S. Department of Energy (DOE). By 2030, wind could supply as much as 20% of the country's electricity.

The largest installed base by far is in Texas. Not only does Texas enjoy vast stretches of open land that have strong steady winds, it also is home to an extremely efficient, statewide electricity distribution grid that is well suited to deliver wind power from rural areas to the major cities where it is needed.

Wind projects, like other renewable power initiatives, benefit from tax credits and subsidies from government. At the end of December 2020, the U.S. Congress extended the production tax credit (PTC) at 60% of the full credit amount, or $0.018 per kilowatt hour ($18 per megawatt hour), for another year through December 31, 2021. In 2020, the credit was 60% of the full credit amount. Under PTC legislation, qualifying wind projects had to begin construction by December 31, 2021.

The Inflation Reduction Act, passed by the U.S. Congress in 2022, extended PTC for wind projects that begin production by the end of 2024. The Inflation Reduction Act also established a tax credit of 30% of total investment in stand-alone energy storage projects regardless of the energy source. Previously, the credit applied to energy storage paired with solar only. The credit could expand to 50%, if the project is built with at least 40% U.S. manufactured components (which tacks on another 10% tax credit); and if the project is located in areas previously major employers in the fossil fuel sectors (the other 10% credit). Some wind projects may qualify for a 100% PTC. To do so, the project must pay prevailing wages at the local rate (to be determined by the Secretary of Labor) for construction or repairs of the facility and ensure that no less than the applicable percentage of total labor hours is performed by qualified apprentices (10% for projects that begin construction in 2022, 12.5% for those beginning in 2023 and 15% for those beginning in 2024 or later). The intent of these wage and labor provisions is to boost the use of union workers.

Internet Research Tip: Wind Power
For the latest on wind-powered electricity generation in the U.S., see the American Clean Power Association at cleanpower.org.

Meanwhile, wind power installation in Europe and Asia has been progressing at a strong pace. Global wind generation cumulative capacity reached 824.9 gigawatts in 2021, up from 733.3 gigawatts in 2020 and 622 gigawatts in 2019, according to BP. China had the highest total capacity installed with 329.0 gigawatts, followed by the U.S. with 132.7 gigawatts and Germany with 63.8 gigawatts.

Offshore wind farms are being emphasized in some locations, particularly where winds are strong and steady, and space for land installations is limited. The UK hopes to raise its share of electricity generated by renewable resources from 7% in 2010 to 30% over the next several years. Britain installed a major wind farm off the coasts of Kent and Essex to the southeast of London in December 2012. Called the London Array, the first phase produces 630 megawatts and has 175 turbines. By the end of 2020, wind power capacity in the UK reached a record 24 gigawatts (both onshore and offshore), largely due to the expansion of the Orsted Walney wind farm in the Irish Sea, which has 87 turbines and a capacity of 659 megawatts.

Formosa 3, a $10 billion offshore wind power project in Taiwan promises to have two gigawatts of capacity, making it three times as powerful as Orsted Walney. Formosa 3 is expected to reach completion between 2026 and 2030.

In early 2017, construction was completed on the first U.S. offshore wind farm. Located near Block Island, Rhode Island, the farm has five 560-foot-tall windmills, each with a six-megawatt capacity (capable of powering about 17,000 homes). The $300 million, privately financed project is backed by Deepwater Wind. A second project, the Coastal Virginia Offshore Wind Project, received state approval in August 2022. The 176-wind turbine project is expected to generate 14.7 megawatts of electricity and will be located 27 miles off the coast of Virginia Beach. Dominion Energy Virginia is spending $9.8 billion to build it, and completion is expected in 2026. Nonetheless, opposition by local property owners remains strong in many locales, and such resistance could potentially lead to increased total costs and delayed or scrapped projects in some instances.

However, many proposed new offshore wind farms are in planning stages, primarily located off the Northeastern coast of the U.S. in federally designated wind energy areas created to avoid lawsuits like those that plagued Cape Wind. Those projects face many obstacles.

New technology has enabled wind turbines to grow to massive size, offering greater operating and maintenance efficiencies. One of the world's largest floating wind turbines is the 344-foot, seven-megawatt structure anchored to the seabed 12 miles off the coast of Fukushima, Japan. The tower is designed to withstand 65-foot waves and tsunamis. It is part of as many as 25 new 10,000-megawatt wind farms to be built over a 25-year period. The first three turbines are being funded by the Japanese government at a cost of $226 million. Later projects will hopefully be funded by a consortium of 11 companies including Hitachi and Mitsubishi Heavy Industries.

Two large wind projects by Orsted, formerly Dong Energy, a major Danish wind developer, are to be built in the German sector of the North Sea. The projects will receive no government subsidies, with a number of major corporations' electricity purchase agreements enabling funding. Both projects will utilize Siemens Gamesa offshore wind turbines, each with a capacity of 11 megawatts and a 200-meter rotor diameter. The two projects, Borkum Riffgrund 3 (900-megawatt capacity) and Gode Wind 3 (242 megawatts) will be commissioned in 2025 and 2024 respectively.

Wind farms may be planned for deeper water and further distances from shore than ever before, posing serious technical challenges. Scientists are hoping to find a way to anchor the platforms in deeper water past current limits. A professor at the Massachusetts Institute of Technology proposes using offshore oil well technology to anchor wind platforms to the ocean floor using tense metal cables. The process would save on building materials and makes installation far easier than the "monopiles" currently used to support offshore wind turbines. With the cable technology, wind platforms might be used in water of up to 600 feet. German wind equipment manufacturer VDMA Power Systems builds turbines using steel foundations almost 100 feet deep. While deeper and more remote offshore farms are becoming more achievable, the cost to build and maintain them can be three times that for onshore farms.

A new $5 billion wind farm and electricity superhighway is on the drawing board called the Chokecherry and Sierra Madre Wind Energy Project, backed by billionaire Phillip Anschutz. The 3,000-megawatt farm will be in rural Wyoming (the largest constructed in the U.S. to date) and connect to a 730-mile transmission line ending in Las Vegas, Nevada where it can connect to the grid supplying the West Coast. The project is expected to be completed as early as 2025.

In 2021, a $2.8 billion wind farm project called Vineyard Wind received U.S. federal approval. The 84-turbine project will lie 12 miles off the coast of Nantucket and have a capacity of up to 800 megawatts. Completion is expected in 2023.

SPOTLIGHT: NextEra Energy, Inc.
NextEra Energy, Inc. is one of the largest electric power companies in North America and a leader in the renewable energy industry. The firm has approximately 55,700 megawatts (MW) of generating capacity, with electric generation capacity across 38 states in the U.S., four provinces in Canada and in Spain. NextEra provides retail and wholesale electric services to more than 10 million customers. It owns generation, transmission and distribution facilities to support its services. The company also has investments in gas infrastructure assets. NextEra's business strategy emphasizes the development, acquisition and operation of renewable, nuclear and natural gas-fired generation facilities in response to long-term federal policy trends supportive of zero and low air emission sources of power. Nearly 100% of the company's generation comes from renewable, nuclear and natural gas-fired facilities. The firm conducts its operations principally through two wholly owned subsidiaries: Florida Power & Light Company (FPL) and NextEra Energy Resources, LLC (NEER). In addition, subsidiary NextEra Energy Capital Holdings, Inc. owns and provides funding for NEER and all NextEra subsidiaries other than FPL. FPL is the largest electric utility in the state of Florida and one of the largest electric utilities in the U.S. NEER is the world's largest operator of wind and solar projects. Additionally, NextEra also operates the recently acquired Gulf Power Company. In March 2021, the firm completed its acquisition of GridLiance Holdco, LP and GridLiance GP, LLC from Blackstone for approximately $660 million.

6) Hydroelectric Power

Of all renewable energy sources, hydroelectric has proven to be one of the most reliable, controllable and cost-effective, as well as the most viable alternative fossil fuel energy. BP reports that global hydroelectric consumption grew from 37.64 exajoules in 2019 to 38.16 exajoules in 2020 and 40.26 exajoules in 2021.

In the U.S., there were 762.9 terawatt-hours of net electrical for power generation from renewable sources in 2021, down from 792.5 terawatt-hours in 2020, according to the U.S. Department of Energy (DOE). During 2021, hydroelectric accounted for 20% of U.S. renewable energy consumption. Costs are extremely low, in the two cent per kilowatt hour range. Unfortunately, potential locations for new hydrodams are limited, and there is little projected growth in large installations in the U.S. However, microhydro power has been of long term interest to landowners and investors. That is the use of small turbines installed on creeks and streams that have reliable flow.

About 60% of America's hydro power is owned and managed by the U.S. Army Corp of Engineers. Washington State is the largest American hydro power producer, primarily on the Columbia and Snake Rivers. Elsewhere in North America, Canada generates about 60% of its electricity via hydroelectric means.

In other countries, there is much new hydro development under consideration or construction. Although most industrialized countries have already realized their full potential for hydro generation, many developing countries are just getting started. For example, China, already a major producer of hydropower, completed the enormous Three Gorges Dam. In 2012, the dam became fully operational at its peak generation capacity of 22.5 gigawatts, and it is one of the largest single sources of electricity in the world by total capacity. Due to China's intense modernization and rapidly growing thirst for energy, this project is of great importance to the future development of the nation. Nonetheless, there was worldwide protest over the fact that 1.3 million people were displaced from homes in the path of the reservoir created by the dam.

Brazil, long a world leader in hydropower, gets about 60% of its total electricity generation from hydroelectricity. Brazil's Belo Monte plant, which was completed in November 2019, has maximum output of 11,233 megawatts (placing it third in the world with regard to capacity behind Three Gorges and Itaipu, which is on the Brazil-Paraguay border).

However, this maximum output can only be reached during peak water flow, and output on a typical day is more like 4,571 megawatts.

Meanwhile, over the mid-term, China plans to triple its total national hydroelectric generation to 300 gigawatts as part of its long-term goal to get 15% of the nation's energy from renewable sources by that year. The International Energy Agency (IEA) released a report in late 2012 that stated that global hydroelectricity production could double by 2050 if certain environmental issues are resolved and public acceptance increases.

7) Geothermal Power

Like hydroelectric power, geothermal energy can be extremely reliable and cost-effective, and is one of the cleanest possible sources of renewable power. It is a well-established technology that uses several different methods to harvest heat from underneath the earth's surface. Potential sites for traditional geothermal generation include areas with volcanic activity, tectonic shifting, major hot springs or geysers, where the earth's heat is very near the surface. In the United States, most geothermal resources are located in the western portion of the country, along the numerous fault lines on the western seaboard and in the Rocky Mountains. The U.S. is a world leader in geothermal energy, with roughly 210 trillion Btus of potential capacity. (Nonetheless, geothermal generation is only 2% of renewable electric power consumption in the U.S.) In many parts of the U.S., smaller geothermal resources are used to heat buildings or to provide commercial quantities of hot water but are not used to generate electricity.

According to the U.S. Department of Energy, operating and maintenance costs for geothermal plants are extremely low, ranking from one to three cents per kilowatt hour. Such plants are much more reliable than renewable power based on wind or solar and can operate at about 90% availability.

However, there is a major obstacle facing significant expansion of geothermal drilling. The possibility of earthquake activity near test wells has led to cancelled projects in the U.S and in Europe. Observers are concerned that the drilling is causing dangerous reactions underground. The cancelled projects typically used technology based on fracturing underground rock, enabling water to penetrate the rock. The water turns to steam, which is then captured to turn a turbine-driven generator. It is possible that the fracturing process can result in tremors. This issue may be difficult to impossible to resolve, and much further study will be required.

New technologies may be required in order to safely drill, particularly if the site is anywhere near a highly populated area. After technical problems forced AltaRock Energy, Inc. to shut down operations at a location called the Geysers in Northern California, the DOE investigated. The result was the imposition of new safeguards, including the use of ground-motion sensors, a federally approved plan for shut down in the event of earthquakes and the filing of estimates by the drilling company of expected earthquake activity for review by outside experts.

There are two predominant techniques for traditional geothermal electricity generation, depending on the type of heat resource: flash steam and binary cycle. High temperature locations can be tapped directly, using steam coming out of the ground to drive a turbine in a technique known as flash steam generation. This is the most common plant type in use. Where lower-temperature geothermal sources are tapped, hot water is used to heat another liquid with a lower boiling point (such as isobutene or isopentane), which then drives the turbine. This technique is known as binary cycle generation. The drawback of binary cycle generation is that it is much less efficient than flash generation. Engineers have also begun combining flash and binary generation, which together increase the efficiency of a plant. Binary cycle technology enables the construction of a plant at a geothermal water source that is substantially cooler than that used in flash steam generation.

Technology developed at Los Alamos National Labs (LANL) in New Mexico may create new opportunities for the utilization of geothermal plants. In a 26-year-long project, LANL was able to develop the tools necessary to harvest heat from almost anywhere on earth. Called Hot Dry Rock Geothermal Energy Technology (HDR), the technique drills holes into the ground until they reach rock that is suitably hot at about 15,000 feet. (Such a system is also referred to as an Enhanced Geothermal System or EGS.) Then, pipes are installed in a closed loop. Water is pumped down one pipe, where it is heated to appropriately high temperatures. The resulting hot water shoots up to the surface. This is used to create steam that drives a turbine to power an electric generating plant. (This may be either a flash steam or binary cycle plant.) As the water cools, it is pumped back into the ground. ReNu Energy, formerly Geodynamics, Ltd., renuenergy.com.au, based in Milton, Queensland, Australia, has high hopes for this technology. It has built plants in New South Wales, Tasmania and elsewhere.

In the U.S., AltaRock Energy, Inc. (altarockenergy.com) is using a next generation version of EGS called SuperHot Rock (SHR) at its dormant Newberry volcano site in Oregon. Water is circulated to mine heat of 400 degrees Celsius (675 degrees Fahrenheit) in rock deep in the Earth's crust and bring it to the surface in the form of superheated steam. The steam drives a turbine to generate electricity. The company believes its Newberry SHR Project could eventually generate up to 10 gigawatts of electricity.

Binary cycle generation makes it possible to produce power from hot springs that were previously thought too cool to efficiently use for geothermal efforts. The Chena hot springs in Alaska average about 109 degrees Fahrenheit, but the springs' owners and engineering conglomerate Raytheon Technologies (formerly United Technologies) have devised a method using a refrigerant called R134a (tetrafluoroethane) to drive turbines. Water from the hot springs is used to heat R134a, which has a relatively low boiling point. A gas similar to steam is produced, which drives the turbines. Cooler temperatures yield smaller amounts of gas, so the designers of the Chena plant compensated by slashing operating costs. Mass-produced air conditioner parts were substituted for standard geothermal components, a scheme that might be adopted by geothermal plants the world over.

Yet another geothermal technology is that developed by Bob Potter of Potter Drilling and Jefferson Tester of MIT called spallation. Superheated steam hits rock, causing crystalline grains to expand, thereby causing tiny fractures. Small particles, called spalls, break off as the grains expand. The technology effectively uses steam as a kind of drill to melt rock. It is similar to air spallation drilling previously used for mining ore.

Iceland is a respected leader in geothermal and hydroelectric power. Even though the country's capacity for both is less than that of some other countries, the low-population island nation of Iceland supplies more than 50% of its energy needs with geothermal energy and another 17% by hydroelectric. Generating such a massive amount of energy with these sources is made possible by the island nation's incredible natural resources but was brought to bear by a concentrated effort by the government and the people.

The Iceland Deep Drilling Project (IDDP), funded by a consortium of three Icelandic energy companies, hopes to tap extremely hot steam in an existing geothermal well at depths of up to 2.5 miles, which is close enough to the Earth's layer of magma to produce steam of over 1,100 degrees Fahrenheit. The drilling and collecting equipment necessary is more expensive than standard geothermal machinery, due to the higher pressures and temperatures found at great depths. However, proponents of the project believe that the extra costs (which might double or triple) will be easily regained because the amount of electricity produced is expected to multiply by as much as 10 times. (For additional information, see www.iddp.is.)

The next big thing in geothermal technology may be to utilize fracking to vastly increase access to heat in the Earth's crust. By drilling horizontally once an initial heat-seeking depth is achieved, some researchers believe that electricity generation could be enhanced by a factor of one thousand or more. Startups Geothermix (geothermixenergy.com), Sage Geosystems (www.sagegeosystems.com) and Fervo Energy (www.fervoenergy.com) are working on the technology.

Yet another new technology is "deep geothermal." Quaise Energy (www.quaise.energy), an MIT university spinoff, recently raised $75 million to develop deep geothermal, which extends drilling as far as 12 miles below the Earth's surface. Drillers use standard drill bits to a depth of about three miles, and then switch to a gyrotron, a radio-wave-emitting device, to vaporize rocks and increase drilling speed. Quaise hopes to drill near abandoned coal power plants and convert them to geothermal power, with steam powered turbines capable of generating 300 megawatts of clean electricity. The cost to repurpose a coal plant in this manner would run about $500 million, which is cheaper than building a new geothermal plant.

8) Biomass, Waste-to-Energy, Waste Methane and Biofuels from Algae

Biomass energy is the term describing the conversion of certain types of organic material into usable energy, either by burning it directly or by harvesting combustible gases or liquids. In some cases, it can be referred to as "waste-to-energy," because a common application is the burning of a city's garbage or an industrial plant's production scrap, such as wood chips or sawdust. Agricultural residues, such as rice straw, nutshells or wheat straw, are also useful as biomass fuels. Waste-to-energy plants have been in use in the U.S. for decades, frequently operating in tandem. A significant advantage of waste-to-energy is the fact that it reduces the amount of material placed in overburdened landfills. The production of ethanol or biodiesel is another way to utilize biomass to create fuel.

Today, several factors are creating heightened interest in waste-to-energy. One of the most important aspects of generating electricity in this manner is the fact that burning garbage takes up a lot less space than compacting it in a landfill. Many municipalities are faced with severe restraints and high costs in their landfill operations. Also, industrial sites are extremely interested in capturing their on-site waste and excess heat as a way of generating electricity, sometimes referred to as co-generation. In comparing landfill gas harvesting and waste incineration, a recent study by the Environmental Protection Agency (EPA), the Energy Information Administration and the DOE found incineration to be far more efficient. Incineration produces 590 kilowatt-hours of electricity per ton of waste compared to the 65 kilowatt-hours produced from landfill gas.

Quantities of waste, such as sewage, manure heaps at feedlots and the garbage filling landfills, create large amounts of methane gas as they decompose. One form of biomass energy generation that utilizes this phenomenon has been affectionately named "cow power." In this method of energy production, cow manure is placed in a holding tank, where it is heated to around 100 degrees Fahrenheit. This allows naturally occurring bacteria to break down the material, releasing methane, which is collected and burned in a generator. By this method, the manure from one cow can produce about 1,200 kilowatt-hours per year, meaning ten cows can power an average American house. Not only can cow power produce electricity, it can also be used to produce high quality (and noticeably less smelly) fertilizer.

In late 2019, Dominion Energy, Inc. and Smithfield Foods announced plans to increase their joint venture to $500 million to build anaerobic digesters across the U.S. Facilities are planned for Arizona, Virginia, North Carolina and California. By 2029, the projects collectively are expected to produce approximately 5 billion cubic feet of gas per year.

A leading waste disposal firm, Waste Management, Inc., is capitalizing on waste methane at a handful of the numerous landfills that it operates.

For example, working with energy management firm Ameresco, it is providing waste methane energy to a BMW automobile plant in Spartanburg, South Carolina via a pipeline to a landfill ten miles away. Of the approximately 1,900 landfills in the U.S., about 636 collect methane gas for energy use according to the EPA.

Both bioethanol and biodiesel are considered to be biomass energy sources. Many types of organic fats are currently used worldwide to make biodiesel, including soybean oil, grapeseed oil (the same oil that is commonly sold as canola), palm oil and beef tallow. Unfortunately, the refining of biodiesel is not a sure way to profits. Costs of capital investment are high, and feedstocks, particularly vegetable oils, can be extremely expensive.

From an environmental impact point-of-view, salvaging chicken fat from a meat packing plant to use in fuels may be reasonably efficient. However, dramatically altering the usage of vast swaths of land to grow plants, such as corn, for fuel is another matter. Land displacement for biofuel use has turned into a global problem and a huge controversy. Farmers from the Americas to Brazil to Indonesia have been converting land that was previously used for food agriculture into acreage used for biofuel plant growth. At the same time, farmers elsewhere have been incentivized by high demand in the marketplace to destroy rain forest, woodlands or open plains in order to plant food crops to take up the slack in the market, or to plant high-value plants for biodiesel or bioethanol feedstock.

When woodlands or prairies are cleared and burned to make way for crops, vast amounts of carbon are released into the atmosphere. Among the biggest culprits are farmers clearing rain forest in Indonesia in order to plant palms for the harvesting of palm oil for biodiesel, and those clearing rain forest in Brazil for planting of soy for biodiesel. (Clearing grassland in the U.S. in order to plant corn for bioethanol is another problem.) Studies found that these activities create immense carbon emission problems, which may be far in excess of any carbon saved over the short term by burning a plant-based fuel as opposed to a petroleum-based fuel in cars and trucks.

In June 2022, Chevron completed the acquisition of Renewable Energy Group, a biomass company with 11 refineries that source predominantly from waste products such as used cooking oil or tallow. Chevron spent $3.15 billion to buy the company and plans to acquire additional renewable energy producers.

Landfills are attracting growing attention as potential natural gas producers. As of 2022, Project Assai, a major trash-fed gas plant operated by Archaea Energy, Inc. in Pennsylvania, was producing natural gas at a rate capable of fueling more than 65,000 homes daily. Landfill operator Waste Management, Inc. is spending $825 million on gas projects at its properties. NextEra Energy, Inc., a renewable power company, is investing $1.1 billion for a collection of landfill facilities.

SPOTLIGHT: FastOx Pathfinder
Sierra Energy (www.sierraenergy.com) has tested a waste-to-energy system called the FastOx Pathfinder that already has a $3 million contract from the U.S. Defense Department. The system is based on a modified blast furnace that heats almost any kind of trash to extreme temperatures without combustion. The resulting materials include hydrogen and synthetic natural gas that can be utilized for making ethanol or diesel fuel, or can be burned for electricity.

9) Ethanol Production Soared, But U.S. Federal Subsidy Expires

High gasoline prices, effective lobbying by agricultural and industrial interests, and a growing interest in cutting reliance on imported oil put a high national focus on bioethanol in America in recent years. Corn and other organic materials, including agricultural waste, can be converted into ethanol through the use of engineered bacteria and superenzymes manufactured by biotechnology firms. This trend gave a boost to the biotech, agriculture and alternative energy sectors. At present, corn is almost the exclusive source for bioethanol in America. This is a shift of a crop from use in the food chain to use in the energy chain that is unprecedented in all of agricultural history—a shift that had profound effects on prices of corn for consumers, livestock growers (where corn has long been a traditional animal feed) and food processors.

Ethanol is an alcohol produced by a distilling process similar to that used to produce liquors. A small amount of ethanol is added to much of the gasoline sold in America, and most U.S. autos are capable of burning "E10," a gasoline blend that contains 10% ethanol. E85 is an 85% ethanol blend that may grow in popularity due to a shift in automotive manufacturing.

Yet, despite the millions of vehicles on the road that can run on E85 and billions of dollars in federal subsidies to participating refiners, many oil companies seem unenthusiastic about the adoption of the higher ethanol mix. E85 requires separate gasoline pumps, trucks and storage tanks, as well as substantial cost to the oil companies (the pumps alone cost about $200,000 per gas station to install). The plants needed to create ethanol cost $500 million or more to build. Many drivers who have tried filling up with E85 once revert to regular unleaded when they find as much as a 25% loss in fuel economy when burning the blend.

Ethanol is a very popular fuel source in Brazil. In fact, Brazil is one of the world's largest producers of ethanol, which provides a significant amount of the fuel used in Brazil's cars. This is due to a concerted effort by the government to reduce dependency on petroleum product imports. After getting an initial boost due to government subsidies and fuel tax strategies beginning in 1975, Brazilian producers developed methods (typically using sugar cane) that enable them to produce ethanol at moderate cost. The fact that Brazil's climate is ideally suited for sugarcane is a great asset. Also, sugar cane can be converted with one less step than corn, which is the primary source for American ethanol. Brazilian automobiles are typically equipped with engines that can burn pure ethanol or a blend of gasoline and ethanol. Brazilian car manufacturing plants operated by Ford, GM and Volkswagen all make such cars.

In America, partly in response to the energy crisis of the 1970s, Congress instituted federal ethanol production subsidies in 1979. Corn-based grain ethanol production picked up quickly, and federal subsidies amounted to several billion dollars. The size of these subsidies and environmental concerns about the production of grain ethanol produced a steady howl of protest from observers through the years. Nonetheless, the Clean Air Act of 1990 further boosted ethanol production by increasing the use of ethanol as an additive to gasoline. Meanwhile, the largest producers of ethanol, such as Archer Daniels Midland (ADM), have reaped significant subsidies from Washington for their output. However, Congress allowed the subsidy to expire on December 31, 2011.

In March 2014, the United Nations Intergovernmental Panel on Climate Change released two Working Group reports that questioned biofuels' cost to the environment, the food chain and ultimately their direct and indirect production of harmful emissions. Ethanol production requires enormous amounts of water. To produce one gallon of ethanol, up to four gallons of water are consumed by ethanol refineries. Add in the water needed to grow the corn in the first place, and the number grows to as much as 1,700 gallons of water for each gallon of ethanol. Meanwhile, Brazil has clear-cut as much as 1 million acres of tropical forest per year to produce sugarcane for ethanol.

A bright note for ethanol proponents is an increase in production efficiency, due to improvements in process technology (such as finer corn grinding to release more starch) and improved temperature control of fermentation to optimize yeast productivity. Better enzymes and yeast strains are also boosting output per bushel of corn.

On the negative side, other concerns regarding the use of corn to manufacture ethanol include the fact that a great deal of energy is consumed in planting, reaping and transporting the corn in trucks. In Brazil alone, the devastation of the rainforest and the need to ship ethanol to other countries emits about 50% more carbon than using petroleum fuels, according to agricultural nonprofit Food First.

10) Cellulosic Ethanol Makes Slow Commercial Progress

Traditional grain ethanol is typically made from corn or sugarcane. In contrast to grain ethanol, "cellulosic" ethanol is typically made from agricultural waste like corncobs, wheat husks, stems, stalks and leaves, which are treated with specially engineered enzymes to break the waste down into its component sugars. The sugars (or sucrose) are used to make ethanol. Since agricultural waste is plentiful, turning it into energy seems a good strategy. Cellulosic ethanol can also be made from certain types of plants and grasses.

The trick to cellulosic ethanol production is the creation of efficient enzymes to treat the agricultural waste. Another challenge lies in efficient collection and delivery of cellulosic material to the refinery. It may be more costly to make cellulosic ethanol than to make it from corn. In any event, the U.S. remains far behind Brazil in cost-efficiency, as Brazil's use of sugar cane refined in smaller, nearby biorefineries creates ethanol at much lower costs per gallon.

> **SPOTLIGHT: Biofuels**
> Corn and sugar cane are not the only sources for creating biofuels.
> **Municipal/Agricultural Waste**: Might be cheaply produced but could be in limited supply compared to the billions of gallons of fuel needed in the marketplace.
> **Wood**: Easily harvested and in somewhat healthy supply; however, cellulose can be more difficult to extract from wood than from other biosources.
> **Algae**: The slimy green stuff does have the potential for high yields per acre, but the process for distilling its cellulose is complex, requiring a source of carbon dioxide to permeate the algae.
> **Grasses/Wheat**: Including switchgrass, miscanthus and wheat straw, the supply could be almost limitless. The challenge here is creating efficient methods for harvesting and infrastructure for delivering it to biorefineries.
> **Vegetable Oils**: Including soybean, canola, sunflower, rapeseed, palm or hemp. It is difficult to keep production costs of these oils low.

11) Tidal Power

The enormous potential of harnessing the movement of the tides to provide electrical power is leading to the development of many tidal generating facilities. Much of recent development has been centered in Europe and the UK. One of the largest projects is located in the La Rance estuary in France. Completed in 1966, the project generates 600 million kilowatt-hours per year.

The Orkney Islands off the coast of Scotland rim the Scapa Flow, an underwater formation that is almost ideal for harvesting tidal power and the site of several installations. The Scottish Government hopes to generate 1,600 megawatts of tidal power over the mid-term.

The main benefit of tidal power, in comparison with other forms of renewable energy, is its predictability. The timing and force of tides can be predicted with great accuracy, and thus so can the power produced by a plant. The main drawback of this power source is its high initial equipment cost, which runs many times that of conventional power sources.

In a traditional tidal energy plant, a dam is constructed that opens temporarily in order to capture tides as they flow inward. When the tidal flow has stopped, the dam closes. When the tide goes out, water behind the dam is released which powers a turbine in a manner similar to traditional hydroelectric power generation. These systems work best when there is a dramatic difference, at least 16 feet, between low tide and high tide.

The HS1000 tidal turbine is a radical design from ANDRITZ HYDRO Hammerfest of Norway. It is a tidal mill that looks a lot like a land-based wind turbine. This tidal mill consists of three 30-foot-long blades and weighs 180 tons. This design offers several benefits, including minimal interference with sea life.

ScottishPower Renewables (a subsidiary of wind energy company Iberdrola) received approval from the Scottish Government and is developing a 10-megawatt tidal power array in The Sound of Islay using 10 of the HS1000 tidal turbines. The firm is also testing its tidal turbines at the European Marine Energy Centre (EMEC) in Orkney. Meanwhile, EMEC is partnering with the Energy Research Institute at Nanyang Technological University in Singapore to develop tidal power in Southeast Asia. The partnership is the fifth signed between EMEC and universities and organizations in Asia.

Another tidal power development with potential is the Archimedes Wave Swing (AWS), a large, submersed telescopic cylinder filled with air. Inside is a "floater" that moves up and down as pressure surrounding the cylinder changes due to waves. That movement, which corresponds with the ebb and flow of the tide, is converted to electricity via a linear generator. Each AWS unit is about 39 feet in diameter and has an average output of 2.5 megawatts in a rough sea (producing about 5 gigawatts per year). The system has been tested in a pilot plant off the coast of Portugal. A company called AWS Ocean Energy Ltd. (www.awsocean.com) tested a small-scale model of its ASW-III prototype on Loch Ness in Scotland, and completed a large-scale installation at Lyness Pier, Orkney. The firm's 16-kilowatt AWS converter was created by joining two sub-assemblies in Glasgow, Scotland in 2021. The converter was tested in 2022, generating more than 10 kilowatts of power during a period of moderate wave conditions, with peaks of 80 kilowatts. AWS Ocean Energy says the AWS unit can operate in up to Force 10 gales. More testing is planned for 2023 and beyond.

Another ocean-driven technology uses "wave energy converters," which have been tested in waters near New Jersey, Hawaii, Scotland, England and Western Australia. The converters are semi-submerged cylinders of almost 400 feet in length and more than 11 feet in diameter. The cylinders are jointed and undulate in wave action like snakes. The energy of the wave action is resisted by hydraulic rams in the joints. The rams then pump high-pressure fluid into chambers that feed the fluid to a motor. The motor, in turn, drives a generator that creates electricity. Power from all the joints is transported down an umbilical cable connecting the cylinder to a junction on the sea floor that consolidates the power and sends it to shore via another cable connection. The cylinders are designed to work in concert, connected by mooring lines, forming a wave "farm."

Irish firm OpenHydro installed a 16-meter turbine off the French coast near Paimpol-Brehat in Brittany. Each turbine weighs 850 tons, with enough capacity to power 4,000 French homes. French nuclear technology and defense company DCNS owns a controlling interest in OpenHydro.

Australian company Carnegie Clean Energy (www.carnegiece.com), formerly Carnegie Wave Energy, has developed large buoys using its CETO technology than can generate 240-kilowatts each. Measuring 11-meters across, the buoys are made of steel. They are filled with seawater and foam that allows them to float well below the surface. This is critical to efficient tidal power technology, since equipment that floats on top of the ocean is vulnerable to damage by storms and constant wave battering.

Another breakthrough in wave power is Oregon-based Northwest Energy Innovations' Azura, a 20-kilowatt wave energy converter that absorbs energy through up-and-down wave motion, as well as back-and-forth motion. Azura was undergoing testing at the U.S. Navy's Wave Energy Test Site in Hawaii. Azura consists of a hull submerged at a depth of 30 meters, which is topped on the surface by a float that rotates 360 degrees, reducing mechanical stress and making failures less likely. See www.azurawave.com for more details.

The latest in energy generation underwater is the adoption of inverted wind turbines for use below the surface of the ocean. The turbines are connected to a rotor with variable pitch blades that are powered by ocean currents. Aquantis (www.aquantistech.com), a Santa Barbara, California company, plans to begin deployment of a 200-megawatt field of underwater turbines in the Gulf Stream off the coast of Florida. The Gulf Stream's constant flow may increase cost effectiveness, and a variety of turbine designs may be applicable to sea currents.

For shallower water, Eco Wave Power Ltd. (www.ecowavepower.com) developed 10-foot floating devices that attach to marine structures such as piers and jetties. The devices use the rise and fall of waves to generate electricity. The firm had a 100-kilowatt facility in Gibraltar that was expected to be upgraded and moved to Los Angeles in 2022. Eco Wave Power has an additional pilot program in Israel.

A variation on the tidal theme is energy capture from tidal streams. The technology utilizes underwater turbines similar to wind turbines which can be secured to the seabed or attached in an inverted position to the bottom of a floating platform. The technology is more advanced than wave systems, with installations in the East River in New York City, Canada's Bay of Fundy, and in waters in China, France, Japan, the Netherlands and the UK. Enel Green Power (www.enelgreenpower.com) is active in tidal stream technology, producing three-bladed horizontal-axis turbines. Orbital Marine Power (orbitalmarine.com) developed a floating turbine called Orbital O2. It is a 236-foot turbine anchored near the Orkney Islands in Scotland. The Orbital O2 can power 2,000 homes and offset more than 2,400 tons of carbon per year.

12) Fuel Cell and Hydrogen Power Research Continue/Fuel Cell Cars Enter Market

The fuel cell is nothing new, despite the excitement it is now generating. It has been around since 1839, when Welsh physics professor William Grove created an operating model based on platinum and zinc components. Much later, the U.S. Apollo space program used fuel cells for certain power needs in the Apollo space vehicles that traveled from the Earth to the Moon.

In basic terms, a fuel cell consists of quantities of hydrogen and oxygen separated by a catalyst. Inside the cell, a chemical reaction within the catalyst generates electricity. Byproducts of this reaction include heat and water. Several enhancements to basic fuel cell technology are under research and development at various firms worldwide. These include fuel cell membranes manufactured with advanced nanotechnologies and "solid oxide" technologies that could prove efficient enough to use on aircraft. Another option for fuel cell membranes are those made of hydrocarbon, which cost about one-half a much as membranes using fluorine compounds.

Fuel cells require a steady supply of hydrogen. Therein lies the biggest problem in promoting the widespread use of fuel cells: how to create, transport and store the hydrogen. At present, no one has been able to put a viable plan in place that would create a network of hydrogen fueling stations substantial enough to meet the needs of everyday motorists in the U.S. or anywhere else.

Many current fuel cells burn hydrogen extracted from such sources as gasoline, natural gas or methanol. Each source has its advantages and disadvantages. Unfortunately, burning a hydrocarbon such as oil, natural gas or coal to produce the energy necessary to create hydrogen results in unwanted emissions. Ideally, hydrogen would be created using renewable, non-polluting means, such as solar power or wind power. Also, nuclear or renewable sources could be used to generate electricity that would be used to extract hydrogen molecules from water.

The potential market for fuel cells encompasses diverse uses in fixed applications (such as providing an electric generating plant for a home or a neighborhood), portable systems (such as portable generators for construction sites) or completely mobile uses (powering anything from small hand-held devices to automobiles). The likely advantages of fuel cells as clean, efficient energy sources are enormous. The fuel cell itself is a proven technology—fuel cells are already in use, powering a U.S. Post Office in Alaska, for example. (This project, in Chugach, Alaska, is the result of a joint venture between the local electric association and the U.S. Postal Service to install a one-megawatt fuel cell facility.) Tiny fuel cells are also on the market for use in powering cellular phones and laptop computers.

Oil companies including BP PLC, Royal Dutch Shell PLC and TotalEnergies SE are spending millions of dollars on green hydrogen projects. The Hydrogen Council reported 244 large-scale green hydrogen projects planned as of June 2021.

In July 2020, Hanwha Energy (www.hanwha.com) completed a 114-fuel cell plant in the Daesan Industrial Complex in Seosan, Korea with a capacity of up to 400,000 megawatts of electricity per year. It was the largest industrial hydrogen fuel cell plant in the world to date.

In Bridgeport, Connecticut, a 14.9-megawatt fuel-cell complex generates enough electricity to power 15,000 homes (out of a total 51,000 in the city). In April 2015, a 1.4-megawatt cell went online at the University of Bridgeport.

U.S. industrial gas supplier Air Products & Chemicals (www.airproducts.com) built a "green hydrogen" plant in Saudi Arabia. Hydrogen is manufactured utilizing electricity from nearby wind and solar farms. This plant has a capacity of four gigawatts. Similar green hydrogen plants are under development elsewhere in the world.

GM invested $1 billion in fuel cell vehicle research. The company leased 199 fuel cell-equipped Equinox crossover vehicles to customers as a test called Project Driveway in three U.S. markets, starting in early 2008. Despite the setback of the financial problems of 2008-09 that led to bankruptcy and a government bailout, GM managed to keep Project Driveway going, in which more than 5,000 drivers provided feedback on Chevrolet Equinox FCV sedans. Some of those vehicles accumulated more than 120,000 miles each. Meanwhile, Hyundai Motor Co. began limited sales of a hydrogen-powered SUV in California in mid-2014.

Toyota unveiled a fuel cell car prototype at the Tokyo automobile show in November 2013. The vehicle, a $57,500 FVC sedan with a 312-mile range called the Mirai, saw delivery of a small number of vehicles in Japan and in California in the U.S. in 2015.

The trucking industry is becoming a new market for hydrogen-fueled transportation. Nikola Corp. (nikolamotor.com) designs and manufactures heavy-duty commercial battery-electric vehicles (BEV) and fuel cell electric vehicles (FCEV). The company was founded in 2015, and is headquartered in Phoenix, Arizona with manufacturing facilities in Arizona and in Germany. Trucking firm U.S. Xpress Enterprises has made reservations for possible future purchases from Nikola.

$38 billion is being invested by a consortium of South Korean conglomerates (including Hyundai) in hydrogen projects by 2030. For the 2022 Beijing Winter Olympics, China planned to have hundreds of hydrogen-powered buses on the roads.

The aviation industry (a massive user of fossil fuels) is also experimenting with hydrogen. Unlike electric batteries, which are too heavy at present to be feasible in long-range aircraft, hydrogen delivers power even more efficiently than jet fuel when calculated by weight. Jet fuel delivers 40 megajoules per kilogram of weight, while hydrogen delivers 140 megajoules per kilogram. Universal Hydrogen (hydrogen.aero) and ZeroAvia (www.zeroavia.com) are using hydrogen fuel cells to power light and regional aircraft.

> **SPOTLIGHT: Sunhydrogen, Inc.**
> Sunhydrogen, Inc. (www.sunhydrogen.com) is a pioneer in large scale solar-to-hydrogen plants. It states that it has developed a "low-cost method" to harness solar cells to power hydrolysis—splitting water molecules so that hydrogen and oxygen are separated. Part of the firm's technology is based on nanotechnology. See the YouTube video: www.youtube.com/watch?v=dkIDRZH273A.

Yet another breakthrough is the ability for wind turbines to create the energy needed to produce hydrogen. (A strategy referred to as "green hydrogen.") Siemens Gamesa Renewable Energy is working with its parent company, Siemens Energy, to develop the technology onshore in Denmark. Offshore projects are also under consideration.

A looming issue is that many people still have concerns about the safety of hydrogen. Naturally gaseous at room temperature, storing hydrogen involves using pressurized tanks that can leak and, if punctured, could cause explosions. It is also difficult to store enough hydrogen in a vehicle to take it the 300+ miles that drivers are used to getting on a tank of gasoline. To do so, hydrogen must be compressed to 10,000 pounds per square inch and stored on board in bulky pressure tanks.

> **SPOTLIGHT: Green Hydrogen**
> Hydrogen is one of the most abundant substances on Earth, and can readily be used as a clean burning fuel. Challenges facing the technology include first generating the hydrogen, and then storing it under pressure for future use. Green hydrogen is made by using renewable energy sources (such as solar or wind) to split water into hydrogen and oxygen, instead of creating hydrogen from fossil fuels (known as gray or blue hydrogen). The process is known as electrolysis, and it is more expensive than producing gray or blue hydrogen. However, green hydrogen could provide long-term storage for renewable energy. Recent hikes in natural gas prices, exacerbated by the war in Ukraine, is spurring many countries to pursue new energy sources. Wood Mackenzie reported a 50-fold increase in announced green hydrogen projects in the second half of 2021. BP PLC is a 40.5% stake holder in a $30 billion green hydrogen project in Australia called the Asian Renewable Energy Hub. The project will cover 2,500 square miles in the Outback and generate up to 26 gigawatts of power (about a third of the total power generated in Australia in all of 2020).

> The South African country of Namibia, famous for strong winds and sunlight, created a project development company called Hyphen Hydrogen Energy (Pty) Ltd. to create and operate green hydrogen production facilities, including a $9.4 billion project that it is hoped will produce 300,000 metric tons per year from five gigawatts of renewable energy by 2030.

13) Electric Cars and Plug-in Hybrids (PHEVs) to See Massive New Investments by Auto Makers

By 2021, most automotive manufacturers in the U.S. and around the world were investing heavily in new electric vehicles of all types. This includes fully electric cars and trucks as well as hybrids. Plug-in hybrids (PHEVs) are similar to standard hybrids, but they enable the owner the option of plugging-in at home overnight to recharge the battery. This will eliminate the need to run the car's gasoline engine, using only battery power as long as the relatively short range isn't exceeded. (Standard hybrids recharge only by running the gasoline-powered side of the car, and by drawing on the drag produced by using the brakes.)

According to the U.S. Bureau of Transportation Statistics, sales of hybrid electric vehicles rose from 380,794 in 2019 to 454,890 in 2020. Sales of all-electric vehicles rose from 233,822 in 2019 to 240,053 in 2020. Sales of PHEVs fell from 85,791 in 2019 to 66,157.

While sales have grown overall, electric cars accounted for only 5.3% of 2020's vehicle sales in the U.S. However, that is changing rapidly. Roughly 630,000 all-electric or plug-in hybrid vehicles were registered in the U.S. during 2021, according to the Energy Information Agency. The state of California (America's largest car market) announced the ban of the sale of gasoline-powered vehicles by 2035.

Worldwide, there were about 16.5 million electric and plug-in hybrid cars on the road in 2021, about three times the number of 2018. This growth, plus government mandates and incentives, is spurring global car manufacturers to invest billions in electric vehicle and battery development over the mid-term. General Motors (GM) is investing $27 billion in electric and autonomous technology (including 20 new electric models by 2023). New vehicles include an all-electric Hummer SUV. GM is building a $2.3 billion battery plant in partnership with LG Chem Ltd. in Ohio and has plans for a third electric truck plant. In addition, GM is partnering with Honda to jointly develop new vehicles including a driverless shuttle and two electric Honda vehicles using GM's technology. The company hopes to reach sales of 400,000 electric vehicles in North America in 2022, up from only 25,000 EVs in 2021.

Electric pickups are garnering the lion's share of EV attention in the U.S. Plug-in versions of the Chevy Silverado and the Ford F-150 have hit the market. Production of the $105,000 fully loaded electric Silverado sold out in 12 minutes in 2021, while Ford logged more than 200,000 customers who spent $100 to reserve the electric F-150 Lightning pickup before it hit the market in the spring of 2022. Tesla is working on its Cybertruck while Rivian Automotive hoped to deliver the first of its R1T pickups by late 2022 or early 2023.

Ford is launching new electric models, including a Mustang SUV. In September 2021, Ford announced that it is partnering with South Korean firm SK Innovation to invest $11.4 billion to build an electric F-150 assembly plant and three battery plants in the United States in Kentucky and Tennessee. Ford now expects to have 40% to 50% of its global vehicle volume to be all-electric by 2030, up from its prior forecast of 40%. These new plants are expected to open by 2025. Meanwhile, U.S. auto manufacturers are launching electric pickup trucks in large numbers.

SPOTLIGHT: EVs Transform Detroit
The shift away from internal combustion engines (ICEs) is changing the face of automotive manufacturing in America and elsewhere. Vehicles that run on batteries require fewer parts than ICEs, making them less labor intensive to produce (needing about 30% fewer manufacturing workhours from start to finish). This adversely impacts traditional automotive manufacturing jobs. On the other hand, EVs rely on electrical engineers, software developers and other technicians and researchers, which may offset some of the job losses. Plants are undergoing major conversions. For example, GM's Factory Zero, a renamed 40-year-old plant in Hamtramck, received $2.2 billion in funding to revamp facilities and equipment to build the Chevrolet Silverado and the GMC Hummer electric pickups. Ford invested $700 million to retool its part of its Rouge plant to build the F-150 Lightning truck and $185 million to build a battery laboratory called Ford Ion Park. The state of Michigan is providing grants for educational groups to develop training curriculums for EV occupations.

Leading tech companies want to be an integral part of the EV revolution as well. Apple and Google are investing in EV-focused technology training programs.

Mercedes-Benz announced plans to go all electric by 2030, investing more than $47 billion in this strategy over the mid-term. Volkswagen is investing in standardizing electric components such as batteries and software across its brands, including Audi and Porsche. It is investing $40 billion with the goal of selling 28 million electric cars worldwide by 2028.

Tesla is the rock star of the electric car industry. Its sales have been impressive, despite the relatively high price of its initial models, and the company's own stock has soared, thrilling early investors. Tesla's high-end Model S sedan has a range of 370 miles per charge and can go from zero to 60 miles per hour in 2.4 seconds. It also offers the Model X SUV and has a Model Y compact crossover that was released in 2020. The Model 3 sedan, first released in 2017, has a base price significantly lower than its luxury models. The company has also announced plans to launch an electric pickup truck.

A Shanghai Tesla plant opened in record time and is producing Model 3 sedans and a Model Y crossover designed specifically for the Chinese market. The company also has a head start on infrastructure for charging stations. As of September 2021, Tesla's Supercharger network (where Tesla owners can get a rapid recharge of batteries) had more than 25,000 stations worldwide, including 1,120 in the U.S. Another player in this sector, Electrify America, had 635 charging stations in operation by July 2021. The U.S. Government is providing massive financial incentives to qualified installations of new charging stations in America, both in homes and at commercial facilities.

In addition, Tesla has hopes to develop heavy-duty electric trucks capable of hauling major loads up to 600 miles at a price of $180,000 (about twice what a traditional diesel-powered truck costs). Other firms such as Cummins, are developing their own electric heavy trucks. Daimler delivered its first Freightliner eCascadia all-electric semi in August 2019. The problem with electrifying 18-wheeled trucks is weight. A diesel-powered engine weighs about two tons while an electric version with its batteries would weigh between four and nine tons, depending on range.

Volvo, which is owned by China's Geely Holding Group, started taking orders for its all-electric XC40 SUV in late 2019. It joined six other new Volvo electric models. Going forward, all cars manufactured by Volvo will be either all-electric or hybrids.

Stellantis NV, a firm created by the merger of Fiat Chrysler Automobiles NV and PSA Group, is investing more than $35.5 billion through 2025 on new plug-in models. Stellantis plans to focus on battery development and sourcing.

China has imposed an increasingly strict mandate boosting zero-emission vehicles due to a massive air pollution problem. For many years, foreign auto makers were required to operate in China through joint ventures with Chinese firms. This restriction was lifted for the development if electric vehicles in 2018 and is expected to be lifted for other vehicles by 2022. Tesla was the first foreign car maker to take advantage of the change. It began exporting is China-made Model 3 to several EU countries in late 2020. The nation of India is also boosting sales of electric vehicles. India, China and the EU are all likely to see very high ratios of electric car sales by 2030.

Improvements in EV technology are enabling the development of larger electric vehicles. According to AlixPartners, by 2022, there will be 78 plug-in hybrid and battery-electric SUVs on the market, compared to 38 in 2019.

Retail giant Amazon is purchasing electric delivery vehicles from Rivian Automotive. Amazon hopes to have 100,000 EVs on the road by 2030.

Electric vans are also being developed. GM created a new company, BrightDrop, in early 2021 to manufacture the vehicles. FedEx and Verizon were early customers. Startup electric van manufacturer Canoo hopes to launch an electric minivan.

Yet another facet to the EV industry is the relative ease of production compared to that of internal combustion engines. According to Volkswagen, EV production takes 30% less effort that internal combustion vehicles. Ford concurs, saying that the simplified production of EVs could lead to a 30% reduction in labor hours per vehicle (which is not good news for the United Autoworkers Union).

Internet Research Tip: Electric Cars
For the latest on electric car manufacturers see:
Electric Drive Transportation Association, www.goelectricdrive.org
Global Electric Motorcars, www.gemcar.com
Tesla Motors, www.teslamotors.com

14) Major Research and Advancements in Lithium Batteries/Tesla and Panasonic Operate the Gigafactory

There remain many obstacles to all-electric vehicles: a shortage of battery charging stations available to the driving public, battery cost and driving range. Another challenge is the increasing demand for lithium. Cobalt is also used in lithium-ion batteries.

There is concern as to whether lithium producers can keep up with demand. Most manufacturers enter into long-term contracts with lithium miners including Ganfreng Lithium, Kidman Resources, Nemaska Lithium and Pilbara Minerals. Ganfreng, for example, had long-term contracts with Tesla, BMW and Volkswagen as of 2019. Chilean lithium producer SQM reported that global lithium demand was expected to grow by at least 20% in 2019 compared to 2018's approximately 270,000 metric tons.

For electrics to gain such high market share, there are several logistical challenges. Electric vehicles in such massive numbers would not only require vastly higher numbers of charging stations but could also require a very significant increase in the generation and distribution of electricity.

The biggest news in advanced batteries for automobiles is being made at Tesla, the U.S.-based maker of high end, all-electric vehicles. Tesla's automobiles are unique on several counts. To begin with, the firm has been very successful in attracting buyers for its Model S sedan and Model X crossover, as well as its Model 3, launched in 2017. Next, Tesla's unique technology ties together thousands of small lithium-ion batteries, similar to cellphone batteries, in each car, as opposed to the normal use of one or two giant batteries per vehicle. This has enabled Tesla's cars to have more power and a range in the neighborhood of 200 to 300 miles per charge. Tesla has also increased the power density of its batteries, meaning more storage per kilogram.

In 2014, Tesla broke ground on a massive battery factory, known as the Gigafactory, near Reno, Nevada. The long-term plan is for a 10 million square foot plant capable of manufacturing enough batteries to power 500,000 cars per year. The factory had a soft opening in 2016 and began commercial production in early 2017. A facility known as Gigafactory 2 in the state of New York manufactures solar panels and solar roof tiles.

The company's next major project was the construction of the world's largest lithium-ion system in Australia. The 100-megawatt system will collect power from a wind farm built by Neoen that will be three times more powerful than any other battery system. CEO Elon Musk made headlines when announcing the project, promising to complete it within 100 days of signing an agreement or it would be paid for with $50 million of his own money. The battery bank was completed in November 2017, 40 days before deadline, and will supply power to more than 30,000 homes. This was a significant proof-of-concept for large-scale energy storage systems.

Toyota is spending $9 million to build lithium-ion battery manufacturing plants in several locations around the world. The company plans to have 10 production lines in place by 2025 (a single plant can house several production lines).

Mitsubishi Hitachi Power Systems is working on battery technology for a 1,000-watt project in Utah. In the UK, ScottishPower is investing $7.2 billion between 2018 and 2022 on renewable energy, battery storage and grid upgrades. Likewise, the World Bank Group is investing $1 billion in battery projects. Overall spending on high-capacity batteries is expected to grow six-fold between 2019 and 2024, reaching $71 billion.

Guidehouse Insights estimated that U.S. businesses would deploy 220 megawatts of energy storage at or near their facilities in 2021, up from 77 megawatts in 2020. Capital Dynamics, a Swiss asset manager, broke ground in mid-2020 in Nevada on a new battery system that will store solar power and manage electricity costs for Switch, Inc., a data-center firm. Switch will use to power to cool a 1.3 million square foot data center at a cost of about five cents per kilowatt hour, several cents less than purchasing power from NV Energy, the local utility. The batteries are part of Capital Dynamics' $1.3 billion solar power storage portfolio.

A Chinese leader in advanced batteries is BYD Company Limited. BYD is already a global leader in contract manufacturing of batteries and handsets for mobile phones. For example, BYD manufactures batteries for iPhones and iPods.

However, another Chinese leader in battery manufacturing is CATL (Contemporary Amperex Technology Ltd). Its strategy includes a vast increase in production capacity through the opening of a new megafactory in southeast China.

South Korea firms plan to dramatically boost their share of the electric vehicle batter market in the U.S. Three companies, LG Energy, SK Innovation and Samsung SDI, are collectively investing $15 billion to expand production in the U.S. As of 2022, the three firms provided about one-tenth of EV battery capacity in the U.S. The firms plan to increase their market share to 70% by 2025, according to the Korea Battery Industry Association.

There is an advanced battery technology called lithium ferrophosphate (LFP) which has a relatively lower risk of catching fire and uses iron instead of cobalt or nickel, making it cheaper to produce. Tesla is using the battery in one version of its Model 3 made in China.

Yet another battery technology under development is a solid-state battery, which has the potential to delivery faster charging times and is far less flammable than lithium-ion batteries. Toyota is working in-house on the technology, while Volkswagen, Ford and BMW are backing solid-state battery startups. Development of solid-state batteries is in the early stages, with perhaps a decade of research and development needed to produce a viable battery.

The holy grail of electric car research is the development of battery technology that will enable a car to go 400 to 500 miles between recharges, while maintaining a competitive retail price for the car. The expensive Tesla Model S already claims a relatively long range of 348 miles.

Wireless Battery Charging for Electric Buses
In the city of Gumi, South Korea, a small number of electric buses are utilizing exciting new technology that enables to them to recharge their batteries, while moving or parked, wirelessly—that is, without being plugged in. The technology is capable of focusing an electromagnetic field towards a specific direction (the bus). The field recharges the battery with little energy loss during transmission. While expensive (Gumi's small system cost nearly $5 million, including two advanced, carbon fiber buses), the technology is very promising as a means of promoting zero-emission public transit.

IBM is working on a radical new lithium battery that could be far lighter than current batteries and have a vehicle range of as much as 500 miles. The Battery 500 Project is researching a lithium-air battery that, instead of shuttling ions back and forth between two metal electrodes, moves them between one metal electrode and air. The concept is similar to zinc-air batteries used to power hearing aids. The problem is that zinc-air batteries are not rechargeable and limited to a very small size.

Samsung Electronics is working to incorporate graphene into a lithium-ion battery. This ultra-thin form of carbon could increase a battery's capacity by as much as 45% and significantly reduce recharging time.

Startups including Sila Nanotechnologies (silanano.com), Angstron Materials (a unit of Global Graphene Group, www.theglobalgraphenegroup.com), Enovix (enovix.com) and Enevate (www.enevate.com) produce materials for lithium-silicon batteries which have the potential to increase capacity by as much as 40%. German automaker BMW plans to use Sila's silicon anode technology in a plug-in electric vehicle by 2023.

Innolith AG (innolith.com), a Swiss startup, announced in 2019 that it had built the world's first rechargeable battery capable of powering a vehicle for more than 600 miles between charges. The firm hopes to have the battery commercially available by 2022.

> **Top Producers of Lithium-Ion Batteries Include:**
> Panasonic Corporation, www.panasonic.com
> LG Chem. www.lgchem.com
> Samsung SDI Co., www.samsungsdi.com
> BYD, www.byd.com
> CATL, www.catlbattery.com

15) Natural Gas-Powered Vehicles Gain in Popularity/Long Term Potential Is Bright Thanks to Low Shale Gas Prices

Natural gas vehicles (NGVs), that is cars and trucks that run on either compressed natural gas (CNG) or liquid natural gas (LNG), are already in use around the world, especially in municipal fleets and buses. NGV Global's Natural Gas Vehicle Knowledge Base reported more than 30 million NGVs worldwide by year end 2021. A large percentage of all new public transit buses run on natural gas, and 60% of the 8,000 new trash trucks sold annually in the U.S. run on CNG.

Natural gas is an attractive fuel for vehicles, not only because it enjoys a highly developed production and pipeline infrastructure, but also because it is economically and environmentally friendly. While initially costing substantially more per vehicle than standard fuel equivalents, natural gas engines save 30% or more on fuel costs, making the investment potentially very worthwhile over the long term, especially for commercial vehicles that drive long total distances each year. Emissions are significantly lower overall and have much lower concentrations of polluting particles and harmful gases. Recognizing the possible economic benefits, UPS has put natural gas trucks in service to haul its packages, including test trucks running on compressed natural gas, liquefied natural gas or propane. GE, FedEx, AT&T, PepsiCo, Budweiser and Waste Management have converted parts of their fleets to natural gas as well.

As for LNG, Shell Oil is helping to install LNG filling units at dozens of Travel Centers of America and Petro Stopping Center truck stop locations on Interstate highways in the U.S., aimed at the long-haul truck market. Shell is interested also in greater use of LNG for trains and ships in America.

Some proponents, including Clean Energy Fuels, a company that installs natural gas fueling stations, believe natural gas is a viable alternative for diesel fuel for semi-trailer trucks. Unlike switching to electric batteries or fuel cells, natural gas-powered trucks that travel primarily on major highways would not need as many new fueling stations. Clean Energy Fuels had more than 570 LNG and/or CNG fueling stations in 2022, across the U.S. and in British Columbia, Canada.

There are detractors who say that natural gas is as bad a pollutant as crude oil. However, the U.S. Department of Energy sponsored a "well-to-wheel" study which found that total emissions related to natural gas were 6% to 11% lower than gasoline. Another report by the nonprofit Center for Climate and Energy Solutions found that LNG reduces lifecycle carbon emissions by 13% compared with gasoline, and CNG lowers them by 29%.

Up until recently, cost was a factor when considering trucks powered by natural gas, since they were as much as $80,000 more expensive than diesel models. However, costs are dropping, and more filling stations were opening, making it possible for 18-wheel trucks to operate with one tank (as opposed to the two that used to be necessary for the long trips between refueling stations). New LNG heavy trucks are expected to go for $30,000 to $40,000 more than diesels, which can be made up in fuel costs savings within one year for heavily used trucks.

Truck manufacturers are taking notice of the trend. New natural gas engines are hitting the market such several engine options from Cummins Westport, Inc. Heavy duty truck manufacturers Navistar and Volvo are producing 13-liter and 14-liter LNG-fueled engines.

16) Homes and Commercial Buildings Seek Green Certification

In a growing trend, many homebuilders across the U.S. are constructing homes in accordance with the National Association of Home Builders' (NAHB) "green" specifications. The NAHB's green specifications require resource-efficient design, construction and operation, focusing on environmentally friendly materials. An effort to save energy and reduce waste is spurring this trend. In addition, local building codes in many cities, such as Houston, Texas, are requiring that greater energy efficiency be incorporated in designs before a building permit will be issued.

There are several advantages to building along eco-sensitive lines. Lower operating costs are incurred because buildings built with highly energy-efficient components have superior insulation and require less heating and/or cooling. These practices include the use of oriented strand board instead of plywood; vinyl and fiber-cement sidings instead of wood products; and well insulated foundations, windows and doors. Heating and cooling equipment with greater efficiency is being installed, as well as dishwashers, refrigerators and washing machines that use between 40% and 70% less energy than their 1970s counterparts. Some builders are opting for high efficiency geothermal heating and cooling, while some home and building owners want solar electricity generation.

In addition to energy concerns, plumbing and water efficiency are vital goals in green buildings. This trend will accelerate due to deep concerns about the availability of water in populous regions ranging from California to China. Wastewater heat recovery systems use wastewater to heat incoming water. Toilets are more efficient. Current models use a mere 1.28 gallons of water per flush, as opposed to four gallons in the 70's. Landscaping is likewise being designed for much lower water usage.

The U.S. Environmental Protection Agency (EPA) established the WaterSense certification, a voluntary program to promote water-efficient products and services. For example, WaterSense certifies low-flow toilets that use a mere 1.28 gallons per flush, creates standards for bathroom-sink faucets that flow at no more than 1.5 gallons per minute and offers a certification program for irrigation companies that use water-efficient practices.

The main disadvantage is that green building is more expensive than traditional construction methods. Added building costs often reach 10% to 20% and more per home; however, some homebuyers are willing to pay the increased price for future savings on utilities and maintenance. As energy prices increased over recent decades, builders became more amenable to constructing homes with energy-savings measures. In addition, some consumers are inclined to spend more when they feel they are buying environmentally friendly products, including homes. (Marketing analysts refer to this segment as "LOHAS," a term that stands for "Lifestyles of Health and Sustainability." It refers to consumers who choose to purchase items that are natural, organic, less polluting and so forth. Such consumers may also prefer products powered by alternative energy, such as hybrid cars.)

The U.S. government and all 50 states offer tax incentives in varying amounts to builders using solar technology. Zero Energy Design ("ZED") is slowly catching on. A handful of "zero energy homes ("ZEH")" that produce approximately as much electricity as they use are being built.

Internet Research Tip, Zero Energy Homes:
ZeroEnergy Design zeroenergy.com
Passive House Institute www.phius.org/home-page
HomeInnovation Research Labs
www.homeinnovation.com

By installing photovoltaic panels or other renewable sources to generate electricity and using improved insulation and energy-efficient appliances and lighting, the zero-energy goal may be achieved, at least in sunny climates such as those in the American West and Southwest. The state of California revised its energy efficiency requirements recently, which took effect in 2014. Requirements include solar panels, hot water pipe insulation and the verification by an independent inspector that all air conditioning units are properly installed for maximum efficiency. The state code goes a step farther, recommending whole-house fans to displace warm air with cooler night air in the summer seasons, improved windows and better insulation. State regulators estimate that these changes will make residential and commercial buildings between 25% and 30% more energy efficient.

Researchers at the University of Colorado developed a film in 2017 that can cool buildings without the use of refrigerants such as hydrofluorocarbons. The film uses radiative cooling, a process that converts unwanted heat into infrared of a specific wavelength that can be safely released into the atmosphere. Transparent polymethylpentene is mixed with tiny glass beads and backed with a silver lining. When stretched across a roof, the silver lining on the bottom of the film reflects light back through the plastic, and the glass beads emit the collected heat when they reach a diameter of about eight microns. The research team estimates that 65 square feet of film could reduce an average American home's internal temperature to 68 degrees Fahrenheit when it is 98 degrees outside.

In the commercial sector, businesses may have several reasons to build greener, more energy-efficient buildings. To begin with, long-term operating costs will be lower, which will likely more than offset higher construction costs. Next, many companies see great public relations benefit in the ability to state that their new factory or headquarters building is environmentally friendly. Many office buildings, both public and private, are featuring alternative energy systems, ultra-high-efficiency heating and cooling, or high-efficiency lighting. In California, many public structures are incorporating solar power generation.

Even building maintenance is getting involved—building owners are finding that they can save huge amounts of money by scheduling janitorial service during the day, instead of the usual after-hours, after-dark schedule. In this manner, there is no need to leave lighting, heating or cooling running late at night for the cleaning crews.

An exemplary green office building is Bank of America Tower (formerly One Bryant Park), a 54-story skyscraper on the Avenue of the Americas in New York City. The $1.2-billion project is constructed largely of recycled and recyclable materials. Rainwater and wastewater is collected and reused, and a lighting and dimming system reduces electrical light levels when daylight is available. The building supplies about 70% of its own energy needs with an on-site natural gas burning power plant. It was the first skyscraper to rate platinum certification by adhering to the Leadership in Energy and Environmental Design (LEED) standards, set by the U.S. Green Building Council in 2000 (see www.usgbc.org).

The Pearl River Tower, a 71-story skyscraper in Guangzhou, China, was designed to be one of the first major zero-energy buildings. Designed by Chicago architecture firm SOM, the tower was planned to be 58% more energy efficient than traditional skyscrapers by using solar roof panels, novel wind turbines embedded in four openings spaced throughout the tower and walls with eight-inch air gaps that trap heat which then rises to power heat exchangers for use in cooling systems. The building encompasses about 2.3 million square feet of floor space.

A growing number of buildings are being retrofitted to use energy more efficiently. One example is the initiative underway at Citigroup, Inc. The banking firm is turning off lobby escalators, incorporating more natural light and using recycled materials in dozens of its properties around the world. Citigroup says it can save as much as $1 per square foot of building per year by making its offices more efficient. Elsewhere, Google, Inc. installed a solar rooftop at its California headquarters.

LEED standards have been adopted by companies such as Ford, Pfizer, Nestlé and Toyota, which have all built LEED-certified structures in the U.S. LEED is not without competition. Another green verification program called Green Globes is backed by the Green Building Initiative in the U.S. Green Building Initiative is a group led by a former timber company executive and funded by several timber and wood products firms. Several U.S. states have adopted Green Globes guidelines instead of those supported by LEED for government-subsidized building projects. In Canada, a version of Green Globes for existing buildings is overseen by the Building Owners and Managers Association of Canada (BOMA Canada) under the brand "BOMA Best." Green Globes is more wood friendly than LEED, which is not surprising considering the involvement of the timber industry. It promotes the use of wood and wood products in construction with fewer restrictions than LEED, which approves of wood if it comes from timber grown under sustainable forestry practices approved by the Forest Stewardship Council, an international accrediting group.

In one ambitious project, a $30 million office building in Seattle, Washington spent its first year in a kind of sustainability test. The Living Building Challenge (living-future.org) established and overseen by the International Living Future Institute, will measure the building's sustainability in seven areas: site, water, energy, health, materials, equity and beauty. Those areas were tested by a list of 20 requirements such as net zero use of water and energy, operable windows and car free living. The new six-story building in Seattle is called Bullitt Center.

Retail giant Walmart has attained remarkable achievements in reducing energy use in stores, cutting waste in packaging and increasing the efficiency of its massive trucking and distribution system. It recently announced a goal to double the generation of solar energy on the roof tops of its buildings from 2013 through 2020, when it hopes to be generating 7 billion kWh of renewable energy. Its 2020 commitments will save approximately $1 billion yearly in energy costs. Walmart announced a collaboration with ENGIE North America in 2021 for more than 500 megawatts of wind generated electricity for use in its stores, clubs and distribution centers in Texas, South Dakota and Oklahoma. The firm ultimately hopes to be 100% powered by renewable energy by 2035.

> **SPOTLIGHT: Solar Power Direct from Roofing Shingles**
>
> Dow Chemical has invested $100 million (plus a $10 million grant from the Department of Energy) in researching new plastic photovoltaic roof panels using thin film solar cells. The product, called Powerhouse, costs a homeowner about $31,000, after government subsidies and tax rebates, for approximately 3,000 square feet of roofing material. This compares to about $12,000 for traditional asphalt shingles, but Dow claims that homeowners will save $76,200 in energy costs over 25 years and increase a home's value by $22,000. In addition, the installation of these shingles may qualify for tax credits.

17) Smart Electric Grid Technologies Are Adopted

The Grid: In the U.S., the networks of local electric lines that businesses and consumers depend on every day are connected with and interdependent upon a national system of major lines, power plants and controllers collectively called "the grid." The grid is divided into three major regions, named East, West and Texas. These regions are also known as "interconnects." In total, the grid is a compendium of about 7,000 power plants sending electricity across 450,000 miles of transmission lines and 2.5 million feeder lines, all managed by 3,300 utilities.

The grid's three interconnects are broken down into about 120 control areas, but operators of those control areas have very little authority beyond making requests (but not demands) of utilities participating within their areas. Unfortunately, much of this grid was designed and constructed with technology developed in the 1950s and 1960s, and it was never intended to carry the amazing amount of power that today's electricity-hungry Americans consume. Simply put, much of the grid is out of date.

When a local utility system needs more power than it is generating, it can draw upon the grid. (In fact, many utility companies in America have no generating capacity at all and draw all of their power from the grid and then resell it to end users.) Conversely, when a generating system is producing more power than is needed locally, it can push power into the grid for other areas to use.

Since electricity cannot be easily stored in large volume for future use, the grid is absolutely vital in smoothing out the fluctuations that occur in supply and demand. Unfortunately, the grid suffers from a long list of inadequacies. For example, about 6% of the energy pushed into the grid is lost during transmission, according to the U.S. Energy Information Administration. Also, the grid has bottlenecks, or distribution squeezes, particularly in densely populated areas like New York City and San Francisco. This means that utilities cannot always get all of the electricity they need in order to meet local demand, and blackouts or shortages occur. Today, the rapid growth in renewable power generation is placing new types of strain on the grid, as wind and solar plants that are constructed in remote locations require significant extensions of major power lines in order to get their electricity into the grid for distribution.

In late 2021, President Biden signed a $1 trillion+ "infrastructure" reconciliation bill into law, of which $73 billion is allocated for grid updates, including a $2.5 billion Transmission Facilitation Program. The goal is to modernize the grid, enabling it to carry more power from renewable sources. The Biden administration has a net-zero emissions goal for the U.S. by 2050. However, to meet that goal, electricity transmission systems will have to expand by 60% by the end of 2030 (at a cost of as much as $360 billion , and possibly triple in capacity by 2050 (at a cost of $2.4 trillion), according to research from Princeton University. This translates into thousands of miles of new transmission lines to connect widely spaced wind and solar farms and hydroelectric plants. It remains to be seen whether or not this immense task will be accomplished in a timely or cost-effective manner.

Building Smarter Grids and Microgrids for Distributed Power: The utilities industry is pushing its own vision of the grid's future, via the respected Electric Power Research Institute (EPRI, www.epri.com), an organization of members representing more than 90% of the electricity generated and delivered in the U.S. EPRI envisions creating an environment in which utilities are encouraged to invest heavily in new transmission technologies. Part of its plan is aimed at developing constant communication among the systems pushing power to, and pulling power from, the grid. EPRI hopes the grid will become a self-repairing, intelligent, digital electricity delivery system. As a

result, a system breakdown in one area might be compensated for by users or producers elsewhere, aborting potential blackout situations.

The electric industry, encouraged by the Department of Energy, is slowly moving toward a "smart grid," by using state-of-the-art digital switches and sensors to monitor and manage the grid—a vast improvement over today's equipment. Congress passed Title XIII of the Energy Independence and Security Act (EISA). Several sections of this act are aimed at boosting a national smart grid with interoperability among regions. Such a smart grid would incorporate sensors throughout the entire delivery system, employ instant communications and computing power and use solid-state power electronics to sense and, where needed, control power flows and resolve disturbances instantly. The upgraded system would have the ability to read and diagnose problems. It would be self-repairing, by automatically isolating affected areas and re-routing power to keep the rest of the system running. Another advantage of this smart grid is that it would be able to seamlessly integrate an array of locally installed, distributed power sources, such as fuel cells and solar power, with traditional central-station power generation.

Internet Research Tips:
The GridWise Alliance, www.gridwise.org, is a consortium of public and private utility and energy companies that supports a stronger electricity grid. Members include General Electric (GE), IBM, Duke Energy and Cisco Systems.

The U.S. Department of Energy offers links to a large number of resources from its Smart Grid web page: www.energy.gov/oe/services/technology-development/smart-grid.

18) The Energy Industry Invests in Storage Battery Technologies with an Eye on Distributed Power and Renewables

The development of large-scale storage systems (often in the form of giant batteries) scattered around electric transmission grids would mean that generating companies could create excess power during periods of slow demand, store that electricity and then sell it through the grid a few hours later when demand picks up. It would also mean that spikes in demand, such as that caused by a massive number of air conditioners turned on during an extremely hot summer afternoon, could be served quickly by drawing on stored power. Former U.S. Energy Secretary Steven Chu believes that America must eventually increase storage of all types to provide 10,000 gigawatts of backup electricity, compared to the 25 gigawatts stored today.

Several large battery storage systems are already in place. In mid-2017, electric vehicle manufacturer Tesla installed a massive 100 MW lithium-ion battery system in South Australia, in conjunction with the local government and French energy firm Neoen. This installation, called the Hornsdale Power Reserve, was the largest of its kind as of mid-2018.

California utility PG&E was granted approval from the California Public Utilities Commission in November 2018 to replace three gas plants with two major battery storage projects. One is a project from Vistra Corp. (vistracorp.com) which came online in early 2021. Called the Moss Landing Energy Storage Facility, its capacity was increased in a second phase completed in August 2021, bringing the facility's total capacity to 400 megawatts/1,600 megawatt-hours. A third expansion phase is planned for completion in 2023, which will add another 350 MW/1,400 MWh in capacity. The other project, Elkhorn Battery, was completed in April 2022. It is a 182.5 MW/730 MWh Tesla Megapack battery energy storage system (BESS).

According to the Energy Information Administration (EIA), battery storage capacity in the U.S. reached 1.4 gigawatts by the end of 2020. In 2021, battery storage capacity in the U.S. more than tripled to reach 4.6 gigawatts, according to the EIA. The amount of battery storage capacity was driven by the commissioning of 106 utility-scale systems with 3.2 gigawatts of capacity.

SPOTLIGHT: Form Energy, Inc.
Startup Form Energy (formenergy.com) launched a rechargeable iron-air battery in 2021 capable of delivering electricity for 100 hours at system costs competitive with conventional power plants, and at less than 1/10th the cost of commonly used lithium-ion batteries. Made from iron, this new, front-of-the-meter battery can be used continuously over a multi-day period, at costs of less than $6 per kilowatt-hour of storage.

Battery systems such as these not only add reliability to an electric grid, they also may lower costs and improve efficiency. If advanced batteries are eventually developed that capture significant volumes of solar- and wind-generated electricity for later use, the benefits would be immense. A major battery research effort is underway by multiple companies and government agencies worldwide.

Stem, Inc. (www.stem.com) is a northern California-based provider of batteries and software to corporate customers. The firm's Athena by Stem is an artificial intelligence (AI) system that collects and analyzes energy storage data at a rate of 400 megabytes (MB) per minute. During hours of peak energy demand, Athena uses the data to shift use away from traditional electricity sources to the drawdown of energy stored in batteries, reducing costs for Stem customers, which include Adobe Systems and Whole Foods Market.

SPOTLIGHT: QuantumScape Corporation

QuantumScape Corporation (www.quantumscape.com) is developing next-generation battery technology for electric vehicles (EVs) and other applications. The firm (which is 15.65% owned by the Volkswagen Group) has been developing a proprietary lithium-metal solid-state battery technology to offer greater energy density, longer life, faster charging and greater safety when compared to conventional lithium-ion batteries. During 2021, QuantumScape announced that it agreed with Volkswagen Group of America, Inc. to select the location of their joint venture solid-state battery pilot-line facility, possibly in Germany. The facility, QS-1, will initially be a 1-gigawatt hour (GWh) battery cell commercial production plant for EV batteries. QuantumScape and Volkswagen intend to expand production capacity by a further 20 GWh at the same location.

Super-capacity storage technologies include flywheels, pumped hydro storage and compressed air energy storage. For additional thoughts along these lines, visit the American Clean Power Association at cleanpower.org.

Today, part of the grid-scale electricity storage that exists is in the form of pumped hydro systems. In this technology, water is pumped uphill, during hours of low electricity demand, to a large holding tank or retention pond. Later, when increased electricity is demanded, the water is released to turn a turbine-powered generator. On the negative side, pumped hydro access is limited to areas with appropriate topography and water supplies.

Salt, stored either in the ground or in a specially constructed tower, is widely considered to be an ideal substance for energy storage, since it absorbs and releases heat in a predictable and stable manner. Abengoa, one of the world's largest utility-scale solar power developers, began operation of the Solana project about 70 miles southwest of Phoenix, Arizona in 2013. This 280-megawatt concentrated solar power (CSP) plant includes one of the world's most advanced molten salt energy storage installations. It has proven capable to generate power for six hours after the sun goes down, utilizing heat stored in molten salt during the day in order to power the plant's turbines during the evening. These six hours help to satisfy peak demand during summer evenings and early night-time hours. The $1.45 billion plant, generating power equivalent to that needed to maintain 70,000 homes, was funded under a loan guarantee provided by the U.S. Department of Energy. Atlantica Sustainable Infrastructure acquired the Solana plant from Abengoa in 2019. While salt storage technology has been successful, such solar tower projects have suffered many problems.

Solar energy is being stored in what many believe is one of the world's largest batteries, located in Manatee County, Florida on the Gulf Coast, which opened in late 2021. Florida Power & Light (a subsidiary of NextEra Energy, Inc.) built it, and it provides 409 megawatts of electricity for two hours during peak demand periods, enough to power approximately 329,000 Florida homes. The company also operates a 74.5-megawatt solar farm in the area. The new battery is part of a slow movement away from natural gas-powered "peaker plants" that operate during peak demand periods and toward battery arrays, made possible by the drop in lithium-ion battery costs.

Underwater storage is the focus of startup StEnSea (Storing Energy at Sea). Developed by the Fraunhofer Institute for Wind Energy and Energy System Technology in Kassel, Germany, the technology stores water in 12 cubic-meter vessels placed on the bottom of Lake Constance. The depth of the lake's floor is about 100 meters, which is subject to significant atmospheric pressure exerted by the water. (That is, the pressure on the lake's floor is about 9 times that on the lake's surface.) The rigid concrete vessels are repeatedly filled and drained from the surrounding lake which turns connected turbines. As pressure builds, up to 3 kilowatt hours of energy are stored in each vessel. Cables carry generated power to land. The project is a pilot, and should it prove viable, the company plans to build in the Norwegian trench at a depth of 600 meters, possibly storing 20 megawatts per vessel.

> **SPOTLIGHT: Hydrogen as an Energy Storage Strategy ("Power-to-Gas")**
>
> While advanced batteries are seen by most firms to be the answer to energy storage, a handful see the production of easily stored hydrogen as an alternative answer. A firm called Hydrogenics developed technology that can use excess wind and solar to power equipment that generates hydrogen. That hydrogen can then be stored or transported for later use, including hydrogen filling stations for fuel-cell powered vehicles. Hydrogenics was acquired by Cummins, Inc. for $290 million in late 2019.

The state of California is putting pressure on battery makers with a mandate that, from 2014 to 2024, major utilities must increase energy storage by about 1.3 gigawatts. In addition, California set a priority to encourage distributed generation, focusing on residential or neighborhood-scale solar power rather than large centralized solar farms. Batteries will be a key element in this effort.

> **Tesla Batteries Power Homes and Offices in Addition to Electric Cars:**
>
> Electric automobile maker Tesla Motors has adapted its expertise to create innovative electric storage batteries for residential and commercial/utility use. On the residential side, Tesla's Powerwall is big enough to provide temporary power to a home or small building at modest cost. Powerwall can readily store excess solar energy for use at night or when clouds obscure the sun. The system also provides power when traditional electric grids suffer outages.
>
> On the commercial side, Tesla's Powerpack is a fully integrated energy storage system that connects large scale customers to a building or utility network that enables users to avoid peak power demand charges. It offers peak shaving, load shifting, emergency backup and demand response capabilities through a device housing 16 individual battery pods, a thermal control system and hundreds of sensors that monitor and report on power performance. Tesla also offers a number of distributed energy products for the utilities market. In addition, a Tesla subsidiary offers solar panels and Solar Roof tiles.

> In 2019, Tesla unveiled Megapack, a new large-scale battery technology for major utility-scale storage systems. As of November 2022, Tesla had a backlog of 42 Megapacks per week at its Gigafactory Nevada. In late 2022, Tesla delivered a 196-megawatt battery system for the Pillswood Project near Hull in the UK which was the largest battery system in Europe at the time. It is capable of backing up power to approximately 300,000 homes in the UK for two hours.

19) Nuclear Energy Moves Ahead in India, China and the Middle East

The first man-made nuclear fission was achieved in 1938, unlocking atomic power both for destructive and creative purposes. In 1951, usable electricity was created via a nuclear reactor for the first time, thanks largely to research conducted at the Manhattan Project that developed the first atomic weapons during World War II.

By the 1970s, nuclear energy was in widespread use in the U.S. and abroad as a fuel to heat steam that turns electric generation turbines. As of 2021, nuclear power provided about 19% of the electricity generated in the U.S., created by 92 nuclear reactors, according to the U.S. Energy Information Administration (www.eia.gov). The number has been steadily decreasing in recent years.

Worldwide, there were only 437 nuclear electric plants operating in 33 nations as the end of 2021, according to the *World Nuclear Industry Status Report*. This is down from a high of 450 reactors in 2018. Approximately 59 new plants were under some stage of construction around the world as of mid-2022, including 21 in China. In fact, China is planning to build 150 reactors between 2022 and 2037, investing up to $440 billion.

The potential for accidents, meltdowns and other disasters has never been far from the minds of many consumers (after all, for many of us, the first image that comes to mind upon hearing the word "nuclear" is a nuclear bomb). The 1979 Three Mile Island nuclear power plant accident in the U.S. led to the cancellation of scores of nuclear projects across the nation. This trend was later reinforced by the disaster at Chernobyl in what was then the Soviet Union.

A difficult regulatory gauntlet, environmental backlash and exceptionally high costs for new plants (including a history of immense cost overruns), combined with today's abundance of low-cost natural gas from shale, created an environment in which there was little to no enthusiasm for the construction of new nuclear plants in the U.S. A few American nuclear reactors have been closed in recent years, and many more nuclear plant owners have announced their intention to close existing sites. About 36 of the reactors in operation in the U.S face closings between 2029 and 2035 when their licenses expire. Some will likely seek license extensions. According to the EIA, as of the end of 2019, there were 23 shut-down reactors in the U.S. that were undergoing various stages of decommissioning.

As of mid-2022, the American mindset for nuclear power was changing. The Infrastructure Act passed by Congress in 2021 calls for $3.2 billion for the development of advanced nuclear power plants. New technology developed by TerraPower (an energy company founded by Bill Gates, www.terrapower.com) calls for reactors that are simpler to build, operate at lower pressure and utilize uranium more efficiently (therefore reducing waste). The technology was still under development as of late 2022 and will require large number of highly skilled engineers and technicians as well as the production of a new high-assay low-enriched uranium. The first TerraPower reactor will be installed at a Wyoming coal-fired power plant that was scheduled to close in 2025.

TECHNOLOGY SPOTLIGHT: TerraPower

A unique technology firm based in Bellevue, Washington has proposed a concept it calls TerraPower, www.terrapower.com, a dramatically different type of nuclear power. This technology would use a new class of reactor called TWR or traveling-wave reactor that would solve the current nuclear waste problem. TWRs would use today's stockpiles of depleted uranium from power plants as its primary fuel source. The TWR would essentially be a reactor-reprocessor.

Traditional reactors rely on uranium-235, and their operation leaves a more common uranium-238 as waste. Every year or two, traditional reactors must be opened and refueled, and the "spent" uranium-238 waste is stockpiled. Millions of pounds of it are now in storage.

A TWR could be fed that uranium-238, which it would convert into a desirable fuel, plutonium-239. Similar conversion of U-238 has already been proven, but present technologies for reprocessing into plutonium are expensive and complicated. TWR could represent a significant step forward while reducing the potential of diverting plutonium to use in atomic weapons.

The EIA's U.S. Nuclear Industry At-a-Glance

For an excellent, up-to-date explanation of nuclear power generation in the U.S. visit this page operated by the U.S. Energy Information Administration: www.eia.gov/energyexplained/nuclear/us-nuclear-industry.php .

Only two new U.S. reactors were under construction as of late 2020, the Vogtle 3 and 4 in Waynesboro, Georgia. The Vogtle reactors are being built to advanced designs that promise to be one-tenth as likely to suffer an accident and be easier to operate and maintain. The reactors, the first new nuclear plants built in the U.S. in 30 years, are 45.7% owned by Southern Co. and began with a budget of approximately $14 billion. As of October 2022, the budget had ballooned to $30 billion, and the project was more than six years behind schedule.

Elsewhere, the Virgil C. Summer Nuclear Generating Station in South Carolina abandoned two new, state-of-the-art Westinghouse AP1000 plants (which were scheduled for completion in 2019 and 2020) after Westinghouse Electric Co. filed for bankruptcy in 2017. Westinghouse Electric was acquired by Brookfield Business Partners in August 2018 for approximately $4.6 billion.

Nuclear power plants in many other parts of the world are in jeopardy as high investment costs are difficult to finance and popular opinion turned against the technology in the wake of Fukushima, despite the fact that nuclear power can dramatically reduce a nation's carbon emissions. In 2011, German Chancellor Angela Merkel announced plans to shut down all 17 of its nuclear reactors by 2022. As recently as 2010, these nuclear plants generated 23% of Germany's electricity. The government hoped to have renewable sources make up the difference. German electricity prices rose dramatically as its reliance on renewables increased. By mid-2022 under new Chancellor Olaf Scholz, Germany planned to postpone the closure of its last three reactors due to energy shortages related to the war in Ukraine.

Switzerland also announced plans to phase out existing reactors as they reach the end of their usability. In addition, Italy cancelled all plans to revive its nuclear program in June 2011 after a landslide vote against nuclear development. This may change over the mid-term due to the war in Ukraine.

The nation of France was an early adopter of nuclear power. The French approved a single, very cost-effective nuclear plant design and built it over and over again around the nation. France currently gets more than 70% of its electricity from nuclear sources. As of mid-2022, France was training thousands of workers in nuclear engineering and construction to tackle the building of up to 14 new reactors and possibly other mini reactors.

Many nations are moving ahead with new nuclear reactors. In October 2013, a preliminary agreement was reached by the UK to allow French firms EDF and AREVA, in partnership with China National Nuclear Corporation, to build a new nuclear power plant at Hinkley Point in southwest England. This French-Chinese consortium is using EPR (European Pressurized Reactor) technology. In 2016, construction was underway on two reactor units at Hinkley Point C using EPR technology at an estimated cost of $22.5 billion. After a number of delays (including the need for additional foundation reinforcement), the project's price tag has risen to as much as $33 billion and the startup date pushed back to June 2027. It is hoped that the plant will provide for about 7% of the UK's electricity needs.

A similar French-Chinese partnership is responsible for the development of two EPR plants in Taishan, Guandong Province, China. In June 2018, Unit 1 at Taishan became the world's first EPR to be connected to a power grid, and full-time commercial generation commenced in late 2019. EPR requires about 17% less fuel than earlier technologies. Four safety systems operate alongside each other, each one 100% capable of ensuring the two essential safety functions required to protect people and the environment in shutting down the nuclear reactor and cooling the reactor core. Equipment known as the core catcher has been designed to recover, contain and cool the reactor core in the event of an accident.

The UK further strengthened ties to China with an agreement in October 2015 to allow Chinese companies to be minority investors and suppliers to EDF. The agreement also opened the door for China to play a greater role in future nuclear projects such as Hinkley Point C.

As of late 2022, China had 53 nuclear reactors in operation and at least 21 under construction. Rising costs are an issue. Newer, safer plants such as the U.S.-designed AP1000 and the French-German designed EPR can cost as much as $7.6 billion in China for a two-reactor configuration. Still, energy consumption per person in China is expected to soar through 2030.

Japan's nuclear industry got a boost in late 2016 when the government okayed a plan to sell Japanese nuclear technology to India, which is planning to build 20 new, advanced technology reactors over the next several years (while as many as 55 have been proposed). Japan plans to bring nine reactors back online in 2022 and has a 2030 emissions goal based on restarting 30 reactors.

The history of nuclear reactor construction is littered with cost overruns, delays and complications. A focus on standardized, advanced-technology designs that can be built over and over again was hoped to streamline the regulatory process, reduce financial risks and encourage investment. However, this has proven to be an elusive goal, and costs are so high that new construction is unlikely anywhere in the world without substantial government guarantees and assistance. The U.S. government offers incentives, primarily in the form of loan guarantees, for the construction of reactors. However, the process and cost of actually getting those guarantees, along with environmental approval and regulatory approval, can be so daunting as to make it next to impossible to build a plant.

Nuclear Waste and Uranium Reprocessing: The controversial Yucca Mountain nuclear waste repository project in Nevada was intended to create a permanent location for America's nuclear waste. It was designed to store waste 1,000 feet underground above another 1,000 feet of solid rock. Supporters maintained that one central depository is far safer than the current method of storing waste underwater near each reactor site. Waste would be transported to a central repository by truck and rail, and it would be sealed in armored casks designed to withstand puncturing and exposure to fire or water. As of late 2020, the Yucca Mountain project was still in operation, but continued be a bone of contention among state and federal leaders as to its future.

Meanwhile, the Waste Isolation Pilot Plant (WIPP) near Carlsbad, New Mexico began accepting shipments in 1999. It stores nuclear waste in rooms mined out of a salt formation 2,150 feet below ground. WIPP continues operations, winning recognition by the DOE for improvements in energy, water and fleet efficiency while reducing pollution and waste. However, this site is primarily for the disposal of nuclear waste from research, medical and military uses.

Another underground disposal project is in Finland at the Olkiluoto Nuclear Power Plant. The proposed site will store spent fuel rods in iron canisters sealed in copper shells to resist corrosion. The canisters will be placed in holes surrounded by clay far below ground.

The alternative to the storage of nuclear waste is reprocessing, in which spent fuel is dissolved in nitric acid. The resulting substance is then separated into uranium, plutonium and unusable waste. The positive side of reprocessing is the recycling of uranium for further nuclear power generation. Surplus plutonium can be mixed with uranium to fabricate MOX (mixed oxide fuel) for use in a commercial nuclear power plant. MOX fuel contains 5% plutonium. Commercial MOX-fueled light water reactors are used in France, the United Kingdom, Germany, Switzerland and Belgium. In the U.S., MOX fuel was fabricated and used in several commercial reactors in the 1970s as part of a development program. The negative side of reprocessing is that the resulting plutonium may be used for nuclear weapons and the financial costs are prohibitively high. Additionally, environmentalists are extremely concerned about the potentially high levels of radioactivity produced during reprocessing, as well as the transportation of reprocessed waste.

Safer Nuclear Power Technologies: New technologies may eventually enable construction of nuclear generating plants that are less expensive to build and much safer to operate than those of previous generations. Pebble-bed modular reactor (PBMR) technology is potentially a highly safe nuclear power plant design, but it is a long shot for commercialization. Scientists in Germany operated a 15-megawatt prototype PBMR from 1967 to 1988. Pebble-bed technology utilizes tiny silicon carbide-coated uranium oxide granules sealed in "pebbles" about the size of oranges, made of graphite. Helium is used as the coolant and energy transfer medium. This containment of the radioactive material in small quantities has the potential to achieve an unprecedented level of safety.

The world's current noteworthy pebble bed project is being carried out in China. In September 2021, the Chinese HTR-PM pebble bed reactor went critical for the first time. It is a demonstration reactor that operates at relatively modest temperatures similar to those of coal-fired plants. However, China is still a long way from having a commercially viable project of high electricity output.

Other nuclear technologies will be used elsewhere in China. Westinghouse, a major maker of nuclear power plants, built two of a total of four nuclear plants it had under contract in China, using its AP1000 model. As part of the deal, Westinghouse agreed to provide China with key technical knowledge necessary to enable China to eventually manufacture its own version of the AP1000 reactor, to be named the CAP1400. After Westinghouse took bankruptcy in 2017, the company successfully emerged from bankruptcy and was acquired by Brookfield Business Partners. The first AP1000 reactor, the Sanmen No. 1 in China's Zhejiang province, entered commercial operation in September 2018.

China is now focusing much of its attention on its own reactor, the Hualong One. It is based on the AP1000 design and developed by the China National Nuclear Corporation (CNNC). The first reactors powered by the Hualong One are the Fuqing 5 and 6 in the Chinese province of Fujian which began commercial operation in January and March 2021 respectively. CNNC then installed two units in Pakistan, the Karachi 2 and Karachi 3. Both were in commercial operation by mid-2022.

The AP1000 is considered a generation 3+ reactor technology. Advanced generation reactors feature higher operating efficiency, greater safety and design that uses fewer pumps and other moving parts in order to simplify construction and operation and make emergency responses more dependable. "Passive" safety systems are built-in that require no outside support, such as external electric power and human action, to kick in. For example, the AP1000 features systems for passive core cooling, passive leak containment cooling and leak containment isolation. Passive systems rely on the use of gravity, natural circulation and/or compressed gas in order to react to emergencies.

Several firms are pursuing mini-reactor designs, including NuScale Power. The hope is to reduce complexity and cost. NuScale Power has been in discussion with several potential customers.

Yet another alternative to traditional nuclear reactors is thorium liquid fuel reactors, which are fueled by molten fluoride salt containing thorium. Thorium is far more abundant than uranium and it creates uranium 223 continuously, resulting in approximately 90 times as much energy from the same quantity of uranium. In addition, it generates less waste, which itself has a much shorter half-life than uranium. India has significant reserves of thorium (about 319,999 tons or 13% of the world's total) and has been working on the technology since the 1950s. Since then, about one ton of thorium oxide fuel has been irradiated experimentally in pressurized heavy water reactors and has been reprocessed, according to the Bhabha Atomic Research Centre (BARC). A reprocessing center for thorium fuels is being built at Kalpakkam.

In the EU, a partnership of laboratories and universities are researching a safer nuclear technology based on the "molten salt fast reactor." The technology is based on blending molten salt with nuclear fuel and can work with either uranium-based fuels or thorium. The reactors don't require large containment structures and use less fuel, making them viable for mass production in factories and potentially combined in arrays to create larger power plants. The end goal is a cleaner, safer and more cost-effective reactor. China is also actively researching a liquid-thorium fuel reactor.

The Middle East, where industrial and residential need for electricity is set to soar, is a ripe area for nuclear power plant development. Saudi Arabia hopes to build 17 gigawatts of nuclear energy after 2040, beginning the process to issue a license to build in late 2022. Nearby in the UAE, the government has awarded a South Korean consortium called Korea Electric Power Corporation (Kepco) with a contract for the construction of four new nuclear plants at a cost of $18.6 billion. Three were in operation as of October 2022 with a fourth under construction.

Kepco and an affiliate, KHNP, developed its own reactor design in 1995, based on an American reactor, which was replicated over and over instead of customizing new plants. The result was a gain in expertise and efficiency and prices fell. As of late 2022, South Korea had 25 operable reactors and three under construction. President Yoon Suk-yeol set a target for nuclear power to provide 30% of South Korea's electricity by 2030.

While many truly revolutionary technologies for nuclear power are under consideration, research or development, actual commercialization of a concept would take many years, and many will not succeed. The challenges of finding investors and government subsidies, developing and testing prototypes or demonstration units, and getting through the regulatory and licensing maze are enormous.

20) Nuclear Fusion Technologies Might Create Unlimited, Emission-Free Power

As opposed to nuclear fission (the technology utilized in today's nuclear electricity generation plants that is based on literally splitting atoms), nuclear fusion is the reaction when two light atomic nuclei (often described as "plasma," which occurs when a gas is heated and some of its electrons change state and become a plasma containing ions, neutral atoms and electrons) fuse together, forming a heavier nucleus. That nucleus releases energy—a lot of it.

Unfortunately, the process requires massive amounts of heat, specifically 100 million+ degrees Celsius. There are various ways to achieve this reaction, including intense heat from an array of powerful lasers that are focused on the substance to be fused, as well as superconducting, high-intensity magnetic fields. The Holy Grail in nuclear fusion research is to create a continuous reaction that generates significantly more power than the energy consumed in creating the heat or the magnetic field needed for the process. If this can be done efficiently and safely, some scientists think fusion power could eventually create limitless, emission-free energy, without any nuclear waste, essentially "harnessing the power of the stars."

In early tests, fusion power generators consumed more energy than they created. However, that is changing, with developments including a 2022 breakthrough, and the long-term potential of major research facilities, including a long-awaited site that is now under construction, the International Thermonuclear Experimental Reactor (ITER) in Southern France (www.iter.org). To be operational as early as 2035 to 2040, at a cost of about $15 billion (up from an initial $11.7 billion), the reactor is a pilot project to demonstrate the feasibility of full-scale fusion power. Initial (early-stage) testing could begin as early as 2025.

In the U.S., a project run by the Lawrence Livermore National Laboratory is testing the use of lasers to ignite fusion. The lab's National Ignition Facility (NIF) is conducting experiments designed to demonstrate ignition, or fusion, that results in a net gain of energy, using a massive laser.

Also, a large-scale project collaboration is underway in America, referred to as US ITER. It is a Department of Energy project, hosted by the Oak Ridge National Laboratory, with a wide array of research partners, both domestic and foreign.

Meanwhile, there are several private fusion initiatives underway. These projects are generally developed on a smaller scale and rely on a technology called low-energy nuclear reaction (LENR). Heat is produced when metals such as nickel and palladium absorb hydrogen or deuterium and are exposed to external stimuli (which is similar to cold fusion). See lenr-canr.org.

In December 2022, researchers at the Lawrence Livermore National Laboratory in Washington, D.C. made a very significant breakthrough in nuclear fusion. The experiment used 192 lasers to heat and compress hydrogen atoms, reaching a temperature of 180 million degrees Fahrenheit. The resulting reaction released 3.15 megajoules of energy for every 2.05 megajoules of laser input, the first-time output ever outpaced input. However, the lasers that were utilized are far from reaching acceptable levels of efficiency, and commercial use of the process remains a long way off. The problem is that the lasers that were utilized are not energy efficient. That is, the lasers themselves convert only about 95% of the power that they consume into heat. Nonetheless, this experiment is very encouraging, and future advances in lasers and other technologies lie ahead.

Plasma confinement refers to technology that contains plasma in an extreme environment (such as high heat or a magnetic field) that are necessary for nuclear fusion. Similar conditions exist in the stars above us.

Magnetic Confinement Fusion (MCF) is one of the more promising technologies for nuclear fusion and is a different approach than the use of lasers. Researchers at MIT and elsewhere are making great strides in MCF. Strong magnetic fields confine plasma at extremely high pressures and temperatures during this process. This technology relies on ultrapowerful, high-temperature superconducting magnets to cause the atomic nuclei to fuse. A startup working in this area in conjunction with MIT's Plasma Science and Fusion Center is Commonwealth Fusion Systems.

No matter which technologies prove to be best over the long-term, it is likely to be many decades before fusion power generation can be commercially used as an everyday power source. While the research costs and challenges are great, nuclear fusion (along with advanced, high-safety-low nuclear waste reactors like those being developed by TerraPower, a startup backed by Microsoft co-founder Bill Gates) is one of the most promising technologies for a low- to no-emissions energy future.

21) New Display Technologies with PLEDs

State of the art LEDs (light emitting diodes) have the potential to greatly reduce energy usage while providing very high-quality lighting and displays. In addition, solar power is now being combined with the latest LEDs to create fully-renewable energy light sources. Now PLEDs, based on polymers, are receiving significant focus in manufacture of displays.

The LED was first developed in 1962 at the University of Illinois at Urbana-Champaign. LEDs are important to a wide variety of industries, from wireless telephone handsets to signage to displays for medical equipment, because they provide a very high quality of light with very low power requirements. They also have an extremely long useful life and produce little heat output. All of these characteristics are great improvements over a conventional incandescent bulb or the LCD (liquid crystal display).

On a groundbreaking day in 1989 at Cambridge University, researchers discovered that organic LEDs (OLEDs) could be manufactured using polymers. The plastic substance known as PPV (polyphenylenevinylene) emits light when layered between electrodes. The resulting product is referred to as a PLED (polymer light emitting diode). Soon, many industries realized the advantages of PLEDs as display devices that emit their own light. In contrast, the older LCD (liquid crystal display) technology works on a system whereby a separate light source has to be filtered in several stages to create the desired image. PLED is more direct, more efficient and much higher quality. It is also an excellent system for the manufacture of extremely thin displays that can work at very low voltage. The useful life of a PLED can be 40,000 hours. Advanced displays utilizing PLED can be viewed at angles approaching 180 degrees, and they can produce quality images in flat panels, even at very low temperatures.

Cambridge Display Technology (CDT, www.cdtltd.co.uk), a subsidiary of Sumitomo Chemical Group, points out several exciting uses for these polymer LEDs that may develop over the mid-term. For example, the low energy requirements of PLEDs could be used to create packaging for consumer or business goods that have a display incorporated into the front of the package. This display could provide a changing, entertaining and highly informative description of the product to be found within the package. Since PLEDs can be incorporated into flexible substrates, displays for advertising or information purposes can be built in the shape of curves. The possibilities are nearly endless. Most likely, new uses will develop as larger and larger numbers of PLEDs are manufactured and higher volume leads to lower prices.

For example, Canadian technology firm Carmanah Technologies Corp. (www.carmanah.com) combined LEDs with solar panels for use in marine buoys. It has expanded further into lighting products for airfields, railways and general outdoor illumination, providing lights that are easy to install as well as powered entirely by renewable solar energy.

22) Electric Utilities Adopt Coal Emissions Scrubbers While the Industry Tests Carbon Capture and Clean Coal Technologies

While coal is an abundant resource in many parts of the world, it is generally burned in a manner that creates significant amounts of air pollution. On a global scale, the burning of coal produces more carbon dioxide than any other fossil fuel source. "Clean coal" technologies have been developed, but advanced technologies are enormously expensive.

In the U.S., coal comes from several different regions. The Northern Appalachian area of the Eastern U.S. and the Illinois Basin in the Midwest produce coal that is high in sulfur, which emits more pollutants. In contrast are the enormous stores of coal in Wyoming and Montana, which burn at lower temperatures and produce less energy than high sulfur coal, but create less pollution. Coal from the Illinois Basin burns in an efficient manner at very high temperatures.

Advanced filtering units called scrubbers are in use by U.S. coal-fired electric generating plants. Scrubbers are multistory facilities that are built adjacent to smokestacks. They capture sulfur as the coal exhaust billows through the smokestack and sequester it for storage before it can be cleaned. Unfortunately, scrubbers are extremely expensive. Costs of $400 million and more for a single scrubber are common.

Multiple clean coal technologies are in development. Scientists at the University of Texas are developing a new technology that blasts sound waves into the flue ducts of coal-fired power plants. The noise, which registers at more than 150 decibels (about as loud as a jet engine at takeoff) causes tiny ash particles in the emission stream to vibrate and stick to larger ones, thereby making larger particles that are easier to capture by pollution control equipment like scrubbers.

Yet another technology to reduce emissions is the use of photosynthesis to capture exhaust gases, such as CO_2, from power plants. A company called GS CleanTech (now a part of GreenShift Corporation, cleantech-alpha.com) developed a CO_2 Bioreactor that converts a concentrated supply of carbon dioxide into oxygen and biomass in the form of algae, which can then be converted into fuel.

Coal-gasification plants could conceivably become a trend for electric generation plant construction over the long term. However, costs remain a significant obstacle. Such plants use a process that first converts coal into a synthetic gas, later burning that gas to power the electric generators. The steam produced in the process is further used to generate electricity. The process is called Integrated Gasification Combined Cycle (IGCC). While these plants are much more expensive to construct than traditional coal-burning plants, they produce much less pollution. Since the coal isn't actually burnt, these plants can use lower-cost coal that is high in sulfur. In addition, such plants reduce the amount of mercury emitted from the use of coal by as much as 95%. Several demonstration plants have been constructed using IGCC technology, typically with government funding. U.S. plants include those in Mulberry, Florida and West Terre Haute, Indiana. Japan has constructed a demonstration plant, the Nakoso Power Station at Iwaki City. Other demonstration plants have been in operation or under consideration in Europe, Asia and Australia. However, high costs and the difficulty of funding continue to create challenges. Siemens, a leading global firm in the power equipment industry, has been involved in multiple projects.

American Electric Power (AEP), a Columbus, Ohio electric utility, shelved plans to build an IGCC carbon-capture plant in West Virginia. This was due to the company's concerns that state regulators would not allow it to be reimbursed (through utility bill increases) for $668 million in related costs. Without substantial government support on the federal and state levels, power companies are unlikely to be able to afford IGCC efforts.

Due to cost overruns associated with the attempt to implement state-of-the-art IGCC clean coal technologies, a plant in Mississippi quickly became one of the most expensive fossil fuel projects ever built. Mississippi Power Co.'s Kemper County plant's price tag was expected to reach $6.4 billion, more than two and one-half times its original budget of $2.4 billion. In 2017, Mississippi Power abandoned its coal gasification efforts and switched to burning natural gas only.

An additional step that can be added to IGCC plants is the capture or "sequestration" (CCS) of carbon dioxide (also referred to as carbon capture use and sequestration (CCUS)). The technology to do so already exists. For example, Norway's Statoil has used it for years at its natural-gas wells in the North Sea. The sequestered carbon dioxide can be pumped underground. Fortunately, carbon dioxide can be used in oil and gas wells to enhance recovery in a process known as CO_2 flooding.

> ***Internet Research Tip: Carbon Capture and Sequestration (CCS)***
>
> For an excellent discussion of carbon capture and sequestration technologies, research and demonstration projects, see the U.S. Department of Energy's web site for the NETL (National Energy Technology Laboratory) netl.doe.gov.

Carbon capture technologies could possibly have wide use outside of the electric utilities industry. As of early 2021, almost 1,400 companies had promised to cut their net carbon dioxide emissions to zero in the coming decades. The Skyonic plant near San Antonio, Texas, which opened in late 2014, captures carbon emitted during the manufacture of cement, and uses it to produce sodium bicarbonate and hydrochloric acid by its reaction to rock salt. The plant received $28 million in funding from the U.S. Department of Energy. It can capture 83,000 tons of carbon dioxide per year, and because it saves carbon emissions made using traditional chemical production processes, it claims an additional 220,000 tons per year. A July 2022 energy bill passed by the U.S. Congress provided new incentives to utility companies that institute effective carbon capture technologies.

In 2021, Exxon announced plans to form a new subsidiary to commercialize carbon capture and storage, planning to invest $3 billion in this area through 2025. The firm forecasted a $2 trillion global market for the technology by 2040. Exxon reported the capture of more than 120 million metric tons of carbon over the past 30 year, or 40% of all captured emissions on a global basis. (Nearly all came from the Shute Creek Treating Facility in Wyoming, which processes natural gas.) Carbon dioxide is separated from other gases and then sold to oil producers that use it in enhanced oil recovery. This kind of recovery pumps carbon into established oil and gas reservoirs to increase pressure. Chevron was forming partnerships in 2021 to develop storage projects, and BP was working on storage projects in the UK and Australia.

Another popular choice to absorb CO_2 is reforestation. French oil and gas giant Total SE announced plans in early 2021 to plant a 40,000-hectare forest in the Democratic Republic of Congo to sequester 10 million tons of CO_2 through 2041. Other companies focused on reforestation include Italian oil and gas firm Eni, as well as IAG, which owns British Airways.

Regenerative farming is also in use to limit CO_2 emissions, which is critical since agriculture generates approximately one-fifth of global emissions. Techniques include reduced soil tillage, cover-crop planting and cyclical grazing of livestock. The National Academy of Sciences estimated that regenerative farming in the U.S. could capture 250 million tons of greenhouse gases per year (an amount equal to about 5% of 2019 U.S. emissions).

23) Superconductivity Provides Advanced Electricity Distribution Technology

Superconductivity is based on the use of super-cooled cable to distribute electricity over distance, with little of the significant loss of electric power incurred during traditional transmission over copper wires. It is one of the most promising technologies for upgrading the ailing electricity grid.

Superconductivity dates back to 1911, when a Dutch physicist determined that the element mercury, when cooled to minus 452 degrees Fahrenheit, has virtually no electrical resistance. That is, it lost zero electric power when used as a means to distribute electricity from one spot to another. Two decades later, in 1933, a German physicist named Walther Meissner discovered that superconductors have no interior magnetic field. This property enabled superconductivity to be put to commercial use by 1984, when magnetic resonance imaging machines (MRIs) were commercialized for medical imaging.

In 1986, IBM researchers K. Alex Muller and Georg Bednorz paved the path to superconductivity at slightly higher temperatures using a ceramic alloy as a medium. Shortly thereafter, a team led by University of Houston physicist Paul Chu created a ceramic capable of superconductivity at temperatures high enough to encourage true commercialization.

In May 2001, the Danish city of Copenhagen established a first when it implemented a 30-meter-long "high temperature" superconductivity (HTS) cable in its own energy grids. Other small but successful implementations have occurred in the U.S.

Today, the Holy Grail for researchers is a quest for materials that will permit superconductivity at temperatures above the freezing point, even at room temperature. There are two types of super-conductivity: "low-temperature" superconductivity (LTS), which requires temperatures lower than minus 328 degrees Fahrenheit; and "high-temperature" superconductivity (HTS), which operates at any temperature higher than that. The former type requires the use of liquid helium to maintain these excessively cold temperatures, while the latter type can reach the required temperatures with much cheaper liquid nitrogen. Liquid nitrogen is pumped through HTS cable assemblies, chilling thin strands of ceramic material that can carry electricity with no loss of power as it travels through the super-cooled cable. HTS wires are capable of carrying more than 130 times the electrical current of conventional copper wire of the same dimension. Consequently, the weight of such cable assemblies can be one-tenth the weight of old-fashioned copper wire. HTS wiring is improving substantially thanks to the development of second-generation technologies.

While cable for superconductivity is both exotic and expensive, the cost is decreasing as production ramps up, and the advantages can be exceptional. Increasing production to commercial levels at an economic cost, as well as producing lengths suitable for transmission purposes remain among the largest hurdles for the superconductor industry. Applications that are currently being implemented include use in electric transmission bottlenecks and in expensive engine systems such as those found in submarines.

Another major player in HTS components is Sumitomo Electric Industries, the largest cable and wire manufacturer in Japan. The firm has begun commercial production of HTS wire at a facility in Osaka. In addition, Sumitomo has developed electric motors based on HTS coil. The superconducting motors are much smaller and lighter than conventional electric motors, at about 90% less volume and 80% less weight.

Another leading firm, AMSC, formerly American Superconductor, sells technology to wind turbine makers, enabling them to design full 10-megawatt class superconductor wind turbines that will operate with higher efficiency than traditional models. It is also participating in advanced-technology electric transmission projects.

Advanced-generation HTS cable has been developed at American Superconductor, utilizing multiple coatings on top of a 100-millimeter substrate, a significant improvement over its earlier 40-millimeter technology. The goal is to achieve the highest level of alignment of the atoms in the superconductor material resulting in higher electrical current transmission capacity. This will increase manufacturing output while increasing efficiency. This is a convergence of nanotechnology with superconductivity since it deals with materials at the atomic level. The company is well set up to increase production as demand increases.

Leading Firms in Superconductivity Technology:
Sumitomo Electric Industries, http://global-sei.com
AMSC, www.amsc.com
Nexans, www.nexans.com
SuperPower, Inc., www.superpower-inc.com

24) Lower Energy Intensity Is a Prime Focus in China/U.S. Achieves Dramatic Energy Intensity Reductions

In a global sense, energy efficiency may advance at the creeping pace of a turtle, but over the years the compounding results are exceptional. "Energy intensity," by one popular measure, refers to the amount of energy required for a nation to produce a unit of GDP (gross domestic product—a basic measure of economic output). A nation's goal should be to make intensity as low as possible.

A table of this progress, as published by the U.S. Energy Information Administration (EIA), shows steady improvements in energy intensity, year by year, for the past 60 years. According to the EIA, America's energy intensity will continue to plummet, and will stand 37% lower in 2050 than in 2019.

This drop in energy used per unit of economic output is not limited to America by any means but is more of a global phenomenon. China, the world's largest consumer of energy and a major concern in terms of pollution and emissions, is showing steady improvement, cutting its energy intensity by about 50% from 1980 through 2004. Its five-year plan for 2011 through 2015 resulted in a 18.2% improvement in energy intensity. China is clearly focusing both government investment and regulation on reducing energy consumption per GDP while improving its infamous air and water pollution problems. It's subsequent five-year plan for 2016 through 2020 called for further energy intensity improvement of 15%.

The increase is almost entirely comprised of consumer use while industrial consumption fell.) The challenge is to make efficient technologies inexpensive, widespread and readily adoptable in emerging nations. This is especially important in light of the fact that there will be big increases in the total demand for energy as the world's population and middle classes grow and emerging nations become more industrial.

Global demand for energy will continue to soar for many decades, along with expanding global middle classes and steady increases in the total global population, particularly in Africa. Most of the increased energy use will occur in emerging nations, particularly India and China. Renewable methods of electricity generation will soar. At the same time, accelerating improvements in energy and conservation technologies will be at work to an increasing degree, reducing total demand, lessening the impact of emissions and greatly boosting efficiency. This is a massive market opportunity for innovative firms that develop significant conservation technologies and services in this regard.

Chapter 2

SOLAR POWER, WIND POWER & RENEWABLE ENERGY INDUSTRY STATISTICS

Contents:	
Global Alternative Energy Industry Statistics and Market Size Overview	46
U.S. Alternative Energy Industry Statistics and Market Size Overview	47
Approximate Energy Unit Conversion Factors	48
Biomass Energy Resource Hierarchy	49
Comparison of Alternative Fuels with Gasoline & Diesel	50
World Total Primary Energy Consumption by Region: 2017-2050	52
Share of Electricity Generation by Energy Source, U.S.: Projections, 2021-2050	53
Energy Consumption by Source & Sector, U.S.: 2021	54
Primary Energy Flow by Source & Sector, U.S.: 2021	55
Net Electrical Power Generation by Fuel Type, U.S.: 2021	56
Net Electrical Power Generation by Fuel Type, U.S.: 1990-July 2022	57
Energy Production by Renewable Energy, U.S.: Selected Years, 1955-2021	58
U.S. Renewable Energy Consumption by Energy Source, 2015 vs. 2021	59
Fuel Ethanol Production & Consumption, U.S.: 1981- July 2022	60
Biodiesel Production & Consumption, U.S.: 2001- July 2022	61
Top 10 Countries by Installed Wind Generating Capacity: 2021	62
Top 15 U.S. States by Installed Wind Generating Capacity: 2nd Quarter 2022	63
U.S. Department of Energy Funding for Science & Energy Programs: 2021-2023	64
Federal R&D & R&D Plant Funding for Energy, U.S.: Fiscal Years 2020-2022	65

Global Alternative Energy Industry Statistics and Market Size Overview

	Number	Unit	Year	Source
Global Wind Power				
Cumulative Installed Wind Turbine Capacity, End of Year (2023 figure is a projection.)	908,000	MW	2023	GWEC
	824,874	MW	2021	BP
	733,300	MW	2020	BP
	621,421	MW	2019	BP
	567,592	MW	2018	BP
	514,402	MW	2017	BP
Global Geothermal Power				
Cumulative Installed Geothermal Power Capacity, End of Year	85,400	MW	2021	BP
	14,601	MW	2020	BP
	14,034	MW	2019	BP
	13,568	MW	2018	BP
	13,126	MW	2017	BP
Global Biofuels Production				
Production	604,280	TTOE	2021	BP
	89,682	TTOE	2020	BP
	95,486	TTOE	2019	BP
	91,820	TTOE	2018	BP
	83,319	TTOE	2017	BP
Global Hydroelectric Power Consumption				
Consumption*	40.26	EJ	2021	BP
	38.16	EJ	2020	BP
	37.64	EJ	2019	BP
	37.32	EJ	2018	BP
	36.59	EJ	2017	BP
Global Nuclear Power Consumption				
Consumption*	604.5	MTOE	2021	BP
	572.8	MTOE	2020	BP
	595.2	MTOE	2019	BP
	611.3	MTOE	2018	BP
	597.1	MTOE	2017	BP
Global Solar Power				
Cumulative Installed Photovoltaic (PV) Power, End of Year	1032.5	MW	2021	BP
	855.7	MW	2020	BP
	707.9	MW	2019	BP
	577.0	MW	2018	BP
	446.1	MW	2017	BP

* Based on gross generation and not accounting for cross-border electricity supply. Converted on the basis of thermal equivalence assuming 38% conversion efficiency in a modern thermal power station.

MW = Megawatts
TTOE = Thousand Tonnes Oil Equivalent
MTOE = Million Tonnes Oil Equivalent

GWEC = Global Wind Energy Council
BP = British Petroleum
EJ = Exajoules

Source: Plunkett Research, Ltd. Copyright© 2022, All Rights Reserved
www.plunkettresearch.com

U.S. Alternative Energy Industry Statistics and Market Size Overview

	Number	Unit	Year	Source
Energy Production	98,337	Tril. Btu	2021	DOE
By Renewable Energy Power Sources	12,172	Tril. Btu	2021	DOE
Biomass (Wood, Waste, Biofuels)	4,850	Tril. Btu	2021	DOE
Conventional Hydroelectric Power	2,283	Tril. Btu	2021	DOE
Wind	3,332	Tril. Btu	2021	DOE
Geothermal	206	Tril. Btu	2021	DOE
Solar	1,246	Tril. Btu	2021	DOE
Energy Consumption (Includes Imports)	93,134	Tril. Btu	2021	DOE
By Fossil Fuels	77,473	Tril. Btu	2021	DOE
By Renewable Energy Power Sources	12,171	Tril. Btu	2021	DOE
Biomass (Wood, Waste, Biofuels)	4,850	Tril. Btu	2021	DOE
Conventional Hydroelectric Power	2,283	Tril. Btu	2021	DOE
Wind	3,332	Tril. Btu	2021	DOE
Geothermal	206	Tril. Btu	2021	DOE
Solar	1,501	Tril. Btu	2021	DOE
By Nuclear	8,129	Tril. Btu	2021	DOE
Renewable Source as a Percent of all Renewable Energy Consumption				
Biomass (Wood, Waste, Biofuels)	43	%	2021	DOE
Hydroelectric	20	%	2021	DOE
Wind	16	%	2021	DOE
Geothermal	18	%	2021	DOE
Solar	3	%	2021	DOE
Net Electricity Generation from Renewable Energy Sources	762.9	TWhs	2021	DOE
Conventional Hydroelectric	260.2	TWhs	2021	DOE
Wind	349.8	TWhs	2021	DOE
Geothermal	16.2	TWhs	2021	DOE
Solar	136.7	TWhs	2021	DOE
U.S. Wind Generating Capacity, 2001	4,195	MW	2001	AWEA
U.S. Wind Generating Capacity, 2019	114,200	MW	2019	AWEA
Light-Duty Alternative-Fuel Vehicle Stock Projection, 2021	10.2	Mil. Vehicles	2021	DOE
Light-Duty Alternative-Fuel Vehicle Stock Projection, 2050	22.1	Mil. Vehicles	2050	DOE
Total Electric Drive Vehicle on U.S. Roads*	6.9	Mil. Vehicles	2020	ElectricDrive.org

DOE = U.S. Department of Energy
AWEA = American Wind Energy Association
MW = Megawatts
Btu = British Thermal Unit
TWhs = Terawatt-Hours
MSW = Municipal Solid Waste
* Includes Hybrids and Plug-ins.
Source: Plunkett Research, Ltd. Copyright© 2022, All Rights Reserved
www.plunkettresearch.com

Approximate Energy Unit Conversion Factors

Crude oil[1]

From	To convert into:				
	tonnes[2]	kilolitres	barrels	US gallons	tonnes/year
	Multiply by:				
Tonnes[2]	1	1.165	7.33	307.86	–
Kilolitres	0.8581	1	6.2898	264.17	–
Barrels	0.1364	0.159	1	42	–
US gallons	0.00325	0.0038	0.0238	1	–
Barrels per day	–	–	–	–	49.8

[1] Based on worldwide average gravity. [2] tonnes = metric tons

Products

From	To convert:			
	barrels to tonnes	tonnes to barrels	kilolitres to tonnes	tonnes to kilolitres
	Multiply by:			
Liquefied Petroleum Gas (LPG)	0.059	16.85	0.373	2.679
Gasoline	0.086	11.60	0.541	1.849
Kerosene	0.120	8.35	0.753	1.328
Gas oil/diesel	0.127	7.88	0.798	1.253
Residual Fuel oil	0.134	7.46	0.843	1.186
Product basket	0.157	6.35	0.991	1.010

Natural Gas (NG) and Liquefied Natural Gas (LNG)

From	To convert to:					
	billion cubic meters NG	billion cubic feet NG	million tonnes oil equivalent	million tonnes LNG	trillion British thermal units	million barrels oil equivalent
	Multiply by:					
1 billion cubic meters NG	1	35.32	0.86	0.74	34.12	5.88
1 billion cubic feet NG	0.03	1	0.02	0.02	0.97	0.17
1 million tonnes oil equivalent	1.16	41.07	1	0.86	39.68	6.84
1 million tonnes LNG	1.36	48.03	1.17	1	46.41	8.00
1 trillion British thermal units	0.03	1.04	0.03	0.02	1	0.17
1 million barrels oil equivalent	0.17	6.00	0.15	0.13	5.80	1

Units

1 metric tonne = 2204.62 lb.	1 kilocalorie (kcal) = 4.187 kJ = 3.968 Btu
1 metric tonne = 1.1023 short tons	1 kilojoule (kJ) = 0.239 kcal = 0.948 Btu
1 kilolitre = 6.2898 barrels	1 British thermal unit (Btu) = 0.252 kcal = 1.055 kJ
1 kilolitre = 1 cubic meter	1 kilowatt-hour (kWh) = 860 kcal = 3600 kJ = 3412 Btu

Calorific equivalents:

One tonne of oil equivalent equals approximately:

Heat units	10 million kilocalories	Solid fuels	1.5 tonnes of hard coal
	42 gigajoules		3 tonnes of lignite
	40 million Btu	Gaseous fuels	See Natural gas and LNG table
		Electricity	12 megawatt-hours

Note: One million tonnes of oil or oil equivalent produces about 4,400 gigawatt-hours (= 4.4 terawatt-hours) of electricity in a modern power station.

Source: BP, *Statistical Review of Energy, June 2022*
Plunkett Research, ® Ltd.
www.plunkettresearch.com

Biomass Energy Resource Hierarchy

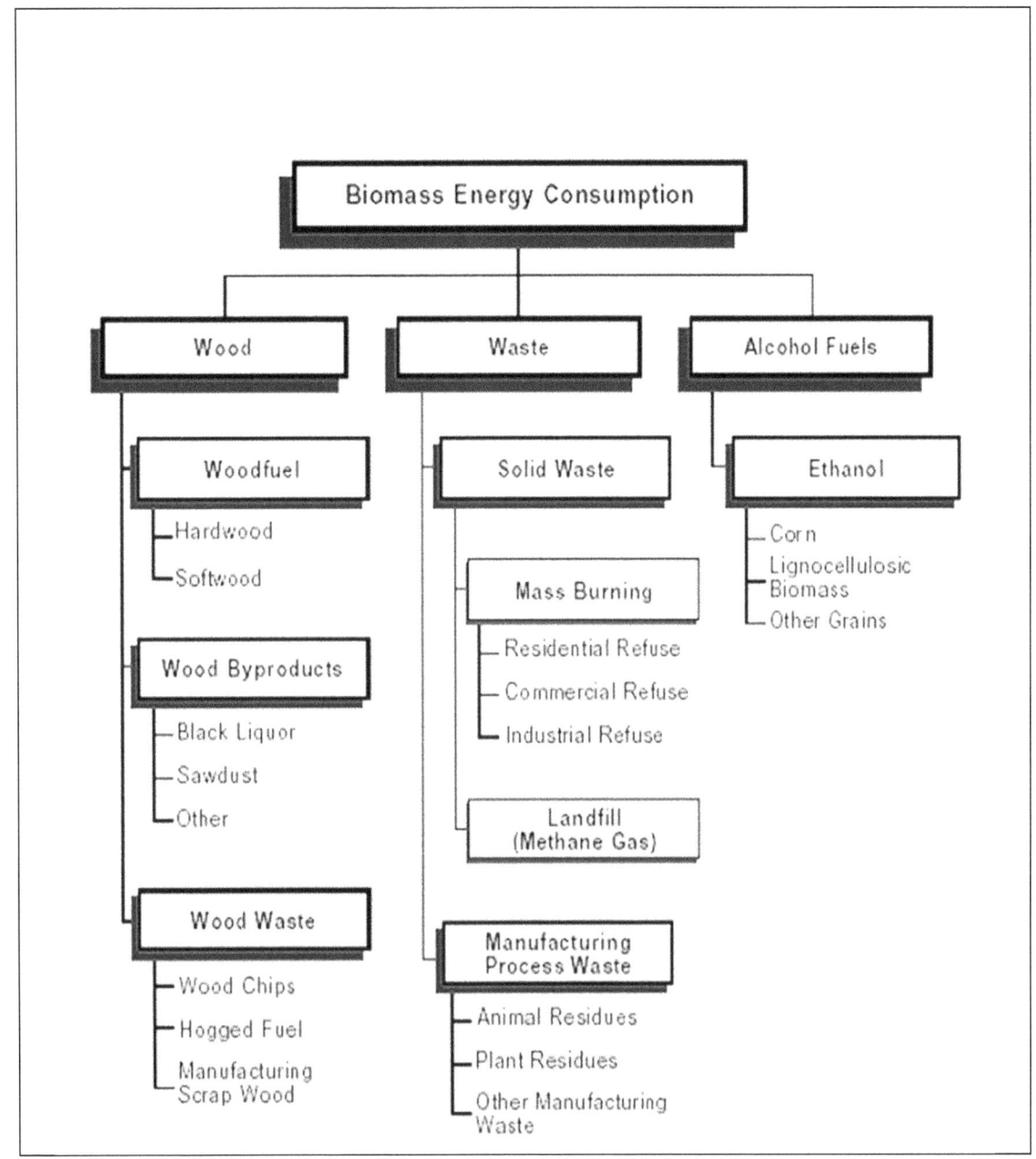

- **Biomass Energy Consumption**
  - **Wood**
    - Woodfuel
      - Hardwood
      - Softwood
    - Wood Byproducts
      - Black Liquor
      - Sawdust
      - Other
    - Wood Waste
      - Wood Chips
      - Hogged Fuel
      - Manufacturing Scrap Wood
  - **Waste**
    - Solid Waste
      - Mass Burning
        - Residential Refuse
        - Commercial Refuse
        - Industrial Refuse
      - Landfill (Methane Gas)
    - Manufacturing Process Waste
      - Animal Residues
      - Plant Residues
      - Other Manufacturing Waste
  - **Alcohol Fuels**
    - Ethanol
      - Corn
      - Lignocellulosic Biomass
      - Other Grains

Source: U.S. Department of Energy, Energy Information Administration
Plunkett Research, ® Ltd.
www.plunkettresearch.com

Comparison of Alternative Fuels with Gasoline & Diesel

(Average Prices as of July 2021)

	Gasoline	Low Sulfur Diesel	Biodiesel (B20)	Compressed Natural Gas (CNG)	Electricity
Octane Number	84 to 93	N/A	N/A	120+	N/A
Cetane Number	N/A	40 to 55	48 to 65	N/A	N/A
Main Fuel Source	Crude Oil	Crude Oil	Soy bean oil, waste cooking oil, animal fats and rapeseed oil	Underground reserves and renewable biogas	Coal; however, nuclear, natural gas, hydroelectric and renewable resources can also be used.
Energy Content per Gallon	112,114 - 116,090 Btu	128,488 Btu	119,550 Btu for B100	20,160 Btu	3,414 Btu
Energy Ratio Compared to Gasoline	97%-100%	One gallon of diesel has 113% of the energy of one gallon of gasoline.	B20 has 109% of the energy of one gallon of gasoline or 99% of the energy of one gallon of diesel.	5.66 pounds or 123.57 cu ft. of CNG has 100% of the energy of one gallon of gasoline	33.70 kWh has 100% of the energy of one gallon of gasoline.
Physical State	Liquid	Liquid	Liquid	Compressed Gas	Electricity
Environmental Impacts of Burning Fuel	Produces harmful emissions; however, gasoline and gasoline vehicles are rapidly improving and emissions are being reduced.	Produces harmful emissions; however, diesel and diesel vehicles are rapidly improving and emissions are being reduced, especially with after-treatment devices.	Reduces particulate matter and global warming gas emissions compared to conventional diesel; however, NOx emissions may be increased.	CNG vehicles can demonstrate a reduction in ozone-forming emissions compared to some conventional fuels; however, HC emissions may be increased.	Electric vehicles have zero tailpipe emissions; however, some amount of emissions can be contributed to power generation.
Fuel Availability (Station data as of 11/16/2020)	Available at all fueling stations.	Available at most fueling stations.	Available in bulk from an increasing number of suppliers. Most states currently have some biodiesel stations available to the public, for a U.S. total of about 713. Minnesota has the highest concentration of stations, with 146.	Roughly 1,556 CNG stations can be found across the country. Minnesota has the highest concentration of CNG stations, with 415. Home fueling has also been available since 2005.	Most homes, gov't facilities, fleet garages, and businesses have adequate electrical capacity for charging, but special upgrades may be required. There are over 101,365 charging outlets nationwide, with over 32,625 of these in California.
Average Retail Price (US$ per GGE)	4.70	3.26	5.34	2.76	NA

(Continued on next page)

Comparison of Alternative Fuels with Gasoline & Diesel (cont.)

(Average Prices as of July 2021)

	Ethanol (E85)	Hydrogen	Liquefied Natural Gas (LNG)	Liquefied Petroleum Gas (Propane, LPG)	Methanol (M85)
Octane Number	110	130+	120+	105	112
Cetane Number	0 to 54	N/A	N/A	N/A	N/A
Main Fuel Source	Corn, grains or agricultural waste	Natural Gas, Methanol and other electrolysis of water.	Underground reserves and renewable biogas	A by-product of petroleum refining or natural gas processing	Natural gas, coal or woody biomass
Energy Content per Gallon	76,330 Btu for E100	51,585 Btu	21,240 Btu	84,250 Btu	57,250 Btu
Energy Ratio Compared to Gasoline	1 gallon of E85 has 73%-83% of the energy of 1 gallon gasoline.	1 kg or 2.198 lbs. of H_2 has 100% of the energy of one gallon of gasoline.	5.38 pounds of LNG has 100% of one gallon of gasoline	1 gallon of propane has 73% of the energy of one gallon of gasoline.	1 gallon of methanol has 49% of the energy of one gallon of gasoline.
Physical State	Liquid	Compressed Gas or Liquid	Cryogenic Liquid	Pressurized Liquid	Liquid
Environmental Impacts of Burning Fuel	E-85 vehicles can demonstrate a 25% reduction in ozone-forming emissions compared to reformulated gasoline.	Zero regulated emissions for fuel cell-powered vehicles, and only NOx emissions possible for internal combustion engines operating on hydrogen.	LNG vehicles can demonstrate a reduction in ozone-forming emissions compared to some conventional fuels; however, HC emissions may be increased.	LPG vehicles can demonstrate a 60% reduction in ozone-forming emissions compared to reformulated gasoline.	M-85 vehicles can demonstrate a 40% reduction in ozone-forming emissions compared to reformulated gasoline.
Fuel Availability (Station data as of 11/16/2020)	U.S. E-85 fueling stations are most heavily concentrated in the Midwest, but, in all, 3,834 stations are available.	There are currently only 63 hydrogen stations across the country, 49 of which are in California. Most are available for public use only.	Public LNG stations are limited (only about 111 nationally, mostly in California), and LNG is also available through several suppliers of cryogenic liquids.	Propane is one of the most accessible alternative fuels in the U.S. There are 2,998 filling stations nationwide, with high concentrations in Texas (426 stations) and California (268 stations).	Though still considered a qualified alternative fuel, the use of Methanol has dramatically declined since the early 1990s. It is used to a greater degree in racing cars, as well as in Chinese automobiles.
Average Retail Price (US$ per GGE)	3.93	N/A	3.54	5.84	N/A

GGE = Gasoline Gallon Equivalent.
N/A = Not applicable or not available.

Source: U.S. Department of Energy, Alternative Fuels Data Center
Plunkett Research, ® Ltd.
www.plunkettresearch.com

World Total Primary Energy Consumption by Region: 2017-2050

(Quadrillion Btu)

Region/Country	History 2017	2018	2019	2020	Projections 2025	2030	2035	2040	2045	2050	Average Annual Percent Change 2020-2050
OECD											
OECD Americas	122.6	125.2	125.3	118.2	126.0	127.5	130.9	134.6	139.7	145.2	0.7%
United States	97.4	99.8	99.9	92.9	98.4	98.6	100.0	101.9	105.0	108.7	0.5%
Canada	15.6	15.8	15.9	14.6	15.4	16.1	16.8	17.5	18.3	19.0	0.9%
Mexico/Chile	9.6	9.6	9.6	10.6	12.1	12.9	14.1	15.1	16.4	17.6	1.7%
OECD Europe	82.9	83.3	83.7	77.6	82.1	83.3	85.9	88.0	90.7	94.1	0.6%
OECD Asia	41.0	40.9	40.8	37.2	39.9	40.5	41.0	41.2	41.5	42.0	0.4%
Japan	20.4	20.2	19.9	18.3	18.7	18.4	18.1	17.7	17.4	17.2	-0.2%
South Korea	13.2	13.0	12.9	12.0	13.5	13.9	14.2	14.3	14.5	14.7	0.7%
Australia/New Zealand	7.5	7.7	7.9	6.9	7.7	8.2	8.7	9.1	9.6	10.1	1.3%
Total OECD	246.5	249.4	249.8	232.9	248.0	251.3	257.7	263.8	272.0	281.3	0.6%
Non-OECD											
Non-OECD Europe & Eurasia	48.9	49.1	49.0	52.6	54.8	56.9	59.5	61.9	64.1	66.0	0.8%
Russia	31.7	31.8	31.6	34.4	36.3	37.6	39.2	40.5	41.6	42.3	0.7%
Other	17.1	17.3	17.4	18.2	18.5	19.2	20.3	21.4	22.5	23.7	0.9%
Non-OECD Asia	220.8	227.4	232.8	230.3	267.2	292.8	320.8	349.4	378.5	402.8	1.9%
China	145.0	149.1	152.7	156.4	169.2	174.6	180.7	187.1	193.5	196.9	0.8%
India	33.9	35.2	36.2	31.5	46.5	59.8	74.4	89.3	105.2	119.8	4.6%
Other	41.9	43.1	43.9	42.5	51.6	58.5	65.7	73.0	79.8	86.1	2.4%
Middle East	36.9	37.3	38.2	35.2	40.3	41.7	43.3	46.1	47.6	48.3	1.1%
Africa	23.9	24.5	24.9	22.9	26.6	29.6	33.2	37.0	41.1	46.0	2.4%
Non-OECD America	32.5	32.3	32.2	27.6	30.8	32.9	35.0	37.2	39.5	42.0	1.4%
Brazil	16.3	16.4	16.6	14.9	16.7	17.7	18.7	19.6	20.2	20.8	1.1%
Other	16.3	15.9	15.6	12.7	14.1	15.1	16.2	17.7	19.4	21.2	1.7%
Total Non-OECD	363.0	370.6	377.2	368.6	419.6	453.9	491.7	531.7	570.8	605.1	1.7%
Total World	609.5	620.0	627.0	601.5	667.5	705.2	749.5	795.4	842.8	886.3	1.3%

Btu = British Thermal Unit

OECD = Organization for Economic Co-Operation and Development (A membership group of 30+ highly developed nations)

Notes: Energy totals include net imports of coal coke and electricity generated from biomass in the U.S. Totals may not equal sum of components due to independent rounding. The electricity portion of the national fuel consumption values consists of generation for domestic use plus an adjustment for electricity trade based on a fuel's share of total generation in the exporting country.

Source: U.S. Department of Energy, Energy Information Administration

Plunkett Research, ® Ltd.

www.plunkettresearch.com

Share of Electricity Generation by Energy Source, U.S.: Projections, 2021-2050

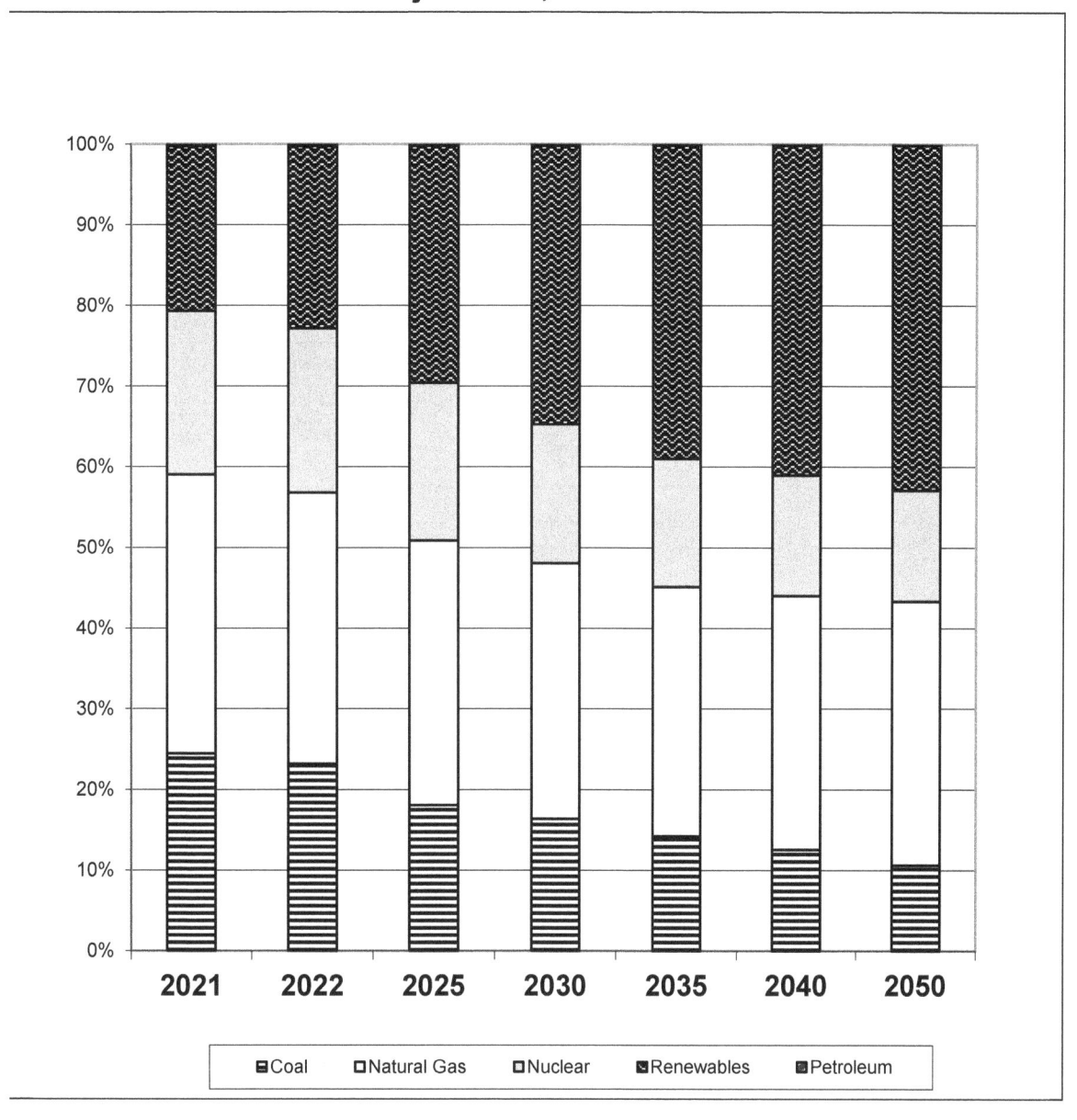

Source: U.S. Department of Energy, Energy Information Administration
Plunkett Research, ® Ltd.
www.plunkettresearch.com

Energy Consumption by Source & Sector, U.S.: 2021

(By Percent; Latest Year Available; Total Energy: 97.3 Quadrillion Btu)

Sector, by Source		Source, by Sector	
Petroleum[1]: 35.1 Quad. Btu		**Transportation: 26.9 Quad. Btu**	
Transportation	69%	Petroleum	90%
Industrial	25%	Natural Gas	4%
Residential & Commercial	3%	Renewable Energy	5%
Electric Power	1%	Electric Power	<1%
Natural Gas[2]: 31.3 Quad. Btu		**Industrial[5]: 25.9 Quad. Btu**	
Transportation	3%	Petroleum	34%
Industrial	33%	Natural Gas	40%
Residential & Commercial	26%	Coal	4%
Electric Power	37%	Renewable Energy	9%
Coal[3]: 10.5 Quad. Btu		Electric Power	13%
Industrial	9%	**Residential: 11.6 Quad. Btu**	
Electric Power	<1%	Petroleum	8%
Commercial	90%	Natural Gas	42%
Renewable Energy[4]: 12.2 Quad. Btu		Renewable Energy	7%
Transportation	12%	Electric Power	43%
Industrial	19%	**Commercial: 9.1 Quad. Btu**	
Residential & Commercial	10%	Petroleum	10%
Electric Power	59%	Natural Gas	37%
Nuclear Electric Power: 8.1 Quad. Btu		Coal	<1%
Electric Power	100%	Renewable Energy	3%
		Electric Power	50%
		Electric Power[7]: 36.7 Quad. Btu	
		Petroleum	1%
		Natural Gas	32%
		Coal	26%
		Renewable Energy	19%
		Nuclear Electric Power	22%

Note: Sum of components may not equal 100 percent due to independent rounding.

[1] Does not include biofuels that have been blended with petroleum, which are included in "Renewable Energy."

[2] Excludes natural gas plant liquids

[3] Includes -0.03 quadrillion Btu of coal coke net imports.

[4] Conventional hydroelectric power, geothermal, solar, wind, and biomass.

[5] Electricity retail sales to ultimate customers reported by electric utilities and, beginning in 1996, other energy service providers.

[6] Includes industrial combined-heat-and-power (CHP) and industrial electricity-only plants.

[7] Electricity-only and combined-heat-and-power (CHP) plants whose primary business is to sell electricity, or electricity and heat, to the public. Includes 0.15 quadrillion Btu of electricity net imports not shown under "Source."

Source: U.S. Department of Energy, U.S. Energy Information Administration
Plunkett Research, ® Ltd.
www.plunkettresearch.com

Primary Energy Flow by Source & Sector, U.S.: 2021

(Latest Year Available; Total Energy: 97.3 Quadrillion Btu)

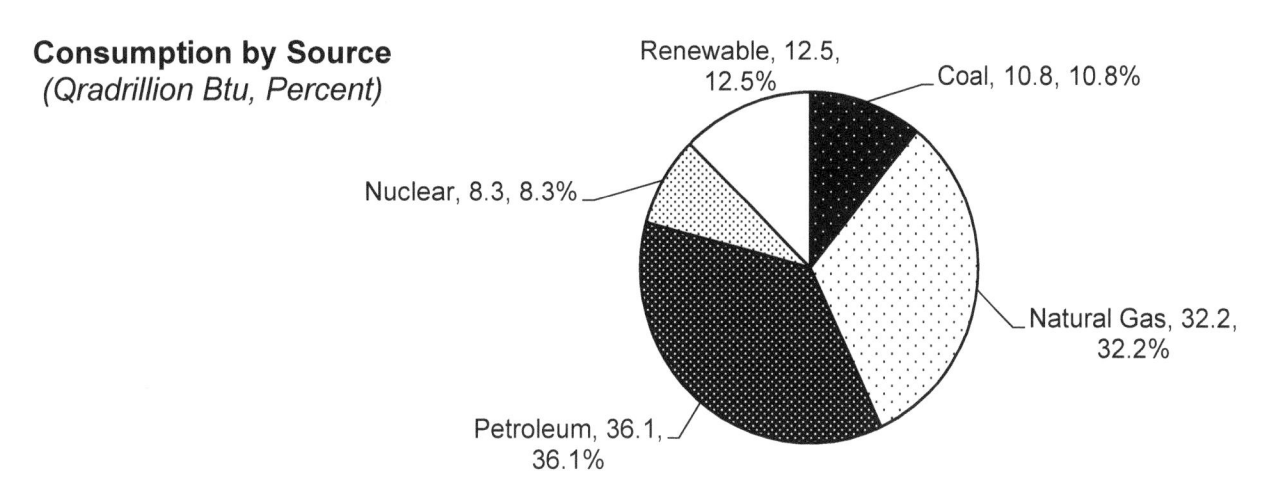

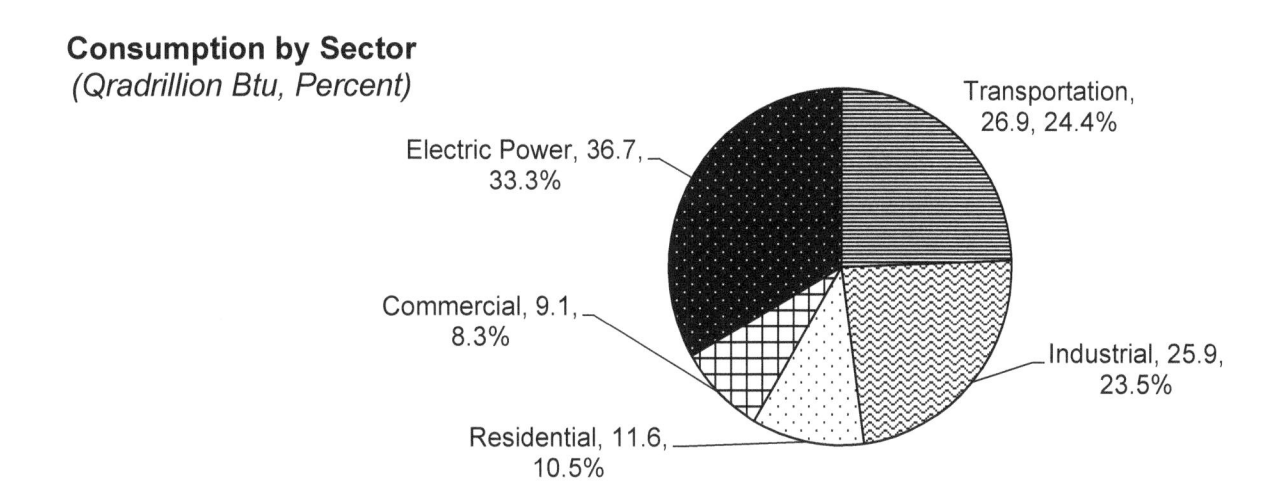

Consumption by Source
(Qradrillion Btu, Percent)

- Renewable, 12.5, 12.5%
- Coal, 10.8, 10.8%
- Natural Gas, 32.2, 32.2%
- Petroleum, 36.1, 36.1%
- Nuclear, 8.3, 8.3%

Consumption by Sector
(Qradrillion Btu, Percent)

- Transportation, 26.9, 24.4%
- Industrial, 25.9, 23.5%
- Residential, 11.6, 10.5%
- Commercial, 9.1, 8.3%
- Electric Power, 36.7, 33.3%

Notes: Sum of components may not equal 100 percent due to independent rounding.
Petroleum: Does not include biofuels that have been blended with petroleum, which are included in "Renewable Energy."
Natural Gas: Excludes supplemental gaseous fuels.
Coal: Includes less than 0.3 quadrillion Btu of coal coke net exports.
Renewable Energy: Includes conventional hydroelectric power, geothermal, solar/PV, wind, and biomass.
Industrial: Includes industrial combined-heat-and-power (CHP) and industrial electricity-only plants.
Residential & Commercial: Includes commercial combined-heat-and-power (CHP) and commercial electricity-only plants.
Electric Power: Includes electricity-only and combined-heat-and-power (CHP) plants whose primary business is to sell electricity, or electricity and heat, to the public.

Source: U.S. Department of Energy, U.S. Energy Information Administration
Plunkett Research, ® Ltd.
www.plunkettresearch.com

Net Electrical Power Generation by Fuel Type, U.S.: 2021

(Latest Year Available; Total Generation: 4,009 Million Megawatt-hours)

Total Generation-All Sources
(Thousand MWh, Percent)

- Coal, 898,679, 22%
- Petroleum, 18,782, 1%
- Natural Gas, 1,575,230, 38%
- Nuclear Energy, 778,152, 19%
- Renewables*, 836,004, 20%

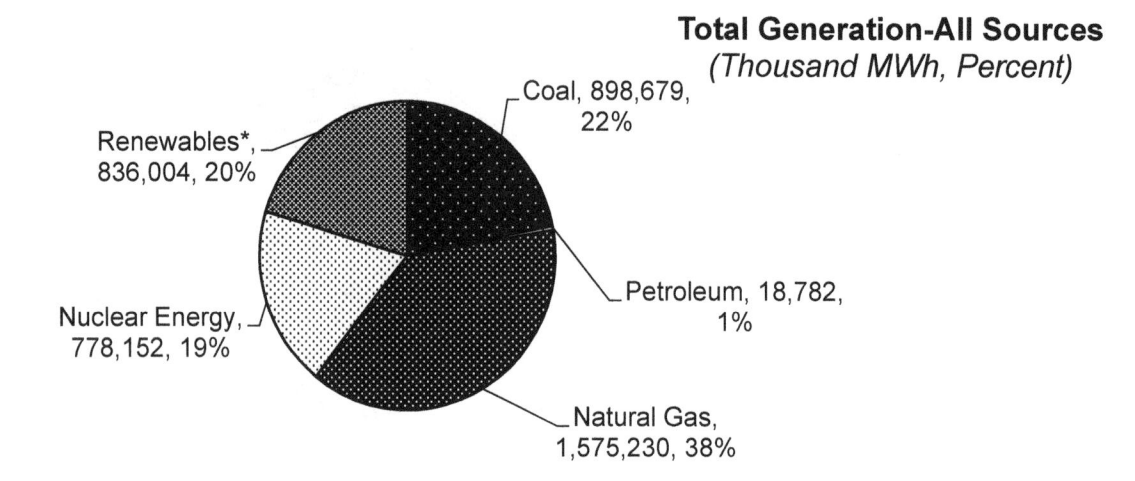

Renewable Sources
(Thousand MWh, Percent)

- Conventional Hydroelectric, 260,225, 31%
- Wood, 37,710, 4%
- Waste, 8,361, 1%
- Geothermal, 16,238, 2%
- Solar, 163,703, 20%
- Wind, 349,767, 42%

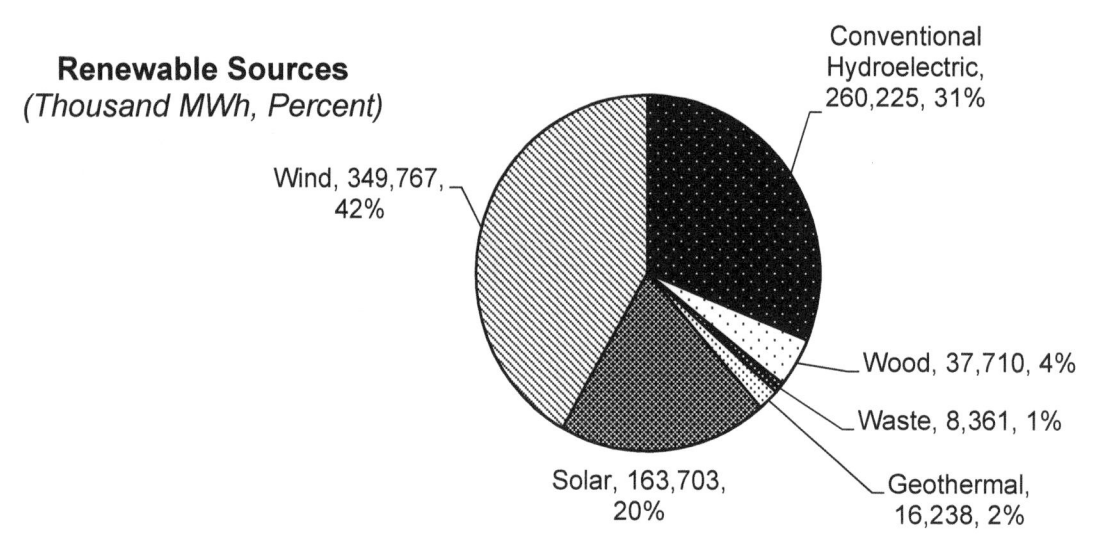

Notes: Sum of components may not equal 100 percent due to independent rounding.

* Renewables include conventional hydroelectric, as well as wind, solar, waste, wood and geothermal energy sources.

Source: U.S. Department of Energy, U.S. Energy Information Administration
Plunkett Research, ® Ltd.
www.plunkettresearch.com

Net Electrical Power Generation by Fuel Type, U.S.: 1990-July 2022

(Thousands of Megawatthours; Latest Year Available)

Year	Coal[1]	Petroleum[2]	Natural Gas	Other Gas[3]	Nuclear Energy	Hydro-electric	Other Renewables[4]	Total
1990	1,594,011	126,621	372,765	10,383	576,862	292,866	15,434	3,037,988
1991	1,590,623	119,752	381,553	11,336	612,565	288,994	15,966	3,073,799
1992	1,621,206	100,154	404,074	13,270	618,776	253,088	16,138	3,083,882
1993	1,690,070	112,788	414,927	12,956	610,291	280,494	16,789	3,197,191
1994	1,690,694	105,901	460,219	13,319	640,440	260,126	15,535	3,247,522
1995	1,709,426	74,554	496,058	13,870	673,402	310,833	73,965	3,353,487
1996	1,795,196	81,411	455,056	14,356	674,729	347,162	75,796	3,444,188
1997	1,845,016	92,555	479,399	13,351	628,644	356,453	77,183	3,492,172
1998	1,873,516	128,800	531,257	13,492	673,702	323,336	77,088	3,620,295
1999	1,881,087	118,061	556,396	14,126	728,254	319,536	79,423	3,694,810
2000	1,966,265	111,221	601,038	13,955	753,893	275,573	80,906	3,802,105
2001	1,903,956	124,880	639,129	9,039	768,826	216,961	70,769	3,736,644
2002	1,933,130	94,568	691,006	11,463	780,064	264,329	79,109	3,858,452
2003	1,973,737	119,406	649,908	15,600	763,733	275,806	79,487	3,883,185
2004	1,978,301	121,145	710,100	15,252	788,528	268,417	83,067	3,970,555
2005	2,012,873	122,225	760,960	13,464	781,986	270,321	87,329	4,055,423
2006	1,990,511	64,166	816,441	14,177	787,219	289,246	96,525	4,064,702
2007	2,016,456	65,739	896,590	13,453	806,425	247,510	105,238	4,156,745
2008	1,985,801	46,242	882,981	11,707	806,208	254,831	126,101	4,119,388
2009	1,755,904	38,937	920,979	10,632	798,855	273,445	144,279	3,950,331
2010	1,847,290	37,061	987,697	11,313	806,968	260,203	167,173	4,125,060
2011	1,733,430	30,182	1,013,689	11,566	790,204	319,355	193,981	4,100,141
2012	1,514,043	23,190	1,225,894	11,898	769,331	276,240	218,333	4,047,765
2013	1,581,115	27,164	1,124,836	12,853	789,016	268,565	253,508	4,065,964
2014	1,581,710	30,232	1,126,609	12,022	797,166	259,367	279,213	4,093,606
2015	1,352,398	28,249	1,333,482	13,117	797,178	249,080	295,161	4,077,601
2016	1,239,149	24,205	1,378,307	12,807	805,694	267,812	341,633	4,076,675
2017	1,207,901	21,091	1,272,864	14,159	804,950	300,045	387,245	4,014,804
2018	1,146,393	24,302	1,480,204	12,191	807,078	291,724	421,049	4,177,810
2019	1,063,184	20,223	1,531,957	13,550	804,219	282,765	707,349	4,134,766
2020	773,805	17,496	1,616,749	11,181	789,917	291,111	501,388	4,009,085
2021	898,679	20,977	1,575,230	11,283	778,152	260,225	451,484	4,115,540
2022*	839,483	20,282	1,651,023	11,376	772,578	278,984	503,938	4,221,809

* Year to date, through August. NA = Not available.

[1] Anthracite, bituminous, subbituminous, lignite, waste coal, and coal synfuel.

[2] Petroleum liquids including distillate fuel oil, residual fuel oil, jet fuel, kerosene, and waste oil; and petroleum coke.

[3] Blast furnace gas and other manufactured and waste gases derived from fossil fuels. Prior to 2011, Other Gas included propane and synthesis gases.

[4] Includes wind; solar thermal and photovoltaic; wood and wood-derived fuels; geothermal; and other biomass. Category realignments are responsible for the dramatic increase in 1995.

Source: U.S. Department of Energy, Energy Information Administration

Plunkett Research, ® Ltd.

www.plunkettresearch.com

Energy Production by Renewable Energy, U.S.: Selected Years, 1955-2021

(In Trillions of Btus; Latest Year Available)

Year	Conventional Hydroelectric Power	Geothermal	Solar/PV	Wind	Biomass	Total Renewable	Total, Renewable & Non-Renewable
1955	1,359.8	NA	NA	NA	1,424.1	2,784.0	40,147.7
1960	1,608.0	0.4	NA	NA	1,319.9	2,928.2	42,803.3
1965	2,059.1	2.0	NA	NA	1,334.8	3,395.8	50,673.9
1970	2,633.5	5.5	NA	NA	1,431.0	4,070.0	63,495.4
1975	3,154.6	33.8	NA	NA	1,498.7	4,687.1	61,320.2
1980	2,900.1	52.7	NA	NA	2,475.5	5,428.3	67,175.4
1985	2,970.2	97.4	0.1	0.1	3,016.2	6,084.0	67,698.3
1990	3,046.4	170.7	58.8	29.0	2,735.1	6,040.0	70,704.0
1991	3,015.9	177.6	61.6	30.8	2,781.8	6,067.8	70,361.6
1992	2,617.4	178.7	62.9	29.9	2,931.7	5,820.5	69,954.8
1993	2,891.6	185.7	65.2	31.0	2,908.4	6,081.9	68,314.5
1994	2,683.5	173.5	67.1	35.6	3,027.5	5,987.1	70,724.6
1995	3,205.3	152.1	68.2	32.6	3,099.1	6,557.3	71,172.9
1996	3,589.7	163.4	69.1	33.4	3,155.3	7,010.9	72,484.8
1997	3,640.5	166.7	68.1	33.6	3,107.9	7,016.8	72,470.5
1998	3,297.1	168.5	67.4	30.9	2,928.9	6,492.7	72,874.6
1999	3,267.6	170.9	66.0	45.9	2,965.1	6,515.6	71,740.3
2000	2,811.1	164.4	63.4	57.1	3,005.7	6,101.7	71,330.0
2001	2,241.9	164.5	61.6	69.6	2,624.2	5,161.8	71,731.9
2002	2,689.0	171.2	59.9	105.3	2,705.4	5,730.9	70,709.9
2003	2,792.5	173.4	58.4	113.3	2,804.8	5,942.5	69,934.8
2004	2,688.5	178.1	58.3	141.7	2,996.0	6,062.7	70,227.7
2005	2,702.9	180.7	57.8	178.1	3,101.2	6,220.8	69,430.7
2006	2,869.0	181.2	60.6	263.7	3,211.5	6,586.2	70,734.5
2007	2,446.4	185.8	65.4	340.5	3,472.1	6,510.4	71,397.7
2008	2,511.1	192.4	73.8	545.5	3,868.3	7,191.5	73,204.6
2009	2,668.8	200.2	77.7	721.1	3,956.6	7,624.9	72,636.6
2010	2,538.5	208.0	90.5	923.4	4,552.5	8,313.8	74,868.4
2011	3,102.9	212.3	111.1	1,167.6	4,704.3	9,299.5	78,060.1
2012	2,628.7	211.6	156.8	1,340.1	4,546.7	8,886.0	79,261.9
2013	2,562.4	214.0	224.5	1,601.4	4,815.6	9,417.9	81,870.8
2014	2,466.6	214.5	336.9	1,727.5	5,020.4	9,766.4	87,754.0
2015	2,321.2	211.8	425.7	1,777.3	4,991.6	9,728.5	88,246.8
2016	2,472.4	209.6	568.7	2,095.6	5,080.5	10,428.2	84,261.9
2017	2,770.0	211.0	774.3	2,347.3	5,203.7	11,300.7	88,117.2
2018	2,687.7	217.6	951.4	2,533.1	5,332.2	11,722.0	95,774.0
2019	2,563.5	201.2	1,017.1	2,634.8	5,178.3	11,595.1	101,400.9
2020	2,592.3	214.2	1,245.7	3,005.5	4,796.1	11,853.9	95,845.2
2021	2,283.0	206.0	1,501.0	3,332.0	4,850.0	12,172.0	98,337.0

NA = Not available

Note: Most data are estimates. Totals may not equal sum of components due to independent rounding.

Source: U.S. Department of Energy, Energy Information Administration

Plunkett Research, ® Ltd.
www.plunkettresearch.com

Plunkett Research, Ltd.   59

U.S. Renewable Energy Consumption by Energy Source, 2015 vs. 2021

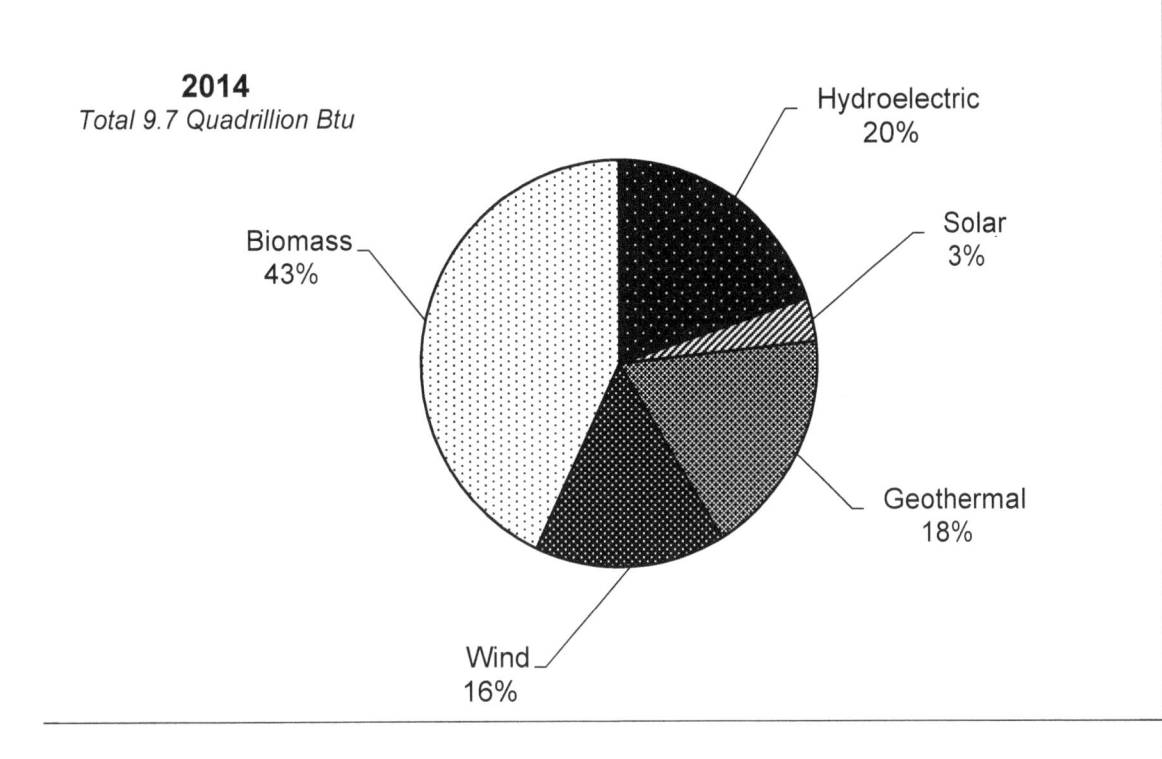

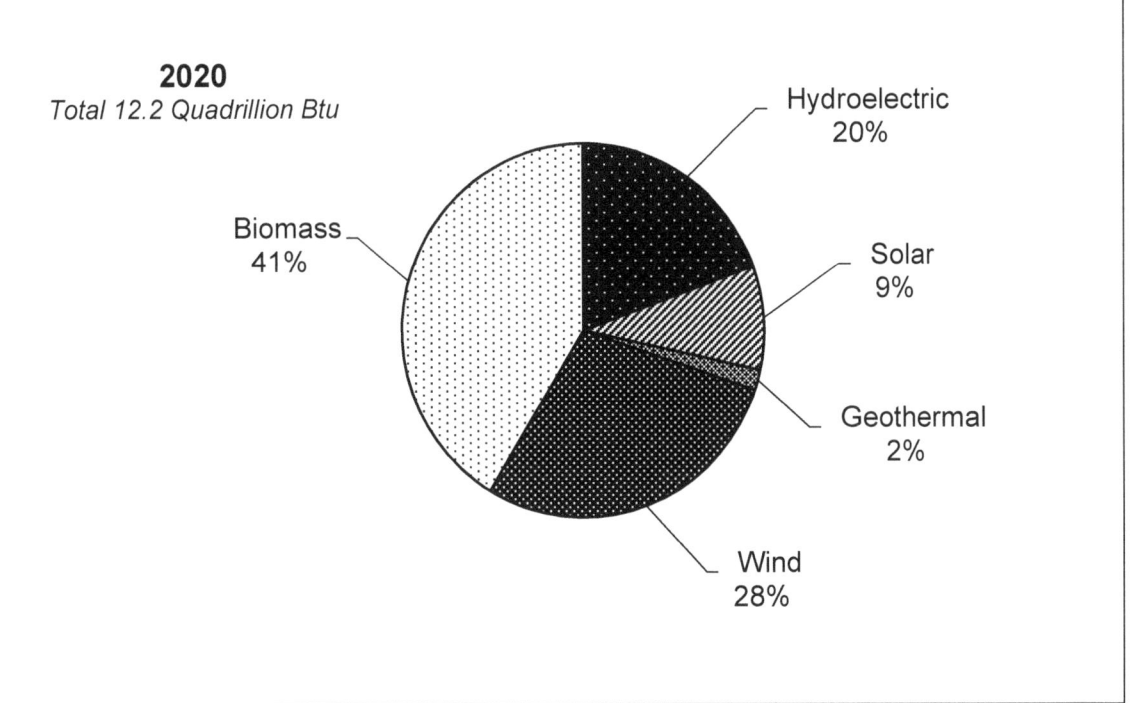

2014
Total 9.7 Quadrillion Btu

- Hydroelectric 20%
- Solar 3%
- Geothermal 18%
- Wind 16%
- Biomass 43%

2020
Total 12.2 Quadrillion Btu

- Hydroelectric 20%
- Solar 9%
- Geothermal 2%
- Wind 28%
- Biomass 41%

Source: U.S. Energy Information Administration

Plunkett Research, ® Ltd.
www.plunkettreasearch.com

Fuel Ethanol Production & Consumption, U.S.: 1981- July 2022

Year	Fuel Ethanol Production (Thous. Barrels)	Fuel Ethanol Production (Mil. Gallons)	Fuel Ethanol Net Imports (Thous. Barrels)	Fuel Ethanol Stocks (Thous. Barrels)	Fuel Ethanol Consumption (Thous. Barrels)	Fuel Ethanol Consumption (Mil. Gallons)
1981	1,978	83	N/A	N/A	1,978	83
1982	5,369	225	N/A	N/A	5,369	225
1983	9,890	415	N/A	N/A	9,890	415
1984	12,150	510	N/A	N/A	12,150	510
1985	14,693	617	N/A	N/A	14,693	617
1986	16,954	712	N/A	N/A	16,954	712
1987	19,497	819	N/A	N/A	19,497	819
1988	19,780	831	N/A	N/A	19,780	831
1989	20,062	843	N/A	N/A	20,062	843
1990	17,802	748	N/A	N/A	17,802	748
1991	20,627	866	N/A	N/A	20,627	866
1992	23,453	985	N/A	1,791	23,453	985
1993	27,484	1,154	244	2,114	27,405	1,151
1994	30,689	1,289	279	2,393	30,689	1,289
1995	32,325	1,358	387	2,186	32,919	1,383
1996	23,178	973	313	2,065	23,612	992
1997	30,674	1,288	85	2,925	29,899	1,256
1998	33,453	1,405	66	3,406	33,038	1,388
1999	34,881	1,465	87	4,024	34,350	1,443
2000	38,627	1,622	116	3,400	39,367	1,653
2001	42,028	1,765	315	4,298	41,445	1,741
2002	50,956	2,140	306	6,200	49,360	2,073
2003	66,772	2,804	292	5,978	67,286	2,826
2004	81,058	3,404	3,542	6,002	84,576	3,552
2005	92,961	3,904	3,234	5,563	96,634	4,059
2006	116,294	4,884	17,408	8,760	130,505	5,481
2007	155,263	6,521	10,457	10,535	163,945	6,886
2008	221,637	9,309	12,610	14,226	230,556	9,683
2009	260,424	10,938	4,720	16,594	262,776	11,037
2010	316,617	13,298	-9,115	17,941	306,155	12,858
2011	331,646	13,929	-24,365	18,238	306,984	12,893
2012	314,714	13,218	-5,891	20,350	306,711	12,882
2013	316,493	13,293	-5,761	16,424	314,658	13,216
2014	340,781	14,313	-18,371	18,739	320,095	13,444
2015	352,553	14,807	-17,632	21,596	332,064	13,947
2016	366,981	15,413	-27,002	19,758	341,817	14,356
2017	379,435	15,936	-31,268	23,043	344,882	14,485
2018	383,127	16,091	-39,410	23,418	343,342	14,420
2019	375,678	15,778	-30,276	22,352	346,468	14,552
2020	331,928	13,941	-27,692	24,663	301,925	12,681
2021	357,517	15,016	-28,135	22,036	332,010	13,944
2022*	215,125	9,036	-21,753	24,165	191,245	8,032

* January to July. N/A = Not Available.

Source: U.S. Department of Energy, Energy Information Administration

Plunkett Research,® Ltd.

www.plunkettresearch.com

Biodiesel Production & Consumption, U.S.: 2001- July 2022

Year	Biodiesel Production (Thous. Barrels)	Biodiesel Production (Mil. Gallons)	Biodiesel Imports (Thous. Barrels)	Biodiesel Exports (Thous. Barrels)	Biodiesel Net Imports (Thous. Barrels)	Biodiesel Consumption (Thous. Barrels)	Biodiesel Consumption (Mil. Gallons)
2001	204.20	8.58	80.92	40.65	40.28	244.48	10.27
2002	249.62	10.48	197.34	57.43	139.92	389.54	16.36
2003	338.32	14.21	96.80	113.47	-16.66	321.66	13.51
2004	666.24	27.98	100.54	127.72	-27.18	639.06	26.84
2005	2,161.59	90.79	213.69	212.71	0.98	2,162.57	90.83
2006	5,962.84	250.44	1,105.32	855.62	249.70	6,212.53	260.93
2007	11,662.50	489.83	3,454.96	6,695.84	-3,240.88	8,421.62	353.71
2008	16,145.38	678.11	7,755.03	16,672.90	-8,917.87	7,227.51	303.56
2009	12,281.07	515.81	1,905.88	6,546.09	-4,640.21	7,662.67	321.83
2010	8,177.26	343.45	563.96	2,587.97	-2,024.01	6,192.26	260.08
2011	23,035.26	967.48	890.37	1,798.62	-908.25	21,099.30	886.17
2012	23,588.36	990.71	853.00	3,055.76	-2,202.76	21,405.86	899.05
2013	32,368.00	1,359.46	8,152.00	4,674.66	3,477.34	34,019.99	1,428.84
2014	30,451.87	1,278.98	4,578.00	1,974.27	2,603.73	33,734.69	1,416.86
2015	30,079.68	1,263.35	8,399.00	2,090.76	6,308.24	35,575.25	1,494.16
2016	37,326.89	1,567.73	16,879.00	2,098.19	14,780.81	49,653.27	2,085.44
2017	37,993.07	1,595.71	9,374.00	2,228.25	7,145.75	47,268.61	1,985.28
2018	44,240.78	1,858.11	3,969.00	2,470.30	1,498.71	45,330.11	1,903.87
2019	41,060.00	1,021.96	4,078.00	2,730.36	1,347.64	43,162.92	1,812.84
2020	24,337.00	1,022.00	2,418.00	1,905.00	513.00	25,425.00	1,068.00
2021	40,686.00	1,709.00	5,005.00	4,452.00	553.00	40,717.00	11,710.00
2022*	21,753.00	914.00	2,762.00	4,414.00	-1,652.00	21,241.00	892.00

* January to July.

Source: U.S. Department of Energy, Energy Information Administration
Plunkett Research, ® Ltd.
www.plunkettresearch.com

Top 10 Countries by Installed Wind Generating Capacity: 2021

(Latest Year Available)

Rank	Country	Total Installed Capacity (MW)	% of Total World Capacity
1	China	328,973	39.9%
2	U.S.A	132,738	16.1%
3	Germany	63,762	7.7%
4	India	400,677	48.6%
5	Spain	274,497	33.3%
6	United Kingdom	27,130	3.3%
7	Brazil	21,161	2.6%
8	France	18,676	2.3%
9	Canada	14,304	1.7%
10	Sweden	12,080	1.5%
Total World		**824,874**	**100.0%**

MW = Megawatts

Source: BP, *Statistical Review of World Energy*, June 2020

Plunkett Research, ® Ltd.

www.plunkettresearch.com

Top 15 U.S. States by Installed Wind Generating Capacity: 2nd Quarter 2022

Rank	State	Total Installed Capacity (MW)	% of Total U.S. Capacity
1	Texas	37,422	26.8%
2	Iowa	12,427	8.9%
3	Oklahoma	11,991	8.6%
4	Kansas	8,224	5.9%
5	Illinois	7,037	5.0%
6	California	6,117	4.4%
7	Colorado	5,197	3.7%
8	Minnesota	4,577	3.3%
9	North Dakota	4,301	3.1%
10	New Mexico	4,235	3.0%
11	Oregon	4,043	2.9%
12	Indiana	3,469	2.5%
13	Washington	3,395	2.4%
14	Nebraska	3,219	2.3%
15	Wyoming	3,176	2.3%
	Total	139,635	100.0%

MW = Megawatts

Source: U.S. Department of Energy

Plunkett Research, ® Ltd.

www.plunkettresearch.com

U.S. Department of Energy
Funding for Science & Energy Programs: 2021-2023

(In Thousands of US$; Latest Year Available)

Area of Scientific Research	FY 20201 Enacted	FY 2022 Annualized CR*	FY 2023 Congressional Request	FY 2023 vs. FY 21 Enacted Dollar	Percent
Energy Programs	**14,467,492**	**12,295,025**	**18,640,430**	**6,345,405**	**52%**
Energy Efficiency and Renewable Energy	2,861,760	3,200,000	4,018,885	818,885	26%
Sustainable transportation	805,500	839,500	128,732	289,231	34%
Vehicle technologies	400,000	42,000	602,731	182,731	43%
Bioenergy technologies	255,000	262,000	340,000	78,000	29%
Hydrogen and fuel cell technologies	150,000	157,500	186,000	28,500	18%
Renewable power	646,000	715,000	1,330,195	614,965	85%
Solar energy technologies	280,000	290,000	534,575	244,575	83%
Wind energy technologies	110,000	114,000	345,390	231,390	202%
Water power technologies	150,000	162,000	190,500	28,500	17%
Geothermal technologies	106,000	108,500	202,000	92,500	84%
Energy efficiency	1,103,500	1,190,500	974,500	-216,000	-18%
Advanced Manufacturing	396,000	416,000	582,500	166,500	40%
Federal energy management program	40,000	40,000	0	-40,000	-100%
Building Technologies	290	307,500	392,000	84,500	27%
Weatherization and intergovernmental programs	0	15,000	0	-15,000	-100%
Corporate support programs	309,500	377,453	585,459	208,006	55%
Electricity	211,720	277,000	297,386	20,386	7%
Transmission Reliability and Resilience	48,220	26,000	37,300	11,300	43%
Energy storage	80,000	120,000	81,000	-39,000	-32%
Program direction	18,000	20,000	17,586	-2,414	-12%
Cybersecurity, Energy Security, and Emergency Response	156,000	185,804	202,143	16,339	8%
Nuclear Energy	1,507,600	1,654,800	1,675,060	20,260	1%
Fossil Energy Programs	750,000	825,000	893,160	68,160	8%
Uranium Enrichment D&D Fund	841,000	860,000	822,421	-37,579	-4%
Energy Information Administration	126,800	129,087	144,480	15,393	11%
Non-Defense Environmental Cleanup	319,200	333,863	323,249	-10,614	-3%
Science	7,026,000	7,475,000	7,799,211	324,211	4%
Advanced Research Projects Agency - Energy.	427,000	450,000	397,203	157,203	65%
Advanced Research Projects Agency - Climate.	0	0	200,000	200,000	NA
Departmental Administration	166,000	240,000	397,203	157,203	65%
Inspector General	57,739	78,000	106,808	28,808	36%
Credit Programs	36,000	36,000	179,866	143,866	399%

NA = Not Available

Source: U.S. Department of Energy, Office of Science
Plunkett Research, ® Ltd.
www.plunkettresearch.com

Federal R&D & R&D Plant Funding for Energy, U.S.: Fiscal Years 2020-2022

(In Millions of US$; Latest Year Available)

	2020 Actual	2021 Prelim.[1]	2022 Proposed	Change, 2021-22 Dollar	Change, 2021-22 Percent
Total	13,603	12,114	15,643	3,529	8%
Energy Programs	4,462	4,066	5,416	1,350	44%
Energy Efficiency and Renewable Energy	2,009	2,043	2,980	937	33%
Electricity Delivery and Energy Reliability	1,248	155	175	20	13%
Fossil Energy	709	721	868	147	20%
Nuclear Energy	1,161	1,068	1,261	193	18%
Electricity Delivery	NA	NA	NA	NA	NA
Cybersecurity, Energy Security, and Emergency Response	36	63	70	7	11%
Advanced Research Projects Agency-Energy (ARPA-E)	390	392	463	71	18%
Department of Agriculture	2,674	2,655	3,245	590	22%
National Institute of Food and Agriculture: Biomass R&D[2]	914	951	1,165	214	22%

Note: Detail may not add to total because of rounding. Percent change is calculated on unrounded data.

[1] The FY 2018 data are official estimates reflecting continuing resolution funding for FY 2018 and not the enacted omnibus spending bill for that year (Consolidated Appropriations Act, 2018, signed 23 March 2018). Most federal agencies did not prepare R&D estimates for FY 2018 based on the final spending figures in the omnibus.

[2] The Biomass R&D program is a mandatory program last authorized in the Agricultural Act of 2014 (Farm Bill).

NA = Not Available

Source: EOP, OMB, Analytical Perspectives, Budget of the United States Government, Fiscal Year 2020
Plunkett Research, ® Ltd.
www.plunkettresearch.com

Plunkett Research, Ltd. 67

Chapter 3

IMPORTANT SOLAR POWER, WIND POWER & RENEWABLE ENERGY INDUSTRY CONTACTS

Addresses, Telephone Numbers and Internet Sites

Contents:

1) Agriculture Industry Associations
2) Alternative Energy-Biomass
3) Alternative Energy-Clean Coal
4) Alternative Energy-Clean Transportation
5) Alternative Energy-Ethanol
6) Alternative Energy-Fuel Cells
7) Alternative Energy-General
8) Alternative Energy-Geothermal
9) Alternative Energy-Hydroelectric
10) Alternative Energy-Solar
11) Alternative Energy-Storage
12) Alternative Energy-Wind
13) Battery Industry Associations
14) Brazilian Government Agencies-Scientific
15) Careers-First Time Jobs/New Grads
16) Careers-General Job Listings
17) Careers-Job Reference Tools
18) Chemicals Industry Associations
19) Computer & Electronics Industry Associations
20) Construction Resources-Energy Efficient Buildings
21) Corporate Information Resources
22) Distillery Industry Associations
23) Economic Data & Research
24) Emissions Cap & Trade Associations
25) Energy Associations-China, General
26) Energy Associations-Electric Power
27) Energy Associations-International
28) Energy Associations-Natural Gas
29) Energy Associations-Nuclear
30) Energy Associations-Oil Sands
31) Energy Associations-Other
32) Energy Education Resources
33) Energy Industry Resources
34) Engineering, Research & Scientific Associations
35) Environmental Organizations
36) Environmental Resources
37) Gasification Industry Associations
38) Hybrid & Electric Vehicles
39) Industry Research/Market Research
40) MBA Resources
41) Metals & Steel Industry Associations
42) Natural Gas Vehicles
43) Nuclear Energy Associations
44) Nuclear Energy Asssociations
45) Renewable Energy Associations
46) Renewable Energy Resources
47) Research & Development, Laboratories
48) Science & Technology Resources
49) Stocks & Financial Markets Data
50) Sustainable Development Organizations
51) Technology Transfer Associations
52) Trade Associations-General
53) Trade Associations-Global
54) Trade Resources
55) U.S. Government Agencies

1) Agriculture Industry Associations

International Sugar Organization (ISO)
1 Canada Sq.
Canary Wharf
London, E14 5AA UK
Phone: 44 (0)20 7513 1144
Fax: 44 (0)20 7513 1146
E-mail Address: info@isosugar.org
Web Address: www.isosugar.org
ISO is focused on conferences, seminars and studies for the global sugar industry, both for human consumption and for the ethanol sector.

Iowa Corn Growers
5505 NW 88th St.
Johnston, IA 50131 USA
Phone: 515-225-9242
E-mail Address: corninfo@iowacorn.org
Web Address: www.iowacorn.org
Iowa Corn Growers provides news and information about the corn industry and works toward long-term corn farming profitability.

National Corn Growers Association (NCGA)
632 Cepi Dr.
Chesterfield, MO 63005 USA
Phone: 636-733-9004
Fax: 636-733-9005
E-mail Address: corninfo@ncga.com
Web Address: www.ncga.com
The National Corn Growers Association (NCGA) represents corn growers across the U.S. It develops and implements programs and policies that protect or advance the interests of corn growers and lobbies Congress on behalf of its members.

2) Alternative Energy-Biomass

Biofuels Association of Australia (BAA)
C5, Level 1, 2 Main St.
Point Cook, VIC 3030 Australia
Web Address: www.biofuelsassociation.com.au
The Biofuels Association of Australia (BAA) is an organization that works to represent the interests of the biofuels industry. In February 2007, the group merged with Renewable Fuels Australia and incorporated.

Biomass Research and Development (BR&D)
Web Address: www.biomassboard.gov
Biomass Research & Development (BRD) is a multi-agency effort to coordinate and accelerate all federal bio-based products and bioenergy research and development.

Centre for the Development of Renewable Energy Sources (CEDER)
Autovia de Navarra A15, Salida 56
Lubia, 42290 Spain
Phone: 975-281-013
Fax: 975-281-051
E-mail Address: contacto.cedar@ciemat.es
Web Address: www.ceder.es
The Centre for the Development of Renewable Energy Sources (CEDER) is a unit of Spain's CIEMAT (Research Centre for Energy, Environment and Technology). CEDER focuses on biomass energy, wind energy and energy efficiency.

EERE Bioenergy Technologies Office
1000 Independence Ave. SW
EE-3B, 5H-021
Washington, DC 20585 USA
Phone: 202-586-5188
E-mail Address: eere_bioenergy@ee.doe.gov
Web Address: www.energy.gov/eere/bioenergy
The Bioenergy Technology Office of the Office of Energy Efficiency and Renewable Energy (EERE), a division of the U.S. Department of Energy, provides information on biomass and biodiesel technology.

National Biodiesel Board (NBB)
605 Clark Ave.
Jefferson City, MO 65110 USA
Phone: 573-635-3893
Fax: 573-635-7913
Toll Free: 800-941-5849
E-mail Address: info@biodiesel.org
Web Address: www.biodiesel.org
The National Biodiesel Board (NBB) is a national trade association that promotes the biodiesel industry.

Northeast Regional Biomass Program (NRBP)
400 N. Capitol St. NW, Ste. 382
Washington, DC 20001 USA
Phone: 202-624-8450
Fax: 202-624-8463
E-mail Address: nrbp@sso.org
Web Address: www.energy.gov/eere/bioenergy/state-regional-resources#Northeast
The Northeast Regional Biomass Program (NRBP) is one of five Regional Biomass Energy Programs established and funded by the U.S. Department of

Energy. The Northeast region consists of 11 states: Connecticut, Delaware, Maine, Maryland, Massachusetts, New Hampshire, New Jersey, New York, Pennsylvania, Rhode Island and Vermont. The NRBP is administered by the CONEG Policy Research Center, Inc.

3) Alternative Energy-Clean Coal

Department of Energy Clean Coal Program
1000 Independence Ave. SW
Washington, DC 20585 USA
Phone: 202-586-7920
Toll Free: 202-586-6660
Web Address: www.fossil.energy.gov/programs/powersystems/cleancoal
The Department of Energy's Clean Coal Program provides information about new technologies and policies to reduce air emissions and other pollutants from coal-burning power plants.

Illinois Clean Coal Institute (ICCI)
5776 Coal Dr., Ste. 200
Carterville, IL 62918 USA
Phone: 618-985-3500
Fax: 618-985-6166
Web Address: www.isgs.illinois.edu/node/34201
The Illinois Clean Coal Institute (ICCI) is a research branch of the Illinois Office of Coal Development that promotes and develops clean coal technology.

International Energy Agency (IEA) Clean Coal Centre
176 Upper Richmond Rd.
London, SW15 2SH UK
Phone: 44-(0)20-3905-3870
E-mail Address: mail@iea-coal.org
Web Address: www.iea-coal.org/
The International Energy Agency (IEA) Clean Coal Centre was established to promote clean coal in its 24 member countries.

National Research Center for Coal & Energy (NRCCE)
1272 Evansdale Dr.
P.O. Box 6064
Morgantown, WV 26506 USA
Phone: 304-293-2867
Fax: 304-293-3749
E-mail Address: NRCCE@mail.wvu.edu
Web Address: www.nrcce.wvu.edu
The National Research Center for Coal & Energy (NRCCE) at West Virginia University promotes the coal industry through research and service programs.

World Coal Association
149-151 Regent St.
Heddon House, 5th Fl.
London, W1B 4JD UK
Phone: 44-20-3745-2760
Fax: 44-20-7851-0061
E-mail Address: info@worldcoal.org
Web Address: www.worldcoal.org
The World Coal Association, formerly known as the World Coal Institute (WCI) is a nonprofit organization that represents the coal industry worldwide.

4) Alternative Energy-Clean Transportation

ACEEE's Green Book Online
529 14th St. NW, Ste. 600
Washington, DC 20045 USA
Phone: 202-507-4000
Fax: 202-429-2248
Web Address: www.greenercars.org
ACEEE's Green Book Online is the official web site for the American Council for an Energy-Efficient Economy (ACEEE)'s Green Book publication, which rates cars on how they impact the environment.

Clean Cities Program
1000 Independence Ave. SW, Rm. 5G-030
Washington, DC 20585 USA
Phone: 202-586-8055
Fax: 202-586-7409
E-mail Address: eere_bioenergy@ee.doe.gov
Web Address: cleancities.energy.gov
The Clean Cities Program, sponsored by the U.S. Department of Energy, is a federal program to promote the use of alternative transportation fuels in U.S. cities.

International Council on Clean Transportation (ICCT)
1500 K St. NW, Ste. 650
Washington, DC 20005 USA
Phone: 202-798-3986
Web Address: www.theicct.org
The International Council on Clean Transportation is an assembly of about 30 top government officials and policymakers from the 10 largest motor vehicle markets. Together, it accounts for 85% of the world's

new car and truck sales, providing them and other interested parties with accurate information about research, best practices, and technical resources for improving the efficiency and environmental performance of cars, trucks and other vehicles. The Council hopes to support sustainable transportation.

WestStart-CALSTART
48 S. Chester Ave.
Pasadena, CA 91106 USA
Phone: 626-744-5600
Fax: 626-744-5610
E-mail Address: calstart@calstart.org
Web Address: www.calstart.org
CALSTART is a nonprofit organization that works to help in the development of advanced transportation technologies and to foster companies that will help clean the air, lessen dependence on foreign oil, reduce global warming and create jobs.

5) Alternative Energy-Ethanol

American Coalition for Ethanol (ACE)
5000 S. Broadband Ln., Ste. 224
Sioux Falls, SD 57108 USA
Phone: 605-334-3381
E-mail Address: cbeck@ethanol.org
Web Address: www.ethanol.org
The American Coalition for Ethanol (ACE) is a nonprofit organization representing farmers, commodity organizations, ethanol producers and other businesses in the ethanol industry.

Brazilian Sugarcane Industry Association
Av. Brigadeiro Faria Lima, 2179
Fl. 10, Jardim Paulistano
Sao Paulo, SP 01452-000 Brazil
Phone: 55-11-3093-4949
Fax: 55-11-3812-1416
E-mail Address: unica@unica.com.br
Web Address: unica.com.br
The Brazilian Sugarcane Industry Association (Uniao da Industria de Cana-de-Acucar, or UNICA), created in 1997, is the country's largest trade association representing producers of sugar, ethanol and bioelectricity. Its member companies are responsible for approximately 50% of Brazil's ethanol production and 60% of the country's sugar production. UNICA maintains a number of international offices, including one in Washington D.C.

Ethanol India
E-5, Royal Prestige, 1127, E Ward
Sykes Extension
Kolhapur, 416 012 India
Phone: 91-231-252-98-13
Fax: 91-231-252-56-84
E-mail Address: info@ethanolindia.net
Web Address: www.ethanolindia.net
Ethanol India provides information and links to the ethanol industry in India and abroad.

Governors' Biofuels Coalition (GBC)
1111 O St., Ste. 223
Lincoln, NE 68509 USA
Phone: 402-651-2948
Web Address: www.governorsbiofuelscoalition.org
The Governors' Biofuels Coalition (GBC), formerly the Governors' Ethanol Coalition, is a group of governors from 33 states in the United States and six foreign that work together to promote the biofuels industry.

Growth Energy Market Development
701 8th St. NW, Ste. 450
Washington, DC 20001 USA
Phone: 202-545-4000
E-mail Address: SBrenden@growthenergy.org
Web Address: www.growthenergy.org
Growth Energy Market Development, created through the 2009 merger of the National Ethanol Vehicle Coalition and Growth Energy, is a nonprofit organization that is one of the leading advocates in the U.S. for expanding the use of 85% (E85) ethanol motor fuel. It also advocates the production of so-called flexible fuel vehicles, which can run on higher than conventional 10% ethanol fuels. Additionally, the firm promotes the installation of ethanol blender pumps, or flex fuel pumps.

Nebraska Ethanol Board
301 Centennial Mall S., Fl. 4
P.O. Box 94922
Lincoln, NE 68509 USA
Phone: 402-471-2941
E-mail Address: roger.berry@nebraska.gov
Web Address: www.ethanol.nebraska.gov
The Nebraska Ethanol Board is a state agency that establishes and promotes standards and procedures for marketing and manufacturing of ethanol in Nebraska.

Renewable Fuels Association (RFA)
425 3rd St. SW, Ste. 1150
Washington, DC 20024 USA
Phone: 202-289-3835

Fax: 202-289-7519
Web Address: www.ethanolrfa.org
The Renewable Fuels Association (RFA) is a trade organization representing the ethanol industry. It publishes a wealth of useful information, including a listing of biorefineries and monthly U.S. fuel ethanol production and demand.

Renewable Industries Canada
54 Murray St., Ste. 450
Ottawa, ON K1N 9M5 Canada
Phone: 613-594-5528
Fax: 613-594-3076
Toll Free: 1-833-4-76-3835
E-mail Address: info@rRICanada.org
Web Address: www.ricanada.org/
Renewable Industries Canada is a nonprofit organization that represent producers of renewable fuels and value-added products that reduce GHG emissions and provide economic opportunity to the benefit of all Canadians. Its mandate is to promote the use of value-added products made from renewable resources through consumer awareness and government liaison activities.

6) Alternative Energy-Fuel Cells

California Fuel Cell Partnership (CaFCP)
3300 Industrial Blvd., Ste. 1000
West Sacramento, CA 95691 USA
Phone: 916-371-2870
Fax: 916-375-2008
E-mail Address: info@cafcp.org
Web Address: cafcp.org
The California Fuel Cell Partnership (CaFCP) is a collaboration of 33 organizations that are committed to promoting commercialized hydrogen fuel cells for automotive applications.

Canadian Hydrogen and Fuel Cell Association (CHFCA)
Ste. 660-475 W Georgia St.
Vancouver, BC V6B 4M9 Canada
Phone: 604-283-1040
Fax: 604-683-6345
E-mail Address: info@chfca.ca
Web Address: www.chfca.ca
The Canadian Hydrogen and Fuel Cell Association (CHFCA) is a nonprofit organization that provides information relating to hydrogen and fuel cell technology and seeks to raise awareness of the positive impact of these technologies. It was formed following the merger of the Canadian Hydrogen Association (CHA) and Hydrogen & Fuel Cells Canada (H2FCC).

EERE Hydrogen, Fuel Cells & Infrastructure Technologies Program
1000 Independence Ave. SW
Washington, DC 20585 USA
Phone: 202-586-3388
E-mail Address: fuelcells@ee.doe.gov
Web Address: www1.eere.energy.gov/hydrogenandfuelcells
The Hydrogen, Fuel Cells & Infrastructure Technologies Program of the Energy Efficiency and Renewable Energy (EERE), a division of the U.S. Department of Energy (DOE), works to develop and successfully introduce fuel cell technologies to the global market.

Fuel Cell and Hydrogen Energy Association (FCHEA)
1211 Connecticut Ave. NW, Ste. 650
Washington, DC 20036 USA
Phone: 202-261-1331
E-mail Address: info@fchea.org
Web Address: www.fchea.org
The Fuel Cell and Hydrogen Energy Association (FCHEA) is an industry association dedicated to fostering the commercialization of fuel cells and hydrogen energy technologies in the U.S.

National Fuel Cell Research Center (NFCRC)
University of California-Irvine
National Fuel Cell Research Center
Irvine, CA 92697-3550 USA
Phone: 949-824-1999
Fax: 949-824-7423
E-mail Address: ivz@nfcrc.uci.edu
Web Address: www.nfcrc.uci.edu
The National Fuel Cell Research Center (NFCRC) promotes the development of efficient fuel cell systems and encourages partnerships to advance fuel cell technology.

Ohio Fuel Cell Coalition (OFCC)
151 Innovation Dr., Ste. 320 D
Elyria, OH 44035 USA
Phone: 440-336-4230
E-mail Address: info@fuelcellcorridor.com
Web Address: www.fuelcellcorridor.com
The Ohio Fuel Cell Coalition (OFCC) is a group of industry, academic and government leaders from throughout the State of Ohio who are dedicated to

developing a forward-looking plan to advance the fuel cell industry in Ohio.

Smithsonian Fuel Cell Project
National Museum of American History
Room 5128, MRC631
Washington, DC 20013-7012 USA
E-mail Address: FUEL-CELL@si.edu
Web Address: americanhistory.si.edu/fuelcells
The Smithsonian Fuel Cell Project presents a historical view of fuel cell technology.

7) Alternative Energy-General

Alliance to Save Energy (ASE)
1850 M St. NW, Ste. 610
Washington, DC 20036 USA
Phone: 202-857-0666
E-mail Address: info@ase.org
Web Address: www.ase.org
The Alliance to Save Energy (ASE) promotes energy-efficiency worldwide to achieve a healthier economy, a cleaner environment and energy security.

American Council for an Energy-Efficient Economy (ACEEE)
529 14th St. NW, Ste. 600
Washington, DC 20045 USA
Phone: 202-507-4000
Fax: 202-429-2248
Web Address: www.aceee.org
The American Council for an Energy-Efficient Economy (ACEEE) is a nonprofit organization dedicated to advancing energy-efficiency as a means of promoting both economic prosperity and environmental protection.

American Council on Renewable Energy (ACORE)
1150 Connecticut Ave. NW, Ste. 401
Washington, DC 20036 USA
Phone: 202-393-0001
E-mail Address: info@acore.org
Web Address: www.acore.org
The American Council on Renewable Energy (ACORE) is a nonprofit organization focused on accelerating the adoption of renewable energy technologies into the mainstream of American society. With an interest in trade, finance and policy, ACORE promotes all renewable energy options for the production of electricity, hydrogen, fuels and end-use energy.

Bloomberg New Energy Finance
New York, NY USA
Phone: 212-617-4050
E-mail Address: bnef-media@bloomberg.net
Web Address: www.bnef.com
Bloomberg New Energy Finance, a unit of media giant Bloomberg LP, publishes white papers and podcasts, produces conferences and presentations, and provides in-depth coverage of alternative energy projects and investments.

Business Council for Sustainable Energy (BCSE)
805 15th St. NW, Ste. 708
Washington, DC 20005 USA
Phone: 202-785-0507
Fax: 202-785-0514
E-mail Address: bcse@bcse.org
Web Address: www.bcse.org
The Business Council for Sustainable Energy (BCSE) strives to realize goals for the nation's economic, environmental and national security. The Council focuses on the promotion of clean energy technologies as solutions to certain environmental challenges.

Center for Energy Efficiency and Renewable Technologies (CEERT)
1100 11th St., Ste. 311
Sacramento, CA 95814 USA
Phone: 916-442-7785
E-mail Address: info@ceert.org
Web Address: www.ceert.org
The Center for Energy Efficiency and Renewable Technologies (CEERT) provides technical support to environmental advocates and clean technology developers.

Chinese Renewable Energy Industries Association (CREIA)
No. A2105-2107 Wuhua Plaza
A4 Che GongZhuang, Xi Cheng District
Beijing, 100044 China
Phone: 86-10-68002617
Fax: 86-10-68002674
E-mail Address: creia@creia.net
Web Address: www.creia.net
The Chinese Renewable Energy Industries Association (CREIA) was established in 2000 under official government sanction to promote the use of renewable energy sources within China.

Clean Energy Council
222 Exhibition St., Lvl. 15

Melbourne, VIC 3000 Australia
Phone: 61-3-9929-4100
Fax: 61-3-9929-4101
E-mail Address: info@cleanenergycouncil.org.au
Web Address: www.cleanenergycouncil.org.au
The Clean Energy Council is an amalgamation of the Australian Wind Energy Industry Association (Auswind) and the Australian Business Council for Sustainable Energy (BCSE). It includes businesses covering a quarter of Australia's total electricity production including gas, wind, hydro and bioenergy; and in the spectrum of business in the low-emission energy and energy efficiency sectors including solar PV, solar hot water, biomass, geothermal and cogeneration.

EUROSOLAR (European Association for Renewable Energy)
Kaiser-Friedrich-Strabe 11
Bonn, 53113 Germany
Phone: 49-228-362373
Fax: 49-228-361213
E-mail Address: info@eurosolar.org
Web Address: www.eurosolar.de
EUROSOLAR (the European Association for Renewable Energy) was founded in 1988. It is a registered non-profit making organization that is dedicated to the cause of substituting nuclear and fossil energy through renewable energy.

Fresh Energy
408 St. Peter St., Ste. 220
St. Paul, MN 55102 USA
Phone: 651-225-0878
Fax: 651-225-0870
E-mail Address: info@fresh-energy.org
Web Address: www.fresh-energy.org
Fresh Energy is a nonprofit organization that works to promote clean electricity, energy efficiency, transportation policy, global warming solutions and energy justice.

Illinois Renewable Energy Association (IREA)
1230 E. Honey Creek Rd.
Oregon, IL 61061 USA
Phone: 815-732-7332
E-mail Address: sonia.vogl@gmail.com
Web Address: www.illinoisrenew.org
The Illinois Renewable Energy Association (IREA) supports sustainable energy development in Illinois.

Interstate Renewable Energy Council
P.O. Box 1156
Latham, NY 12110-1156 USA
Phone: 518-621-7379
E-mail Address: info@irecusa.org
Web Address: www.irecusa.org
Interstate Renewable Energy Council (IREC), formed in 1982 as a nonprofit organization, supports market-oriented services promoting renewable energy, aimed at education, coordination, procurement, the adoption and implementation of uniform guidelines and standards, workforce development, and consumer protection.

Ministry of New and Renewable Energy-Gov. of India
Lodhi Rd.
Block-14, CGO Complex
New Delhi, 110 003 India
Phone: 91-11-24360707
Fax: 91-11-24360404
Web Address: www.mnre.gov.in
The Ministry of New and Renewable Energy is the website for the Government of India's sustainable energy programs. The website provides recent developments and public information regarding various renewable energy issues.

National Energy Foundation (NEF)
Sherwood Dr., Ste. 2.15
Milton Keynes, MK3 6DP UK
Phone: 44-01908-665555
Fax: 44-01908-665577
E-mail Address: info@nef.org.uk
Web Address: www.nef.org.uk
The National Energy Foundation (NEF) aims to help people and businesses throughout the UK reduce their carbon emissions through the use of energy efficiency measures and renewable energy sources.

Northeast Sustainable Energy Association (NESEA)
20 Federal St., Ste. 8
Greenfield, MA 01301 USA
Phone: 413-774-6051
Web Address: www.nesea.org
The Northeast Sustainable Energy Association (NESEA) is a regional membership organization that promotes the everyday application of clean electricity, green transportation, and healthy, efficient buildings.

REN21 (Renewable Energy Policy Network for the 21st Century)
1 rue Miollis

Paris, 75015 France
Phone: 33-1-44-37-42-63
Fax: 33-1-44-3750-95 Read more at:
http://www.ren21.net/contact/
E-mail Address: secretariat@ren21.net
Web Address: www.ren21.net
REN21 (Renewable Energy Policy Network for the 21st Century) is a global organization that promotes the development of renewable energy. The goal of REN21 is the promotion of policies that will increase the wise use of renewable energy worldwide. In order to achieve this objective, REN21 encourages action in three areas: policy, advocacy and knowledge exchange. REN21 convenes and engages key leaders and stakeholders in national legislation and international processes. REN21 and its participants encourage the inclusion of renewable energy matters in the deliberations of appropriate meetings and venues and target relevant political processes.

Renewable Energy & Energy Efficiency Partnership (REEEP)
Wagramer Strasse 5
Vienna Int'l Ctr., Rm. D-1861
Vienna, A-1400 Austria
Phone: 43-1-26026-3425
E-mail Address: info@reeep.org
Web Address: www.reeep.org
The Renewable Energy and Energy Efficiency Partnership (REEEP) is a global, non-profit organization that structures policy and regulatory initiatives for clean energy, and facilitates financing for energy projects. Backed by more than 200 national governments, businesses, development banks and NGOs, REEEP hopes to contribute to international, national and regional policy dialogues. Its aim is to accelerate the integration of renewables into the energy mix and to advocate energy efficiency as a path to improved energy security and reduced carbon emissions, ensuring socio-economic benefits.

RenewableUK
22 Chapter St.
London, SW1P 4NP UK
Phone: 44-020-7901-3000
Fax: 44-020-7901-3001
E-mail Address: info@renewable-uk.com
Web Address: www.renewableuk.com/
RenewableUK (formerly the British Wind Energy Association, or BWEA) is the leading trade and professional body representing the UK's wind, wave and tidal power generation industry.

Sustainable Energy Association of Singapore (SEAS)
180 Kitchener Rd.
#06-10 City Square Mall
Singapore, 208539 Singapore
Phone: 65-6338-8578
Fax: 65-6834-3089
E-mail Address: info@seas.org.sg
Web Address: www.seas.org.sg
The Sustainable Energy Association of Singapore (SEAS) represents the interests of companies in renewable energy, carbon trading, energy efficiency, clean development mechanism projects and their financial institutions.

8) Alternative Energy-Geothermal

EERE Geothermal Technologies Program
1000 Independence Ave. SW, Room 5E-066
Washington, DC 20585 USA
Phone: 202-287-1818
E-mail Address: geothermal@ee.doe.gov
Web Address: www1.eere.energy.gov/geothermal
The Geothermal Technologies Program of the Office of Energy Efficiency and Renewable Energy (EERE), a division of the U.S. Department of Energy, works with U.S. industries to develop geothermal energy into an economically competitive contributor to the U.S. energy supply.

Geothermal Education Office
664 Hilary Dr.
Tiburon, CA 94920 USA
Fax: 415-435-7737
E-mail Address: 24hrcleanpower@gmail.com
Web Address: www.geothermaleducation.org
The Geothermal Education Office works to promote public understanding of geothermal resources.

Geothermal Exchange Organization (The)
312 S. 4th St., Ste. 100
Springfield, IL 62701 USA
Toll Free: 1-888-255-4436
Web Address: www.geoexchange.org
The Geothermal Exchange Organization, formerly known as GeoExchange Heat Pump Consortium (GHPC) offers information on how geothermal heating and cooling can provide energy efficiency and reliability in the field of interior climate control. It also promotes the design, production and installation of GEOExchange systems.

Geothermal Heat Pump Consortium (GeoExchange)
312 S 4th St., Ste. 100
Springfield, IL 62701 USA
Phone: 888-255-4436
E-mail Address: info@ghpc
Web Address: www.geoexchange.org
Geothermal Heat Pump Consortium (GeoExchange) offers information on how geothermal heating and cooling can provide energy efficiency and reliability in the field of interior climate control.

Geothermal Resources Council (GRC)
1120 Rte. 73, Ste. 200
Mount Laurel, NJ 08054 USA
Phone: 530-758-2360
Fax: 856-439-0525
E-mail Address: grc@geothermal.org
Web Address: www.geothermal.org
The Geothermal Resources Council (GRC) is an association that encourages the development of geothermal resources and provides information on geothermal energy.

International Geothermal Association (IGA)
Charles-de-Gaulle-Str. 5
Bonn, D-53113 Germany
Phone: 49-234-3210712
Fax: 49-234-3214809
E-mail Address: iga@lovegeothermal.org
Web Address: www.geothermal-energy.org
The International Geothermal Association (IGA) is a scientific, educational and cultural organization that has more than 5000 members in 65 countries. The IGA is a nonprofit, non-governmental organization in within the Economic and Social Council of the United Nations.

International Ground Source Heat Pump Association (IGSHPA)
312 S. 4th St., Ste. 100
Springfield, IL 62701 USA
Phone: 405-744-5175
Fax: 405-744-5283
Toll Free: 800-626-4747
E-mail Address: info@igshpa.org
Web Address: www.igshpa.org
The International Ground Source Heat Pump Association (IGSHPA), which is affiliated with Oklahoma State University, promotes geothermal energy technology on the local, state, national and global levels.

9) Alternative Energy-Hydroelectric

British Hydropower Association
Manor Farm Business Ctr., Unit 6B
Gussage St. Michael
Dorset, BH21 5HT UK
Phone: 44-1258-840934
E-mail Address: info@british-hydro.org
Web Address: www.british-hydro.org
The British Hydropower Association is the trade association representing the hydropower industry in the UK.

Hydroelectric.com
Phone: 212-845-9579
Web Address: www.hydroelectric.com
Hydroelectric.com, operated by WorldNews (WN) Network, provides news and opinions on hydroelectric power.

International Journal on Hydropower & Dams
P.O. Box 285
Little Woodcote Estate
Wallington, Surrey SM6 6AN UK
Phone: 44-20-8773-7244
E-mail Address: edit@hydropower-dams.com
Web Address: www.hydropower-dams.com
The International Journal on Hydropower & Dams is an online journal with detailed information about the hydropower segment of the energy industry.

National Hydropower Association (NHA)
601 New Jersey Ave. NW, Ste. 660
Washington, DC 20001 USA
Phone: 202-682-1700
Fax: 202-682-9478
E-mail Address: info@hydro.org
Web Address: www.hydro.org
The National Hydropower Association (NHA) is the only national trade association dedicated exclusively to representing the interests of the hydropower industry. Its members span the breadth of the industry and all related fields.

Northwest Hydroelectric Association (NWHA)
P.O. Box 441
Lake Oswego, OR 97034 USA
Phone: 503-502-7262
Fax: 503-253-9172
E-mail Address: info@nwhydro.org
Web Address: www.nwhydro.org

The Northwest Hydroelectric Association (NWHA) represents the hydroelectric industry in the Northwest.

Waterpower Canada
1402 - 150 Metcalfe St.
Ottawa, ON K2P 1P1 Canada
Phone: 613-751-6655
Fax: 613-751-4465
E-mail Address: info@watercanada.ca
Web Address: www.waterpowercanada.ca
Waterpower Canada is the national trade association dedicated to representing the interests of the hydropower industry. Its members span the breadth of the industry and, with nearly 50 members, include hydropower producers, manufacturers, developers, engineering firms, organizations and individuals interested in the field of hydropower. Waterpower Canada members represent more than 95% of the hydropower capacity in Canada.

10) Alternative Energy-Solar

American Solar Energy Society (ASES)
2525 Arapahoe Ave., Ste. E4-253
Boulder, CO 80302 USA
Phone: 303-443-3130
Fax: 303-443-3212
E-mail Address: info@ases.org
Web Address: www.ases.org
The American Solar Energy Society (ASES) is a nonprofit association committed to advancing the use of solar energy to benefit citizens and the global environment, promoting widespread solar energy use in the near future and long-term.

California Solar and Storage Association
1107 9th St., Ste. 820
Sacramento, CA 95814 USA
Phone: 916-228-4567
E-mail Address: info@calssa.org
Web Address: www.calseia.org
The California Solar Energy Industry Association promotes the use of solar thermal and photovoltaic systems in California and changed to the California Solar and Storage Association.

California Solar Center
7966 Mill Station Rd.
Sebastopol, CA 95472 USA
Phone: 707-829-3154
Fax: 707-827-8361
E-mail Address: info@rahus.org
Web Address: http://rahus.org/california-solar-center/
California Solar Center provides news and information on California's solar industry. It is a project of the Rahus Institute, which is focused on the implementation of renewable resource technologies.

Canadian Renewable Energy Association
240 Bank St., Ste. 400
Ottawa, Ontario K2P 1X4 Canada
Phone: 613-234-8716
Toll Free: 800-922-6932
E-mail Address: info@renewablesassociation.ca
Web Address: www.renewablesassociation.ca
The Canadian Renewable Energy Association, the byproduct of the Canadian Solar Industries Association and the Canadian Wind Energy Association, represents wind energy, solar, and energy storage solutions for Canada.

EERE Solar Energy Technologies Program
1000 Independence Ave. SW
Washington, DC 20585 USA
Phone: 202-287-1862
E-mail Address: solar@ee.doe.gov
Web Address: www1.eere.energy.gov/solar
The Solar Energy Technologies Program of the Office of Energy Efficiency and Renewable Energy (EERE), a division of the U.S. Department of Energy, works with industry participants, universities, federal and state government, and other non-governmental agencies to develop economically competitive photovoltaic materials.

European Solar Thermal Electricity Association (ESTELA)
Rue de l'Industrie 10
Brussels, B-1000 Belgium
Phone: 32 (0) 2-893-2596
E-mail Address: contact@estelasolar.org
Web Address: www.estelasolar.org
The European Solar Thermal Electricity Association (ESTELA) was created in 2007 to promote solar thermal electricity (STE) in Europe and worldwide. ESTELA supports its members by fostering market penetration of solar thermal power.

IEA Photovoltaic Power Systems Programme (PVPS)
Waldweg 8
St. Ursen, CH 1717 Switzerland
Phone: 41-26-494-0030
Fax: 41-26-494-0034
E-mail Address: mary.brunisholz@netenergy.ch

Web Address: www.iea-pvps.org
The Photovoltaic Power Systems Programme (PVPS) is a collaborative R&D agreement, established within the International Energy Agency (IEA), that conducts projects regarding solar photovoltaic electricity. IEA PVPS operates worldwide via a network of national teams in member countries. Its website provides information about the results of the IEA PVPS program including publications and other project results.

Institute of Solar Energy (IES)
Instituto de Energia Solar
Avenida Complutense s/n
Madrid, 28040 Spain
Phone: 34-91-544-1060
Fax: 34-91-544-6341
Web Address: www.ies.upm.es
The IES is a unit of Spain's Polytechnic University of Madrid that focuses on the development of photovoltaic solar energy.

International Solar Energy Society (ISES)
Wiesentalstr. 50
Villa Tannheim
Freiburg, 79115 Germany
Phone: 49-761-45906-50
Fax: 49-761-45906-99
E-mail Address: hq@ises.org
Web Address: www.ises.org
The International Solar Energy Society (ISES) is an international nonprofit group promoting the advancement of renewable energy technology, implementation and education worldwide. ISES maintains a presence in over 50 countries worldwide.

New Mexico Solar Energy Association (NMSEA)
P.O. Box 3434
Albuquerque, NM 87190 USA
Phone: 505-246-0400
Fax: 505-246-2251
Toll Free: 888-886-6765
E-mail Address: info@nmsolar.org
Web Address: www.nmsea.org
The New Mexico Solar Energy Association (NMSEA) is a nonprofit organization that promotes solar power in New Mexico.

Northern California Solar Energy Association (NorCal Solar)
1569 Solano Ave., Ste. 185
Berkeley, CA 94707 USA
Phone: 510-592-7136
E-mail Address: info@norcalsolar.org
Web Address: www.norcalsolar.org
The Northern California Solar Energy Association (NorCal Solar) is a volunteer organization that promotes solar power. The group's web site offers step by step information transitioning to photovoltaics and regulations by municipality.

Solar Electric Power Association (SEPA)
1220 19th St. NW, Ste. 800
Washington, DC 20036-2405 USA
Phone: 202-857-0898
Web Address: www.solarelectricpower.org
The Solar Electric Power Association (SEPA) is a nonprofit organization consisting of more than 900 electric utilities, solar and other companies associated with solar electricity. It aims to help energy utilities add solar energy to their generation portfolios.

Solar Energy Industries Association (SEIA)
1425 K St. NW, Ste. 1000
Washington, DC 20005 USA
Phone: 202-682-0556
E-mail Address: info@seia.org
Web Address: www.seia.org
Established in 1974, the Solar Energy Industries Association is the American trade association of the solar energy industry. Among its operations is a web site that provides news for the solar energy industry, links to related products and companies and solar energy statistics.

Solar Platform of Almeria (PSA)
Carretera de Senes, km. 4.5
Paraje Los Retamares
Tabernas, Almeria 04200 Spain
Phone: 34-950-387-900
Fax: 34-950-365-300
E-mail Address: info@psa.es
Web Address: www.psa.es
The Solar Platform of Almeria (Plataforma Solar de Almeria), a dependency of Spain's Center for Energy, Environment and Technological Research (CIEMAT), is the largest center for research, development and testing of concentrating solar power (CSP) technologies in Europe. PSA activities form an integral part of the CIEMAT Department of Renewable Energies as one of its lines of R&D.

Spanish Photovoltaic Union (UNEF)
Calle de Velazquez, 18
7 Izquierda
Madrid, 28001 Spain

Phone: 34-917-817-512
Fax: 34-917-816-443
E-mail Address: info@unef.es
Web Address: unef.es
Formerly the Spanish Photovoltaic Industry Association, known as Union Espanola Fotovoltaica (UNEF), it represents manufacturers and users of photovoltaic energy in Spain.

11) Alternative Energy-Storage

EERE Energy Storage
1000 Independence Ave. SW, MS EE-2F
Washington, DC 20585 USA
Phone: 202-586-1411
Fax: 202-586-1472
E-mail Address: OEwebmaster@hq.doe.gov
Web Address:
http://energy.gov/oe/services/technology-development/energy-storage
The Industrial Distributed Energy Program of the Office of Energy Efficiency and Renewable Energy (EERE), a division of the U.S. Department of Energy, provides a web page with information on energy storage technologies, such as batteries, superconducting magnetic energy storage, flywheels, supercapacitors, compressed air energy storage and pumped hydropower storage.

Energy Storage Association
901 New York Ave. NW, Ste. 510
Washington, DC 20001 USA
Phone: 202-293-0537
E-mail Address: info@energystorage.org
Web Address: www.energystorage.org
The Energy Storage Association promotes the development and commercialization of improved energy storage delivery systems for use by electricity suppliers and their customers. Its web site provides information on advanced storage technologies such as flywheels, pumped hydro storage, flow cell batteries and compressed air energy storage.

12) Alternative Energy-Wind

American Wind Energy Association (AWEA)
1501 M St. NW, Ste. 900
Washington, DC 20005 USA
Phone: 202-383-2500
Fax: 202-383-2505
E-mail Address: stats@awea.org
Web Address: www.awea.org

The American Wind Energy Association (AWEA) promotes wind energy as a clean source of electricity worldwide. Its website provides excellent resources for research, including an online library, discussions of legislation, and descriptions of wind technologies.

Danish Wind Industry Association (DWIA)
Vester Voldgade 106
Copenhagen, DK-1552 Denmark
Phone: 45-3373-0330
Fax: 45-3373-0333
E-mail Address: danish@windpower.org
Web Address: www.xn--drmstrre-64ad.dk/wp-content/wind/miller/windpower%20web/core.htm
The Danish Wind Industry Association (DWIA) is a nonprofit association whose purpose is to promote wind energy.

EERE Wind Program
1000 Independence Ave. SW
Office of Energy Efficiency and Renewable Energy
Washington, DC 20585 USA
Phone: 202-586-5348
E-mail Address: liz.hartman@ee.doe.gov
Web Address: www1.eere.energy.gov/wind
The Wind Program of the Office of Energy Efficiency and Renewable Energy (EERE), a division of the U.S. Department of Energy, works with the U.S wind industry to develop clean, domestic wind energy technologies that can compete with traditional sources.

German WindEnergy Association (BWE)
EUREF-Campus 16
Berlin, 10829 Germany
Phone: 49-30-212341-210
Fax: 49-30-212341-410
E-mail Address: info@wind-energie.de
Web Address: www.wind-energie.de/en
The German WindEnergy Association (BWE) is one of the largest renewable energy associations in the world, with over 20,000 members. Its members include wind turbine manufacturers, operators and their shareholders, planning offices, financiers, scientists, engineers, technicians and lawyers, as well as early conservationists and students. BWE pools expertise and experience from the entire industry. One of BWE's goals is to be an important contact for politicians, business, science and the media.

Global Wind Energy Council (GWEC)
Rue Belliard 51-53,
Brussels, 1000 Belgium

Phone: 32-490-56-81-39
E-mail Address: info@gwec.net
Web Address: www.gwec.net
The Global Wind Energy Council (GWEC) was established in early 2005 to provide a credible and representative forum for the entire wind energy sector at an international level. GWEC's mission is to ensure that wind power establishes itself as one of the world's leading energy sources, providing substantial environmental and economic benefits.

Indian Wind Energy Association
Fl.2 AIFD Building
12-13, Special Institution Area, Shaheed Jeet Singh Marg
New Delhi, 110067 India
Phone: 91-11-4652-3042
Fax: 91-11-4652-3041
E-mail Address: manish@inwea.org
Web Address: www.inwea.org
The Indian Wind Energy Association was organized to promote and develop wind power in India.

Indian Wind Turbine Manufacturers Association (IWTMA)
C-1, Fl.2, Soami Nagar
New Delhi, 110017 India
Phone: 91-011-4181-4744
E-mail Address: secretarygeneral@indianwindpower.com
Web Address: www.indianwindpower.com
An industry association that promotes the use of wind power in India and Indian manufactured wind turbine products.

Japanese Wind Energy Association (JWEA)
Chiyoda-ku Kita 2-1
Fl. 4, Dainichi Kanda Building
Tokyo, 101-0021 Japan
Phone: 81-03-3526-3400
Fax: 81-03-3526-3410
E-mail Address: info@jwea.or.jp
Web Address: www.jwea.or.jp
The Japanese Wind Energy Association (JWEA) is an organization of Japanese energy companies that research, design and promote wind energy technology.

Wind Energy Market
Neustaedtische Kirchstrasse 6
Berlin, 10117 Germany
Fax: 49-30-212341-410
E-mail Address: service@wind-energie.de
Web Address: www.wind-energy-market.com
Operated by the German WindEnergy Association, Wind Energy Market is a website that offers a wealth of information on hundreds of wind energy firms as well as reviews of wind turbines, small and large.

Wind Europe
Rue Belliard 40
Brussels, B-1040 Belgium
Phone: 32-2-213-1811
Fax: 32-2-213-1890
E-mail Address: info@windeurope.org
Web Address: www.windeurope.org
Wind Europe, formerly The European Wind Energy Association (EWEA), co-ordinates international policy, communications, research and analysis from its headquarters in Brussels. EWEA manages European programs, hosts events and supports the needs of its members.

13) Battery Industry Associations

Consortium for Battery Innovation
2530 Meridian Pkwy., Ste. 115
Durham, NC 27713 USA
Phone: 919-361-4647
Fax: 919-361-1957
Web Address: www.batteryinnovation.org
The Consortium for Battery Innovation, formerly known as ALABC, has been carrying out research into lead batteries for a quarter of a century. Members have commissioned research into advanced lead batteries to help meet the needs of global energy storage.

14) Brazilian Government Agencies-Scientific

National Council for Scientific & Technological Development
SHIS QI 1 Conjunto B - Blocos A, B, C & D
Edificio Santos Dumont
Brasilia, DF 71605-001 Brazil
Toll Free: 800-61-96-97
Web Address: www.cnpq.br
The National Council for Scientific & Technological Development (Conselho Nacional de Desenvolvimento Cientifico e Tecnologico, or CNPq) is a Brazilian government agency affiliated with the country's Ministry of Science and Technology. CNPq works to promote scientific and technological research in Brazil through grants and

other support services. The organization also seeks to encourage the development of Brazilian scientists and researchers through the awarding of scholarships and fellowships to students in the sciences.

15) Careers-First Time Jobs/New Grads

CollegeGrad.com, Inc.
950 Tower Ln., Fl. 6
Foster City, CA 94404 USA
E-mail Address: info@quinstreet.com
Web Address: www.collegegrad.com
CollegeGrad.com, Inc. offers in-depth resources for college students and recent grads seeking entry-level jobs.

National Association of Colleges and Employers (NACE)
62 Highland Ave.
Bethlehem, PA 18017-9085 USA
Phone: 610-868-1421
E-mail Address: customerservice@naceweb.org
Web Address: www.naceweb.org
The National Association of Colleges and Employers (NACE) is a premier U.S. organization representing college placement offices and corporate recruiters who focus on hiring new grads.

16) Careers-General Job Listings

CareerBuilder, Inc.
200 N La Salle Dr., Ste. 1100
Chicago, IL 60601 USA
Phone: 773-527-3600
Fax: 773-353-2452
Toll Free: 800-891-8880
Web Address: www.careerbuilder.com
CareerBuilder, Inc. focuses on the needs of companies and also provides a database of job openings. The site has over 1 million jobs posted by 300,000 employers and receives an average 23 million unique visitors monthly. The company also operates online career centers for 140 newspapers and 9,000 online partners. Resumes are sent directly to the company, and applicants can set up a special e-mail account for job-seeking purposes. CareerBuilder is primarily a joint venture between three newspaper giants: The McClatchy Company, Gannett Co., Inc. and Tribune Company.

CareerOneStop
Toll Free: 877-872-5627
E-mail Address: info@careeronestop.org
Web Address: www.careeronestop.org
CareerOneStop is operated by the employment commissions of various state agencies. It contains job listings in both the private and government sectors, as well as a wide variety of useful career resources and workforce information. CareerOneStop is sponsored by the U.S. Department of Labor.

LaborMarketInfo (LMI)
Employment Development Dept.
P.O. Box 826880, MIC 57
Sacramento, CA 94280-0001 USA
Phone: 916-262-2162
Fax: 916-262-2352
Web Address: www.labormarketinfo.edd.ca.gov
LaborMarketInfo (LMI) provides job seekers and employers a wide range of resources, namely the ability to find, access and use labor market information and services. It provides statistics for employment demographics on both a local and regional level, as well as career searching tools for California residents. The web site is sponsored by California's Employment Development Office.

Recruiters Online Network
E-mail Address: rossi.tony@comcast.net
Web Address: www.recruitersonline.com
The Recruiters Online Network provides job postings from thousands of recruiters, Careers Online Magazine, a resume database, as well as other career resources.

USAJOBS
USAJOBS Program Office
1900 E St. NW, Ste. 6500
Washington, DC 20415-0001 USA
Phone: 818-934-6600
Web Address: www.usajobs.gov
USAJOBS, a program of the U.S. Office of Personnel Management, is the official job site for the U.S. Federal Government. It provides a comprehensive list of U.S. government jobs, allowing users to search for employment by location; agency; type of work; or by senior executive positions. It also has special employment sections for individuals with disabilities, veterans and recent college graduates; an information center, offering resume and interview tips and other information; and allows users to create a profile and post a resume.

17) Careers-Job Reference Tools

Vault.com, Inc.
132 W. 31st St., Fl. 16
New York, NY 10001 USA
Fax: 212-366-6117
Toll Free: 800-535-2074
E-mail Address: customerservice@vault.com
Web Address: www.vault.com
Vault.com, Inc. is a comprehensive career web site for employers and employees, with job postings and valuable information on a wide variety of industries. Its features and content are largely geared toward MBA degree holders.

18) Chemicals Industry Associations

American Chemical Society (ACS)
1155 16th St. NW
Washington, DC 20036 USA
Phone: 202-872-4600
Toll Free: 800-333-9511
E-mail Address: service@acs.org
Web Address: www.acs.org
The American Chemical Society (ACS) is a nonprofit organization aimed at promoting the understanding of chemistry and chemical sciences. It represents a wide range of disciplines including chemistry, chemical engineering and other technical fields.

Brazilian Chemical Industry Association
Av. Chedid Jafet, 222, Bloco C, Fl. 4
Vila Olimpia
Sao Paulo, SP 04551-065 Brazil
Phone: 55-11-2148-4700
Fax: 55-11-2148-4760
Web Address: www.abiquim.org.br
The Brazilian Chemical Industry Association (Associacao Brasileira da Industria Quimica, ABIQUIM) represents Brazilian manufacturers of chemical products and assists with a variety of issues related to the industry, including product quality; environmental and safety issues; human resource development; product advocacy; tariff negotiations; and trade agreements. ABIQUIM runs a 24-hour hotline for chemical transportation safety issues and is also involved with plastics recycling efforts.

Chemical Industries Association (CIA)
Kings Bldg.
Smith Sq.
London, SW1P 3JJ UK
Phone: 44-20-7834-3399
Fax: 44-20-7834-4469
E-mail Address: enquiries@cia.org.uk
Web Address: www.cia.org.uk
The Chemical Industries Association (CIA) is the UK's leading trade association for the chemical and chemistry-related industries, representing members both nationally and internationally.

Council for Chemical Research (CCR)
120 Wall St., Fl. 23
New York, NY 10005-4020 USA
Phone: 856-439-0500
Fax: 856-439-0525
E-mail Address: info@ccrhq.org
Web Address: www.ccrhq.org
The Council for Chemical Research (CCR) represents industry, academia and government members involved in the chemical sciences and engineering.

International Council of Chemical Associations (ICCA)
Web Address: www.icca-chem.org
The International Council of Chemical Associations (ICCA) is a virtual organization that represents chemical manufacturers and producers all over the world.

Singapore Chemical Industry Council (SCIC)
8 Jurong Town Hall
#25-04, The JTC Summit
Singapore, 609434 Singapore
Phone: 65-6267-8891
E-mail Address: secretariat@scic.sg
Web Address: www.scic.sg
The Singapore Chemical Industry Council (SCIC) is the official body representing the chemical industry of Singapore in the private sector. Its membership comprises key companies, logistics service providers and traders.

Society of Chemical Industry (SCI)
14/15 Belgrave Sq.
London, SW1X 8PS UK
Phone: 44-20-7598-1500
Fax: 44-20-7598-1545
E-mail Address: secretariat@soci.org
Web Address: www.soci.org
The Society of Chemical Industry (SCI) is a professional association for networking and problem solving in the international chemical industry. Established in 1881, SCI has members in over 70

countries. Its international headquarters are in London, with additional offices in the U.S., Canada, Continental Europe, India and Australia.

UIC (Union des Industries Chimiques)
Le Diamant A
14 Rue de la Republique
Puteaux, 92909 France
Phone: 33-1-46-53-11-00
Web Address: www.uic.fr
UIC, the Union des Industries Chimiques (Union of French Chemical Industries), represents chemicals manufacturers in France, including basic, fine, specialty and pharmaceuticals. It provides support to its members in six areas: technical, economic, social, innovation, communication and legal.

19) Computer & Electronics Industry Associations

Canadian Advanced Technology Alliances (CATAAlliance)
207 Bank St., Ste. 416
Ottawa, ON K2P 2N2 Canada
Phone: 613-236-6550
E-mail Address: info@cata.ca
Web Address: www.cata.ca
The Canadian Advanced Technology Alliances (CATAAlliance) is one of Canada's leading trade organizations for the research, development and technology sectors.

20) Construction Resources-Energy Efficient Buildings

Building Green
122 Birge St., Ste. 30
Brattleboro, VT 05301 USA
Phone: 802-257-7300
Toll Free: 800-861-0954
Web Address: http://www2.buildinggreen.com/
BuildingGreen provides research and information on energy-efficient buildings.

Efficient Windows Collaborative (EWC)
21629 Zodiac St., N.E.
Wyoming, MN 55092 USA
E-mail Address: efficientwindowscollaborative@gmail.com
Web Address: www.efficientwindows.org
The Efficient Windows Collaborative (EWC) web site provides unbiased information on the benefits of energy-efficient windows, descriptions of how they work and recommendations for their selection and use. The web site is sponsored by the U.S. Department of Energy's Windows and Glazings Program and the participation of industry members.

Energy Efficiency Programme Office (E2PO)
40 Scotts Rd.
Environmental Bldg. #13-00
Singapore, 228231 Singapore
Fax: 65-6235-2611
Toll Free: 800-2255-632
E-mail Address: contact_NEA@nea.gov.sg
Web Address: www.e2singapore.gov.sg
To drive energy efficiency improvement in Singapore, the Energy Efficiency Programme Office (E2PO) has been established. The website includes information about energy programs, publications, incentives and development opportunities for power generation, industry, transport, green buildings and the public sector of Singapore.

Green Building Initiative (GBI)
7805 SW 40th Ave., Ste. 80010
Portland, OR 97219 USA
Phone: 503-274-0448
E-mail Address: info@thegbi.org
Web Address: www.thegbi.org
The Green Building Initiative (GBI) is a nonprofit network of building industry leaders committed to bringing green to mainstream residential and commercial construction. The GBI believes in building approaches that are environmentally progressive, but also practical and affordable for builders to implement.

International Self-Powered Building Council (ISPBC)
Web Address: www.ispbc.org
International Self-Powered Building Council (ISPBC) is a non-profit organization based in Washington, D.C. with worldwide chapters comprised of developers, architects, builders, property owners, renewable energy companies, engineers, designers, green building material manufacturers and suppliers. ISPBC is dedicated to the global deployment of Self-Powered-Building (SPB), a power generating, energy-efficient and economically superior Building 2.0 with a sophisticated approach to urban design. ISPBC seeks to achieve this by combining the most advanced photovoltaic (PV) and other renewable energy

technologies with cutting edge design to provide stylish and seamlessly integrated modern buildings.

National Institute of Building Sciences (NIBS)
1090 Vermont Ave. NW, Ste. 700
Washington, DC 20005 USA
Phone: 202-289-7800
Fax: 202-289-1092
E-mail Address: nibs@nibs.org
Web Address: www.nibs.org
The National Institute of Building Sciences (NIBS) is a representative company that supports advances in building science and technology.

U.S. Green Building Council (USGBC)
2101 L St. NW, Ste. 500
Washington, DC 20037 USA
Phone: 202-742-3792
Toll Free: 800-795-1747
Web Address: www.usgbc.org
The United States Green Building Council (USGBC) is a coalition of building industry leaders working to promote environmentally responsible commercial and residential structures.

21) Corporate Information Resources

Business Journals (The)
120 W. Morehead St., Ste. 400
Charlotte, NC 28202 USA
Toll Free: 866-853-3661
E-mail Address: gmurchison@bizjournals.com
Web Address: www.bizjournals.com
Bizjournals.com is the online media division of American City Business Journals, the publisher of dozens of leading city business journals nationwide. It provides access to research into the latest news regarding companies both small and large. The organization maintains 42 websites and 64 print publications and sponsors over 700 annual industry events.

Business Wire
101 California St., Fl. 20
San Francisco, CA 94111 USA
Phone: 415-986-4422
Fax: 415-788-5335
Toll Free: 800-227-0845
E-mail Address: info@businesswire.com
Web Address: www.businesswire.com
Business Wire offers news releases, industry- and company-specific news, top headlines, conference calls, IPOs on the Internet, media services and access to tradeshownews.com and BW Connect On-line through its informative and continuously updated web site.

Edgar Online, Inc.
35 W. Wacker Dr.
Chicago, IL 60601 USA
Phone: 301-287-0300
Fax: 301-287-0390
Toll Free: 800-823-5304
Web Address: www.edgar-online.com
Edgar Online, Inc. is a gateway and search tool for viewing corporate documents, such as annual reports on Form 10-K, filed with the U.S. Securities and Exchange Commission.

PR Newswire Association LLC
200 Vesey St., Fl. 19
New York, NY 10281 USA
Fax: 800-793-9313
Toll Free: 800-776-8090
E-mail Address: mediainquiries@cision.com
Web Address: www.prnewswire.com
PR Newswire Association LLC provides comprehensive communications services for public relations and investor relations professionals, ranging from information distribution and market intelligence to the creation of online multimedia content and investor relations web sites. Users can also view recent corporate press releases from companies across the globe. The Association is owned by United Business Media plc.

Silicon Investor
E-mail Address: si.admin@siliconinvestor.com
Web Address: www.siliconinvestor.com
Silicon Investor is focused on providing information about technology companies. Its web site serves as a financial discussion forum and offers quotes, profiles and charts.

22) Distillery Industry Associations

Online Distillery Network-Distillers & Fuel Ethanol Plants Worldwide
2710 Clark Pl.
Eau Claire, WI 54701 USA
Phone: 715-831-8151
Fax: 715-831-8151
E-mail Address: murtagh@distill.com
Web Address: www.distill.com
The Online Distillery Network for Distillers and Fuel Ethanol Plants Worldwide is a website, built and

sponsored by Murtagh & Associates, for distilleries producing alcohol (ethyl alcohol or ethanol) for beverage, fuel and industrial uses. It provides links to the home pages of distilleries and fuel-ethanol plants located in various countries around the world, and to related organizations and other services, including distillery auctions and used-equipment dealers.

23) Economic Data & Research

Centre for European Economic Research (The, ZEW)
L 7, 1
Mannheim, 68161 Germany
Phone: 49-621-1235-01
Fax: 49-621-1235-224
E-mail Address: empfang@zew.de
Web Address: www.zew.de/en
Zentrum fur Europaische Wirtschaftsforschung, The Centre for European Economic Research (ZEW), distinguishes itself in the analysis of internationally comparative data in a European context and in the creation of databases that serve as a basis for scientific research. The institute maintains a special library relevant to economic research and provides external parties with selected data for the purpose of scientific research. ZEW also offers public events and seminars concentrating on banking, business and other economic-political topics.

Economic and Social Research Council (ESRC)
Polaris House
North Star Ave.
Swindon, SN2 1UJ UK
Phone: 44-01793 413000
E-mail Address: esrcenquiries@esrc.ac.uk
Web Address: www.esrc.ac.uk
The Economic and Social Research Council (ESRC) funds research and training in social and economic issues. It is an independent organization, established by Royal Charter. Current research areas include the global economy; social diversity; environment and energy; human behavior; and health and well-being.

Eurostat
5 Rue Alphonse Weicker
Joseph Bech Bldg.
Luxembourg, L-2721 Luxembourg
Phone: 352-4301-1
E-mail Address: eurostat-pressoffice@ec.europa.eu
Web Address: ec.europa.eu/eurostat
Eurostat is the European Union's service that publishes a wide variety of comprehensive statistics on European industries, populations, trade, agriculture, technology, environment and other matters.

Federal Statistical Office of Germany
Gustav-Stresemann-Ring 11
Wiesbaden, D-65189 Germany
Phone: 49-611-75-2405
Fax: 49-611-72-4000
Web Address: www.destatis.de
Federal Statistical Office of Germany publishes a wide variety of nation and regional economic data of interest to anyone who is studying Germany, one of the world's leading economies. Data available includes population, consumer prices, labor markets, health care, industries and output.

India Brand Equity Foundation (IBEF)
Fl. 20, Jawahar Vyapar Bhawan
Tolstoy Marg
New Delhi, 110001 India
Phone: 91-11-43845500
Fax: 91-11-23701235
E-mail Address: info.brandindia@ibef.org
Web Address: www.ibef.org
India Brand Equity Foundation (IBEF) is a public-private partnership between the Ministry of Commerce and Industry, the Government of India and the Confederation of Indian Industry. The foundation's primary objective is to build positive economic perceptions of India globally. It aims to effectively present the India business perspective and leverage business partnerships in a globalizing marketplace.

National Bureau of Statistics (China)
57, Yuetan Nanjie, Sanlihe
Xicheng District
Beijing, 100826 China
Fax: 86-10-6878-2000
E-mail Address: info@gj.stats.cn
Web Address: www.stats.gov.cn/english
The National Bureau of Statistics (China) provides statistics and economic data regarding China's economy and society.

Organization for Economic Co-operation and Development (OECD)
2 rue Andre Pascal
Cedex 16
Paris, 75775 France
Phone: 33-1-45-24-82-00
Fax: 33-1-45-24-85-00

Planning (Japan)
19-1 Wakamatsu-cho
Shinjuku-ku
Tokyo, 162-8668 Japan
Phone: 81-3-5273-2020
E-mail Address: toukeisoudan@soumu.go.jp
Web Address: www.stat.go.jp/english
The Statistics Bureau, Director-General for Policy Planning (Japan) and Statistical Research and Training Institute, a part of the Japanese Ministry of Internal Affairs and Communications, plays the central role of producing and disseminating basic official statistics and coordinating statistical work under the Statistics Act and other legislation.

Statistics Canada
150 Tunney's Pasture Driveway
Ottawa, ON K1A 0T6 Canada
Phone: 514-283-8300
Fax: 514-283-9350
Toll Free: 800-263-1136
E-mail Address: STATCAN.infostats-infostats.STATCAN@canada.ca
Web Address: www.statcan.gc.ca
Statistics Canada provides a complete portal to Canadian economic data and statistics. Its conducts Canada's official census every five years, as well as hundreds of surveys covering numerous aspects of Canadian life.

24) Emissions Cap & Trade Associations

International Emissions Trading Association (IETA)
24, Rue Merle d'Aubigne
Geneva, CH-1207 Switzerland
Phone: 41-22-737-05-00
Fax: 41-22-737-05-08
E-mail Address: secretariat@ieta.org
Web Address: www.ieta.org
IETA is a leading association in the carbon emissions cap and trade industry. It sponsors research, publications and conferences on a worldwide basis.

UK Emissions Trading Group (ETG)
8 Duncannon St.
Golden Cross House
London, WC2N 4JF UK
Phone: 44-20-7484-5274
E-mail Address: John.Craven@etg.uk.com
Web Address: www.etg.uk.com
The business-led UK Emissions Trading Group (ETG) offers a forum for discussion and resolution of all aspects of emissions trading and enables communication to take place between commerce and industry, and the UK Government.

25) Energy Associations-China, General

China Energy Association (CEA)
7 Nanlishi Road, Toutiao
Xicheng District
Beijing, 100045 China
Phone: 86-010-68051807
Fax: 86-010-68051799
E-mail Address: hzt1008@hotmail.com
Web Address: www.zhnx.org.cn
The China Energy Association (CEA) is a membership organization that represents the energy sources sector and energy industry. The organization publishes the Energy Resource World magazine.

26) Energy Associations-Electric Power

American Public Power Association (APPA)
2451 Crystal Dr., Ste. 1000
Arlington, VA 22202-4804 USA
Phone: 202-467-2900
E-mail Address: info@PublicPower.org
Web Address: www.publicpower.org
The American Public Power Association (APPA) is a nonprofit service organization for the country's community-owned electric utilities, dedicated to advancing the public policy interests of its members and their consumers.

Edison Electric Institute (EEI)
701 Pennsylvania Ave. NW
Washington, DC 20004-2696 USA
Phone: 202-508-5000
E-mail Address: feedback@eei.org
Web Address: www.eei.org

The Edison Electric Institute (EEI) is an association of U.S. shareholder-owned electric companies as well as worldwide affiliates and industry associates. Its web site provides energy news and a link to Electric Perspectives magazine.

Electric Power Service Provider Association
1401 New York Ave. NW, Ste. 1230
Washington, DC 20005-2110 USA
Phone: 202-628-8200
Fax: 202-628-8260
Web Address: www.epsa.org
The Electric Power Service Provider Association promotes the interests of the electric power generation and distribution industry.

Institute of Public Utilities
Owen Graduate Hall
735 E. Shaw Ln., Rm. W157
East Lansing, MI 48825-1109 USA
Phone: 517-355-1876
Fax: 517-355-1854
E-mail Address: ipu@msu.edu
Web Address: www.ipu.msu.edu
The Institute of Public Utilities, of Michigan State University, is committed to a mission of supporting informed, effective and efficient utility regulation by providing educational programs and applied research to the regulatory policy community.

National Rural Electric Cooperative Association (NRECA)
4301 Wilson Blvd.
Arlington, VA 22203-1860 USA
Phone: 703-907-5500
Web Address: www.nreca.coop
The National Rural Electric Cooperative Association (NRECA) is the national service organization dedicated to representing the interests of consumer-owned cooperative electric utilities and the consumers they serve.

Public Utility Research Center (PURC)
University of Florida, 100 Bryan Hall
P.O. Box 117150
Gainesville, FL 32611-7150 USA
Phone: 352-392-2397
Fax: 352-392-2086
Web Address: warrington.ufl.edu/purc/
Public Utility Research Center (PURC) at the University of Florida, provides international training and strategic research in public utility regulation, market rules, and infrastructure management in the energy, telecommunications, and water industries.

Western Energy Institute (WEI)
1050 SW 6th Ave., Ste. 325
Portland, OR 97204 USA
Phone: 503-231-1994
Fax: 503-231-2595
Web Address: www.westernenergy.org
The Western Energy Institute (WEI) serves the electric and gas industries throughout the western U.S. and Canada.

Women's International Network of Utility Professionals (WINUP)
2795 E. Bidwell St., Ste. 100-209
Folsom, CA 95630 USA
Phone: 916-425-8780
E-mail Address: winup@att.net
Web Address: www.winup.org
The Women's International Network of Utility Professionals (WINUP) provides networking and support for women in the utility industry.

27) Energy Associations-International

International Association for Energy Economics (IAEE)
28790 Chagrin Blvd., Ste. 350
Cleveland, OH 44122 USA
Phone: 216-464-5365
E-mail Address: iaee@iaee.org
Web Address: www.iaee.org
The International Association for Energy Economics (IAEE) provides members with an opportunity to exchange ideas and information relevant to professionals involved in energy economics.

International Energy Agency (IEA)
9 rue de la Federation
Paris Cedex 15, 75739 France
Phone: 33-1-40-57-65-00
Fax: 33-1-40-57-65-09
E-mail Address: info@iea.org
Web Address: www.iea.org
The International Energy Agency (IEA) is the energy forum for its members' countries and is committed to taking joint measures to meet oil supply emergencies. It shares energy information, coordinates energy policies and helps in the development of national energy programs. The agency publishes a wealth of information each year, including statistics of fuel usage and emissions.

28) Energy Associations-Natural Gas

Gas Technology Institute (GTI)
1700 S. Mount Prospect Rd.
Des Plaines, IL 60018 USA
Phone: 847-768-0500
Fax: 847-768-0501
E-mail Address: publicrelations@gti.org
Web Address: www.git.energy
The Gas Technology Institute (GTI) is a not-for-profit research and development organization and works to develop and deploy technologies related to affordable energy production, sustainable energy development and the efficient use of energy resources. Its network of partners, investors and clients includes state and federal government agencies; natural gas utilities and pipeline companies; industrial companies; electric utilities; independent power producers; technology developers; and national laboratories. In addition to its Illinois headquarters (which houses 28 specialized laboratories working on various advanced energy technologies), GTI also maintains smaller offices and facilities in locations including Houston, Texas; Sacramento, California; and Washington D.C.

29) Energy Associations-Nuclear

Canadian Nuclear Association
130 Albert St., Ste. 1610
Ottawa, ON K1P 5G4 Canada
Phone: 613-237-4262
Fax: 613-237-0989
E-mail Address: info@cna.ca
Web Address: www.cna.ca
The Canadian Nuclear Association is a nonprofit organization that promotes nuclear technologies and power in Canada.

European Nuclear Society
Ave. des Arts 56
Brussels, 1000 Belgium
Phone: 32-2-505-30-50
Fax: 32-2-502-39-02
E-mail Address: info@euronuclear.org
Web Address: www.euronuclear.org
The European Nuclear Society promotes the science and application of nuclear technology in Europe.

International Atomic Energy Agency (IAEA)
P.O. Box 100
Vienna Int'l Ctr.
Vienna, A-1400 Austria
Phone: 43-1-2600-0
Fax: 43-1-2600-7
Web Address: www.iaea.org
The International Atomic Energy Agency (IAEA), which is a part of United Nations and known as Atoms for Peace, focuses on global nuclear energy developments and promotes safe and peaceful use of nuclear technologies.

Japan Atomic Industrial Forum
1-2-8 Toranomon, Minato-ku
Kotohira Twr., Fl. 9
Tokyo, 105-8605 Japan
Phone: 81-3-6812-7100
Fax: 81-3-6812-7110
Web Address: www.jaif.or.jp/english
The Japan Atomic Industrial Forum, Inc. is a non-profit industry organization that promotes the use of safe nuclear power.

Nuclear Energy Institute (NEI)
1201 F St. NW, Ste. 1100
Washington, DC 20004-1218 USA
Phone: 202-739-8000
Fax: 202-785-4019
E-mail Address: webmaster@nei.org
Web Address: www.nei.org
The Nuclear Energy Institute (NEI) is a policy organization for the national nuclear technologies industry.

Societe Francaise D'Energie Nucleaire (SFEN)
103 rue Reaumur
Paris, 75002 France
Phone: 33-01-53-58-32-10
Fax: 33-01-53-58-32-11
E-mail Address: sfen@sfen.org
Web Address: www.sfen.org
The Societe Francaise D'Energie Nucleaire (SFEN) or the French Nuclear Energy Society is a non-profit organization that publishes and provides information on nuclear energy and its applications.

United Kingdom Atomic Energy Authority (UKAEA)
Culham Science Ctr.
Abingdon
Oxfordshire, OX14 3DB UK
Phone: 44-1235-52882
E-mail Address: foienquiries@ukaea.uk

Web Address:
www.gov.uk/government/organisations/uk-atomic-energy-authority
The United Kingdom Atomic Energy Authority (UKAEA) is a researcher in the field of fusion technologies and is responsible for the decommissioning of nuclear reactors in the United Kingdom.

World Council of Nuclear Workers (WONUC)
49 rue Lauriston
Paris, 75116 France
Phone: 33-1-39-48-52-20
Fax: 33-1-39-48-51-51
E-mail Address: cchaubardwillm@cogema.fr
Web Address:
www.inis.iaea.org/search/search.aspx?orig_q=RN:39122922
The World Council of Nuclear Workers (WONUC) is a nonprofit trade union for workers in the nuclear industry.

World Nuclear Association
10 Southampton St.
Tower House
London, WC2E 7HA UK
Phone: 44-20-7451-1520
Fax: 44-20-7839-1501
E-mail Address: info@world-nuclear.org
Web Address: www.world-nuclear.org
The World Nuclear Association promotes the peaceful worldwide use of nuclear power as a sustainable energy resource.

World Nuclear Transport Institute
125 Kingsway
Aviation House
London, WC2B 6NH UK
Phone: 44-207-580-1144
Fax: 44-207-580-5365
E-mail Address: wnti@wnti.co.uk
Web Address: www.wnti.co.uk
The World Nuclear Transport Institute is dedicated to the safe and efficient transportation of nuclear materials.

30) Energy Associations-Oil Sands

Oil Sands Community Alliance (OSCA)
512 Snow Eagle Dr.
Fort McMurray, AGB T9H 4GB Canada
Phone: 780-790-1999
Fax: 780-790-1971
E-mail Address: info@oscaalberta.ca
Web Address: www.oscaalberta.ca
The Oil Sands Community Alliance (OSCA), formerly known as the Oil Sand Developers Group, on behalf of its members, works closely with oil sands operators and developers, related industries, governments, Aboriginal people, and other organizations active in Alberta's oil sands deposit region to define and address regional issues related to oil sands development.

31) Energy Associations-Other

National Association of State Energy Officials (NASEO)
1300 North 17th St., Ste. 1275
Arlington, VA 22209 USA
Phone: 703-299-8800
Fax: 703-299-6208
Web Address: www.naseo.org
The National Association of State Energy Officials (NASEO) provides a forum for energy officials, policymakers and others to trade information and discuss issues with regional and national implications.

U.S. Energy Association (USEA)
1300 Pennsylvania Ave. NW
Ste. 550, Mailbox 142
Washington, DC 20004-3022 USA
Phone: 202-312-1230
E-mail Address: reply@usea.org
Web Address: www.usea.org
The U.S. Energy Association (USEA) represents the interests of the U.S. energy sector by increasing understanding in domestic and international energy issues. USEA is the U.S. member committee of the World Energy Counsel (WEC).

Women's Council on Energy and the Environment (WCEE)
P.O. Box 33211
Washington, DC 20033 USA
Phone: 202-997-4512
Fax: 202-478-2098
Web Address: www.wcee.org
The Women's Council on Energy and the Environment (WCEE) is dedicated to promoting professional and educational opportunities for women in the fields of energy and environment in the Washington, D.C. area.

32) Energy Education Resources

National Energy Education Development (NEED)
8408 Kao Cir.
Manassas, VA 20110 USA
Phone: 703-257-1117
Fax: 703-257-0037
Toll Free: 800-875-5029
E-mail Address: info@need.org
Web Address: www.need.org
National Energy Education Development (NEED) is devoted to developing and disseminating hands-on energy education programs to schools nationwide.

33) Energy Industry Resources

BP Statistical Review of World Energy
1 St. James Sq.
London, SW1Y 4PD UK
Phone: 44-20-7496-4000
Fax: 44-20-7496-4630
Web Address: www.bp.com/statisticalreview
BP Statistical Review of World Energy, a publication of BP plc, is an excellent source of the world's current and historical energy trends.

California Energy Commission
1516 Ninth St., MS-29
Sacramento, CA 95814-5512 USA
Phone: 916-654-4287
E-mail Address: renewable@energy.ca.gov
Web Address: www.energy.ca.gov
The California Energy Commission is the state's primary energy policy and planning agency.

Canadian Energy Research Institute (CERI)
3512-33 St. NW, Ste. 150
Calgary, AB T2L 2A6 Canada
Phone: 403-282-1231
Fax: 403-284-4181
E-mail Address: info@ceri.ca
Web Address: www.ceri.ca
The Canadian Energy Research Institute (CERI) represents various Canadian governmental departments, the University of Calgary and over 100 private sector energy-related companies. It seeks to provide analysis of energy economics and related government issues in the fields of energy production, transportation and consumption.

ElectricNet
5340 Fryling Rd., Ste. 300
Erie, PA 16510 USA
Phone: 814-897-7700
Fax: 814-897-9555
E-mail Address: info@electricnet.com
Web Address: www.electricnet.com
ElectricNet is a gateway to valuable industry information pertinent to those who design, manufacture, construct, startup, test, repair, service, calibrate, maintain or sell electrical equipment, power apparatus, plant electrical facilities or generation, transmission or distribution equipment or systems.

Enerdata
47 Ave. Alsace Lorraine
Grenoble, 38000 France
Phone: 33-4-76-42-25-46
Fax: 33-4-76-51-61-45
E-mail Address: info@enerdata.net
Web Address: www.enerdata.net
Enerdata publishes an annual, online Global Energy Statistical Yearbook. It is an excellent way to study energy consumption and production, as well as emissions and other factors.

Energy Central
6105 S. Main St., Ste. 200
Aurora, CO 80016 USA
Phone: 303-782-5510
Toll Free: 800-459-2233
E-mail Address: service@energycentral.com
Web Address: www.energycentral.com
Energy Central provides a large number of news releases related to the energy industry as well as other industry information.

Energy Charter Secretariat
Boulevard de la Woluwe, 56
Brussels, B-1200 Belgium
Phone: 32-2-775-98-00
Fax: 32-2-775-98-01
E-mail Address: info@encharter.org
Web Address: www.energycharter.org
The Energy Charter Treaty, an international agreement, plays an important role as part of an effort to build a legal foundation for energy security, based on the principles of open, competitive markets and sustainable development. The group holds conferences and publishes excellent reports on such topics as LNG, renewable energy and investments. More than 50 nations are members.

Energy Policy Research Foundation Inc. (EPRINC)
1031 31st St. NW
Washington, DC 20007-4401 USA
Phone: 202-944-3339
Fax: 202-944-9830
E-mail Address: contact@eprinc.org
Web Address: www.eprinc.org
The Energy Policy Research Foundation, Inc. (EPRINC), formerly PIRINC was incorporated in 1944 and is a not-for-profit organization that studies energy economics with special emphasis on oil. It is known internationally for providing objective analysis of energy issues. Its website offers a wealth of up-to-the-minute white papers on energy production and energy issues.

India Energy Portal (IEP)
Lodhi Rd.
Darbari Seth Block, IHC Complex
New Delhi, 110 003 India
Phone: 91-11-2468-2100
Fax: 91-11-2468-2144
E-mail Address: mailbox@teri.res.in
Web Address: www.indiaenergyportal.org
The India Energy Portal (IEP), built upon public-private partnership, provides access to information and knowledge on various aspects of energy.

Power Online
5340 Fryling Rd., Ste. 300
Erie, PA 16510 USA
Phone: 814-897-7700
Fax: 814-897-9555
E-mail Address: info@poweronline.com
Web Address: www.poweronline.com
Power Online is an energy industry web site offering a global newswire and energy job postings, as well as a Web Resource Center link.

34) Engineering, Research & Scientific Associations

American Association for the Advancement of Science (AAAS)
1200 New York Ave. NW
Washington, DC 20005 USA
Phone: 202-326-6400
Web Address: www.aaas.org
The American Association for the Advancement of Science (AAAS) is the world's largest scientific society and the publisher of Science magazine. It is an international nonprofit organization dedicated to advancing science around the globe.

American Geophysical Union (AGU)
2000 Florida Ave. NW
Washington, DC 20009 USA
Phone: 202-462-6900
Fax: 202-328-0566
Toll Free: 800-966-2481
E-mail Address: service@agu.org
Web Address: www.agu.org
The American Geophysical Union (AGU) is an international scientific community that performs research and provides information about the interdisciplinary field of geophysics.

American Institute of Chemical Engineers (AIChE)
120 Wall St., Fl. 23
New York, NY 10005-4020 USA
Phone: 203-702-7660
Fax: 203-775-5177
Toll Free: 800-242-4363
Web Address: www.aiche.org
The American Institute of Chemical Engineers (AIChE) provides leadership in advancing the chemical engineering profession. The organization, which is comprised of more than 50,000 members from over 100 countries, provides informational resources to chemical engineers.

American Institute of Mining, Metallurgical and Petroleum Engineers (AIME)
12999 E. Adam Aircraft Cir.
Englewood, CO 80112 USA
Phone: 303-948-4255
Fax: 888-702-0049
E-mail Address: aime@aimehq.org
Web Address: www.aimehq.org
The American Institute of Mining, Metallurgical and Petroleum Engineers (AIME) is a trade association devoted to the science of the production and use of minerals, metals, energy sources and materials.

American Nuclear Society (ANS)
555 N. Kensington Ave.
La Grange Park, IL 60526 USA
Phone: 708-352-6611
Fax: 708-579-8314
Toll Free: 800-323-3044
Web Address: www.ans.org
The American Nuclear Society (ANS) is a nonprofit organization unifying professional activities within

the nuclear science and technology fields. ANS seeks to promote the awareness and understanding of the application of nuclear science and technology.

American Physical Society (APS)
One Physics Ellipse
College Park, MD 20740-3844 USA
Phone: 301-209-3200
Fax: 301-209-0865
Web Address: www.aps.org
The American Physical Society (APS) develops and implements effective programs in physics education and outreach. APS publishes a number of research journals dedicated to physics research, including Physical Review, Physical Review Letters and Reviews of Modern Physics.

American Society of Civil Engineers (ASCE)
1801 Alexander Bell Dr.
Reston, VA 20191-4400 USA
Phone: 703-295-6300
Toll Free: 800-548-2723
Web Address: www.asce.org
The American Society of Civil Engineers (ASCE) is a leading professional organization serving civil engineers. It ensures safer buildings, water systems and other civil engineering works by developing technical codes and standards.

China Academy of Building Research (CABR)
30, Bei San Huan Dong Lu
Beijing, 100013 China
Phone: 010-84272233
Fax: 010-84281369
E-mail Address: office@cabr.com.cn
Web Address: www.cabr.com.cn
CABR is responsible for the development and management of the major engineering construction and product standards of China and is also the largest comprehensive research and development institute in the building industry in China. Some related institutes include Institute of Earthquake Engineering, Institute of Building Fire Research, Institute of Building Environment and Energy Efficiency (Building Physics), Institute of Foundation Engineering as well as many others.

CIEMAT
Avenida Complutense 40
Madrid, 28040 Spain
Phone: 91-346-60-00
Fax: 91-346-64-80
E-mail Address: contacto@ciemat.es
Web Address: www.ciemat.es
The CIEMAT, a unit of Spain's Ministry of Education and Science, is a public research agency. Its areas of focus include solar energy, biomass energy, wind energy, environment, basic research, fusion by magnetic confinement, nuclear safety, and technology transfer. Primary operations include PSA, the Solar Platform of Almeria, where concentrating solar power (CSP) is researched; CEDER, the Centre for the Development of Renewable Energy Sources; and CETA-CIEMAT, a center for information technology research.

Industrial Research Institute (IRI)
P.O. Box 13968
Arlington, VA 22219 USA
Phone: 703-647-2580
Fax: 703-647-2581
E-mail Address: information@iriweb.org
Web Address: www.iriweb.org
The Innovation Research Interchange (IRI) is a nonprofit organization of over 200 leading industrial companies, representing industries such as aerospace, automotive, chemical, computers and electronics, which carry out industrial research efforts in the U.S. manufacturing sector. IRI helps members improve research and development capabilities.

Institute of Electrical and Electronics Engineers (IEEE)
3 Park Ave., Fl. 17
New York, NY 10016-5997 USA
Phone: 212-419-7900
Fax: 212-752-4929
Toll Free: 800-678-4333
E-mail Address: society-info@ieee.org
Web Address: www.ieee.org
The Institute of Electrical and Electronics Engineers (IEEE) is a nonprofit, technical professional association of more than 430,000 individual members in approximately 160 countries. The IEEE sets global technical standards and acts as an authority in technical areas ranging from computer engineering, biomedical technology and telecommunications to electric power, aerospace and consumer electronics.

International Standards Organization (ISO)
Chemin de Blandonnet 8
1214 Vernier
Geneva, CP 401 Switzerland
Phone: 41-22-749-01-11
Fax: 41-22-733-34-30
E-mail Address: central@iso.org

Web Address: www.iso.org
The International Standards Organization (ISO) is a global consortium of national standards institutes from 162 countries. The established International Standards are designed to make products and services more efficient, safe and clean.

Minerals, Metals & Materials Society (The) (TMS)
5700 Corporate Dr., Ste. 750
Pittsburgh, PA 15237 USA
Phone: 724-776-9000
Fax: 724-776-3770
Toll Free: 800-759-4867
E-mail Address: tmsgeneral@tms.org
Web Address: www.tms.org
The Minerals Metals & Materials Society (TMS) is an organization of professionals and students involved in metallurgy and material engineering, promoting the exchange of information, education and technology.

Research in Germany, German Academic Exchange Service (DAAD)
Kennedyallee 50
Bonn, 53175 Germany
Phone: 49-228-882-743
Web Address: www.research-in-germany.de
The Research in Germany portal, German Academic Exchange Service (DAAD), is an information platform and contact point for those looking to find out more about Germany's research landscape and its latest research achievements. The portal is an initiative of the Federal Ministry of Education and Research.

Royal Society (The)
6-9 Carlton House Ter.
London, SW1Y 5AG UK
Phone: 44-20-7451-2500
E-mail Address: science.policy@royalsociety.org
Web Address: royalsociety.org
The Royal Society, originally founded in 1660, is the UK's leading scientific organization and the oldest scientific community in continuous existence. It operates as a national academy of science, supporting scientists, engineers, technologists and researchers. Its web site contains a wealth of data about the research and development initiatives of its fellows and foreign members.

Society of Exploration Geophysicists (SEG)
8801 S. Yale, Ste. 500
Tulsa, OK 74137-3575 USA
Phone: 918-497-5581
Fax: 918-497-5558
Toll Free: 877-778-5463
E-mail Address: members@seg.org
Web Address: www.seg.org
The Society of Exploration Geophysicists (SEG) promotes the science of geophysics. The website provides access to their foundation, online publications and employment and education services.

35) Environmental Organizations

Global Footprint Network
1528 Webster St.
Ste. 11
Oakland, CA 94612 USA
Phone: 510-839-8879
Fax: 510-251-2410
E-mail Address: media@footprintnetwork.org
Web Address: www.footprintnetwork.org
Global Footprint Network publishes regional studies of human demands on the ecology which it calls an Ecological Footprint. The Footprint takes into consideration human use of land, water and other resources to fill needs for housing, agriculture, energy and more, along with nature's ability to fulfill those demands. The organization's analysis creates a scale by which one nation may compare its footprint against that of others.

Pembina Institute (The)
219 19 St. NW
Calgary, AB T2N 2H9 Canada
Phone: 403-269-3344
Fax: 403-269-3377
Web Address: www.pembina.org
The Pembina Institute is an independent, not-for-profit environmental policy research and education organization. The Pembina Institute's major policy research and education programs are in the areas of sustainable energy, climate change, environmental governance, ecological fiscal reform, sustainability indicators, and the environmental impacts of the energy industry.

36) Environmental Resources

Center for Clean Air Policy (CCAP)
750 First St. NE, Ste. 1025
Washington, DC 20002 USA
Phone: 202-408-9260

Fax: 202-408-8896
Web Address: www.ccap.org
The Center for Clean Air Policy (CCAP) promotes and applies solutions to key environmental and energy problems.

Center for Climate and Energy Solutions (C2ES)
3100 Clarendon Blvd., Ste. 800
Arlington, VA 22201 USA
Phone: 703-516-4146
Fax: 703-516-9551
E-mail Address: press@c2es.org
Web Address: www.c2es.org
The Center for Climate and Energy Solutions (C2ES), the successor to the Pew Center on Global Climate Change, was established in 2011 as a nonprofit, non-partisan and independent organization. C2ES' mission is to provide credible information, straight answers, and innovative solutions in the effort to address global climate change.

German Federal Environmental Foundation
Deutsche Bundesstiftung Umwelt
An der Bornau 2
Osnabruck, 49090 Germany
Phone: 49-541-9633-0
Fax: 49-541-9633-190
E-mail Address: info@dbu.de
Web Address: www.dbu.de
The German Federal Environmental Foundation's projects and activities concentrate on environmental technology and research, nature conservation, environmental communication and cultural assets. It is an initiative of the German Government.

37) Gasification Industry Associations

Global Syngas Technologies Council (GSTC)
P.O. Box 18456
Sugar Land, TX 77496 USA
Phone: 713-703-8196
E-mail Address: info@globalsyngas.org
Web Address: www.globalsyngas.org
Global Syngas Technologies Council (GSTC) promotes the role that syngas technologies play in helping improve the energy, power, chemical, refining, fuel and waste management industries. GSTC encourages the use of economically competitive and environmentally conscious technologies to produce electricity, fuels, chemicals, fertilizers, substitute natural gas and hydrogen from a variety of feedstocks, including coal, petroleum coke, natural gas, refinery liquids, biomass and waste.

GSTC also facilitates relationships among technology, equipment and service providers, as well as plant owners and operators.

38) Hybrid & Electric Vehicles

Electric Drive Transportation Association (EDTA)
1250 Eye St. NW, Ste. 902
Washington, DC 20005 USA
Phone: 202-408-0774
E-mail Address: info@electricdrive.org
Web Address: www.electricdrive.org
The Electric Drive Transportation Association (EDTA) is an industry association working to advance electric vehicle transportation technologies and supporting infrastructure through policy, information and market development initiatives.

High-Efficiency Truck Users Forum (HTUF)
48 S. Chester Ave.
Pasadena, CA 91106 USA
Phone: 626-744-5600
Fax: 626-744-5610
E-mail Address: calstart@calstart.org
Web Address: www.calstart.org/Projects/htuf.aspx
The High-Efficiency Truck Users Forum, formerly known as the Hybrid Truck Users Forum (HTUF), operated by CALSTART, offers a wealth of information on technologies, pilot projects, test results, fleet purchasing plans and much more.

Vehicle Technologies Program
1000 Independence Ave. SW
EE-3V, Rm. 5G-030
Washington, DC 20585 USA
Phone: 202-586-8055
Fax: 202-586-7409
E-mail Address: connie.bezanson@ee.doe.gov
Web Address:
www1.eere.energy.gov/vehiclesandfuels
Vehicle Technologies Program of the Office of Energy Efficiency and Renewable Energy (EERE), a division of the U.S. Department of Energy, works with U.S. industries toward the development of emission- and petroleum-free cars and light trucks. The program focuses on high-risk technological research for fuel cells and advanced hybrid propulsion systems.

39) Industry Research/Market Research

Forrester Research
60 Acorn Park Dr.
Cambridge, MA 02140 USA
Phone: 617-613-5730
Toll Free: 866-367-7378
E-mail Address: press@forrester.com
Web Address: www.forrester.com
Forrester Research is a publicly traded company that identifies and analyzes emerging trends in technology and their impact on business. Among the firm's specialties are the financial services, retail, health care, entertainment, automotive and information technology industries.

Gartner, Inc.
56 Top Gallant Rd.
Stamford, CT 06902 USA
Phone: 203-964-0096
E-mail Address: info@gartner.com
Web Address: www.gartner.com
Gartner, Inc. is a publicly traded IT company that provides competitive intelligence and strategic consulting and advisory services to numerous clients worldwide.

MarketResearch.com
6116 Executive Blvd., Ste. 550
Rockville, MD 20852 USA
Phone: 240-747-3093
Fax: 240-747-3004
Toll Free: 800-298-5699
E-mail Address: customerservice@marketresearch.com
Web Address: www.marketresearch.com
MarketResearch.com is a leading broker for professional market research and industry analysis. Users are able to search the company's database of research publications including data on global industries, companies, products and trends.

Plunkett Research, Ltd.
P.O. Drawer 541737
Houston, TX 77254-1737 USA
Phone: 713-932-0000
Fax: 713-932-7080
E-mail Address: customersupport@plunkettresearch.com
Web Address: www.plunkettresearch.com
Plunkett Research, Ltd. is a leading provider of market research, industry trends analysis and business statistics. Since 1985, it has served clients worldwide, including corporations, universities, libraries, consultants and government agencies. At the firm's web site, visitors can view product information and pricing and access a large amount of basic market information on industries such as financial services, InfoTech, ecommerce, health care and biotech.

40) MBA Resources

MBA Depot
Web Address: www.mbadepot.com
MBA Depot is an online community and information portal for MBAs, potential MBA program applicants and business professionals.

41) Metals & Steel Industry Associations

Society for Mining, Metallurgy and Exploration (SME)
12999 E. Adam Aircraft Cir.
Englewood, CO 80112 USA
Phone: 720-738-4085
Toll Free: 800-958-1550
E-mail Address: cs@smenet.org
Web Address: www.smenet.org
The Society for Mining, Metallurgy and Exploration (SME) advances the worldwide mining and minerals community through information exchange and professional development.

42) Natural Gas Vehicles

Asia Pacific Natural Gas Vehicles Association (ANGVA)
Lvl. 2, Block A, Lot 3288 & 3289,
Off Jalan Ayer Itam, Kawasan Institusi Bangi
Kajang, Selangor 43000 Malaysia
Phone: 603-2166-5137
Fax: 603-2166-5135
E-mail Address: leegs@angva.org
Web Address: www.angva.org
Asia Pacific Natural Gas Vehicles Association (ANGVA) serves the needs of fleet operators, vehicle manufacturers, gas suppliers, equipment suppliers, refueling equipment providers, consultants, government representatives, non-governmental organizations (NGO) and others involved with the natural gas vehicles industry by promoting the use of natural gas as the fuel for the transportation sector.

Natural Gas Vehicles for America (NGVAmerica)
400 N. Capitol St. NW
Washington, DC 20001 USA
Phone: 202-824-7360
E-mail Address: Syborra@ngvamerica.org
Web Address: www.ngvamerica.org
Natural Gas Vehicle for America (NGVAmerica) is a national organization dedicated to the development of a growing, sustainable and profitable market for vehicles powered by natural gas or hydrogen. NGVAmerica represents more than 230 companies interested in the promotion and use of natural gas and hydrogen as transportation fuels, including: engine, vehicle and equipment manufacturers; fleet operators and service providers; natural gas companies; and environmental groups and government organizations.

43) Nuclear Energy Associations

EUROfusion
Boltzmannstr. 2
Garching, BY 85748 Germany
Phone: +49 89 3299-01
E-mail Address: contact@euro-fusion.org
Web Address: https://www.euro-fusion.org/
EUROfusion supports and funds fusion research activities on behalf of the European Commission's Euratom program. EUROfusion, the European Consortium for the Development of Fusion Energy, is a collaboration composed of fusion research bodies from European Union member states and Switzerland. EUROfusion's mission is to pave the way for fusion power reactors.

44) Nuclear Energy Associations

Fusion Industry Association (FIA)
800 Maine Ave. SW, Ste. 223
Washington, DC 20024 USA
Web Address: www.fusionindustryassociation.org
The Fusion Industry Association (FIA) is working to transform the energy system with commercially viable fusion power, founded as an initiative in 2018.

45) Renewable Energy Associations

RE100
Phone: 646-233-0550
Web Address: www.there100.org
RE100 is a group of major corporations committed to be 100% renewable energy-powered by the middle of the 21st Century. It publishes data and news on energy use by large corporations. It is managed by an international non-profit called the Climate Group.

46) Renewable Energy Resources

International Renewable Energy Agency (IRENA)
Masdar City, P.O. Box 236
Abu Dhabi, UAE
Phone: 971-2417-9000
E-mail Address: info@irena.org
Web Address: irena.org
The International Renewable Energy Agency (IRENA) is an intergovernmental organisation that supports countries in their transition to a sustainable energy future, and serves as the principal platform for international cooperation, a centre of excellence and a repository of policy, technology, resource and financial knowledge on renewable energy. IRENA promotes the widespread adoption and sustainable use of all forms of renewable energy, including bioenergy, geothermal, hydropower, ocean, solar and wind energy in the pursuit of sustainable development, energy access, energy security and low-carbon economic growth and prosperity.

47) Research & Development, Laboratories

Argonne National Laboratory, Nuclear Engineering Division (ANL)
9700 S. Cass Ave.
Argonne, IL 60439-4814 USA
E-mail Address: neinfo@anl.gov
Web Address: www.ne.anl.gov
The Argonne National Laboratory-Nuclear Engineering Division (ANL) is engaged in research and development in the area of applied nuclear technologies such as nonproliferation, environmental remediation, fusion power and new initiatives.

Commonwealth Scientific and Industrial Research Organization (CSRIO)
CSIRO Enquiries
Private Bag 10
Clayton South, Victoria 3169 Australia
Phone: 61-3-9545-2176
Toll Free: 1300-363-400
Web Address: www.csiro.au
The Commonwealth Scientific and Industrial Research Organization (CSRIO) is Australia's national science agency and a leading international research agency. CSRIO performs research in

Australia over a broad range of areas including agriculture, minerals and energy, manufacturing, communications, construction, health and the environment.

Fraunhofer-Gesellschaft (FhG) (The)
Fraunhofer-Gesellschaft zur Forderung der angewandten Forschung e.V.
Postfach 20 07 33
Munich, 80007 Germany
Phone: 49-89-1205-0
Fax: 49-89-1205-7531
Web Address: www.fraunhofer.de
The Fraunhofer-Gesellschaft (FhG) institute focuses on research in health, security, energy, communication, the environment and mobility. FhG includes over 80 research units in Germany. Over 70% of its projects are derived from industry contracts.

Hanford Nuclear Site
2420 Stevens Center Pl., H520
Richland, WA 99352 USA
Phone: 509-376-7411
E-mail Address: Webmaster@rl.gov
Web Address: www.hanford.gov
The Hanford Nuclear Site is designed to solve critical problems related to the environment, energy production and use, U.S. economic competitiveness and national security.

Helmholtz Association
Anna-Louisa-Karsch-Strasse 2
Berlin, 10178 Germany
Phone: 49-30-206329-0
E-mail Address: info@helmholtz.de
Web Address: www.helmholtz.de/en
The Helmholtz Association is a community of 18 scientific-technical and biological-medical research centers. Helmholtz Centers perform top-class research in strategic programs in several core fields: energy, earth and environment, health, key technologies, structure of matter, aeronautics, space and transport.

Idaho National Laboratory (INL)
1955 N. Fremont Ave.
Idaho Falls, ID 83415 USA
Toll Free: 866-495-7440
Web Address: www.inl.gov
Idaho National Laboratory (INL) is a multidisciplinary, multiprogram laboratory that specializes in developing nuclear energy with research concerning the environment, energy, science and national defense.

Los Alamos National Laboratory (LANL)
P.O. Box 1663
Los Alamos, NM 87545 USA
Phone: 505-667-5061
E-mail Address: community@lanl.gov
Web Address: www.lanl.gov
The Los Alamos National Laboratory (LANL), a national energy lab in New Mexico, was originally built as a work site for the team that designed the first atomic bomb during World War II. Currently, it provides a continual stream of research in physics and energy matters. Much of that research is put to use in the commercial sector.

Max Planck Society (MPG)
Hofgartenstr. 8
Munich, 80539 Germany
Phone: 49-89-2108-0
Fax: 49-89-2108-1111
E-mail Address: post@gv.mpg.de
Web Address: www.mpg.de
The Max Planck Society (MPG) currently maintains 83 institutes, research units and working groups that are devoted to basic research in the natural sciences, life sciences, social sciences, and the humanities. Max Planck Institutes work largely in an interdisciplinary setting and in close cooperation with universities and research institutes in Germany and abroad.

National Renewable Energy Laboratory (NREL)
15013 Denver W. Pkwy.
Golden, CO 80401 USA
Phone: 303-275-3000
Web Address: www.nrel.gov
The National Renewable Energy Laboratory (NREL) reduces nuclear danger, transfers applied environmental technology to government and non-government entities and forms economic and industrial alliances.

National Research Council Canada (NRC)
1200 Montreal Rd.
Bldg. M-58
Ottawa, ON K1A 0R6 Canada
Phone: 613-993-9101
Fax: 613-952-9907
Toll Free: 877-672-2672
E-mail Address: info@nrc-cnrc.gc.ca
Web Address: www.nrc-cnrc.gc.ca

National Research Council Canada (NRC) is comprised of 12 government organization, research institutes and programs that carry out multidisciplinary research. It maintains partnerships with industries and sectors key to Canada's economic development.

Oak Ridge National Laboratory (ORNL)
1 Bethel Valley Rd.
P.O. Box 2008
Oak Ridge, TN 37831 USA
Phone: 865-576-7658
Web Address: www.ornl.gov
The Oak Ridge National Laboratory (ORNL) is a multi-program science and technology laboratory managed for the U.S. Department of Energy by U.T.-Battelle, LLC. It conducts basic and applied research and development to create scientific knowledge and technological solutions.

Sandia National Laboratories
1515 Eubank SE
Albuquerque, NM 87125 USA
Phone: 505-844-8066
Web Address: www.sandia.gov
Sandia National Laboratories is a national security laboratory operated for the U.S. Department of Energy by the Sandia Corporation. It designs all nuclear components for the nation's nuclear weapons and performs a wide variety of energy research and development projects.

Savannah River Site (SRS)
U.S. Dept. of Energy, P.O. Box A
Savannah River Operations Office
Aiken, SC 29802 USA
Phone: 803-952-7697
E-mail Address: will.callicott@srs.gov
Web Address: www.srs.gov
The Savannah River Site (SRS) is a nuclear fuel storage and production site that works to protect the people and the environment of the U.S. through safe, secure, cost-effective management of the country's nuclear weapons stockpile and nuclear materials. While the site is owned by the U.S. Department of Energy, it is operated by the subsidiaries of Washington Savannah River Company, LLC (WSRC), itself a wholly-owned subsidiary of Washington Group International.

48) Science & Technology Resources

Technology Review
1 Main St., Fl. 13
Cambridge, MA 02142 USA
Phone: 617-475-8000
Fax: 617-475-8000
Web Address: www.technologyreview.com
Technology Review, an MIT enterprise, publishes tech industry news, covers innovation and writes in-depth articles about research, development and cutting-edge technologies.

49) Stocks & Financial Markets Data

SiliconValley.com
4 N. Second St., Ste. 700
San Jose, CA 95113 USA
Phone: 408-920-5000
Fax: 408-228-8060
E-mail Address: svfeedback@mercurynews.com
Web Address: www.siliconvalley.com
SiliconValley.com, run by San Jose Mercury News and owned by MediaNews Group, offers a summary of current financial news and information regarding the field of technology.

50) Sustainable Development Organizations

International Institute for Sustainable Development (IISD)
111 Lombard Ave., Ste. 325
Winnipeg, Manitoba R3B 0T4 Canada
Phone: 204-958-7700
Fax: 204-958-7710
E-mail Address: info@iisd.org
Web Address: www.iisd.org
The International Institute for Sustainable Development (IISD) is dedicated to advancing sustainable development on a global basis. It publishes public policy recommendations on international trade and investment, economic policy, climate change, energy and the management of natural and social assets.

51) Technology Transfer Associations

Association of University Technology Managers (AUTM)
111 W. Jackson Blvd., Ste. 1412
Chicago, IL 60604 USA

Phone: 847-686-2244
Fax: 847-686-2253
E-mail Address: info@autm.net
Web Address: www.autm.net
The Association of University Technology Managers (AUTM) is a nonprofit professional association whose members belong to over 300 research institutions, universities, teaching hospitals, government agencies and corporations. The association's mission is to advance the field of technology transfer and enhance members' ability to bring academic and nonprofit research to people around the world.

Federal Laboratory Consortium for Technology Transfer
111 W. Jackson Blvd., Ste. 1412
Chicago, IL 60604 USA
Phone: 847-686-2298
E-mail Address: info@federallabs.org
Web Address: www.federallabs.org
In keeping with the aims of the Federal Technology Transfer Act of 1986 and other related legislation, the Federal Laboratory Consortium (FLC) works to facilitate the sharing of research results and technology developments between federal laboratories and the mainstream U.S. economy. FLC affiliates include federal laboratories, large and small businesses, academic and research institutions, state and local governments and various federal agencies. The group has regional support offices and local contacts throughout the U.S.

Licensing Executives Society (USA and Canada), Inc.
11130 Sunrise Valley Dr., Ste. 350
Reston, VA 20191 USA
Phone: 703-234-4058
Fax: 703-435-4390
E-mail Address: info@les.org
Web Address: www.lesusacanada.org
Licensing Executives Society (USA and Canada), Inc., established in 1965, is a professional association composed of about 3,000 members who work in fields related to the development, use, transfer, manufacture and marketing of intellectual property. Members include executives, lawyers, licensing consultants, engineers, academic researchers, scientists and government officials. The society is part of the larger Licensing Executives Society International, Inc. (same headquarters address), with a worldwide membership of some 12,000 members from approximately 80 countries.

State Science and Technology Institute (SSTI)
5015 Pine Creek Dr.
Westerville, OH 43081 USA
Phone: 614-901-1690
E-mail Address: contactus@ssti.org
Web Address: www.ssti.org
The State Science and Technology Institute (SSTI) is a national nonprofit group that serves as a resource for technology-based economic development. In addition to the information on its web site, the Institute publishes a free weekly digest of news and issues related to technology-based economic development efforts, as well as a members-only publication listing application information, eligibility criteria and submission deadlines for a variety of funding opportunities, federal and otherwise.

52) Trade Associations-General

BUSINESSEUROPE
168 Ave. de Cortenbergh 168
Brussels, 1000 Belgium
Phone: 32-2-237-65-11
Fax: 32-2-231-14-45
E-mail Address: main@businesseurope.eu
Web Address: www.businesseurope.eu
BUSINESSEUROPE is a major European trade federation that operates in a manner similar to a chamber of commerce. Its members are the central national business federations of the 34 countries throughout Europe from which they come. Companies cannot become direct members of BUSINESSEUROPE, though there is a support group which offers the opportunity for firms to encourage BUSINESSEUROPE objectives in various ways.

53) Trade Associations-Global

World Trade Organization (WTO)
Centre William Rappard
Rue de Lausanne 154
Geneva 21, CH-1211 Switzerland
Phone: 41-22-739-51-11
Fax: 41-22-731-42-06
E-mail Address: enquiries@wto.og
Web Address: www.wto.org
The World Trade Organization (WTO) is a global organization dealing with the rules of trade between nations. To become a member, nations must agree to abide by certain guidelines. Membership increases a nation's ability to import and export efficiently.

54) Trade Resources

BrazilBiz
Web Address: www.brazilbiz.com.br
The BrazilBiz web site serves as a clearinghouse of general contact information for Brazilian companies; registration on the site is free and allows users to search within the BrazilBiz database for firms across a range of industries.

Made-in-China.com - China Manufacturers Directory
Block A, Software Bldg. No. 9, Xinghuo Rd.
Nanjing New & High Technology Industry Development Zone
Nanjing, Jiangsu 210032 China
Fax: 86-25-6667-0000
Web Address: www.made-in-china.com
Made-in-China.com - China Manufacturers Directory, one of the largest business to business portals in China, helps to connect Chinese manufacturers, suppliers and traders with international buyers. Made-in-China.com contains additional information on trade shows and important laws and regulations about business with China.

55) U.S. Government Agencies

Bureau of Economic Analysis (BEA)
4600 Silver Hill Rd.
Washington, DC 20233 USA
Phone: 301-278-9004
E-mail Address: customerservice@bea.gov
Web Address: www.bea.gov
The Bureau of Economic Analysis (BEA), is an agency of the U.S. Department of Commerce, is the nation's economic accountant, preparing estimates that illuminate key national, international and regional aspects of the U.S. economy.

Bureau of Labor Statistics (BLS)
2 Massachusetts Ave. NE
Washington, DC 20212-0001 USA
Phone: 202-691-5200
Fax: 202-691-7890
Toll Free: 800-877-8339
E-mail Address: blsdata_staff@bls.gov
Web Address: stats.bls.gov
The Bureau of Labor Statistics (BLS) is the principal fact-finding agency for the Federal Government in the field of labor economics and statistics. It is an independent national statistical agency that collects, processes, analyzes and disseminates statistical data to the American public, U.S. Congress, other federal agencies, state and local governments, business and labor. The BLS also serves as a statistical resource to the Department of Labor.

Bureau of Reclamation
1849 C St. NW
Washington, DC 20240-0001 USA
Phone: 202-513-0501
Fax: 202-513-0309
Web Address: www.usbr.gov
The Bureau of Reclamation is best known for the dams, power plants and canals it constructed in 17 western states including Hoover Dam and Grand Coulee Dam.

Energy Efficiency and Renewable Energy (EERE)
1000 Independence Ave. SW
Forrestal Building
Washington, DC 20585 USA
Phone: 202-586-5000
Fax: 202-586-4403
E-mail Address: The.Secretary@hq.doe.gov
Web Address: energy.gov/eere/office-energy-efficiency-renewable-energy
The Energy Efficiency and Renewable Energy (EERE), an office of the U.S. Department of Energy, provides information on bioenergy, geothermal, hydrogen, hydropower, tidal, hydropower, solar, wind and energy conservation methods. The Office also works with U.S. industries to advance the development of various alternative energy technologies.

Energy Information Administration (EIA)
1000 Independence Ave. SW
Washington, DC 20585 USA
Phone: 202-586-8800
E-mail Address: infoctr@eia.gov
Web Address: www.eia.gov
The Energy Information Administration (EIA) is a vast source of useful information on every branch of the industry. It is operated by the U.S. Department of Energy (DOE). The site includes links to a number of other helpful energy industry web sites.

Federal Energy Regulatory Commission (FERC)
888 First St. NE
Washington, DC 20426 USA
Phone: 202-502-6088
Toll Free: 866-208-3372
E-mail Address: customer@ferc.gov

Web Address: www.ferc.gov
The Federal Energy Regulatory Commission (FERC) regulates and oversees energy industries in the economic, environmental and safety interests of the American public.

National Institute of Standards and Technology (NIST)
100 Bureau Dr.
Gaithersburg, MD 20899-1070 USA
Phone: 301-975-6478
Toll Free: 800-877-8339
E-mail Address: inquiries@nist.gov
Web Address: www.nist.gov
The National Institute of Standards and Technology (NIST) is an agency of the U.S. Department of Commerce that works with various industries to develop and apply technology, measurements and standards.

National Science Foundation (NSF)
2415 Eisenhower Ave.
Alexandria, VA 22314 USA
Phone: 703-292-5111
Toll Free: 800-877-8339
E-mail Address: info@nsf.gov
Web Address: www.nsf.gov
The National Science Foundation (NSF) is an independent U.S. government agency responsible for promoting science and engineering. The foundation provides colleges and universities with grants and funding for research into numerous scientific fields.

Office of Scientific and Technical Information (OSTI)
1 Science.gov Way
Oak Ridge, TN 37830 USA
Phone: 865-576-1188
Fax: 865-576-2865
E-mail Address: OSTIWebmaster@osti.gov
Web Address: www.osti.gov
The U.S. Department of Energy's Office of Scientific and Technical Information (OSTI) provides access to a wealth of energy, science, and technology research and development information from the Manhattan Project to the present.

U.S. Census Bureau
4600 Silver Hill Rd.
Washington, DC 20233-8800 USA
Phone: 301-763-4636
Toll Free: 800-923-8282
E-mail Address: pio@census.gov
Web Address: www.census.gov
The U.S. Census Bureau is the official collector of data about the people and economy of the U.S. Founded in 1790, it provides official social, demographic and economic information. In addition to the Population & Housing Census, which it conducts every 10 years, the U.S. Census Bureau conducts numerous other surveys annually.

U.S. Department of Commerce (DOC)
1401 Constitution Ave. NW
Washington, DC 20230 USA
Phone: 202-482-2000
E-mail Address: publicaffairs@doc.gov
Web Address: www.commerce.gov
The U.S. Department of Commerce (DOC) regulates trade and provides valuable economic analysis of the economy.

U.S. Department of Energy (DOE)
1000 Independence Ave. SW
Washington, DC 20585 USA
Phone: 202-586-5000
Fax: 202-586-4403
E-mail Address: The.Secretary@hq.doe.gov
Web Address: www.energy.gov
U.S. Department of Energy (DOE) web site is the best way to gain information from the U.S. Government regarding its many agencies, bureaus and operations in energy. Through the site, users can gain access to government agencies such as Los Alamos National Laboratory, the strategic oil reserves and the agencies that regulate nuclear, geothermal and other types of power.

U.S. Department of Labor (DOL)
200 Constitution Ave. NW
Washington, DC 20210 USA
Phone: 202-693-4676
Toll Free: 866-487-2365
E-mail Address: m-DOLPublicAffairs@dol.gov
Web Address: www.dol.gov
The U.S. Department of Labor (DOL) is the government agency responsible for labor regulations. The Department of Labor's goal is to foster, promote, and develop the welfare of the wage earners, job seekers, and retirees of the United States; improve working conditions; advance opportunities for profitable employment; and assure work-related benefits and rights.

U.S. Environmental Protection Agency (EPA) On-road Vehicles and Engines
U.S. EPA, OAR/OTAQ/CISD.
2000 Traverwood Dr.
Ann Arbor, MI 48105 USA
Phone: 734-214-4200
E-mail Address: otaq@epa.gov
Web Address: www.epa.gov/vehicles-and-engines
The U.S. Environmental Protection Agency (EPA) On-road Vehicles and Engines site, part of the EPA's Office of Transportation and Air Quality (OTAQ), provides details about the best and worst cars and trucks in terms of exhaust emissions. Its web site allows people to instantly check the emission rating of any vehicle. The site also contains information about industry emission trends and goals.

U.S. Geological Survey (USGS)
12201 Sunrise Valley Dr.
Reston, VA 20192 USA
Phone: 703-648-5953
Toll Free: 888-275-8747
Web Address: www.usgs.gov
The U.S. Geological Survey (USGS) conducts research on geography, geology, biology and related hazards and benefits in the United States.

U.S. Nuclear Regulatory Commission (NRC)
11555 Rockville Pike
Rockville, MD 20852 USA
Phone: 301-415-7000
Fax: 301-415-3716
Toll Free: 800-368-5642
E-mail Address: OPA.Resource@nrc.gov
Web Address: www.nrc.gov
The U.S. Nuclear Regulatory Commission (NRC) is an independent agency established by Congress to ensure adequate protection of public health and safety, common defense and security and the environment in use of nuclear materials in the United States.

U.S. Patent and Trademark Office (PTO)
600 Dulany St.
Madison Bldg.
Alexandria, VA 22314 USA
Phone: 571-272-1000
Toll Free: 800-786-9199
E-mail Address: usptoinfo@uspto.gov
Web Address: www.uspto.gov
The U.S. Patent and Trademark Office (PTO) administers patent and trademark laws for the U.S. and enables registration of patents and trademarks.

U.S. Securities and Exchange Commission (SEC)
100 F St. NE
Washington, DC 20549 USA
Phone: 202-942-8088
Fax: 202-772-9295
Toll Free: 800-732-0330
E-mail Address: help@sec.gov
Web Address: www.sec.gov
The U.S. Securities and Exchange Commission (SEC) is a nonpartisan, quasi-judicial regulatory agency responsible for administering federal securities laws. These laws are designed to protect investors in securities markets and ensure that they have access to disclosure of all material information concerning publicly traded securities. Visitors to the web site can access the EDGAR database of corporate financial and business information.

Chapter 4

THE RENEWABLE ENERGY 250: WHO THEY ARE AND HOW THEY WERE CHOSEN

Includes Indexes by Company Name, Industry & Location

The companies chosen to be listed in PLUNKETT'S SOLAR POWER, WIND POWER & RENEWABLE ENERGY INDUSTRY ALMANAC comprise a unique list. THE RENEWABLE ENERGY 250 were chosen specifically for their dominance in the many facets of the alternative energy industry in which they operate. Complete information about each firm can be found in the "Individual Profiles," beginning at the end of this chapter. These profiles are in alphabetical order by company name.

THE RENEWABLE ENERGY 250 includes leading companies from all parts of the United States as well as many other nations, and from all alternative energy and related industry segments, such as wind, solar, geothermal, hydroelectric and special services relating to the industry.

Simply stated, the list contains the most successful, fastest growing firms in alternative and renewable energy and related industries in the world. To be included in our list, the firms had to meet the following criteria:

1) Generally, these are corporations based in the U.S., however, the headquarters of many firms are located in other nations.
2) Prominence, or a significant presence, in alternative energy and supporting fields. (See the following Industry Codes section for a complete list of types of businesses that are covered).
3) The companies in THE RENEWABLE ENERGY 250 do not have to be exclusively in the alternative energy field.
4) Financial data and vital statistics must have been available to the editors of this book, either directly from the company being written about or from outside sources deemed reliable and accurate by the editors. A small number of companies that we would like to have included are not listed because of a lack of sufficient, objective data.

INDEXES TO THE RENEWABLE ENERGY 250, AS FOUND IN THIS CHAPTER AND IN THE BACK OF THE BOOK:	
Index of Companies Within Industry Groups	p. 104
Alphabetical Index	p. 112
Index of Headquarters Location by U.S. State	p. 114
Index of Non-U.S. Headquarters Location by Country	p. 116
Index of Firms Noted as "Hot Spots for Advancement" for Women/Minorities	p. 372
Index by Subsidiaries, Brand Names and Selected Affiliations	p. 373

INDEX OF COMPANIES WITHIN INDUSTRY GROUPS

The industry codes shown below are based on the 2012 NAIC code system (NAIC is used by many analysts as a replacement for older SIC codes because NAIC is more specific to today's industry sectors, see www.census.gov/NAICS). Companies are given a primary NAIC code, reflecting the main line of business of each firm.

Industry Group/Company	Industry Code	2021 Sales	2021 Profits
Aircraft Engine and Engine Parts Manufacturing			
Raytheon Technologies Corporation	336412	64,388,001,792	3,864,000,000
ATV, Snowmobile, Golf Cart, Go-cart and Race Car Equipment Manufacturing			
Spruce Power Holdings Corp	336999	15,600,000	28,790,000
Automobile (Car) and Truck Parts, Components and Systems Manufacturing, Including Gasoline Engines, Interiors and Electronics,			
Cummins Inc	336300	24,021,000,192	2,131,000,064
Modine Manufacturing Company	336300	1,808,400,000	-210,700,000
Quantum Fuel Systems LLC	336300	40,273,000	
Automobile (Car) Manufacturing (incl. Autonomous or Self-Driving)			
Tesla Inc	336111	53,823,000,576	5,519,000,064
Basic Inorganic Chemicals Manufacturing, Including Acids, Carbides and Alkalies			
Cabot Corporation	325180	3,408,999,936	250,000,000
Centrus Energy Corp	325180	298,300,000	175,000,000
Battery Manufacturing, Including Automobile (Car) and Truck Storage Batteries			
LG Energy Solution Ltd	335910		
Battery Manufacturing, Including Energy Storage Technologies			
A123 Systems LLC	335911	461,448,000	
Active Power Inc	335911	70,000,000	
Ambri Incorporated	335911		
APC by Schneider Electric	335911	3,400,000,000	
Arotech Corporation	335911	104,000,000	
Beacon Power LLC	335911		
EnerDel Inc	335911	44,625,000	
Energy Vault Holdings Inc	335911		
Envision AESC SDI Co Ltd	335911	687,011,818	
Exide Technologies LLC	335911	2,853,401,200	
Primearth EV Energy Co Ltd	335911	1,640,481,430	
Stryten Energy LLC	335911		
Ultralife Corporation	335911	98,267,000	-234,000
Biomass Electric Power Generation (Biomass Energy)			
Falck Renewables SpA	221117	570,929,403	61,274,642
IronClad Energy Partners LLC	221117		
Boilers and Condensers (Including Nuclear Reactors) and Heat Exchangers Manufacturing			
Babcock & Wilcox Enterprises Inc	332410	723,363,008	30,894,000
Commonwealth Fusion Systems LLC	332410		
Orano SA	332410	4,819,400,192	691,399,296
Talbott's Biomass Energy Systems Ltd	332410	7,082,500	426,354

Industry Group/Company	Industry Code	2021 Sales	2021 Profits
Westinghouse Electric Company LLC	332410	4,334,575,000	
Chemical Manufacturing, Cyclic Crude, Intermediate and Gum & Wood			
Atlantic Methanol Production Company LLC	325194	952,000,000	
Methanex Corporation	325194	4,414,559,232	482,358,016
Coal Mining			
China Shenhua Energy Company Limited	212110	47,113,981,952	7,065,214,464
Computer Manufacturing, Including PCs, Laptops, Mainframes and Tablets			
Hitachi Limited	334111	60,277,841,920	3,463,795,456
Construction Equipment and Machinery Manufacturing			
Caterpillar Inc	333120	50,971,000,832	6,488,999,936
Construction of Telecommunications Lines and Systems & Electric Power Lines and Systems			
Abengoa SA	237130	1,438,078,108	
Carmanah Technologies Corporation	237130	30,000,000	
Consumer Electronics Manufacturing, Including Audio and Video Equipment, Stereos, TVs and Radios			
Panasonic Corporation	334310	46,257,278,976	1,139,908,608
Samsung Electronics Co Ltd	334310	194,273,886,208	27,267,213,312
Sharp Corporation	334310	16,751,671,296	367,797,760
Contract Electronics Manufacturing Services (CEM) and Printed Circuits Assembly			
Wurth Elektronik GmbH & Co KG	334418	1,004,420,000	
Crude Petroleum and Natural Gas Extraction, Exploration and Production			
BP plc	211111	157,739,008,000	7,565,000,192
Chevron Corporation	211111	155,606,007,808	15,624,999,936
Eni SpA	211111	74,987,511,808	5,700,324,352
Equinor ASA	211111	88,744,001,536	8,562,999,808
Exxon Mobil Corporation (ExxonMobil)	211111	276,692,008,960	23,040,000,000
Shell Oil Company	211111	6,871,700,000	
Shell plc	211111	261,504,008,192	20,100,999,168
Suncor Energy Inc	211111	29,833,975,808	2,987,532,032
Syncrude Canada Ltd	211111	4,200,000,000	
TotalEnergies SE	211111	184,633,999,360	16,032,000,000
Electric Power Distribution			
Alliander NV	221122	2,120,000,000	354,000,000
Electric Power Generation			
GE Vernova	221110		
Electric Power Transmission and Control			
ENGIE Global Energy Management & Sales	221121		
Zorlu Enerji Elektrik Uretim AS	221121	625,603,626	148,941,825
Electrical Contractors and Other Wiring Installation Contractors			
GRID Alternatives	238210	91,000,000	
Electricity Control Panels, Circuit Breakers and Power Switches Equipment (Switchgear) Manufacturing			
ABB Ltd	335313	28,945,000,448	4,545,999,872

Industry Group/Company	Industry Code	2021 Sales	2021 Profits
Engineering Services, Including Civil, Mechanical, Electronic, Computer and Environmental Engineering			
Ameresco Inc	541330	1,215,697,024	70,458,000
Atomic Energy of Canada Limited (AECL)	541330	824,109,962	5,196,241
BIOS-BIOENERGYSYSTEME GmbH	541330	6,386,869	
Black & Veatch Holding Company	541330	3,801,451,500	
ENGlobal Corporation	541330	36,410,000	-5,685,000
McDermott International Ltd	541330	6,507,280,000	
Environmental Control and Automation Manufacturing			
Ducon Technologies Inc	334512		
Ethanol (Bioethanol) Refining or Manufacturing			
Alto Ingredients Inc	325193	1,207,891,968	46,082,000
Amyris Inc	325193	341,816,992	-270,968,992
Cosan SA	325193		
Green Plains Inc	325193	2,827,168,000	-65,992,000
Iogen Corporation	325193		
REX American Resources Corporation	325193	372,664,000	3,001,000
Factory Automation, Robots (Robotics) Industrial Process, Thermostat, Flow Meter and Environmental Quality Monitoring and Control Manufacturing (incl. Artificial Intelligence, AI)			
Siemens AG	334513	60,974,174,208	6,033,275,392
Flour, Grain & Corn Milling and Cooking Oils (Including Vegetable, Canola, Olive, Peanut & Soy) Manufacturing			
AG Processing Inc	311200	4,148,301,305	
Archer-Daniels-Midland Company (ADM)	311200	85,248,999,424	2,708,999,936
Cargill Incorporated	311200	134,400,000,000	
Peter Cremer North America LP	311200		
Fluid Power Valve and Hose Fitting Manufacturing			
Entegris Inc	332912	2,298,893,056	409,126,016
Fossil Fuel Electric Power Generation			
AES Corporation (The)	221112	11,141,000,192	-409,000,000
Arizona Public Service Company	221112	3,803,835,000	649,503,000
Berkshire Hathaway Energy Company	221112	25,150,000,000	6,189,000,000
Calpine Corporation	221112	8,000,000,000	
CEZ AS	221112	9,419,863,040	390,574,528
CK Infrastructure Holdings Limited	221112	897,873,280	957,366,272
Dominion Energy Inc	221112	13,964,000,256	3,288,000,000
Enel SpA	221112	94,545,469,440	3,122,888,192
Entergy Corporation	221112	11,742,896,128	1,118,718,976
FirstEnergy Corporation	221112	11,132,000,256	1,283,000,064
Iberdrola SA	221112	38,303,121,408	3,804,459,520
Ontario Power Generation Inc	221112	6,877,000,000	1,344,000,000
PacifiCorp	221112		
PNM Resources Inc	221112	1,779,873,024	196,356,992
Reliance Power Limited	221112	1,143,307,460	31,160,669
RWE AG	221112	24,017,547,264	706,052,864
Scottish and Southern Energy plc (SSE)	221112	7,604,999,680	2,535,816,960
Southern California Edison Company	221112	14,905,000,000	925,000,000

Industry Group/Company	Industry Code	2021 Sales	2021 Profits
Southern Company	221112	23,113,000,960	2,408,000,000
Tata Power Co Ltd	221112		
Tennessee Valley Authority (TVA)	221112	10,503,000,000	1,512,000,000
Uniper SE	221112	160,578,551,808	-4,082,571,776
UNS Energy Corporation	221112	2,334,000,000	
Vattenfall AB	221112	16,745,930,000	704,630,700
WEC Energy Group Inc	221112	8,316,000,256	1,301,500,032
Fuel Cells Manufacturing			
Ballard Power Systems Inc	335999A	104,505,000	-114,233,000
Bloom Energy Corporation	335999A	972,176,000	-164,444,992
Electrochem	335999A		
FuelCell Energy Inc	335999A	69,585,000	-101,055,000
Nuvera Fuel Cells LLC	335999A	-320,000	
Plug Power Inc	335999A	502,342,016	-459,964,992
SFC Energy AG	335999A	62,986,868	-5,708,606
Soluna Holdings Inc	335999A	14,345,000	-5,261,000
Fuel Dealers, Including Propane and Bottled Gas			
Clean Energy Fuels Corp	454310	255,646,000	-93,146,000
Generators, and Wind, Steam and Gas Turbine Equipment Manufacturing			
Alstom SA	333611	8,602,876,928	241,879,408
American Superconductor Corporation	333611	87,125,000	-22,678,000
Capstone Green Energy Corporation	333611	67,636,000	-18,387,000
Clipper Windpower LLC	333611		
ENERCON GmbH	333611	5,038,800,000	
GE Power	333611	16,903,000,000	726,000,000
Nordex SE	333611	5,331,090,944	-225,384,608
Siemens Gamesa Renewable Energy SA	333611	9,986,405,376	-613,649,024
Sinovel Wind Group Co Ltd	333611	94,000,000	
Suzlon Energy Limited	333611	458,708,000	14,118,600
Vestas Wind Systems A/S	333611	15,263,863,808	163,537,904
Xinjiang Goldwind Science & Technology Co Ltd	333611	7,107,620,864	485,868,160
Geothermal Electric Power Generation (Geothermal Energy)			
Ormat Technologies Inc	221116	663,084,032	62,092,000
Heavy Construction, Including Civil Engineering-Construction, Major Construction Projects, Land Subdivision, Infrastructure, Utilities, Highways and Bridges			
Bechtel Group Inc	237000	19,360,000,000	
Fluor Corporation	237000	12,434,879,488	-440,169,984
Fomento de Construcciones y Contratas SA (FCC)	237000	6,521,228,288	568,108,096
HOCHTIEF AG	237000	20,934,686,720	203,610,544
Webuild SpA	237000	5,853,894,144	-298,627,040
Highway, Street, Tunnel & Bridge Construction (Infrastructure)			
Acciona SA	237310	7,936,292,352	325,164,256
Aecon Group Inc	237310	2,884,772,096	36,034,608
VINCI SA	237310	49,188,675,584	2,543,161,088

Industry Group/Company	Industry Code	2021 Sales	2021 Profits
HVAC (Cooling, Heating, Ventilation and Air Conditioning) and Refrigeration Equipment Manufacturing			
Trane Technologies plc	333400	14,136,399,872	1,423,399,936
Hydroelectric Power Generation			
Avista Corporation	221111	1,438,936,064	147,334,000
Bonneville Power Administration	221111	3,823,000,000	245,747,000
British Columbia Hydro and Power Authority	221111	5,085,243,690	545,470,480
Companhia Energetica de Minas Gerais SA (CEMIG)	221111	6,214,284,288	692,795,008
Companhia Paranaense de Energia - Copel	221111	4,429,804,032	914,720,768
Guangxi Guiguan Electric Power Co Ltd	221111	1,150,468,000	188,013,176
Hydro-Quebec	221111	10,769,620,000	2,642,360,000
IDACORP Inc	221111	1,458,083,968	245,550,000
Itaipu Binacional	221111	3,700,000,000	
Manitoba Hydro-Electric	221111	2,236,587,535	92,761,695
New York Power Authority	221111	2,741,000,000	13,900,000
Newfoundland and Labrador Hydro	221111	752,334,840	53,472,960
PG&E Corporation	221111	20,642,000,896	-88,000,000
Portland General Electric Company	221111	2,396,000,000	244,000,000
Puget Energy Inc	221111	3,805,661,000	260,849,000
Sacramento Municipal Utility District	221111	1,791,000,000	341,000,000
Western Area Power Administration	221111	1,444,898,840	
Industrial & Commercial Fan, Blower, Filter and Air Purification Equipment Manufacturing			
Porvair plc	333413	200,000,000	
Industrial Gas (i.e. Helium, Nitrogen, Oxygen, Neon) Manufacturing			
Air Liquide US LLC	325120	17,338,776,000	
Air Products and Chemicals Inc	325120	10,323,000,320	2,099,100,032
Light Truck and Utility Vehicle Manufacturing			
Lordstown Motors Corp	336112	0	-410,368,000
Machine Tool and Laser Manufacturing (for Bending, Buffing, Boring, Pressing, Grinding or Forming)			
ATS Automation Tooling Systems Inc	333517	1,037,224,064	46,486,256
Umicore SA	333517	23,555,764,224	606,127,232
Machinery and Engines Manufacturing, Including Construction, Agricultural, Mining, Industrial, Commercial and HVAC (Broad-Based)			
General Electric Company (GE)	333000	74,196,000,768	-6,520,000,000
Mitsubishi Corporation	333000	88,971,673,600	1,191,511,936
Measuring and Dispensing Pump Manufacturing			
Flowserve Corporation	333913	3,541,060,096	125,949,000
Medical Equipment and Supplies Manufacturing			
3M Company	339100	35,355,000,832	5,920,999,936
Nuclear Electric Power Generation			
EDF Energy Nuclear Generation Group Limited	221113	4,010,666,400	
Electricite de France SA (EDF)	221113	82,710,028,288	5,007,001,600
Exelon Corporation	221113	36,346,998,784	1,706,000,000
Green Mountain Power Corporation	221113	744,793,000	
Oil and Gas Field Services			
Halliburton Company	213112	15,294,999,552	1,456,999,936

Industry Group/Company	Industry Code	2021 Sales	2021 Profits
Paints and Coatings Manufacturing			
Sulzer AG	325510	3,201,237,760	1,437,325,696
Petrochemicals Manufacturing			
Evonik Industries AG	325110	14,644,965,376	730,534,592
Photographic and Photocopying Equipment Manufacturing			
Kyocera Corporation	333316	10,543,704,064	622,956,032
Power, Distribution and Specialty Transformer Manufacturing			
Mitsubishi Electric Corporation	335311	28,943,163,392	1,333,637,248
Primary Battery Manufacturing			
Contemporary Amperex Technology Co Limited (CATL)	335912	17,920,623,000	2,198,318,690
Enovix Corp	335912	0	-125,874,000
Freyr Battery SA	335912	0	-93,378,000
Group14 Technologies Inc	335912		
Ion Storage Systems Inc	335912		
Lithium Werks BV	335912		
Nanosys Inc	335912		
Northvolt AB	335912		
QuantumScape Corporation	335912	0	-45,966,000
Radar, Navigation, Sonar, Space Vehicle Guidance, Flight Systems and Marine Instrument Manufacturing			
Teledyne Technologies Inc	334511	4,614,300,160	445,300,000
Real Estate Rental, Leasing, Development and Management, including REITs			
Brookfield Asset Management Inc	531100	75,731,001,344	3,966,000,128
Recycling and Materials Recovery Facilities			
Cory Group (Cory Topco Limited)	562920	161,924,210	-198,645,000
Scientific Research and Development (R&D) in Physics, Engineering, Telecommunications and Computers			
GE Global Research	541712		
Luna Innovations Incorporated	541712	87,513,000	1,382,000
Semiconductor and Solar Cell Manufacturing, Including Chips, Memory, LEDs, Transistors and Integrated Circuits, Artificial Intelligence (AI), & Internet of Things (IoT)			
EMCORE Corporation	334413	158,444,000	25,643,000
Motech Industries Inc	334413	184,470,930	3,360,870
Toshiba Corporation	334413	21,091,420,160	787,074,624
Semiconductor Manufacturing Equipment and Systems (Including Etching, Wafer Processing & Surface Mount) Manufacturing			
Applied Materials Inc	333242	23,062,999,040	5,888,000,000
Eternalsun Spire	333242		
Sewage Treatment Facilities			
Companhia de Saneamento Basico do Estado de Sao Paulo (SABESP)	221320	3,599,922,688	425,884,960
Software (Business and Consumer), Packaged Software and Software as a Service (SaaS)			
Enel X North America Inc	511200	310,277,600	

Industry Group/Company	Industry Code	2021 Sales	2021 Profits
Solar Cell Manufacturing			
AVANCIS GmbH	334413A		
Blueleaf Energy	334413A	1,200,000,000	
Canadian Solar Inc	334413A	5,277,169,152	95,248,000
Central Electronics Limited	334413A	36,713,245	3,170,175
CSUN Solar Tech Co Ltd	334413A	598,000,000	
CubicPV	334413A	87,000,000	
First Solar Inc	334413A	2,923,376,896	468,692,992
Global Solar Energy Inc	334413A		
Hanwha Q Cells	334413A	3,450,000,000	
Hanwha Solutions Corporation	334413A	7,792,000,000	
JA Solar Technology Co Ltd	334413A	5,679,944,000	281,361,610
JinkoSolar Holding Co Ltd	334413A	5,738,091,520	101,337,728
MiaSole Hi-Tech Corp	334413A		
Photowatt International SAS	334413A		
PowerFilm Solar Inc	334413A	12,500,000	
Spectrolab Inc	334413A		
SunPower Corporation	334413A	1,323,492,992	-37,358,000
Trina Solar Co Ltd	334413A	7,030,000,000	297,000,000
United Renewable Energy LLC	334413A	449,225,820	-40,456,080
Wuxi Suntech Power Co Ltd	334413A	1,601,374,000	
Yingli Energy (China) Co Ltd	334413A		
Solar Electric Power Generation (Solar Energy)			
Adani Green Energy Limited	221114	425,779,332	24,941,619
BrightSource Energy Inc	221114	550,000,000	
Duke Energy Sustainable Solutions	221114	196,270,000	
Fotowatio Renewable Ventures SLU	221114		
Lightsource BP	221114		
Silicon Ranch Corporation	221114		
SkyPower Limited	221114		
Sunrun Inc	221114	1,609,954,048	-79,423,000
Swell Energy Inc	221114		
TerraForm Power Operating LLC	221114	1,280,000,000	
Trinity Solar Inc	221114	310,000,000	
Solid Waste Combustors and Incinerators			
Covanta Holding Corporation	562213	2,000,000,000	
Specialized Commercial and Service Machinery Manufacturing, Including Cleaning, Laundry and Automobile (Car) Washing Equipment			
Energy Recovery Inc	333318	103,904,000	14,269,000
Specialty Chemicals Manufacturing, Including Fragrances, Silicones, Biodiesel and Enzymes			
BASF SE	325199	76,968,566,784	5,408,501,760
Dow Inc	325199	54,968,000,512	6,311,000,064
Imperial Western Products Inc	325199		
Renewable Energy Group Inc	325199	3,200,000,000	
SeQuential	325199		
Viridos Inc	325199		
World Energy LLC	325199	110,000,000	

Industry Group/Company	Industry Code	2021 Sales	2021 Profits
Steam and Air-Conditioning Utilities			
ReNu Energy Limited	221330	120,000	-736,713
Uranium, Radium and Vanadium Mining and Production			
Cameco Corporation	212291	1,069,813,440	-74,399,624
Vaccines, Skin Replacement Products and Biologicals Manufacturing			
IFF Nutrition & Biosciences	325414	11,655,999,488	268,000,000
Novozymes A/S	325414	1,968,920,704	414,301,664
Venture Capital, Private Equity Investment and Hedge Funds			
Chevron Technology Ventures LLC	523910		
Waste Collection, Recycling, Treatment and Remediation Services			
Waste Management Inc	562000	17,930,999,808	1,816,000,000
Water Meters, Fluid Metering, Fluid Measurement and Control Instruments			
Badger Meter Inc	334514	505,198,016	60,884,000
Water Utilities and Supply Systems			
Veolia Environnement SA	221310	27,917,094,912	395,918,400
Wind Electric Power Generation (Wind Energy)			
AGL Energy Limited	221115	6,858,225,152	-1,321,433,216
China Longyuan Power Group Corporation Limited	221115	5,229,583,872	900,095,424
Clearway Energy Inc	221115	1,286,000,000	51,000,000
Enel Green Power SpA	221115	9,568,104,920	4,836,282,300
Essent NV	221115	6,000,000,000	
GE Renewable Energy	221115	15,697,000,000	-795,000,000
Invenergy	221115		
NextEra Energy Inc	221115	17,068,999,680	3,572,999,936
NextEra Energy Resources LLC	221115	3,053,000,000	-147,000,000
Orsted A/S	221115	9,105,022,976	1,443,603,072
Renewable Energy Systems Ltd	221115	83,208,112	
Shell WindEnergy Inc	221115		
SSE Airtricity Limited	221115	1,746,981,600	
Tri Global Energy LLC	221115		

ALPHABETICAL INDEX

3M Company
A123 Systems LLC
ABB Ltd
Abengoa SA
Acciona SA
Active Power Inc
Adani Green Energy Limited
Aecon Group Inc
AES Corporation (The)
AG Processing Inc
AGL Energy Limited
Air Liquide US LLC
Air Products and Chemicals Inc
Alliander NV
Alstom SA
Alto Ingredients Inc
Ambri Incorporated
Ameresco Inc
American Superconductor Corporation
Amyris Inc
APC by Schneider Electric
Applied Materials Inc
Archer-Daniels-Midland Company (ADM)
Arizona Public Service Company
Arotech Corporation
Atlantic Methanol Production Company LLC
Atomic Energy of Canada Limited (AECL)
ATS Automation Tooling Systems Inc
AVANCIS GmbH
Avista Corporation
Babcock & Wilcox Enterprises Inc
Badger Meter Inc
Ballard Power Systems Inc
BASF SE
Beacon Power LLC
Bechtel Group Inc
Berkshire Hathaway Energy Company
BIOS-BIOENERGYSYSTEME GmbH
Black & Veatch Holding Company
Bloom Energy Corporation
Blueleaf Energy
Bonneville Power Administration
BP plc
BrightSource Energy Inc
British Columbia Hydro and Power Authority
Brookfield Asset Management Inc
Cabot Corporation
Calpine Corporation
Cameco Corporation
Canadian Solar Inc
Capstone Green Energy Corporation
Cargill Incorporated
Carmanah Technologies Corporation
Caterpillar Inc
Central Electronics Limited
Centrus Energy Corp

CEZ AS
Chevron Corporation
Chevron Technology Ventures LLC
China Longyuan Power Group Corporation Limited
China Shenhua Energy Company Limited
CK Infrastructure Holdings Limited
Clean Energy Fuels Corp
Clearway Energy Inc
Clipper Windpower LLC
Commonwealth Fusion Systems LLC
Companhia de Saneamento Basico do Estado de Sao Paulo (SABESP)
Companhia Energetica de Minas Gerais SA (CEMIG)
Companhia Paranaense de Energia - Copel
Contemporary Amperex Technology Co Limited (CATL)
Cory Group (Cory Topco Limited)
Cosan SA
Covanta Holding Corporation
CSUN Solar Tech Co Ltd
CubicPV
Cummins Inc
Dominion Energy Inc
Dow Inc
Ducon Technologies Inc
Duke Energy Sustainable Solutions
EDF Energy Nuclear Generation Group Limited
Electricite de France SA (EDF)
Electrochem
EMCORE Corporation
Enel Green Power SpA
Enel SpA
Enel X North America Inc
ENERCON GmbH
EnerDel Inc
Energy Recovery Inc
Energy Vault Holdings Inc
ENGIE Global Energy Management & Sales
ENGlobal Corporation
Eni SpA
Enovix Corp
Entegris Inc
Entergy Corporation
Envision AESC SDI Co Ltd
Equinor ASA
Essent NV
Eternalsun Spire
Evonik Industries AG
Exelon Corporation
Exide Technologies LLC
Exxon Mobil Corporation (ExxonMobil)
Falck Renewables SpA
First Solar Inc
FirstEnergy Corporation
Flowserve Corporation
Fluor Corporation
Fomento de Construcciones y Contratas SA (FCC)
Fotowatio Renewable Ventures SLU
Freyr Battery SA

FuelCell Energy Inc
GE Global Research
GE Power
GE Renewable Energy
GE Vernova
General Electric Company (GE)
Global Solar Energy Inc
Green Mountain Power Corporation
Green Plains Inc
GRID Alternatives
Group14 Technologies Inc
Guangxi Guiguan Electric Power Co Ltd
Halliburton Company
Hanwha Q Cells
Hanwha Solutions Corporation
Hitachi Limited
HOCHTIEF AG
Hydro-Quebec
Iberdrola SA
IDACORP Inc
IFF Nutrition & Biosciences
Imperial Western Products Inc
Invenergy
Iogen Corporation
Ion Storage Systems Inc
IronClad Energy Partners LLC
Itaipu Binacional
JA Solar Technology Co Ltd
JinkoSolar Holding Co Ltd
Kyocera Corporation
LG Energy Solution Ltd
Lightsource BP
Lithium Werks BV
Lordstown Motors Corp
Luna Innovations Incorporated
Manitoba Hydro-Electric
McDermott International Ltd
Methanex Corporation
MiaSole Hi-Tech Corp
Mitsubishi Corporation
Mitsubishi Electric Corporation
Modine Manufacturing Company
Motech Industries Inc
Nanosys Inc
New York Power Authority
Newfoundland and Labrador Hydro
NextEra Energy Inc
NextEra Energy Resources LLC
Nordex SE
Northvolt AB
Novozymes A/S
Nuvera Fuel Cells LLC
Ontario Power Generation Inc
Orano SA
Ormat Technologies Inc
Orsted A/S
PacifiCorp
Panasonic Corporation

Peter Cremer North America LP
PG&E Corporation
Photowatt International SAS
Plug Power Inc
PNM Resources Inc
Portland General Electric Company
Porvair plc
PowerFilm Solar Inc
Primearth EV Energy Co Ltd
Puget Energy Inc
Quantum Fuel Systems LLC
QuantumScape Corporation
Raytheon Technologies Corporation
Reliance Power Limited
Renewable Energy Group Inc
Renewable Energy Systems Ltd
ReNu Energy Limited
REX American Resources Corporation
RWE AG
Sacramento Municipal Utility District
Samsung Electronics Co Ltd
Scottish and Southern Energy plc (SSE)
SeQuential
SFC Energy AG
Sharp Corporation
Shell Oil Company
Shell plc
Shell WindEnergy Inc
Siemens AG
Siemens Gamesa Renewable Energy SA
Silicon Ranch Corporation
Sinovel Wind Group Co Ltd
SkyPower Limited
Soluna Holdings Inc
Southern California Edison Company
Southern Company
Spectrolab Inc
Spruce Power Holdings Corp
SSE Airtricity Limited
Stryten Energy LLC
Sulzer AG
Suncor Energy Inc
SunPower Corporation
Sunrun Inc
Suzlon Energy Limited
Swell Energy Inc
Syncrude Canada Ltd
Talbott's Biomass Energy Systems Ltd
Tata Power Co Ltd
Teledyne Technologies Inc
Tennessee Valley Authority (TVA)
TerraForm Power Operating LLC
Tesla Inc
Toshiba Corporation
TotalEnergies SE
Trane Technologies plc
Tri Global Energy LLC
Trina Solar Co Ltd

Trinity Solar Inc
Ultralife Corporation
Umicore SA
Uniper SE
United Renewable Energy LLC
UNS Energy Corporation
Vattenfall AB
Veolia Environnement SA
Vestas Wind Systems A/S
VINCI SA
Viridos Inc
Waste Management Inc
Webuild SpA
WEC Energy Group Inc
Western Area Power Administration
Westinghouse Electric Company LLC
World Energy LLC
Wurth Elektronik GmbH & Co KG
Wuxi Suntech Power Co Ltd
Xinjiang Goldwind Science & Technology Co Ltd
Yingli Energy (China) Co Ltd
Zorlu Enerji Elektrik Uretim AS

INDEX OF HEADQUARTERS LOCATION BY U.S. STATE

To help you locate members of THE RENEWABLE ENERGY 250 geographically, the city and state of the headquarters of each company are in the following index.

ARIZONA
Arizona Public Service Company; Phoenix
First Solar Inc; Tempe
Global Solar Energy Inc; Tucson
UNS Energy Corporation; Tucson

CALIFORNIA
Amyris Inc; Emeryville
Applied Materials Inc; Santa Clara
Bloom Energy Corporation; San Jose
BrightSource Energy Inc; Oakland
Capstone Green Energy Corporation; Van Nuys
Chevron Corporation; San Ramon
Clean Energy Fuels Corp; Newport Beach
Duke Energy Sustainable Solutions; San Luis Obispo
EMCORE Corporation; Alhambra
Energy Recovery Inc; San Leandro
Energy Vault Holdings Inc; Westlake Village
Enovix Corp; Fremont
GRID Alternatives; Oakland
Imperial Western Products Inc; Coachella
MiaSole Hi-Tech Corp; Santa Clara
Nanosys Inc; Milpitas
PG&E Corporation; San Francisco
Quantum Fuel Systems LLC; Lake Forest
QuantumScape Corporation; San Jose
Sacramento Municipal Utility District; Sacramento
Southern California Edison Company; Rosemead
Spectrolab Inc; Sylmar
SunPower Corporation; San Jose
Sunrun Inc; San Francisco
Swell Energy Inc; Santa Monica
Teledyne Technologies Inc; Thousand Oaks
Tesla Inc; Palo Alto
Viridos Inc; La Jolla

COLORADO
Western Area Power Administration; Lakewood

CONNECTICUT
FuelCell Energy Inc; Danbury

FLORIDA
NextEra Energy Inc; Juno Beach
NextEra Energy Resources LLC; Juno Beach

GEORGIA
Southern Company; Atlanta

Stryten Energy LLC; Alpharetta
United Renewable Energy LLC; Cumming

IDAHO
IDACORP Inc; Boise

ILLINOIS
Alto Ingredients Inc; Pekin
Archer-Daniels-Midland Company (ADM); Chicago
Caterpillar Inc; Deerfield
Exelon Corporation; Chicago
Invenergy; Chicago
IronClad Energy Partners LLC; Lombard

INDIANA
Cummins Inc; Columbus
EnerDel Inc; Anderson

IOWA
Berkshire Hathaway Energy Company; Des Moines
Clipper Windpower LLC; Cedar Rapids
IFF Nutrition & Biosciences; Cedar Rapids
PowerFilm Solar Inc; Ames
Renewable Energy Group Inc; Ames

KANSAS
Black & Veatch Holding Company; Overland Park

LOUISIANA
Entergy Corporation; New Orleans

MASSACHUSETTS
Ambri Incorporated; Marlborough
Ameresco Inc; Framingham
American Superconductor Corporation; Ayer
APC by Schneider Electric; Boston
Beacon Power LLC; Tyngsboro
Cabot Corporation; Boston
Commonwealth Fusion Systems LLC; Cambridge
CubicPV; Bedford
Electrochem; Raynham
Enel X North America Inc; Boston
Entegris Inc; Billerica
GE Vernova; Boston
General Electric Company (GE); Boston
Nuvera Fuel Cells LLC; Billerica
Raytheon Technologies Corporation; Waltham
World Energy LLC; Boston

MARYLAND
Centrus Energy Corp; Bethesda
Ion Storage Systems Inc; Beltsville

MICHIGAN
A123 Systems LLC; Novi
Arotech Corporation; Ann Arbor

Dow Inc; Midland

MINNESOTA
3M Company; St. Paul
Cargill Incorporated; Minneapolis

NEBRASKA
AG Processing Inc; Omaha
Green Plains Inc; Omaha

NEVADA
Ormat Technologies Inc; Reno

NEW JERSEY
Clearway Energy Inc; Princeton
Covanta Holding Corporation; Morristown
Trinity Solar Inc; Wall

NEW MEXICO
PNM Resources Inc; Albuquerque

NEW YORK
Ducon Technologies Inc; New York
GE Global Research; Niskayuna
GE Power; Schenectady
New York Power Authority; White Plains
Plug Power Inc; Latham
Soluna Holdings Inc; Albany
TerraForm Power Operating LLC; New York
Ultralife Corporation; Newark

OHIO
Babcock & Wilcox Enterprises Inc; Akron
FirstEnergy Corporation; Akron
Lordstown Motors Corp; Lordstown
Peter Cremer North America LP; Cincinnati
REX American Resources Corporation; Dayton

OREGON
Bonneville Power Administration; Portland
PacifiCorp; Portland
Portland General Electric Company; Portland
SeQuential; Portland

PENNSYLVANIA
Air Products and Chemicals Inc; Allentown
Westinghouse Electric Company LLC; Cranberry Township

TENNESSEE
Silicon Ranch Corporation; Nashville
Tennessee Valley Authority (TVA); Knoxville

TEXAS
Active Power Inc; Austin
Air Liquide US LLC; Houston

Atlantic Methanol Production Company LLC; Houston
Calpine Corporation; Houston
Chevron Technology Ventures LLC; Houston
ENGlobal Corporation; Houston
Exxon Mobil Corporation (ExxonMobil); Irving
Flowserve Corporation; Irving
Fluor Corporation; Irving
Halliburton Company; Houston
McDermott International Ltd; Houston
Shell Oil Company; Houston
Shell WindEnergy Inc; Houston
Spruce Power Holdings Corp; Boston
Tri Global Energy LLC; Dallas
Waste Management Inc; Houston

VERMONT
Green Mountain Power Corporation; Colchester

VIRGINIA
AES Corporation (The); Arlington
Bechtel Group Inc; Reston
Dominion Energy Inc; Richmond
Luna Innovations Incorporated; Roanoke

WASHINGTON
Avista Corporation; Spokane
Group14 Technologies Inc; Woodinville
Puget Energy Inc; Bellevue

WISCONSIN
Badger Meter Inc; Milwaukee
Modine Manufacturing Company; Racine
WEC Energy Group Inc; Milwaukee

INDEX OF NON-U.S. HEADQUARTERS LOCATION BY COUNTRY

AUSTRALIA
AGL Energy Limited; North Sydney
ReNu Energy Limited; Milton

AUSTRIA
BIOS-BIOENERGYSYSTEME GmbH; Graz

BELGIUM
Umicore SA; Brussels

BRAZIL
Companhia de Saneamento Basico do Estado de Sao Paulo (SABESP); Sao Paulo
Companhia Energetica de Minas Gerais SA (CEMIG); Belo Horizonte
Companhia Paranaense de Energia - Copel; Mossungue
Cosan SA; Sau Paulo
Itaipu Binacional; Parana

CANADA
Aecon Group Inc; Toronto
Atomic Energy of Canada Limited (AECL); Chalk River
ATS Automation Tooling Systems Inc; Cambridge
Ballard Power Systems Inc; Burnaby
British Columbia Hydro and Power Authority; Vancouver
Brookfield Asset Management Inc; Toronto
Cameco Corporation; Saskatoon
Canadian Solar Inc; Kitchener
Carmanah Technologies Corporation; Victoria
Hydro-Quebec; Montreal
Iogen Corporation; Ottawa
Manitoba Hydro-Electric; Winnipeg
Methanex Corporation; Vancouver
Newfoundland and Labrador Hydro; St. John's
Ontario Power Generation Inc; Toronto
SkyPower Limited; Toronto
Suncor Energy Inc; Calgary
Syncrude Canada Ltd; Calgary

CHINA
China Longyuan Power Group Corporation Limited; Beijing
China Shenhua Energy Company Limited; Beijing
Contemporary Amperex Technology Co Limited (CATL); Ningde
CSUN Solar Tech Co Ltd; Jiangning
Guangxi Guiguan Electric Power Co Ltd; Nanning
JA Solar Technology Co Ltd; Beijing
JinkoSolar Holding Co Ltd; Shangrao
Sinovel Wind Group Co Ltd; Beijing
Trina Solar Co Ltd; Changzhou
Wuxi Suntech Power Co Ltd; Wuxi

Xinjiang Goldwind Science & Technology Co Ltd; Urumqi
Yingli Energy (China) Co Ltd; Baoding

CZECH REPUBLIC
CEZ AS; Praha 4

DENMARK
Novozymes A/S; Bagsvaerd
Orsted A/S; Fredericia
Vestas Wind Systems A/S; Aarhus

FRANCE
Alstom SA; Paris
Electricite de France SA (EDF); Paris
Exide Technologies LLC; Gennevilliers
GE Renewable Energy; Boulogne-Billancourt
Orano SA; Issy-les-Moulineaux
Photowatt International SAS; Bourgoin-Jallieu
TotalEnergies SE; Courbevoie
Veolia Environnement SA; Aubervilliers
VINCI SA; Nanterre Cedex

GERMANY
AVANCIS GmbH; Torgau
BASF SE; Ludwigshafen am Rhein
ENERCON GmbH; Bremen
Evonik Industries AG; Essen
HOCHTIEF AG; Essen
Nordex SE; Hamburg
RWE AG; Essen
SFC Energy AG; Brunnthal
Siemens AG; Munich
Uniper SE; Dusseldorf
Wurth Elektronik GmbH & Co KG; Niedernhall

HONG KONG
CK Infrastructure Holdings Limited; Hong Kong

INDIA
Adani Green Energy Limited; Ahmedabad
Central Electronics Limited; Sahibabad
Reliance Power Limited; Mumbai
Suzlon Energy Limited; Pune
Tata Power Co Ltd; Mumbai

IRELAND
SSE Airtricity Limited; Dublin
Trane Technologies plc; Dublin

ITALY
Enel Green Power SpA; Rome
Enel SpA; Rome
Eni SpA; Rome
Falck Renewables SpA; Sesto San Giovanni
Webuild SpA; Milan

JAPAN
Envision AESC SDI Co Ltd; Kanagawa
Hitachi Limited; Tokyo
Kyocera Corporation; Kyoto
Mitsubishi Corporation; Tokyo
Mitsubishi Electric Corporation; Tokyo
Panasonic Corporation; Osaka
Primearth EV Energy Co Ltd; Shizuoka-ken
Sharp Corporation; Sakai City, Osaka
Toshiba Corporation; Tokyo

KOREA
Hanwha Q Cells; Seoul
Hanwha Solutions Corporation; Seoul
LG Energy Solution Ltd; Seoul
Samsung Electronics Co Ltd; Suwon-si

LUXUMBOURG
Freyr Battery SA; Luxembourg

NORWAY
Equinor ASA; Stavanger

SINGAPORE
Blueleaf Energy; Singapore

SPAIN
Abengoa SA; Sevilla
Acciona SA; Madrid
Fomento de Construcciones y Contratas SA (FCC); Madrid
Fotowatio Renewable Ventures SLU; Madrid
Iberdrola SA; Bilbao
Siemens Gamesa Renewable Energy SA; Zamudio

SWEDEN
Northvolt AB; Stockholm
Vattenfall AB; Solna

SWITZERLAND
ABB Ltd; Zurich
Sulzer AG; Winterthur

TAIWAN
Motech Industries Inc; Tainan

THE NETHERLANDS
Alliander NV; Arnhem
Essent NV; Hertogenbosch
Eternalsun Spire; The Hague
Lithium Werks BV; Enschede
Shell plc; The Hague

TURKEY
Zorlu Enerji Elektrik Uretim AS; Istanbul

UNITED KINGDOM
BP plc; London
Cory Group (Cory Topco Limited); London
EDF Energy Nuclear Generation Group Limited; London
ENGIE Global Energy Management & Sales; London
Lightsource BP; London
Porvair plc; Norfolk
Renewable Energy Systems Ltd; Hertfordshire
Scottish and Southern Energy plc (SSE); Perth
Talbott's Biomass Energy Systems Ltd; Stone

Individual Profiles
On Each Of
THE RENEWABLE ENERGY 250

3M Company

NAIC Code: 339100

www.3m.com

TYPES OF BUSINESS:
Health Care Products
Specialty Materials & Textiles
Industrial Products
Safety, Security & Protection Products
Display & Graphics Products
Consumer & Office Products
Electronics & Communications Products
Fuel Cell Technology

BRANDS/DIVISIONS/AFFILIATES:
Scotch
Post-it
Nexcare
Filtrete
Command
Futuro
Littmann
Ace

GROWTH PLANS/SPECIAL FEATURES:

3M is a multinational conglomerate that has operated since 1902, when it was known as Minnesota Mining and Manufacturing. The company is well known for its research and development laboratory and leverages its science and technology across multiple product categories. As of 2020, 3M is organized into four business segments: safety and industrial, transportation and electronics, healthcare, and consumer. Nearly 50% of the company's revenue comes from outside the Americas, with the safety and industrial segment constituting a plurality of net sales. Many of the company's 60,000-plus products touch and concern a variety of consumers and end markets.

3M offers its employees medical and dental insurance, tuition reimbursement, flexible spending accounts, disability coverage, a 401(k), adoption assistance and more.

CONTACTS:
Note: Officers with more than one job title may be intentionally listed here more than once.

Michael Roman, CEO
Denise Rutherford, Sr. VP, Divisional
Monish Patolawala, CFO
Theresa Reinseth, Chief Accounting Officer
Ivan Fong, Chief Legal Officer
John Banovetz, Chief Technology Officer
Michael Vale, Executive VP, Divisional
Ashish Khandpur, Executive VP, Divisional
Mojdeh Poul, Executive VP, Divisional
Jeffrey Lavers, Executive VP, Divisional
Eric Hammes, President, Divisional
Kristen Ludgate, Senior VP, Divisional
Veena Lakkundi, Senior VP, Divisional

FINANCIAL DATA:
Note: Data for latest year may not have been available at press time.

In U.S. $	2021	2020	2019	2018	2017	2016
Revenue	35,355,000,000	32,184,000,000	32,136,000,000	32,765,000,000	31,657,000,000	30,109,000,000
R&D Expense	1,994,000,000	1,878,000,000	1,911,000,000	1,821,000,000	1,870,000,000	1,764,000,000
Operating Income	7,666,000,000	6,906,000,000	6,059,000,000	6,733,000,000	7,234,000,000	7,112,000,000
Operating Margin %	.22%	.21%	.19%	.21%	.23%	.24%
SGA Expense	6,900,000,000	6,795,000,000	7,030,000,000	7,529,000,000	6,498,000,000	6,115,000,000
Net Income	5,921,000,000	5,449,000,000	4,517,000,000	5,349,000,000	4,858,000,000	5,050,000,000
Operating Cash Flow	7,454,000,000	8,113,000,000	7,070,000,000	6,439,000,000	6,240,000,000	6,662,000,000
Capital Expenditure	1,603,000,000	1,501,000,000	1,699,000,000	1,577,000,000	1,373,000,000	1,420,000,000
EBITDA	9,607,000,000	9,235,000,000	7,684,000,000	8,838,000,000	9,414,000,000	8,726,000,000
Return on Assets %	.13%	.12%	.11%	.14%	.14%	.15%
Return on Equity %	.42%	.48%	.45%	.50%	.44%	.46%
Debt to Equity	1.11%	1.453	1.812	1.377	1.051	1.041

CONTACT INFORMATION:
Phone: 651 733-1110   Fax: 651 733-9973
Toll-Free: 800-364-3577
Address: 3M Center, St. Paul, MN 55144-1000 United States

SALARIES/BONUSES:
Top Exec. Salary: $1,337,487   Bonus: $
Second Exec. Salary: $934,096   Bonus: $

STOCK TICKER/OTHER:
Stock Ticker: MMM   Exchange: NYS
Employees: 95,000   Fiscal Year Ends: 12/31
Parent Company:

OTHER THOUGHTS:
Estimated Female Officers or Directors: 7
Hot Spot for Advancement for Women/Minorities: Y

Sales, profits and employees may be estimates. Financial information, benefits and other data can change quickly and may vary from those stated here.

Plunkett Research, Ltd.

A123 Systems LLC
NAIC Code: 335911

www.a123systems.com

TYPES OF BUSINESS:
Batteries, Design & Manufacture
Lithium Ion Solutions
Battery Systems
Thermal Management Systems
Software
Technology
Manufacturing

BRANDS/DIVISIONS/AFFILIATES:
Wanxiang Group Corporation
Ultraphosphate

GROWTH PLANS/SPECIAL FEATURES:
A123 Systems, LLC develops and manufactures advanced lithium ion solutions at the system, module and cell level. The company designs and innovates battery systems, and specializes in supporting the development and validation of advanced cell designs, software, electronics and thermal management systems that power electrified vehicles, including low-voltage hybrids, plug-ins, commercial vehicles and high-performance motorsports. A123 Systems' trademarked Ultraphosphate technology was specifically engineered to maximize power by reducing resistance across the entire range of operating temperatures, resulting with benefits for every power application. Today, the firm spends the majority of its scientific talent on programs to extract maximum driving range from the smallest and lightest package possible, primarily using the nickel manganese cobalt family of chemistries. A123 Systems' manufacturing sites are located in the U.S., China, Germany and Czech Republic. The firm operates as a subsidiary of Wanxiang Group Corporation.

CONTACTS: Note: Officers with more than one job title may be intentionally listed here more than once.

Peter W. Cirino, CEO
Robert Johnson, VP-Energy Solutions Group
Mujeeb Ijaz, VP-Cell Products Group

FINANCIAL DATA: Note: Data for latest year may not have been available at press time.

In U.S. $	2021	2020	2019	2018	2017	2016
Revenue	461,448,000	443,700,000	522,000,000	515,000,000	500,000,000	450,000,000
R&D Expense						
Operating Income						
Operating Margin %						
SGA Expense						
Net Income						
Operating Cash Flow						
Capital Expenditure						
EBITDA						
Return on Assets %						
Return on Equity %						
Debt to Equity						

CONTACT INFORMATION:
Phone: 734-772-0300 Fax:
Toll-Free:
Address: 27101 Cabaret Dr., Novi, MI 48377 United States

STOCK TICKER/OTHER:
Stock Ticker: Subsidiary Exchange:
Employees: 1,958 Fiscal Year Ends: 12/31
Parent Company: Wanxiang Group Corporation

SALARIES/BONUSES:
Top Exec. Salary: $ Bonus: $
Second Exec. Salary: $ Bonus: $

OTHER THOUGHTS:
Estimated Female Officers or Directors:
Hot Spot for Advancement for Women/Minorities:

Sales, profits and employees may be estimates. Financial information, benefits and other data can change quickly and may vary from those stated here.

ABB Ltd

NAIC Code: 335313

www.abb.com

TYPES OF BUSINESS:
Diversified Engineering Services
Power Transmission & Distribution Systems
Control & Automation Technology Products
Industrial Robotics
Energy Trading Software
Artificial Intelligence

BRANDS/DIVISIONS/AFFILIATES:

GROWTH PLANS/SPECIAL FEATURES:
ABB is a global supplier of electrical equipment and automation products. Founded in the late 19th century, the company was created out of the merger of two old industrial companies: ASEA and BBC. The company is the number-one or number-two supplier in all of its core markets and the number-two robotic arm supplier globally. In automation, it offers a full suite of products for discrete and process automation (continuous processes like chemical production) as well as industrial robotics.

CONTACTS: Note: Officers with more than one job title may be intentionally listed here more than once.
Bjorn Rosengren, CEO
Timo Ihamuotila, CFO
Sylvia Hill, Chief Human Resources Officer
Diane de Saint Victor, General Counsel
Brice Koch, Head-Power Systems Div.
Bernhard Jucker, Head-Power Prod. Div.
Veli-Matti Reinikkala, Head-Process Automation Div.
Tarak Mehta, Head-Low Voltage Prod. Div.
Peter Voser, Chmn.
Frank Duggan, Head-Global Markets

FINANCIAL DATA: Note: Data for latest year may not have been available at press time.

In U.S. $	2021	2020	2019	2018	2017	2016
Revenue	28,945,000,000	26,134,000,000	27,978,000,000	27,662,000,000	25,196,000,000	24,929,000,000
R&D Expense	1,219,000,000	1,127,000,000	1,198,000,000	1,147,000,000	1,013,000,000	967,000,000
Operating Income	3,348,000,000	2,007,000,000	2,261,000,000	2,102,000,000	2,068,000,000	2,034,000,000
Operating Margin %	.12%	.08%	.08%	.08%	.08%	.08%
SGA Expense	5,162,000,000	4,895,000,000	5,447,000,000	5,295,000,000	4,765,000,000	4,532,000,000
Net Income	4,546,000,000	5,146,000,000	1,439,000,000	2,173,000,000	2,213,000,000	1,899,000,000
Operating Cash Flow	3,330,000,000	1,693,000,000	2,325,000,000	2,924,000,000	3,799,000,000	3,843,000,000
Capital Expenditure	820,000,000	694,000,000	762,000,000	772,000,000	752,000,000	632,000,000
EBITDA	6,828,000,000	1,996,000,000	3,038,000,000	3,297,000,000	3,172,000,000	2,832,000,000
Return on Assets %	.11%	.12%	.03%	.05%	.05%	.05%
Return on Equity %	.29%	.35%	.10%	.15%	.16%	.14%
Debt to Equity	.31%	0.354	0.554	0.472	0.451	0.433

CONTACT INFORMATION:
Phone: 41-43-317-7111 Fax: 41-43-317-4420
Toll-Free:
Address: Affolternstrasse 44, Zurich, CH-8050 Switzerland

STOCK TICKER/OTHER:
Stock Ticker: ABB
Employees: 105,000
Parent Company:

Exchange: NYS
Fiscal Year Ends: 12/31

SALARIES/BONUSES:
Top Exec. Salary: $1,526,040 Bonus: $991,919
Second Exec. Salary: $915,648 Bonus: $708,705

OTHER THOUGHTS:
Estimated Female Officers or Directors: 2
Hot Spot for Advancement for Women/Minorities: Y

Sales, profits and employees may be estimates. Financial information, benefits and other data can change quickly and may vary from those stated here.

Abengoa SA

NAIC Code: 237130

www.abengoa.com/web

TYPES OF BUSINESS:
Specialty Engineering and Construction
Ethanol Production
Recycling & Waste Management Services
Bioenergy
IT Services
Construction-Plants & Infrastructure
Solar Energy Generation

BRANDS/DIVISIONS/AFFILIATES:

CONTACTS: Note: Officers with more than one job title may be intentionally listed here more than once.
Joaquin Fernandez De Pierola Marin, CEO
Alfonso Gonzalez Dominguez, Exec. VP-Eng. & Industrial Construction
Luis Fernandez Mateo, Dir.-Organization, Quality & Budgets
M.A. Jimenez-Velasco Mazario, General Sec.
Izaskun Artucha Corta, Dir.-Strategy & Corp. Dev.
Barbara Zubiria Furest, Dir.-Investor Rel.
Vicente Jorro de Inza, Dir.-Finance
Javier Garoz Neira, Exec. VP-Biofuels
Javier Molina Montes, Exec. VP-Industrial Recycling
Santiago Seage Medela, Exec. VP-Solar
Juan Carlos Jimenez Lora, Dir.-Planning & Control
Gonzalo Fernandez De Araoz, Chmn.
Alfonso Gonzalez Dominguez, Pres., Latin America Bus. Group

GROWTH PLANS/SPECIAL FEATURES:
Abengoa SA is a Spanish technology company that offers solutions for sustainability in the transmission, infrastructure, energy and water sectors. For transmission and infrastructure sectors, the firm provides engineering and construction services and solutions in relation to: energy transmission, energy distribution, rail electrification, singular installations and all types of industrial plants. This division is also engaged in the manufacture of steel structures, electrical ancillary and electronic equipment. Within the energy sector, Abengoa creates facilities that convert energy from renewable sources into electricity, as well as from conventional energy sources. This division comprises open cycle and combined cycle technologies, cogeneration, wind farms, solar thermal, photovoltaic and biomass plants. Within the water sector, the company recycles and recovers industrial and urban waste, preventing the need for extracting natural resources. It specializes in water management and treatment; and designs, constructs and operates facilities for treating water, making it potable or for water desalination. This division also provides related water services and solutions for other water infrastructures worldwide. Abengoa provides operation services and implementation of predictive, preventive and corrective maintenance of renewable, conventional and water treatment plants.

FINANCIAL DATA: Note: Data for latest year may not have been available at press time.

In U.S. $	2021	2020	2019	2018	2017	2016
Revenue	1,438,078,108	1,382,767,412	1,686,333,824	1,471,225,472	1,599,541,760	1,782,383,360
R&D Expense						
Operating Income						
Operating Margin %						
SGA Expense						
Net Income		-143,069,840	-620,135,040	-1,691,600,000	4,624,016,384	-9,004,917,760
Operating Cash Flow						
Capital Expenditure						
EBITDA						
Return on Assets %						
Return on Equity %						
Debt to Equity						

CONTACT INFORMATION:
Phone: 34 954937000 Fax:
Toll-Free:
Address: 1 Energia Solar St., Sevilla, 41014 Spain

STOCK TICKER/OTHER:
Stock Ticker: ABG.A Exchange: Madrid
Employees: 13,502 Fiscal Year Ends: 03/31
Parent Company:

SALARIES/BONUSES:
Top Exec. Salary: $ Bonus: $
Second Exec. Salary: $ Bonus: $

OTHER THOUGHTS:
Estimated Female Officers or Directors: 4
Hot Spot for Advancement for Women/Minorities: Y

Acciona SA

NAIC Code: 237310

www.acciona.es

TYPES OF BUSINESS:
Heavy Construction
Energy Solutions
Infrastructure Transport Solutions
Water Solutions
Social Solutions
Efficient Cities
Sustainable Real Estate
Asset Management

BRANDS/DIVISIONS/AFFILIATES:
Bestinver Gestion
Bestinver Securities

GROWTH PLANS/SPECIAL FEATURES:
Acciona SA is an engineering and construction firm providing sustainable solutions for infrastructure and renewable energy projects across the world. It works in various phases, from design and construction to operations and maintenance. The company operates two business divisions energy and infrastructure. The infrastructure division encompasses construction, water treatment, industrial, and service business lines. Projects may be granted under concessions from governments or acquired independently when Acciona identifies an opportunity. Energy developments focus on renewable technologies and primarily revolve around wind, solar, hydro, and biomass. The company has a presence on five continents and utilizes an organizational structure to ensure availability.

CONTACTS:
Note: Officers with more than one job title may be intentionally listed here more than once.

Jose Manuel Entrecanales, CEO
Jorge Vega-Penichet, General Counsel
Juan Muro-Lara, Chief Corp. Dev. Officer
Joaquin Mollinedo, Chief Institutional Rel. Officer
Juan Muro-Lara, Chief Investor Rel. Officer
Alfonso Callejo, Chief Corp. Resources Officer
Pedro Martinez, Pres., Acciona Infrastructure
Luis Castilla, Pres., Acciona Agua
Rafael Mateo, CEO-Acciona Energy
Carmen Becerril, Chief Int'l Officer

FINANCIAL DATA:
Note: Data for latest year may not have been available at press time.

In U.S. $	2021	2020	2019	2018	2017	2016
Revenue	7,936,292,000	6,347,594,000	7,041,520,000	7,353,849,000	7,103,591,000	5,853,500,000
R&D Expense						
Operating Income	654,304,400	357,713,200	678,417,900	593,121,600	597,823,000	403,834,800
Operating Margin %	.08%	.06%	.10%	.08%	.08%	.07%
SGA Expense	3,450,896,000	2,462,655,000	2,707,304,000	2,860,731,000	2,869,941,000	2,205,577,000
Net Income	325,164,300	379,028,000	344,387,300	321,229,600	215,567,400	344,684,000
Operating Cash Flow	561,103,400	947,465,200	770,971,500	622,474,200	480,906,200	805,940,200
Capital Expenditure	928,719,000	886,961,000	1,289,065,000	631,337,500	752,830,500	773,853,500
EBITDA	1,493,289,000	1,302,356,000	1,409,407,000	1,459,858,000	1,328,317,000	1,990,387,000
Return on Assets %	.02%	.02%	.02%	.02%	.01%	.02%
Return on Equity %	.09%	.11%	.10%	.09%	.06%	.10%
Debt to Equity	1.13	1.581	1.649	1.245	1.406	1.467

CONTACT INFORMATION:
Phone: 34 916632850   Fax: 34 916632851
Toll-Free:
Address: Ave. De Europa, 18, Parque Empresarial La Moreleja, Madrid, 28108 Spain

STOCK TICKER/OTHER:
Stock Ticker: ACXIF
Employees: 39,699
Parent Company:

Exchange: PINX
Fiscal Year Ends: 12/31

SALARIES/BONUSES:
Top Exec. Salary: $ Bonus: $
Second Exec. Salary: $ Bonus: $

OTHER THOUGHTS:
Estimated Female Officers or Directors: 2
Hot Spot for Advancement for Women/Minorities:

Sales, profits and employees may be estimates. Financial information, benefits and other data can change quickly and may vary from those stated here.

Plunkett Research, Ltd.   125

Active Power Inc

NAIC Code: 335911

www.activepower.com

TYPES OF BUSINESS:
Manufacturing-Power Supplies
Battery-Free Backup Power Systems
Flywheel Energy Systems
Product Design and Manufacture
Product Sales and Marketing
Power Technology
Flywheel Technology

BRANDS/DIVISIONS/AFFILIATES:
Langley Holdings PLC
Piller Group GmbH
Piller Power Systems Inc
CleanSource
PowerHouse

CONTACTS: *Note: Officers with more than one job title may be intentionally listed here more than once.*
Jack Pearce, CEO
James Powers, CFO
Daryl Dulaney, Director
Lee Higgins, Other Corporate Officer

GROWTH PLANS/SPECIAL FEATURES:
Active Power, Inc., a division of Piller Power Systems, Inc., designs, manufactures and markets battery-free uninterrupted power solutions (UPS) that provide backup electric power in the event of voltage fluctuations or power disturbances. Piller Power Systems, Inc. is the U.S. subsidiary of Piller Group GmbH, itself a subsidiary of U.K.-based engineering and industrial group Langley Holdings PLC. The firm is headquartered in Texas, USA, with international offices in Australia, Austria, Canada, China, France, Germany, Iberica, India, Italy, Latin America, Netherlands, Singapore, South Korea, Taiwan and the U.K. Active Power has more than 100 issued patents, including one covering its flywheel technology. The company focuses on improving system reliability and energy and space efficiency while lowering the cost of electric power for broad industry users, including broadcasting, data center, health care, leisure, industrial, manufacturing and transportation sectors. Active Power markets its flywheels under the CleanSource name. The CleanSource flywheel generator provides a highly reliable, low-cost and non-toxic replacement for lead-acid batteries. It stores kinetic energy in its constantly spinning flywheel. The flywheel apparatus converts its rotary motion into electricity and powers the critical load during utility disturbances or until a standby generator takes over. CleanSource Plus offers 20% more power for the same footprint and is available in single- and multi-module configurations. Active Power's PowerHouse product is a factory-built enclosed uninterruptible power supply system designed for all types of environments, deployable almost anywhere in the world.

FINANCIAL DATA: *Note: Data for latest year may not have been available at press time.*

In U.S. $	2021	2020	2019	2018	2017	2016
Revenue	70,000,000	65,000,000	72,000,000	70,000,000	65,000,000	60,000,000
R&D Expense						
Operating Income						
Operating Margin %						
SGA Expense						
Net Income						
Operating Cash Flow						
Capital Expenditure						
EBITDA						
Return on Assets %						
Return on Equity %						
Debt to Equity						

CONTACT INFORMATION:
Phone: 512 836-6464   Fax: 512 836-4511
Toll-Free:
Address: 2128 W. Braker Ln., Austin, TX 78758 United States

STOCK TICKER/OTHER:
Stock Ticker: Subsidiary   Exchange:
Employees: 1,000   Fiscal Year Ends: 12/31
Parent Company: Langley Holdings plc

SALARIES/BONUSES:
Top Exec. Salary: $ Bonus: $
Second Exec. Salary: $ Bonus: $

OTHER THOUGHTS:
Estimated Female Officers or Directors:
Hot Spot for Advancement for Women/Minorities: Y

Sales, profits and employees may be estimates. Financial information, benefits and other data can change quickly and may vary from those stated here.

Adani Green Energy Limited

NAIC Code: 221114

www.adanigreenenergy.com

TYPES OF BUSINESS:
Solar Electric Power Generation
Renewable Energy
Project Management
Utility Projects
Solar Power
Wind Power
Hybrid Power
Solar Parks

BRANDS/DIVISIONS/AFFILIATES:
SB Energy Holdings Ltd
SB Energy India
Adani Hybrid Energy Jaisalmer One Ltd

GROWTH PLANS/SPECIAL FEATURES:
Adani Green Energy Limited is a leading renewable company in India, with a current project portfolio of 20,434 megawatts (MW), as of late-2022. Adani Green develops, builds, owns, operates and maintains utility-scale grid-connected solar and wind farm projects. The electricity generated is supplied to central and state government entities and government-backed corporations. The firm is present across 11 Indian states, with a portfolio of 54 operational projects and 12 projects under construction. Adani Green's projects include solar power, wind power, hybrid power and solar parks. During 2022, Adani Green announced that its subsidiary Adani Hybrid Energy Jaisalmer One Limited commissioned a 390 MW wind-solar hybrid power plant in Rajasthan, claiming to be the first wind and solar hybrid power generation plant in India.

CONTACTS: Note: Officers with more than one job title may be intentionally listed here more than once.

Vneet S. Jaain, Managing Dir.
Gautam Adani, Chmn.

FINANCIAL DATA: Note: Data for latest year may not have been available at press time.

In U.S. $	2021	2020	2019	2018	2017	2016
Revenue	425,779,332	349,428,000	306,301,000			
R&D Expense						
Operating Income						
Operating Margin %						
SGA Expense						
Net Income	24,941,619	70,311,000	113,839,000			
Operating Cash Flow						
Capital Expenditure						
EBITDA						
Return on Assets %						
Return on Equity %						
Debt to Equity						

CONTACT INFORMATION:
Phone: 91 79-2555-5555   Fax: 91 79-2555-6490
Toll-Free:
Address: Adani House, Shantigram near Vaishnodevi Cir., S G Hwy, Ahmedabad, Gujarat 382421 India

STOCK TICKER/OTHER:
Stock Ticker: 541450
Employees: 1,569
Parent Company: Adani Group

Exchange: Bombay
Fiscal Year Ends: 03/31

SALARIES/BONUSES:
Top Exec. Salary: $ Bonus: $
Second Exec. Salary: $ Bonus: $

OTHER THOUGHTS:
Estimated Female Officers or Directors:
Hot Spot for Advancement for Women/Minorities:

Sales, profits and employees may be estimates. Financial information, benefits and other data can change quickly and may vary from those stated here.

Aecon Group Inc

NAIC Code: 237310

www.aecon.com

TYPES OF BUSINESS:
Highway, Street, Tunnel & Bridge Construction (Infrastructure)
Infrastructure Development
Civil Infrastructure
Urban Transportation
Nuclear Power Infrastructure
Conventional Industrial Infrastructure
Private Finance Solutions
Operations Management

BRANDS/DIVISIONS/AFFILIATES:
Groupe Aecon Quebec Ltee

GROWTH PLANS/SPECIAL FEATURES:
Aecon Group Inc is a Canada-based company that operates in two segments: Construction and Concessions. The Construction segment includes various aspects of the construction of public and private infrastructure projects, mainly in the transportation sector. Its concessions segment is engaged in the development, financing, construction, and operation of infrastructure projects. Aecon generates the majority of its revenue from the Construction segment.

Aecon Group offers medical and dental insurance, an employee stock purchase program, a pension plan and tuition reimbursement.

CONTACTS:
Note: Officers with more than one job title may be intentionally listed here more than once.

Jean-Louis Servranckx, CEO
David Smales, CFO
John Beck, Chairman of the Board
Yonni Fushman, Chief Legal Officer
Mark Scherer, Executive VP, Divisional
Steven Nackan, Executive VP
Michael Derksen, Other Corporate Officer
Marty Harris, Other Corporate Officer
Thomas Clochard, Other Corporate Officer
Manuel Rivaya, Senior VP, Divisional
Eric MacDonald, Senior VP, Divisional
Gordana Terkalas, Senior VP, Divisional

FINANCIAL DATA:
Note: Data for latest year may not have been available at press time.

In U.S. $	2021	2020	2019	2018	2017	2016
Revenue	2,884,772,000	2,642,735,000	2,509,859,000	2,369,058,000	2,035,009,000	2,330,502,000
R&D Expense						
Operating Income	69,751,140	92,221,100	65,308,650	54,228,160	28,241,210	45,940,830
Operating Margin %	.02%	.03%	.03%	.02%	.01%	.02%
SGA Expense	132,209,300	132,308,700	133,045,600	129,482,900	135,297,000	134,229,300
Net Income	36,034,610	63,848,610	52,840,660	42,803,160	20,436,200	33,913,090
Operating Cash Flow	-22,781,830	197,977,900	142,122,800	267,404,800	143,187,600	19,500,550
Capital Expenditure	30,184,300	101,019,000	148,918,200	155,630,200	123,133,600	29,004,230
EBITDA	150,708,300	175,954,000	147,569,100	141,079,100	107,401,700	109,842,400
Return on Assets %	.02%	.03%	.02%	.02%	.01%	.02%
Return on Equity %	.06%	.10%	.09%	.07%	.04%	.06%
Debt to Equity	.76%	0.768	0.788	0.743	0.587	0.34

CONTACT INFORMATION:
Phone: 416 293-7004 Fax: 416 293-0271
Toll-Free: 877-232-2677
Address: 20 Carlson Court, Ste. 800, Toronto, ON M9W 7K6 Canada

STOCK TICKER/OTHER:
Stock Ticker: ARE Exchange: TSE
Employees: 5,900 Fiscal Year Ends: 12/31
Parent Company:

SALARIES/BONUSES:
Top Exec. Salary: $ Bonus: $
Second Exec. Salary: $ Bonus: $

OTHER THOUGHTS:
Estimated Female Officers or Directors: 2
Hot Spot for Advancement for Women/Minorities:

Sales, profits and employees may be estimates. Financial information, benefits and other data can change quickly and may vary from those stated here.

AES Corporation (The)

NAIC Code: 221112

www.aes.com

TYPES OF BUSINESS:
Utilities-Electricity
Wind Generation
Contract Power Generation

GROWTH PLANS/SPECIAL FEATURES:
AES is a global power company operating across 14 countries and 4 continents. Its current generation portfolio consists of over 31 gigawatts of generation, with the generation mix composed of renewables (43%), gas (32%), coal (23%), and oil (2%). The company has 3.5 gigawatts of generation under construction. AES has majority ownership and operates six electric utilities distributing power to 2.6 million customers.

BRANDS/DIVISIONS/AFFILIATES:
AES Tiete SA

CONTACTS: Note: Officers with more than one job title may be intentionally listed here more than once.
Andres Gluski, CEO
Gustavo Pimenta, CFO
John Morse, Chairman of the Board
Sherry Kohan, Chief Accounting Officer
Bernerd Santos, COO
Paul Freedman, Executive VP
Letitia Mendoza, Executive VP
Lisa Krueger, Executive VP
Stephen Coughlin, Vice President, Divisional

FINANCIAL DATA: Note: Data for latest year may not have been available at press time.

In U.S. $	2021	2020	2019	2018	2017	2016
Revenue	11,141,000,000	9,660,000,000	10,189,000,000	10,736,000,000	10,530,000,000	10,281,000,000
R&D Expense						
Operating Income	2,556,000,000	2,528,000,000	2,153,000,000	2,374,000,000	2,250,000,000	2,137,000,000
Operating Margin %	.23%	.26%	.21%	.22%	.21%	.21%
SGA Expense	155,000,000	165,000,000	196,000,000	192,000,000	215,000,000	194,000,000
Net Income	-409,000,000	46,000,000	303,000,000	1,203,000,000	-1,161,000,000	-1,130,000,000
Operating Cash Flow	1,902,000,000	2,755,000,000	2,466,000,000	2,343,000,000	2,504,000,000	2,897,000,000
Capital Expenditure	2,116,000,000	1,900,000,000	2,405,000,000	2,121,000,000	2,177,000,000	2,345,000,000
EBITDA	903,000,000	2,594,000,000	3,096,000,000	4,077,000,000	3,110,000,000	2,497,000,000
Return on Assets %	-.01%	.00%	.01%	.04%	-.03%	-.03%
Return on Equity %	-.18%	.02%	.10%	.42%	-.44%	-.38%
Debt to Equity	8.78%	7.005	6.11	5.498	7.222	6.586

CONTACT INFORMATION:
Phone: 703 522-1315 Fax:
Toll-Free:
Address: 4300 Wilson Blvd., Arlington, VA 22203 United States

STOCK TICKER/OTHER:
Stock Ticker: AES
Employees: 8,450
Parent Company:

Exchange: NYS
Fiscal Year Ends: 12/31

SALARIES/BONUSES:
Top Exec. Salary: $1,241,000 Bonus: $
Second Exec. Salary: $570,000 Bonus: $

OTHER THOUGHTS:
Estimated Female Officers or Directors: 2
Hot Spot for Advancement for Women/Minorities: Y

Sales, profits and employees may be estimates. Financial information, benefits and other data can change quickly and may vary from those stated here.

AG Processing Inc

NAIC Code: 311200

www.agp.com

TYPES OF BUSINESS:
Grain Transportation & Marketing
Soybean Operations
Biodiesel Operations
Animal Feed
Production Facilities
Soybean Oil
Product Export and Merchandising
Grains and Processed Commodities

BRANDS/DIVISIONS/AFFILIATES:
AminoPlus

CONTACTS: *Note: Officers with more than one job title may be intentionally listed here more than once.*
Chris Schaffer, CEO
Lou Rickers, COO
Kyle Droescher, CFO
Mark Sandeen, CMO
Matt Bendler, VP-Human Resources
Greg Cassalia, VP-IT
Mark Craigmile, Sr. VP-Oper.
Michael L. Maranell, Sr. VP-Corp. & Member Rel.
Robert Flack, VP-Animal Nutrition
John Campbell, Sr. VP-Gov't Rel. & Renewable Fuels
Lowell Wilson, Chmn.

GROWTH PLANS/SPECIAL FEATURES:
AG Processing, Inc. (AGP) is a U.S. agribusiness engaged in soybean and biodiesel operations, with owners including local and regional cooperatives representing approximately 200,000 farmers throughout the country. AGP operates 10 soybean processing plants in Iowa, Minnesota, Missouri, Nebraska and South Dakota; and four soybean oil refineries; and three biodiesel production facilities. Soybeans are process into two primary products: soybean meal, which is used as animal feed, and crude soybean oil, which is further processed for the food sector and industrial uses, including biofuels. The company's refined vegetable oils serve a variety of sectors, including food service, food manufacturing, packaged products, consumer retail, renewable fuels production and industrial uses. AGP's biodiesel production plants have a combined annual capacity of 175 million gallons. In addition to these commodity-based products, AGP produces and markets AminoPlus, a high-performance soy bypass protein product for the dairy industry. AG's products group is comprised of AGP's export, centralized rail and grain merchandising businesses, and works closely with its soy processing division. Exports include a complete line of grains and processed commodities including soybean meal, soybean hulls, AminoPlus, distillers dried grains, wheat, corn and soybeans. Grains are merchandised on a regional, national and global basis.

AGP offers its employees life, medical, dental and long-term disability insurance; tuition reimbursement; and a 401(k) and retirement plan.

FINANCIAL DATA: *Note: Data for latest year may not have been available at press time.*

In U.S. $	2021	2020	2019	2018	2017	2016
Revenue	4,148,301,305	4,066,962,064	3,987,217,710	3,797,350,200	3,616,524,000	3,410,986,000
R&D Expense						
Operating Income						
Operating Margin %						
SGA Expense						
Net Income						
Operating Cash Flow						
Capital Expenditure						
EBITDA						
Return on Assets %						
Return on Equity %						
Debt to Equity						

CONTACT INFORMATION:
Phone: 402-496-7809 Fax: 402-498-2215
Toll-Free: 800-247-1345
Address: 12700 W. Dodge Rd., Omaha, NE 68154 United States

SALARIES/BONUSES:
Top Exec. Salary: $ Bonus: $
Second Exec. Salary: $ Bonus: $

STOCK TICKER/OTHER:
Stock Ticker: Private   Exchange:
Employees: 1,100   Fiscal Year Ends: 08/31
Parent Company:

OTHER THOUGHTS:
Estimated Female Officers or Directors:
Hot Spot for Advancement for Women/Minorities:

Sales, profits and employees may be estimates. Financial information, benefits and other data can change quickly and may vary from those stated here.

AGL Energy Limited

NAIC Code: 221115

www.agl.com.au

TYPES OF BUSINESS:
Wind Electric Power Generation
Energy Production
Gas Services
Electricity Services
Telecommunications Services
Renewable Sources and Systems
Solar Solutions
Smart Home Solutions

BRANDS/DIVISIONS/AFFILIATES:
Accel Energy Limited
AGL Australia Limited

GROWTH PLANS/SPECIAL FEATURES:
AGL Energy is one of Australia's largest retailers of electricity and gas. It services 3.7 million retail electricity and gas accounts in the eastern and southern Australian states, or about one third of the market. Profit is dominated by energy generation, underpinned by its low-cost coal-fired generation fleet. Founded in 1837, it is the oldest company on the ASX. Generation capacity comprises a portfolio of peaking, intermediate, and base-load electricity generation plants, with a combined capacity of 10,500 megawatts.

CONTACTS:
Note: Officers with more than one job title may be intentionally listed here more than once.

Graeme Hunt, CEO
Markus Brokhof, COO
Damien Nicks, CFO
Joanne Fox, Exec. Gen. Mngr.-People & Culture
John Chambers, Exec. Gen. Mngr.-Technology & Future Bus.

FINANCIAL DATA:
Note: Data for latest year may not have been available at press time.

In U.S. $	2021	2020	2019	2018	2017	2016
Revenue	6,858,225,000	7,672,402,000	8,379,351,000	8,229,100,000	7,935,662,000	
R&D Expense						
Operating Income	382,689,100	692,179,300	922,049,600	1,039,553,000	846,924,400	
Operating Margin %	.06%	.09%	.11%	.13%	.11%	
SGA Expense	607,422,700	603,570,000	579,170,400	602,285,900	523,950,200	
Net Income	-1,321,433,000	651,727,200	581,096,700	1,019,006,000	346,089,600	
Operating Cash Flow						
Capital Expenditure	446,256,600	486,708,600	587,517,600	462,309,000	319,763,700	
EBITDA	-1,108,899,000	1,511,494,000	1,346,475,000	1,946,834,000	953,512,300	
Return on Assets %	-.14%	.07%	.06%	.11%	.04%	
Return on Equity %	-.30%	.12%	.11%	.20%	.07%	
Debt to Equity	.52%	0.38	0.326	0.336	0.419	

CONTACT INFORMATION:
Phone: 61 299212999 Fax: 61 299212552
Toll-Free:
Address: Level 22, 101 Miller St., North Sydney, NSW C3 - 2060 Australia

STOCK TICKER/OTHER:
Stock Ticker: AGLNF
Employees: 4,186
Parent Company:

Exchange: PINX
Fiscal Year Ends: 12/31

SALARIES/BONUSES:
Top Exec. Salary: $ Bonus: $
Second Exec. Salary: $ Bonus: $

OTHER THOUGHTS:
Estimated Female Officers or Directors:
Hot Spot for Advancement for Women/Minorities:

Sales, profits and employees may be estimates. Financial information, benefits and other data can change quickly and may vary from those stated here.

Air Liquide US LLC

NAIC Code: 325120

www.airliquide.com/united-states-america

TYPES OF BUSINESS:
Industrial Gas Manufacturing
Liquefied Atmospheric Gases
Oil and Gas
Chemicals
Metals
Hydrogen Energy
Gas Supply
Welding

BRANDS/DIVISIONS/AFFILIATES:
Air Liquide USA
Airgas
Air Liquide Electronics US
Air Liquide Global E&C Solutions US Inc
Air Liquide Advanced Technologies US LLC
SEPPIC Inc
Alizent
Innovation Campus Delaware

GROWTH PLANS/SPECIAL FEATURES:
Air Liquide US LLC is a subsidiary of the French company Air Liquide SA and was one of the first companies to develop a viable process to liquefy atmospheric gases for industrial applications. Air Liquide US is comprised of two main entities: Air Liquide USA, which manages the oil/gas, chemicals, metals, electronics and hydrogen energy activities; and Airgas, which supplies gases, welding equipment and supplies, as well as related safety products. Airgas serves multiple industries across the healthcare and industrial merchant sectors. Subsidiaries of Air Liquide US include Air Liquide Electronics US (electronics), Air Liquide Global E&C Solutions US Inc. (engineering and construction), Air Liquide Advanced Technologies US LLC (technologies), SEPPIC Inc. (healthcare), Alizent (digital and information technology), and Innovation Campus Delaware (innovation/research and development).

CONTACTS:
Note: Officers with more than one job title may be intentionally listed here more than once.

John Buckley, CEO-Air Liquide USA LLC
Benoit Potier, Chmn.

FINANCIAL DATA:
Note: Data for latest year may not have been available at press time.

In U.S. $	2021	2020	2019	2018	2017	2016
Revenue	17,338,776,000	16,671,900,000	17,850,000,000	17,000,000,000	16,625,000,000	17,500,000,000
R&D Expense						
Operating Income						
Operating Margin %						
SGA Expense						
Net Income						
Operating Cash Flow						
Capital Expenditure						
EBITDA						
Return on Assets %						
Return on Equity %						
Debt to Equity						

CONTACT INFORMATION:
Phone: 713-624-8000   Fax: 713-624-8085
Toll-Free: 877-855-9533
Address: 9811 Katy Freeway, Ste. 100, Houston, TX 77024 United States

STOCK TICKER/OTHER:
Stock Ticker: Subsidiary   Exchange:
Employees: 20,000   Fiscal Year Ends: 12/31
Parent Company: Air Liquide SA

SALARIES/BONUSES:
Top Exec. Salary: $ Bonus: $
Second Exec. Salary: $ Bonus: $

OTHER THOUGHTS:
Estimated Female Officers or Directors:
Hot Spot for Advancement for Women/Minorities:

Sales, profits and employees may be estimates. Financial information, benefits and other data can change quickly and may vary from those stated here.

Air Products and Chemicals Inc

NAIC Code: 325120

www.airproducts.com

TYPES OF BUSINESS:
Industrial Gases & Chemicals
Respiratory Therapy & Home Medical Equipment
Specialty Resins
Hydrogen Refinery
Natural Gas Liquefaction
Semiconductor Materials
Gasification Technology

GROWTH PLANS/SPECIAL FEATURES:
Since its founding in 1940, Air Products has become one of the leading industrial gas suppliers globally, with operations in 50 countries and 19,000 employees. The company is the largest supplier of hydrogen and helium in the world. It has a unique portfolio serving customers in a number of industries, including chemicals, energy, healthcare, metals, and electronics. Air Products generated $10.3 billion in revenue in fiscal 2021.

BRANDS/DIVISIONS/AFFILIATES:

CONTACTS:
Note: Officers with more than one job title may be intentionally listed here more than once.

Seifollah Ghasemi, CEO
Melissa Schaeffer, CFO
Russell Flugel, Chief Accounting Officer
Samir Serhan, COO
Sean Major, Executive VP

FINANCIAL DATA:
Note: Data for latest year may not have been available at press time.

In U.S. $	2021	2020	2019	2018	2017	2016
Revenue	10,323,000,000	8,856,300,000	8,918,900,000	8,930,200,000	8,187,600,000	7,503,700,000
R&D Expense	93,500,000	83,900,000	72,900,000	64,500,000	57,600,000	71,800,000
Operating Income	2,267,800,000	2,237,600,000	2,169,800,000	1,965,600,000	1,786,000,000	1,612,500,000
Operating Margin %	.22%	.25%	.24%	.22%	.22%	.21%
SGA Expense	828,400,000	742,100,000	750,000,000	760,800,000	713,500,000	683,800,000
Net Income	2,099,100,000	1,886,700,000	1,760,000,000	1,497,800,000	3,000,400,000	631,100,000
Operating Cash Flow	3,341,900,000	3,264,700,000	2,969,900,000	2,534,400,000	1,562,200,000	2,660,700,000
Capital Expenditure	2,464,200,000	2,509,000,000	1,989,700,000	1,568,400,000	1,039,700,000	907,700,000
EBITDA	3,970,500,000	3,718,100,000	3,509,300,000	3,116,200,000	2,402,500,000	2,524,400,000
Return on Assets %	.08%	.09%	.09%	.08%	.16%	.04%
Return on Equity %	.16%	.16%	.16%	.14%	.35%	.09%
Debt to Equity	.57%	0.643	0.292	0.309	0.337	0.552

CONTACT INFORMATION:
Phone: 610 481-4911   Fax: 610 481-5900
Toll-Free:
Address: 7201 Hamilton Blvd., Allentown, PA 18195 United States

STOCK TICKER/OTHER:
Stock Ticker: APD
Employees: 19,275
Parent Company:

Exchange: NYS
Fiscal Year Ends: 09/30

SALARIES/BONUSES:
Top Exec. Salary: $1,401,923   Bonus: $
Second Exec. Salary: $713,462   Bonus: $

OTHER THOUGHTS:
Estimated Female Officers or Directors: 4
Hot Spot for Advancement for Women/Minorities: Y

Sales, profits and employees may be estimates. Financial information, benefits and other data can change quickly and may vary from those stated here.

Alliander NV

NAIC Code: 221122

www.alliander.com

TYPES OF BUSINESS:
Electric & Gas Utility
Sustainable Energy Development
Sustainable Energy Management
Solar Energy
Wind Energy
Electric Vehicle Charging Systems
Energy Distribution and Metering
Sustainable Technologies

BRANDS/DIVISIONS/AFFILIATES:
Liander
Kenter
Stam Heerhugowaard Holding
Alliander Telecom
CDMA Utilities

GROWTH PLANS/SPECIAL FEATURES:
Alliander NV is made up of a group of companies engaged in the development and management of sustainable energy throughout the Netherlands. Types of energy include solar, wind and green gas, as well as vehicle charging systems. Grid Manager Liander is responsible for distributing energy across all Alliander grids. Qirion develops sustainable technologies and intelligent energy infrastructures. Kenter is a metering business that offers innovative solutions for energy metering and energy management. Other technical activities pursued by Alliander are organized in Stam Heerhugowaard Holding, Alliander Telecom and CDMA Utilities. All shares in Alliander NV are directly or indirectly held by Dutch provincial authorities and municipalities.

CONTACTS:
Note: Officers with more than one job title may be intentionally listed here more than once.

Maarten Otto, CEO
Walter Bien, CFO
J. Reezigt, Dir.-General Affairs

FINANCIAL DATA:
Note: Data for latest year may not have been available at press time.

In U.S. $	2021	2020	2019	2018	2017	2016
Revenue	2,120,000,000	2,462,630,000	2,305,884,000	2,196,080,000	2,204,070,000	1,831,080,000
R&D Expense						
Operating Income						
Operating Margin %						
SGA Expense						
Net Income	354,000,000	275,127,000	401,127,300	382,026,000	243,166,000	299,690,000
Operating Cash Flow						
Capital Expenditure						
EBITDA						
Return on Assets %						
Return on Equity %						
Debt to Equity						

CONTACT INFORMATION:
Phone: 31-26-844-2266 Fax:
Toll-Free:
Address: Utrechtseweg 68, Arnhem, 6812 AH Netherlands

STOCK TICKER/OTHER:
Stock Ticker: Private Exchange:
Employees: 5,991 Fiscal Year Ends: 12/31
Parent Company:

SALARIES/BONUSES:
Top Exec. Salary: $ Bonus: $
Second Exec. Salary: $ Bonus: $

OTHER THOUGHTS:
Estimated Female Officers or Directors: 3
Hot Spot for Advancement for Women/Minorities: Y

Sales, profits and employees may be estimates. Financial information, benefits and other data can change quickly and may vary from those stated here.

Alstom SA

NAIC Code: 333611

www.alstom.com

TYPES OF BUSINESS:
Equipment-Electric Power Distribution
High-Speed Trains
Monorails
Trams
Integrated Systems
Signaling Products and Solutions
Digital Mobility Solutions
Manufacture

BRANDS/DIVISIONS/AFFILIATES:
Shunter
Bombardier Transportation
Helion Hydrogen Power
Flertex

GROWTH PLANS/SPECIAL FEATURES:
Alstom develops and markets systems, equipment and services for the railway transport sector including rolling stock, maintenance and modernization services, signaling and infrastructure, which are offered separately, bundled, or as fully integrated solutions. The company is one of the key international players in the industry with a strong position in European markets.

CONTACTS:
Note: Officers with more than one job title may be intentionally listed here more than once.

Henri Poupart-Lafarge, CEO
Danny Di Perna, Exec. VP-Operations
Laurent Martinez, CFO
Thierry Best, CCO
Anne-Sophie Chauveau-Galas, Chief Human Resources Officer
Alexandre Domingues, Chief Digital Transformation Officer
Keith Carr, Group General Counsel
Jerome Pecresse, Exec. VP
Philippe Cochet, Exec. VP
Gregoire Poux-Guillaume, Exec. VP
Henri Poupart-Lafarge, Chmn.

FINANCIAL DATA:
Note: Data for latest year may not have been available at press time.

In U.S. $	2021	2020	2019	2018	2017	2016
Revenue	8,602,877,000	8,030,984,000	7,904,658,000	7,193,709,000	7,154,538,000	
R&D Expense	311,407,500	295,739,200	284,967,200	246,775,700	171,372,000	
Operating Income	425,002,700	556,224,700	559,162,500	388,769,700	412,272,200	
Operating Margin %	.05%	.07%	.07%	.05%	.06%	
SGA Expense	619,877,200	578,747,900	557,204,000	558,183,200	527,825,900	
Net Income	241,879,400	457,318,600	666,882,100	357,433,100	283,008,700	
Operating Cash Flow	-445,567,300	466,132,000	416,189,200	409,334,400	392,686,800	
Capital Expenditure	259,506,200	268,319,700	269,298,900	286,925,800	215,439,200	
EBITDA	658,068,700	812,793,200	567,975,900	404,438,000	476,903,900	
Return on Assets %	.01%	.04%	.05%	.03%	.02%	
Return on Equity %	.04%	.13%	.18%	.10%	.08%	
Debt to Equity	.25%	0.378	0.07	0.345	0.436	

CONTACT INFORMATION:
Phone: 33 14149200   Fax: 33 14149248
Toll-Free:
Address: 48, rue Albert Dhalenne, Paris, 93400 France

STOCK TICKER/OTHER:
Stock Ticker: ALSMY   Exchange: PINX
Employees: 74,100   Fiscal Year Ends: 03/31
Parent Company:

SALARIES/BONUSES:
Top Exec. Salary: $ Bonus: $
Second Exec. Salary: $ Bonus: $

OTHER THOUGHTS:
Estimated Female Officers or Directors: 4
Hot Spot for Advancement for Women/Minorities: Y

Sales, profits and employees may be estimates. Financial information, benefits and other data can change quickly and may vary from those stated here.

Alto Ingredients Inc

NAIC Code: 325193

www.altoingredients.com

TYPES OF BUSINESS:
Ethanol Distribution
Specialty Alcohol Production
Essential Ingredients
Yeast
Corn Gluten Meal
Distillers Grains
Liquid Feed
Product Marketing

BRANDS/DIVISIONS/AFFILIATES:
Pacific Ethanol Inc

GROWTH PLANS/SPECIAL FEATURES:
Alto Ingredients Inc is a producer of specialty alcohols and essential ingredients. The company serves five markets: Health, Home & Beauty, Food & Beverage, Essential Ingredients, and Renewable Fuels. Its customers include major food and beverage companies and consumer products manufacturers and distributors. The company operates under three segments: Marketing and distribution, Pekin Campus production, and Other production. The Marketing and distribution segment participates in marketing and merchant trading for alcohols and essential ingredients; Pekin Campus produces and sells products produced at the company's Pekin, Illinois, campus, and about half of the firm's revenue flows from this segment. Other production makes and sells from the company's other production facilities.

CONTACTS:
Note: Officers with more than one job title may be intentionally listed here more than once.

Michael Kandris, CEO
Bryon McGregor, CFO
William Jones, Chairman of the Board
Christopher Wright, General Counsel
James Sneed, Other Executive Officer

FINANCIAL DATA:
Note: Data for latest year may not have been available at press time.

In U.S. $	2021	2020	2019	2018	2017	2016
Revenue	1,207,892,000	897,023,000	1,424,881,000	1,515,371,000	1,632,255,000	1,624,758,000
R&D Expense						
Operating Income	38,599,000	20,879,000	-45,391,000	-51,537,000	-25,585,000	23,509,000
Operating Margin %	.03%	.02%	-.03%	-.03%	-.02%	.01%
SGA Expense	29,185,000	31,980,000	35,453,000	36,373,000	31,516,000	30,849,000
Net Income	46,082,000	-15,116,000	-88,949,000	-60,273,000	-34,964,000	1,419,000
Operating Cash Flow	26,821,000	71,681,000	-31,227,000	1,566,000	36,509,000	37,228,000
Capital Expenditure	16,384,000	6,580,000	3,281,000	15,154,000	20,866,000	19,171,000
EBITDA	74,430,000	30,912,000	-33,187,000	-10,517,000	13,194,000	58,392,000
Return on Assets %	.09%	-.03%	-.14%	-.09%	-.05%	.00%
Return on Equity %	.14%	-.06%	-.35%	-.19%	-.10%	.00%
Debt to Equity	.17%	0.272	0.919	0.283	0.642	0.486

CONTACT INFORMATION:
Phone: 916 403-2123   Fax: 916 446-3937
Toll-Free:
Address: 1300 S. Second St., Pekin, IL 61554 United States

STOCK TICKER/OTHER:
Stock Ticker: ALTO
Employees: 417
Parent Company:

Exchange: NAS
Fiscal Year Ends: 12/31

SALARIES/BONUSES:
Top Exec. Salary: $509,856   Bonus: $
Second Exec. Salary: $336,130   Bonus: $

OTHER THOUGHTS:
Estimated Female Officers or Directors:
Hot Spot for Advancement for Women/Minorities:

Sales, profits and employees may be estimates. Financial information, benefits and other data can change quickly and may vary from those stated here.

Ambri Incorporated

NAIC Code: 335911

www.ambri.com

TYPES OF BUSINESS:
Large Storage Batteries
Liquid-Metal Batteries
Electricity Storage
Renewable Energy
Manufacturing Facilities
Battery Cells and Direct Current Systems

BRANDS/DIVISIONS/AFFILIATES:

CONTACTS: *Note: Officers with more than one job title may be intentionally listed here more than once.*
Jim Prueitt, COO
Phil Giudice, Pres.
Nora Murphy, CFO
Adam Briggs, CCO
Donald R. Sadoway, Chief Scientific Advisor
David Bradwell, CTO
Shazad Butt, VP-Mfg. & Eng.
Kristin Brief, Dir.-Corp. Dev.
Dan Leff, Chmn.

GROWTH PLANS/SPECIAL FEATURES:

Ambri Incorporated is a technology company specializing in liquid metal batteries for electricity storage purposes. This technology reduces the price of power, increases system reliability and allows for widespread use of renewable energy sources such as solar or wind energy. The liquid metal battery technology originated at the Massachusetts Institute of Technology (MIT) and consists of self-separating liquid layers which float atop one another depending on density and immiscibility (like oil and water). The batteries are comprised of a liquid calcium alloy anode, a molten salt electrolyte and a cathode comprised of solid particles of antimony, enabling the use of low-cost materials and a low number of steps in the cell assembly process. The battery cells operate at high temperatures and are self-maintained via charging and discharging, making the technology low cost and efficient. Ambri's product is ready to install, complete with the shelves of cells, thermal management features, a weatherproof outer enclosure and a battery management system. The product is convenient for applications that require high-energy capacity, frequent cycling, long life and high efficiency. The system is insulated and self-heating when operated, requiring no external heating/cooling to keep the batteries at operating temperature. For large-scale projects, multiple systems are placed together on site and connected in parallel, enabling unlimited upward scalability. Ambri's commercial systems are factory assembled, shipped to the site and require minimal maintenance. Because they are not lithium-ion batteries, there is no risk of combustion. During 2022, Ambri announced plans to produce cells and complete direct current (DC) systems at its pilot manufacturing site in Massachusetts, and the battery systems would be used for trial deployments and then become commercial products in 2023. Ambri's high volume production facility is planned to produce multiple gigawatt-hours of systems in the US starting in 2024.

FINANCIAL DATA: *Note: Data for latest year may not have been available at press time.*

In U.S. $	2021	2020	2019	2018	2017	2016
Revenue						
R&D Expense						
Operating Income						
Operating Margin %						
SGA Expense						
Net Income						
Operating Cash Flow						
Capital Expenditure						
EBITDA						
Return on Assets %						
Return on Equity %						
Debt to Equity						

CONTACT INFORMATION:
Phone: 617 714-5723   Fax:
Toll-Free:
Address: 53 Brigham St., Unit 8, Marlborough, MA 01752 United States

STOCK TICKER/OTHER:
Stock Ticker: Private   Exchange:
Employees: 40   Fiscal Year Ends:
Parent Company:

SALARIES/BONUSES:
Top Exec. Salary: $ Bonus: $
Second Exec. Salary: $ Bonus: $

OTHER THOUGHTS:
Estimated Female Officers or Directors: 2
Hot Spot for Advancement for Women/Minorities:

Sales, profits and employees may be estimates. Financial information, benefits and other data can change quickly and may vary from those stated here.

Ameresco Inc

NAIC Code: 541330

www.ameresco.com

TYPES OF BUSINESS:
Energy Engineering and Consulting Services
Landfill Gas-to-Energy Generation
Solar Power Technology
Cogeneration

BRANDS/DIVISIONS/AFFILIATES:
Ameresco Canada Inc

GROWTH PLANS/SPECIAL FEATURES:
Ameresco Inc provides energy efficiency solutions for facilities in North America and Europe. It focuses on projects that reduce energy, also focuses on the operation and maintenance costs of governmental, educational, utility, healthcare, and other institutional, commercial, and industrial entities facilities. Ameresco distributes solar energy products and systems, such as PV panels, solar regulators, solar charge controllers, inverters, solar-powered lighting systems, solar-powered water pumps, solar panel mounting hardware, and other system components. The company's segment includes U.S. Regions; U.S. Federal; Canada; Non-Solar DG and All Other. It derives a majority of revenue from the U.S. Regions segment.

CONTACTS:
Note: Officers with more than one job title may be intentionally listed here more than once.

Louis Maltezos, CEO, Subsidiary
George Sakellaris, CEO
Doran Hole, CFO
Mark Chiplock, Chief Accounting Officer
David Corrsin, Director
Michael Bakas, Executive VP, Divisional
Robert Georgeoff, Executive VP, Geographical
Nicole Bulgarino, Executive VP
Britta MacIntosh, Senior VP, Divisional

FINANCIAL DATA:
Note: Data for latest year may not have been available at press time.

In U.S. $	2021	2020	2019	2018	2017	2016
Revenue	1,215,697,000	1,032,275,000	866,933,000	787,138,000	717,152,000	651,227,000
R&D Expense						
Operating Income	96,446,000	73,350,000	51,614,000	59,099,000	36,588,000	23,776,000
Operating Margin %	.08%	.07%	.06%	.08%	.05%	.04%
SGA Expense	134,923,000	116,050,000	116,504,000	114,513,000	107,570,000	110,568,000
Net Income	70,458,000	54,052,000	44,436,000	37,984,000	37,491,000	12,032,000
Operating Cash Flow	-172,296,000	-102,583,000	-196,293,000	-53,201,000	-135,570,000	-52,634,000
Capital Expenditure	183,775,000	182,757,000	141,412,000	129,616,000	88,410,000	76,041,000
EBITDA	141,931,000	116,577,000	92,062,000	87,945,000	62,081,000	48,531,000
Return on Assets %	.04%	.03%	.04%	.04%	.04%	.02%
Return on Equity %	.12%	.12%	.11%	.11%	.12%	.04%
Debt to Equity	.59%	0.704	0.689	0.582	0.515	0.478

CONTACT INFORMATION:
Phone: 508 661-2200 Fax:
Toll-Free: 866-263-7372
Address: 111 Speen St., Ste. 410, Framingham, MA 01701 United States

STOCK TICKER/OTHER:
Stock Ticker: AMRC
Employees: 1,141
Parent Company:

Exchange: NYS
Fiscal Year Ends: 12/31

SALARIES/BONUSES:
Top Exec. Salary: $1,163,462 Bonus: $625,000
Second Exec. Salary: $332,531 Bonus: $322,660

OTHER THOUGHTS:
Estimated Female Officers or Directors: 3
Hot Spot for Advancement for Women/Minorities: Y

Sales, profits and employees may be estimates. Financial information, benefits and other data can change quickly and may vary from those stated here.

American Superconductor Corporation

NAIC Code: 333611

www.amsc.com

TYPES OF BUSINESS:
Turbine and Turbine Generator Set Units Manufacturing
Power Electronic Switches
SMES Systems
Electric Motors & Generators
Superconducting Materials
Electric Transmission Cables
Wind Turbine Design

BRANDS/DIVISIONS/AFFILIATES:
Windtec Solutions
Gridtec Solutions
PowerModule
Amperium
Marinetec Solutions
Northeast Power Systems Inc

GROWTH PLANS/SPECIAL FEATURES:
American Superconductor Corp generates the ideas, technologies, and solutions that meet world's demand for smarter, cleaner and energy. Through its Windtec Solutions, the company enables manufacturers to launch wind turbines quickly, effectively and profitably. Through its Gridtec Solutions, the company provides engineering planning services and grid systems that optimize network reliability, efficiency and performance. The company's segment includes Grid and Wind. It generates maximum revenue from the Grid segment.

CONTACTS:
Note: Officers with more than one job title may be intentionally listed here more than once.
Daniel McGahn, CEO
John Kosiba, CFO

FINANCIAL DATA:
Note: Data for latest year may not have been available at press time.

In U.S. $	2021	2020	2019	2018	2017	2016
Revenue	87,125,000	63,838,000	56,207,000	48,403,000	75,195,000	
R&D Expense	11,015,000	9,565,000	9,874,000	11,594,000	12,540,000	
Operating Income	-20,105,000	-23,129,000	-18,225,000	-30,559,000	-27,542,000	
Operating Margin %	-.23%	-.36%	-.32%	-.63%	-.37%	
SGA Expense	25,322,000	22,669,000	22,028,000	22,577,000	25,688,000	
Net Income	-22,678,000	-17,096,000	26,761,000	-32,776,000	-27,373,000	
Operating Cash Flow	-8,681,000	-16,497,000	42,714,000	-24,827,000	-11,215,000	
Capital Expenditure	1,764,000	4,630,000	952,000	2,534,000	656,000	
EBITDA	-14,753,000	-18,821,000	-13,616,000	-19,100,000	-20,023,000	
Return on Assets %	-.15%	-.14%	.26%	-.35%	-.23%	
Return on Equity %	-.24%	-.22%	.40%	-.58%	-.38%	
Debt to Equity	.03%	0.042				

CONTACT INFORMATION:
Phone: 978 842-3000 Fax: 978 842-3024
Toll-Free:
Address: 114 East Main Street, Ayer, MA 01432 United States

STOCK TICKER/OTHER:
Stock Ticker: AMSC Exchange: NAS
Employees: 326 Fiscal Year Ends: 03/31
Parent Company:

SALARIES/BONUSES:
Top Exec. Salary: $525,000 Bonus: $
Second Exec. Salary: $345,000 Bonus: $

OTHER THOUGHTS:
Estimated Female Officers or Directors: 1
Hot Spot for Advancement for Women/Minorities:

Sales, profits and employees may be estimates. Financial information, benefits and other data can change quickly and may vary from those stated here.

Amyris Inc

NAIC Code: 325193

www.amyris.com

TYPES OF BUSINESS:
Ethanol Production
Artemisinin
Renewable Fuels
Biodiesel
Biochemicals

BRANDS/DIVISIONS/AFFILIATES:
PURECANE
No Compromise
Terasana

GROWTH PLANS/SPECIAL FEATURES:
Amyris Inc is an industrial biotechnology company. It is engaged in the engineering, manufacturing, and sales of products in a variety of consumer and industrial markets, including cosmetics, flavors and fragrances, solvents and cleaners, polymers, lubricants, healthcare products, and fuels. The business operations are spread across the world with the majority of the revenues generated in the United States. The company generates revenue from the sale of renewable products, licenses of and royalties from intellectual property, and grants, and collaborative research and development services.

CONTACTS: Note: Officers with more than one job title may be intentionally listed here more than once.
John Melo, CEO
Hermanus Kieftenbeld, CFO
Geoffrey Duyk, Chairman of the Board
Robin Hughes, Chief Accounting Officer
Eduardo Alvarez, COO
Nicole Kelsey, General Counsel
Kathleen Valiasek, Other Executive Officer

FINANCIAL DATA: Note: Data for latest year may not have been available at press time.

In U.S. $	2021	2020	2019	2018	2017	2016
Revenue	341,817,000	173,137,000	152,557,000	63,604,000	127,671,000	67,192,000
R&D Expense	94,289,000	71,676,000	71,460,000	68,722,000	57,562,000	51,412,000
Operating Income	-165,422,000	-123,422,000	-121,674,000	-132,718,000	-56,051,000	-88,619,000
Operating Margin %	-.48%	-.71%	-.80%	-2.09%	-.44%	-1.32%
SGA Expense	257,811,000	137,071,000	126,586,000	90,902,000	63,853,000	47,721,000
Net Income	-270,969,000	-331,039,000	-242,767,000	-230,235,000	-155,982,000	-97,334,000
Operating Cash Flow	-181,333,000	-175,753,000	-156,933,000	-109,366,000	-101,179,000	-82,367,000
Capital Expenditure	45,636,000	12,781,000	13,080,000	12,472,000	4,412,000	922,000
EBITDA	-234,012,000	-263,773,000	-166,295,000	-182,611,000	-100,666,000	-47,778,000
Return on Assets %	-.46%	-1.99%	-1.87%	-1.66%	-1.49%	-.82%
Return on Equity %	-6.79%					
Debt to Equity	1.31%					

CONTACT INFORMATION:
Phone: 510 450-0761   Fax: 510 225-2645
Toll-Free:
Address: 5885 Hollis St., Ste. 100, Emeryville, CA 94608 United States

STOCK TICKER/OTHER:
Stock Ticker: AMRS
Employees: 980
Parent Company:

Exchange: NAS
Fiscal Year Ends: 12/31

SALARIES/BONUSES:
Top Exec. Salary: $712,500   Bonus: $532,650
Second Exec. Salary: $500,000   Bonus: $164,400

OTHER THOUGHTS:
Estimated Female Officers or Directors: 4
Hot Spot for Advancement for Women/Minorities: Y

Sales, profits and employees may be estimates. Financial information, benefits and other data can change quickly and may vary from those stated here.

APC by Schneider Electric

NAIC Code: 335911

www.apc.com

TYPES OF BUSINESS:
Back-Up Power Supplies
Power Protection & Management Products
Consulting Services
PC Accessories
Power Management Software
Fuel Cell-Based Power Backup

BRANDS/DIVISIONS/AFFILIATES:
Schneider Electric SE
Fuel Cell Extended Run
InfraStruXure

CONTACTS: Note: Officers with more than one job title may be intentionally listed here more than once.
Annett Clayton, CEO
Aamir Paul, Pres.
Fei Tong, CFO
Neil Rasmussen, Sr. VP-Innovation
Randy Amon, Sr. VP-Customer Care, Quality & Process
Leanne Cunnold, Sr. VP-Bus. Dev. & Strategy
Rob McKernan, Pres., Americas
Mike Maiello, Sr. VP-Home & Bus. Networks
Philippe Arsonneau, Pres., Asia Pacific & Japan
Chenhong Huang, Sr. VP-Greater China
Ed Machala, Sr. VP-Supply Chain, Purchasing & Manufacturing

GROWTH PLANS/SPECIAL FEATURES:

APC by Schneider Electric designs, develops, manufactures and markets power protection and management solutions for computer, communications and electronic applications worldwide. APC stands for American power conversion. The company's products include uninterruptible power supply (UPS) products, electrical surge protection devices, power distribution products, precision cooling equipment, power management software and accessories, racks and enclosures and various desktop and notebook personal computer accessories. These products are primarily used with sensitive electronic devices, which rely on electric utility power, such as home electronics, PCs, high-performance computer workstations, servers, networking equipment, communications equipment, internet equipment, data centers, mainframe computers and facilities. APC's UPS products regulate the flow of utility power to the protected equipment and provide seamless back-up power during power interruptions. Back-up power lasts for enough time to continue computer operations, conduct an orderly shutdown, preserve data, work through short power outages or, in some cases, continue operating for several hours or longer. In addition, the firm's Fuel Cell Extended Run (FCXR) product provides hydrogen-based power backup for its proprietary InfraStruXure power, cooling, environmental monitoring and management data center for modular and mobile configurations. The company's security and environmental appliances and accessories protect against environmental or human threats and monitor valuable systems with sensors, cameras and accessories. APC's precision cooling equipment regulates temperature and humidity. Last, the company provides power management software, consulting services and notebook and PC accessories. Its data center software business is responsible for software creation and development, sales, service and marketing programs. APC is a subsidiary of Schneider Electric SE.

APC offers employees comprehensive benefits, retirement and savings options, and employee assistance programs.

FINANCIAL DATA: Note: Data for latest year may not have been available at press time.

In U.S. $	2021	2020	2019	2018	2017	2016
Revenue	3,400,000,000	3,200,000,000	3,046,020,000	2,939,540,000	2,958,720,000	480,000,000
R&D Expense						
Operating Income						
Operating Margin %						
SGA Expense						
Net Income						
Operating Cash Flow						
Capital Expenditure						
EBITDA						
Return on Assets %						
Return on Equity %						
Debt to Equity						

CONTACT INFORMATION:
Phone: 617 904-9422 Fax:
Toll-Free: 877-272-2722
Address: One Boston Pl., 201 Washington St., Ste. 2700, Boston, MA 02108 United States

SALARIES/BONUSES:
Top Exec. Salary: $ Bonus: $
Second Exec. Salary: $ Bonus: $

STOCK TICKER/OTHER:
Stock Ticker: Subsidiary Exchange:
Employees: 7,000 Fiscal Year Ends: 12/31
Parent Company: Schneider Electric SE

OTHER THOUGHTS:
Estimated Female Officers or Directors: 2
Hot Spot for Advancement for Women/Minorities:

Sales, profits and employees may be estimates. Financial information, benefits and other data can change quickly and may vary from those stated here.

Applied Materials Inc

www.appliedmaterials.com

NAIC Code: 333242

TYPES OF BUSINESS:
Semiconductor Manufacturing Equipment
LCD Display Technology Equipment
Automation Software
Energy Generation & Conversion Technologies

GROWTH PLANS/SPECIAL FEATURES:
Applied Materials is the world's largest supplier of semiconductor manufacturing equipment, providing materials engineering solutions to help make nearly every chip in the world. The firm's systems are used in nearly every major process step with the exception of lithography. Key tools include those for chemical and physical vapor deposition, etching, chemical mechanical polishing, wafer- and reticle-inspection, critical dimension measurement, and defect-inspection scanning electron microscopes.

Applied Materials offers comprehensive benefits, retirement options and employee assistance programs.

BRANDS/DIVISIONS/AFFILIATES:

CONTACTS: Note: Officers with more than one job title may be intentionally listed here more than once.
Gary Dickerson, CEO
Daniel Durn, CFO
James Morgan, Chairman Emeritus
Thomas Iannotti, Chairman of the Board
Charles Read, Chief Accounting Officer
Teri Little, Chief Legal Officer
Omkaram Nalamasu, Chief Technology Officer
Ginetto Addiego, Senior VP, Divisional
Ali Salehpour, Senior VP, Divisional
Steve Ghanayem, Senior VP, Divisional
Prabu Raja, Senior VP, Divisional

FINANCIAL DATA: Note: Data for latest year may not have been available at press time.

In U.S. $	2021	2020	2019	2018	2017	2016
Revenue	23,063,000,000	17,202,000,000	14,608,000,000	16,705,000,000	14,698,000,000	10,825,000,000
R&D Expense	2,485,000,000	2,234,000,000	2,054,000,000	2,022,000,000	1,781,000,000	1,540,000,000
Operating Income	7,200,000,000	4,365,000,000	3,350,000,000	4,491,000,000	3,936,000,000	2,152,000,000
Operating Margin %	.31%	.25%	.23%	.27%	.27%	.20%
SGA Expense	1,229,000,000	1,093,000,000	982,000,000	1,004,000,000	895,000,000	819,000,000
Net Income	5,888,000,000	3,619,000,000	2,706,000,000	3,038,000,000	3,519,000,000	1,721,000,000
Operating Cash Flow	5,442,000,000	3,804,000,000	3,247,000,000	3,787,000,000	3,789,000,000	2,566,000,000
Capital Expenditure	668,000,000	422,000,000	441,000,000	622,000,000	345,000,000	253,000,000
EBITDA	7,401,000,000	4,782,000,000	3,869,000,000	5,087,000,000	4,421,000,000	2,557,000,000
Return on Assets %	.24%	.17%	.15%	.16%	.21%	.12%
Return on Equity %	.52%	.39%	.36%	.38%	.42%	.23%
Debt to Equity	.46%	0.533	0.574	0.776	0.567	0.433

CONTACT INFORMATION:
Phone: 408 727-5555   Fax: 408 727-9943
Toll-Free:
Address: 3050 Bowers Ave., Santa Clara, CA 95052-8039 United States

STOCK TICKER/OTHER:
Stock Ticker: AMAT
Employees: 27,000
Parent Company:

Exchange: NAS
Fiscal Year Ends: 10/31

SALARIES/BONUSES:
Top Exec. Salary: $1,049,808   Bonus: $
Second Exec. Salary: $681,635   Bonus: $

OTHER THOUGHTS:
Estimated Female Officers or Directors: 2
Hot Spot for Advancement for Women/Minorities: Y

Sales, profits and employees may be estimates. Financial information, benefits and other data can change quickly and may vary from those stated here.

Archer-Daniels-Midland Company (ADM)

NAIC Code: 311200

www.adm.com

TYPES OF BUSINESS:
Food Processing-Oilseeds, Corn & Wheat
Agricultural Services
Nutraceuticals
Transportation Services
Biodiesel
Natural Plastics
Chocolate
Corn Syrups

BRANDS/DIVISIONS/AFFILIATES:
Pacificor
Wilmar International Limited
Hungrana Ltd
Almidones Mexicanos SA
Neovia SAS
Florida Chemical Company
Ziegler Group (The)
Gleadell Agriculture Ltd

GROWTH PLANS/SPECIAL FEATURES:

Archer-Daniels Midland is a major processor of oilseeds, corn, wheat, and other agricultural commodities. Additionally, the company owns an extensive network of logistical assets to store and transport crops around the globe. ADM also runs a nutrition business that focuses on both human and animal ingredients. The company is also a large producer of corn-based sweeteners, starches, and ethanol.

ADM offers its employees comprehensive health and financial benefits and learning/development opportunities.

CONTACTS: Note: Officers with more than one job title may be intentionally listed here more than once.

Thuy-Nga Vo, Assistant Secretary
Patricia Logan, Other Corporate Officer
Juan Luciano, CEO
Vikram Luthar, CFO, Divisional
John Stott, CFO, Divisional
Ray Young, CFO
Molly Strader Fruit, Chief Accounting Officer
Benjamin Bard, Chief Compliance Officer
Vincent Macciocchi, Chief Marketing Officer
Todd Werpy, Chief Scientific Officer
Ian Pinner, Chief Strategy Officer
Kristy Folkwein, Chief Technology Officer
D. Findlay, General Counsel
Joseph Taets, Other Corporate Officer
Veronica Braker, Other Corporate Officer
Jennifer Weber, Other Executive Officer

FINANCIAL DATA: Note: Data for latest year may not have been available at press time.

In U.S. $	2021	2020	2019	2018	2017	2016
Revenue	85,249,000,000	64,355,000,000	64,656,000,000	64,341,000,000	60,828,000,000	62,346,000,000
R&D Expense						
Operating Income	2,993,000,000	1,766,000,000	1,654,000,000	2,016,000,000	1,540,000,000	1,637,000,000
Operating Margin %	.04%	.03%	.03%	.03%	.03%	.03%
SGA Expense	2,994,000,000	2,687,000,000	2,493,000,000	2,165,000,000	1,978,000,000	1,981,000,000
Net Income	2,709,000,000	1,772,000,000	1,379,000,000	1,810,000,000	1,595,000,000	1,279,000,000
Operating Cash Flow	6,595,000,000	-2,386,000,000	-5,452,000,000	-4,784,000,000	-5,966,000,000	-6,508,000,000
Capital Expenditure	1,169,000,000	823,000,000	828,000,000	842,000,000	1,049,000,000	882,000,000
EBITDA	4,574,000,000	3,198,000,000	2,983,000,000	3,365,000,000	2,863,000,000	3,015,000,000
Return on Assets %	.05%	.04%	.03%	.04%	.04%	.03%
Return on Equity %	.13%	.09%	.07%	.10%	.09%	.07%
Debt to Equity	.39%	0.437	0.44	0.406	0.362	0.379

CONTACT INFORMATION:
Phone: 312-634-8100   Fax:
Toll-Free: 800-637-5843
Address: 77 West Wacker Dr., Ste. 4600, Chicago, IL 60601 United States

STOCK TICKER/OTHER:
Stock Ticker: ADM
Employees: 40,739
Parent Company:

Exchange: NYS
Fiscal Year Ends: 12/31

SALARIES/BONUSES:
Top Exec. Salary: $1,400,004   Bonus: $
Second Exec. Salary: $850,008   Bonus: $

OTHER THOUGHTS:
Estimated Female Officers or Directors: 4
Hot Spot for Advancement for Women/Minorities: Y

Sales, profits and employees may be estimates. Financial information, benefits and other data can change quickly and may vary from those stated here.

Arizona Public Service Company

NAIC Code: 221112

www.aps.com

TYPES OF BUSINESS:
Electric Utility
Electricity Distribution
Clean Energy Generation
Solar Systems

BRANDS/DIVISIONS/AFFILIATES:
Pinnacle West Capital Corporation
APS Solar Communities

GROWTH PLANS/SPECIAL FEATURES:
Arizona Public Service Company (APS), the principal subsidiary of Pinnacle West Capital Corporation, is one of the largest electricity providers in Arizona. The company serves approximately 2.7 million residential and business customers, and is engaged in the generation of clean energy. APS' service territory spans across the state, from Douglas to the Grand Canyon, from the solar fields of Gila Bend to Payson. The firm set a goal to provide 100% clean, carbon-free electricity to customers by 2050, with a target of achieving a resource mix that is 65% clean energy by 2030, with 45% of APS' generation portfolio coming from renewable energy. Coal-fired generation is slated to end at APS by 2031. APS Solar Communities produces rooftop solar systems, which connect directly to its distribution system.

APS offers its employees tuition reimbursement, employee development and training programs, 401(k) pension and retiree health and life insurance plans.

CONTACTS:
Note: Officers with more than one job title may be intentionally listed here more than once.

Jeff Guldner, Pres.
David P. Falck, Exec. VP
Denise R. Danner, Chief Acct. Officer

FINANCIAL DATA:
Note: Data for latest year may not have been available at press time.

In U.S. $	2021	2020	2019	2018	2017	2016
Revenue	3,803,835,000	3,586,982,000	3,471,209,000	3,688,342,000	3,557,652,000	3,498,090,000
R&D Expense						
Operating Income						
Operating Margin %						
SGA Expense						
Net Income	649,503,000	587,521,000	584,764,000	589,758,000	523,802,000	481,634,000
Operating Cash Flow						
Capital Expenditure						
EBITDA						
Return on Assets %						
Return on Equity %						
Debt to Equity						

CONTACT INFORMATION:
Phone: 602-250-1000 Fax: 602-250-3007
Toll-Free: 800-253-9405
Address: 400 N. 5th St., Phoenix, AZ 85004 United States

STOCK TICKER/OTHER:
Stock Ticker: Subsidiary Exchange:
Employees: 6,000 Fiscal Year Ends: 12/31
Parent Company: Pinnacle West Capital Corporation

SALARIES/BONUSES:
Top Exec. Salary: $ Bonus: $
Second Exec. Salary: $ Bonus: $

OTHER THOUGHTS:
Estimated Female Officers or Directors: 2
Hot Spot for Advancement for Women/Minorities: Y

Sales, profits and employees may be estimates. Financial information, benefits and other data can change quickly and may vary from those stated here.

Arotech Corporation

NAIC Code: 335911

www.arotech.com

TYPES OF BUSINESS:
Mobile Electric Power Technology
Engineering and Technology Solutions
Product Development
Power Systems
Amplifier Equipment
Software
Simulation Training Products
Battery Packs and Power Systems

BRANDS/DIVISIONS/AFFILIATES:
UEC Electronics LLC
Aldetec Incorporated
Broadband Wireless Technologies
FAAC Incorporated
MILO
Realtime Technologies
Inter-Coastal Electronics
Epsilor

CONTACTS:
Note: Officers with more than one job title may be intentionally listed here more than once.

Dean M. Krutty, CEO
Christopher Garvey, CFO
Yaakov Har-Oz, General Counsel
Ronen Badichi, General Manager, Divisional
Kurt Flosky, President, Divisional
David Modeen, President, Geographical
Jeffrey Parker, Chmn.

GROWTH PLANS/SPECIAL FEATURES:

Arotech Corporation develops engineering and technology solutions that foster new product innovation. The company operates through three business divisions: advanced electronics, training and simulation, and energy solutions. The advanced electronics division is comprised of: UEC Electronics LLC, a product design and manufacturing company that specializes in power systems, including vehicle power, clean energy power generation, power distribution and power management systems; Aldetec Incorporated provides custom integrated microwave assemblies and radio frequency (RF) amplifier equipment for commercial, military and space flight industry sectors; Broadband Wireless Technologies specializes in high-efficiency power amplifiers, from high frequency (HF) through X-band; and U.S. Technologies designs, engineers, manufactures and services complex, critical electronic components, sub-assemblies and high-performance RF/microwave power applications. The training and simulation division is comprised of: FAAC Incorporated, which provides engineering and software products to the U.S. government and private industry sectors, and conducts tactical land and air combat analysis, and develops analytical models and simulations; MILO, a supplier of interactive, multimedia, fully-digital simulation training products to law enforcement, governmental and commercial clients worldwide; Realtime Technologies, which specializes in multi-body vehicle dynamics modeling and graphical simulation solutions and offers simulation software applications, consulting services, custom engineering solutions and software and hardware development; and Inter-Coastal Electronics, an engineering firm that develops, manufactures, fields and maintains test, telemetry and training instrumentation systems and services for war fighters and first responders. Last, the energy solutions division serves the military, defense, marine, aerospace, industrial, and electric vehicle markets, and comprises: Epsilor, which develops and produces battery packs and chargers; and Epsilor-Electric Fuel Ltd., which develops and produces custom and mobile portable power systems.

FINANCIAL DATA:
Note: Data for latest year may not have been available at press time.

In U.S. $	2021	2020	2019	2018	2017	2016
Revenue	104,000,000	100,000,000	99,497,736	96,599,744	98,722,680	92,975,752
R&D Expense						
Operating Income						
Operating Margin %						
SGA Expense						
Net Income				1,869,955	3,834,136	-2,848,256
Operating Cash Flow						
Capital Expenditure						
EBITDA						
Return on Assets %						
Return on Equity %						
Debt to Equity						

CONTACT INFORMATION:
Phone: 800 281-0356   Fax:
Toll-Free: 800-281-0356
Address: 1229 Oak Valley Dr., Ann Arbor, MI 48108 United States

SALARIES/BONUSES:
Top Exec. Salary: $ Bonus: $
Second Exec. Salary: $ Bonus: $

STOCK TICKER/OTHER:
Stock Ticker: Private   Exchange:
Employees: 514   Fiscal Year Ends: 12/31
Parent Company: Greenbriar Equity Group LP

OTHER THOUGHTS:
Estimated Female Officers or Directors:
Hot Spot for Advancement for Women/Minorities:

Sales, profits and employees may be estimates. Financial information, benefits and other data can change quickly and may vary from those stated here.

Atlantic Methanol Production Company LLC

www.atlanticmethanol.com
NAIC Code: 325194

TYPES OF BUSINESS:
Methyl Alcohol (methanol), Natural, Manufacturing
Methanol Production
Natural Gas Reserves

BRANDS/DIVISIONS/AFFILIATES:
Marathon Oil Corporation
Chevron Corporation
SONAGAS GE
AMPCO Marketing LLC
AMPCO Services LLC
Atlantic Methanol Services BV

GROWTH PLANS/SPECIAL FEATURES:
Atlantic Methanol Production Company, LLC (AMPCO) produces methanol from natural gas reserves on Bioko Island, which lies off the coast of Equatorial Guinea. Methanol, also known as methyl alcohol, is a light, volatile alcohol used for motor gasoline blending, solvents and antifreeze. In its capacity as a fuel, it is most often used as a less flammable replacement for gasoline. Marathon Oil Corporation and Chevron Corporation each own a 45% share of AMPCO; and SONAGAS GE (The National Gas Company of Equatorial Guinea) owns the remaining 10%. Marketing and sales subsidiaries include AMPCO Marketing, LLC and AMPCO Services, LLC in the U.S.; and Atlantic Methanol Services BV in the Netherlands, serving Europe. AMPCO maintains storage at its production site in Punta Europa in Equatorial Guinea, as well as through terminals located in Texas, Louisiana, the Netherlands and the U.K.

CONTACTS:
Note: Officers with more than one job title may be intentionally listed here more than once.

Paul Moschell, Pres.
Jim O'Casek, VP-Oper.
Doug Blackwell, VP-Finance & Acct.
Edson S. Jones, VP-Mktg.
Nancy Ampim Elonga, Mgr.-Human Resources
Brian Jackson, Dir.-Commercial Oper.
Jim O'Casek, Mgr.-Finance & Admin.
Andrew Costa, Gen. Counsel
Juan Antonio, Vice Chmn.
Jose Estevez, Chmn.

FINANCIAL DATA:
Note: Data for latest year may not have been available at press time.

In U.S. $	2021	2020	2019	2018	2017	2016
Revenue	952,000,000	425,040,000	483,000,000	460,000,000	450,000,000	440,000,000
R&D Expense						
Operating Income						
Operating Margin %						
SGA Expense						
Net Income						
Operating Cash Flow						
Capital Expenditure						
EBITDA						
Return on Assets %						
Return on Equity %						
Debt to Equity						

CONTACT INFORMATION:
Phone: 281-872-8324   Fax: 281-872-1084
Toll-Free:
Address: 12600 Northborough Dr., Ste. 150, Houston, TX 77067 United States

STOCK TICKER/OTHER:
Stock Ticker: Joint Venture   Exchange:
Employees: 450   Fiscal Year Ends: 12/31
Parent Company: Marathon Oil Corporation

SALARIES/BONUSES:
Top Exec. Salary: $ Bonus: $
Second Exec. Salary: $ Bonus: $

OTHER THOUGHTS:
Estimated Female Officers or Directors:
Hot Spot for Advancement for Women/Minorities:

Sales, profits and employees may be estimates. Financial information, benefits and other data can change quickly and may vary from those stated here.

Atomic Energy of Canada Limited (AECL)

NAIC Code: 541330

www.aecl.ca

TYPES OF BUSINESS:
Nuclear Reactor Design
Nuclear Waste Management
Research & Laboratories

BRANDS/DIVISIONS/AFFILIATES:

GROWTH PLANS/SPECIAL FEATURES:
Atomic Energy of Canada, Ltd. (AECL) is a global nuclear technology and engineering company owned by the Canadian government. AECL is responsible for enabling nuclear science and technology and to fulfill the Government of Canada's radioactive waste and decommissioning activities. Nuclear science and technology are utilized to sustain and develop the country's capabilities in a cost-effective manner. AECL delivers its services through a long-term contract with Canadian Nuclear Laboratories (CNL) for the management and operation of its nuclear sites. The firm also works with CNL to provide technical services and research and development products for third parties on a commercial basis. AECL's radioactive waste and decommissioning division manages various types of radioactive waste at its sites, including high-level waste (used fuel), intermediate-level waste and low-level waste. AECL receives federal funding to deliver its services and reports to Parliament through the Minister of Natural Resources.

CONTACTS: Note: Officers with more than one job title may be intentionally listed here more than once.
Fred Dermarkar, CEO
Thomas Assimes, CFO
Nancy Chaput, Chief Human Resources Officer
William Kupferschmidt, VP-R&D
Yvonne Penning, General Counsel
Randy Lesco, VP-Oper.
Joan Miller, VP-Waste Mgmt. & Decommissioning
Jon Lundy, Chief Legal Officer
Richard V. Cote, VP-Isotopes Strategy
James Burpee, Chmn.

FINANCIAL DATA: Note: Data for latest year may not have been available at press time.

In U.S. $	2021	2020	2019	2018	2017	2016
Revenue	824,109,962	810,370,000	721,537,000	67,433,500	716,718,000	86,803,700
R&D Expense						
Operating Income						
Operating Margin %						
SGA Expense						
Net Income	5,196,241	-249,781,000	118,230,000	98,554,800	306,110,000	-103,929,000
Operating Cash Flow						
Capital Expenditure						
EBITDA						
Return on Assets %						
Return on Equity %						
Debt to Equity						

CONTACT INFORMATION:
Phone: 613-584-3311   Fax: 613-584-8272
Toll-Free: 888-220-2465
Address: 286 Plant Rd., Station 508A, Chalk River, ON K0J 1J0 Canada

STOCK TICKER/OTHER:
Stock Ticker: Government-Owned   Exchange:
Employees: 45   Fiscal Year Ends: 03/31
Parent Company:

SALARIES/BONUSES:
Top Exec. Salary: $ Bonus: $
Second Exec. Salary: $ Bonus: $

OTHER THOUGHTS:
Estimated Female Officers or Directors: 4
Hot Spot for Advancement for Women/Minorities: Y

Sales, profits and employees may be estimates. Financial information, benefits and other data can change quickly and may vary from those stated here.

ATS Automation Tooling Systems Inc

www.atsautomation.com

NAIC Code: 333517

TYPES OF BUSINESS:
Machine Tool Manufacturing
Testing Equipment
Manufacturing Consulting
Photovoltaic Cells Manufacturing
Photovoltaic Cells Installation & Design
Photovoltaic Cells Research & Development

BRANDS/DIVISIONS/AFFILIATES:

GROWTH PLANS/SPECIAL FEATURES:
ATS Automation Tooling Systems Inc is a Canada-based company that provides automation systems. The company designs and builds customized automated manufacturing and testing systems for customers, and provides pre- and post-automation services. The company's products comprise conveyor systems, automated electrified monorails, tray handlers, laser systems, and other hardware and software products. The company also provides pre-automation solutions, including strategic direction and planning services, as well as aftermarket support. The company's clients primarily come from the life sciences, food & beverage transportation, consumer products and electronics, and energy sectors. The company generates the majority of its sales from the North American and European markets.

CONTACTS:
Note: Officers with more than one job title may be intentionally listed here more than once.

Andrew Hider, CEO
Ryan McLeod, CFO
David McAusland, Chairman of the Board
Joe Metri, Chief Information Officer
Stewart Mccuaig, General Counsel
Heinrich Sielemann, Managing Director, Subsidiary
Simone Volpi, Managing Director, Subsidiary
Angella Alexander, Other Executive Officer
Christian Debus, President, Divisional
Chris Hart, President, Divisional
Udo Panenka, President, Divisional
Jeremy Patten, President, Divisional
Simon Roberts, Senior VP, Divisional
Steve Emery, Vice President, Divisional
Joe Tassone, Vice President, Divisional

FINANCIAL DATA:
Note: Data for latest year may not have been available at press time.

In U.S. $	2021	2020	2019	2018	2017	2016
Revenue	1,037,224,000	1,036,993,000	909,254,100	808,664,500	733,213,900	
R&D Expense						
Operating Income	97,164,780	88,659,130	83,261,400	61,986,030	52,174,820	
Operating Margin %	.09%	.09%	.09%	.08%	.07%	
SGA Expense	181,538,800	173,999,200	155,159,500	147,017,200	129,627,300	
Net Income	46,486,260	38,367,190	51,310,260	34,209,020	25,381,330	
Operating Cash Flow	134,296,800	14,757,780	92,547,490	43,290,560	92,766,530	
Capital Expenditure	22,899,330	41,028,340	29,679,490	18,839,800	12,981,510	
EBITDA	139,365,900	122,634,600	117,712,700	89,975,550	77,718,620	
Return on Assets %	.03%	.03%	.04%	.03%	.03%	
Return on Equity %	.07%	.06%	.09%	.07%	.05%	
Debt to Equity	.55%	0.743	0.416	0.415	0.475	

CONTACT INFORMATION:
Phone: 519 653-4483   Fax: 519 653-6520
Toll-Free:
Address: 730 Fountain Street North, Cambridge, ON N3H 4R7 Canada

STOCK TICKER/OTHER:
Stock Ticker: ATA   Exchange: TSE
Employees: 5,000   Fiscal Year Ends: 03/31
Parent Company:

SALARIES/BONUSES:
Top Exec. Salary: $ Bonus: $
Second Exec. Salary: $ Bonus: $

OTHER THOUGHTS:
Estimated Female Officers or Directors: 2
Hot Spot for Advancement for Women/Minorities: Y

Sales, profits and employees may be estimates. Financial information, benefits and other data can change quickly and may vary from those stated here.

AVANCIS GmbH

NAIC Code: 334413A

www.avancis.de

TYPES OF BUSINESS:
Photovoltaic Cell Manufacturing
Photovoltaic Modules
Product Design and Manufacture
Product Marketing and Customization
Copper Indium Gallium Selenide Technology
Thin-Film Processing
Solar Factories
PV Applications

BRANDS/DIVISIONS/AFFILIATES:
China National Building Materials Group Co Ltd

GROWTH PLANS/SPECIAL FEATURES:
AVANCIS GmbH develops, produces and markets photovoltaic (PV) modules for electricity-producing building facades, roofs and open spaces. The company also offers technical consulting for energy-efficient construction planning. AVANCIS' copper indium gallium selenide (CIGS) technology is among the most powerful and long-term stable thin-film processes available, and the company continues to research and develop its CIGS technology. Other solutions for AVANCIS' products include solar factories, PV applications and custom PV solutions. The firm's products are developed and manufactured in Germany. AVANCIS operates as a subsidiary of CTF Solar GmbH, itself a subsidiary of China National Building Material Group Co. Ltd.

CONTACTS:
Note: Officers with more than one job title may be intentionally listed here more than once.

Thomas Dalibor, CTO
Tom Clarius, Dir.-Quality, Health, Safety & Environment

FINANCIAL DATA:
Note: Data for latest year may not have been available at press time.

In U.S. $	2021	2020	2019	2018	2017	2016
Revenue						
R&D Expense						
Operating Income						
Operating Margin %						
SGA Expense						
Net Income						
Operating Cash Flow						
Capital Expenditure						
EBITDA						
Return on Assets %						
Return on Equity %						
Debt to Equity						

CONTACT INFORMATION:
Phone: 49-3421-7388-0   Fax: 49-3421-7388-111
Toll-Free:
Address: Solarstrasse 3, Torgau, 04860 Germany

STOCK TICKER/OTHER:
Stock Ticker: Subsidiary   Exchange:
Employees: 37   Fiscal Year Ends: 12/31
Parent Company: China National Building Materials Group Co Ltd

SALARIES/BONUSES:
Top Exec. Salary: $ Bonus: $
Second Exec. Salary: $ Bonus: $

OTHER THOUGHTS:
Estimated Female Officers or Directors: 1
Hot Spot for Advancement for Women/Minorities:

Avista Corporation

NAIC Code: 221111

www.avistacorp.com

TYPES OF BUSINESS:
Hydroelectric Power Generation
Gas and Electric Utility
eBusiness & Consulting Services
Energy Marketing
Thermal Power Generation
Venture Fund Investment
Metal Fabrication
Real Estate Investment

BRANDS/DIVISIONS/AFFILIATES:
Alaska Energy and Resources Company
Alaska Electric Light and Power Company

GROWTH PLANS/SPECIAL FEATURES:
Avista Corp is an electric and natural gas utility company headquartered in Spokane, Washington. Avista primarily operates in the Pacific Northwest of the United States along with some operations in Juneau, Alaska. The company has two major business segments including Avista Utilities, which provides electric distribution and transmission, and natural gas distribution services in parts of eastern Washington and northern Idaho and also provides natural gas distribution service in parts of northeastern and southwestern Oregon. Avista Utilities has electric generating facilities in Washington, Idaho, Oregon and Montana. AEL&P is a regulated utility providing electric services in Juneau, Alaska that is a wholly-owned subsidiary and the primary operating subsidiary of AERC.

Avista offers comprehensive benefits, retirement options and employee assistance plans.

CONTACTS:
Note: Officers with more than one job title may be intentionally listed here more than once.

Dennis Vermillion, CEO
Mark Thies, CFO
Scott Morris, Chairman of the Board
Ryan Krasselt, Chief Accounting Officer
Gregory Hesler, Chief Compliance Officer
James Kensok, Chief Information Officer
Edward Schlect, Chief Strategy Officer
Jason Thackston, Other Corporate Officer
Kevin Christie, Other Executive Officer
David Meyer, Other Executive Officer
Heather Rosentrater, Senior VP, Divisional
Bryan Cox, Vice President, Divisional
Latisha Hill, Vice President, Divisional

FINANCIAL DATA:
Note: Data for latest year may not have been available at press time.

In U.S. $	2021	2020	2019	2018	2017	2016
Revenue	1,438,936,000	1,321,891,000	1,345,622,000	1,396,893,000	1,445,929,000	1,442,483,000
R&D Expense						
Operating Income	228,232,000	232,700,000	230,064,000	264,831,000	306,797,000	299,861,000
Operating Margin %	.16%	.18%	.17%	.19%	.21%	.21%
SGA Expense						
Net Income	147,334,000	129,488,000	196,979,000	136,429,000	115,916,000	137,228,000
Operating Cash Flow	267,340,000	331,004,000	398,212,000	361,885,000	410,298,000	358,267,000
Capital Expenditure	439,939,000	404,306,000	442,510,000	424,350,000	412,339,000	406,644,000
EBITDA	493,706,000	461,740,000	534,311,000	446,973,000	467,227,000	464,806,000
Return on Assets %	.02%	.02%	.03%	.02%	.02%	.03%
Return on Equity %	.07%	.07%	.11%	.08%	.07%	.09%
Debt to Equity	.96%	1.072	1.038	1.019	0.892	1.049

CONTACT INFORMATION:
Phone: 509 489-0500   Fax: 509 777-5075
Toll-Free:
Address: 1411 E. Mission Ave., Spokane, WA 99220-2600 United States

STOCK TICKER/OTHER:
Stock Ticker: AVA
Employees: 1,809
Parent Company:

Exchange: NYS
Fiscal Year Ends: 12/31

SALARIES/BONUSES:
Top Exec. Salary: $769,038   Bonus: $
Second Exec. Salary: $461,615   Bonus: $

OTHER THOUGHTS:
Estimated Female Officers or Directors: 7
Hot Spot for Advancement for Women/Minorities: Y

Sales, profits and employees may be estimates. Financial information, benefits and other data can change quickly and may vary from those stated here.

Babcock & Wilcox Enterprises Inc

NAIC Code: 332410

www.babcock.com

TYPES OF BUSINESS:
Power Generation Systems
Steam Generators
Environmental Equipment
Engineering & Construction Services
Power Plants
Emissions Reduction Equipment
Waste-to-Energy & Biomass Energy Systems

BRANDS/DIVISIONS/AFFILIATES:
Fosler Construction Company Inc
VODA A/S

GROWTH PLANS/SPECIAL FEATURES:
Babcock & Wilcox Enterprises is a power generation equipment supplier and servicing company that operates in three segments: B&W Renewable, B&W Environmental, and B&W Thermal. B&W Thermal, which focuses on steam generation products and solutions for plants in the power generation, oil and gas, and industrial sectors, generates the majority of the company's revenue. B&W Renewable focuses on sustainable power and heat generation while B&W Environmental focuses on emissions control. The company's customer base spans the industrial, electrical utility, and municipal industries located predominantly in the United States, Canada, Denmark, and the United Kingdom. Business in the U.S. contributes the vast majority of its revenue.

CONTACTS: Note: Officers with more than one job title may be intentionally listed here more than once.

Kenneth Young, CEO
Louis Salamone, CFO
Jimmy Morgan, COO
John Dziewisz, General Counsel, Subsidiary

FINANCIAL DATA: Note: Data for latest year may not have been available at press time.

In U.S. $	2021	2020	2019	2018	2017	2016
Revenue	723,363,000	566,317,000	859,111,000	1,062,388,000	1,341,429,000	1,420,941,000
R&D Expense	1,595,000	4,379,000	2,861,000	3,780,000	7,614,000	8,849,000
Operating Income	9,953,000	6,849,000	-21,615,000	-356,755,000	-204,541,000	-87,667,000
Operating Margin %	.01%	.01%	-.03%	-.34%	-.15%	-.06%
SGA Expense	167,980,000	154,624,000	179,012,000	223,331,000	221,145,000	217,084,000
Net Income	30,894,000	-10,318,000	-121,974,000	-725,292,000	-379,824,000	-115,649,000
Operating Cash Flow	-111,196,000	-40,806,000	-176,317,000	-281,885,000	-189,833,000	2,273,000
Capital Expenditure	6,679,000	8,230,000	3,804,000	5,473,000	14,278,000	22,450,000
EBITDA	81,049,000	56,212,000	-56,451,000	-497,128,000	-257,749,000	-77,586,000
Return on Assets %	.03%	-.02%	-.18%	-.70%	-.27%	-.07%
Return on Equity %					-1.03%	-.18%
Debt to Equity	11.61%				0.518	0.018

CONTACT INFORMATION:
Phone: 330 753-4511   Fax:
Toll-Free:
Address: 1200 E. Market St., Ste. 650, Akron, OH 44305 United States

STOCK TICKER/OTHER:
Stock Ticker: BW
Employees: 2,100
Parent Company:

Exchange: NYS
Fiscal Year Ends: 12/31

SALARIES/BONUSES:
Top Exec. Salary: $750,000   Bonus: $
Second Exec. Salary: $500,000   Bonus: $50,000

OTHER THOUGHTS:
Estimated Female Officers or Directors: 3
Hot Spot for Advancement for Women/Minorities: Y

Sales, profits and employees may be estimates. Financial information, benefits and other data can change quickly and may vary from those stated here.

Badger Meter Inc

www.badgermeter.com

NAIC Code: 334514

TYPES OF BUSINESS:
Water Meters & Meter Reading
Specialty Meters

BRANDS/DIVISIONS/AFFILIATES:
ORION
BEACON

GROWTH PLANS/SPECIAL FEATURES:
Badger Meter Inc is a manufacturer and marketer of products incorporating flow measurement, control and communication solutions. The company's products measure water, oil, chemicals and other fluids, provide and communicate timely measurement data. Badger's product lines include two categories: sales of water meters and related technologies to municipal water utilities (municipal water), and sales of meters to various industries for water and other fluids (flow instrumentation). It derives most of its revenues from the United States.

CONTACTS: Note: Officers with more than one job title may be intentionally listed here more than once.
Kenneth Bockhorst, CEO
Robert Wrocklage, CFO
Daniel Weltzien, Chief Accounting Officer
William Bergum, General Counsel
Karen Bauer, Treasurer
William Parisen, Vice President, Divisional
Sheryl Hopkins, Vice President, Divisional
Fred Begale, Vice President, Divisional
Kimberly Stoll, Vice President, Divisional
Gregory Gomez, Vice President, Divisional

FINANCIAL DATA: Note: Data for latest year may not have been available at press time.

In U.S. $	2021	2020	2019	2018	2017	2016
Revenue	505,198,000	425,544,000	424,625,000	433,732,000	402,440,000	393,761,000
R&D Expense						
Operating Income	78,723,000	65,156,000	62,148,000	56,869,000	56,595,000	52,672,000
Operating Margin %	.16%	.15%	.15%	.13%	.14%	.13%
SGA Expense	126,761,000	103,093,000	101,380,000	105,480,000	99,151,000	97,904,000
Net Income	60,884,000	49,343,000	47,177,000	27,790,000	34,571,000	32,295,000
Operating Cash Flow	87,510,000	89,578,000	80,714,000	60,350,000	49,751,000	56,185,000
Capital Expenditure	6,746,000	9,059,000	7,496,000	8,643,000	15,069,000	10,596,000
EBITDA	106,585,000	90,372,000	86,294,000	61,324,000	80,020,000	73,207,000
Return on Assets %	.12%	.11%	.12%	.07%	.09%	.09%
Return on Equity %	.16%	.14%	.15%	.10%	.13%	.13%
Debt to Equity						

CONTACT INFORMATION:
Phone: 414 355-0400 Fax:
Toll-Free: 800-876-3837
Address: 4545 W. Brown Deer Rd., Milwaukee, WI 53224 United States

STOCK TICKER/OTHER:
Stock Ticker: BMI
Employees: 1,837
Parent Company:
Exchange: NYS
Fiscal Year Ends: 12/31

SALARIES/BONUSES:
Top Exec. Salary: $640,000 Bonus: $
Second Exec. Salary: $350,000 Bonus: $

OTHER THOUGHTS:
Estimated Female Officers or Directors: 3
Hot Spot for Advancement for Women/Minorities: Y

Sales, profits and employees may be estimates. Financial information, benefits and other data can change quickly and may vary from those stated here.

Ballard Power Systems Inc

NAIC Code: 335999A

www.ballard.com

TYPES OF BUSINESS:
Fuel Cell Manufacturing
Automotive Parts Manufacturing
Carbon Products
Residential Cogeneration Fuel Cells

BRANDS/DIVISIONS/AFFILIATES:
FCgen-H2PM
FCwave
ClearGen II
FCvelocity
FCmove
FCgen
Arcola Energy

CONTACTS:
Note: Officers with more than one job title may be intentionally listed here more than once.

R. MacEwen, CEO
Paul Dobson, CFO
James Roche, Chairman of the Board
Kevin Colbow, Chief Technology Officer
Robert Campbell, Other Executive Officer
Sarabjot Sidhu, Senior VP, Divisional
Jan Laishley, Senior VP, Divisional

GROWTH PLANS/SPECIAL FEATURES:
Ballard is a world leader in proton exchange membrane fuel cell, power system development, and commercialization. The company's principal business is the design, development, manufacture, sale and service of PEM fuel cell products for a variety of applications, focusing on power product markets of heavy-duty motive (consisting of bus, truck, rail, and marine applications), material handling, and stationary power generation. Sales are concentrated in the U.S., Europe, and China.

FINANCIAL DATA:
Note: Data for latest year may not have been available at press time.

In U.S. $	2021	2020	2019	2018	2017	2016
Revenue	104,505,000	103,877,000	105,723,000	96,586,000	121,288,000	85,270,000
R&D Expense	62,162,000	35,519,000	25,259,000	27,039,000	25,022,000	19,827,000
Operating Income	-87,974,000	-41,159,000	-23,886,000	-20,536,000	-4,323,000	-16,137,000
Operating Margin %	-.84%	-.40%	-.23%	-.21%	-.04%	-.19%
SGA Expense	37,880,000	25,124,000	20,965,000	23,171,000	20,901,000	20,494,000
Net Income	-114,233,000	-51,377,000	-39,050,000	-27,323,000	-8,048,000	-21,687,000
Operating Cash Flow	-80,476,000	-42,934,000	-14,230,000	-31,688,000	-9,768,000	-3,904,000
Capital Expenditure	14,701,000	12,866,000	13,934,000	9,854,000	6,444,000	6,881,000
EBITDA	-103,567,000	-40,478,000	-26,323,000	-21,435,000	-681,000	-16,076,000
Return on Assets %	-.09%	-.08%	-.11%	-.10%	-.04%	-.13%
Return on Equity %	-.10%	-.09%	-.15%	-.14%	-.07%	-.18%
Debt to Equity	.01%	0.017	0.069	0.018	0.052	0.051

CONTACT INFORMATION:
Phone: 604 454-0900   Fax: 604 412-4747
Toll-Free:
Address: 9000 Glenlyon Pkwy., Burnaby, BC V5J 5J8 Canada

STOCK TICKER/OTHER:
Stock Ticker: BLDP
Employees: 1,367
Parent Company:

Exchange: NAS
Fiscal Year Ends: 12/31

SALARIES/BONUSES:
Top Exec. Salary: $449,302   Bonus: $434,313
Second Exec. Salary: $277,429   Bonus: $187,478

OTHER THOUGHTS:
Estimated Female Officers or Directors: 1
Hot Spot for Advancement for Women/Minorities:

Sales, profits and employees may be estimates. Financial information, benefits and other data can change quickly and may vary from those stated here.

BASF SE

NAIC Code: 325199

www.basf.com

TYPES OF BUSINESS:
Chemicals Manufacturing
Agricultural Products
Oil & Gas Production
Plastics
Coatings
Nanotechnology Research
Nutritional Products
Agricultural Biotechnology

GROWTH PLANS/SPECIAL FEATURES:
Based in Germany, BASF is the world's largest chemical company, with products spanning the full spectrum of commodities to specialties. In addition, the company is a strong player in agricultural crop protection. Given its sheer size, BASF has a top-three market position in 70% of its businesses.

BRANDS/DIVISIONS/AFFILIATES:

CONTACTS:
Note: Officers with more than one job title may be intentionally listed here more than once.

Hans-Ulrich Engel, CFO
Andreas Kreimeyer, Exec. Dir.-Research
Wayne T. Smith, Head-Chemical Eng.
Margret Suckale, Dir.-Industrial Rel.
Martin Brudermuller, Vice Chmn.-Exec. Board
Martin Brudermuller, Chmn.
Harold Schwager, Head-Procurement

FINANCIAL DATA:
Note: Data for latest year may not have been available at press time.

In U.S. $	2021	2020	2019	2018	2017	2016
Revenue	76,968,570,000	57,922,770,000	58,086,310,000	58,971,570,000	59,953,770,000	56,356,920,000
R&D Expense	2,170,060,000	2,042,755,000	2,113,262,000	1,952,662,000	1,804,793,000	1,824,378,000
Operating Income	7,594,230,000	866,652,900	4,211,835,000	5,928,494,000	7,436,568,000	6,462,195,000
Operating Margin %	.10%	.01%	.07%	.10%	.12%	.11%
SGA Expense	9,618,379,000	8,544,121,000	9,030,817,000	8,882,947,000	9,314,805,000	8,912,326,000
Net Income	5,408,502,000	-1,038,025,000	8,246,423,000	4,609,418,000	5,951,996,000	3,971,914,000
Operating Cash Flow	7,094,803,000	5,300,783,000	7,319,055,000	7,774,415,000	8,602,877,000	7,557,018,000
Capital Expenditure	3,458,778,000	3,064,132,000	3,744,724,000	3,813,273,000	3,913,158,000	4,059,069,000
EBITDA	11,488,780,000	5,745,370,000	8,190,605,000	9,455,821,000	11,522,080,000	10,364,580,000
Return on Assets %	.07%	-.01%	.10%	.06%	.08%	.06%
Return on Equity %	.15%	-.03%	.22%	.14%	.19%	.13%
Debt to Equity	.36%	0.501	0.388	0.442	0.47	0.406

CONTACT INFORMATION:
Phone: 49 621600   Fax: 49 6216042525
Toll-Free: 800-526-1072
Address: Carl-Bosch-Strasse 38, Ludwigshafen am Rhein, 67056 Germany

STOCK TICKER/OTHER:
Stock Ticker: BFFAF
Employees: 111,047
Parent Company:

Exchange: PINX
Fiscal Year Ends: 12/31

SALARIES/BONUSES:
Top Exec. Salary: $1,782,492   Bonus: $4,042,914
Second Exec. Salary: $1,185,357   Bonus: $2,689,334

OTHER THOUGHTS:
Estimated Female Officers or Directors: 2
Hot Spot for Advancement for Women/Minorities: Y

Sales, profits and employees may be estimates. Financial information, benefits and other data can change quickly and may vary from those stated here.

Beacon Power LLC

NAIC Code: 335911

www.beaconpower.com

TYPES OF BUSINESS:
Flywheel Energy Storage Systems
Energy Storage Systems
Product Design and Manufacture
Manufacturing Facility
Flywheel-Based Energy Storage Systems
Smart Energy Matrix Technology

BRANDS/DIVISIONS/AFFILIATES:
RGA Investments LLC

CONTACTS: Note: Officers with more than one job title may be intentionally listed here more than once.
Robert G. Abboud, CEO
Brian Battle, CFO

GROWTH PLANS/SPECIAL FEATURES:
Beacon Power, LLC designs, manufactures and operates flywheel-based energy storage systems for grid-scale frequency regulation services and other utility-scale energy storage applications. The firm incorporates its flywheel-based systems into company-owned frequency regulation plants that serve the electricity grid, utilities, distributed generation and renewable energy markets. The company currently operates three commercial flywheel plants ranging in capacity up to 20 megawatts (MW). Using flywheel technology, Beacon has developed a line of kinetic batteries, which provide: greater reliability; faster response time; and cleaner operation, including zero direct emissions of carbon dioxide, nitrogen oxide, sulfur dioxide and mercury. These batteries also require less maintenance than typical acid and chemical-based batteries. A flywheel battery consists of a high-density spinning disc enclosed in a vacuum-sealed compartment and rotating on magnetic bearings, allowing it to spin with virtually no friction. Beacon's system draws energy from an outside source and stores it as kinetic energy. When fluctuations in demand require extra energy, a generator converts the kinetic energy back to electricity as needed until backup power generators are activated. The company has expanded this technology into a smart energy matrix which links several energy systems together. Beacon's patented flywheel systems are modular and can be configured to meet the power capacity demands of a variety of applications, from 100 kilowatts (kW) to multi-MW systems. Beacon owns more than 40 patents focused on the design and use of its flywheel energy storage systems. The company operates as a subsidiary of RGA Investments, LLC.

FINANCIAL DATA: Note: Data for latest year may not have been available at press time.

In U.S. $	2021	2020	2019	2018	2017	2016
Revenue						
R&D Expense						
Operating Income						
Operating Margin %						
SGA Expense						
Net Income						
Operating Cash Flow						
Capital Expenditure						
EBITDA						
Return on Assets %						
Return on Equity %						
Debt to Equity						

CONTACT INFORMATION:
Phone: 978 661-2000 Fax:
Toll-Free:
Address: 65 Middlesex Rd., Tyngsboro, MA 01879 United States

STOCK TICKER/OTHER:
Stock Ticker: Subsidiary Exchange:
Employees: 73 Fiscal Year Ends: 12/31
Parent Company: RGA Investments LLC

SALARIES/BONUSES:
Top Exec. Salary: $ Bonus: $
Second Exec. Salary: $ Bonus: $

OTHER THOUGHTS:
Estimated Female Officers or Directors: 1
Hot Spot for Advancement for Women/Minorities:

Sales, profits and employees may be estimates. Financial information, benefits and other data can change quickly and may vary from those stated here.

Bechtel Group Inc

www.bechtel.com

NAIC Code: 237000

TYPES OF BUSINESS:
Heavy Construction
Civic Engineering
Procurement
Infrastructure
Defense
Chemicals
Water Solutions
Advanced Energy Solutions

BRANDS/DIVISIONS/AFFILIATES:

CONTACTS: Note: Officers with more than one job title may be intentionally listed here more than once.
Brendan Bechtel, CEO
Craig Albert, Pres.
Keith Hennessey, CFO
Justin Zaccaria, Chief Human Resources Officer
Catherine Hunt Ryan, Pres.-Manufacturing & Technology
Michael Bailey, General Counsel
Charlene Wheeless, Head-Corp. Affairs
Anette Sparks, Controller
Steve Katzman, Pres., Asia
Jose Ivo, Pres., Americas
Charlene Wheeless, Head-Sustainability Svcs.
Michael Wilkinson, Head-Risk Mgmt.
Brendan Bechtel, Chmn.
David Welch, Pres., EMEA

GROWTH PLANS/SPECIAL FEATURES:
Bechtel Group, Inc. is one of the world's largest engineering companies. The privately-owned firm offers engineering, procurement and construction management services (EPC), with a broad project portfolio including road and rail systems, airports and seaports, nuclear power plants, petrochemical facilities, mines, defense and aerospace facilities, environmental cleanup projects, telecommunication networks, pipelines and oil fields development. Bechtel has seven areas of expertise: infrastructure; defense & nuclear security; environmental cleanup; chemicals; water; energy; and mining & metals. The infrastructure segment oversees projects pertaining to wired and wireless telecommunications, power, ports, harbors, bridges, airports and airport systems, commercial and light-industrial buildings, wireless sites, railroads, rapid-transit and rail systems. The defense & nuclear security segment includes missile defense infrastructure, scientific and national security facility operations, commercial and U.S. navy nuclear reactor services and chemical weapons dematerialization projects. The environmental cleanup segment offers cleanup & remediation, waste processing & disposal and decontamination & decommissioning services. The chemicals segment helps customers that create facilities to produce finished polymers and other end-products such as ethylene, polyethylene, polypropylene, butylene, polyester and polyethylene terephthalate (PET), and polyvinyl chloride. It assists with process design packages and technology through licensors for polyethylene, polypropylene, vinyl and other products. The energy segment offers solutions in areas such as advanced fuels, carbon capture, combined/simple cycle, emissions retrofits, energy technologies, hydrogen, liquefied natural gas (LNG), nuclear power and transmission and storage. The water segment offers large-scale conveyance & tunneling, industrial water solutions, water planning for new cities and hydroelectric power & pumped storage solutions. Last, the mining & metal segment encompasses mining and metal projects across six continents, including procurement, construction, engineering and solutions for mining of coal, ferrous, industrial and nonferrous metals. In April 2022, Bechtel announced a new manufacturing and technology business for semiconductor, electric vehicle, synthetic materials and data center sectors.

FINANCIAL DATA: Note: Data for latest year may not have been available at press time.

In U.S. $	2021	2020	2019	2018	2017	2016
Revenue	19,360,000,000	17,600,000,000	21,800,000,000	25,500,000,000	25,900,000,000	32,900,000,000
R&D Expense						
Operating Income						
Operating Margin %						
SGA Expense						
Net Income						
Operating Cash Flow						
Capital Expenditure						
EBITDA						
Return on Assets %						
Return on Equity %						
Debt to Equity						

CONTACT INFORMATION:
Phone: 571-392-6300   Fax:
Toll-Free:
Address: 12011 Sunset Hills Rd, Reston, VA 20190-5918 United States

STOCK TICKER/OTHER:
Stock Ticker: Private   Exchange:
Employees: 38,000   Fiscal Year Ends: 12/31
Parent Company:

SALARIES/BONUSES:
Top Exec. Salary: $ Bonus: $
Second Exec. Salary: $ Bonus: $

OTHER THOUGHTS:
Estimated Female Officers or Directors: 4
Hot Spot for Advancement for Women/Minorities: Y

Sales, profits and employees may be estimates. Financial information, benefits and other data can change quickly and may vary from those stated here.

Berkshire Hathaway Energy Company

www.berkshirehathawayenergyco.com

NAIC Code: 221112

TYPES OF BUSINESS:
Utilities-Electricity & Natural Gas
Energy Generation and Distribution
Electricity
Natural Gas
Natural Gas Pipelines
Energy Storage
Clean Energy Development
Solar, Wind and Geothermal Power

BRANDS/DIVISIONS/AFFILIATES:
Berkshire Hathaway Inc
PacifiCorp
MidAmerican Energy Company
NV Energy Inc
Northern Powergrid
Northern Natural Gas Company
Kern River Gas Transmission Company
BHE Renewables

CONTACTS:
Note: Officers with more than one job title may be intentionally listed here more than once.

William J. Fehrman, CEO
Scott W. Thon, Pres.-Oper.
Calvin D. Haack, CFO
Maureen E. Sammon, Chief Admin. Officer
Douglas L. Anderson, General Counsel
Gregory E. Abel, Chmn.

GROWTH PLANS/SPECIAL FEATURES:

Berkshire Hathaway Energy Company generates, transmits, stores, distributes and supplies energy through its subsidiaries. The company has 11 primary subsidiaries. PacifiCorp serves roughly 2 million customers, operating in two business units: Rocky Mountain Power, which delivers electricity in Wyoming, Utah and Idaho; and Pacific Power, delivering electricity in Oregon, Washington and California. MidAmerican Energy Company generates, transmits and sells electricity, and supplies natural gas to approximately 1.6 million customers in Illinois, Nebraska, Iowa and South Dakota. NV Energy, Inc. has approximately 1.6 million customers in Nevada, serving approximately 90% of the state with electricity. Northern Powergrid offers 3.9 million users' electricity in the northeastern part of England. Northern Natural Gas Company owns a 14,600-mile interstate natural gas pipeline system extending from Texas to Michigan's upper peninsula, serving 81 utility companies. BHE GT&S is an interstate natural gas transmission and storage company based in Virginia that operates more than 5,500 miles of transmission line and 760 billion cubic feet (Bcf) of underground storage capacity in the eastern U.S. Kern River Gas Transmission Company owns 1,700 miles of interstate pipeline and delivers natural gas to Nevada, Utah and California. BHE Renewables' 4,654 megawatts total capacity of owned and under construction clean energy includes: 1,536 MW solar, 1,665 MW wind, 345 MW geothermal and 138 MW hydro. AltaLink is the largest regulated transmission company with an 81,853-square-mile (212,000 square kilometers) service area, supplying electricity to more than 85% of the population in Alberta. BHE U.S. Transmission provides transmission solutions for wholesale customers, owning more than 1,020 miles of lines. Last, HomeServices of America, Inc. is a leading U.S. residential real estate brokerage firm, with 915 sales offices throughout the country. Berkshire Hathaway Energy is a wholly owned subsidiary of Berkshire Hathaway, Inc.

Berkshire offers comprehensive employee benefits.

FINANCIAL DATA:
Note: Data for latest year may not have been available at press time.

In U.S. $	2021	2020	2019	2018	2017	2016
Revenue	25,150,000,000	20,952,000,000	19,844,000,000	19,787,000,000	18,614,000,000	17,422,000,000
R&D Expense						
Operating Income						
Operating Margin %						
SGA Expense						
Net Income	6,189,000,000	6,943,000,000	2,950,000,000	2,568,000,000	2,910,000,000	2,570,000,000
Operating Cash Flow						
Capital Expenditure						
EBITDA						
Return on Assets %						
Return on Equity %						
Debt to Equity						

CONTACT INFORMATION:
Phone: 515-242-3022   Fax:
Toll-Free:
Address: 666 Grand Ave., Des Moines, IA 50306-0657 United States

STOCK TICKER/OTHER:
Stock Ticker: Subsidiary   Exchange:
Employees: 23,600   Fiscal Year Ends: 12/31
Parent Company: Berkshire Hathaway Inc

SALARIES/BONUSES:
Top Exec. Salary: $ Bonus: $
Second Exec. Salary: $ Bonus: $

OTHER THOUGHTS:
Estimated Female Officers or Directors: 1
Hot Spot for Advancement for Women/Minorities:

Sales, profits and employees may be estimates. Financial information, benefits and other data can change quickly and may vary from those stated here.

BIOS-BIOENERGYSYSTEME GmbH

NAIC Code: 541330

www.bios-bioenergy.at

TYPES OF BUSINESS:
Biomass Plant Design & Development
Biomass Fuel Energy Processing
Research and Development
Biomass Power Production
Heat, Cold and Combined Power
Computational Fluid Dynamics
Biomass Combustion, Gasification
Software and Technologies

BRANDS/DIVISIONS/AFFILIATES:
BIOBIL 2020
DATEVAL1.0

CONTACTS:
Note: Officers with more than one job title may be intentionally listed here more than once.
Claudia Benesch, Managing Dir.

GROWTH PLANS/SPECIAL FEATURES:
BIOS-BIOENERGYSYSTEME GmbH is engaged in the research, development, design and optimization of processes and plants for heat, cold and power production via biomass fuels. The company specializes in the computational fluid dynamics (CFD) simulation of biomass combustion, gasification and pyrolysis processes regarding new technologies as well as for the optimization and refurbishment of existing plants. BIOS operates testing and laboratory facilities for its research and development activities, and works in close collaboration with national and international partners along its innovative path. BIOS partners for the planning of innovative and sustainable system solutions for heat generation, combined heat, power and cooling plants, industrial waste heat utilization, energy centers for industry and district heating networks, as well as for pellet production, biomass torrefaction and biorefinery plants based on biomass pyrolysis. Biogenic raw materials and other solid, liquid and gaseous fuels are considered. BIOS' plant monitoring services and solutions provide detailed evaluation of the performance of overall plants and of single plant components, from the start-up phase and the first year of operations through to trouble shooting. BIOS focuses on the sustainable utilization of biomass ashes and the consequent development and improvement of ash utilization processes, serving clients and customers such as municipalities and local authorities, utilities and municipal energy suppliers, heat supply companies, sawmills and wood industry, window/door/furniture industry, hotels, waste treatment/recycling/disposal companies, composting plants and other industries. BIOS' commercially-available software programs and customer-specific software include: BIOBIL 2020, offering detailed mass and energy balance calculations for combustion processes; and DATEVAL 1.0, an application for the evaluation and validation of operating data of biomass combustion and biomass combined heat and power plants. Quality management solutions and services are also provided by BIOS.

FINANCIAL DATA:
Note: Data for latest year may not have been available at press time.

In U.S. $	2021	2020	2019	2018	2017	2016
Revenue	6,386,869	6,141,220	6,100,000	6,000,000	5,700,000	5,600,000
R&D Expense						
Operating Income						
Operating Margin %						
SGA Expense						
Net Income						
Operating Cash Flow						
Capital Expenditure						
EBITDA						
Return on Assets %						
Return on Equity %						
Debt to Equity						

CONTACT INFORMATION:
Phone: 43-316-481-300 Fax: 43-316-481-300-4
Toll-Free:
Address: Hedwig-Katschinka-Straße 4, Graz, A-8020 Austria

STOCK TICKER/OTHER:
Stock Ticker: Private
Employees: 25
Parent Company:

Exchange:
Fiscal Year Ends: 12/31

SALARIES/BONUSES:
Top Exec. Salary: $ Bonus: $
Second Exec. Salary: $ Bonus: $

OTHER THOUGHTS:
Estimated Female Officers or Directors: 3
Hot Spot for Advancement for Women/Minorities: Y

Sales, profits and employees may be estimates. Financial information, benefits and other data can change quickly and may vary from those stated here.

Black & Veatch Holding Company

NAIC Code: 541330

www.bv.com

TYPES OF BUSINESS:
Heavy & Civil Engineering, Construction
Infrastructure & Energy Services
Environmental & Hydrologic Engineering
Consulting Services
IT Services
Power Plant Engineering and Construction
Asset Management
Project Development

BRANDS/DIVISIONS/AFFILIATES:
Black & Veatch Construction Inc
Overland Contracting
Atonix Digital
Diode Ventures

CONTACTS: Note: Officers with more than one job title may be intentionally listed here more than once.
Steven L. Edwards, CEO
Laszlo von Lazar, Pres.-Oper.
Kenneth L. Williams, CFO
Patty Corcoran, Chief Human Resources Officer
Irvin Bishop, Jr., CIO
James R. Lewis, Chief Admin. Officer
Timothy W. Triplett, General Counsel
Cindy Wallis-Lage, Pres., Water
O.H. Oskvig, CEO-Energy Business
William R. Van Dyke, Pres., Federal Svcs.
Steven L. Edwards, Chmn.
Hoe Wai Cheong, Sr. VP-Water-Asia Pacific
John E. Murphy, Pres., Construction & Procurement

GROWTH PLANS/SPECIAL FEATURES:

Black & Veatch Holding Company (B&V) is an employee-owned engineering, procurement, consulting and construction company, with more than 100 offices worldwide. The company specializes in the following markets: commercial, connected communities, data centers, management consulting, food and beverage, industrial and manufacturing, governments, mining, oil/gas, power utilities, telecommunications, transportation and water. B&V divides its service offerings into 10 categories. Asset management services span from single asset evaluation to enterprise optimization and efficiency, with specific services including: ISO 55000 assessment and implementation, enterprise asset management system implementation, capital prioritization and risk management. Consulting services include advanced metering infrastructure, customer engagement, operations, infrastructure investment, infrastructure transactions, utility rates and regulatory support. Engineering solutions ensures project performance in relation to power generation, power delivery, oil/gas, water supply challenges and integrated broadband/telecommunications. Master Planning, offering sustainable infrastructure solutions with data analytics for business-decision purposes about investing and optimization. Program management, providing services for reducing risk and managing large-scale capital programs or multiple-site distributed infrastructure programs. Construction services focus on power, water, telecommunications, non-union shops and more through Black & Veatch Construction, Inc. and Overland Contracting. Data analytic services includes software subsidiary Atonix Digital, which focuses on cloud-based software development, sales and delivery. Environmental services consist of integrated solutions that address current environmental needs and future environmental risks. Procurement provides proposal support, global sourcing, procurement management, preparation of request for proposal packages, evaluation, contract administration and more. Last, project development services include working directly with project developers, entrepreneurs and city and utility planners throughout the development process. Subsidiary Diode Ventures provides end-to-end asset development solutions.

FINANCIAL DATA: Note: Data for latest year may not have been available at press time.

In U.S. $	2021	2020	2019	2018	2017	2016
Revenue	3,801,451,500	3,586,275,000	3,622,500,000	3,500,000,000	3,400,000,000	3,200,000,000
R&D Expense						
Operating Income						
Operating Margin %						
SGA Expense						
Net Income						
Operating Cash Flow						
Capital Expenditure						
EBITDA						
Return on Assets %						
Return on Equity %						
Debt to Equity						

CONTACT INFORMATION:
Phone: 913-458-2000 Fax: 913-458-2934
Toll-Free:
Address: 11401 Lamar Ave., Overland Park, KS 66211 United States

STOCK TICKER/OTHER:
Stock Ticker: Private
Employees: 10,000
Parent Company:

Exchange:
Fiscal Year Ends: 12/31

SALARIES/BONUSES:
Top Exec. Salary: $ Bonus: $
Second Exec. Salary: $ Bonus: $

OTHER THOUGHTS:
Estimated Female Officers or Directors: 4
Hot Spot for Advancement for Women/Minorities: Y

Sales, profits and employees may be estimates. Financial information, benefits and other data can change quickly and may vary from those stated here.

Bloom Energy Corporation

www.bloomenergy.com

NAIC Code: 335999A

TYPES OF BUSINESS:
Fuel Cell Manufacturing

GROWTH PLANS/SPECIAL FEATURES:
Bloom Energy designs, manufactures, sells, and installs solid-oxide fuel cell systems ("Energy Servers") for on-site power generation. Bloom Energy Servers are fuel-flexible and can use natural gas, biogas, and hydrogen to create 24/7 electricity for stationary applications. In 2021, the company announced plans to leverage its technology and enter the electrolyzer market. Bloom primarily sells its systems in the United States and South Korea.

BRANDS/DIVISIONS/AFFILIATES:
Bloom Energy Server

CONTACTS:
Note: Officers with more than one job title may be intentionally listed here more than once.

KR Sridhar, CEO
Gregory Cameron, CFO
Swaminathan Venkataraman, Chief Technology Officer
Shawn Soderberg, Executive VP
Christopher White, Executive VP

FINANCIAL DATA:
Note: Data for latest year may not have been available at press time.

In U.S. $	2021	2020	2019	2018	2017	2016
Revenue	972,176,000	794,247,000	785,177,000	632,648,000	365,623,000	208,540,000
R&D Expense	103,396,000	83,577,000	104,168,000	89,135,000	51,146,000	46,848,000
Operating Income	-114,502,000	-80,785,000	-232,804,000	-165,009,000	-155,072,000	-240,983,000
Operating Margin %	-.12%	-.10%	-.30%	-.26%	-.42%	-1.16%
SGA Expense	208,687,000	163,001,000	226,223,000	181,624,000	87,615,000	90,646,000
Net Income	-164,445,000	-157,553,000	-304,414,000	-273,540,000	-276,362,000	-279,658,000
Operating Cash Flow	-60,681,000	-98,796,000	163,770,000	-91,948,000	-91,966,000	-282,826,000
Capital Expenditure	49,810,000	37,913,000	51,053,000	48,461,000	61,454,000	8,979,000
EBITDA	-69,844,000	-47,763,000	-150,013,000	-129,938,000	-115,712,000	-211,297,000
Return on Assets %	-.10%	-.11%	-.22%	-.20%	-.23%	-.23%
Return on Equity %	-9.53%					
Debt to Equity		9.792				

CONTACT INFORMATION:
Phone: 408-543-1500   Fax: 408-543-1501
Toll-Free:
Address: 4353 N. First St., San Jose, CA 95134 United States

STOCK TICKER/OTHER:
Stock Ticker: BE   Exchange: NYS
Employees: 1,719   Fiscal Year Ends: 12/31
Parent Company:

SALARIES/BONUSES:
Top Exec. Salary: $700,000   Bonus: $1,000,000
Second Exec. Salary: $600,000   Bonus: $

OTHER THOUGHTS:
Estimated Female Officers or Directors:
Hot Spot for Advancement for Women/Minorities:

Sales, profits and employees may be estimates. Financial information, benefits and other data can change quickly and may vary from those stated here.

Blueleaf Energy

NAIC Code: 334413A

www.blueleafenergy.com

TYPES OF BUSINESS:
Photovoltaic Cell Manufacturing
Solar System Development
Solar System Finance
Solar System Delivery
Solar System Operation and Maintenance
Solar System Investment
Photovoltaic Systems and Solar Plants
Wind Farms

BRANDS/DIVISIONS/AFFILIATES:
Macquarie Group Limited

CONTACTS:
Note: Officers with more than one job title may be intentionally listed here more than once.

Raghuram Natarajan, CEO
Roy Tang, CFO
Phyllis Liew, Dir.-HR
Jan Vannerum, Dir.-Investor Rel.
Marc Lohoff, Chief Sales Officer

GROWTH PLANS/SPECIAL FEATURES:

Blueleaf Energy is a downstream solar company specializing in the development, finance, delivery, operation and maintenance of high-performance solar systems for commercial and industrial applications. The company develops, builds, manages, finances and invests in utility-scale solar assets across the Asia Pacific. Blueleaf's operations and maintenance team provides operational and commercial asset management services for utility-scale solar plants (covering traditional photovoltaic (PV), PV + storage, PV hybrid, microgrid PV, floating PV) and wind farms by applying state-of-the-art processes and tools. Blueleaf offers relevant support services for a power plant, from remote monitoring and analysis, technical onsite management, predictive maintenance and commercial asset management. Additionally, Blueleaf provides 24/7 technical support throughout the region. The firm operates as a segregated subsidiary of Macquarie Group Limited, being part of its green investment division. In September 2022, a letter of intent to invest in the Philippines was signed by Macquarie through Blueleaf Energy. Blueleaf would partner with SunAsia to develop an initial portfolio of up to 1.3 GW of floating solar projects in Laguna Lake, creating over 1,000 jobs during peak construction and over 200 jobs for long-term operations.

FINANCIAL DATA:
Note: Data for latest year may not have been available at press time.

In U.S. $	2021	2020	2019	2018	2017	2016
Revenue	1,200,000,000	1,368,000,000	1,200,000,000	1,157,625,000	1,102,500,000	1,050,000,000
R&D Expense						
Operating Income						
Operating Margin %						
SGA Expense						
Net Income						
Operating Cash Flow						
Capital Expenditure						
EBITDA						
Return on Assets %						
Return on Equity %						
Debt to Equity						

CONTACT INFORMATION:
Phone: 65 9030 5770   Fax:
Toll-Free:
Address: 03 Anson Rd., Fuji Xerox Towers 07-01, Singapore, 079907 Singapore

STOCK TICKER/OTHER:
Stock Ticker: Private
Employees: 2,045
Parent Company: Macquarie Group Limited

Exchange:
Fiscal Year Ends: 12/31

SALARIES/BONUSES:
Top Exec. Salary: $ Bonus: $
Second Exec. Salary: $ Bonus: $

OTHER THOUGHTS:
Estimated Female Officers or Directors:
Hot Spot for Advancement for Women/Minorities:

Sales, profits and employees may be estimates. Financial information, benefits and other data can change quickly and may vary from those stated here.

Bonneville Power Administration

NAIC Code: 221111

www.bpa.gov

TYPES OF BUSINESS:
Hydroelectric Power Generation & Transmission
Electricity Marketing
Electricity Transmission
Electric Transmission Maintenance
Nuclear Power Marketing
Electric Service Invoicing and Forms
Electric Payments Services

BRANDS/DIVISIONS/AFFILIATES:

GROWTH PLANS/SPECIAL FEATURES:
Bonneville Power Administration (BPA) is a non-profit federal power marketing administration that markets and transmits wholesale electricity at cost along the Pacific Northwest. BPA operates and maintains more than 15,000 circuit miles of high-voltage transmission in its service territory, and engages in advancing innovative energy-saving solutions that reduce energy use and cuts costs. BPA markets wholesale electrical power from 31 federal hydroelectric projects, one non-federal nuclear plant and several small non-federal power plants. The firm serves residential, commercial, industrial, federal, agricultural and utility distribution energy sectors. BPA offers related services and solutions to commercial customers, contractors and vendors, including buying/selling products or services, submitting invoices, forms, payments and more.

BPA offers its employees health insurance, retirement benefits, life insurance and a variety of employee assistance plans and programs.

CONTACTS: Note: Officers with more than one job title may be intentionally listed here more than once.
John Hairston, CEO
Joel D. Cook, COO
Marcus Harris, CFO
Ben Berry, CIO
Randy Roach, General Counsel
Cathy Ehli, Exec. VP-Corp. Strategy
Elliot Mainzer, Deputy Administrator
Greg Delwiche, Sr. VP-Power Svcs.
Larry Bekkedahl, Sr. VP-Transmission Svcs.
John Hairston, Exec. VP-Internal Bus. Svcs.

FINANCIAL DATA: Note: Data for latest year may not have been available at press time.

In U.S. $	2021	2020	2019	2018	2017	2016
Revenue	3,823,000,000	3,683,700,000	3,655,900,000	3,710,300,000	3,596,800,000	3,432,600,000
R&D Expense						
Operating Income						
Operating Margin %						
SGA Expense						
Net Income	245,747,000	245,700,000	247,600,000	470,600,000	338,600,000	277,200,000
Operating Cash Flow						
Capital Expenditure						
EBITDA						
Return on Assets %						
Return on Equity %						
Debt to Equity						

CONTACT INFORMATION:
Phone: 503-230-3000 Fax: 503-230-5884
Toll-Free: 800-282-3713
Address: 905 NE 11th Ave., Portland, OR 97232 United States

STOCK TICKER/OTHER:
Stock Ticker: Government-Owned   Exchange:
Employees: 2,793   Fiscal Year Ends: 09/30
Parent Company:

SALARIES/BONUSES:
Top Exec. Salary: $ Bonus: $
Second Exec. Salary: $ Bonus: $

OTHER THOUGHTS:
Estimated Female Officers or Directors: 3
Hot Spot for Advancement for Women/Minorities: Y

Sales, profits and employees may be estimates. Financial information, benefits and other data can change quickly and may vary from those stated here.

BP plc
NAIC Code: 211111

www.bp.com

TYPES OF BUSINESS:
Oil & Gas Exploration & Production
Refining
Renewable & Alternative Energy
Fuel Stations
Convenience Stores
Retail

BRANDS/DIVISIONS/AFFILIATES:

GROWTH PLANS/SPECIAL FEATURES:
BP is an integrated oil and gas company that explores for, produces, and refines oil around the world. In 2021, it produced 1.1 million barrels of liquids and 6.5 billion cubic feet of natural gas per day. At end-2020, reserves stood at 7.9 billion barrels of oil equivalent, 53% of which are liquids. The company operates refineries with a capacity of 1.9 million barrels of oil per day. BP also holds a 20% ownership interest in Rosneft, which it plans to exit.

CONTACTS:
Note: Officers with more than one job title may be intentionally listed here more than once.

Bernard Looney, CEO
Murray Auchincloss, CFO
Kerry Dryburgh, Exec. VP-Human Resources
Bernard Looney, COO-Prod.
Rupert Bondy, General Counsel
Andy Hopwood, COO-Strategy & Regions, Upstream
Dev Sanyal, Chief of Staff
Katrina Landis, Exec. VP-Corp. Bus. Activities
Bob Fryer, Exec. VP-Safety & Operational Risk
Lamar McKay, Chief Exec.-Upstream
Helge Lund, Chmn.

FINANCIAL DATA:
Note: Data for latest year may not have been available at press time.

In U.S. $	2021	2020	2019	2018	2017	2016
Revenue	157,739,000,000	105,944,000,000	159,307,000,000	298,756,000,000	240,208,000,000	183,008,000,000
R&D Expense						
Operating Income	10,672,000,000	-573,000,000	16,193,000,000	16,341,000,000	7,919,000,000	-4,418,000,000
Operating Margin %	.07%	-.01%	.10%	.05%	.03%	-.02%
SGA Expense	11,931,000,000	10,397,000,000	11,057,000,000	12,179,000,000	10,508,000,000	10,495,000,000
Net Income	7,565,000,000	-20,305,000,000	4,026,000,000	9,383,000,000	3,389,000,000	115,000,000
Operating Cash Flow	23,612,000,000	12,162,000,000	25,770,000,000	22,873,000,000	18,931,000,000	10,691,000,000
Capital Expenditure	10,887,000,000	12,306,000,000	15,418,000,000	16,707,000,000	16,562,000,000	16,701,000,000
EBITDA	32,744,000,000	-6,884,000,000	29,423,000,000	34,708,000,000	24,838,000,000	13,885,000,000
Return on Assets %	.03%	-.08%		.03%		
Return on Equity %	.10%	-.29%		.09%		
Debt to Equity	.83%	0.992	0.66	0.568	0.564	0.542

CONTACT INFORMATION:
Phone: 44 2074964000   Fax: 44 2074964570
Toll-Free:
Address: 1 St. James's Sq., London, SW1Y 4PD United Kingdom

STOCK TICKER/OTHER:
Stock Ticker: BP
Employees: 64,000
Parent Company:

Exchange: NYS
Fiscal Year Ends: 12/31

SALARIES/BONUSES:
Top Exec. Salary: $1,473,898   Bonus: $2,696,019
Second Exec. Salary: $813,262   Bonus: $1,515,118

OTHER THOUGHTS:
Estimated Female Officers or Directors: 3
Hot Spot for Advancement for Women/Minorities: Y

Sales, profits and employees may be estimates. Financial information, benefits and other data can change quickly and may vary from those stated here.

BrightSource Energy Inc

www.brightsourceenergy.com

NAIC Code: 221114

TYPES OF BUSINESS:
Solar Electric Power Generation
Concentrated Solar Power (CSP)
Solar Power Plants
Solar Thermal Technology
Solar Power Generated Steam
Solar Power Projects
Solar Power Operations
Solar Power Financing Services

BRANDS/DIVISIONS/AFFILIATES:

CONTACTS: *Note: Officers with more than one job title may be intentionally listed here more than once.*
H. David Ramm, CEO
Tom Wray, VP-Bus. Dev.
Eitan Abramovitch, CFO
Israel Kroizer, Exec. VP-R&D
Israel Kroizer, Exec. VP-Eng. & Product Supply
Daniel T. Judge, General Counsel
Joseph Desmond, Sr. VP-Gov't Affairs
Ilan Glanzman, Gen. Mgr.-Product Supply
Gabriel Kaufman, VP-Receiver Dev. Mgmt.
H. David Ramm, Chmn.
Mathew Brett, Sr. VP-Int'l Dev.

GROWTH PLANS/SPECIAL FEATURES:
BrightSource Energy, Inc. is an alternative energy company engaged in financing, designing and operating solar-thermal (concentrated solar power) power plants. The company operates some of the world's largest solar power plants, with operations in the U.S., China, Europe, Israel and South Africa. BrightSource's solar thermal technology generates power by creating high-temperature steam to turn a turbine via solar energy alone. In additional to steam for electric power applications, the company offers solutions for a variety of industrial steam needs, including enhanced oil recovery, mining, manufacturing and agriculture; and integrates its technology through a hybridization process to increase output and reliability. Projects by BrightSource include: Ashalim, in partnership with General Electric and NOY Infrastructure & Energy Investment Fund to build a 121 megawatt (MW) solar thermal power station in Israel's Negev desert; Coalinga, in partnership with Chevron Technology Ventures built a 29-MW thermal solar-to-steam facility to support enhanced oil recovery efforts at Chevron's oil field in Coalinga, California; Delingha, a solar technology project in Qinghai, China, including multiple towers with thermal energy storage; Ivanpah, a solar thermal system operated by BrightSource in California's Mojave Desert, delivering power to PG&E and Southern California Edison; and Solar Energy Development Center (SEDC), a fully operational solar demonstration facility used to test equipment, materials and procedures as well as construction and operating methods, and located in the Negev Desert of Israel.

FINANCIAL DATA: *Note: Data for latest year may not have been available at press time.*

In U.S. $	2021	2020	2019	2018	2017	2016
Revenue	550,000,000	530,000,000	536,000,000	525,000,000	500,000,000	409,500,000
R&D Expense						
Operating Income						
Operating Margin %						
SGA Expense						
Net Income						
Operating Cash Flow						
Capital Expenditure						
EBITDA						
Return on Assets %						
Return on Equity %						
Debt to Equity						

CONTACT INFORMATION:
Phone: 510-550-8161   Fax: 510-550-8165
Toll-Free:
Address: 1999 Harrison St., Ste. 2150, Oakland, CA 94612 United States

STOCK TICKER/OTHER:
Stock Ticker: Private
Employees: 360
Parent Company:

Exchange:
Fiscal Year Ends:

SALARIES/BONUSES:
Top Exec. Salary: $ Bonus: $
Second Exec. Salary: $ Bonus: $

OTHER THOUGHTS:
Estimated Female Officers or Directors: 1
Hot Spot for Advancement for Women/Minorities: Y

Sales, profits and employees may be estimates. Financial information, benefits and other data can change quickly and may vary from those stated here.

British Columbia Hydro and Power Authority

www.bchydro.com

NAIC Code: 221111

TYPES OF BUSINESS:
Electric Utility
Hydroelectric Power Generation & Distribution
Thermal Power Generation
Testing, Consulting & Research Services
Wholesale Electricity
Electric Vehicle Charging Stations

BRANDS/DIVISIONS/AFFILIATES:
Powerex Corporation
Powertech Labs Inc

CONTACTS: Note: Officers with more than one job title may be intentionally listed here more than once.
Chris O'Riley, CEO/Pres.
Charlotte Mitha, Exec. VP-Oper.
David Wong, CFO
Ray Aldeguer, General Counsel
Chris O'Riley, Exec. VP-Generation
Susan Yurkovich, Exec. VP-Site C Clean Energy Project
Teresa Conway, CEO/Pres., Powerex Corp.
Greg Reimer, Exec. VP-Dist. & Transmission

GROWTH PLANS/SPECIAL FEATURES:
British Columbia Hydro and Power Authority (BC Hydro), owned by the Province of British Columbia, is one of the largest electric utilities in Canada. BC Hydro's primary business activities are the generation and distribution of electricity. The company generates 97.4% of its electricity from clean and renewable sources. It operates 30 hydroelectric facilities and two thermal generating plants, with the majority of generation coming from dams on the Peace and Columbia river systems. BC Hydro delivers electricity to customers through a network of more than 49,700 miles (80,000 kilometers) of transmission and distribution lines. Independent power products (including run-of-river hydroelectric, wind and biomass generating projects) account for more than 20% of the firm's domestic supply. BC Hydro subsidiaries include: wholly-owned Powerex Corporation, which is a leading marketer of wholesale energy products and services in western Canada and the western U.S.; and Powertech Labs, Inc., which provides testing, consulting and research services to North American electric and natural gas industries, their customers and suppliers. In September 2022, BC Hydro announced that its electric vehicle fast charging network is being designed to be fully accessible and stations retrofitted over the next three years, including 116 public chargers at 78 sites throughout British Columbia. By the end of 2025, BC Hydro plans to expand its public charging network to 325 units at 145 sites.

FINANCIAL DATA: Note: Data for latest year may not have been available at press time.

In U.S. $	2021	2020	2019	2018	2017	2016
Revenue	5,085,243,690	4,441,172,746	4,156,780,000	4,618,670,000	4,407,860,000	4,518,391,082
R&D Expense						
Operating Income						
Operating Margin %						
SGA Expense						
Net Income	545,470,480	499,445,970	-327,523,000	530,596,000	513,275,000	523,137,921
Operating Cash Flow						
Capital Expenditure						
EBITDA						
Return on Assets %						
Return on Equity %						
Debt to Equity						

CONTACT INFORMATION:
Phone: 604-224-9376 Fax:
Toll-Free: 800-224-9376
Address: 333 Dunsmuir St., Vancouver, BC V6B 5R3 Canada

SALARIES/BONUSES:
Top Exec. Salary: $ Bonus: $
Second Exec. Salary: $ Bonus: $

STOCK TICKER/OTHER:
Stock Ticker: Government-Owned Exchange:
Employees: 3,330 Fiscal Year Ends: 03/31
Parent Company:

OTHER THOUGHTS:
Estimated Female Officers or Directors: 6
Hot Spot for Advancement for Women/Minorities: Y

Brookfield Asset Management Inc

www.brookfield.com

NAIC Code: 531100

TYPES OF BUSINESS:
Real Estate and Industrial Investments
Asset Management
Hydroelectric Generation & Transmission
Paper Production
Agriculture
Financial Services
Timber Development
Wind Power Development

BRANDS/DIVISIONS/AFFILIATES:
Brookfield Renewable Energy Partners LP
Brookfield Property Partners LP
Brookfield Infrastructure Partners LP
Brookfield Business Partners LP
Oaktree Capital Management LLC

GROWTH PLANS/SPECIAL FEATURES:
Brookfield Asset Management Inc owns and manages commercial property, power, and infrastructure assets. Its investment focus includes Real Estate, Infrastructure, Renewable Power and Private Equity. Real Estate is made up of office and retail properties; Renewable power is made up of hydroelectric, wind, solar, and storage generating facilities; Infrastructure is made up of utilities, transport, energy, data infrastructure, and sustainable resource assets; and Private Equity is focused on business services, infrastructure services, and industrial operations. Brookfield has the greatest amount of assets in Real Estate and generates the most revenue through Private Equity. Located around the world, its assets are concentrated in the United States, Canada, Brazil, and Australia.

CONTACTS:
Note: Officers with more than one job title may be intentionally listed here more than once.

Craig Noble, CEO, Divisional
Samuel Pollock, Other Corporate Officer
J. Flatt, CEO
Nicholas Goodman, CFO
Frank McKenna, Chairman of the Board
Sachin Shah, Chief Investment Officer
Justin Beber, Chief Legal Officer
Lori Pearson, COO
Brian Lawson, Director
Jeffrey Blidner, Director
Cyrus Madon, Other Corporate Officer
Brian Kingston, Other Corporate Officer
Connor Teskey, Other Corporate Officer

FINANCIAL DATA:
Note: Data for latest year may not have been available at press time.

In U.S. $	2021	2020	2019	2018	2017	2016
Revenue	75,731,000,000	62,752,000,000	67,826,000,000	56,771,000,000	40,786,000,000	24,411,000,000
R&D Expense						
Operating Income	11,615,000,000	9,474,000,000	10,124,000,000	8,046,000,000	5,958,000,000	4,581,000,000
Operating Margin %	.15%	.15%	.15%	.14%	.15%	.19%
SGA Expense	116,000,000	101,000,000	98,000,000	104,000,000	95,000,000	92,000,000
Net Income	3,966,000,000	-134,000,000	2,807,000,000	3,584,000,000	1,462,000,000	1,651,000,000
Operating Cash Flow	7,874,000,000	8,341,000,000	6,328,000,000	5,159,000,000	4,005,000,000	3,083,000,000
Capital Expenditure	6,881,000,000	4,012,000,000	3,053,000,000	1,962,000,000	1,690,000,000	1,472,000,000
EBITDA	28,753,000,000	14,548,000,000	17,952,000,000	15,196,000,000	11,117,000,000	8,246,000,000
Return on Assets %	.01%	.00%	.01%	.01%	.01%	.01%
Return on Equity %	.10%	-.01%	.09%	.13%	.06%	.07%
Debt to Equity	3.39%	4.011	4.136	4.174	2.808	2.505

CONTACT INFORMATION:
Phone: 416 363-9491   Fax: 416 365-9642
Toll-Free:
Address: 181 Bay St., Brookfield Pl., Ste. 300, Toronto, ON M5J 2T3 Canada

STOCK TICKER/OTHER:
Stock Ticker: BAM
Employees: 181,000
Parent Company:

Exchange: NYS
Fiscal Year Ends: 12/31

SALARIES/BONUSES:
Top Exec. Salary: $478,740   Bonus: $1,087,506
Second Exec. Salary: $750,000   Bonus: $750,000

OTHER THOUGHTS:
Estimated Female Officers or Directors: 3
Hot Spot for Advancement for Women/Minorities: Y

Sales, profits and employees may be estimates. Financial information, benefits and other data can change quickly and may vary from those stated here.

Cabot Corporation

NAIC Code: 325180

www.cabot-corp.com

TYPES OF BUSINESS:
Chemicals Manufacturing
Specialty Chemicals
Performance Materials
Metal Oxides
Carbon Black
Composite Materials
Nanotechnology
Purification Solutions

BRANDS/DIVISIONS/AFFILIATES:

GROWTH PLANS/SPECIAL FEATURES:
Cabot Corp manufactures and sells a variety of chemicals, materials, and chemical-based products. The company organizes itself into three segments based on the product type. The reinforcement materials segment, which generates more revenue than any other segment, sells rubber-grade carbon black products used in hoses and belts in automobiles. The performance chemicals segment sells ink-jet colorants and metal oxides used in the automotive and construction industries. The purification solutions segment sells carbon-based products used to purify air, water, and food and beverages.

CONTACTS:
Note: Officers with more than one job title may be intentionally listed here more than once.

Sean Keohane, CEO
Erica McLaughlin, CFO
Susan Rataj, Chairman of the Board
Lisa Dumont, Chief Accounting Officer
Karen Kalita, General Counsel
Jeff Zhu, President, Divisional
Hobart Kalkstein, President, Divisional

FINANCIAL DATA:
Note: Data for latest year may not have been available at press time.

In U.S. $	2021	2020	2019	2018	2017	2016
Revenue	3,409,000,000	2,614,000,000	3,337,000,000	3,242,000,000	2,717,000,000	2,411,000,000
R&D Expense	56,000,000	57,000,000	60,000,000	66,000,000	57,000,000	53,000,000
Operating Income	454,000,000	151,000,000	335,000,000	398,000,000	338,000,000	247,000,000
Operating Margin %	.13%	.06%	.10%	.12%	.12%	.10%
SGA Expense	289,000,000	292,000,000	290,000,000	308,000,000	262,000,000	275,000,000
Net Income	250,000,000	-238,000,000	157,000,000	-113,000,000	248,000,000	147,000,000
Operating Cash Flow	257,000,000	377,000,000	363,000,000	298,000,000	348,000,000	392,000,000
Capital Expenditure	195,000,000	200,000,000	224,000,000	229,000,000	147,000,000	112,000,000
EBITDA	615,000,000	178,000,000	462,000,000	320,000,000	507,000,000	406,000,000
Return on Assets %	.08%	-.08%	.05%	-.03%	.08%	.05%
Return on Equity %	.30%	-.28%	.14%	-.09%	.18%	.12%
Debt to Equity	.85%	1.712	1.026	0.623	0.439	0.717

CONTACT INFORMATION:
Phone: 617-345-0100   Fax:
Toll-Free:
Address: Two Seaport Lane, Ste 1300, Boston, MA 02210 United States

SALARIES/BONUSES:
Top Exec. Salary: $1,026,250   Bonus: $
Second Exec. Salary: $518,174   Bonus: $

STOCK TICKER/OTHER:
Stock Ticker: CBT   Exchange: NYS
Employees: 4,500   Fiscal Year Ends: 09/30
Parent Company:

OTHER THOUGHTS:
Estimated Female Officers or Directors: 3
Hot Spot for Advancement for Women/Minorities: Y

Sales, profits and employees may be estimates. Financial information, benefits and other data can change quickly and may vary from those stated here.

Calpine Corporation

NAIC Code: 221112

www.calpine.com

TYPES OF BUSINESS:
Wholesale Electric Generation and Distribution
Electric Generation
Natural Gas
Geothermal Power Generation

BRANDS/DIVISIONS/AFFILIATES:
Energy Capital Partners
CPN Management LP
CPN Pipeline
Calpine Energy Solutions
Champion Energy Services

CONTACTS:
Note: Officers with more than one job title may be intentionally listed here more than once.
Thad Hill, CEO
Andrew Novotny, COO
Zamir Rauf, CFO
W. Miller, Director
Charles Gates, Executive VP, Divisional
Caleb Stephenson, Executive VP
Andrew Novotny, Executive VP
Caleb Stephenson, Executive VP
Andrew Novotny, Executive VP
Jim Wood, President, Subsidiary
Jeff Koshkin, Senior VP

GROWTH PLANS/SPECIAL FEATURES:
Calpine Corporation is a leading generator of electricity from natural gas and geothermal resources in North America. The firm operates through three divisions, including power operations, commercial operations and retail operations. Calpine's power operations include: outage services, consisting of coordination of fleet maintenance, outage scheduling, engineering and construction scheduling, equipment and related supply warehousing; engineering and construction services, providing engineering, construction and specialized technical support services to maximize the operational performance and efficiency of Calpine power plants; supply chain services, which supports plants and business units by research procurement options and identifying and qualifying vendors for a range of products and services; and CPN Pipeline, a subsidiary that supports power operations by maintaining pipeline segments that deliver natural gas to Calpine's power plants. Calpine's commercial operations division applies specialized trading and market knowledge to maximize the value of its power plant fleet. This includes long-term bilateral contracts, sport market participation decisions and forward hedging programs. The retail operations division provides retail services for powering businesses and homes. This division's Calpine Energy Solutions supplies power to commercial and industrial retail customers, as well as flexible electricity and natural gas products and services to customers in 20 states and Mexico; and Champion Energy Services provides energy services to residential customers, as well as to governmental, commercial and industrial customers. Calpine is privately owned by CPN Management LP, itself a subsidiary of Energy Capital Partners.

Calpine offers comprehensive benefits, retirement plans and various employee assistance programs.

FINANCIAL DATA:
Note: Data for latest year may not have been available at press time.

In U.S. $	2021	2020	2019	2018	2017	2016
Revenue	8,000,000,000	8,800,000,000	10,072,000,000	9,512,000,000	8,752,000,000	6,716,000,256
R&D Expense						
Operating Income						
Operating Margin %						
SGA Expense						
Net Income			7,700,000,000	10,000,000	-339,000,000	92,000,000
Operating Cash Flow						
Capital Expenditure						
EBITDA						
Return on Assets %						
Return on Equity %						
Debt to Equity						

CONTACT INFORMATION:
Phone: 713 830-2000 Fax:
Toll-Free:
Address: 717 Texas Ave., Ste. 1000, Houston, TX 77002 United States

SALARIES/BONUSES:
Top Exec. Salary: $ Bonus: $
Second Exec. Salary: $ Bonus: $

STOCK TICKER/OTHER:
Stock Ticker: Private Exchange:
Employees: 2,300 Fiscal Year Ends: 12/31
Parent Company: Energy Capital Partners

OTHER THOUGHTS:
Estimated Female Officers or Directors: 3
Hot Spot for Advancement for Women/Minorities: Y

Sales, profits and employees may be estimates. Financial information, benefits and other data can change quickly and may vary from those stated here.

Cameco Corporation

NAIC Code: 212291

www.cameco.com

TYPES OF BUSINESS:
Uranium Exploration & Production
Uranium Marketing & Fuel Services
Nuclear Power Generation

BRANDS/DIVISIONS/AFFILIATES:
Blind River
Port Hope Conversion Facility
Cameco Fuel Manufacturing

GROWTH PLANS/SPECIAL FEATURES:
Cameco is one of the world's largest uranium producers. When operating at normal production, the flagship McArthur River mine in Saskatchewan accounts for roughly 50% of output in normal market conditions. Amid years of uranium price weakness, the company has reduced production, instead purchasing from the spot market to meet contracted deliveries. In the long term, Cameco has the ability increase annual uranium production by restarting shut mines and investing in new ones. In addition to its large uranium mining business, Cameco operates uranium conversion and fabrication facilities.

The company offers comprehensive benefits, flexible spending accounts and more.

CONTACTS:
Note: Officers with more than one job title may be intentionally listed here more than once.

Timothy Gitzel, CEO
Grant Isaac, CFO
Ian Bruce, Chairman of the Board
Sean Quinn, Chief Legal Officer
Brian Reilly, COO
Alice Wong, Other Executive Officer

FINANCIAL DATA:
Note: Data for latest year may not have been available at press time.

In U.S. $	2021	2020	2019	2018	2017	2016
Revenue	1,069,813,000	1,305,602,000	1,351,189,000	1,517,092,000	1,564,376,000	1,763,510,000
R&D Expense	5,198,987	2,875,835	4,393,899	1,274,361	4,105,227	3,591,711
Operating Income	-80,653,930	-29,234,870	68,381,770	52,613,640	172,291,200	176,519,000
Operating Margin %	-.08%	-.02%	.05%	.03%	.11%	.10%
SGA Expense	92,524,270	105,418,800	90,568,130	102,668,400	118,293,600	149,885,800
Net Income	-74,399,620	-38,563,750	53,672,580	120,634,900	-148,645,500	-44,686,780
Operating Cash Flow	332,398,700	41,261,880	382,253,200	484,152,800	432,318,100	226,570,800
Capital Expenditure	71,648,540	56,183,590	54,550,920	40,154,340	82,705,100	157,324,500
EBITDA	106,816,400	164,552,900	358,802,700	336,992,700	158,362,400	226,658,600
Return on Assets %	-.01%	-.01%	.01%	.02%	-.03%	-.01%
Return on Equity %	-.02%	-.01%	.01%	.03%	-.04%	-.01%
Debt to Equity	.21%	0.201	0.20	0.199	0.308	0.284

CONTACT INFORMATION:
Phone: 306 956-6200   Fax: 306 956-6201
Toll-Free:
Address: 2121 11th St. W., Saskatoon, SK S7M 1J3 Canada

SALARIES/BONUSES:
Top Exec. Salary: $769,476   Bonus: $
Second Exec. Salary: $425,319   Bonus: $

STOCK TICKER/OTHER:
Stock Ticker: CCJ   Exchange: NYS
Employees: 1,885   Fiscal Year Ends: 12/31
Parent Company:

OTHER THOUGHTS:
Estimated Female Officers or Directors: 3
Hot Spot for Advancement for Women/Minorities: Y

Sales, profits and employees may be estimates. Financial information, benefits and other data can change quickly and may vary from those stated here.

Plunkett Research, Ltd.   169

Canadian Solar Inc
NAIC Code: 334413A   www.canadian-solar.com

TYPES OF BUSINESS:
Photovoltaic Cell Manufacturing
Custom Engineered Solar Specialty Products
Standard Solar Products
Solar Modules
Solar Ingots
Solar Wafers
Solar Cells

BRANDS/DIVISIONS/AFFILIATES:
Canadian Solar
Recurrent Energy LLC

GROWTH PLANS/SPECIAL FEATURES:
Canadian Solar Inc is a Canadian solar power company. It is an integrated provider of solar power products, services, and system solutions. The company engages in designing, developing and manufacturing solar ingots, wafers, cells, modules and other solar power products. It operates through two business segments CSI Solar and Global Energy segment. The CSI Solar segment design, develop and manufacture solar ingots, wafers, cells, modules and other solar power and battery storage products. Its Energy segment primarily comprises solar and battery storage project development and sale, O&M and asset management services for operational projects, sale of electricity, and investment in retained assets.

CONTACTS: Note: Officers with more than one job title may be intentionally listed here more than once.
Shawn Qu, CEO
Huifeng Chang, CFO
Jianyi Zhang, Chief Compliance Officer
Yan Zhuang, Director

FINANCIAL DATA: Note: Data for latest year may not have been available at press time.

In U.S. $	2021	2020	2019	2018	2017	2016
Revenue	5,277,169,000	3,476,495,000	3,200,583,000	3,744,512,000	3,390,393,000	2,853,078,000
R&D Expense	58,407,000	45,167,000	47,045,000	44,193,000	28,777,000	17,407,000
Operating Income	180,373,000	220,177,000	258,440,000	331,124,000	228,264,000	53,359,000
Operating Margin %	.03%	.06%	.08%	.09%	.07%	.02%
SGA Expense	709,000,000	448,815,000	423,109,000	410,778,000	387,030,000	349,156,000
Net Income	95,248,000	146,703,000	171,585,000	237,070,000	99,572,000	65,249,000
Operating Cash Flow	-408,254,000	-120,541,000	600,111,000	216,280,000	203,920,000	-278,073,000
Capital Expenditure	429,500,000	334,941,000	291,182,000	316,282,000	310,675,000	1,111,488,000
EBITDA	479,386,000	415,476,000	420,722,000	533,780,000	351,767,000	253,227,000
Return on Assets %	.01%	.02%	.03%	.04%	.02%	.01%
Return on Equity %	.06%	.10%	.13%	.21%	.10%	.08%
Debt to Equity	.43%	0.435	0.46	0.321	0.514	0.70

CONTACT INFORMATION:
Phone: 905 530-2334   Fax: 905 530-2001
Toll-Free:
Address: 545 Speedvale Ave. West, Kitchener, ON N1K 1E6 Canada

STOCK TICKER/OTHER:
Stock Ticker: CSIQ
Employees: 12,774
Parent Company:

Exchange: NAS
Fiscal Year Ends: 12/31

SALARIES/BONUSES:
Top Exec. Salary: $ Bonus: $
Second Exec. Salary: $ Bonus: $

OTHER THOUGHTS:
Estimated Female Officers or Directors: 1
Hot Spot for Advancement for Women/Minorities:

Sales, profits and employees may be estimates. Financial information, benefits and other data can change quickly and may vary from those stated here.

Capstone Green Energy Corporation
www.capstonegreenenergy.com

NAIC Code: 333611

TYPES OF BUSINESS:
Microturbines
Turbine & Turbine Generator Set Unit Manufacturing
Turbine Parts & Service

BRANDS/DIVISIONS/AFFILIATES:
Capstone Turbine Corporation

GROWTH PLANS/SPECIAL FEATURES:
Capstone Green Energy Corp is the producer of low-emission microturbine systems. The company develops, manufactures, markets and services microturbine technology solutions for use in stationary distributed power generation applications. Capstone Turbine's products include onboard generation for hybrid electric vehicles; conversion of oil field and biomass waste gases into electricity; combined heat, power, and chilling solutions; capacity addition; and standby power.

CONTACTS: Note: Officers with more than one job title may be intentionally listed here more than once.
Darren Jamison, CEO
Frederick Hencken, CFO
Robert Flexon, Chairman of the Board
Neshan Tavitian, Chief Accounting Officer
James Crouse, Other Executive Officer

FINANCIAL DATA: Note: Data for latest year may not have been available at press time.

In U.S. $	2021	2020	2019	2018	2017	2016
Revenue	67,636,000	68,926,000	83,412,000	82,837,000	77,169,000	
R&D Expense	2,417,000	3,649,000	3,600,000	4,040,000	5,388,000	
Operating Income	-13,953,000	-16,829,000	-15,106,000	-8,668,000	-24,250,000	
Operating Margin %	-.21%	-.24%	-.18%	-.10%	-.31%	
SGA Expense	18,391,000	22,211,000	20,958,000	19,609,000	20,651,000	
Net Income	-18,387,000	-21,898,000	-16,659,000	-10,026,000	-25,244,000	
Operating Cash Flow	1,701,000	-19,698,000	-17,703,000	-8,641,000	-18,546,000	
Capital Expenditure	3,209,000	4,207,000	3,360,000	1,752,000	204,000	
EBITDA	-11,382,000	-14,202,000	-13,888,000	-8,232,000	-23,112,000	
Return on Assets %	-.20%	-.29%	-.24%	-.17%	-.44%	
Return on Equity %	-1.41%	-1.22%	-.68%	-.43%	-1.11%	
Debt to Equity	4.37%	2.537	1.18	0.005	0.001	

CONTACT INFORMATION:
Phone: 818 734-5300   Fax: 818 734-5320
Toll-Free:
Address: 16640 Stagg St., Van Nuys, CA 91406 United States

SALARIES/BONUSES:
Top Exec. Salary: $473,331   Bonus: $
Second Exec. Salary: $239,423   Bonus: $

STOCK TICKER/OTHER:
Stock Ticker: CGRN   Exchange: NAS
Employees: 112   Fiscal Year Ends: 03/31
Parent Company:

OTHER THOUGHTS:
Estimated Female Officers or Directors: 2
Hot Spot for Advancement for Women/Minorities:

Sales, profits and employees may be estimates. Financial information, benefits and other data can change quickly and may vary from those stated here.

Cargill Incorporated

www.cargill.com

NAIC Code: 311200

TYPES OF BUSINESS:
Crop Production, Milling & Distribution
Meat Processing
Food Ingredients
Fertilizers
Steel
Money Markets & Commodity Trading
Supply Chain Solutions
Risk Management & Financial Services

BRANDS/DIVISIONS/AFFILIATES:

CONTACTS: Note: Officers with more than one job title may be intentionally listed here more than once.
David MacLennan, CEO
Brian Sikes, COO
David W. MacLennan, Pres.
Jamie Miller, CFO
Julian Chase, Chief Transformation Officer
Stephanie Lundquist, Chief Human Resources Officer
Christopher P. Mallett, Corp. VP-R&D
Jennifer Hartsock, CIO
Laura Witte, General Counsel
Thomas M. Hayes, Corp. VP-Oper.
Sarena Lin, Corp. VP-Strategy & Bus. Dev.
Michael A. Fernandez, Corp. VP-Corp. Affairs
Kimberly A. Lattu, Controller
Emery N. Koenig, Chief Risk Officer
Jayme D. Olson, Treas.
David MacLennan, Chmn.

GROWTH PLANS/SPECIAL FEATURES:
Cargill, Incorporated, established in 1865, is a leading provider and marketer of food, agricultural, financial and industrial products and services operating in 70 countries worldwide. The company operates through five business segments: food ingredients & bio-industrial, animal nutrition, protein & salt, agricultural supply chain and metals & shipping. The food ingredients & bio-industrial segment serves food and beverage manufacturers, foodservice companies and retailers with food ingredients, as well as food and non-food applications. Non-food applications encompass specialty ingredients for personal care as well as for pharmaceutical applications. Among these products are sustainable, nature-derived ingredients for a range of bio-industrial applications. The animal nutrition segment helps livestock and aquaculture farmers, feed manufacturers and distributors of all sizes to deliver better animal nutrition via innovative feed and pre-mix products and services, as well as digital modeling and formulation solutions. The protein & salt segment processes beef, poultry, value-added meats and egg products to food makers, food service companies and food retailers. This division's salt is used in food, agriculture, water softening and for deicing winter roads. The agricultural supply chain segment connects producers and users of grains and oilseeds worldwide through origination, trading, processing and distribution. This division also offers a range of farmer services and risk management solutions. Last, the metals & shipping segment offers Cargill customers physical supply and risk management solutions in global ferrous markets, including iron ore and steel. This division also provides ocean freight shipping services through its own sizable fleet, enabling customers to ship their products to global ports via Cargill. In May 2022, Cargill announced plans to build a new soybean processing facility in Pemiscot County, Missouri, operational in 2026.

FINANCIAL DATA: Note: Data for latest year may not have been available at press time.

In U.S. $	2021	2020	2019	2018	2017	2016
Revenue	134,400,000,000	114,600,000,000	113,490,000,000	114,695,000,000	109,700,000,000	109,699,000,000
R&D Expense						
Operating Income						
Operating Margin %						
SGA Expense						
Net Income		4,128,040,000	2,564,000,000	3,103,000,000	2,800,000,000	2,835,000,000
Operating Cash Flow						
Capital Expenditure						
EBITDA						
Return on Assets %						
Return on Equity %						
Debt to Equity						

CONTACT INFORMATION:
Phone: 952-742-7575 Fax: 952-742-7393
Toll-Free: 800-227-4455
Address: P.O. Box 9300, Minneapolis, MN 55440-9300 United States

SALARIES/BONUSES:
Top Exec. Salary: $ Bonus: $
Second Exec. Salary: $ Bonus: $

STOCK TICKER/OTHER:
Stock Ticker: Private Exchange:
Employees: 155,000 Fiscal Year Ends: 05/31
Parent Company:

OTHER THOUGHTS:
Estimated Female Officers or Directors: 4
Hot Spot for Advancement for Women/Minorities: Y

Sales, profits and employees may be estimates. Financial information, benefits and other data can change quickly and may vary from those stated here.

Carmanah Technologies Corporation

NAIC Code: 237130

www.carmanah.com

TYPES OF BUSINESS:
LED Lighting Manufacturer
Traffic Beacons
Traffic Signs
LED Lighting
Speedcheck Signs
Monitor Systems

BRANDS/DIVISIONS/AFFILIATES:
Vance Street Capital LLC
StreetHub

CONTACTS:
Note: Officers with more than one job title may be intentionally listed here more than once.

Geoff Wilcox, CEO
James Meekison, Chairman of the Board

GROWTH PLANS/SPECIAL FEATURES:

Carmanah Technologies Corporation manufactures compliant solar and AC-powered systems for traffic safety, with thousands of installations across North America. The company's products are grouped into five categories: crosswalk beacons and signs; school zone beacons and signs; connectivity; warning beacons and 24-hour flashers; and speedcheck signs. Crosswalk beacons and signs include rectangular rapid flashing beacons, circular flashing beacons, LED-enhanced signs and overhead lighting. School zone beacons and signs include flashing beacons, radar speed signs and LED-enhanced signs. Connectivity encompasses the StreetHub portfolio of beacons and signs that leverage cellular technology to allow authorized city personnel to remotely monitor and control all of their Carmanah transportation safety products from a single web-based platform. StreetHub enables users to set and adjust beacon schedules, collect data, manage alerts, monitor battery and lamp health, and more. Warning beacons and 24-hour flashers include 24-hour flashing beacons, LED-enhanced signs, wrong-way driver systems, advisory speed signs and emergency vehicle warning systems. Last, speedcheck signs include Your Speed radar signs, advisory speed signs and variable speed limit signs. During 2022, Carmanah was acquired by Vance Street Capital LLC, a Los Angeles-based private equity firm looking to grow its traffic and pedestrian safety intelligent transportation systems (ITS) platform.

FINANCIAL DATA:
Note: Data for latest year may not have been available at press time.

In U.S. $	2021	2020	2019	2018	2017	2016
Revenue	30,000,000	28,891,220	29,183,050	30,719,000	51,939,000	47,742,000
R&D Expense						
Operating Income						
Operating Margin %						
SGA Expense						
Net Income			895,850	943,000	11,351,000	4,228,000
Operating Cash Flow						
Capital Expenditure						
EBITDA						
Return on Assets %						
Return on Equity %						
Debt to Equity						

CONTACT INFORMATION:
Phone: 250 380-0052 Fax: 250 380-0062
Toll-Free:
Address: 250 Bay St., Victoria, BC V9A 3K5 Canada

STOCK TICKER/OTHER:
Stock Ticker: Private Exchange:
Employees: 80 Fiscal Year Ends: 12/31
Parent Company: Vance Street Capital LLC

SALARIES/BONUSES:
Top Exec. Salary: $ Bonus: $
Second Exec. Salary: $ Bonus: $

OTHER THOUGHTS:
Estimated Female Officers or Directors:
Hot Spot for Advancement for Women/Minorities:

Sales, profits and employees may be estimates. Financial information, benefits and other data can change quickly and may vary from those stated here.

Caterpillar Inc

NAIC Code: 333120

www.cat.com

TYPES OF BUSINESS:
Machinery-Earth Moving & Agricultural
Diesel and Turbine Engines
Financing
Fuel Cell Manufacturing
Rail Car Maintenance
Engine & Equipment Remanufacturing
Locomotive Manufacturing and Maintenance

BRANDS/DIVISIONS/AFFILIATES:
Cat
Caterpillar Financial Services Corporation
Caterpillar Insurance Holdings Inc

GROWTH PLANS/SPECIAL FEATURES:
Caterpillar is an iconic manufacturer of heavy equipment, power solutions, and locomotives. It is currently the world's largest manufacturer of heavy equipment with over 13% market share in 2021. The company is divided into four reportable segments: construction industries, resource industries, energy and transportation, and Caterpillar Financial Services. Its products are available through a dealer network that covers the globe with about 2,700 branches maintained by 160 dealers. Caterpillar Financial Services provides retail financing for machinery and engines to its customers, in addition to wholesale financing for dealers, which increases the likelihood of Caterpillar product sales.

Caterpillar offers its employees health coverage, 401(k), an employee assistance program and flexible spending accounts.

CONTACTS:
Note: Officers with more than one job title may be intentionally listed here more than once.

D. Umpleby, CEO
Andrew Bonfield, CFO
Gary Marvel, Chief Accounting Officer
Suzette Long, Chief Legal Officer
Cheryl Johnson, Other Executive Officer
Joseph Creed, President, Divisional
Denise Johnson, President, Divisional
Bob De Lange, President, Divisional
Anthony Fassino, President, Divisional

FINANCIAL DATA:
Note: Data for latest year may not have been available at press time.

In U.S. $	2021	2020	2019	2018	2017	2016
Revenue	50,971,000,000	41,748,000,000	53,800,000,000	54,722,000,000	45,462,000,000	38,537,000,000
R&D Expense	1,686,000,000	1,415,000,000	1,693,000,000	1,850,000,000	1,842,000,000	1,853,000,000
Operating Income	6,878,000,000	4,553,000,000	8,290,000,000	8,293,000,000	4,460,000,000	1,757,000,000
Operating Margin %	.13%	.11%	.15%	.15%	.10%	.05%
SGA Expense	5,365,000,000	4,642,000,000	5,162,000,000	5,478,000,000	4,999,000,000	4,383,000,000
Net Income	6,489,000,000	2,998,000,000	6,093,000,000	6,147,000,000	754,000,000	-67,000,000
Operating Cash Flow	7,198,000,000	6,327,000,000	6,912,000,000	6,558,000,000	5,706,000,000	5,639,000,000
Capital Expenditure	2,472,000,000	2,115,000,000	2,669,000,000	2,916,000,000	2,336,000,000	2,928,000,000
EBITDA	11,044,000,000	6,941,000,000	10,810,000,000	10,992,000,000	7,490,000,000	3,678,000,000
Return on Assets %	.08%	.04%	.08%	.08%	.01%	.00%
Return on Equity %	.41%	.20%	.43%	.44%	.06%	.00%
Debt to Equity	1.58%	1.696	1.802	1.781	1.741	1.737

CONTACT INFORMATION:
Phone: 309 675-1000   Fax: 309 675-4332
Toll-Free:
Address: 510 Lake Cook Rd., Ste. 100, Deerfield, IL 60015 United States

STOCK TICKER/OTHER:
Stock Ticker: CAT   Exchange: NYS
Employees: 107,700   Fiscal Year Ends: 12/31
Parent Company:

SALARIES/BONUSES:
Top Exec. Salary: $1,637,500   Bonus: $
Second Exec. Salary: $853,000   Bonus: $

OTHER THOUGHTS:
Estimated Female Officers or Directors: 11
Hot Spot for Advancement for Women/Minorities: Y

Sales, profits and employees may be estimates. Financial information, benefits and other data can change quickly and may vary from those stated here.

Central Electronics Limited

NAIC Code: 334413A

www.celindia.co.in

TYPES OF BUSINESS:
Photovoltaic Cell Manufacturing
Electronics Components
Railway Signaling Products
Safety Equipment
Microwave Electronics

BRANDS/DIVISIONS/AFFILIATES:
DACF-710P
DACF-720P
DACF-730P
DAC-E1/BPAC-E1
DAC-RS232

CONTACTS: *Note: Officers with more than one job title may be intentionally listed here more than once.*
Chetan Prakash Jain, CEO

GROWTH PLANS/SPECIAL FEATURES:

Central Electronics Limited (CEL) was established in 1974 by India's Ministry of Science and Technology to develop renewable energy systems and next-generation electronic equipment. The firm divides its products into four groups: solar, railway, strategic electronics, and security and surveillance. The solar group includes the manufacturing of mono-crystalline silicon solar photovoltaic cells and modules via state-of-the-art screen-printing technology, primarily supplying India and abroad with both rural and industrial applications. The railway group products include axle counter systems used in railway signaling for the safe running of trains. These include the single section digital axle counter, DACF-710P; the high availability single section digital counter, DACF-720P; the multi-section digital axle counter, DACF-730P; and interface for axle counters, DAC-E1/BPAC-E1 and DAC-RS232. The strategic electronics group products include piezoelectric ceramics and microwave electronics. Various grades of piezo-ceramic elements are manufactured for low- and high-power applications. Microwave electronics include phase shifters, which are critical elements for electronically-scanned phased array antennas, allowing the antenna beam to be steered in the desired direction without physically re-positioning the antenna. Shifter features include latching, reciprocal, low insertion loss and fast switching. CEL is one of the few companies worldwide that has pioneered the production of the ferrite phase shifters for C- and X-bands. The firm has various production facilities for meeting the bulk demand of its phase shifters. Last, CEL's security and surveillance solutions are customized per customer requirements, with expertise in integrated technology to ensure those requirements are successfully being met. Technology solutions include WiFi/wireline-based networks, GIS info mapping, smart city, command and control room, data centers, smart parking, smart security/surveillance, Internet of Things (IoT), smart logistics, smart education, remote asset tracking, access control, drone-based monitoring and more.

FINANCIAL DATA: *Note: Data for latest year may not have been available at press time.*

In U.S. $	2021	2020	2019	2018	2017	2016
Revenue	36,713,245	33,180,800	34,385,200	341,481,000	444,160,000	308,861,000
R&D Expense						
Operating Income						
Operating Margin %						
SGA Expense						
Net Income	3,170,175	415,593	242,655	33,366,600	25,921,500	16,900,700
Operating Cash Flow						
Capital Expenditure						
EBITDA						
Return on Assets %						
Return on Equity %						
Debt to Equity						

CONTACT INFORMATION:
Phone: 91-120-289-51-55   Fax: 91-120-289-51-42
Toll-Free:
Address: Saur Urja Marg, 4 Industrial Area, Sahibabad, 201010 India

STOCK TICKER/OTHER:
Stock Ticker: Private   Exchange:
Employees: 230   Fiscal Year Ends: 03/31
Parent Company:

SALARIES/BONUSES:
Top Exec. Salary: $ Bonus: $
Second Exec. Salary: $ Bonus: $

OTHER THOUGHTS:
Estimated Female Officers or Directors:
Hot Spot for Advancement for Women/Minorities:

Sales, profits and employees may be estimates. Financial information, benefits and other data can change quickly and may vary from those stated here.

Plunkett Research, Ltd. 175

Centrus Energy Corp

www.centrusenergy.com

NAIC Code: 325180

TYPES OF BUSINESS:
Uranium Enrichment
Spent Fuel Transportation & Storage Systems
Fuel Cycle Consulting Services
Centrifuge Manufacturing

BRANDS/DIVISIONS/AFFILIATES:

GROWTH PLANS/SPECIAL FEATURES:
Centrus Energy Corpis engaged in the supply of nuclear fuel and services for the nuclear power industry. It operates through the Low-Enriched Uranium (LEU) and Technical solutions segments. The LEU segment has two components which include the sale of separative work units and uranium. The Technical Solutions segment provides advanced engineering, design, and manufacturing services to government and private sector customers. The majority of the firm's revenue gets derived from the LEU segment. It has a business presence in the US and other countries, of which prime revenue is generated in the US.

CONTACTS: Note: Officers with more than one job title may be intentionally listed here more than once.
Daniel Poneman, CEO
Philip Strawbridge, CFO
Mikel Williams, Chairman of the Board
Dennis Scott, Chief Compliance Officer
John Donelson, Chief Marketing Officer
John Dorrian, Controller
Larry Cutlip, Senior VP, Divisional

FINANCIAL DATA: Note: Data for latest year may not have been available at press time.

In U.S. $	2021	2020	2019	2018	2017	2016
Revenue	298,300,000	247,200,000	209,700,000	193,000,000	218,400,000	311,300,000
R&D Expense						47,900,000
Operating Income	68,300,000	51,000,000	-19,700,000	-92,700,000	-49,300,000	-61,500,000
Operating Margin %	.23%	.21%	-.09%	-.48%	-.23%	-.20%
SGA Expense	38,100,000	38,800,000	48,300,000	66,000,000	59,400,000	46,200,000
Net Income	175,000,000	54,400,000	-16,500,000	-104,100,000	12,200,000	-67,000,000
Operating Cash Flow	50,000,000	67,100,000	11,300,000	-74,400,000	-16,100,000	37,700,000
Capital Expenditure	1,200,000	1,400,000	100,000	100,000	500,000	3,000,000
EBITDA	144,600,000	60,400,000	-6,200,000	-92,600,000	29,400,000	-34,800,000
Return on Assets %	.26%	.01%	-.05%	-.18%	.01%	-.09%
Return on Equity %						
Debt to Equity						

CONTACT INFORMATION:
Phone: 301 564-3200   Fax:
Toll-Free:
Address: 6901 Rockledge Dr., Ste. 800, Bethesda, MD 20817 United States

STOCK TICKER/OTHER:
Stock Ticker: LEU   Exchange: ASE
Employees: 266   Fiscal Year Ends: 12/31
Parent Company:

SALARIES/BONUSES:
Top Exec. Salary: $750,000   Bonus: $
Second Exec. Salary: $575,000   Bonus: $

OTHER THOUGHTS:
Estimated Female Officers or Directors: 1
Hot Spot for Advancement for Women/Minorities: Y

Sales, profits and employees may be estimates. Financial information, benefits and other data can change quickly and may vary from those stated here.

CEZ AS
NAIC Code: 221112

www.cez.cz

TYPES OF BUSINESS:
Electric Utility
Heat Generation & Distribution
Nuclear Research
Telecommunications
Energy Facility Construction & Maintenance
Raw Materials Mining
Wind Power
Solar Power

BRANDS/DIVISIONS/AFFILIATES:

GROWTH PLANS/SPECIAL FEATURES:
CEZ a.s is a Czech energy company of which the government of the Czech Republic is the majority shareholder. Its core business is the generation, distribution, trade, and sale of electricity and heat. With its subsidiaries, the company operates a portfolio of both conventional and renewable energy power plants. Total energy production is mainly split between facilities utilizing thermal and nuclear inputs. CEZ segments comprise Generation - Traditional Energy; Generation - New Energy; Distribution; Sales; Mining; and Support Services. Most of its revenue gets derived from Generation - Traditional Energy segment.

CONTACTS: Note: Officers with more than one job title may be intentionally listed here more than once.
Daniel Benes, CEO
Ladislav Stepanek, Chief Prod. Officer
Pavel Cyrani, Chief Strategy Officer
Peter Bodnar, Chief Investment Officer
Tomas Pleskac, Chief Foreign Countries Officer
Michaela Chaloupkova, Chief Purchasing Officer

FINANCIAL DATA: Note: Data for latest year may not have been available at press time.

In U.S. $	2021	2020	2019	2018	2017	2016
Revenue	9,419,863,000	8,434,392,000	8,049,282,000	7,232,989,000	7,938,344,000	8,058,377,000
R&D Expense						
Operating Income	1,897,624,000	1,311,064,000	959,781,800	861,330,400	904,572,400	1,169,689,000
Operating Margin %	.20%	.16%	.12%	.12%	.11%	.15%
SGA Expense	35,981,840	32,471,420	29,479,580	27,764,260	26,766,980	
Net Income	390,574,500	216,928,200	573,355,900	411,956,200	748,558,000	569,686,000
Operating Cash Flow	2,359,803,000	2,878,428,000	1,712,568,000	1,410,193,000	1,827,495,000	1,952,793,000
Capital Expenditure						
EBITDA	2,209,333,000	1,899,259,000	2,349,152,000	2,100,669,000	2,439,824,000	2,222,737,000
Return on Assets %	.01%	.01%	.02%	.02%	.03%	.02%
Return on Equity %	.05%	.02%	.06%	.04%	.07%	.05%
Debt to Equity	.60%	0.522	0.569	0.607	0.53	0.554

CONTACT INFORMATION:
Phone: 420 211041111   Fax: 420 211042001
Toll-Free:
Address: Duhova 2/1444, Praha 4, 140 53 Czech Republic

STOCK TICKER/OTHER:
Stock Ticker: CEZYY   Exchange: PINX
Employees: 31,704   Fiscal Year Ends: 12/31
Parent Company:

SALARIES/BONUSES:
Top Exec. Salary: $ Bonus: $
Second Exec. Salary: $ Bonus: $

OTHER THOUGHTS:
Estimated Female Officers or Directors: 1
Hot Spot for Advancement for Women/Minorities:

Sales, profits and employees may be estimates. Financial information, benefits and other data can change quickly and may vary from those stated here.

Chevron Corporation

www.chevron.com

NAIC Code: 211111

TYPES OF BUSINESS:
Oil & Gas Exploration & Production
Power Generation
Petrochemicals
Gasoline Retailing
Coal Mining
Fuel & Oil Additives
Convenience Stores
Pipelines

BRANDS/DIVISIONS/AFFILIATES:
Texaco
Chevron
Havoline
Delo
Ursa
Taro
Caltex
Chevron Phillips Chemical Company LLC

CONTACTS:
Note: Officers with more than one job title may be intentionally listed here more than once.

Pierre Breber, CFO
Michael Wirth, Chairman of the Board
David Inchausti, Chief Accounting Officer
James Johnson, Executive VP, Divisional
Mark Nelson, Executive VP, Divisional
Joseph Geagea, Executive VP
R Pate, General Counsel
Rhonda Morris, Other Executive Officer
Colin Parfitt, Vice President, Divisional

GROWTH PLANS/SPECIAL FEATURES:
Chevron is an integrated energy company with exploration, production, and refining operations worldwide. It is the second-largest oil company in the United States with production of 3.1 million of barrels of oil equivalent a day, including 7.7 million cubic feet a day of natural gas and 1.8 million of barrels of liquids a day. Production activities take place in North America, South America, Europe, Africa, Asia, and Australia. Its refineries are in the U.S. and Asia for total refining capacity of 1.8 million barrels of oil a day. Proven reserves at year-end 2021 stood at 11.3 billion barrels of oil equivalent, including 6.1 billion barrels of liquids and 30.9 trillion cubic feet of natural gas.

FINANCIAL DATA:
Note: Data for latest year may not have been available at press time.

In U.S. $	2021	2020	2019	2018	2017	2016
Revenue	155,606,000,000	94,471,000,000	139,865,000,000	158,902,000,000	134,674,000,000	110,215,000,000
R&D Expense						
Operating Income	16,180,000,000	-6,097,000,000	100,000,000	14,446,000,000	3,128,000,000	-5,471,000,000
Operating Margin %	.10%	-.06%	.00%	.09%	.02%	-.05%
SGA Expense	4,014,000,000	4,213,000,000	4,143,000,000	3,838,000,000	4,110,000,000	4,305,000,000
Net Income	15,625,000,000	-5,543,000,000	2,924,000,000	14,824,000,000	9,195,000,000	-497,000,000
Operating Cash Flow	29,187,000,000	10,577,000,000	27,314,000,000	30,618,000,000	20,338,000,000	12,690,000,000
Capital Expenditure	8,056,000,000	8,922,000,000	14,116,000,000	13,792,000,000	13,404,000,000	18,109,000,000
EBITDA	40,394,000,000	13,788,000,000	35,724,000,000	41,429,000,000	29,075,000,000	17,987,000,000
Return on Assets %	.07%	-.02%	.01%	.06%	.04%	.00%
Return on Equity %	.12%	-.04%	.02%	.10%	.06%	.00%
Debt to Equity	.22%	0.325	0.164	0.186	0.227	0.242

CONTACT INFORMATION:
Phone: 925 842-1000   Fax:
Toll-Free:
Address: 6001 Bollinger Canyon Rd., San Ramon, CA 94583 United States

STOCK TICKER/OTHER:
Stock Ticker: CVX
Employees: 42,595
Parent Company:

Exchange: NYS
Fiscal Year Ends: 12/31

SALARIES/BONUSES:
Top Exec. Salary: $1,650,000   Bonus: $
Second Exec. Salary: $1,210,000   Bonus: $

OTHER THOUGHTS:
Estimated Female Officers or Directors: 5
Hot Spot for Advancement for Women/Minorities: Y

Chevron Technology Ventures LLC

www.chevron.com/technology/technology-ventures
NAIC Code: 523910

TYPES OF BUSINESS:
Venture Capital
Power & Energy Investments
Diversified Technology Investments
Venture Capital
Hydrogen Energy Technology
Wind Farming Technology
Nanofilms
Biodiesel

BRANDS/DIVISIONS/AFFILIATES:
Chevron Corporation
Chevron Venture Capital
Future Energy Fund
Future Energy Fund II

CONTACTS:
Note: Officers with more than one job title may be intentionally listed here more than once.
Jim Gable, Pres.
John Hanten, Venture Exec.
Don Riley, Venture Exec.

GROWTH PLANS/SPECIAL FEATURES:
Chevron Technology Ventures, LLC is the branch of Chevron Corporation that invests in and commercializes new technologies through a corporate venture capital model. Chevron Tech pursues business solutions and technologies with the potential to improve Chevron's base business operations by sponsoring and demonstrating emerging technologies and championing their integration into Chevron to improve business value. The firm searches for companies in the water management, production enhancement, emerging materials, power systems, information technology and subsurface and base business industries. Some technologies may be studied, then shelved for future consideration. Through Chevron Venture Capital (Chevron VC), the company finds, sponsors and demonstrates early-stage technology and aims to champion its integration into Chevron. Chevron VC invests in companies at any phase in the development cycle and helps transfer the technology into the business. Chevron Tech's biofuels business unit develops technologies related to large-scale commercial production and distribution of non-food biofuels in the U.S. The company's first Future Energy Fund was launched in 2018 and has invested in more than 12 companies with more than 150 other investors to support innovations in areas such as carbon capture, emerging mobility and energy storage. Future Energy Fund II launched in 2021, and focuses on industrial decarbonization, emerging mobility, energy decentralization and the circular carbon economy. In January 2022, Chevron Technology led a funding round for Mobilus Labs, securing $2.7 million in funding. Mobilus Labs will use the funds to expand the deployment of its voice communications platform internationally, with a focus on the U.S. and Europe in the energy, construction, chemicals and manufacturing sectors. Other investors included Vinci BV, Ascension Ventures, Schox VC, Entrepreneur First and members of the U.K. Stanford Angels.

FINANCIAL DATA:
Note: Data for latest year may not have been available at press time.

In U.S. $	2021	2020	2019	2018	2017	2016
Revenue						
R&D Expense						
Operating Income						
Operating Margin %						
SGA Expense						
Net Income						
Operating Cash Flow						
Capital Expenditure						
EBITDA						
Return on Assets %						
Return on Equity %						
Debt to Equity						

CONTACT INFORMATION:
Phone: 713-954-6974
Fax: 713-854-6388
Toll-Free:
Address: 1500 Louisiana, Fl. 39, Houston, TX 77002 United States

STOCK TICKER/OTHER:
Stock Ticker: Subsidiary
Employees: 118
Parent Company: Chevron Corporation
Exchange:
Fiscal Year Ends: 12/31

SALARIES/BONUSES:
Top Exec. Salary: $
Second Exec. Salary: $
Bonus: $
Bonus: $

OTHER THOUGHTS:
Estimated Female Officers or Directors: 1
Hot Spot for Advancement for Women/Minorities:

Sales, profits and employees may be estimates. Financial information, benefits and other data can change quickly and may vary from those stated here.

China Longyuan Power Group Corporation Limited

www.clypg.com.cn
NAIC Code: 221115

TYPES OF BUSINESS:
Wind Electric Power Generation
Wind Power Generation
Solar Power Generation
Thermal Power Generation
Geothermal Power Generation
Biomass Power Generation
Power Equipment Manufacturing
Renewable Power Consulting Services

BRANDS/DIVISIONS/AFFILIATES:
China Guodian Corporation

GROWTH PLANS/SPECIAL FEATURES:
Longyuan is China's largest wind farm operator with installed capacity of 24 gigawatts as of the end 2021, representing 7.2% of nationwide wind capacity. It has more than 300 wind farms spread across 29 regions in China, and has also expanded into Canada and South Africa. Longyuan also owns two coal-fired power plants in Jiangsu and operates other renewable assets such as solar, geothermal, and tidal energy on a limited scale. The power generation volume mix is about 89% wind, 7% thermal, and the remainder in other renewables. China Energy Investment, which was created through the merger of China Guodian and China Shenhua Group, is the major shareholder with a controlling stake of 57%.

CONTACTS:
Note: Officers with more than one job title may be intentionally listed here more than once.
Jian Tang, Pres.
Zhongjun Li, Chmn.

FINANCIAL DATA:
Note: Data for latest year may not have been available at press time.

In U.S. $	2021	2020	2019	2018	2017	2016
Revenue	5,229,584,000	4,048,787,000	3,876,206,000	3,718,147,000	3,456,048,000	3,068,397,000
R&D Expense	19,695,760	10,818,150	8,983,614	1,194,548	462,951	
Operating Income	1,827,105,000	1,503,730,000	1,386,264,000	1,357,664,000	1,178,958,000	960,092,400
Operating Margin %	.35%	.37%	.36%	.37%	.34%	.31%
SGA Expense	18,637,450	51,445,560	50,157,500	50,761,290	34,560,280	39,804,670
Net Income	900,095,400	699,561,200	636,158,500	596,455,600	544,928,500	504,220,600
Operating Cash Flow	2,354,886,000	1,724,975,000	1,758,146,000	2,003,582,000	1,782,495,000	1,613,856,000
Capital Expenditure	2,490,036,000	2,765,595,000	1,535,931,000	1,225,642,000	1,272,582,000	1,701,523,000
EBITDA	2,810,323,000	2,484,046,000	2,450,012,000	1,836,347,000	1,646,145,000	2,014,847,000
Return on Assets %	.04%	.03%	.03%	.03%	.03%	.03%
Return on Equity %	.11%	.09%	.09%	.09%	.09%	.09%
Debt to Equity	.88%	0.908	0.924	0.975	0.915	0.82

CONTACT INFORMATION:
Phone: 86 1066579988 Fax: 86 1066091661
Toll-Free:
Address: Fl. 20, Tower C, 6-9 Fuchengmen N. St., Beijing, 100034 China

STOCK TICKER/OTHER:
Stock Ticker: CLPXY Exchange: PINX
Employees: 8,053 Fiscal Year Ends:
Parent Company: China Guodian Corporation

SALARIES/BONUSES:
Top Exec. Salary: $ Bonus: $
Second Exec. Salary: $ Bonus: $

OTHER THOUGHTS:
Estimated Female Officers or Directors:
Hot Spot for Advancement for Women/Minorities:

Sales, profits and employees may be estimates. Financial information, benefits and other data can change quickly and may vary from those stated here.

China Shenhua Energy Company Limited

NAIC Code: 212110

www.csec.com

TYPES OF BUSINESS:
Coal Mining
Coal Mining
Transportation Logistics
Coal Sales
Chemicals Production
Shipping Services
Electricity

BRANDS/DIVISIONS/AFFILIATES:
Shenhua Shendong Coal Group Co Ltd
Shenhua Baotou Energy Co Ltd
Shenhua Sales Group Co Ltd
Shenhua Baoshen Railway Group Co Ltd
Shenhua Logistics Group Co Ltd
Shenhua Information Technology Co Ltd

GROWTH PLANS/SPECIAL FEATURES:
With annual production of over 280 million metric tons and marketable coal reserves of 14.6 billion metric tons, China Shenhua is the largest coal producer in China. The company runs a balanced portfolio of assets compared with other coal producers, with integrated coal, coal-fired power generation, and coal transportation network that comprises railway, port and shipping businesses. As of 2020, the coal, power, and transportation segments accounted for 56%, 14%, and 28% of the company's gross profit, respectively. Its 53%-owned Shuohuang Line is one of the most important coal rail-transport corridors, delivering coal from western China to the coast.

CONTACTS: Note: Officers with more than one job title may be intentionally listed here more than once.
Wang Jinli, VP-Coal Prod.
Huang Qing, Sec.
Wang Pingang, Sr. VP-Power Oper.
Hao Gui, Sr. VP-Safety, Health & Environmental Mgmt.
Zhang Yuzhuo, Vice Chmn.
Xue Jilian, Sr. VP-Transportation Oper.
Xiangxi Wang, Chmn.

FINANCIAL DATA:
Note: Data for latest year may not have been available at press time.

In U.S. $	2021	2020	2019	2018	2017	2016
Revenue	47,113,980,000	32,784,680,000	33,994,520,000	37,118,910,000	34,960,790,000	25,738,160,000
R&D Expense	351,229,800	191,426,600	132,115,200	63,808,860	95,853,830	56,219,260
Operating Income	11,611,240,000	8,953,338,000	9,616,725,000	10,935,350,000	10,633,730,000	6,590,864,000
Operating Margin %	.25%	.27%	.28%	.29%	.30%	.26%
SGA Expense	306,676,100	-909,627,600	390,723,800	434,574,800	321,714,700	334,785,700
Net Income	7,065,214,000	5,505,270,000	6,078,707,000	6,165,425,000	6,329,866,000	3,192,130,000
Operating Cash Flow	13,292,340,000	11,425,020,000	8,869,430,000	12,403,090,000	13,373,440,000	11,508,500,000
Capital Expenditure	3,353,900,000	2,905,552,000	2,671,679,000	2,942,375,000	2,848,630,000	4,084,048,000
EBITDA	13,993,960,000	11,779,620,000	12,556,850,000	13,722,000,000	13,913,700,000	9,393,957,000
Return on Assets %	.09%	.07%	.08%	.08%	.08%	.04%
Return on Equity %	.14%	.11%	.13%	.14%	.15%	.08%
Debt to Equity	.14%	0.15	0.117	0.166	0.235	0.236

CONTACT INFORMATION:
Phone: 86 10-58131088   Fax: 86 10-58131804
Toll-Free:
Address: 22 W. Binhe Rd., Andingmen, Dongcheng Dist., Beijing, 100011 China

STOCK TICKER/OTHER:
Stock Ticker: CSUAY
Employees: 76,182
Parent Company:

Exchange: PINX
Fiscal Year Ends: 12/31

SALARIES/BONUSES:
Top Exec. Salary: $ Bonus: $
Second Exec. Salary: $ Bonus: $

OTHER THOUGHTS:
Estimated Female Officers or Directors: 1
Hot Spot for Advancement for Women/Minorities:

Sales, profits and employees may be estimates. Financial information, benefits and other data can change quickly and may vary from those stated here.

CK Infrastructure Holdings Limited

NAIC Code: 221112

www.cki.com.hk

TYPES OF BUSINESS:
Electric Utility
Energy Infrastructure
Transportation Infrastructure
Water Infrastructure
Waste Management
Waste-to-Energy
Household Infrastructure
Investments

BRANDS/DIVISIONS/AFFILIATES:
Shen-Shan Highway
Green Island Cement
SA Power Networks
Powercor
Wellington Electricity
UK Power Networks
Northumbrian Water
Reliance Home Comfort

GROWTH PLANS/SPECIAL FEATURES:
CK Infrastructure Holdings Ltd is a leading global utility and infrastructure investment company with a focus on regulated utility assets. It is part of the CK Hutchison group of companies, holding the bulk of the group infrastructure businesses. CKI's investments stretch across Hong Kong, the U.K., Australia, Europe, Canada, and New Zealand. The U.K. division contributes about half of total group net profit. The company also owns an infrastructure materials business in Hong Kong and mainland China, producing cement, concrete, asphalt, and aggregates.

CONTACTS:
Note: Officers with more than one job title may be intentionally listed here more than once.

Hing Lam Kam, Managing Dir.
Loi Shun Chan, CFO
Eirene Yeung, Corp. Sec.
Ivan Chan Kee Ham, Chief Planning & Investment Officer
Wendy Tong Barnes Wai Che, Chief Corp. Affairs Officer
Edmond Ip Tak Chuen, Deputy Chmn.
Canning Fok Kin Ning, Deputy Chmn.
Andrew John Hunter, Deputy Managing Dir.
Joanna Chen Tsien Hua, Head-Bus. Dev.
Victor Li Tzar Kuoi, Chmn.
Duncan Nicholas Macrae, Head-Intl Bus.

FINANCIAL DATA:
Note: Data for latest year may not have been available at press time.

In U.S. $	2021	2020	2019	2018	2017	2016
Revenue	897,873,300	914,944,100	857,744,200	910,740,100	766,402,600	677,863,700
R&D Expense						
Operating Income	308,421,000	404,221,300	390,845,000	410,973,200	246,252,700	171,854,600
Operating Margin %	.34%	.44%	.46%	.45%	.32%	.25%
SGA Expense						
Net Income	957,366,300	932,524,500	1,338,402,000	1,330,376,000	1,306,553,000	1,227,569,000
Operating Cash Flow	389,188,800	359,888,200	412,247,100	494,543,700	378,232,900	320,396,000
Capital Expenditure	46,753,620	26,243,170	55,925,990	53,887,680	33,122,450	41,020,880
EBITDA	1,138,775,000	1,181,707,000	1,588,476,000	1,577,648,000	1,513,951,000	1,397,258,000
Return on Assets %	.05%	.04%	.07%	.07%	.07%	.07%
Return on Equity %	.06%	.06%	.08%	.09%	.09%	.09%
Debt to Equity	.15%	0.221	0.216	0.235	0.204	0.065

CONTACT INFORMATION:
Phone: 852 21223133   Fax: 852 25014550
Toll-Free:
Address: Fl. 12 Cheung Kong Ctr., 2 Queen's Road Central, Hong Kong, Central 999077 Hong Kong

STOCK TICKER/OTHER:
Stock Ticker: CKISY   Exchange: PINX
Employees: 2,365   Fiscal Year Ends: 12/31
Parent Company:

SALARIES/BONUSES:
Top Exec. Salary: $ Bonus: $
Second Exec. Salary: $ Bonus: $

OTHER THOUGHTS:
Estimated Female Officers or Directors: 7
Hot Spot for Advancement for Women/Minorities: Y

Sales, profits and employees may be estimates. Financial information, benefits and other data can change quickly and may vary from those stated here.

Clean Energy Fuels Corp

NAIC Code: 454310

www.cleanenergyfuels.com

TYPES OF BUSINESS:
Automotive Natural Gas Retailing
LNG, Liquefied Natural Gas Production & Sales
CNG, Compressed Natural Gas Production & Sales
Renewable Natural Gas

BRANDS/DIVISIONS/AFFILIATES:
Clean Energy Renewables
Redeem
Clean Energy Cryogenics
NG Advantage LLC

GROWTH PLANS/SPECIAL FEATURES:
Clean Energy Fuels Corp is a natural gas marketer and retailer operating in the United States and Canada. The company supplies compressed natural gas, liquefied natural gas, and renewable natural gas as an alternative fuel for vehicles. The majority of revenue is generated within the U.S. and mostly consists of compressed natural gas. The company operates by purchasing natural gas from local utilities; compressing, cooling, or liquefying it at company-owned plants; and selling natural gas products through company-owned or customer-owned fueling stations. The company also builds, operates, and maintains natural gas fueling stations for customers. The company's target markets include heavy-duty trucking, airports, public transit, institutional energy users, and government fleets.

CONTACTS:
Note: Officers with more than one job title may be intentionally listed here more than once.

Andrew Littlefair, CEO
Robert Vreeland, CFO
Stephen Scully, Chairman of the Board
Mitchell Pratt, COO
Barclay Corbus, Senior VP, Divisional

FINANCIAL DATA:
Note: Data for latest year may not have been available at press time.

In U.S. $	2021	2020	2019	2018	2017	2016
Revenue	255,646,000	291,724,000	344,065,000	346,419,000	341,599,000	402,656,000
R&D Expense						
Operating Income	-95,048,000	-9,884,000	8,889,000	4,438,000	-66,559,000	-17,659,000
Operating Margin %	-.37%	-.03%	.03%	.01%	-.19%	-.04%
SGA Expense	89,906,000	68,516,000	73,444,000	77,207,000	95,715,000	105,503,000
Net Income	-93,146,000	-9,864,000	20,421,000	-3,790,000	-79,237,000	-12,153,000
Operating Cash Flow	41,298,000	61,041,000	12,279,000	37,982,000	-4,317,000	46,288,000
Capital Expenditure	28,905,000	13,273,000	27,088,000	25,263,000	36,307,000	23,640,000
EBITDA	-44,422,000	43,810,000	71,316,000	58,932,000	-8,940,000	76,472,000
Return on Assets %	-.11%	-.01%	.03%	-.01%	-.09%	-.01%
Return on Equity %	-.15%	-.02%	.04%	-.01%	-.18%	-.03%
Debt to Equity	.09%	0.211	0.116	0.155	0.282	0.654

CONTACT INFORMATION:
Phone: 949-437-1000 Fax: 562 493-4532
Toll-Free:
Address: 4675 MacArthur Court, Ste 800, Newport Beach, CA 92660 United States

STOCK TICKER/OTHER:
Stock Ticker: CLNE   Exchange: NAS
Employees: 465   Fiscal Year Ends: 12/31
Parent Company:

SALARIES/BONUSES:
Top Exec. Salary: $700,812   Bonus: $
Second Exec. Salary: $519,769   Bonus: $

OTHER THOUGHTS:
Estimated Female Officers or Directors: 1
Hot Spot for Advancement for Women/Minorities:

Plunkett Research, Ltd. 183

Clearway Energy Inc
NAIC Code: 221115

www.clearwayenergy.com

TYPES OF BUSINESS:
Wind Electric Power Generation
Solar Electric Power Generation

GROWTH PLANS/SPECIAL FEATURES:
Clearway Energy Inc is an electric utility company that owns, operates, and acquires contracted renewable and conventional energy generation and thermal infrastructure assets across the U.S. The company segments its operations into conventional power generation, renewables and thermal divisions. Together, these groups control a portfolio of natural gas, oil, solar, and wind-fueled power-producing facilities. most of the energy produced by the NRG Yield can be derived from its renewable assets. Almost all of the revenue generated by the company comes from selling energy and capacity under long-term, fixed-price agreements to local utilities. NRG Yield's conventional generation, renewables, and thermal business segments each contribute significantly to the firm's total income.

BRANDS/DIVISIONS/AFFILIATES:

CONTACTS: Note: Officers with more than one job title may be intentionally listed here more than once.
Christopher Sotos, CEO
Chad Plotkin, CFO
Jonathan Bram, Chairman of the Board
Kevin Malcarney, General Counsel

FINANCIAL DATA: Note: Data for latest year may not have been available at press time.

In U.S. $	2021	2020	2019	2018	2017	2016
Revenue	1,286,000,000	1,199,000,000	1,032,000,000	1,053,000,000	1,009,000,000	1,035,000,000
R&D Expense	6,000,000	5,000,000	5,000,000	3,000,000		
Operating Income	280,000,000	366,000,000	260,000,000	367,000,000	330,000,000	408,000,000
Operating Margin %	.22%	.31%	.25%	.35%	.33%	.39%
SGA Expense	40,000,000	34,000,000	29,000,000	20,000,000	19,000,000	16,000,000
Net Income	51,000,000	25,000,000	-11,000,000	48,000,000	-16,000,000	57,000,000
Operating Cash Flow	701,000,000	545,000,000	477,000,000	498,000,000	517,000,000	577,000,000
Capital Expenditure	151,000,000	124,000,000	228,000,000	83,000,000	190,000,000	20,000,000
EBITDA	904,000,000	879,000,000	772,000,000	827,000,000	759,000,000	664,000,000
Return on Assets %	.00%	.00%	.00%	.01%	.00%	.01%
Return on Equity %	.03%	.01%	-.01%	.03%	-.01%	.03%
Debt to Equity	4.09%	3.797	2.803	2.99	3.239	3.095

CONTACT INFORMATION:
Phone: 609 608-1525   Fax:
Toll-Free:
Address: 300 Carnegie Center Suite 300, Princeton, NJ 08540 United States

STOCK TICKER/OTHER:
Stock Ticker: CWEN
Employees: 301
Parent Company:

Exchange: NYS
Fiscal Year Ends: 12/31

SALARIES/BONUSES:
Top Exec. Salary: $638,260   Bonus: $
Second Exec. Salary: $396,954   Bonus: $

OTHER THOUGHTS:
Estimated Female Officers or Directors:
Hot Spot for Advancement for Women/Minorities:

Sales, profits and employees may be estimates. Financial information, benefits and other data can change quickly and may vary from those stated here.

Clipper Windpower LLC

NAIC Code: 333611

www.clipperwind.com

TYPES OF BUSINESS:
Turbine Manufacturing
Wind Project Development & Maintenance
Turbine Parts
New and Used Assembly and Repair Services
Hardware Kitting
Pitch Motor Repair
Remediation Services
Manufacturing Facilities

BRANDS/DIVISIONS/AFFILIATES:
Platinum Equity LLC
Liberty

GROWTH PLANS/SPECIAL FEATURES:
Clipper Windpower, LLC designs and manufactures wind turbine parts, and develops wind energy projects. The firm is owned by Platinum Equity, LLC. From a 330,000-square-foot facility in Iowa, Clipper specializes in new and used gearbox assembly and repair, wind turbine hub assembly and repair, matrix assembly and repair, hardware kitting and pitch motor repair. Clipper focuses on remediation and maintenance services of its already-in-use Liberty 2.5-megawatt wind turbine fleets. The company provides specialized kits comprised of various parts and hardware to make complete components for turbine builds. Clipper is headquartered in Cedar Rapids, Iowa, along with its manufacturing plant, and has customer sites in the U.S. and Mexico.

CONTACTS:
Note: Officers with more than one job title may be intentionally listed here more than once.

Robert Skeers, Dir.-Manufacturing Oper.
Matt Shaffer, Corporate Controller
Jeff Evans, Mngr.-Engineering, Quality & Compliance
Robert T. Loyd, Plant Mgr.-Cedar Rapids Mfg. Facility

FINANCIAL DATA:
Note: Data for latest year may not have been available at press time.

In U.S. $	2021	2020	2019	2018	2017	2016
Revenue						
R&D Expense						
Operating Income						
Operating Margin %						
SGA Expense						
Net Income						
Operating Cash Flow						
Capital Expenditure						
EBITDA						
Return on Assets %						
Return on Equity %						
Debt to Equity						

CONTACT INFORMATION:
Phone: 319-364-2860   Fax: 319-364-2960
Toll-Free:
Address: 4601 Bowling St. SW, Cedar Rapids, IA 52404 United States

STOCK TICKER/OTHER:
Stock Ticker: Private
Employees: 600
Parent Company: Platinum Equity LLC
Exchange:
Fiscal Year Ends: 12/31

SALARIES/BONUSES:
Top Exec. Salary: $ Bonus: $
Second Exec. Salary: $ Bonus: $

OTHER THOUGHTS:
Estimated Female Officers or Directors:
Hot Spot for Advancement for Women/Minorities:

Sales, profits and employees may be estimates. Financial information, benefits and other data can change quickly and may vary from those stated here.

Commonwealth Fusion Systems LLC

www.cfs.energy

NAIC Code: 332410

TYPES OF BUSINESS:
Nuclear Power Plant Equipment
Fusion Energy
Superconducting Magnets
Tokamak Fusion Systems
Net Energy Production
Fusion Power Plant

BRANDS/DIVISIONS/AFFILIATES:
SPARC
ARC

CONTACTS:
Note: Officers with more than one job title may be intentionally listed here more than once.

Robert Mumgaard, Pres.

GROWTH PLANS/SPECIAL FEATURES:
Commonwealth Fusion Systems, LLC (CFS) is a startup that combines science with magnet technology to create a path for commercializing fusion energy. Fusion power is a proposed form of power generation that would generate electricity by using heat from nuclear fusion reactions. In the fusion process, two lighter atomic nuclei combine to form a heavier nucleus and therefore release energy. CFS is using high-temperature superconducting magnets to build small and low-cost tokamak fusion systems along with a net energy-producing fusion machine, referred to as SPARC. SPARC will pave the way for the first commercially viable fusion power plant, referred to as ARC. CFS has assembled a team working to design and build fusion machines that will provide limitless, clean, fusion energy. CFS has raised more than $2 billion in funding since its 2018 founding. In mid-2022, CFS and the United Kingdom Atomic Energy Authority announced a collaborative agreement that comprises a five-year series of work projects for leveraging innovative fusion energy research and supporting a fast path to clean commercial fusion energy.

FINANCIAL DATA:
Note: Data for latest year may not have been available at press time.

In U.S. $	2021	2020	2019	2018	2017	2016
Revenue						
R&D Expense						
Operating Income						
Operating Margin %						
SGA Expense						
Net Income						
Operating Cash Flow						
Capital Expenditure						
EBITDA						
Return on Assets %						
Return on Equity %						
Debt to Equity						

CONTACT INFORMATION:
Phone: 610-909-5219
Fax:
Toll-Free:
Address: 148 Sidney St., Cambridge, MA 02139 United States

STOCK TICKER/OTHER:
Stock Ticker: Private
Employees:
Parent Company:
Exchange:
Fiscal Year Ends:

SALARIES/BONUSES:
Top Exec. Salary: $
Bonus: $
Second Exec. Salary: $
Bonus: $

OTHER THOUGHTS:
Estimated Female Officers or Directors:
Hot Spot for Advancement for Women/Minorities:

Sales, profits and employees may be estimates. Financial information, benefits and other data can change quickly and may vary from those stated here.

Companhia de Saneamento Basico do Estado de Sao Paulo (SABESP)

NAIC Code: 221320

www.sabesp.com.br

TYPES OF BUSINESS:
Water Treatment
Sewage Services
Wastewater Systems
Sanitation
Water Supply
Water Treatment
Advisory Services

BRANDS/DIVISIONS/AFFILIATES:

GROWTH PLANS/SPECIAL FEATURES:
Companhia De Saneamento Basico Do Estado De Sao Paulo is Brazilian water and waste management company. SABESP is one of the largest waste management companies in the world, and the state of Sao Paulo is the company's majority stakeholder. The company generates revenue through exclusive long-term agreements with municipal governments. It is not uncommon for SABESP to serve the vast majority of the market. The company operates in a single segment, which is Sanitation services.

CONTACTS:
Note: Officers with more than one job title may be intentionally listed here more than once.

Benedito Pinto Ferreira Braga, Jr., CEO
Rui de Britto Alvares Affonso, Chief Investor Rel. Officer
Manuelito Pereira Magalhaes, Jr., Corp. Mgmt. Officer
Luiz Paulo de Almeida Neto, Regional Systems Officer
Paulo Massato Yoshimoto, Metropolitan Officer
Mario Engler Pinto, Jr., Chmn.

FINANCIAL DATA:
Note: Data for latest year may not have been available at press time.

In U.S. $	2021	2020	2019	2018	2017	2016
Revenue	3,599,923,000	3,287,136,000	3,321,510,000	2,970,854,000	2,698,083,000	2,603,884,000
R&D Expense						
Operating Income	752,728,900	827,112,800	1,054,231,000	954,905,500	730,640,700	632,559,500
Operating Margin %	.21%	.25%	.32%	.32%	.27%	.24%
SGA Expense	326,892,700	300,943,600	337,878,800	283,098,800	291,837,000	262,175,200
Net Income	425,885,000	179,768,000	621,967,200	523,625,900	465,306,700	544,317,400
Operating Cash Flow	722,854,800	919,455,400	775,214,700	709,772,200	609,844,700	554,751,700
Capital Expenditure	9,286,704	7,832,407	14,435,660	9,353,933	3,494,450	394,473,500
EBITDA	1,137,421,000	760,038,200	1,314,467,000	1,072,843,000	963,077,500	1,078,591,000
Return on Assets %	.04%	.02%	.07%	.07%	.07%	.08%
Return on Equity %	.10%	.04%	.16%	.15%	.15%	.20%
Debt to Equity	.64%	0.624	0.48	0.565	0.591	0.695

CONTACT INFORMATION:
Phone: 55 1133888000 Fax: 55 1138154465
Toll-Free:
Address: 300 Rua Costa Carvalho Pinheiros, Sao Paulo, SP 05429-900 Brazil

STOCK TICKER/OTHER:
Stock Ticker: SBS
Employees: 12,515
Parent Company:

Exchange: NYS
Fiscal Year Ends: 12/31

SALARIES/BONUSES:
Top Exec. Salary: $ Bonus: $
Second Exec. Salary: $ Bonus: $

OTHER THOUGHTS:
Estimated Female Officers or Directors:
Hot Spot for Advancement for Women/Minorities: S

Sales, profits and employees may be estimates. Financial information, benefits and other data can change quickly and may vary from those stated here.

Companhia Energetica de Minas Gerais SA (CEMIG)

www.cemig.com.br
NAIC Code: 221111

TYPES OF BUSINESS:
Hydroelectric Power Generation
Electricity Generation
Natural Gas Distribution
Hydro Power Plants
Wind Farms
Photovoltaic Plant
Transmission Network
Electricity Distribution

BRANDS/DIVISIONS/AFFILIATES:
Cemig Distribuicao SA
Gasmig

GROWTH PLANS/SPECIAL FEATURES:
Energy Company of Minas Gerais is a Brazilian power company that generates, transmits, and distributes electricity. As one of the largest power companies in Brazil, the firm operates across most Brazilian states and Chile. The company has various subsidiaries and operates chiefly through its generation, transmission, distribution, and gas segments. The majority of the company's revenue is derived from electricity sales to consumers. The company generates power primarily through hydroelectric resources and secondarily through thermal and wind resources.

CONTACTS:
Note: Officers with more than one job title may be intentionally listed here more than once.

Reynaldo Passanezi Filho, CEO
Maria Celeste Morais Guimaraes, Chief Counsel
Fernando Henrique Schuffner Neto, Chief Bus. Dev. Officer
Luiz Henrique Michalick, Chief Comm. & Institutional Rel. Officer
Luiz Fernando Rolla, Chief Investor Rel. Officer
Luiz Henrique de Castro Carvalho, Chief Generation & Transmission Officer
Frederico Pacheco de Medeiros, Chief Corp. Mgmt. Officer
Ricardo Jose Charbel, Chief Energy Dist. & Commercialization Officer
Jose Carlos de Mattos, Chief Gas Div. Officer

FINANCIAL DATA:
Note: Data for latest year may not have been available at press time.

In U.S. $	2021	2020	2019	2018	2017	2016
Revenue	6,214,284,000	4,659,512,000	4,707,164,000	4,118,538,000	4,010,121,000	3,467,300,000
R&D Expense						
Operating Income	1,038,731,000	793,823,700	556,304,600	531,740,000	534,510,500	513,639,800
Operating Margin %	.17%	.17%	.12%	.13%	.13%	.15%
SGA Expense	132,242,400	134,828,100	162,532,500	172,875,500	186,727,700	193,746,200
Net Income	692,795,000	528,969,600	589,919,200	318,046,700	184,880,800	61,688,490
Operating Cash Flow	680,605,100	1,589,679,000	376,041,200	186,173,600	107,123,700	224,036,300
Capital Expenditure	43,034,190	31,952,420	185,065,500	162,163,200	206,305,520	210,738,200
EBITDA	1,380,788,000	1,114,825,000	1,264,983,000	779,232,800	756,145,800	596,937,700
Return on Assets %	.07%	.05%	.06%	.03%	.02%	.01%
Return on Equity %	.20%	.17%	.21%	.12%	.07%	.03%
Debt to Equity	.52%	0.752	0.76	0.854	0.84	0.80

CONTACT INFORMATION:
Phone: 55 3135063711 Fax:
Toll-Free:
Address: Ave. Barbacena, 1200, Belo Horizonte, MG 30190-131 Brazil

STOCK TICKER/OTHER:
Stock Ticker: CIG
Employees: 5,025
Parent Company:

Exchange: NYS
Fiscal Year Ends: 12/31

SALARIES/BONUSES:
Top Exec. Salary: $ Bonus: $
Second Exec. Salary: $ Bonus: $

OTHER THOUGHTS:
Estimated Female Officers or Directors: 2
Hot Spot for Advancement for Women/Minorities:

Sales, profits and employees may be estimates. Financial information, benefits and other data can change quickly and may vary from those stated here.

Companhia Paranaense de Energia - Copel

www.copel.com/hpcweb

NAIC Code: 221111

TYPES OF BUSINESS:
Utilities-Electric
Hydroelectric & Thermoelectric Generation
Telecommunications Services
Information Technology
Utilities-Gas

BRANDS/DIVISIONS/AFFILIATES:
Copel Geracao Y Transmissao SA
Copel Distribuicao SA
Copel Telecomunicacoes SA
Copel Comercializacao SA
Copel Renovaveis SA

GROWTH PLANS/SPECIAL FEATURES:
Companhia Paranaense De Energia Copel is primarily involved in the production of power in the Brazilian state of Parana. Specifically, the company's operating segments include power generation and transmission, gas, power distribution, power sale, and telecommunications. Most of the company's revenue is derived from the sale of electricity. It generates electricity through renewable energy sources such as hydroelectric, wind plants, and thermoelectric plants. The company was designed to allow Parana to manage the distribution of power and related services, so the state is a major shareholder.

CONTACTS:
Note: Officers with more than one job title may be intentionally listed here more than once.

Jorge Andriguetto, Jr., Chief Eng. Officer
Yara Christina Eisenbach, Chief Corp. Mgmt. Officer
Julio Jacob, Jr., Chief Legal Officer
Luiz Eduardo da Veiga Sebastiani, Chief Investor Rel. Officer
Henrique Jose Ternes Neto, Chief New Energies Officer
Jaime de Oliveira Kuhn, Chief Power Generation & Transmission Officer
Adir Hannouche, Chief Telecomm. Officer
Jonel Nazareno Iurk, Chief Environment & Corp. Citizenship Officer
Marcel Martins Malczewski, Chmn.
Vlademir Santo Daleffe, Chief Dist. Officer

FINANCIAL DATA:
Note: Data for latest year may not have been available at press time.

In U.S. $	2021	2020	2019	2018	2017	2016
Revenue	4,429,804,000	3,441,488,000	2,930,988,000	2,687,414,000	2,590,284,000	2,419,843,000
R&D Expense						
Operating Income	638,090,000	903,549,100	577,944,300	398,344,000	368,366,300	329,091,500
Operating Margin %	.14%	.26%	.20%	.15%	.14%	.14%
SGA Expense	197,410,900	169,970,300	155,859,700	132,574,500	151,941,200	177,548,900
Net Income	914,720,800	721,090,800	367,535,200	259,879,000	190,906,700	165,445,600
Operating Cash Flow	625,534,600	727,858,400	543,931,100	327,091,400	182,702,500	272,762,500
Capital Expenditure	63,292,210	43,689,860	68,816,650	224,611,500	371,562,000	408,762,500
EBITDA	1,148,406,000	1,134,403,000	707,517,900	477,662,300	408,196,100	396,999,400
Return on Assets %	.10%	.09%	.05%	.04%	.03%	.03%
Return on Equity %	.24%	.21%	.12%	.09%	.07%	.06%
Debt to Equity	.42%	0.373	0.592	0.521	0.487	0.424

CONTACT INFORMATION:
Phone: 55 4133223535 Fax: 55 4133314376
Toll-Free:
Address: Rua Jose Izidoro Biazetto, 158, Mossungue, PR 81200-240 Brazil

STOCK TICKER/OTHER:
Stock Ticker: ELP
Employees: 6,538
Parent Company:

Exchange: NYS
Fiscal Year Ends: 12/31

SALARIES/BONUSES:
Top Exec. Salary: $ Bonus: $
Second Exec. Salary: $ Bonus: $

OTHER THOUGHTS:
Estimated Female Officers or Directors: 2
Hot Spot for Advancement for Women/Minorities:

Contemporary Amperex Technology Co Limited (CATL)

www.catl.com/en/
NAIC Code: 335912

TYPES OF BUSINESS:
Lithium Batteries, Primary, Manufacturing
Electric Vehicle Batteries
Energy Storage Batteries
Technology
Research and Development

BRANDS/DIVISIONS/AFFILIATES:
Contemporary Amperex Technology (USA) Inc
Contemporary Amperex Technology Canada Limited
Contemporary Amperex Technology France
Contemporary Amperex Technology GmbH
United Auto Battery Co
Guangdong Brunp Recycling Technology Limited
CATL Xiamen Institute of New Energy

CONTACTS: Note: Officers with more than one job title may be intentionally listed here more than once.
Yuqun Zeng, Chmn.

GROWTH PLANS/SPECIAL FEATURES:
Contemporary Amperex Technology Co., Limited (CATL) is a Chinese battery products manufacturing giant engaged in related research and technology development. CATL's technologies cover the full industry chains of vehicle and energy storage batteries, including materials, batter cells, modules, battery management systems, battery recycling and reuse. The firm's business focuses on research and development (R&D), production and sales of electric vehicle and energy storage battery systems. CATL's lithium-ion battery can be applied to electric passenger vehicles, buses, trucks and diversified special vehicles. Battery and storage systems include cells, modules, electric boxes and battery cabinets, all of which provide the flow and/or storage of new energy. The company has manufacturing facilities, branch offices and R&D centers located in China and Germany, and branch offices in China, Canada, the U.S., the U.K., Germany, Hong Kong and Japan. Subsidiaries include: Contemporary Amperex Technology (USA), Inc.; Contemporary Amperex Technology Canada Limited; Contemporary Amperex Technology France; Contemporary Amperex Technology GmbH; United Auto Battery Co.; and Guangdong Brunp Recycling Technology Limited, among others. In addition, CATL Xiamen Institute of New Energy, co-established with Xiamen University, plans and organizes sci-tech industrial projects in key areas such as intelligent energy, energy storage technologies, high-power devices and next-generation power batteries.

FINANCIAL DATA: Note: Data for latest year may not have been available at press time.

In U.S. $	2021	2020	2019	2018	2017	2016
Revenue	17,920,623,000	7,709,190,000	6,552,410,000	4,305,100,000	3,070,450,000	
R&D Expense						
Operating Income						
Operating Margin %						
SGA Expense						
Net Income	2,198,318,690	7,709,190,000	717,329,000	611,327,000	643,984,000	
Operating Cash Flow						
Capital Expenditure						
EBITDA						
Return on Assets %						
Return on Equity %						
Debt to Equity						

CONTACT INFORMATION:
Phone: 86-593-2583668 Fax: 86-593-2583667
Toll-Free:
Address: No. 2 Xingang Rd., Zhangman Twon, Jiaocheng Dist., Ningde, Fujian 352100 China

STOCK TICKER/OTHER:
Stock Ticker: 300750   Exchange: Shenzhen
Employees: 33,000   Fiscal Year Ends: 12/31
Parent Company:

SALARIES/BONUSES:
Top Exec. Salary: $ Bonus: $
Second Exec. Salary: $ Bonus: $

OTHER THOUGHTS:
Estimated Female Officers or Directors:
Hot Spot for Advancement for Women/Minorities:

Sales, profits and employees may be estimates. Financial information, benefits and other data can change quickly and may vary from those stated here.

Cory Group (Cory Topco Limited)

NAIC Code: 562920

www.coryenergy.com

TYPES OF BUSINESS:
Waste Management
Recycling
Landfills & Transfer Stations
Street Cleaning
Electric Generation-Landfill Gas
Resource Management
Energy Recovery Services

BRANDS/DIVISIONS/AFFILIATES:
Cory Environmental Holdings Ltd
Cory Riverside (Holdings) Ltd
Riverside Resource Recovery Ltd
Riverside (Thames) Ltd
Cory Environmental Ltd
Cory Ship Repair Services Ltd
Riverside Energy Park Ltd

CONTACTS: *Note: Officers with more than one job title may be intentionally listed here more than once.*
Dougie Sutherland, CEO
Ben Butler, CFO
Bernard Kauhold, Dir.-Dev.
Richard Milnes-James, Group Dir.-Finance
Andy Pike, Dir.-Riverside Resource Recovery
Alistair Holl, Dir.-Resource Mgmt.
Chris Jones, Dir.-Risk Mgmt. & Compliance
John Barry, Chmn.
Jon Steggles, Dir.-Resource Logistics

GROWTH PLANS/SPECIAL FEATURES:

Cory Topco Limited and its subsidiaries, operating as Cory Group, are engaged in resource management, recycling and energy recovery. The firm operates the largest energy-from-waste facility in the U.K., with up to 785,000 tons of London's waste turned into electricity and recycling product annually. Approximately 160,000 households are supplied with energy generated by Cory Riverside. Up to 200,000 tons of ash is recycled as construction aggregate, and up to 10,000 tons of air pollution control residue is recycled to create building blocks for use in construction. Nearly 150,000 tons of carbon is saved by not sending waste to landfills. The group's energy-from-waste process works like this: waste is tipped into one of the tipping bays, the bays open into a waste bunker, overhead waste cranes mix the waste to ensure it maintains a similar heating value, the waste travels down chutes and onto a horizontal feeder table where ram feeders push the waste onto a stoker grate, the stoker grates tumbles the waste down the burning waste bed and dries the waste, secondary swirling air mixes the gases off the burning waste back into the waste, ammonia is injected into the flue gas to reduce nitrogen oxide levels, heat from the flue gases boils the water to create steam, the steam drives the turbine that drives the generator and produces electricity. Any resulting burned-out product (ash) falls into a quench bath and is then loaded onto trucks for recycling and re-use. Subsidiaries within Cory Group include Cory Environmental Holdings Ltd., Cory Riverside (Holdings) Ltd., Riverside Resource Recovery Ltd., Riverside (Thames) Ltd., Cory Environmental Ltd., Cory Ship Repair Services Ltd. and Riverside Energy Park Ltd. Cory Riverside is privately-owned by a consortium of infrastructure investors.

FINANCIAL DATA: *Note: Data for latest year may not have been available at press time.*

In U.S. $	2021	2020	2019	2018	2017	2016
Revenue	161,924,210	174,300,000	151,388,000	150,000,000	143,315,550	136,491,000
R&D Expense						
Operating Income						
Operating Margin %						
SGA Expense						
Net Income	-198,645,000	-37,949,700	19,018,300			
Operating Cash Flow						
Capital Expenditure						
EBITDA						
Return on Assets %						
Return on Equity %						
Debt to Equity						

CONTACT INFORMATION:
Phone: 020-7417-5200 Fax: 0844-854-1001
Toll-Free:
Address: 10 Dominion St., Fl. 5, London, EC2M 2EF United Kingdom

SALARIES/BONUSES:
Top Exec. Salary: $ Bonus: $
Second Exec. Salary: $ Bonus: $

STOCK TICKER/OTHER:
Stock Ticker: Private Exchange:
Employees: 314 Fiscal Year Ends: 12/31
Parent Company:

OTHER THOUGHTS:
Estimated Female Officers or Directors:
Hot Spot for Advancement for Women/Minorities:

Sales, profits and employees may be estimates. Financial information, benefits and other data can change quickly and may vary from those stated here.

Cosan SA

NAIC Code: 325193

www.cosan.com.br

TYPES OF BUSINESS:
Sugar & Ethanol Production
Gas Stations
Sugar & Ethanol Export
Natural Gas Distribution
Agricultural Development
Lubricants

BRANDS/DIVISIONS/AFFILIATES:
Cosan SA
Cosan Logistica SA
Raizen Combustiveis SA
Raizen Energia SA
Companhia de Gas de Sao Paulo (Comgas)
Moove
Rumo SA

GROWTH PLANS/SPECIAL FEATURES:
Cosan Limited invests in strategic business industries including agribusiness, fuel and natural gas distribution, lubricants and logistics. The company's direct subsidiaries are Cosan SA and Cosan Logistica SA, each of which operate through their respective subsidiaries and jointly-controlled entities, including: Raizen Combustiveis SA, a leading fuel distributor in Brazil, managing a fuel distribution network of approximately 7,300 Shell branded service stations; Raizen Energia SA, a producer of sugarcane ethanol in Brazil, and the world's largest individual exporter of cane sugar; Companhia de Gas de Sao Paulo (known as Comgas), currently Brazil's largest natural gas distributor and present in more than 175 cities throughout the state of Sao Paulo; Moove, which produces and distributes Mobil branded lubricant and base oil products and Comma branded lubricant products, globally; and Rumo SA, a rail-based logistics operator in Latin America, offering a full range of rail transport, port lifting and warehousing logistics services.

CONTACTS: Note: Officers with more than one job title may be intentionally listed here more than once.
Luis Henrique Cals de Beauclair Guimaraes, CEO
Marcelo Eduardo Martins, CFO
Marcos Marinho Lutz, Chief Commercial Officer
Marcelo E. Martins, Investor Rel. Officer
Rubens Ometto Silveira Mello, Chmn.

FINANCIAL DATA: Note: Data for latest year may not have been available at press time.

In U.S. $	2021	2020	2019	2018	2017	2016
Revenue	4,777,164,000	3,774,788,000	3,806,846,000	1,900,511,000	1,416,762,000	1,392,940,000
R&D Expense						
Operating Income	737,311,600	594,369,000	778,882,000	216,844,600	184,680,000	249,687,500
Operating Margin %	.15%	.16%	.20%	.11%	.13%	.18%
SGA Expense	424,020,800	415,885,000	351,324,400	301,447,300	302,393,100	296,133,900
Net Income	1,165,827,000	158,742,900	243,123,000	305,177,200	242,935,200	191,360,800
Operating Cash Flow	950,666,000	1,044,809,000	1,162,983,000	497,536,900	331,143,300	412,839,700
Capital Expenditure	881,894,000	745,191,000	510,303,600	116,646,700	75,446,310	90,737,300
EBITDA	2,414,890,000	1,354,051,000	1,603,151,000	717,193,200	662,970,600	628,702,300
Return on Assets %	.07%	.01%	.04%	.06%	.05%	.04%
Return on Equity %	.63%	.11%	.13%	.17%	.14%	.12%
Debt to Equity	3.00%	7.565	1.046	0.886	0.854	0.915

CONTACT INFORMATION:
Phone: 55 1138979797 Fax:
Toll-Free:
Address: Av. Faria Lima, 4100, 16/Fl, Sau Paulo, SP 04543-011 Brazil

STOCK TICKER/OTHER:
Stock Ticker: CSAN
Employees: 10,581
Parent Company:

Exchange: NYS
Fiscal Year Ends: 03/31

SALARIES/BONUSES:
Top Exec. Salary: $ Bonus: $
Second Exec. Salary: $ Bonus: $

OTHER THOUGHTS:
Estimated Female Officers or Directors:
Hot Spot for Advancement for Women/Minorities:

Sales, profits and employees may be estimates. Financial information, benefits and other data can change quickly and may vary from those stated here.

Covanta Holding Corporation

NAIC Code: 562213

www.covanta.com

TYPES OF BUSINESS:
Solid Waste Combustors and Incinerators
Waste-to-Energy Services
Recycling Services
Composting
Product Destruction Services
Transportation and Logistics Services

BRANDS/DIVISIONS/AFFILIATES:
EQT AB Group
EQT Infrastructure V Fund
Miller Environmental Transfer
Biologic Environmental Services and Waste

CONTACTS: Note: Officers with more than one job title may be intentionally listed here more than once.
Azeez Mohammed, CEO
Adel Omrani, Exec. VP-Oper, Safety & Engineering
Gregg Kam, CFO
Derek W. Veenhof, CCO
Ginny Angilello, Chief Human Resources Officer
Gagan Sood, CTO
Derek Veenhof, Executive VP, Divisional
Michael de Castro, Executive VP, Divisional
Matthew Mulcahy, Executive VP
Virginia Angilello, Other Executive Officer
Paul Stauder, President, Subsidiary
Timothy Simpson, Secretary
Howard Lance, Chmn.

GROWTH PLANS/SPECIAL FEATURES:

Covanta Holding Corporation is a leader in sustainable materials management, providing environmental solutions to businesses and communities throughout North America. Covanta's waste-to-energy services can be customized to meet specific needs. The company diverts waste from being disposed in landfills by reusing and repurposing materials, recycling and composting, and recovering energy from the materials that remain after these processes. Services include renewable waste-to-energy, secure product destruction, liquid waste management, pharmaceutical and medical waste, metals recycling, plastic and packaged goods recycling, electronic waste recycling, universal waste recycling, on-site services, advisory services, field and industrial services, transportation services and logistics services. Industries served span agriculture, chemical manufacturing, energy/utilities, engineering, construction, government, healthcare, manufacturing, municipalities, pharmaceutical, biotechnology, retail, consumer brands and transportation. Covanta operates as a subsidiary of EQT Infrastructure V Fund, the infrastructure arm of EQT AB Group. During 2022, Covanta acquired Miller Environmental Transfer (MET), a provider of environmental services across the south-central U.S. specializing in a variety of waste services; and acquired Biologic Environmental Services and Waste Solutions, and environmental management firm offering comprehensive waste management services.

Covanta offers its employees comprehensive health benefits, retirement plans, flexible savings and health accounts and other plans and programs.

FINANCIAL DATA: Note: Data for latest year may not have been available at press time.

In U.S. $	2021	2020	2019	2018	2017	2016
Revenue	2,000,000,000	1,904,000,000	1,870,000,000	1,868,000,000	1,752,000,000	1,699,000,064
R&D Expense						
Operating Income						
Operating Margin %						
SGA Expense						
Net Income		-28,000,000	10,000,000	152,000,000	57,000,000	-4,000,000
Operating Cash Flow						
Capital Expenditure						
EBITDA						
Return on Assets %						
Return on Equity %						
Debt to Equity						

CONTACT INFORMATION:
Phone: 862-345-5000   Fax:
Toll-Free:
Address: 445 South St., Fl. 4, Morristown, NJ 07960 United States

STOCK TICKER/OTHER:
Stock Ticker: Subsidiary   Exchange:
Employees: 4,000   Fiscal Year Ends: 12/31
Parent Company: EQT AB Group

SALARIES/BONUSES:
Top Exec. Salary: $ Bonus: $
Second Exec. Salary: $ Bonus: $

OTHER THOUGHTS:
Estimated Female Officers or Directors:
Hot Spot for Advancement for Women/Minorities:

Sales, profits and employees may be estimates. Financial information, benefits and other data can change quickly and may vary from those stated here.

CSUN Solar Tech Co Ltd

NAIC Code: 334413A

www.csunsolartech.com

TYPES OF BUSINESS:
Photovoltaic Cell Manufacturing
Photovoltaic Materials
Solar Panels
Solar Modules
Solar Storage Systems
Manufacturing Facilities
Research and Development

BRANDS/DIVISIONS/AFFILIATES:
China Electric Equipment Group Co Ltd (CEEG)

GROWTH PLANS/SPECIAL FEATURES:
CSUN Solar Tech Co., Ltd., part of China Electric Equipment Group Co., Ltd (CEEG), is a global research and development and manufacturing company of high-performance photovoltaic (PV) materials and solar panels. CSUN has supplied more than 15 gigawatts (GW) of solar panels worldwide. The firm has a 2.5GW design production capacity of solar panels with seven manufacturing centers in China, South Korea, Turkey, Vietnam and the U.S. Products include half- and full-cell solar modules, bifacial modules and related energy storage systems.

CONTACTS:
Note: Officers with more than one job title may be intentionally listed here more than once.

Zhuo Wang, Gen. Mngr.-CEEG
Aihua Wang, VP

FINANCIAL DATA:
Note: Data for latest year may not have been available at press time.

In U.S. $	2021	2020	2019	2018	2017	2016
Revenue	598,000,000	584,480,000	562,000,000	550,000,000	540,000,000	520,000,000
R&D Expense						
Operating Income						
Operating Margin %						
SGA Expense						
Net Income						
Operating Cash Flow						
Capital Expenditure						
EBITDA						
Return on Assets %						
Return on Equity %						
Debt to Equity						

CONTACT INFORMATION:
Phone: 86 2552766890   Fax: 86 2552766886
Toll-Free:
Address: No. 6 Shuge Rd., Jiangning, Nanjing 211100 China

STOCK TICKER/OTHER:
Stock Ticker: Subsidiary   Exchange:
Employees: 2,791   Fiscal Year Ends: 12/31
Parent Company: China Electric Equipment Group Co Ltd (CEEG)

SALARIES/BONUSES:
Top Exec. Salary: $ Bonus: $
Second Exec. Salary: $ Bonus: $

OTHER THOUGHTS:
Estimated Female Officers or Directors: 3
Hot Spot for Advancement for Women/Minorities: Y

CubicPV

NAIC Code: 334413A

cubicpv.com

TYPES OF BUSINESS:
Photovoltaic Cell Manufacturing
Solar Panels
Solar Wafers
Solar Technologies
Silicon Modules
Perovskite Modules
Direct Wafer Technology
Tandem Module Stacking

BRANDS/DIVISIONS/AFFILIATES:
Direct Wafer

CONTACTS: Note: Officers with more than one job title may be intentionally listed here more than once.
Frank van Mierlo, CEO
Craig Lund, VP-Bus. Dev.

GROWTH PLANS/SPECIAL FEATURES:
CubicPV is a solar energy technology firm that primarily develops and builds multi-crystalline solar wafers for the photovoltaics (PV) industry. The Cubic name refers to the shared cubic crystal structure of both silicon and perovskite, as well as the exponential increase in power delivered by the tandem modules built from both materials. CubicPV's Direct Wafer technology is capable of producing a multi-crystalline wafer directly from molten silicon every 20 seconds. This process, by comparison to conventional casting and sawing ingot-based methods, reduces costs significantly, provides high-performance and is aesthetically pleasing. The Direct Wafer process has demonstrated the ability to grow a three-dimensional wafer, or a thin wafer with a thick border, which is impossible via conventional ingot-based production technologies. CubicPV's perovskite technology develops highly-stable and efficient metal halide perovskite materials for use in single-junction and tandem PV solar panels for the utility-scale market. CubicPV's tandem modules offer enhanced efficiency and works by stacking two solar cells on top of each other, and are made of different semiconductor materials. Silicon is the material for the bottom cell and is powered by Direct Wafer technology. Perovskite is the top layer material. Headquartered in Massachusetts, CubicPV has an additional office located in Dallas, Texas.

FINANCIAL DATA: Note: Data for latest year may not have been available at press time.

In U.S. $	2021	2020	2019	2018	2017	2016
Revenue	87,000,000	81,000,000	72,000,000	74,000,000	75,000,000	70,000,000
R&D Expense						
Operating Income						
Operating Margin %						
SGA Expense						
Net Income						
Operating Cash Flow						
Capital Expenditure						
EBITDA						
Return on Assets %						
Return on Equity %						
Debt to Equity						

CONTACT INFORMATION:
Phone: 781-861-1611 Fax:
Toll-Free:
Address: 6-8 Preston Ct., Bedford, MA 01730 United States

STOCK TICKER/OTHER:
Stock Ticker: Private Exchange:
Employees: 180 Fiscal Year Ends: 12/31
Parent Company:

SALARIES/BONUSES:
Top Exec. Salary: $ Bonus: $
Second Exec. Salary: $ Bonus: $

OTHER THOUGHTS:
Estimated Female Officers or Directors:
Hot Spot for Advancement for Women/Minorities:

Sales, profits and employees may be estimates. Financial information, benefits and other data can change quickly and may vary from those stated here.

Cummins Inc

www.cummins.com

NAIC Code: 336300

TYPES OF BUSINESS:
Automotive Products, Motors & Parts Manufacturing
Engines
Filtration Systems
Power Generation Systems
Alternators
Air Handling Systems
Filtration & Emissions Solutions
Fuel Systems

BRANDS/DIVISIONS/AFFILIATES:

GROWTH PLANS/SPECIAL FEATURES:
Cummins is the top manufacturer of diesel engines used in commercial trucks, off-highway equipment, and railroad locomotives, in addition to standby and prime power generators. The company also sells powertrain components, which include filtration products, transmissions, turbochargers, aftertreatment systems, and fuel systems. Cummins is in the unique position of competing with its primary customers, heavy-duty truck manufacturers, who make and aggressively market their own engines. Despite robust competition across all its segments and increasing government regulation of diesel emissions, Cummins has maintained its leadership position in the industry.
Cummins offers employees life, medical and dental insurance; and various employee assistance programs.

CONTACTS: Note: Officers with more than one job title may be intentionally listed here more than once.
N. Linebarger, CEO
Norbert Nusterer, Pres., Divisional
Mark Smith, CFO
Christopher Clulow, Chief Accounting Officer
Marya Rose, Chief Administrative Officer
Sherry Aaholm, Chief Information Officer
Walter Fier, Chief Technology Officer
Livingston Satterthwaite, COO
Sharon Barner, General Counsel
Jill Cook, Other Executive Officer
Jennifer Rumsey, President, Divisional
Tracy Embree, President, Divisional
Amy Rochelle Davis, President, Divisional
Peter Anderson, Vice President, Divisional
Thaddeaus Ewald, Vice President, Divisional

FINANCIAL DATA: Note: Data for latest year may not have been available at press time.

In U.S. $	2021	2020	2019	2018	2017	2016
Revenue	24,021,000,000	19,811,000,000	23,571,000,000	23,771,000,000	20,428,000,000	17,509,000,000
R&D Expense	1,090,000,000	906,000,000	1,001,000,000	902,000,000	754,000,000	637,000,000
Operating Income	2,214,000,000	1,847,000,000	2,489,000,000	2,392,000,000	1,977,000,000	1,733,000,000
Operating Margin %	.09%	.09%	.11%	.10%	.10%	.10%
SGA Expense	2,374,000,000	2,125,000,000	2,454,000,000	2,437,000,000	2,429,000,000	2,099,000,000
Net Income	2,131,000,000	1,789,000,000	2,260,000,000	2,141,000,000	999,000,000	1,394,000,000
Operating Cash Flow	2,256,000,000	2,722,000,000	3,181,000,000	2,378,000,000	2,277,000,000	1,939,000,000
Capital Expenditure	786,000,000	575,000,000	775,000,000	784,000,000	587,000,000	594,000,000
EBITDA	3,524,000,000	3,111,000,000	3,615,000,000	3,478,000,000	3,029,000,000	2,529,000,000
Return on Assets %	.09%	.08%	.12%	.12%	.06%	.09%
Return on Equity %	.26%	.23%	.30%	.29%	.14%	.20%
Debt to Equity	.46%	0.488	0.259	0.217	0.219	0.228

CONTACT INFORMATION:
Phone: 812 377-5000   Fax:
Toll-Free:
Address: 500 Jackson St., Columbus, IN 47202 United States

STOCK TICKER/OTHER:
Stock Ticker: CMI   Exchange: NYS
Employees: 59,900   Fiscal Year Ends: 12/31
Parent Company:

SALARIES/BONUSES:
Top Exec. Salary: $1,575,000   Bonus: $
Second Exec. Salary: $740,000   Bonus: $

OTHER THOUGHTS:
Estimated Female Officers or Directors: 2
Hot Spot for Advancement for Women/Minorities: Y

Dominion Energy Inc

NAIC Code: 221112

www.dom.com

TYPES OF BUSINESS:
Utilities-Electricity & Natural Gas
Energy Production
Nuclear Energy
Solar Energy
Natural Gas
Electricity
Coal
Hydroelectricity

GROWTH PLANS/SPECIAL FEATURES:
Based in Richmond, Virginia, Dominion Energy is an integrated energy company with over 30 gigawatts of electric generation capacity and more than 90,000 miles of electric transmission and distribution lines. Dominion owns a liquefied natural gas export facility in Maryland and is constructing a 5.2 GW wind farm off the Virginia Beach coast.

BRANDS/DIVISIONS/AFFILIATES:
Birdseye

CONTACTS:
Note: Officers with more than one job title may be intentionally listed here more than once.

Robert Blue, CEO
James Chapman, CFO
Thomas Farrell, Chairman of the Board
Michele Cardiff, Chief Accounting Officer
Carlos Brown, Chief Compliance Officer
Diane Leopold, COO
Daniel Stoddard, Other Executive Officer
Edward Baine, President, Divisional
Phillip Blevins, President, Divisional
Donald Raikes, President, Divisional
William Murray, Senior VP, Divisional

FINANCIAL DATA:
Note: Data for latest year may not have been available at press time.

In U.S. $	2021	2020	2019	2018	2017	2016
Revenue	13,964,000,000	14,172,000,000	14,401,000,000	11,199,000,000	12,586,000,000	11,737,000,000
R&D Expense						
Operating Income	3,322,000,000	4,099,000,000	2,912,000,000	2,760,000,000	3,805,000,000	3,412,000,000
Operating Margin %	.24%	.29%	.20%	.25%	.30%	.29%
SGA Expense						
Net Income	3,288,000,000	-401,000,000	1,358,000,000	2,447,000,000	2,999,000,000	2,123,000,000
Operating Cash Flow	4,037,000,000	5,227,000,000	5,204,000,000	4,773,000,000	4,502,000,000	4,151,000,000
Capital Expenditure	5,960,000,000	6,020,000,000	4,980,000,000	4,254,000,000	5,504,000,000	6,085,000,000
EBITDA	6,090,000,000	6,935,000,000	5,889,000,000	5,040,000,000	6,007,000,000	5,261,000,000
Return on Assets %	.03%	.00%	.01%	.03%	.04%	.03%
Return on Equity %	.13%	-.02%	.05%	.13%	.19%	.16%
Debt to Equity	1.47%	1.431	0.979	1.549	1.805	2.07

CONTACT INFORMATION:
Phone: 804 819-2000   Fax: 804 775-5819
Toll-Free:
Address: 120 Tredegar St., Richmond, VA 23219 United States

STOCK TICKER/OTHER:
Stock Ticker: D
Employees: 17,300
Parent Company:

Exchange: NYS
Fiscal Year Ends: 12/31

SALARIES/BONUSES:
Top Exec. Salary: $1,225,000   Bonus: $
Second Exec. Salary: $871,250   Bonus: $

OTHER THOUGHTS:
Estimated Female Officers or Directors: 4
Hot Spot for Advancement for Women/Minorities: Y

Sales, profits and employees may be estimates. Financial information, benefits and other data can change quickly and may vary from those stated here.

Dow Inc

NAIC Code: 325199

www.dow.com/en-us.html

TYPES OF BUSINESS:
Specialty Chemicals Manufacturer
Manufacturing
Coatings & Infrastructure
Packaging Products
Industrial Intermediates
Performance Materials
Innovation

GROWTH PLANS/SPECIAL FEATURES:
Dow Inc is a diversified chemical manufacturing company. It combining science and technology to develop innovative solutions that are essential to human progress. Dow's portfolio is comprised of six global business units, organized into three operating segments: Packaging & Specialty Plastics, Industrial Intermediates & Infrastructure, and Performance Materials & Coatings.

BRANDS/DIVISIONS/AFFILIATES:

CONTACTS: Note: Officers with more than one job title may be intentionally listed here more than once.
James Fitterling, CEO
Howard Ungerleider, CFO
Ronald Edmonds, Chief Accounting Officer
Attiganal Sreeram, Chief Technology Officer
Amy Wilson, General Counsel
Karen Carter, Other Executive Officer
Mauro Gregorio, President, Divisional
Jane Palmieri, President, Divisional
Diego Donoso, President, Divisional
Jack Broodo, President, Divisional
John Sampson, Senior VP, Divisional

FINANCIAL DATA: Note: Data for latest year may not have been available at press time.

In U.S. $	2021	2020	2019	2018	2017	2016
Revenue	54,968,000,000	38,542,000,000	42,951,000,000	49,604,000,000	43,730,000,000	48,158,000,000
R&D Expense	857,000,000	768,000,000	765,000,000	800,000,000	803,000,000	1,593,000,000
Operating Income	7,887,000,000	2,556,000,000	3,520,000,000	5,479,000,000	4,382,000,000	4,287,000,000
Operating Margin %	.14%	.07%	.08%	.11%	.10%	.09%
SGA Expense	1,645,000,000	1,471,000,000	1,590,000,000	1,782,000,000	1,795,000,000	4,066,000,000
Net Income	6,311,000,000	1,225,000,000	-1,359,000,000	4,641,000,000	465,000,000	4,318,000,000
Operating Cash Flow	7,009,000,000	6,226,000,000	5,930,000,000	4,254,000,000	-4,929,000,000	-2,957,000,000
Capital Expenditure	2,324,000,000	1,387,000,000	1,970,000,000	2,137,000,000	2,994,000,000	3,991,000,000
EBITDA	11,718,000,000	5,772,000,000	2,624,000,000	7,721,000,000	3,697,000,000	8,133,000,000
Return on Assets %	.10%	.02%	-.02%	.06%	.01%	
Return on Equity %	.41%	.09%	-.06%	.16%	.02%	
Debt to Equity	.85%	1.448	1.308	0.593	0.765	

CONTACT INFORMATION:
Phone: 989 636-1000   Fax: 989 636-3518
Toll-Free: 800-422-8193
Address: 2211 H.H. Dow Way, Midland, MI 48674 United States

STOCK TICKER/OTHER:
Stock Ticker: DOW
Employees: 35,700
Parent Company:

Exchange: NYS
Fiscal Year Ends: 12/31

SALARIES/BONUSES:
Top Exec. Salary: $1,555,000   Bonus: $
Second Exec. Salary: $1,207,771   Bonus: $

OTHER THOUGHTS:
Estimated Female Officers or Directors: 3
Hot Spot for Advancement for Women/Minorities: Y

Sales, profits and employees may be estimates. Financial information, benefits and other data can change quickly and may vary from those stated here.

Ducon Technologies Inc

NAIC Code: 334512

www.ducon.com

TYPES OF BUSINESS:
Air Pollution & Environmental Control Products
Infrastructure Engineering
Environmental Control Solutions
Renewable Energy Solutions
Infrastructure and Plant Maintenance
Environmental Control Technologies
Consulting Services

BRANDS/DIVISIONS/AFFILIATES:

CONTACTS: Note: Officers with more than one job title may be intentionally listed here more than once.
Aron Devendra Govil, Chmn.
Aron Govil, Pres.
Renato dela Rama, Controller

GROWTH PLANS/SPECIAL FEATURES:
Ducon Technologies, Inc. is a global engineering and construction firm that provides custom engineered solutions in environmental control, renewable energy, infrastructure and plant maintenance. The firm's environmental systems division provides advanced technologies for air pollution control equipment, and environmental consulting services. It supplies equipment to a wide variety of industries and processes, including chemicals/additives, synthetic rubber, plastics, ammonium sulfate fertilizers, refineries, cement manufacturing, industrial minerals and ores, glass manufacturing, power generation, battery manufacturing, chrome plating, mining and ore processing, pulp/paper, pharmaceutical, food, steel and wastewater treatment. Ducon Technologies supplies custom engineered solar power plants, which utilize innovative photovoltaic solar technology and solar thermal plant design capabilities to deliver clean and reliable electricity. The firm provides site fabrication and field erection for mechanical structures and complete plants on a turn-key basis. This division offers project management services for civil construction, steel support structures, pipeline installation, electrical and controls, and installation of heavy machineries for business sectors like steel, power, cement, mining, petrochemical and others worldwide. Ducon is headquartered in New York, with additional offices in New York and Florida.

FINANCIAL DATA: Note: Data for latest year may not have been available at press time.

In U.S. $	2021	2020	2019	2018	2017	2016
Revenue						
R&D Expense						
Operating Income						
Operating Margin %						
SGA Expense						
Net Income						
Operating Cash Flow						
Capital Expenditure						
EBITDA						
Return on Assets %						
Return on Equity %						
Debt to Equity						

CONTACT INFORMATION:
Phone: 631-694-1700   Fax: 631-420-4985
Toll-Free:
Address: 5 Penn Plaza, New York, NY 10001 United States

STOCK TICKER/OTHER:
Stock Ticker: Private   Exchange:
Employees: Fiscal Year Ends: 12/31
Parent Company:

SALARIES/BONUSES:
Top Exec. Salary: $ Bonus: $
Second Exec. Salary: $ Bonus: $

OTHER THOUGHTS:
Estimated Female Officers or Directors:
Hot Spot for Advancement for Women/Minorities:

Sales, profits and employees may be estimates. Financial information, benefits and other data can change quickly and may vary from those stated here.

Duke Energy Sustainable Solutions

sustainablesolutions.duke-energy.com

NAIC Code: 221114

TYPES OF BUSINESS:
Solar Electric Power Generation
Renewables Financing
Energy Infrastructure Services
Energy-Efficient Infrastructure Lighting
Distributed Energy Generation
Solar Energy Solutions
Energy Storage Solutions
Microgrids

BRANDS/DIVISIONS/AFFILIATES:
Duke Energy Corporation
Duke Energy Commercial Enterprises Inc
Duke Energy One Inc
Duke Energy Renewables Inc
Duke Energy Renewables Storage LLC
Duke Energy Renewables Wind LLC
REC Solar Commercial Corporation

CONTACTS:
Note: Officers with more than one job title may be intentionally listed here more than once.

Chris Fallon, Pres.
Ken Ambur, General Counsel
Ethan Miller, VP
Paul Detering, Sr. VP

GROWTH PLANS/SPECIAL FEATURES:

Duke Energy Sustainable Solutions is a commercial brand that unifies products and services offered by several Duke Energy Corporation subsidiaries under one comprehensive brand. These unregulated subsidiaries include Duke Energy Commercial Enterprises Inc., Duke Energy One Inc., Duke Energy Renewables Inc., Duke Energy Renewables Commercial LLC, Duke Energy Renewables Services LLC, Duke Energy Renewables Solar LLC, Duke Energy Renewables Storage LLC, Duke Energy Renewables Wind LLC and REC Solar Commercial Corporation. Duke Energy services include renewables financing, energy infrastructure-as-a-service, operations and maintenance and full lifecycle management. Solutions by Duke Energy are grouped into five categories, and include: energy solutions, such as energy infrastructure as a service, renewables financing, central utility plant and energy-efficient lighting; distributed generation, including solar energy, central utility plant, energy storage, combined heat and power, and community solar; off-site renewables, including wind energy, solar energy, virtual power purchase agreement (VPPA) and operations and maintenance services; energy resilience, including microgrids, backup power generators, uninterruptible power supply and emergency storm preparedness; and fleet electrification. Industries served by Duke Energy include manufacturing, pharmaceutical, healthcare, education, transportation, retail and distribution, state and local government, and federal government.

Duke Energy offers its employees comprehensive health benefits, retirement benefits, wellness programs and other plans and programs.

FINANCIAL DATA:
Note: Data for latest year may not have been available at press time.

In U.S. $	2021	2020	2019	2018	2017	2016
Revenue	196,270,000	190,000,000	176,904,000	170,100,000	162,000,000	150,000,000
R&D Expense						
Operating Income						
Operating Margin %						
SGA Expense						
Net Income						
Operating Cash Flow						
Capital Expenditure						
EBITDA						
Return on Assets %						
Return on Equity %						
Debt to Equity						

CONTACT INFORMATION:
Phone: 844-732-7652 Fax: 805-54808661
Toll-Free:
Address: 3450 Broad St., Ste. 105, San Luis Obispo, CA 93401 United States

STOCK TICKER/OTHER:
Stock Ticker: Subsidiary   Exchange:
Employees: 700   Fiscal Year Ends: 12/31
Parent Company: Duke Energy Corporation

SALARIES/BONUSES:
Top Exec. Salary: $ Bonus: $
Second Exec. Salary: $ Bonus: $

OTHER THOUGHTS:
Estimated Female Officers or Directors: 1
Hot Spot for Advancement for Women/Minorities:

Sales, profits and employees may be estimates. Financial information, benefits and other data can change quickly and may vary from those stated here.

EDF Energy Nuclear Generation Group Limited

www.edfenergy.com
NAIC Code: 221113

TYPES OF BUSINESS:
Nuclear Electric Power Generation
Renewable Energy Generation
Nuclear Power
Wind Farms
Solar Farms
Solar Panels
Battery Storage
Nuclear Power Stations

BRANDS/DIVISIONS/AFFILIATES:
Electricite de France SA (EDF)

CONTACTS: Note: Officers with more than one job title may be intentionally listed here more than once.
Simone Rossi, CEO
Rob Guyler, CFO
Carol McArthur, Chief People Officer
Jean-Bernard Levy, Chmn.

GROWTH PLANS/SPECIAL FEATURES:
EDF Energy Nuclear Generation Group Limited is a subsidiary of French energy company Electricite de France SA (EDF), and one of the U.K.'s largest generators and suppliers of low-carbon electricity. EDF builds and runs wind farms across the U.K., including onshore and offshore. The company has an operational portfolio of 36 wind farms, including two offshore wind farms. EDF Energy's solar division builds solar farms and installs photovoltaic (PV) solar panels on land and on roof tops. The firm's battery storage sites provide up to 2 gigawatts (GW) of flexible capacity, with a goal of offering 25GW of battery storage by 2050. Currently, the firm is building two nuclear power stations, Hinkley Point C and Sizewell C, each of which will provide low-carbon electricity for approximately 6 million homes in the U.K. EDF Energy's eight nuclear power stations generate enough low carbon electricity for approximately 44% of U.K. homes. EDF's Tees Green Hydrogen project is developing a hydrogen electrolyzer using green electricity produced by Teesside Offshore Wind Farm and a new solar farm at the same location. In addition, EDF works with a wide range of suppliers to provide wind farm technology, engineering expertise and specialized services to businesses via power purchase agreements, enabling businesses to generate their own electricity.

FINANCIAL DATA: Note: Data for latest year may not have been available at press time.

In U.S. $	2021	2020	2019	2018	2017	2016
Revenue	4,010,666,400	3,856,410,000	3,726,000,000	3,600,000,000	3,557,100,000	4,521,272,816
R&D Expense						
Operating Income						
Operating Margin %						
SGA Expense						
Net Income			207,196,132	197,329,650	187,933,000	754,514,575
Operating Cash Flow						
Capital Expenditure						
EBITDA						
Return on Assets %						
Return on Equity %						
Debt to Equity						

CONTACT INFORMATION:
Phone: 44-1355-846000   Fax: 44-1355-846001
Toll-Free:
Address: 40 Grosvenor Pl., London, SW1X 7AW United Kingdom

STOCK TICKER/OTHER:
Stock Ticker: Subsidiary   Exchange:
Employees: 5,000   Fiscal Year Ends: 03/31
Parent Company: Electricite de France SA (EDF)

SALARIES/BONUSES:
Top Exec. Salary: $ Bonus: $
Second Exec. Salary: $ Bonus: $

OTHER THOUGHTS:
Estimated Female Officers or Directors:
Hot Spot for Advancement for Women/Minorities:

Sales, profits and employees may be estimates. Financial information, benefits and other data can change quickly and may vary from those stated here.

Electricite de France SA (EDF)

NAIC Code: 221113

www.edf.fr

TYPES OF BUSINESS:
Electric Utility
Nuclear Generation
Hydroelectric Generation
Wind Generation
Thermal Generation
Boiler Maintenance
Photovoltaic Cells
Renewable Energy

BRANDS/DIVISIONS/AFFILIATES:

GROWTH PLANS/SPECIAL FEATURES:
Electricite de France is one of the world's largest energy companies, controlling the French power grid along with a massive global generation fleet. Its French nuclear fleet comprises 58 plants. It operates the largest power supply business in France, which acts as a broker between generators and retail end users, is a major renewable developer, and holds stakes in other energy businesses globally, including a small but growing Chinese footprint. With the acquisition of Areva's nuclear reactor unit in 2017, EDF became an integrated nuclear developer.

CONTACTS: Note: Officers with more than one job title may be intentionally listed here more than once.
Jean-Bernard Levy, CEO
Xavier Girre, Exec. VP-Finance
Christophe Carval, Sr. VP-Human Resources
Alain Tchernonog, Gen. Sec.
Thomas Piquemal, Sr. Exec. VP-Corp. Finance
Vincent de Rivas, CEO-EDF Energy
Pierre Lederer, Sr. Exec. VP-Customers, Optimization & Trading
Herve Machenaud, Sr. Exec. VP-Generation

FINANCIAL DATA: Note: Data for latest year may not have been available at press time.

In U.S. $	2021	2020	2019	2018	2017	2016
Revenue	82,710,030,000	67,599,910,000	69,867,900,000	67,124,960,000	63,546,710,000	69,726,880,000
R&D Expense						
Operating Income	6,260,466,000	5,145,079,000	6,184,082,000	5,704,241,000	4,774,915,000	7,842,964,000
Operating Margin %	.08%	.08%	.09%	.08%	.08%	.11%
SGA Expense	13,596,170,000	12,559,120,000	12,690,340,000	12,817,650,000	11,435,900,000	10,945,290,000
Net Income	5,007,002,000	636,524,700	5,048,131,000	1,152,599,000	3,107,220,000	2,791,896,000
Operating Cash Flow	12,385,790,000	12,673,700,000	13,731,310,000	13,086,950,000	11,421,210,000	10,894,370,000
Capital Expenditure	17,379,080,000	16,189,270,000	16,448,780,000	15,683,970,000	14,441,280,000	14,098,530,000
EBITDA	19,562,850,000	19,052,650,000	20,207,210,000	17,959,790,000	17,327,180,000	18,490,550,000
Return on Assets %	.01%	.00%	.02%	.00%	.01%	.01%
Return on Equity %	.10%	.00%	.10%	.01%	.07%	.07%
Debt to Equity	1.07%	1.171	1.20	1.13	1.182	1.508

CONTACT INFORMATION:
Phone: 33 140422222 Fax: 33 140427940
Toll-Free:
Address: 22-30, Ave. de Wagram, Paris, 75382 France

STOCK TICKER/OTHER:
Stock Ticker: ECIFY
Employees: 162,208
Parent Company:

Exchange: PINX
Fiscal Year Ends: 12/31

SALARIES/BONUSES:
Top Exec. Salary: $ Bonus: $
Second Exec. Salary: $ Bonus: $

OTHER THOUGHTS:
Estimated Female Officers or Directors: 4
Hot Spot for Advancement for Women/Minorities: Y

Sales, profits and employees may be estimates. Financial information, benefits and other data can change quickly and may vary from those stated here.

Electrochem

NAIC Code: 335999A

www.electrochemsolutions.com

TYPES OF BUSINESS:
Fuel Cell Manufacturing
Customized Power Solutions
Environmental Catastrophe Monitoring
Geologic Formation Exploration Solutions
Lithium Power Cells
Custom Battery Packs
Advanced Battery Technologies
Ultracapacitors

BRANDS/DIVISIONS/AFFILIATES:
Integer Holdings Corporation

GROWTH PLANS/SPECIAL FEATURES:
Electrochem is an Integer Holdings Corporation company and provider of custom power solutions for critical applications. Electrochem's power solutions enable products to monitor potential environmental catastrophes, support troops on the battlefield or explore geologic formations miles below the earth's surface. The company's portfolio of cells come in various sizes, temperature ranges and rate capabilities, with products including lithium cells, custom battery packs, advanced battery technologies and ultracapacitors. Electrochem primarily serves the energy, military and environmental markets. The firm offers battery consulting, engineering, quality and manufacturing capabilities for its customized solutions.

CONTACTS:
Note: Officers with more than one job title may be intentionally listed here more than once.

Carter Houghton, Pres.
Michael S. Pien, VP-R&D
Steven A. Lis, Sr. Scientist

FINANCIAL DATA:
Note: Data for latest year may not have been available at press time.

In U.S. $	2021	2020	2019	2018	2017	2016
Revenue						
R&D Expense						
Operating Income						
Operating Margin %						
SGA Expense						
Net Income						
Operating Cash Flow						
Capital Expenditure						
EBITDA						
Return on Assets %						
Return on Equity %						
Debt to Equity						

CONTACT INFORMATION:
Phone: 781-830-5800 Fax:
Toll-Free:
Address: 670 Paramount Dr., Raynham, MA 02767 United States

STOCK TICKER/OTHER:
Stock Ticker: Subsidiary Exchange:
Employees: 10 Fiscal Year Ends: 12/31
Parent Company: Integer Holdings Corporation

SALARIES/BONUSES:
Top Exec. Salary: $ Bonus: $
Second Exec. Salary: $ Bonus: $

OTHER THOUGHTS:
Estimated Female Officers or Directors: 1
Hot Spot for Advancement for Women/Minorities:

Sales, profits and employees may be estimates. Financial information, benefits and other data can change quickly and may vary from those stated here.

EMCORE Corporation

www.emcore.com

NAIC Code: 334413

TYPES OF BUSINESS:
Nanotechnology-Semiconductors
Navigation Sensors
Lasers
Optical Subsystems
Cable TV
Fiber-to-the-Premise
Broadband
Aerospace and Defense

BRANDS/DIVISIONS/AFFILIATES:

GROWTH PLANS/SPECIAL FEATURES:
EMCORE Corp is engaged in the manufacturing of sensors, lasers, and optical subsystems. The company operates in two segments: Aerospace & Defense and Broadband. It's Aerospace & Defense segment comprises of two product lines that are Navigation & Inertial Sensing and Defense Optoelectronic. The broadband segment includes CATV Lasers & Transmitters, Chip Devices, and Other products. The company operates in four geographical segments that include the United States and Canada, which is the key revenue generator; Asia; Europe; and Other.

EMCORE offers its employees medical, dental and vision insurance; retirement planning benefits; paid time off; and employee assistance programs.

CONTACTS: Note: Officers with more than one job title may be intentionally listed here more than once.
Jeffrey Rittichier, CEO
Thomas Minichiello, CFO
Stephen Domenik, Chairman of the Board
Albert Lu, Senior VP, Divisional
Iain Black, Senior VP, Divisional

FINANCIAL DATA: Note: Data for latest year may not have been available at press time.

In U.S. $	2021	2020	2019	2018	2017	2016
Revenue	158,444,000	110,128,000	87,265,000	85,617,000	122,895,000	91,998,000
R&D Expense	17,448,000	20,269,000	19,443,000	15,387,000	12,542,000	9,921,000
Operating Income	19,496,000	-9,318,000	-36,434,000	-18,277,000	7,791,000	2,898,000
Operating Margin %	.12%	-.08%	-.42%	-.21%	.06%	.03%
SGA Expense	24,544,000	24,631,000	32,080,000	21,377,000	22,246,000	20,734,000
Net Income	25,643,000	-7,000,000	-35,984,000	-17,453,000	8,235,000	8,266,000
Operating Cash Flow	11,153,000	-3,892,000	-15,151,000	1,470,000	11,701,000	-5,552,000
Capital Expenditure	5,358,000	4,516,000	10,790,000	6,583,000	9,600,000	5,779,000
EBITDA	23,557,000	-3,834,000	-29,292,000	-12,660,000	11,548,000	5,404,000
Return on Assets %	.17%	-.06%	-.30%	-.13%	.06%	.06%
Return on Equity %	.24%	-.09%	-.39%	-.15%	.07%	.07%
Debt to Equity	.09%	0.273				

CONTACT INFORMATION:
Phone: 626-293-3400   Fax: 626-293-3428
Toll-Free:
Address: 2015 W. Chestnut St., Alhambra, CA 91803 United States

SALARIES/BONUSES:
Top Exec. Salary: $468,750   Bonus: $
Second Exec. Salary: $361,250   Bonus: $

STOCK TICKER/OTHER:
Stock Ticker: EMKR
Employees: 365
Parent Company:

Exchange: NAS
Fiscal Year Ends: 09/30

OTHER THOUGHTS:
Estimated Female Officers or Directors: 1
Hot Spot for Advancement for Women/Minorities:

Sales, profits and employees may be estimates. Financial information, benefits and other data can change quickly and may vary from those stated here.

Enel Green Power SpA

NAIC Code: 221115

www.enelgreenpower.com

TYPES OF BUSINESS:
Wind Electric Power Generation
Photovoltaic Cell Production
Renewable Energy
Solar Power
Geothermal Power
Wind Power

BRANDS/DIVISIONS/AFFILIATES:
Enel SpA

GROWTH PLANS/SPECIAL FEATURES:
Enel Green Power SpA, based in Italy and a subsidiary of Enel SpA, develops and operates renewable energy generation facilities all over the world. With a managed capacity of approximately 55 gigawatts (GW) and 1,200+ plants worldwide, the firm is present with assets in operation or under construction in more than 20 countries, and manages development activities in an additional six countries. Enel Green's power generation is comprised of wind, solar, hydroelectric and geothermal renewable resources. In addition, the firm has developed related technologies and solutions, including the construction of off-grid solutions and storage systems in order to improve flexibility and performance in its power plants. Parent company Enel SpA is one of the world's top renewable energy producers. Enel plans to invest $85 billion in new renewable energy production capacity between 2020 and 2030. During 2022, Enel Green began commercial operations at its hybrid renewable industrial-scale power plant in Chile, began building a solar power station in Soria, obtained authorization to begin commercial operation of the Sol de Lila solar power park in Chile, and began building more than 1,130MW of new renewable projects in Spain.

CONTACTS: Note: Officers with more than one job title may be intentionally listed here more than once.
Salvatore Bernabei, CEO
Renato Mastroianni, Operation & Maintenance
Javier Vaquerizo Alonso, Commercial Office
Antonio Scala, People and Organization
Vittorio Vagliasindi, Head-Eng. & Construction
Giulio Carone, Head-Admin.
Giulio Fazio, Head-Legal Affairs
Ingmar Wilhelm, Head-Bus. Dev.
Francesca Romana Napolitano, Head-Corp. Affairs
Giulio Carone, Head-Finance & Control
Felice Egidi, Head-Regulatory Affairs
Attilio Cherubini, Head-Safety & Environment
Silvia Fiori, Head-Internal Audit
Maurizio Bezzeccheri, Head-Iberia & Latin America
Francesco Venturini, Head-North America
Dino Marcozzi, Head-Procurement

FINANCIAL DATA: Note: Data for latest year may not have been available at press time.

In U.S. $	2021	2020	2019	2018	2017	2016
Revenue	9,568,104,920	9,447,660,000	8,641,970,000	2,383,660,000	2,182,510,000	2,400,000,000
R&D Expense						
Operating Income						
Operating Margin %						
SGA Expense						
Net Income	4,836,282,300	4,741,866,820				
Operating Cash Flow						
Capital Expenditure						
EBITDA						
Return on Assets %						
Return on Equity %						
Debt to Equity						

CONTACT INFORMATION:
Phone: 39 683057767   Fax: 39 683053659
Toll-Free:
Address: Viale Regina Margherita 125, Rome, 00198 Italy

STOCK TICKER/OTHER:
Stock Ticker: Subsidiary   Exchange:
Employees: 8,289   Fiscal Year Ends: 12/31
Parent Company: Enel SpA

SALARIES/BONUSES:
Top Exec. Salary: $ Bonus: $
Second Exec. Salary: $ Bonus: $

OTHER THOUGHTS:
Estimated Female Officers or Directors: 4
Hot Spot for Advancement for Women/Minorities: Y

Sales, profits and employees may be estimates. Financial information, benefits and other data can change quickly and may vary from those stated here.

Enel SpA

NAIC Code: 221112

www.enel.it

TYPES OF BUSINESS:
Fossil Fuel Electric Power Generation
Hydroelectricity
Solar Generation
Wind Power Generation
Geothermal Generation
Smart Meters
Smart Cities
Energy Trading

BRANDS/DIVISIONS/AFFILIATES:
Enel Green Power
Enel X

GROWTH PLANS/SPECIAL FEATURES:
Enel is a diversified energy company domiciled in Italy. Operations are concentrated in Italy, Spain, and Latin America. The firm's primary activities are electric generation, electric networks, and gas and electricity marketing. Around 50% of the company's EBITDA is derived from its regulated networks. Taking into account power sold through power purchase agreements in Latin America, around 70% of EBITDA is quasi-regulated. Enel is a giant in global power generation with 86 gigawatts of capacity, of which 39 GW is renewables, including a large share of hydro.

CONTACTS:
Note: Officers with more than one job title may be intentionally listed here more than once.

Francesco Starace, CEO
Paolo Andrea Colombo, Pres.
Alberto De Paoli, CFO
Roberto Deambrogio, Dir.-Communications
Guido Stratta, Dir.-People & Organization
Claudio Sartorelli, Sec.
Gianluca Comin, Head-External Rel.
Claudio Machetti, Head-Risk Mgmt.
Simone Mori, VP-Regulation, Environment & Innovation
Luigi Ferraris, CEO-Enel Green Power
Michele Crisostomo, Chmn.
Andrea Brentan, Dir.-Iberia & Latin America

FINANCIAL DATA:
Note: Data for latest year may not have been available at press time.

In U.S. $	2021	2020	2019	2018	2017	2016
Revenue	94,545,470,000	62,988,530,000	72,286,680,000	74,866,080,000	71,909,670,000	67,962,240,000
R&D Expense						
Operating Income	17,779,600,000	10,023,800,000	6,383,854,000	12,072,430,000	9,582,146,000	9,730,015,000
Operating Margin %	.19%	.16%	.09%	.16%	.13%	.14%
SGA Expense						
Net Income	3,122,888,000	2,555,891,000	2,128,931,000	4,689,719,000	3,700,657,000	2,516,721,000
Operating Cash Flow	9,860,258,000	11,269,430,000	11,017,750,000	10,845,400,000	9,915,097,000	9,642,861,000
Capital Expenditure	11,948,060,000	9,350,059,000	9,067,050,000	8,087,781,000	8,322,806,000	8,658,695,000
EBITDA	16,211,800,000	14,643,010,000	16,249,010,000	17,316,410,000	15,189,440,000	17,610,190,000
Return on Assets %	.02%	.02%	.01%	.03%	.02%	.02%
Return on Equity %	.11%	.09%	.07%	.14%	.11%	.08%
Debt to Equity	1.84%	1.748	1.783	1.544	1.22	1.188

CONTACT INFORMATION:
Phone: 39 0685091 Fax:
Toll-Free:
Address: Viale Regina Margherita, 137, Rome, 00198 Italy

STOCK TICKER/OTHER:
Stock Ticker: ESOCF
Employees: 66,279
Parent Company:

Exchange: PINX
Fiscal Year Ends: 12/31

SALARIES/BONUSES:
Top Exec. Salary: $ Bonus: $
Second Exec. Salary: $ Bonus: $

OTHER THOUGHTS:
Estimated Female Officers or Directors:
Hot Spot for Advancement for Women/Minorities:

Sales, profits and employees may be estimates. Financial information, benefits and other data can change quickly and may vary from those stated here.

Enel X North America Inc

NAIC Code: 511200

www.enelx.com

TYPES OF BUSINESS:
Software, Energy Conservation and Management
Renewable Energy Technology
Renewable Energy Solutions
Renewable Energy Development
Electric Vehicle Charging Stations
EV Software
Battery Storage
Energy Maintenance Solutions

BRANDS/DIVISIONS/AFFILIATES:
Enel SpA

CONTACTS:
Note: Officers with more than one job title may be intentionally listed here more than once.

Enrico Viale, Pres.
William Sorenson, CFO
Matthew Cushing, General Counsel
Micah Remley, Senior VP, Divisional
Holly Lynch, Senior VP, Divisional
Eric Erston, Senior VP, Divisional

GROWTH PLANS/SPECIAL FEATURES:
Enel X North America, Inc. is a developer and provider of technological solutions in regards to renewable energy and recyclable materials, enabling customers to meet their energy goals. The firm's products and services are grouped into four industry categories: consumers, businesses, utilities and public sector. Products and solutions for consumers include electric vehicle (EV) smart charging stations and related software. Products and solutions for businesses span energy transition via facility load and on-site resources, energy storage and battery systems for facilities, renewable energy production/storage and dispatch from solar arrays, advisory services, utility bill management, energy supply management, and smart charging stations and infrastructure to support electric vehicles. Products and solutions for utilities include distributed energy resource deployment to address peak demand and congestion, designing/developing and enrolling megawatts of curtailment from large customers into demand response programs, auction-based wholesale energy purchasing through an automated process, and smart EV charging programs. Last, products and solutions for the public sector include smart charging stations and infrastructure to support EVs, route analysis and charging infrastructure for bus electrification, intelligent charging infrastructure fleet management solutions for fleet electrification, on-site distributed energy resource investing for energy transition during peak demands, battery systems for energy storage, renewable energy production/storage and dispatch via solar arrays, renewable advisory services, technology services, utility bill management and energy supply management. Enel X is the advanced energy services arm of Enel SpA.

FINANCIAL DATA: Note: Data for latest year may not have been available at press time.

In U.S. $	2021	2020	2019	2018	2017	2016
Revenue	310,277,600	235,822,080	367,314,080	386,601,020		
R&D Expense						
Operating Income						
Operating Margin %						
SGA Expense						
Net Income						
Operating Cash Flow						
Capital Expenditure						
EBITDA						
Return on Assets %						
Return on Equity %						
Debt to Equity						

CONTACT INFORMATION:
Phone: 617 224-9900 Fax: 617 224-9910
Toll-Free:
Address: 101 Seaport Blvd., Fl. 12, Boston, MA 02210 United States

STOCK TICKER/OTHER:
Stock Ticker: Subsidiary Exchange:
Employees: 1,600 Fiscal Year Ends: 12/31
Parent Company: Enel SpA

SALARIES/BONUSES:
Top Exec. Salary: $ Bonus: $
Second Exec. Salary: $ Bonus: $

OTHER THOUGHTS:
Estimated Female Officers or Directors: 2
Hot Spot for Advancement for Women/Minorities:

Sales, profits and employees may be estimates. Financial information, benefits and other data can change quickly and may vary from those stated here.

Plunkett Research, Ltd.

ENERCON GmbH
NAIC Code: 333611

www.enercon.de

TYPES OF BUSINESS:
Wind Turbine Manufacturing
Wind Turbine Manufacture
Technologies
Wind Energy Conversion Solutions
Integrated Solutions
Wind Farm Data Acquisition Solutions
Wind Farm Remote Monitoring Solutions
Wind Farm Towers

BRANDS/DIVISIONS/AFFILIATES:
SCANA Server
SCADA Remote
ENERCON SCADA Metro

CONTACTS: Note: Officers with more than one job title may be intentionally listed here more than once.
Jurgen Zeschky, CEO
Jost Backhaus, COO
Stefan Lükemeyer, Chief Sales Officer
Martin Prillmann, Chief Restructuring Officer
Jorg Scholle, CTO
Bernard Fink, Manager-Sales
Stefan Hartage, Head-Electrical Engineering Development

GROWTH PLANS/SPECIAL FEATURES:
ENERCON GmbH, founded in 1984, designs and manufactures wind turbines. The company's technology primarily consists of drive technology, grid technology and wind energy converter (WEC) components. ENERCON'S drive technology features a gearless drive concept for its wind energy converters. This technology offers integrated solutions for compliance with international grid codes. Its Supervisory Control and Data Acquisition (SCADA) system comprises all components for data acquisition, remote monitoring and control of a wind farm. The SCADA Server is connected to the WEC through the wind farm's fiber optical data bus, and fulfills functions relating to communication, data recording and control in the wind farm. SCADA Remote software enables customers to connect directly to the SCADA server of a wind farm from anywhere in the world. The ENERCON SCADA Metro option is available for integration of meteorological data from a wind mast in the ENERCON SCADA system. This division's annular generator includes a rotor and stator and forms the key component of the ENERCON WEC design, providing optimal energy flow, minimal vibration during operation, low sound emissions and long service life. All fixed-position nacelle components are housed in the machine house to withstand the highest dynamic stresses. Yaw drives ensure optimal yaw control of the nacelle. The E-module is the wind energy converter's control base. The hub is the link between the rotor blade and wind energy converter. The rotor blade comprises an innovative aerodynamic design, offering maximum power, low noise emissions and minimal structural loads. ENERCON towers are designed for optimal load dynamic and manufactured in both steel and pre-cast concrete tower sections. The turbine's foundation bears all static and dynamic loads from the wind turbine. ENERCON'S service info portal enables users to retrieve relevant wind energy converter data easily and swiftly.

FINANCIAL DATA: Note: Data for latest year may not have been available at press time.

In U.S. $	2021	2020	2019	2018	2017	2016
Revenue	5,038,800,000	4,845,000,000	5,100,000,000	5,147,060,000	6,708,040,000	5,267,800,000
R&D Expense						
Operating Income						
Operating Margin %						
SGA Expense						
Net Income				-217,320,000	367,145,000	
Operating Cash Flow						
Capital Expenditure						
EBITDA						
Return on Assets %						
Return on Equity %						
Debt to Equity						

CONTACT INFORMATION:
Phone: 49 421 24415100 Fax: 49 421 2441539
Toll-Free:
Address: Terrhof 59, Bremen, D-28199 Germany

STOCK TICKER/OTHER:
Stock Ticker: Private Exchange:
Employees: 20,000 Fiscal Year Ends: 12/31
Parent Company:

SALARIES/BONUSES:
Top Exec. Salary: $ Bonus: $
Second Exec. Salary: $ Bonus: $

OTHER THOUGHTS:
Estimated Female Officers or Directors:
Hot Spot for Advancement for Women/Minorities:

Sales, profits and employees may be estimates. Financial information, benefits and other data can change quickly and may vary from those stated here.

EnerDel Inc

NAIC Code: 335911

www.enerdel.com

TYPES OF BUSINESS:
Battery Development & Manufacturing
Lithium-Ion Energy Solutions
Storage Solutions
Battery Solutions
Cells and Modules
Battery Packs
Next-Generation Technologies
Heavy Duty Vehicle Batteries

BRANDS/DIVISIONS/AFFILIATES:
PLH Energy LLC
MOXIE+
VIGOR+

CONTACTS:
Note: Officers with more than one job title may be intentionally listed here more than once.

Steve Heir, CEO
James Bowman, Sr. VP-Operations
Chris Bardsley, VP-Finance
Michael O'Neill, VP-Mktg. & Sales
Tiara Hicks, VP-Human Resources
Bob Hong, Sr. Dir.-Engineering
Sean Hendrix, VP-Eng.
Kev Adjemian, Chief Strategy Officer
Michael Alma, Sr. VP-Asia Business
Ben Wrightsman, Dir.-Procurement

GROWTH PLANS/SPECIAL FEATURES:
EnerDel, Inc. designs and manufactures lithium-ion energy storage solutions and battery systems. The company's products and solutions are primarily for heavy-duty transportation, on/off grid electrical, mass transit and task-oriented applications. Products by EnerDel are grouped into three categories, including cells and modules, battery packs and next-generation technologies. Cells and modules include the MOXIE+ line of battery modules, which are designed as building blocks and offer versatility across a variety of uses. MOXIE+ offers pack designers and integrators a flexible solution for product development all the way through final assembly. This division's power cell provides a balance between energy and power and is made of lithium nickel, manganese and cobalt oxide (NMC) hard carbon or graphite. Its energy cell is made of NMC graphite and comprises over 40% greater capacity than the power cell, designed for a variety of applications requiring long run times. EnerDel's VIGOR+ brand of battery packs can be used for a variety of applications, including transportation, heavy-duty buses and trucks, industrial equipment, trolley buses, trams, construction, agricultural machines and military and civilian mobile hybrid power systems. This division's lithium-ion products offer industry-leading life spans and come with a warranty. Last, EnerDel's next-generation technologies leverages VDA modules (conforming with the German Association of Automotive Industry Standard) as the building block of its next-generation battery packs, providing cost-effective solutions that meet market demands. Prototype packs were scheduled to launch by the end of 2022, and customer samples were scheduled to be available in 2023. EnerDel's headquarters and manufacturing sites are located in Indiana, and its advanced engineering tech center is located in California. In mid-2022, EnerDel was acquired by PLH Energy, LLC, becoming an American owned and managed company.

FINANCIAL DATA:
Note: Data for latest year may not have been available at press time.

In U.S. $	2021	2020	2019	2018	2017	2016
Revenue	44,625,000	42,500,000	50,000,000	51,000,000	50,000,000	50,000,000
R&D Expense						
Operating Income						
Operating Margin %						
SGA Expense						
Net Income						
Operating Cash Flow						
Capital Expenditure						
EBITDA						
Return on Assets %						
Return on Equity %						
Debt to Equity						

CONTACT INFORMATION:
Phone: 317-703-1800   Fax:
Toll-Free:
Address: 3619 W. 73rd St., Anderson, IN 46011 United States

STOCK TICKER/OTHER:
Stock Ticker: Private   Exchange:
Employees: 164   Fiscal Year Ends: 12/31
Parent Company: PLH Energy LLC

SALARIES/BONUSES:
Top Exec. Salary: $ Bonus: $
Second Exec. Salary: $ Bonus: $

OTHER THOUGHTS:
Estimated Female Officers or Directors: 1
Hot Spot for Advancement for Women/Minorities:

Sales, profits and employees may be estimates. Financial information, benefits and other data can change quickly and may vary from those stated here.

Energy Recovery Inc

NAIC Code: 333318

www.energyrecovery.com

TYPES OF BUSINESS:
Seawater Desalination Products
Pumps

BRANDS/DIVISIONS/AFFILIATES:
Pressure Exchanger
PX
VorTeq
IsoBoost
IsoGen
AquaBold
ERI
Pump Engineering

GROWTH PLANS/SPECIAL FEATURES:
Energy Recovery Inc is an engineering-driven technology company. It is engaged in engineering, designing, manufacturing and supplying solutions that make industrial processes more efficient and sustainable. The company operates in two segments, Water and Emerging Technologies. It offers energy recovery devices (ERDs) and pumps as well as related products and services to the global reverse osmosis desalination market. The company derives a majority of the revenue from the Water segment. Geographically, the company operates in the U.S. and other international countries.
ERI offers its employees comprehensive health benefits, life and disability insurance, 401(k), employee development opportunities and assistance programs.

CONTACTS:
Note: Officers with more than one job title may be intentionally listed here more than once.

Robert Mao, CEO
Joshua Ballard, CFO
William Yeung, Chief Legal Officer
Farshad Ghasripoor, Chief Technology Officer
Rodney Clemente, Senior VP, Divisional

FINANCIAL DATA:
Note: Data for latest year may not have been available at press time.

In U.S. $	2021	2020	2019	2018	2017	2016
Revenue	103,904,000	118,986,000	86,942,000	74,515,000	69,129,000	57,784,000
R&D Expense	20,069,000	23,449,000	23,402,000	17,012,000	13,443,000	10,136,000
Operating Income	13,831,000	33,626,000	10,364,000	9,978,000	9,249,000	3,426,000
Operating Margin %	.13%	.28%	.12%	.13%	.13%	.06%
SGA Expense	37,322,000	33,646,000	32,266,000	29,022,000	26,745,000	25,742,000
Net Income	14,269,000	26,387,000	10,913,000	22,093,000	18,354,000	3,719,000
Operating Cash Flow	13,526,000	16,870,000	5,268,000	7,565,000	2,895,000	4,965,000
Capital Expenditure	6,679,000	6,785,000	7,382,000	5,235,000	7,376,000	1,112,000
EBITDA	19,770,000	38,925,000	14,759,000	15,310,000	13,597,000	7,396,000
Return on Assets %	.07%	.13%	.06%	.13%	.12%	.02%
Return on Equity %	.08%	.17%	.09%	.22%	.23%	.06%
Debt to Equity	.08%	0.096	0.085	0.111	0.019	0.00

CONTACT INFORMATION:
Phone: 510 483-7370 Fax: 510 483-7371
Toll-Free:
Address: 1717 Doolittle Dr., San Leandro, CA 94577 United States

STOCK TICKER/OTHER:
Stock Ticker: ERII
Employees: 222
Parent Company:

Exchange: NAS
Fiscal Year Ends: 12/31

SALARIES/BONUSES:
Top Exec. Salary: $514,423 Bonus: $
Second Exec. Salary: $342,735 Bonus: $

OTHER THOUGHTS:
Estimated Female Officers or Directors: 2
Hot Spot for Advancement for Women/Minorities: Y

Sales, profits and employees may be estimates. Financial information, benefits and other data can change quickly and may vary from those stated here.

Energy Vault Holdings Inc

NAIC Code: 335911

www.energyvault.com

TYPES OF BUSINESS:
Storage Battery Manufacturing
Grid-Scale Energy Storage Solutions
Energy Storage Technologies
Gravity-based Energy Storage Technology
Energy Storage System Development
Energy Storage Operations
Energy Management Software
Research and Development

BRANDS/DIVISIONS/AFFILIATES:
Energy Vault SA

GROWTH PLANS/SPECIAL FEATURES:
Energy Vault Holdings, Inc. develops sustainable, grid-scale energy storage solutions designed to advance the transition to a carbon-free power grid. The firm aims to accelerate decarbonization through energy storage technologies, including its proprietary gravity-based energy storage technology. Energy Vault's product platform helps utilities, independent power producers and large energy users to reduce their cost of energy while maintaining power reliability. The company's business model is comprised of the following product and service categories: building, operating and transferring energy storage projects to customers; building, operating and holding energy storage systems as an equity sponsor or co-sponsor; selling energy management software as a service; and entering into intellectual property license and royalty agreements associated with the company's energy storage technologies. Wholly-owned Energy Vault SA is based in Lugano, Switzerland and serves as the company's research and development hub.

CONTACTS:
Note: Officers with more than one job title may be intentionally listed here more than once.

Robert Allen Piconi, CEO
Chris Wiese, COO
David Hitchcock, CFO
Laurence Alexander, CMO
Gonca Icoren, Chief People Officer
Marco Terruzzin, Chief Product Officer
Robert Allen Piconi, Chmn.

FINANCIAL DATA:
Note: Data for latest year may not have been available at press time.

In U.S. $	2021	2020	2019	2018	2017	2016
Revenue						
R&D Expense		8,519,541	2,064,590			
Operating Income		-14,505,430	-10,012,660			
Operating Margin %						
SGA Expense		5,985,891	7,948,068			
Net Income		-24,171,000	-10,141,450			
Operating Cash Flow		-16,700,300	-14,833,340			
Capital Expenditure		1,754,504	1,156,148			
EBITDA		-23,987,390	-8,940,820			
Return on Assets %		-.70%	-.26%			
Return on Equity %						
Debt to Equity						

CONTACT INFORMATION:
Phone: 805 852-0000 Fax:
Toll-Free:
Address: 4360 Park Terrace Dr., Ste. 100, Westlake Village, CA 91361 United States

STOCK TICKER/OTHER:
Stock Ticker: NRGV
Employees:
Parent Company:

Exchange: NYS
Fiscal Year Ends:

SALARIES/BONUSES:
Top Exec. Salary: $ Bonus: $
Second Exec. Salary: $ Bonus: $

OTHER THOUGHTS:
Estimated Female Officers or Directors:
Hot Spot for Advancement for Women/Minorities:

Sales, profits and employees may be estimates. Financial information, benefits and other data can change quickly and may vary from those stated here.

ENGIE Global Energy Management & Sales

gems.engie.com

NAIC Code: 221121

TYPES OF BUSINESS:
Wholesale Electricity Generation
Energy Asset Management Solutions
Energy Supply Solutions
Energy Transition Services and Solutions
Risk Management Solutions
Energy Market Access Services and Solutions
Hedging Energy Strategies

BRANDS/DIVISIONS/AFFILIATES:
ENGIE

CONTACTS:
Note: Officers with more than one job title may be intentionally listed here more than once.

Edouard Neviaski, CEO
Sebastien Hubau, CFO
Stephanie Massart, Chief Human Resources Officer
Francois Graux, General Counsel
Philip De Chudde, Exec. VP-Bus. Dev. Oversight
Penny Chalmers, Exec. VP-Strategy & Comm.
Steve Riley, CEO-U.K.-Europe
Tony Concannon, CEO-Australia
Shankar Krishnamoorthy, CEO-Middle East, Turkey & Africa
Willem Van Twembeke, CEO-Asia
Zin Smati, CEO-North America

GROWTH PLANS/SPECIAL FEATURES:
ENGIE Global Energy Management & Sales, a business unit of ENGIE, is a global energy player in electricity, natural gas and energy services. The firm groups its services and expertise into four categories: power asset management, energy supply, energy transition services, and risk management and market access. Power asset management solutions range from demand-side management solutions to power purchase agreements and battery storage services to offer options for optimizing power assets and profit from energy markets. Energy supply solutions consist of tailor-made gas and electricity supply solutions, including price formulation and volume pattern, as well as turn-key delivery to sites throughout Europe. Energy transition services consist of a wide range of low-carbon energy transition solutions, including power purchase agreements (PPAs), power optimization agreements and other options. Risk management and market access solutions help customers design and execute tailored hedging energy strategies across ENGIE Global's more than 20 platforms on three continents, and provides expertise on cross markets, products and areas.

FINANCIAL DATA:
Note: Data for latest year may not have been available at press time.

In U.S. $	2021	2020	2019	2018	2017	2016
Revenue						
R&D Expense						
Operating Income						
Operating Margin %						
SGA Expense						
Net Income						
Operating Cash Flow						
Capital Expenditure						
EBITDA						
Return on Assets %						
Return on Equity %						
Debt to Equity						

CONTACT INFORMATION:
Phone: 44-20-7320-8600   Fax: 44-20-7320-8700
Toll-Free:
Address: 85 Queen Victoria St., Senator House, London, EC4V 4DP United Kingdom

STOCK TICKER/OTHER:
Stock Ticker: Subsidiary
Employees: 13,500
Parent Company: ENGIE

Exchange:
Fiscal Year Ends: 12/31

SALARIES/BONUSES:
Top Exec. Salary: $ Bonus: $
Second Exec. Salary: $ Bonus: $

OTHER THOUGHTS:
Estimated Female Officers or Directors: 2
Hot Spot for Advancement for Women/Minorities:

Sales, profits and employees may be estimates. Financial information, benefits and other data can change quickly and may vary from those stated here.

ENGlobal Corporation

NAIC Code: 541330

www.englobal.com

TYPES OF BUSINESS:
Engineering Services
Renewables
Automation
Refining
Transportation
Upstream Oil and Gas
Government Services
Engineering

BRANDS/DIVISIONS/AFFILIATES:

GROWTH PLANS/SPECIAL FEATURES:
ENGlobal Corp engages in providing engineering and professional services to the energy industry. The company operates through two segments Engineering, Procurement and Construction Management (EPCM) and Automation. The EPCM segment provides services relating to the development, management, and execution of projects across the United States. In addition, it also includes the government services group, which provides engineering, design, installation, operation, and maintenance of various government, public sector, and international facilities. The Automation segment offers services related to the design, fabrication, and implementation of process distributed control and analyzer systems, information technology and electrical projects across the United States and Central Asia.

ENGlobal offers its employees medical, dental and vision coverage; life insurance; flexible spending accounts; and educational reimbursement.

CONTACTS:
Note: Officers with more than one job title may be intentionally listed here more than once.
Mark Hess, CEO
Darren Spriggs, CFO
William Coskey, Chairman of the Board
Roger Westerlind, President
Bruce Williams, Senior VP, Divisional

FINANCIAL DATA:
Note: Data for latest year may not have been available at press time.

In U.S. $	2021	2020	2019	2018	2017	2016
Revenue	36,410,000	64,449,000	56,446,000	53,996,000	55,765,000	59,224,000
R&D Expense						
Operating Income	-13,476,000	-383,000	-1,401,000	-3,097,000	-6,143,000	-3,238,000
Operating Margin %	-.37%	-.01%	-.02%	-.06%	-.11%	-.05%
SGA Expense	12,833,000	8,834,000	9,317,000	10,030,000	12,581,000	13,350,000
Net Income	-5,685,000	-625,000	-1,466,000	-5,671,000	-16,258,000	-2,342,000
Operating Cash Flow	-13,664,000	-519,000	2,665,000	-3,428,000	-5,104,000	9,565,000
Capital Expenditure	240,000	428,000	345,000	107,000	713,000	64,000
EBITDA	-4,852,000	80,000	-963,000	-5,079,000	-5,097,000	-2,053,000
Return on Assets %	-.16%	-.02%	-.06%	-.22%	-.44%	-.05%
Return on Equity %	-.27%	-.05%	-.10%	-.31%	-.56%	-.06%
Debt to Equity	.18%	0.245	0.104			0.00

CONTACT INFORMATION:
Phone: 281 878-1000   Fax: 281 821-5488
Toll-Free:
Address: 654 N. Sam Houston Pkwy E., Ste. 400, Houston, TX 77060
United States

STOCK TICKER/OTHER:
Stock Ticker: ENG
Employees: 198
Parent Company:

Exchange: NAS
Fiscal Year Ends: 12/31

SALARIES/BONUSES:
Top Exec. Salary: $260,205   Bonus: $60,385
Second Exec. Salary: $270,210   Bonus: $30,192

OTHER THOUGHTS:
Estimated Female Officers or Directors: 2
Hot Spot for Advancement for Women/Minorities: Y

Eni SpA

NAIC Code: 211111

www.eni.com/en-it

TYPES OF BUSINESS:
Oil & Gas-Exploration & Production
Hydrocarbons
Oil Refining
Biofuels
Electric Generation
Renewable Energy
Bio-Based Products
Gas Stations

BRANDS/DIVISIONS/AFFILIATES:
enjoy

GROWTH PLANS/SPECIAL FEATURES:
Eni is an integrated oil and gas company that explores for, produces, and refines oil around the world. In 2021, the company produced 0.8 million barrels of liquids and 4.6 billion cubic feet of natural gas per day. At end-2021, Eni held reserves of 6.6 billion barrels of oil equivalent, 49% of which are liquids. The Italian government owns a 30.1% stake in the company. Eni is placing its renewable and low-carbon business in a separate entity, Plentitude; it plans to list publicly in 2022.

CONTACTS: Note: Officers with more than one job title may be intentionally listed here more than once.

Claudio Descalzi, CEO
Massimo Mantovani, General Counsel
Stefano Lucchini, Sr. Exec. VP-Public Affairs & Comm.
Roberto Ulissi, Sr. Exec. VP-Corp. Affairs & Governance
Claudio Descalzi, COO-Exploration & Prod.
Angelo Fanelli, COO-Refining & Mktg.
Marco Petracchini, Sr. Exec. VP-Internal Audit
Lucia Calvosa, Chmn.
Marco Alvera, Sr. Exec. VP-Midstream

FINANCIAL DATA: Note: Data for latest year may not have been available at press time.

In U.S. $	2021	2020	2019	2018	2017	2016
Revenue	74,987,510,000	43,075,100,000	68,432,290,000	74,250,120,000	65,531,690,000	54,605,990,000
R&D Expense						
Operating Income	10,845,400,000	263,423,300	7,741,120,000	9,909,221,000	4,834,650,000	1,890,968,000
Operating Margin %	.14%	.01%	.11%	.13%	.07%	.03%
SGA Expense	2,828,129,000	2,803,647,000	2,933,890,000	3,028,879,000	2,889,822,000	2,931,931,000
Net Income	5,700,324,000	-8,455,986,000	144,931,800	4,040,463,000	3,304,053,000	-1,433,650,000
Operating Cash Flow	12,594,380,000	4,722,035,000	12,135,100,000	13,364,080,000	9,907,263,000	7,513,930,000
Capital Expenditure	5,127,452,000	4,547,724,000	8,202,356,000	8,929,952,000	8,501,033,000	8,989,688,000
EBITDA	21,508,660,000	6,153,726,000	17,559,270,000	21,306,930,000	19,902,660,000	14,399,170,000
Return on Assets %	.05%	-.07%	.00%	.04%	.03%	-.01%
Return on Equity %	.14%	-.20%	.00%	.08%	.07%	-.03%
Debt to Equity	.63%	0.697	0.495	0.394	0.418	0.388

CONTACT INFORMATION:
Phone: 39 252041730 Fax: 39 252041765
Toll-Free:
Address: Piazzale Enrico Mattei, 1, Rome, 00144 Italy

STOCK TICKER/OTHER:
Stock Ticker: E Exchange: NYS
Employees: 32,689 Fiscal Year Ends: 12/31
Parent Company:

SALARIES/BONUSES:
Top Exec. Salary: $379,956 Bonus: $
Second Exec. Salary: $82,000 Bonus: $

OTHER THOUGHTS:
Estimated Female Officers or Directors: 1
Hot Spot for Advancement for Women/Minorities: Y

Sales, profits and employees may be estimates. Financial information, benefits and other data can change quickly and may vary from those stated here.

Enovix Corp

NAIC Code: 335912

www.enovix.com

TYPES OF BUSINESS:
Lithium Batteries, Primary, Manufacturing

GROWTH PLANS/SPECIAL FEATURES:
Enovix Corp is engaged in the business of advanced silicon-anode lithium-ion battery development and production. It is also developing its 3D cell technology and production process for the electric vehicle and energy storage markets to help enable the widespread utilization of renewable energy.

BRANDS/DIVISIONS/AFFILIATES:

CONTACTS:
Note: Officers with more than one job title may be intentionally listed here more than once.

Harrold Rust, CEO
Steffen Pietzke, CFO
Thurman Rodgers, Chairman of the Board
Edward Hejlek, Chief Legal Officer
Ashok Lahiri, Chief Technology Officer
Cameron Dales, Other Executive Officer

FINANCIAL DATA:
Note: Data for latest year may not have been available at press time.

In U.S. $	2021	2020	2019	2018	2017	2016
Revenue						
R&D Expense	37,850,000	14,442,000				
Operating Income	-69,522,000	-23,530,000				
Operating Margin %						
SGA Expense	29,705,000	5,713,000				
Net Income	-125,874,000	-39,650,000				
Operating Cash Flow	-51,306,000	-20,050,000				
Capital Expenditure	43,584,000	26,953,000				
EBITDA	-124,172,000	-38,964,000				
Return on Assets %	-.46%	-.61%				
Return on Equity %	-.69%	-1.09%				
Debt to Equity	.03%					

CONTACT INFORMATION:
Phone: 510 687-1330 Fax:
Toll-Free:
Address: 3501 W. Warren Ave., Fremont, CA 94538 United States

STOCK TICKER/OTHER:
Stock Ticker: ENVX Exchange: NAS
Employees: Fiscal Year Ends:
Parent Company:

SALARIES/BONUSES:
Top Exec. Salary: $338,536 Bonus: $180,000
Second Exec. Salary: $308,369 Bonus: $73,125

OTHER THOUGHTS:
Estimated Female Officers or Directors:
Hot Spot for Advancement for Women/Minorities:

Sales, profits and employees may be estimates. Financial information, benefits and other data can change quickly and may vary from those stated here.

Entegris Inc

NAIC Code: 332912

www.entegris.com

TYPES OF BUSINESS:
Fuel Cell Materials & Components
Semiconductor Material Handling Technology
Fluid Handling Products
Maintenance Services

BRANDS/DIVISIONS/AFFILIATES:

GROWTH PLANS/SPECIAL FEATURES:
Entegris Inc is a supplier of advanced materials and process solutions for the semiconductor and other high-technology industries. The company's reportable segments include Specialty Chemicals & Engineered Materials (SCEM), Microcontamination Control (MC), and Advanced Materials Handling (AMH). The SCEM segment provides high-performance & high-purity process chemistries, gases, & materials, and safe & efficient delivery systems. The Microcontamination Control (MC) segment includes solutions to purify critical liquid chemistries and process gases used in semiconductor manufacturing processes and other high-technology industries. Its geographical segments are Taiwan, North America, South Korea, Japan, China, Europe, and Southeast.

Entegris offers its employees medical, dental and life insurance; disability coverage; a 401(k) plan; an employee stock purchase plan; flexible spending accounts; and an employee assistance program.

CONTACTS:
Note: Officers with more than one job title may be intentionally listed here more than once.

Bertrand Loy, CEO
Gregory Graves, CFO
Paul Olson, Chairman of the Board
Michael Sauer, Chief Accounting Officer
Jim O'Neill, Chief Technology Officer
Todd Edlund, COO
Joe Colella, General Counsel
Stuart Tison, General Manager
Clint Haris, General Manager
William Shaner, General Manager
Bruce Beckman, Senior VP, Divisional
Susan Rice, Senior VP, Divisional
Corey Rucci, Senior VP, Divisional

FINANCIAL DATA:
Note: Data for latest year may not have been available at press time.

In U.S. $	2021	2020	2019	2018	2017	2016
Revenue	2,298,893,000	1,859,313,000	1,591,066,000	1,550,497,000	1,342,532,000	1,175,270,000
R&D Expense	167,632,000	136,057,000	121,140,000	118,456,000	106,951,000	106,991,000
Operating Income	551,768,000	395,445,000	239,278,000	292,689,000	241,817,000	155,536,000
Operating Margin %	.24%	.21%	.15%	.19%	.18%	.13%
SGA Expense	292,408,000	265,128,000	284,807,000	246,534,000	216,194,000	201,901,000
Net Income	409,126,000	294,969,000	254,860,000	240,755,000	85,066,000	97,147,000
Operating Cash Flow	400,454,000	446,674,000	382,298,000	312,576,000	293,373,000	207,555,000
Capital Expenditure	210,626,000	131,752,000	112,355,000	110,153,000	93,597,000	65,260,000
EBITDA	658,483,000	539,409,000	506,414,000	415,794,000	319,305,000	256,731,000
Return on Assets %	.13%	.11%	.11%	.11%	.05%	.06%
Return on Equity %	.26%	.23%	.23%	.24%	.09%	.11%
Debt to Equity	.58%	0.816	0.837	0.924	0.578	0.539

CONTACT INFORMATION:
Phone: 978 436-6500 Fax: 952 556-1880
Toll-Free: 800-394-4083
Address: 129 Concord Rd., Billerica, MA 01821 United States

STOCK TICKER/OTHER:
Stock Ticker: ENTG
Employees: 5,800
Parent Company:

Exchange: NAS
Fiscal Year Ends: 12/31

SALARIES/BONUSES:
Top Exec. Salary: $981,250   Bonus: $
Second Exec. Salary: $565,000   Bonus: $

OTHER THOUGHTS:
Estimated Female Officers or Directors:
Hot Spot for Advancement for Women/Minorities:

Sales, profits and employees may be estimates. Financial information, benefits and other data can change quickly and may vary from those stated here.

Entergy Corporation

NAIC Code: 221112

www.entergy.com

TYPES OF BUSINESS:
Utilities-Electric
Energy Management
Energy Trading
Nuclear Generation
Hydroelectric Generation
Wind Generation

GROWTH PLANS/SPECIAL FEATURES:
Entergy is a holding company with five regulated integrated utilities that generate and distribute electricity to about 3 million customers in Arkansas, Louisiana, Mississippi, and Texas. It is one of the largest power producers in the country with approximately 23 gigawatts of regulated utility-owned power generation capacity. Entergy was the second-largest nuclear owner in the U.S. before it began retiring and selling its merchant plants in 2014.
Entergy offers comprehensive benefits, retirement options and employee assistance programs.

BRANDS/DIVISIONS/AFFILIATES:
Entergy Arkansas LLC
Entergy Louisiana LLC
Entergy Mississippi LLC
Entergy New Orleans LLC
Entergy Texas Inc
System Energy Resources Inc

CONTACTS:
Note: Officers with more than one job title may be intentionally listed here more than once.

David Ellis, CEO, Subsidiary
Peter Norgeot, Senior VP, Divisional
Roderick West, CEO, Subsidiary
Haley Fisackerly, CEO, Subsidiary
Sallie Rainer, CEO, Subsidiary
Phillip May, CEO, Subsidiary
Laura Landreaux, CEO, Subsidiary
Leo Denault, CEO
Andrew Marsh, CFO
Kimberly Fontan, Chief Accounting Officer
Paul Hinnenkamp, COO
Marcus Brown, Executive VP
A. Bakken, Executive VP
Kathryn Collins, Other Executive Officer
Julie Harbert, Senior VP, Divisional

FINANCIAL DATA:
Note: Data for latest year may not have been available at press time.

In U.S. $	2021	2020	2019	2018	2017	2016
Revenue	11,742,900,000	10,113,640,000	10,878,670,000	11,009,450,000	11,074,480,000	10,845,640,000
R&D Expense						
Operating Income	2,109,251,000	1,795,818,000	1,680,524,000	1,001,686,000	1,898,779,000	-815,231,000
Operating Margin %	.18%	.18%	.15%	.09%	.17%	-.08%
SGA Expense						
Net Income	1,118,719,000	1,406,653,000	1,258,244,000	862,555,000	425,353,000	-564,503,000
Operating Cash Flow	2,300,713,000	2,689,866,000	2,816,627,000	2,385,247,000	2,623,500,000	2,998,699,000
Capital Expenditure	6,422,112,000	5,156,861,000	4,631,505,000	4,271,217,000	4,001,618,000	4,044,257,000
EBITDA	4,387,731,000	4,328,560,000	4,013,157,000	2,573,632,000	3,708,844,000	1,407,899,000
Return on Assets %	.02%	.03%	.02%	.02%	.01%	-.01%
Return on Equity %	.10%	.13%	.13%	.10%	.05%	-.07%
Debt to Equity	2.12%	1.935	1.665	1.755	1.794	1.793

CONTACT INFORMATION:
Phone: 504 576-4000   Fax: 504 576-4428
Toll-Free: 800-368-3749
Address: 639 Loyola Ave., New Orleans, LA 70113 United States

STOCK TICKER/OTHER:
Stock Ticker: ETR
Employees: 12,369
Parent Company:

Exchange: NYS
Fiscal Year Ends: 12/31

SALARIES/BONUSES:
Top Exec. Salary: $1,289,538   Bonus: $
Second Exec. Salary: $748,087   Bonus: $

OTHER THOUGHTS:
Estimated Female Officers or Directors: 5
Hot Spot for Advancement for Women/Minorities: Y

Sales, profits and employees may be estimates. Financial information, benefits and other data can change quickly and may vary from those stated here.

Envision AESC SDI Co Ltd

NAIC Code: 335911

www.envision-aesc.com/en/aboutus

TYPES OF BUSINESS:
Batteries for Electric Automobiles
Battery Technology
Artificial Intelligence of Things
Renewable Energy
Lithium-Ion Batteries
Battery Production Plants
Research and Development Center

BRANDS/DIVISIONS/AFFILIATES:
Envision Group

GROWTH PLANS/SPECIAL FEATURES:
Envision AESC SDI Co., Ltd. is a world-leading battery technology company. The firm utilizes Artificial Intelligence of Things (AIoT) to develop its battery technology and multidisciplinary applications, which enable electric vehicles to participate in the renewable energy eco-system. Envision AESC's lithium-ion batteries have been installed in more than 600,000 electric vehicles, with a zero rate of critical malfunction. The AIoT battery systems collect and monitor a large number of processes and battery status parameters during the production process. The data covers the entire production chain. Each cell has more than 2,000 data collection points, with the data being monitored and traceable in real time. The data can correspond to more than 800 quality control projects. Envision AESC has battery production plants in Kanagawa, Japan; Sunderland, U.K.; Tennessee, USA; and Douai, France. Envision AESC also has another three production bases and a research and development center in China. Envision Group is the parent company of Envision AESC SDI Co., Ltd.

CONTACTS:
Note: Officers with more than one job title may be intentionally listed here more than once.

Lei Zhang, CEO

FINANCIAL DATA:
Note: Data for latest year may not have been available at press time.

In U.S. $	2021	2020	2019	2018	2017	2016
Revenue	687,011,818	660,588,287	629,131,702	599,173,050	570,641,000	332,108,979
R&D Expense						
Operating Income						
Operating Margin %						
SGA Expense						
Net Income						
Operating Cash Flow						
Capital Expenditure						
EBITDA						
Return on Assets %						
Return on Equity %						
Debt to Equity						

CONTACT INFORMATION:
Phone: 81 46-252-3211 Fax:
Toll-Free:
Address: 2-10-1 Hironodai, Zama-city, Kanagawa, 252-0012 Japan

STOCK TICKER/OTHER:
Stock Ticker: Joint Venture Exchange:
Employees: 531 Fiscal Year Ends: 03/31
Parent Company: Envision Group

SALARIES/BONUSES:
Top Exec. Salary: $ Bonus: $
Second Exec. Salary: $ Bonus: $

OTHER THOUGHTS:
Estimated Female Officers or Directors:
Hot Spot for Advancement for Women/Minorities:

Sales, profits and employees may be estimates. Financial information, benefits and other data can change quickly and may vary from those stated here.

Equinor ASA
NAIC Code: 211111

www.equinor.com

TYPES OF BUSINESS:
Oil & Gas Exploration & Production
Refining
Pipelines
Energy Marketing
Oil and Gas
Wind Power
Solar Power

BRANDS/DIVISIONS/AFFILIATES:

GROWTH PLANS/SPECIAL FEATURES:
Equinor is a Norway-based integrated oil and gas company. It has been publicly listed since 2001, but the government retains a 67% stake. Operating primarily on the Norwegian Continental Shelf, the firm produced 2.1 million barrels of oil equivalent per day in 2021 (52% oil) and ended the year with 5.4 billion barrels of proven reserves (49% oil). Operations also include offshore wind, solar, oil refineries and natural gas processing, marketing, and trading.

Equinox offers its employees comprehensive benefits.

CONTACTS: Note: Officers with more than one job title may be intentionally listed here more than once.
Anders Opedal, CEO
Ulrica Fearn, CFO
Tim Dodson, Exec. VP-Exploration
John Knight, Exec. VP-Bus. Dev. & Global Strategy
William Maloney, Exec. VP-Dev. & Prod., North America
Oystein Michelsen, Exec. VP-Dev. & Prod., Norway
Jon Erik Reinhardsen, Chmn.
Lars Christian Bacher, Exec. VP-Int'l Dev. & Prod.

FINANCIAL DATA: Note: Data for latest year may not have been available at press time.

In U.S. $	2021	2020	2019	2018	2017	2016
Revenue	88,744,000,000	45,753,000,000	62,911,000,000	78,555,000,000	60,971,000,000	45,688,000,000
R&D Expense						
Operating Income	33,404,000,000	-3,888,000,000	8,679,000,000	19,384,000,000	13,169,000,000	-222,000,000
Operating Margin %	.38%	-.08%	.14%	.25%	.22%	.00%
SGA Expense	780,000,000	706,000,000	809,000,000	758,000,000	738,000,000	762,000,000
Net Income	8,563,000,000	-5,510,000,000	1,843,000,000	7,535,000,000	4,590,000,000	-2,922,000,000
Operating Cash Flow	28,816,000,000	10,386,000,000	13,749,000,000	19,694,000,000	14,802,000,000	8,818,000,000
Capital Expenditure	8,040,000,000	8,476,000,000	10,204,000,000	11,367,000,000	10,755,000,000	12,191,000,000
EBITDA	44,525,000,000	11,955,000,000	23,489,000,000	28,701,000,000	22,554,000,000	11,995,000,000
Return on Assets %	.06%	-.05%	.02%	.07%	.04%	-.03%
Return on Equity %	.23%	-.15%	.04%	.18%	.12%	-.08%
Debt to Equity	.77%	0.955	0.606	0.541	0.607	0.798

CONTACT INFORMATION:
Phone: 47 51990000   Fax: 47 51990050
Toll-Free:
Address: Forusbeen 50, Stavanger, 4035 Norway

SALARIES/BONUSES:
Top Exec. Salary: $1,370,000   Bonus: $
Second Exec. Salary: $988,000   Bonus: $

STOCK TICKER/OTHER:
Stock Ticker: EQNR   Exchange: NYS
Employees: 21,126   Fiscal Year Ends: 12/31
Parent Company:

OTHER THOUGHTS:
Estimated Female Officers or Directors: 6
Hot Spot for Advancement for Women/Minorities: Y

Sales, profits and employees may be estimates. Financial information, benefits and other data can change quickly and may vary from those stated here.

Essent NV

NAIC Code: 221115

www.essent.nl

TYPES OF BUSINESS:
Wind Electric Power Generation
Electricity Distribution
Natural Gas Distribution
Smart Solutions
Energy Trading
Renewable Power Generation
Solar Products
Boilers

BRANDS/DIVISIONS/AFFILIATES:
E.ON SE
Energiedirect.nl
Vandebron
Powerhouse

GROWTH PLANS/SPECIAL FEATURES:
Essent NV is a Netherlands-based energy company. Electricity and gas are supplied to clients in the Netherlands under the Essent brand name. Bundled packages, as well as related smart solutions are offered as well to both residential and business customers. Energiedirect.nl arranges energy supply to customers, with a goal of providing the best rates available. Entrepreneurs can trade directly on the energy market through the company's Powerhouse brand. Subsidiary Vandebron sells power generated from independent wind, solar and biomass projects. Other products offered by Essent include solar panels, central heating boilers and more. Essent operates as a subsidiary of E.ON SE.

CONTACTS:
Note: Officers with more than one job title may be intentionally listed here more than once.

Resi Becker, CEO
Stephan Segbers, COO
Christopher Borger, CFO
M. G. Edens, Sec.

FINANCIAL DATA:
Note: Data for latest year may not have been available at press time.

In U.S. $	2021	2020	2019	2018	2017	2016
Revenue	6,000,000,000	5,648,283,900	4,954,635,000	4,630,500,000	4,410,000,000	4,200,000,000
R&D Expense						
Operating Income						
Operating Margin %						
SGA Expense						
Net Income						
Operating Cash Flow						
Capital Expenditure						
EBITDA						
Return on Assets %						
Return on Equity %						
Debt to Equity						

CONTACT INFORMATION:
Phone: 31-88-8511000 Fax:
Toll-Free:
Address: Willemsplein 4, Hertogenbosch, 5211 AK Netherlands

STOCK TICKER/OTHER:
Stock Ticker: Subsidiary Exchange:
Employees: 400 Fiscal Year Ends: 12/31
Parent Company: E.ON SE

SALARIES/BONUSES:
Top Exec. Salary: $ Bonus: $
Second Exec. Salary: $ Bonus: $

OTHER THOUGHTS:
Estimated Female Officers or Directors:
Hot Spot for Advancement for Women/Minorities:

Sales, profits and employees may be estimates. Financial information, benefits and other data can change quickly and may vary from those stated here.

Eternalsun Spire

NAIC Code: 333242

eternalsunspire.com/about-us

TYPES OF BUSINESS:
Photovoltaic Manufacturing Equipment
Solar Measurement Products and Solutions
Solar Testing
Solar Testing Technology
Temperature-controlled Lab Flasher
Temperature-controlled Chamber
Module Performance Measurement

BRANDS/DIVISIONS/AFFILIATES:

CONTACTS: Note: Officers with more than one job title may be intentionally listed here more than once.
Florian van Rijn van Alkemade, CEO
Mark Roelofs, Mgr.-Oper.
Rodger Lafavre, COO
Erik Bentschap Knook, CCO
Priscilla Lim, Mgr.-HR
Stefan Roest, CTO
Stephen Hogan, Executive VP
Roger Little, Founder

GROWTH PLANS/SPECIAL FEATURES:
Eternalsun Spire, created by the merger of Eternal Sun with Spire Solar LLC, enables solar measurement control via high-end solar testing advice, technology and services. The firm's temperature-controlled lab flasher (TCLF) consists of the A+A+A+ Xenon Single Long Pulse Spire solar simulator and temperature-controlled chamber. The lab flasher provides measurement accuracy and precision for critical module performance measurements. Its single pulse duration supports maximum module power determination of high-efficiency silicon, thin-film, PERC, HIT and multi-junction modules; and the add-on temperature control chamber enables accurate temperature-related tests. Performance and degradation of various photovoltaic (PV) technologies over time can be studied with EternalSun Spire's temperature-controlled A-class steady-state solar simulator, referred to as a light soaker. The chamber can be added to existing Spire flashers. EternalSun Spire offers a micro uniformity measurement tool for calibrating flash solar simulators swiftly and accurately; and its uniformity calibration robot measures the uniformity of steady state solar simulators. The company develops solutions based on customers' goals and needs, with applications addressing high-end research for PV module research groups, testing services for PV module buyers, certification and testing according to IEC norms, and maximum power determination for PV manufacturers. Eternalsun Spire headquarters are located in the Netherlands, with an international office in Shanghai, China, and representative offices worldwide.

FINANCIAL DATA: Note: Data for latest year may not have been available at press time.

In U.S. $	2021	2020	2019	2018	2017	2016
Revenue						
R&D Expense						
Operating Income						
Operating Margin %						
SGA Expense						
Net Income						
Operating Cash Flow						
Capital Expenditure						
EBITDA						
Return on Assets %						
Return on Equity %						
Debt to Equity						

CONTACT INFORMATION:
Phone: 31-157440161   Fax:
Toll-Free:
Address: Wolga 11, The Hague, 2491BK Netherlands

STOCK TICKER/OTHER:
Stock Ticker: Private   Exchange:
Employees: 86   Fiscal Year Ends: 12/31
Parent Company:

SALARIES/BONUSES:
Top Exec. Salary: $ Bonus: $
Second Exec. Salary: $ Bonus: $

OTHER THOUGHTS:
Estimated Female Officers or Directors:
Hot Spot for Advancement for Women/Minorities:

Sales, profits and employees may be estimates. Financial information, benefits and other data can change quickly and may vary from those stated here.

Evonik Industries AG

NAIC Code: 325110

www.evonik.com

TYPES OF BUSINESS:
Petrochemicals
Industrial Engineering
Electricity Generation
Real Estate
Renewable Energy-Biomass
Paints and Coatings

BRANDS/DIVISIONS/AFFILIATES:
Evonik Nutrition & Care GmbH
Evonik Resource Efficiency GmbH
Evonik Performance Materials GmbH
Evonik Technology & Infrastructure GmbH
RAG Foundation
PeroxyChem
Porocel Group

GROWTH PLANS/SPECIAL FEATURES:
Evonik Industries is a German chemical company offering a mix of specialty and commodity chemical products. It has a number-one to -three market position in 80% of its businesses. Around 45% of sales are generated in Europe, while the key markets of North America and Asia account for roughly 25% each. The company is organized into four major segments: specialty additives, smart materials, nutrition and care, and performance materials.

CONTACTS:
Note: Officers with more than one job title may be intentionally listed here more than once.

Christian Kullmann, CEO
Ute Wolf, CFO
Thomas Wessel, Chief Human Resources Officer

FINANCIAL DATA:
Note: Data for latest year may not have been available at press time.

In U.S. $	2021	2020	2019	2018	2017	2016
Revenue	14,644,970,000	11,946,100,000	12,836,260,000	12,991,960,000	14,084,820,000	12,468,050,000
R&D Expense	454,380,700	424,023,400	419,127,100	427,940,500	466,132,000	428,919,700
Operating Income	1,204,501,000	823,565,100	1,147,703,000	1,104,615,000	1,244,651,000	1,331,806,000
Operating Margin %	.08%	.07%	.09%	.09%	.09%	.11%
SGA Expense	2,216,086,000	1,989,874,000	2,035,900,000	2,117,179,000	2,359,059,000	2,155,371,000
Net Income	730,534,600	455,360,000	2,062,340,000	912,678,600	698,218,700	826,502,900
Operating Cash Flow	1,777,373,000	1,691,197,000	1,293,614,000	1,723,513,000	1,518,846,000	1,732,327,000
Capital Expenditure	867,632,200	936,181,000	861,756,600	928,346,900	1,018,440,000	928,346,900
EBITDA	2,239,588,000	1,834,170,000	2,114,242,000	1,842,005,000	2,142,640,000	2,056,465,000
Return on Assets %	.03%	.02%	.10%	.05%	.04%	.05%
Return on Equity %	.09%	.05%	.25%	.12%	.09%	.11%
Debt to Equity	.37%	0.442	0.413	0.477	0.497	0.422

CONTACT INFORMATION:
Phone: 49-201-177-01 Fax: 49-201-177-3475
Toll-Free:
Address: Rellinghauser Strasse 1-11, Essen, NW 45128 Germany

STOCK TICKER/OTHER:
Stock Ticker: EVKIY   Exchange: PINX
Employees: 33,004   Fiscal Year Ends: 12/31
Parent Company:

SALARIES/BONUSES:
Top Exec. Salary: $ Bonus: $
Second Exec. Salary: $ Bonus: $

OTHER THOUGHTS:
Estimated Female Officers or Directors: 1
Hot Spot for Advancement for Women/Minorities:

Sales, profits and employees may be estimates. Financial information, benefits and other data can change quickly and may vary from those stated here.

Exelon Corporation

NAIC Code: 221113

www.exeloncorp.com

TYPES OF BUSINESS:
Electric Power Generation-Nuclear
Energy Generation
Electricity
Natural Gas
Renewable Energy
Distribution
Marketing
Retail

BRANDS/DIVISIONS/AFFILIATES:
Exelon Generation Company LLC
Constellation
Commonwealth Edison Company
PECO Energy Company
Baltimore Gas and Electric Company
Pepco Holdings LLC
Potomac Electric Power Company
Delmarva Power & Light

GROWTH PLANS/SPECIAL FEATURES:
Exelon serves approximately 10 million power and gas customers at its six regulated utilities in Illinois, Pennsylvania, Maryland, New Jersey, Delaware, and Washington, D.C. Exelon is a Fortune 200 company and one of the largest energy delivery companies in the U.S. The firm operates six fully regulated transmission and distribution utilities, Atlantic City Electric (ACE), Baltimore Gas and Electric (BGE), Commonwealth Edison (ComEd), Delmarva Power & Light (DPL), PECO Energy Company (PECO) and Potomac Electric Power Company (Pepco).

CONTACTS: Note: Officers with more than one job title may be intentionally listed here more than once.
Christopher Crane, CEO
Joseph Nigro, CFO
Matthew Bauer, Chief Accounting Officer, Subsidiary
Steven Cichocki, Chief Accounting Officer, Subsidiary
Caroline Fulginiti, Chief Accounting Officer, Subsidiary
Jason Jones, Chief Accounting Officer, Subsidiary
Julie Giese, Chief Accounting Officer, Subsidiary
Fabian Souza, Chief Accounting Officer
William Von Hoene, Chief Strategy Officer
Terence Donnelly, COO, Subsidiary
Stephen Woerner, COO, Subsidiary
William Swahl, COO, Subsidiary
J. Anthony, COO, Subsidiary

FINANCIAL DATA: Note: Data for latest year may not have been available at press time.

In U.S. $	2021	2020	2019	2018	2017	2016
Revenue	36,347,000,000	33,039,000,000	34,438,000,000	35,978,000,000	33,558,000,000	31,366,000,000
R&D Expense						
Operating Income	2,522,000,000	2,799,000,000	4,342,000,000	3,835,000,000	3,939,000,000	3,260,000,000
Operating Margin %	.07%	.08%	.13%	.11%	.12%	.10%
SGA Expense						
Net Income	1,706,000,000	1,963,000,000	2,936,000,000	2,005,000,000	3,779,000,000	1,121,000,000
Operating Cash Flow	3,012,000,000	4,235,000,000	6,659,000,000	8,644,000,000	7,480,000,000	8,461,000,000
Capital Expenditure	7,981,000,000	8,048,000,000	7,248,000,000	7,594,000,000	7,584,000,000	8,553,000,000
EBITDA	11,352,000,000	10,495,000,000	11,381,000,000	9,750,000,000	10,762,000,000	9,085,000,000
Return on Assets %	.01%	.02%	.02%	.02%	.03%	.01%
Return on Equity %	.05%	.06%	.09%	.07%	.14%	.04%
Debt to Equity	1.04%	1.089	0.984	1.121	1.089	1.247

CONTACT INFORMATION:
Phone: 312 394-7398 Fax: 312 394-7945
Toll-Free: 800-483-3220
Address: 10 S. Dearborn St., Chicago, IL 60680-5379 United States

STOCK TICKER/OTHER:
Stock Ticker: EXC Exchange: NAS
Employees: 32,713 Fiscal Year Ends: 12/31
Parent Company:

SALARIES/BONUSES:
Top Exec. Salary: $1,303,595 Bonus: $
Second Exec. Salary: $820,906 Bonus: $

OTHER THOUGHTS:
Estimated Female Officers or Directors: 6
Hot Spot for Advancement for Women/Minorities: Y

Sales, profits and employees may be estimates. Financial information, benefits and other data can change quickly and may vary from those stated here.

Exide Technologies LLC

NAIC Code: 335911

www.exide.com

TYPES OF BUSINESS:
Automotive Battery Technology
Battery Storage Solutions
Energy Storage Solutions
Battery Production
Research and Development
Manufacturing Facilities
Recycling Plants

BRANDS/DIVISIONS/AFFILIATES:

GROWTH PLANS/SPECIAL FEATURES:
Exide Technologies, LLC is a global provider of stored electrical energy solutions for the transportation and industrial markets. The company produces a range of battery and energy storage systems and specialty applications for the transportation, network power and motive power markets, and industries including agricultural, automotive, electric, light- and heavy-duty truck, marine, materials handling, military, mining, powersport, railroad, security, telecommunications, utility and uninterruptible power supply, among others. Exide Technologies has two research and development facilities, nine production plants and three recycling plants in Europe.

CONTACTS:
Note: Officers with more than one job title may be intentionally listed here more than once.

Stefan Stubing, CEO
Michael Geiger, Sr. VP-Sales & Mktg.
Sharon Cottam, VP-Human Resources
Martin Gaessl, VP-IT
Carla Chaney, Executive VP, Divisional
Bruce Cole, Executive VP, Divisional
Barbara Hatcher, Executive VP
Michael Ostermann, Executive VP
Brad Kalter, Other Corporate Officer
Ed Mosley, Other Executive Officer

FINANCIAL DATA:
Note: Data for latest year may not have been available at press time.

In U.S. $	2021	2020	2019	2018	2017	2016
Revenue	2,853,401,200	2,743,655,000	2,855,000,000	2,800,000,000	2,700,000,000	2,650,000,000
R&D Expense						
Operating Income						
Operating Margin %						
SGA Expense						
Net Income		228,900,000	-218,000,000			
Operating Cash Flow						
Capital Expenditure						
EBITDA						
Return on Assets %						
Return on Equity %						
Debt to Equity						

CONTACT INFORMATION:
Phone: 331-41-21-23-00   Fax:
Toll-Free:
Address: 5 Allee des Pierres Mayettes, Gennevilliers, 92636 France

STOCK TICKER/OTHER:
Stock Ticker: Private   Exchange:
Employees: 8,986   Fiscal Year Ends: 03/31
Parent Company:

SALARIES/BONUSES:
Top Exec. Salary: $ Bonus: $
Second Exec. Salary: $ Bonus: $

OTHER THOUGHTS:
Estimated Female Officers or Directors: 2
Hot Spot for Advancement for Women/Minorities: Y

Sales, profits and employees may be estimates. Financial information, benefits and other data can change quickly and may vary from those stated here.

Exxon Mobil Corporation (ExxonMobil)

NAIC Code: 211111

www.exxonmobil.com

TYPES OF BUSINESS:
Oil & Gas Exploration & Production
Gas Refining & Supply
Fuel Marketing
Power Generation
Chemicals
Petroleum Products
Convenience Stores

BRANDS/DIVISIONS/AFFILIATES:
ExxonMobil
Esso
Exxon
XTO
Mobil

GROWTH PLANS/SPECIAL FEATURES:
ExxonMobil is an integrated oil and gas company that explores for, produces, and refines oil around the world. In 2021, it produced 2.3 million barrels of liquids and 8.5 billion cubic feet of natural gas per day. At the end of 2021, reserves were 18.5 billion barrels of oil equivalent, 66% of which were liquids. The company is the world's largest refiner with a total global refining capacity of 4.6 million barrels of oil per day and one of the world's largest manufacturers of commodity and specialty chemicals.

85% of Exxon Mobil's employees are covered by its health program, its benefits vary across global offices, but build on categories such as health, finance and life.

CONTACTS:
Note: Officers with more than one job title may be intentionally listed here more than once.

Darren Woods, CEO
Neil Chapman, Sr. VP
Andrew Swiger, CFO
Len Fox, Chief Accounting Officer
Craig Morford, General Counsel
James Spellings, Other Corporate Officer
Neil Duffin, President, Subsidiary
Linda DuCharme, President, Subsidiary
Stephen Littleton, Secretary
Jack Williams, Senior VP
Liam Mallon, Vice President
Karen McKee, Vice President

FINANCIAL DATA:
Note: Data for latest year may not have been available at press time.

In U.S. $	2021	2020	2019	2018	2017	2016
Revenue	276,692,000,000	178,574,000,000	255,583,000,000	279,332,000,000	237,162,000,000	200,628,000,000
R&D Expense						
Operating Income	24,019,000,000	-29,448,000,000	12,766,000,000	22,124,000,000	13,819,000,000	2,771,000,000
Operating Margin %	.09%	-.16%	.05%	.08%	.06%	.01%
SGA Expense	9,574,000,000	10,168,000,000	11,398,000,000	11,480,000,000	10,649,000,000	10,443,000,000
Net Income	23,040,000,000	-22,440,000,000	14,340,000,000	20,840,000,000	19,710,000,000	7,840,000,000
Operating Cash Flow	48,129,000,000	14,668,000,000	29,716,000,000	36,014,000,000	30,066,000,000	22,082,000,000
Capital Expenditure	12,076,000,000	17,282,000,000	24,361,000,000	19,574,000,000	15,402,000,000	16,163,000,000
EBITDA	52,788,000,000	18,284,000,000	39,884,000,000	50,464,000,000	39,168,000,000	30,730,000,000
Return on Assets %	.07%	-.06%	.04%	.06%	.06%	.02%
Return on Equity %	.14%	-.13%	.07%	.11%	.11%	.05%
Debt to Equity	.26%	0.30	0.137	0.107	0.13	0.173

CONTACT INFORMATION:
Phone: 972 444-1000   Fax: 972 444-1348
Toll-Free:
Address: 5959 Las Colinas Blvd., Irving, TX 75039 United States

STOCK TICKER/OTHER:
Stock Ticker: XOM
Employees: 74,900
Parent Company:

Exchange: NYS
Fiscal Year Ends: 12/31

SALARIES/BONUSES:
Top Exec. Salary: $1,615,000   Bonus: $3,142,000
Second Exec. Salary: $1,068,000   Bonus: $1,932,000

OTHER THOUGHTS:
Estimated Female Officers or Directors: 2
Hot Spot for Advancement for Women/Minorities: Y

Sales, profits and employees may be estimates. Financial information, benefits and other data can change quickly and may vary from those stated here.

Plunkett Research, Ltd.

Falck Renewables SpA
NAIC Code: 221117

www.falckrenewables.com

TYPES OF BUSINESS:
Biomass Electric Power Generation
Wind Farm Design and Construction
Wind Farm Operation
Waste and Biomass Power Plants
Waste Burning Plants
Composting Facility
Waste-to-Energy Technologies

BRANDS/DIVISIONS/AFFILIATES:
Green Bidco SpA

GROWTH PLANS/SPECIAL FEATURES:
Falck Renewables SpA is a renewable energy service firm. Falck builds wind farms, with projects throughout Europe with an installed capacity of more than 1,400 megawatts (MW) and a total 4,800 MW managed. Falck Renewables also designs, constructs and operates waste and biomass fueled power plants and operates three waste burning plants and a composting facility in Italy. Falck produces more than 2.81 billion kilowatt hours (KWh) of energy per year, generated by wind, solar, biomass and waste-to-energy technologies. Based in Milan, Italy, Falck Renewables has locations in Rome, the U.K., France, Spain, Sweden, Holland, the U.S. Japan and Australia. In early-2022, Green Bidco SpA acquired the 60% share of Falck Renewables held by Falk SpA, becoming the firms new majority shareholder.

CONTACTS: Note: Officers with more than one job title may be intentionally listed here more than once.
Toni Volpe, CEO
Lucia Giancaspro, Head-Legal Affairs
Luciano Cavalli, Manager-Bus. Dev.
Giorgio Botta, Investor Rel. Officer
Guido Corbetta, Vice Chmn.
Piero Manzoni, Managing Dir.
Marco Cavenaghi, Head-Procurement
Umberto De Servi, Head-Environment Health & Safety
Olov Mikael Kramer, Chmn.

FINANCIAL DATA: Note: Data for latest year may not have been available at press time.

In U.S. $	2021	2020	2019	2018	2017	2016
Revenue	570,929,403	472,137,000	419,388,000	384,187,000	345,726,000	291,009,000
R&D Expense						
Operating Income						
Operating Margin %						
SGA Expense						
Net Income	61,274,642	73,479,700	70,753,900	66,608,700	35,365,700	-4,016,170
Operating Cash Flow						
Capital Expenditure						
EBITDA						
Return on Assets %						
Return on Equity %						
Debt to Equity						

CONTACT INFORMATION:
Phone: 39-02-2433-1   Fax: 39-02-2433-2394
Toll-Free:
Address: Via Alberto Falck 4-16, Sesto San Giovanni, Milan 20099 Italy

STOCK TICKER/OTHER:
Stock Ticker: FKR   Exchange: Milan
Employees: 693   Fiscal Year Ends: 12/31
Parent Company: Green Bidco SpA

SALARIES/BONUSES:
Top Exec. Salary: $ Bonus: $
Second Exec. Salary: $ Bonus: $

OTHER THOUGHTS:
Estimated Female Officers or Directors:
Hot Spot for Advancement for Women/Minorities: Y

Sales, profits and employees may be estimates. Financial information, benefits and other data can change quickly and may vary from those stated here.

First Solar Inc

NAIC Code: 334413A

www.firstsolar.com

TYPES OF BUSINESS:
Photovoltaic Cell Manufacturing
Thin-Film Solar Modules
Solar Module Collection & Recycling
Photovoltaic Site Operation & Maintenance
Solar Project Engineering, Procurement & Construction
Project Development & Financing

BRANDS/DIVISIONS/AFFILIATES:

GROWTH PLANS/SPECIAL FEATURES:
First Solar designs and manufactures solar photovoltaic panels, modules, and systems for use in utility-scale development projects. The company's solar modules use cadmium telluride to convert sunlight into electricity. This is commonly called thin-film technology. First Solar is the world's largest thin-film solar module manufacturer. It has production lines in Vietnam, Malaysia, and Ohio. It plans to add a large factory in India.

First Solar offers comprehensive employee benefits, which may differ by employee position and office location.

CONTACTS: Note: Officers with more than one job title may be intentionally listed here more than once.
Mark Widmar, CEO
Alexander Bradley, CFO
Michael Ahearn, Chairman of the Board
Byron Jeffers, Chief Accounting Officer
Markus Gloeckler, Chief Technology Officer
Philip deJong, COO
Jason Dymbort, General Counsel
Michael Koralewski, Other Executive Officer
Kuntal Verma, Other Executive Officer
Patrick Buehler, Other Executive Officer
Georges Antoun, Other Executive Officer
Caroline Stockdale, Other Executive Officer

FINANCIAL DATA: Note: Data for latest year may not have been available at press time.

In U.S. $	2021	2020	2019	2018	2017	2016
Revenue	2,923,377,000	2,711,332,000	3,063,117,000	2,244,044,000	2,941,324,000	2,904,563,000
R&D Expense	99,115,000	93,738,000	96,611,000	84,472,000	88,573,000	124,762,000
Operating Income	439,467,000	323,489,000	201,215,000	40,113,000	215,032,000	250,641,000
Operating Margin %	.15%	.12%	.07%	.02%	.07%	.09%
SGA Expense	170,320,000	222,918,000	205,471,000	176,857,000	202,699,000	261,994,000
Net Income	468,693,000	398,355,000	-114,933,000	144,326,000	-165,615,000	-416,112,000
Operating Cash Flow	237,559,000	37,120,000	174,201,000	-326,809,000	1,340,677,000	206,753,000
Capital Expenditure	540,291,000	416,635,000	668,717,000	739,838,000	514,357,000	229,452,000
EBITDA	845,169,000	550,151,000	112,412,000	269,804,000	343,193,000	-285,773,000
Return on Assets %	.06%	.05%	-.02%	.02%	-.02%	-.06%
Return on Equity %	.08%	.08%	-.02%	.03%	-.03%	-.08%
Debt to Equity	.06%	0.077	0.111	0.088	0.083	0.036

CONTACT INFORMATION:
Phone: 602 414-9300 Fax: 602 414-9400
Toll-Free: 877-850-3757
Address: 350 W. Washington St., Ste. 600, Tempe, AZ 85281 United States

STOCK TICKER/OTHER:
Stock Ticker: FSLR
Employees: 5,100
Parent Company:

Exchange: NAS
Fiscal Year Ends: 12/31

SALARIES/BONUSES:
Top Exec. Salary: $900,309   Bonus: $
Second Exec. Salary: $575,000   Bonus: $

OTHER THOUGHTS:
Estimated Female Officers or Directors: 3
Hot Spot for Advancement for Women/Minorities: Y

FirstEnergy Corporation

www.firstenergycorp.com

NAIC Code: 221112

TYPES OF BUSINESS:
Electric Utility
Power Generation
Electricity Transmission
Electricity Distribution
Coal Facilities
Hydro Facilities

GROWTH PLANS/SPECIAL FEATURES:
FirstEnergy is one of the largest investor-owned utilities in the United States with 10 regulated distribution companies across six mid-Atlantic and Midwestern states. FirstEnergy also owns and operates one of the nation's largest electric transmission systems with 24,000 miles of lines.

BRANDS/DIVISIONS/AFFILIATES:
Ohio Edison
Illuminating Company (The)
Met-Ed
Penelec
West Penn Power
Jersey Central Power & Light
Mon Power
Potomac Edison

CONTACTS:
Note: Officers with more than one job title may be intentionally listed here more than once.

Steven Strah, CEO
K. Taylor, CFO
Jason Lisowski, Chief Accounting Officer
Hyun Park, Chief Legal Officer
Donald Misheff, Director
John Somerhalder, Director
Christine Walker, Other Executive Officer
Samuel Belcher, President, Subsidiary
Gary Benz, Senior VP, Subsidiary

FINANCIAL DATA:
Note: Data for latest year may not have been available at press time.

In U.S. $	2021	2020	2019	2018	2017	2016
Revenue	11,132,000,000	10,790,000,000	11,035,000,000	11,261,000,000	10,928,000,000	10,700,000,000
R&D Expense						
Operating Income	2,229,000,000	1,685,000,000	1,836,000,000	2,358,000,000	2,326,000,000	1,995,000,000
Operating Margin %	.20%	.16%	.17%	.21%	.21%	.19%
SGA Expense	-382,000,000	477,000,000	674,000,000	144,000,000	102,000,000	102,000,000
Net Income	1,283,000,000	1,079,000,000	912,000,000	1,348,000,000	-1,724,000,000	-6,177,000,000
Operating Cash Flow	2,811,000,000	1,423,000,000	2,467,000,000	1,410,000,000	3,808,000,000	3,383,000,000
Capital Expenditure	2,445,000,000	2,657,000,000	2,665,000,000	2,675,000,000	2,841,000,000	3,067,000,000
EBITDA	4,226,000,000	3,316,000,000	3,296,000,000	3,947,000,000	4,079,000,000	3,970,000,000
Return on Assets %	.03%	.02%	.02%	.02%	-.04%	-.13%
Return on Equity %	.16%	.15%	.13%	.18%	-.34%	-.66%
Debt to Equity	2.56%	3.058	2.813	2.633	4.761	2.915

CONTACT INFORMATION:
Phone: 800 736-3402 Fax:
Toll-Free: 800-633-4766
Address: 76 S. Main St., Akron, OH 44308 United States

STOCK TICKER/OTHER:
Stock Ticker: FE
Employees: 12,395
Parent Company:

Exchange: NYS
Fiscal Year Ends: 12/31

SALARIES/BONUSES:
Top Exec. Salary: $686,209   Bonus: $750,000
Second Exec. Salary: $1,076,236   Bonus: $

OTHER THOUGHTS:
Estimated Female Officers or Directors: 6
Hot Spot for Advancement for Women/Minorities: Y

Sales, profits and employees may be estimates. Financial information, benefits and other data can change quickly and may vary from those stated here.

Flowserve Corporation

NAIC Code: 333913

www.flowserve.com

TYPES OF BUSINESS:
Pump, Valve & Seal Manufacturing
Aftermarket Servicing, Installation and Retrofitting
Fluid Motion Control Systems
Production
Manufacturing
Fluid Pumps
Valves
Industrial Internet of Things

BRANDS/DIVISIONS/AFFILIATES:

GROWTH PLANS/SPECIAL FEATURES:
Flowserve Corp is a manufacturer and aftermarket service provider of comprehensive flow control systems. It develops precision-engineered flow control equipment to monitor movement and protect customers' materials and processes. It offers an extensive range of pumps, valves, seals, and services for several global industries, including oil and gas, chemical, power generation, and water management. In addition, Flowserve has a worldwide network of Quick Response Centers to provide aftermarket equipment services. The aftermarket services help customers with installation, advanced diagnostics, repair, and retrofitting. Sales are roughly split across many global regions, with North America and Europe contributing the majority of total revenue.

CONTACTS:
Note: Officers with more than one job title may be intentionally listed here more than once.

R. Rowe, CEO
Amy Schwetz, CFO
Roger Fix, Chairman of the Board
Scott Vopni, Chief Accounting Officer
Lanesha Minnix, Chief Legal Officer
Elizabeth Burger, Other Executive Officer
Keith Gillespie, Other Executive Officer
Kirk Wilson, President, Divisional
Tamara Morytko, President, Divisional
Sanjay Chowbey, President, Divisional
John Roueche, Treasurer

FINANCIAL DATA: Note: Data for latest year may not have been available at press time.

In U.S. $	2021	2020	2019	2018	2017	2016
Revenue	3,541,060,000	3,728,134,000	3,939,697,000	3,835,699,000	3,660,831,000	3,990,487,000
R&D Expense						
Operating Income	252,649,000	238,524,000	376,140,000	224,285,000	187,226,000	271,422,000
Operating Margin %	.07%	.06%	.10%	.06%	.05%	.07%
SGA Expense	797,076,000	878,245,000	913,203,000	966,584,000	901,727,000	965,376,000
Net Income	125,949,000	130,420,000	238,828,000	104,508,000	2,652,000	132,455,000
Operating Cash Flow	250,119,000	310,537,000	324,097,000	190,831,000	311,066,000	240,476,000
Capital Expenditure	54,936,000	57,405,000	75,716,000	83,993,000	61,602,000	89,699,000
EBITDA	291,027,000	359,230,000	483,317,000	327,070,000	441,191,000	389,801,000
Return on Assets %	.03%	.03%	.05%	.02%	.00%	.03%
Return on Equity %	.07%	.08%	.14%	.06%	.00%	.08%
Debt to Equity	.79	1.094	.869	.861	.906	.919

CONTACT INFORMATION:
Phone: 972 443-6500   Fax: 972 443-6800
Toll-Free:
Address: 5215 N. O'Connor Blvd., Ste. 700, Irving, TX 75039 United States

STOCK TICKER/OTHER:
Stock Ticker: FLS
Employees: 16,000
Parent Company:

Exchange: NYS
Fiscal Year Ends: 12/31

SALARIES/BONUSES:
Top Exec. Salary: $1,133,000   Bonus: $
Second Exec. Salary: $664,250   Bonus: $

OTHER THOUGHTS:
Estimated Female Officers or Directors: 3
Hot Spot for Advancement for Women/Minorities: Y

Sales, profits and employees may be estimates. Financial information, benefits and other data can change quickly and may vary from those stated here.

Fluor Corporation

NAIC Code: 237000

www.fluor.com

TYPES OF BUSINESS:
Heavy Construction and Engineering
Engineering
Procurement
Fabrication
Construction
Energy Solutions
Urban Solutions
Mission Solutions

BRANDS/DIVISIONS/AFFILIATES:

GROWTH PLANS/SPECIAL FEATURES:
Fluor is one of the largest global providers of engineering, procurement, construction, fabrication, operations, and maintenance services. The firm serves a wide range of end markets including oil and gas, chemicals, mining, metals, and transportation. The company's business is organized into three core segments: urban solutions, mission solutions, and energy solutions. Fluor employs over 40,000 workers in more than 60 countries. The company generated $12.4 billion in revenue in 2021.

Fluor offers its employees health, dental, vision, life and accident insurance; disability coverage; savings and retirement plans; a tax savings account; and educational assistance.

CONTACTS: Note: Officers with more than one job title may be intentionally listed here more than once.
David Constable, CEO
Joseph Brennan, CFO
Alan Boeckmann, Chairman of the Board
John Regan, Chief Accounting Officer
John Reynolds, Chief Legal Officer
Taco de Haan, Executive VP
Stacy Dillow, Executive VP
Alvin Collins, President, Divisional
James Breuer, President, Divisional
Terry Towle, President, Divisional
Thomas DAgostino, President, Divisional
Mark Fields, President, Divisional

FINANCIAL DATA: Note: Data for latest year may not have been available at press time.

In U.S. $	2021	2020	2019	2018	2017	2016
Revenue	12,434,880,000	14,157,930,000	15,454,480,000	18,851,010,000	14,806,510,000	19,036,520,000
R&D Expense						
Operating Income	195,144,000	198,004,000	-345,871,000	448,216,000	94,032,000	599,243,000
Operating Margin %	.02%	.01%	-.02%	.02%	.01%	.03%
SGA Expense	216,451,000	201,522,000	139,819,000	121,164,000	183,697,000	191,073,000
Net Income	-440,170,000	-435,046,000	-1,522,164,000	173,468,000	153,671,000	281,401,000
Operating Cash Flow	25,332,000	185,884,000	219,018,000	162,164,000	601,971,000	705,919,000
Capital Expenditure	75,073,000	113,442,000	180,842,000	210,998,000	283,107,000	235,904,000
EBITDA	31,132,000	174,438,000	-604,098,000	679,549,000	346,536,000	842,202,000
Return on Assets %	-.06%	-.06%	-.18%	.02%	.02%	.03%
Return on Equity %	-.38%	-.35%	-.70%	.06%	.05%	.09%
Debt to Equity	.84%	1.651	1.11	0.586	0.476	0.486

CONTACT INFORMATION:
Phone: 469 398-7000 Fax: 469 398-7255
Toll-Free:
Address: 6700 Las Colinas Blvd., Irving, TX 75039 United States

STOCK TICKER/OTHER:
Stock Ticker: FLR
Employees: 43,717
Parent Company:

Exchange: NYS
Fiscal Year Ends: 12/31

SALARIES/BONUSES:
Top Exec. Salary: $1,350,045 Bonus: $
Second Exec. Salary: $514,692 Bonus: $273,769

OTHER THOUGHTS:
Estimated Female Officers or Directors: 3
Hot Spot for Advancement for Women/Minorities: Y

Sales, profits and employees may be estimates. Financial information, benefits and other data can change quickly and may vary from those stated here.

Fomento de Construcciones Y Contratas SA (FCC)
www.fcc.es

NAIC Code: 237000

TYPES OF BUSINESS:
Heavy & Civil Engineering Construction
Alternative Energy Development
Integrated Water Management
Cement Manufacturing
Logistics Services
Engineering Services
Railway Concessions

BRANDS/DIVISIONS/AFFILIATES:
Control Empresarial de Capitales SA de CV
FCC Aqualia
FCC Construction
FACC Industrial
FCC Concessiones
Cementos Portland Valderrivas

GROWTH PLANS/SPECIAL FEATURES:
Fomento de Construcciones Y Contratas SA is in the business of environmental services, end to end water management, construction and cement. The company's activities include services related to urban water treatment, waste recovery, end to end water cycle and also infrastructure construction projects, building construction, manufacturing of cement and concrete and operation of quarries and mineral deposits. The firm derives majority of its revenues from environmental services segment. It carries out international operations in European, the US and Latin American markets.

CONTACTS:
Note: Officers with more than one job title may be intentionally listed here more than once.

Pablo Colio Abril, CEO
Antonio Gomez Ciria, Gen. Dir.-Admin.
Jose Manuel Velasco Guardado, Gen. Dir.-Comm.
Juan Bejar, Exec. Chmn.-Cementos Portland Valderrivas SA
Eric Marotel, Managing Dir.-Cemusa
Eduardo Gonzalez Gomez, Gen Dir.-Energy
Miguel Hernanz Sanjuan, Gen. Dir.-Internal Audit
Esther Alcocer Koplowitz, Chairperson

FINANCIAL DATA:
Note: Data for latest year may not have been available at press time.

In U.S. $	2021	2020	2019	2018	2017	2016
Revenue	6,521,228,000	6,030,360,000	6,146,118,000	5,865,630,000	5,681,750,000	5,828,208,000
R&D Expense						
Operating Income	660,520,800	547,497,500	559,115,500	467,528,400	435,547,500	409,544,000
Operating Margin %	.10%	.09%	.09%	.08%	.08%	.07%
SGA Expense						
Net Income	568,108,100	256,743,700	261,174,900	246,353,700	115,593,900	-158,225,400
Operating Cash Flow	730,775,500	592,530,100	617,478,000	479,265,900	752,924,500	1,003,655,000
Capital Expenditure	379,360,900	399,476,100	321,606,600	284,526,600	266,758,700	296,522,600
EBITDA	1,338,899,000	1,029,939,000	1,070,165,000	900,387,800	785,076,900	584,121,100
Return on Assets %	.04%	.02%	.02%	.02%	.01%	-.01%
Return on Equity %	.22%	.12%	.15%	.20%	.14%	-.30%
Debt to Equity	1.21%	1.696	2.484	2.30	4.925	5.789

CONTACT INFORMATION:
Phone: 34-934-964900 Fax: 34 913594923
Toll-Free:
Address: Federico Salmon, 13, Madrid, 28016 Spain

STOCK TICKER/OTHER:
Stock Ticker: FMOCY Exchange: PINX
Employees: 58,640 Fiscal Year Ends: 12/31
Parent Company: Control Empresarial de Capitales SA de CV

SALARIES/BONUSES:
Top Exec. Salary: $ Bonus: $
Second Exec. Salary: $ Bonus: $

OTHER THOUGHTS:
Estimated Female Officers or Directors: 2
Hot Spot for Advancement for Women/Minorities: Y

Sales, profits and employees may be estimates. Financial information, benefits and other data can change quickly and may vary from those stated here.

Fotowatio Renewable Ventures SLU

NAIC Code: 221114

www.frv.com

TYPES OF BUSINESS:
Solar Electric Power Generation
Solar Panels
Solar Plant Maintenance Services
Solar Plant Construction
Finance Services
Technologies

BRANDS/DIVISIONS/AFFILIATES:
Abdul Latif Jameel Energy and Environmental Srvcs
OMERS Infrastructure Management Inc

CONTACTS: Note: Officers with more than one job title may be intentionally listed here more than once.
Daniel Sagi-Vela, CEO

GROWTH PLANS/SPECIAL FEATURES:
Fotowatio Renewable Ventures SLU is a Spanish firm specializing in the management of solar power generation facilities. FRV focuses on the design, development, construction, financing, operation and maintenance of solar plants. The company's geographic diversification includes plants developed across five continents, operating under business and regulatory environments. The firm utilizes the latest technologies and solutions to design and deliver optimal results; and its in-house team researches and develops innovative solutions including battery storage, hybrid technology and financing. The company is experienced in engineering, procurement and construction (EPC) regarding the development of its own projects. It operates in the following areas of financial management: technical, accounting, finance, administration, and legal and corporate services. FRV encompasses trained professionals who are solely dedicated to the operation and maintenance (O&M) and management of its solar and wind arms. The firm's asset management provides full-cycle services for third-party projects, local authorities and financial entities, from development to construction and into operations. This division manages the O&M contract to reach stated goals. Assets are monitored through FRV's state-of-the-art system, which offers 24-hour supervision worldwide. Headquartered in Spain, FRV has global offices in Mexico, Italy, Australia and Chile. Fotowatio Renewables is a joint venture between Abdul Latif Jameel Energy and Environmental Services (51%) and OMERS Infrastructure Management Inc. (49%).

FINANCIAL DATA: Note: Data for latest year may not have been available at press time.

In U.S. $	2021	2020	2019	2018	2017	2016
Revenue						
R&D Expense						
Operating Income						
Operating Margin %						
SGA Expense						
Net Income						
Operating Cash Flow						
Capital Expenditure						
EBITDA						
Return on Assets %						
Return on Equity %						
Debt to Equity						

CONTACT INFORMATION:
Phone: 34-913-191290   Fax:
Toll-Free:
Address: Maria de Molina 40, Fl. 5, Madrid, 28006 Spain

STOCK TICKER/OTHER:
Stock Ticker: Joint Venture   Exchange:
Employees: 120   Fiscal Year Ends:
Parent Company: Abdul Latif Jameel Energy and Environmental Srvcs

SALARIES/BONUSES:
Top Exec. Salary: $ Bonus: $
Second Exec. Salary: $ Bonus: $

OTHER THOUGHTS:
Estimated Female Officers or Directors:
Hot Spot for Advancement for Women/Minorities:

Freyr Battery SA

NAIC Code: 335912

www.freyrbattery.com

TYPES OF BUSINESS:
Primary Battery Manufacturing
Lithium-Ion Battery Production
Battery Cell Facilities
Renewable Power
Hydro Power
Wind Power

GROWTH PLANS/SPECIAL FEATURES:
FREYR Battery is an emerging producer of clean battery solutions for a better planet. It designs and manufactures high-density and cost-competitive lithium-ion batteries with a reduced carbon footprint for the global markets for electric mobility, stationary energy storage, marine and aviation applications.

BRANDS/DIVISIONS/AFFILIATES:

CONTACTS:
Note: Officers with more than one job title may be intentionally listed here more than once.

Tom Elinar Jensen, CEO
Jan Arve Jaugan, COO
Steffen Foreid, CFO
Gery Bonduelle, Exec. VP-Sales
Hege Marie Norheim, Exec. VP-Human Resources
Ryuta Kawaguchi, CTO
Torstein Dale Sjotveit, Chmn.

FINANCIAL DATA:
Note: Data for latest year may not have been available at press time.

In U.S. $	2021	2020	2019	2018	2017	2016
Revenue						
R&D Expense	13,816,000	1,865,000				
Operating Income	-75,571,000	-8,923,000				
Operating Margin %						
SGA Expense	61,635,000	7,043,000				
Net Income	-93,378,000	-9,605,000				
Operating Cash Flow	-63,136,000	-7,336,000				
Capital Expenditure	13,775,000	71,000				
EBITDA	-93,255,000	-9,537,000				
Return on Assets %	-.29%	-.60%				
Return on Equity %	-.34%	-1.94%				
Debt to Equity						

CONTACT INFORMATION:
Phone: 352 466 111 3721   Fax:
Toll-Free:
Address: 412F, route D'Esch, Luxembourg, L-2086 Luxembourg

STOCK TICKER/OTHER:
Stock Ticker: FREY
Employees: 119
Parent Company:

Exchange: NYS
Fiscal Year Ends: 12/31

SALARIES/BONUSES:
Top Exec. Salary: $600,719   Bonus: $4,467,802
Second Exec. Salary: $581,843   Bonus: $350,561

OTHER THOUGHTS:
Estimated Female Officers or Directors:
Hot Spot for Advancement for Women/Minorities:

Sales, profits and employees may be estimates. Financial information, benefits and other data can change quickly and may vary from those stated here.

Plunkett Research, Ltd.

FuelCell Energy Inc

NAIC Code: 335999A

www.fuelcellenergy.com

TYPES OF BUSINESS:
Fuel Cell Manufacturing
Fuel Cell Power Plants
Fuel Cell Technology
Thermal Energy
Power Generation Solutions

BRANDS/DIVISIONS/AFFILIATES:

GROWTH PLANS/SPECIAL FEATURES:
FuelCell Energy Inc is a fuel-cell power company. FuelCell designs manufactures, sells, installs, operates, and services fuel cell products, which efficiently convert chemical energy in fuels into electricity through a series of chemical reactions. It serves various industries such as Industrial, Wastewater treatment, Commercial and Hospitality, Data centers and Communications, Education and Healthcare, and others. Geographically, the company generates a majority of its revenue from the United States followed by South Korea.

CONTACTS:
Note: Officers with more than one job title may be intentionally listed here more than once.

Jason Few, CEO
Michael Bishop, CFO
James England, Chairman of the Board
Anthony Leo, Chief Technology Officer
Michael Lisowski, COO
Joshua Dolger, General Counsel

FINANCIAL DATA:
Note: Data for latest year may not have been available at press time.

In U.S. $	2021	2020	2019	2018	2017	2016
Revenue	69,585,000	70,871,000	60,752,000	89,437,000	95,666,000	108,252,000
R&D Expense	11,315,000	4,797,000	13,786,000	22,817,000	20,398,000	20,846,000
Operating Income	-64,902,000	-39,166,000	-66,929,000	-44,632,000	-43,580,000	-46,353,000
Operating Margin %	-.93%	-.55%	-1.10%	-.50%	-.46%	-.43%
SGA Expense	37,948,000	26,644,000	31,874,000	24,908,000	25,916,000	25,150,000
Net Income	-101,055,000	-89,107,000	-77,568,000	-47,334,000	-53,903,000	-50,957,000
Operating Cash Flow	-70,438,000	-36,781,000	-30,572,000	16,322,000	-71,845,000	-46,595,000
Capital Expenditure	6,353,000	382,000	2,151,000	10,028,000	12,351,000	7,726,000
EBITDA	-73,788,000	-54,390,000	-54,483,000	-32,646,000	-36,170,000	-40,782,000
Return on Assets %	-.15%	-.22%	-.30%	-.17%	-.16%	-.18%
Return on Equity %	-.25%	-.68%	-1.27%	-.68%	-.53%	-.52%
Debt to Equity	.13%	0.825	1.19	0.871	0.63	0.707

CONTACT INFORMATION:
Phone: 203 825-6000   Fax: 203 825-6100
Toll-Free:
Address: 3 Great Pasture Rd., Danbury, CT 06813 United States

STOCK TICKER/OTHER:
Stock Ticker: FCEL
Employees: 382
Parent Company:

Exchange: NAS
Fiscal Year Ends: 10/31

SALARIES/BONUSES:
Top Exec. Salary: $512,211   Bonus: $
Second Exec. Salary: $397,735   Bonus: $

OTHER THOUGHTS:
Estimated Female Officers or Directors:
Hot Spot for Advancement for Women/Minorities:

Sales, profits and employees may be estimates. Financial information, benefits and other data can change quickly and may vary from those stated here.

GE Global Research

NAIC Code: 541712

www.ge.com/research

TYPES OF BUSINESS:
Research & Development
Nuclear & Fossil Fuel Energy Technology
Wind, Solar, Hydroelectric & Biomass Technology
Fuel Cell & Energy Storage Technology
Nanotechnology
Photonics & Optoelectronics
Engine Technology
Biotechnology

BRANDS/DIVISIONS/AFFILIATES:
General Electric Company

CONTACTS:
Note: Officers with more than one job title may be intentionally listed here more than once.

Hema Achanta, Research Engineer
Mark M. Little, Sr. VP-Global Research
Janith Samarasinghe, Research Engineer
Michael Idelchik, VP-Advanced Tech. Programs
Xiangli Chen, Gen. Mgr.-GE China Tech. Center
Terry K. Lieb, Dir.-Global Tech., Chemistry & Chemical Eng.
Christine M. Furstoss, Dir.-Global Tech., Mfg. & Materials Tech.
Kenneth G. Herd, Gen. Mgr.-Brazil Tech. Center
James R. Maughan, Dir.-Global Tech. & Research, Americas
A. Nadeem Ishaque, Dir.-Global Tech., Diagnostics & Biomedical Tech.
Danielle Merfield, Dir.-Global Tech., Electrical Tech. & Systems
Michael Ming, Gen. Mgr.-Oil & Gas Tech. Center
Gopi Katragadda, Managing Dir.-GE India Tech. Center
Carlos Hartel, Managing Dir.-GE Global Research Center-Europe

GROWTH PLANS/SPECIAL FEATURES:
GE Global Research (GE Global) is the research and development arm of General Electric Company. GE Global researches and develops advance horizontal technologies across 13 core areas. Additive manufacturing makes metal additive manufacturing faster, reliable and pervasive. Artificial Intelligence (AI) enables the smart industrial internet by connecting human expertise with industrial machines to enable intelligent and user-friendly products. Biology and applied physics creates and builds tools and imaging solutions for the healthcare, biomanufacturing, biotechnology and related industries. Controls and optimization leverages controls, estimation, optimization, operations research and risk management to increase customer outcomes. Digital technologies deliver business value with foundational systems and applications that make up the ecosystem to digitally manage critical business data and operations. Edge computing pushes data collection, analytics and compute capability to the Edge in order to manage industrial machines more dynamically with security and safety. Electric power technology accelerates not only the generation and delivery of electricity, but the electrification of products. Electronics and sensing solutions are focused on extreme integration across technologies, form factors and harsh environments. Materials deliver advanced, disruptive material solutions to drive performance, cost and durability across diverse product lines. Mechanics and design technology improves durability, affordability, efficiency and power density of industrial products and services. Robotics and autonomous systems address redundant, dangerous and other types of work on behalf of humans. Software and analytics harness the power of computing, data and analytics to enable the optimization of industrial assets. Last, thermosciences invents innovative aerodynamic, thermal management and combustion solutions for improved performance, reliability, cost and environmental impact. GE Global offers commercial services, digital solutions and intellectual property solutions. The firm serves GE's company-wide business divisions, related partners and government agencies.

FINANCIAL DATA:
Note: Data for latest year may not have been available at press time.

In U.S. $	2021	2020	2019	2018	2017	2016
Revenue						
R&D Expense						
Operating Income						
Operating Margin %						
SGA Expense						
Net Income						
Operating Cash Flow						
Capital Expenditure						
EBITDA						
Return on Assets %						
Return on Equity %						
Debt to Equity						

CONTACT INFORMATION:
Phone: 518-387-5000 Fax: 518-387-6696
Toll-Free:
Address: 1 Research Cir., Niskayuna, NY 12309 United States

STOCK TICKER/OTHER:
Stock Ticker: Subsidiary Exchange:
Employees: 1,000 Fiscal Year Ends: 12/31
Parent Company: General Electric Company (GE)

SALARIES/BONUSES:
Top Exec. Salary: $ Bonus: $
Second Exec. Salary: $ Bonus: $

OTHER THOUGHTS:
Estimated Female Officers or Directors: 2
Hot Spot for Advancement for Women/Minorities:

Sales, profits and employees may be estimates. Financial information, benefits and other data can change quickly and may vary from those stated here.

GE Power

NAIC Code: 333611

www.ge.com/power

TYPES OF BUSINESS:
Generation Equipment-Turbines & Generators
Gas Power Solutions
Steam Power Solutions
Nuclear Power Solutions
Power Conversion Solutions
Energy Consulting Services

BRANDS/DIVISIONS/AFFILIATES:
General Electric Company (GE)
GE Gas Power
GE Steam Power
GE Hitachi Nuclear Energy
GE Power Conversion
GE Energy Consulting

CONTACTS:
Note: Officers with more than one job title may be intentionally listed here more than once.
Scott Strazik, CEO
Jeffery R. Immelt, CEO-GE

GROWTH PLANS/SPECIAL FEATURES:
GE Power, a business division of the General Electric Company (GE), operates in five business segments: gas, steam, nuclear, power conversion and energy consulting. The GE Gas Power segment offers gas turbines and power plant solutions, including power plants, steam turbines, generators, heat recovery steam generators, digitals, controls and cybersecurity solutions. Industries served include cement, data centers, oil and gas, metals, mining, large facilities and paper/pulp. The GE Steam Power segment offers products and solutions that help customers lower their carbon path, with products including steam turbines, air quality and pollution control systems, boilers, generators and synchronous condensers. This division's services include equipment services and produce life cycle solutions. The GE Hitachi Nuclear Energy segment is a global leader in new plant technology, fuel and services, with solutions spanning decommissioning and dismantling, dose reduction, life extension, long-term asset management, parts and plant performance. This division's digital solutions offer virtual reality solutions, outage planning solutions and analytics. The GE Power Conversion segment designs and delivers advanced power conversion technologies for industrial processes across marine, oil and gas, power generation, hydro, metals, mining, research and testing, and energy transition sectors. This division's services include contact center, training, contracts, digital solutions, drives, rotating machines and spare parts. Last, the GE Energy Consulting segment aim to solve global technical and economic problems, enabling technology integration and energy transition. Practice areas within this division include power economics, power systems planning power systems operation, generation products and related software. Consulting solutions span renewables integration, energy investments, global forecasting, microgrid, digital energy, distributed energy, integrated wind/solar/battery storage power plant, and grid code modeling and testing. During 2022, General Electric Company announced plans to spin off the combined GE Renewable Energy/GE Power/GE Digital businesses in a single global public company by early-2024.

FINANCIAL DATA: *Note: Data for latest year may not have been available at press time.*

In U.S. $	2021	2020	2019	2018	2017	2016
Revenue	16,903,000,000	17,589,000,000	18,625,000,000			
R&D Expense						
Operating Income						
Operating Margin %						
SGA Expense						
Net Income	726,000,000	274,000,000	291,000,000			
Operating Cash Flow						
Capital Expenditure						
EBITDA						
Return on Assets %						
Return on Equity %						
Debt to Equity						

CONTACT INFORMATION:
Phone: 518-385-2211 Fax:
Toll-Free:
Address: 1 River Rd., Schenectady, NY 12345 United States

SALARIES/BONUSES:
Top Exec. Salary: $ Bonus: $
Second Exec. Salary: $ Bonus: $

STOCK TICKER/OTHER:
Stock Ticker: Subsidiary Exchange:
Employees: 32,000 Fiscal Year Ends: 12/31
Parent Company: General Electric Company (GE)

OTHER THOUGHTS:
Estimated Female Officers or Directors:
Hot Spot for Advancement for Women/Minorities:

Sales, profits and employees may be estimates. Financial information, benefits and other data can change quickly and may vary from those stated here.

GE Renewable Energy

NAIC Code: 221115

www.ge.com/renewableenergy

TYPES OF BUSINESS:
Wind Electric Power Generation
Hydroelectric Power Generation
Solar Electric Power Generation

BRANDS/DIVISIONS/AFFILIATES:
General Electric Co. (GE)
LM Wind Power
GE Vernova

CONTACTS:
Note: Officers with more than one job title may be intentionally listed here more than once.

Jerome Pecresse, CEO

GROWTH PLANS/SPECIAL FEATURES:

GE Renewable Energy, a subsidiary of General Electric Company (GE), brings together one of the broadest product and service portfolios of the renewable energy industry. The firm has a large clean energy footprint, more than 400 gigawatts (GW), utilizing wind energy, hydroelectric power, solar energy and hybrid solutions. GE Renewable's wind energy comes from a portfolio of nearly 50,000 onshore and offshore wind turbines. GE subsidiary LM Wind Power in-sources wind turbine blade design and manufacturing for GE Renewable. The hydroelectric power solutions of the firm represent more than 25% of the total installed worldwide capacity. The firm's portfolio of solutions for hydropower generation includes a broad range of hydro solutions and services: from water to wire, from individual equipment to complete turnkey solutions, for new plants and the installed base. GE Renewables solar energy offerings include both concentrated solar power (CSP) plants and photovoltaic solar solutions. Hybrid power plants combine various sources of power generation and storage to accentuate the positive aspects and address the challenges of a specific generation type. GE Renewable is a global leader in grid infrastructure products and services, offering a broad set of utility applications ranging from medium voltage to high and ultra-high voltage power equipment, including transformers, gas-insulated solutions, circuit breakers, disconnectors, voltage regulators, bushings, post insulators, surge arresters, capacitors and reactors. The company also offers related digital solutions across its product portfolio, including digital wind, digital hydro, digital solar and digital grid solutions. In late-2022, parent GE announced plans to unite its energy business, including renewables, power, digital and energy financial services, under a single banner: GE Vernova.

FINANCIAL DATA:
Note: Data for latest year may not have been available at press time.

In U.S. $	2021	2020	2019	2018	2017	2016
Revenue	15,697,000,000	15,666,000,000	9,620,000,000	9,533,000,000	9,205,000,000	
R&D Expense						
Operating Income						
Operating Margin %						
SGA Expense						
Net Income	-795,000,000	-715,000,000	293,000,000	287,000,000	583,000,000	
Operating Cash Flow						
Capital Expenditure						
EBITDA						
Return on Assets %						
Return on Equity %						
Debt to Equity						

CONTACT INFORMATION:
Phone: 33-1-85-32-20-00 Fax:
Toll-Free:
Address: 204, Rond Point du Pont De Sevres, Boulogne-Billancourt, 92100 France

SALARIES/BONUSES:
Top Exec. Salary: $ Bonus: $
Second Exec. Salary: $ Bonus: $

STOCK TICKER/OTHER:
Stock Ticker: Subsidiary Exchange:
Employees: 38,000 Fiscal Year Ends:
Parent Company: General Electric Co (GE)

OTHER THOUGHTS:
Estimated Female Officers or Directors:
Hot Spot for Advancement for Women/Minorities:

Sales, profits and employees may be estimates. Financial information, benefits and other data can change quickly and may vary from those stated here.

GE Vernova

NAIC Code: 221110

www.gevernova.com

TYPES OF BUSINESS:
Electric Power Generation
Energy Production
Renewable Energy
Wind and Hydro Solutions
Gas and Steam Power Production
Nuclear Power
Power Conversion
Energy Digital Technology and Software

BRANDS/DIVISIONS/AFFILIATES:
General Electric Company

CONTACTS:
Note: Officers with more than one job title may be intentionally listed here more than once.

Scott Strazik, CEO

GROWTH PLANS/SPECIAL FEATURES:
GE Vernova operates the energy businesses of General Electric Company. Vernova's energy divisions include renewable energy, power, digital and energy financial services. The renewable energy division consists of onshore and offshore wind projects, turbines and related equipment and services; offshore grid equipment, services and solutions; and hydro and hybrid solutions. The power division consists of gas turbines, heavy-duty gas turbines and aero-derivatives, along with related equipment and services. This division produces gas power, steam power and nuclear power, and also engages in power conversion for specialized sectors. The digital division designs and produces software and technologies that enable renewable energy to take place on the grid, reduce emissions, increase plant productivity, adapt to consumer demand and keep power producers and utilities safe. Last, the energy financial services division supports GE's energy customers by offering finance solutions across onshore, offshore and re-powering, as well as for financing global power projects in regards to thermal power generation, and offering access to domestic and global capital markets, and funding sources across public and private sectors.

FINANCIAL DATA: *Note: Data for latest year may not have been available at press time.*

In U.S. $	2021	2020	2019	2018	2017	2016
Revenue						
R&D Expense						
Operating Income						
Operating Margin %						
SGA Expense						
Net Income						
Operating Cash Flow						
Capital Expenditure						
EBITDA						
Return on Assets %						
Return on Equity %						
Debt to Equity						

CONTACT INFORMATION:
Phone: 617-443-3000 Fax:
Toll-Free:
Address: 5 Necco St., Boston, MA 02210 United States

STOCK TICKER/OTHER:
Stock Ticker: Subsidiary Exchange:
Employees: Fiscal Year Ends:
Parent Company: General Electric Company

SALARIES/BONUSES:
Top Exec. Salary: $ Bonus: $
Second Exec. Salary: $ Bonus: $

OTHER THOUGHTS:
Estimated Female Officers or Directors:
Hot Spot for Advancement for Women/Minorities:

Sales, profits and employees may be estimates. Financial information, benefits and other data can change quickly and may vary from those stated here.

General Electric Company (GE)

NAIC Code: 333000

www.ge.com

TYPES OF BUSINESS:
Machinery and Equipment Manufacturing
Industrial Technology
Financial Services
Power
Renewable Energy
Aviation
Healthcare

BRANDS/DIVISIONS/AFFILIATES:

GROWTH PLANS/SPECIAL FEATURES:
GE was formed through the combination of two companies in 1892, including one with historical ties to American inventor Thomas Edison. Today, GE is a global leader in air travel, precision health, and in the energy transition. The company is known for its differentiated technology and its massive industrial installed base of equipment sprawled throughout the world. That installed base most notably includes aerospace engines, gas and steam turbines, onshore and offshore wind turbines, as well as medical diagnostic and mobile equipment. GE earns most of its profits on the service revenue of that equipment, which is generally higher-margin. The company is led by former Danaher alum Larry Culp who is leading a multi-year turnaround of the storied conglomerate based on Lean principles.

CONTACTS:
Note: Officers with more than one job title may be intentionally listed here more than once.

Russell Stokes, CEO, Subsidiary
Jerome Pecresse, CEO, Subsidiary
Kieran Murphy, CEO, Subsidiary
John Slattery, CEO, Subsidiary
Scott Strazik, CEO, Subsidiary
H. Culp, CEO
Carolina Dybeck Happe, CFO
Thomas Timko, Chief Accounting Officer
Michael Holston, General Counsel
L. Cox, Other Executive Officer
David Joyce, Vice Chairman

FINANCIAL DATA:
Note: Data for latest year may not have been available at press time.

In U.S. $	2021	2020	2019	2018	2017	2016
Revenue	74,196,000,000	75,834,000,000	90,221,000,000	97,012,000,000	99,279,000,000	119,468,000,000
R&D Expense	2,497,000,000	2,565,000,000	3,118,000,000	3,415,000,000		
Operating Income	3,813,000,000	409,000,000	5,151,000,000	6,761,000,000	-2,739,000,000	14,178,000,000
Operating Margin %	.05%	.01%	.06%	.07%	-.03%	.12%
SGA Expense	13,990,000,000	14,989,000,000	17,100,000,000	17,433,000,000	26,425,000,000	17,638,000,000
Net Income	-6,520,000,000	5,704,000,000	-4,979,000,000	-22,355,000,000	-8,484,000,000	7,500,000,000
Operating Cash Flow	3,332,000,000	3,568,000,000	8,734,000,000	4,978,000,000	6,554,000,000	1,160,000,000
Capital Expenditure	1,361,000,000	1,730,000,000	2,498,000,000	6,947,000,000	7,096,000,000	7,948,000,000
EBITDA	1,202,000,000	12,949,000,000	6,414,000,000	-9,639,000,000	-496,000,000	19,125,000,000
Return on Assets %	-.03%	.02%	-.02%	-.07%	-.02%	.02%
Return on Equity %	-.18%	.16%	-.18%	-.52%	-.14%	.08%
Debt to Equity	.84%	2.064	2.375	2.932	1.962	1.387

CONTACT INFORMATION:
Phone: 203-373-2211 Fax:
Toll-Free:
Address: 5 Necco St., Boston, MA 02210 United States

STOCK TICKER/OTHER:
Stock Ticker: GE   Exchange: NYS
Employees: 168,000   Fiscal Year Ends: 12/31
Parent Company:

SALARIES/BONUSES:
Top Exec. Salary: $2,500,000   Bonus: $4,200,000
Second Exec. Salary: $1,500,000 Bonus: $2,100,000

OTHER THOUGHTS:
Estimated Female Officers or Directors: 10
Hot Spot for Advancement for Women/Minorities: Y

Global Solar Energy Inc

globalsolar.com

NAIC Code: 334413A

TYPES OF BUSINESS:
Photovoltaic Cell Manufacturing
Photovoltaic Cells
Solar Plant Design & Installation

BRANDS/DIVISIONS/AFFILIATES:
Hanergy Holding Group Limited
PowerFLEX
PoweFLEX+
PowerFLEX + FG-M1

CONTACTS:
Note: Officers with more than one job title may be intentionally listed here more than once.

Timothy Teich, VP-Oper.
Jeffrey S. Britt, Pres.
Greg Decker, Dir.-Sales & Mktg.
Timothy Teich, VP-Oper.

GROWTH PLANS/SPECIAL FEATURES:
Global Solar Energy, Inc. manufactures thin-film copper indium gallium diSelenide (CIGS) solar solutions. The company's lightweight and flexible solar power has been integrated into commercial, residential, off-grid and mobile applications worldwide. Among Global Solar's most innovative contributions are solutions for the Building Applied Photovoltaic (BAPV) and transportation markets. Branded as PowerFLEX and PowerFLEX+, these CIGS thin film modules range from 90 to 315 Watts dc (direct current). No racking system is required when bonding the modules with a simple peel-and-stick process to clean thermoplastic polyolefin (TPO) and EPDM (ethylene propylene diene terpolymer) membranes, coated steels and elastomeric-coated modified bitumen. This installation process provides high wind resistance and no penetrations for roofs with at least a 2-degree slope, curved roofs and roofs that can only handle a light load. The solar modules have the ability to provide 25 years of reliable power. The company offers solar mobility to the recreational marine and RV markets, as well as to the commercial trucking market, with its PowerFLEX mobile kits. These 100 W and 200 W kits come with instruction manuals and all the accessories needed for a complete system solution. The PowerFLEX + FG-M1 solar panel is 55 W and designed to fit off-grid, mobile, marine and RV installations. Global Solar also provides off-grid power generation for remote purposes; and provides original equipment manufacturers with ICI technology with its FG-SM series of solar submodules. Its thin-film material allows it to partner with other industries to create innovative, efficient and effective products. Global Solar operates in Tucson, Arizona, and is a subsidiary of Hanergy Holding Group Limited.

FINANCIAL DATA:
Note: Data for latest year may not have been available at press time.

In U.S. $	2021	2020	2019	2018	2017	2016
Revenue						
R&D Expense						
Operating Income						
Operating Margin %						
SGA Expense						
Net Income						
Operating Cash Flow						
Capital Expenditure						
EBITDA						
Return on Assets %						
Return on Equity %						
Debt to Equity						

CONTACT INFORMATION:
Phone: 520-546-6313   Fax: 520-546-6318
Toll-Free:
Address: 8500 South Rita Rd., Tucson, AZ 85747 United States

STOCK TICKER/OTHER:
Stock Ticker: Subsidiary   Exchange:
Employees: 95   Fiscal Year Ends: 12/31
Parent Company: Hanergy Holding Group Limited

SALARIES/BONUSES:
Top Exec. Salary: $ Bonus: $
Second Exec. Salary: $ Bonus: $

OTHER THOUGHTS:
Estimated Female Officers or Directors:
Hot Spot for Advancement for Women/Minorities:

Sales, profits and employees may be estimates. Financial information, benefits and other data can change quickly and may vary from those stated here.

Green Mountain Power Corporation

www.greenmountainpower.com

NAIC Code: 221113

TYPES OF BUSINESS:
Utilities-Electric & Natural Gas
Hydroelectric Power Generation
Nuclear Power Generation
Solar Power Generation

BRANDS/DIVISIONS/AFFILIATES:
Energir Inc
Nothern New Englang Energy Corporation

GROWTH PLANS/SPECIAL FEATURES:
Green Mountain Power Corporation is a Vermont-based utility company that provides electricity and energy products and services based primarily through renewable fuels. The company's energy supply is 100% carbon free and nearly 80% renewable. Most of the firm's energy supply is hydro power, from small local hydro facilities in Vermont and large sources in Quebec. Green Mountain Power's fuel mix is comprised of over 68.2% large hydro, 21.2% nuclear, 7.2% Vermont hydro and the remainder new renewables (including solar). Green Mountain serves residential and business customers. The firm operates as a subsidiary of Northern New England Energy Corporation, itself a subsidiary of Energir Inc.

CONTACTS:
Note: Officers with more than one job title may be intentionally listed here more than once.

Mari McClure, CEO
Mike Burke, VP-Oper.
Mathieu Lepage, CFO
Mark Dincecco, CTO
Donald J. Rendall, Jr., General Counsel

FINANCIAL DATA:
Note: Data for latest year may not have been available at press time.

In U.S. $	2021	2020	2019	2018	2017	2016
Revenue	744,793,000	721,000,000	700,000,000	693,000,000	660,000,000	652,855,260
R&D Expense						
Operating Income						
Operating Margin %						
SGA Expense						
Net Income						
Operating Cash Flow						
Capital Expenditure						
EBITDA						
Return on Assets %						
Return on Equity %						
Debt to Equity						

CONTACT INFORMATION:
Phone: 802-864-5731   Fax: 802-655-8419
Toll-Free: 888-835-4672
Address: 163 Acorn Ln., Colchester, VT 05446 United States

STOCK TICKER/OTHER:
Stock Ticker: Subsidiary
Employees: 510
Parent Company: Energir Inc

Exchange:
Fiscal Year Ends: 12/31

SALARIES/BONUSES:
Top Exec. Salary: $ Bonus: $
Second Exec. Salary: $ Bonus: $

OTHER THOUGHTS:
Estimated Female Officers or Directors: 3
Hot Spot for Advancement for Women/Minorities: Y

Sales, profits and employees may be estimates. Financial information, benefits and other data can change quickly and may vary from those stated here.

Green Plains Inc

www.gpreinc.com

NAIC Code: 325193

TYPES OF BUSINESS:
Ethanol Production
Agri-Technology
Renewable Crops
Feed Ingredients
Specialty Alcohols
Low-Carbon Fuel
Technologies

BRANDS/DIVISIONS/AFFILIATES:
Project 24

GROWTH PLANS/SPECIAL FEATURES:
Green Plains Inc manufactures and sells ethanol and ethanol byproducts in four segments based on function. The ethanol production segment, which generates the majority of revenue, includes the production of ethanol, grains, and corn oil. The agribusiness and energy services segment includes the grain procurement and commodity marketing business, which markets, sells, and distributes ethanol, distillers grains, and corn oil. The food and ingredients segment includes cattle feeding operations. The partnership segment provides fuel storage and transportation services.

CONTACTS: Note: Officers with more than one job title may be intentionally listed here more than once.
Todd Becker, CEO
Patrich Simpkins, CFO
Wayne Hoovestol, Chairman of the Board
Paul Kolomaya, Chief Accounting Officer
Michelle Mapes, Chief Administrative Officer
Alain Treuer, Director
Mark Hudak, Executive VP, Divisional

FINANCIAL DATA: Note: Data for latest year may not have been available at press time.

In U.S. $	2021	2020	2019	2018	2017	2016
Revenue	2,827,168,000	1,923,719,000	2,417,238,000	2,983,932,000	3,289,475,000	3,410,881,000
R&D Expense						
Operating Income	-4,093,000	-77,745,000	-142,570,000	-60,397,000	23,748,000	91,688,000
Operating Margin %	.00%	-.04%	-.06%	-.02%	.01%	.03%
SGA Expense	91,139,000	84,932,000	77,077,000	108,259,000	107,515,000	104,677,000
Net Income	-65,992,000	-108,775,000	-166,860,000	15,923,000	61,061,000	10,663,000
Operating Cash Flow	4,246,000	98,895,000	-9,532,000	38,967,000	-182,163,000	100,701,000
Capital Expenditure	187,195,000	110,579,000	75,481,000	40,529,000	44,594,000	58,113,000
EBITDA	116,095,000	-42,893,000	-60,615,000	191,351,000	132,128,000	174,428,000
Return on Assets %	-.04%	-.07%	-.09%	.01%	.02%	.00%
Return on Equity %	-.08%	-.16%	-.20%	.02%	.07%	.01%
Debt to Equity	.59%	0.521	0.375	0.315	0.814	0.907

CONTACT INFORMATION:
Phone: 402 884-8700   Fax: 402 884-8776
Toll-Free:
Address: 1811 Aksarben Dr., Omaha, NE 68106 United States

STOCK TICKER/OTHER:
Stock Ticker: GPRE
Employees: 859
Parent Company:

Exchange: NAS
Fiscal Year Ends: 12/31

SALARIES/BONUSES:
Top Exec. Salary: $729,167   Bonus: $
Second Exec. Salary: $414,583   Bonus: $

OTHER THOUGHTS:
Estimated Female Officers or Directors: 1
Hot Spot for Advancement for Women/Minorities:

Sales, profits and employees may be estimates. Financial information, benefits and other data can change quickly and may vary from those stated here.

GRID Alternatives

NAIC Code: 238210

www.gridalternatives.org

TYPES OF BUSINESS:
Solar Panel Installation
Renewable Efficiency Solutions
Solar Panels
Solar Installation
Job Training
Clean Mobility Solutions
EV Charging Stations

BRANDS/DIVISIONS/AFFILIATES:

CONTACTS: Note: Officers with more than one job title may be intentionally listed here more than once.
Erica Mackie, CEO
Tim Sears, COO
Zach Franklin, Chief Strategy Officer
Anna Bautista, Dir.-Construction
Zach Franklin, VP-Dev.
Zach Franklin, VP-Comm.
Stanley Greschner, VP-Gov't Rel.
Maura McKnight, Mgr.-Corp. & Foundation Dev.
Mary Spinelli, Mgr.-Events
Julian Foley, Mgr.-Comm.
Ben Passer, Chmn.

GROWTH PLANS/SPECIAL FEATURES:
GRID Alternatives is a 501(c) (3) certified nonprofit organization that develops and implements renewable energy projects for off-grid communities throughout the world. GRID installs solar projects that serve low-income households and communities, and enables the communities to access a variety of clean mobility and battery storage incentive programs. The organization partners with affordable housing organizations, job training groups, government agencies, municipalities, utilities, tribes and local communities to offer its clean energy programs. Solar installations for qualified households are provided free of charge, and hands-on solar training helps connect people to clean energy jobs. Technical assistance and solar installation for multi-family affordable housing is also provided. GRID provides home Level 2 electric vehicle charging stations to eligible consumers throughout California via partnerships, while also providing employment and training opportunities for community members. For many renters and other EV drivers unable to charge at home, GRID has developed subsidized access to certain Level 2 and DC Fast Charging public charging stations. Other programs include shared mobility, solar program policies, and solar program design and administration. The firm is based in Oakland, California, with eight affiliate offices serving all of California, Colorado, Delaware, Maryland and Washington DC, USA; and in Mexico, Nepal and Nicaragua.

FINANCIAL DATA: Note: Data for latest year may not have been available at press time.

In U.S. $	2021	2020	2019	2018	2017	2016
Revenue	91,000,000	58,917,982	51,682,440	54,244,197	58,238,179	43,141,477
R&D Expense						
Operating Income						
Operating Margin %						
SGA Expense						
Net Income			-9,360,744	1,291,145		2,976,325
Operating Cash Flow						
Capital Expenditure						
EBITDA						
Return on Assets %						
Return on Equity %						
Debt to Equity						

CONTACT INFORMATION:
Phone: 510-731-1310   Fax: 510-225-2585
Toll-Free:
Address: 1171 Ocean Ave., Ste. 200, Oakland, CA 94608 United States

STOCK TICKER/OTHER:
Stock Ticker: Nonprofit
Employees:
Parent Company:

Exchange:
Fiscal Year Ends: 12/31

SALARIES/BONUSES:
Top Exec. Salary: $ Bonus: $
Second Exec. Salary: $ Bonus: $

OTHER THOUGHTS:
Estimated Female Officers or Directors: 6
Hot Spot for Advancement for Women/Minorities: Y

Group14 Technologies Inc

NAIC Code: 335912

group14.technology

TYPES OF BUSINESS:
Primary Battery Manufacturing
Silicon-Carbon Composite Anode Materials
Nanomaterials
Manufacturing

BRANDS/DIVISIONS/AFFILIATES:
SCC55
Dryolysis
Siligenesis

CONTACTS: *Note: Officers with more than one job title may be intentionally listed here more than once.*
Erik Luebbe, CEO
Chris Piercy, VP-Bus. Dev.
Mike Willis, CFO
Grant Ray, VP-Mktg.
Henry Costantino, CTO
Chris Timmons, VP-Engineering

GROWTH PLANS/SPECIAL FEATURES:
Group14 Technologies, Inc. commercializes cost-effective, advanced silicon-carbon composite anode materials for lithium-ion batteries. The company derives its name from the Periodic Table column listing both silicon and carbon. Group14 cells contain silicon material built on the foundation of enerG2's advanced carbon manufacturing capability. The silicon-carbon anode materials are manufactured with increased energy capacity while maintaining the low cost and high cycle life of graphite. The firm's expertise in nanomaterials and manufacturing has enabled the development of novel approaches to producing and incorporating silicon into carbon to produce a class of silicon-carbon composites for battery applications. The U.S. Department of Energy supported this project with a $2.8 million grant designed to help Group14 Technologies scale its low-cost manufacturing process to the plant level. SCC55 is Group14's flagship, a micronized silicon-carbon powder that has five times the capacity and affords up to 50% more energy density than conventional graphite for lithium battery anodes. Its hard-carbon-based scaffolding keeps the silicon amorphous, nano-sized and carbon-encased. SCC55 is drop-in ready. Group 14's Dryolysis process is an approach to synthesizing carbon to create a highly scalable carbon scaffold, removing the need for solvent by combining dry polymerization with thermal processing. This platform yields the carbon scaffold for silicon-carbon composite, which is ideal for retaining amorphous, nano-sized silicon. Dryrolysis is accomplished in a single step and in a single reactor. Siligenesis is how Group 14 makes its silicon anode material, and employs a non-exotic precursor that converts into silicon within the porous carbon scaffold. Siligenesis also supports silicon's expansion and contraction within remaining intraparticle void spaces of the composite, further boosting electromechanical performance. During 2022, Group14 announced it had raised $400 million in Series C funding led by Porsche AG with participation from other large institutional investors.

FINANCIAL DATA: *Note: Data for latest year may not have been available at press time.*

In U.S. $	2021	2020	2019	2018	2017	2016
Revenue						
R&D Expense						
Operating Income						
Operating Margin %						
SGA Expense						
Net Income						
Operating Cash Flow						
Capital Expenditure						
EBITDA						
Return on Assets %						
Return on Equity %						
Debt to Equity						

CONTACT INFORMATION:
Phone: 206-547-0445 Fax:
Toll-Free:
Address: 8502 Maltby Rd., Woodinville, WA 98072 United States

STOCK TICKER/OTHER:
Stock Ticker: Subsidiary Exchange:
Employees: Fiscal Year Ends:
Parent Company: EnerG2

SALARIES/BONUSES:
Top Exec. Salary: $ Bonus: $
Second Exec. Salary: $ Bonus: $

OTHER THOUGHTS:
Estimated Female Officers or Directors:
Hot Spot for Advancement for Women/Minorities:

Sales, profits and employees may be estimates. Financial information, benefits and other data can change quickly and may vary from those stated here.

Guangxi Guiguan Electric Power Co Ltd

en.china-cdt.ex1.ipv6.china-cdt.com/dtwzen/dtwzen_site_html/aboutus/LISTEDCOMPANYPROFILE/2020/dtwzen_site-ABOUTUS_LISTEDCOMPANYPROFILE-20200619-Fb9O.html

NAIC Code: 221111

TYPES OF BUSINESS:
Hydroelectric Power Generation
Wind Electric Power Generation
Thermal Electric Power Generation
Hydro Power Generation
Electric Generation and Distribution

GROWTH PLANS/SPECIAL FEATURES:
Guangxi Guiguan Electric Power Co., Ltd. engages in the generation and distribution of electricity in China. The company's in-service installed capacity is made up of hydropower, thermal power and wind power. The firm also provides financial technology consulting services in regards to electrical power. Guangxi Guiguan Electric operates as a subsidiary of China Datang Corporation.

BRANDS/DIVISIONS/AFFILIATES:
China Datang Corporation

CONTACTS:
Note: Officers with more than one job title may be intentionally listed here more than once.

Kai Li, Chmn.

FINANCIAL DATA:
Note: Data for latest year may not have been available at press time.

In U.S. $	2021	2020	2019	2018	2017	2016
Revenue	1,150,468,000	1,374,850,000	1,294,140,000	1,414,759,500	1,347,390,000	1,232,520,000
R&D Expense						
Operating Income						
Operating Margin %						
SGA Expense						
Net Income	188,013,176	382,183,000	343,271,000	430,723,000	430,723,000	418,204,000
Operating Cash Flow						
Capital Expenditure						
EBITDA						
Return on Assets %						
Return on Equity %						
Debt to Equity						

CONTACT INFORMATION:
Phone: 86-771-6118880 Fax: 86-771-6118899
Toll-Free:
Address: No. 126 Minzu Ave, Qingxiu Dist., Nanning, Guangxi Zhuang 530029 China

STOCK TICKER/OTHER:
Stock Ticker: 600236 Exchange: Shanghai
Employees: 3,775 Fiscal Year Ends:
Parent Company: China Datang Corporation

SALARIES/BONUSES:
Top Exec. Salary: $ Bonus: $
Second Exec. Salary: $ Bonus: $

OTHER THOUGHTS:
Estimated Female Officers or Directors:
Hot Spot for Advancement for Women/Minorities:

Sales, profits and employees may be estimates. Financial information, benefits and other data can change quickly and may vary from those stated here.

Halliburton Company

NAIC Code: 213112

www.halliburton.com

TYPES OF BUSINESS:
Oil Field Services
Software Information Systems
Project Management Consulting
Well Drilling Services
Oil and Natural Gas Services
Well Completion Services
Well Production Services
Advanced Technology

BRANDS/DIVISIONS/AFFILIATES:
Baroid
Landmark
Sperry
Halliburton Labs

GROWTH PLANS/SPECIAL FEATURES:
Halliburton is one of the three largest oilfield service firms in the world, offering superior expertise in a number of business lines, including completion fluids, wireline services, cementing, and countless others. It's the number one pressure pumper in North America, and has been a leading innovator in hydraulic fracturing over the last two decades.

Employee benefits include retirement and savings plans; an employee stock purchase program; life, disability and AD&D insurance; comprehensive health benefits; and a wellness program.

CONTACTS:
Note: Officers with more than one job title may be intentionally listed here more than once.

Jeffrey Miller, CEO
Lance Loeffler, CFO
Charles Geer, Chief Accounting Officer
Van Beckwith, Chief Legal Officer
Eric Carre, Executive VP, Divisional
Lawrence Pope, Executive VP, Divisional
Joe Rainey, President, Geographical
Mark Richard, President, Geographical
Myrtle Jones, Senior VP, Divisional
Anne Beaty, Senior VP, Divisional
Timothy McKeon, Vice President

FINANCIAL DATA:
Note: Data for latest year may not have been available at press time.

In U.S. $	2021	2020	2019	2018	2017	2016
Revenue	15,295,000,000	14,445,000,000	22,408,000,000	23,995,000,000	20,620,000,000	15,887,000,000
R&D Expense						
Operating Income	1,776,000,000	1,363,000,000	2,058,000,000	2,732,000,000	2,021,000,000	644,000,000
Operating Margin %	.12%	.09%	.09%	.11%	.10%	.04%
SGA Expense	204,000,000	182,000,000	227,000,000	254,000,000	256,000,000	226,000,000
Net Income	1,457,000,000	-2,945,000,000	-1,131,000,000	1,656,000,000	-463,000,000	-5,763,000,000
Operating Cash Flow	1,911,000,000	1,881,000,000	2,445,000,000	3,157,000,000	2,468,000,000	-1,703,000,000
Capital Expenditure	799,000,000	728,000,000	1,530,000,000	2,026,000,000	1,373,000,000	798,000,000
EBITDA	2,625,000,000	-1,657,000,000	1,072,000,000	3,974,000,000	2,831,000,000	-5,483,000,000
Return on Assets %	.07%	-.13%	-.04%	.06%	-.02%	-.18%
Return on Equity %	.25%	-.45%	-.13%	.19%	-.05%	-.46%
Debt to Equity	1.49%	1.988	1.391	1.083	1.253	1.298

CONTACT INFORMATION:
Phone: 281 871-2699 Fax: 713 759-2635
Toll-Free: 888-669-3920
Address: 3000 N. Sam Houston Pkwy. E., Houston, TX 77032 United States

STOCK TICKER/OTHER:
Stock Ticker: HAL
Employees: 40,000
Parent Company:

Exchange: NYS
Fiscal Year Ends: 12/31

SALARIES/BONUSES:
Top Exec. Salary: $1,500,000 Bonus: $
Second Exec. Salary: $910,000 Bonus: $

OTHER THOUGHTS:
Estimated Female Officers or Directors:
Hot Spot for Advancement for Women/Minorities: Y

Sales, profits and employees may be estimates. Financial information, benefits and other data can change quickly and may vary from those stated here.

Hanwha Q Cells

www.hanwha.com/en/products_and_services/affiliates/hanwha_q_cells.solar_energy.html

NAIC Code: 334413A

TYPES OF BUSINESS:
Photovoltaic Cell Manufacturing
Photovoltaic Cell Manufacturing
Silicon Ingot Production
Solar Power
Solar Modules
Solar Storage

BRANDS/DIVISIONS/AFFILIATES:
Hanwha Solutions Corporation
Q.ANTUM

CONTACTS: Note: Officers with more than one job title may be intentionally listed here more than once.
Min-Su Kim, Pres.
Jeong-Eui Hong, CTO
Ray (Inbok) Park, VP-Admin. & General Affairs
Seung Youn Kim, Chmn.
Ray (Inbok) Park, VP-Purchasing

GROWTH PLANS/SPECIAL FEATURES:

Hanwha Q Cells manufactures and sells photovoltaic (PV) cells, silicon ingots, silicon wafers and PV modules. Sunlight creates electromagnetic radiation on the solar cell, which initiates a physical response where the solar cells generate a direct current. Hanwha's solar panel is made up of 60 solar cells that are electrically connected and comprise a tough glass panel and frame. Several modules together make a power and efficient solar system. The electrical current produced at the terminals of the solar modules flows through the connected cable to the inverter where it is converted to alternating current so it can be used by electrical equipment. Q Cells' products are used for residential, commercial, industrial and utility purposes. The company developed Q.ANTUM technology to maximize the efficiency of conventional solar panels, which guarantees high performances in winter or summer and under clear or cloud skies. Hanwha Q Cells operates as a subsidiary of Hanwha Solutions Corporation, and based at its parent's Seoul, Korea headquarters. The firm's research and development headquarter is located in Thalheim, Germany, and its R&D network covers China, Malaysia and South Korea.

FINANCIAL DATA: Note: Data for latest year may not have been available at press time.

In U.S. $	2021	2020	2019	2018	2017	2016
Revenue	3,450,000,000	3,355,000,000	3,050,000,000	2,298,345,100	2,188,900,096	2,425,900,032
R&D Expense						
Operating Income						
Operating Margin %						
SGA Expense						
Net Income						
Operating Cash Flow						
Capital Expenditure						
EBITDA						
Return on Assets %						
Return on Equity %						
Debt to Equity						

CONTACT INFORMATION:
Phone: 82 1600 3400   Fax: 82 2 729 4503
Toll-Free:
Address: Fl. 24, 86, Cheonggyecheon-ro, Jung-gu, Seoul, 04541 South Korea

STOCK TICKER/OTHER:
Stock Ticker: Subsidiary   Exchange:
Employees: 8,003   Fiscal Year Ends: 12/31
Parent Company: Hanwha Solutions Corporation

SALARIES/BONUSES:
Top Exec. Salary: $ Bonus: $
Second Exec. Salary: $ Bonus: $

OTHER THOUGHTS:
Estimated Female Officers or Directors:
Hot Spot for Advancement for Women/Minorities:

Plunkett Research, Ltd.   247

Hanwha Solutions Corporation
NAIC Code: 334413A   www.hanwhasolutions.com/en

TYPES OF BUSINESS:
Photovoltaic Cell Manufacturing
Chemicals and Petrochemicals
Solar Cells
Solar Modules
Lightweight Composite Materials
Photovoltaic Materials
Malls and Shopping Centers
Sustainable Energy Innovation

BRANDS/DIVISIONS/AFFILIATES:
Hanwha Q Cells

CONTACTS: Note: Officers with more than one job title may be intentionally listed here more than once.
Jochen Endle, Contact-Corp. Comm
Oliver Beckel, Specialist-Public Affairs
Koo Yung Lee, Chmn.

GROWTH PLANS/SPECIAL FEATURES:
Hanwha Solutions Corporation is the parent company of subsidiaries that deliver sustainable solutions, advanced materials, shopping retail sites and industrial land development. The company operates through five business segments: chemical, Q Cells, advanced materials, galleria and insight. The chemical segment develops innovative technology in regards to serving the petrochemical industry with products and solutions. This division produces polyvinyl chloride, an array of linear low-density polyethylene, chlor-alkali, alkali water soluble resin and toluene diisocyanate. It is expanding its assets to include chlorinated polyvinyl chloride, hydrogenated resins and xylylene diisocyanate. The Q Cells segment designs, develops and sells solar solutions such as solar cells, solar panels, solar energy storage solutions, modules, ingots and more, and retails electricity. This division also actively pursues businesses in major global markets by building and operating power plants in the mid-stream sector, and has subsidiaries throughout the world. The advanced materials segment is a technology company that innovates products and technology in the fields of lightweight composite materials, photovoltaic materials and electronic materials. This division has production centers in North America, Europe, China and Korea. The galleria segment is a leading retailer of shopping malls comprised of stores and restaurants that offer apparel and food and beverages. Last, the insight segment engages in innovation through three divisions: Qcells Energy for green energy, Premium Lifestyle for developing luxury residential facilities as well as related amenities and programs, and City Development for developing sustainable solutions for complex development projects.

FINANCIAL DATA: Note: Data for latest year may not have been available at press time.

In U.S. $	2021	2020	2019	2018	2017	2016
Revenue	7,792,000,000	8,447,680,000	8,166,970,000	8,097,790,000	8,747,930,000	7,674,790,000
R&D Expense						
Operating Income						
Operating Margin %						
SGA Expense						
Net Income		277,455,000	-215,034,000	143,229,000	781,902,000	639,082,000
Operating Cash Flow						
Capital Expenditure						
EBITDA						
Return on Assets %						
Return on Equity %						
Debt to Equity						

CONTACT INFORMATION:
Phone: 82-1600-3400   Fax: 82-02-729-4503
Toll-Free:
Address: Fl. 24, 86, Cheonggyecheon-ro, Jung gu, Seoul, 04541 South Korea

STOCK TICKER/OTHER:
Stock Ticker: 9830   Exchange: Seoul
Employees: 7,510   Fiscal Year Ends: 12/31
Parent Company: Hanwha Grou

SALARIES/BONUSES:
Top Exec. Salary: $ Bonus: $
Second Exec. Salary: $ Bonus: $

OTHER THOUGHTS:
Estimated Female Officers or Directors:
Hot Spot for Advancement for Women/Minorities:

Sales, profits and employees may be estimates. Financial information, benefits and other data can change quickly and may vary from those stated here.

Hitachi Limited

NAIC Code: 334111

www.hitachi.com

TYPES OF BUSINESS:
Computer & Electronics Manufacturing
Information Technology
Nuclear Energy
Industrial Manufacturing
Transportation Mobility
Smart Life Products and Solutions
Automotive Systems
Automotive Components

BRANDS/DIVISIONS/AFFILIATES:
Hitachi Astemo Ltd
Hitachi Solutions Technology Ltd
Hitachi GE Nuclear Ltd
Hitachi Industry & Control Solutions Ltd
Hitachi Rail STS Mobilinx Hurontario GP Inc
Hitachi High-tech Amata Smart Services Co Ltd

GROWTH PLANS/SPECIAL FEATURES:
Hitachi Ltd provides IT services and has an expertise in the range of business fields, including financial services. The company's main products and services include system integration, consulting, cloud services, servers, storage, software, telecommunications and networks, and ATMs. Hitachi operates in various segments namely, Information and Telecommunication Systems; Social Infrastructure and Industrial Systems; Electronic Systems and Equipment; Construction Machinery; High Functional Materials and Components; Automotive Systems; Smart Life and Ecofriendly Systems; Financial Services; and Others.

CONTACTS:
Note: Officers with more than one job title may be intentionally listed here more than once.

Toshiaki Higashihara, CEO
Shigeru Azuhata, Gen. Mgr.-R&D
Toyoaki Nakamura, Gen. Mgr.-Consumer Bus.
Koji Tanaka, Exec. VP-Power Systems Bus.
Nobuo Mochida, Exec. VP-Prod. Eng.
Tatsuro Ishizuka, CEO-Power Systems Group
Junzo Nakajima, CEO-Asia Pacific

FINANCIAL DATA:
Note: Data for latest year may not have been available at press time.

In U.S. $	2021	2020	2019	2018	2017	2016
Revenue	60,277,840,000	60,540,710,000	65,466,660,000	64,693,230,000	63,268,320,000	
R&D Expense						
Operating Income	3,419,374,000	4,570,510,000	5,213,347,000	4,934,745,000	4,055,553,000	
Operating Margin %	.06%	.08%	.08%	.08%	.06%	
SGA Expense	11,739,910,000	11,797,630,000	12,160,310,000	12,342,990,000	12,376,240,000	
Net Income	3,463,795,000	604,878,000	1,536,750,000	2,506,546,000	1,596,930,000	
Operating Cash Flow	5,476,798,000	3,873,329,000	4,212,414,000	5,021,324,000	4,347,462,000	
Capital Expenditure	2,575,302,000	2,909,043,000	3,261,028,000	3,063,025,000	4,903,415,000	
EBITDA	9,383,521,000	4,401,517,000	6,249,807,000	7,068,398,000	6,237,488,000	
Return on Assets %	.05%	.01%	.02%	.04%	.02%	
Return on Equity %	.15%	.03%	.07%	.12%	.08%	
Debt to Equity	.48%	0.339	0.217	0.248	0.266	

CONTACT INFORMATION:
Phone: 81 332581111   Fax: 81 332582375
Toll-Free:
Address: 6-6, Marunouchi 1-chome, Chiyoda-ku, Tokyo, 100-8280 Japan

STOCK TICKER/OTHER:
Stock Ticker: HTHIF
Employees: 295,941
Parent Company:

Exchange: PINX
Fiscal Year Ends: 03/31

SALARIES/BONUSES:
Top Exec. Salary: $ Bonus: $
Second Exec. Salary: $ Bonus: $

OTHER THOUGHTS:
Estimated Female Officers or Directors: 1
Hot Spot for Advancement for Women/Minorities:

Sales, profits and employees may be estimates. Financial information, benefits and other data can change quickly and may vary from those stated here.

HOCHTIEF AG

NAIC Code: 237000

www.hochtief.de

TYPES OF BUSINESS:
Heavy Construction
Airport Management & Consulting Services
Infrastructure Development
Geothermal Plant Construction
Green Building Engineering Services

GROWTH PLANS/SPECIAL FEATURES:
Hochtief AG develops and constructs building and infrastructure projects. It works on complex projects in transportation, energy, urban infrastructure, and mining markets. It expands transportation networks with roads, bridges, and tunnels, or designs and constructs office buildings, hospitals, and power plants. The company leans on expertise and technical know-how in developing, financing, building, and operating in designated business areas. Also, it will partner with external groups to work on specific components of a project. Hochtief reports operating segments by regional divisions: Americas, Asia Pacific, and Europe. The Americas and the Asia Pacific account for the majority of sales and are where most of the company's assets are located.

BRANDS/DIVISIONS/AFFILIATES:
Turner
Flatiron
HOCHTIEF PPP
HOCHTIEF Infrastructure
CIMIC Group
CPB Contractors
Leighton Asia
Abertis

CONTACTS:
Note: Officers with more than one job title may be intentionally listed here more than once.

Peter Sassenfeld, CFO
Marcelino Fernandez Verdes, Chmn.

FINANCIAL DATA:
Note: Data for latest year may not have been available at press time.

In U.S. $	2021	2020	2019	2018	2017	2016
Revenue	20,934,690,000	22,477,900,000	25,315,920,000	23,387,180,000	22,161,780,000	19,495,600,000
R&D Expense						
Operating Income	368,920,900	-614,402,100	874,802,400	783,046,800	717,044,200	448,536,500
Operating Margin %	.02%	-.03%	.03%	.03%	.03%	.02%
SGA Expense	389,931,100	534,411,500	487,785,600	453,672,700	404,531,100	401,785,200
Net Income	203,610,500	418,383,800	-201,971,300	531,738,100	412,013,700	313,839,000
Operating Cash Flow	379,169,000	692,664,300	1,093,855,000	1,539,655,000	1,343,645,000	1,149,065,000
Capital Expenditure	77,594,330	389,020,400	576,780,500	402,844,800	349,964,200	266,924,200
EBITDA	879,260,000	1,744,428,000	2,662,622,000	1,705,258,000	1,358,844,000	1,058,570,000
Return on Assets %	.01%	.02%	-.01%	.04%	.03%	.02%
Return on Equity %	.28%	.44%	-.13%	.44%	.35%	.16%
Debt to Equity	5.22%	6.25	2.827	0.29	0.811	0.90

CONTACT INFORMATION:
Phone: 49 2018240 Fax: 49 2018242777
Toll-Free:
Address: Alfredstrasse 236, Essen, NW 45133 Germany

STOCK TICKER/OTHER:
Stock Ticker: HOCFF
Employees: 33,835
Parent Company: ACS Group

Exchange: PINX
Fiscal Year Ends: 12/31

SALARIES/BONUSES:
Top Exec. Salary: $ Bonus: $
Second Exec. Salary: $ Bonus: $

OTHER THOUGHTS:
Estimated Female Officers or Directors: 1
Hot Spot for Advancement for Women/Minorities:

Hydro-Quebec

NAIC Code: 221111

www.hydroquebec.com

TYPES OF BUSINESS:
Electric Utility-Hydroelectric
Hydroelectric & Wind Power
Hybrid Drive Train Systems
Construction & Engineering
Technical Consulting & Services
Technology & Research
PEV Charging Stations

BRANDS/DIVISIONS/AFFILIATES:
Hydro-Quebec TransEnergie

GROWTH PLANS/SPECIAL FEATURES:
Hydro-Quebec, owned by the government of Quebec, is one of the largest generators and distributors of electric power in Canada and the largest supplier of electricity to Quebec. The company operates approximately 60 hydroelectric generating stations, of which nearly 100% of Hydro-Quebec's electricity is generated using water. This energy is delivered to customers throughout Quebec and to export markets. Hydro-Quebec's transmission system consists of more than 21,100 miles (34,000 km) of high-voltage lines running from large generating stations in remote areas to the province's more populated areas. The lines are supported by towers for the transportation and transmission of electric power. Hydro-Quebec delivers electricity through 161,556 miles (260,000 km) of extension line. Subsidiary Hydro-Quebec TransEnergie operates the company's transmission system. Hydro-Quebec also engages in developing and enhancing technological innovations for electricity providers worldwide, including safe battery materials, energy storage systems, electrical powertrain systems, network maintenance robots and more.

CONTACTS: Note: Officers with more than one job title may be intentionally listed here more than once.

Sophie Brochu, CEO
Eric Filion, COO
Jean-Hugues Lafleur, CFO
Pierre Despars, Exec. VP-Strategy & Dev.
Nathalie Dubois, VP-Talent & Culture
Jean-Francois Morin, VP-Digital Technologies
Elie Saheb, Exec. VP-Tech.
Marie-Jose Nadeau, Exec. VP-Corp. Affairs
Marie-Jose Nadeau, Sec.
Lise Croteau, VP-Acct. & Control
Richard Cacchione, Pres., Hydro-Quebec Prod.
Andre Boulanger, Pres., Hydro-Quebec TransEnergie
Daniel Richard, Pres., Hydro-Quebec Dist.
Real Laporte, Pres., Hydro-Quebec Equipment et Svcs. partages
Jacynthe Cote, Chmn.

FINANCIAL DATA: Note: Data for latest year may not have been available at press time.

In U.S. $	2021	2020	2019	2018	2017	2016
Revenue	10,769,620,000	10,634,300,000	10,729,400,000	10,532,800,000	10,728,500,000	10,656,166,374
R&D Expense						
Operating Income						
Operating Margin %						
SGA Expense						
Net Income	2,642,360,000	1,801,590,000	2,236,800,000	2,339,650,000	22,671,000,000	2,285,575,530
Operating Cash Flow						
Capital Expenditure						
EBITDA						
Return on Assets %						
Return on Equity %						
Debt to Equity						

CONTACT INFORMATION:
Phone: 514-289-2211 Fax: 514-289-5440
Toll-Free:
Address: 75, Blvd. Rene-Levesque W., Montreal, QC H2Z 1A4 Canada

STOCK TICKER/OTHER:
Stock Ticker: Government-Owned Exchange:
Employees: 21,168 Fiscal Year Ends: 12/31
Parent Company:

SALARIES/BONUSES:
Top Exec. Salary: $ Bonus: $
Second Exec. Salary: $ Bonus: $

OTHER THOUGHTS:
Estimated Female Officers or Directors: 10
Hot Spot for Advancement for Women/Minorities: Y

Sales, profits and employees may be estimates. Financial information, benefits and other data can change quickly and may vary from those stated here.

Iberdrola SA

NAIC Code: 221112

www.iberdrola.es

TYPES OF BUSINESS:
Renewable Power Generation
Wind Generation
Hydroelectric Generation
Engineering & Construction
Solar Power Generation
Electric Utility
Electricity Distribution

BRANDS/DIVISIONS/AFFILIATES:
Iberdrola Renovables Energia
ScottishPower Renewable Energy
Avangrid Renewables
Iberdrola Distribucion Electrica
ScottishPower Energy Networks
Generacion Espana
ScottishPower Generation Holdings
Iberdrola Generacion Mexico

GROWTH PLANS/SPECIAL FEATURES:
Iberdrola is one of the largest utilities in the world with electric utility operations in nearly 40 countries. The company has a 52 gigawatt portfolio of hydro, wind, natural gas, and nuclear power plants. It is the largest owner of wind farms in the world, representing nearly 40% of its portfolio. Although the company has recently developed or acquired distribution and power generation assets in other geographic areas, Spain is still home to around 50% of its power generation capacity. Iberdrola also owns and operates electricity and distribution networks in Spain, the U.K., Brazil, and the U.S.

CONTACTS:
Note: Officers with more than one job title may be intentionally listed here more than once.

Ignacio S. Galan, CEO
Jose S. Armada, CFO
Juan Carlos Rebollo Liceaga, Dir.-Admin. & Control
Julian Martinez-Simancas Sanchez, Sec.
Fernando Becker Zuazua, Dir.-Corp. Resources
Javier Villalba Sanchez, Dir.-Energy Networks
Francisco Martinez Corcoles, Dir.-Liberalized Bus.
Xabier Viteri Solaun, Dir.-Property

FINANCIAL DATA:
Note: Data for latest year may not have been available at press time.

In U.S. $	2021	2020	2019	2018	2017	2016
Revenue	38,303,120,000	32,457,870,000	35,682,600,000	34,348,710,000	30,615,140,000	28,162,940,000
R&D Expense						
Operating Income	7,579,541,000	5,873,655,000	6,027,400,000	5,616,063,000	3,988,821,000	4,550,581,000
Operating Margin %	.20%	.18%	.17%	.16%	.13%	.16%
SGA Expense	2,875,133,000	2,782,103,000	2,784,061,000	2,739,186,000	2,525,194,000	2,216,962,000
Net Income	3,804,460,000	3,536,140,000	3,394,146,000	2,951,567,000	2,745,864,000	2,648,906,000
Operating Cash Flow	7,937,953,000	8,173,957,000	6,771,644,000	7,428,977,000	5,567,587,000	6,580,573,000
Capital Expenditure	6,774,582,000	5,729,702,000	5,464,321,000	5,577,481,000	5,998,378,000	4,806,567,000
EBITDA	12,256,530,000	10,465,450,000	10,150,120,000	9,273,014,000	7,750,374,000	7,988,071,000
Return on Assets %	.03%	.03%	.03%	.03%	.03%	.03%
Return on Equity %	.10%	.10%	.09%	.08%	.08%	.07%
Debt to Equity	.83%	0.915	0.847	0.845	0.799	0.715

CONTACT INFORMATION:
Phone: 34-944-151-411   Fax: 34-944-663-194
Toll-Free:
Address: Plaza Euskadi Number 5, Bilbao, 48009 Spain

STOCK TICKER/OTHER:
Stock Ticker: IBDSF
Employees: 38,702
Parent Company:

Exchange: PINX
Fiscal Year Ends: 12/31

SALARIES/BONUSES:
Top Exec. Salary: $ Bonus: $
Second Exec. Salary: $ Bonus: $

OTHER THOUGHTS:
Estimated Female Officers or Directors: 5
Hot Spot for Advancement for Women/Minorities: Y

Sales, profits and employees may be estimates. Financial information, benefits and other data can change quickly and may vary from those stated here.

IDACORP Inc

NAIC Code: 221111

www.idacorpinc.com

TYPES OF BUSINESS:
Hydroelectric Power Generation
Electric Utility
Energy Solutions & Marketing
Housing & Real Estate Investments
Hydroelectric Power Plants
Natural Gas Plants
Coal Generating Stations

BRANDS/DIVISIONS/AFFILIATES:
Idaho Power Company
Ida-West Energy Company
IDACORP Financial Services Inc

GROWTH PLANS/SPECIAL FEATURES:
Idacorp Inc is a holding company that, through its subsidiaries, acts as an electric utility engaged in the generation, transmission, distribution, sale, and purchase of electric energy and capacity. To do this, Idacorp owns and operates a portfolio of hydroelectric, coal-fired, gas-fired, and diesel-fired power plants located across the Northwestern United States. The company's hydroelectric and coal-fired plants are responsible for Most of its total energy production. Idacorp primarily generates revenue from the sale of electricity to retail and wholesale customers. Most of the company's customers are residential consumers living in the Northwestern United States, while commercial and industrial consumers also represent significant revenue streams.

CONTACTS:
Note: Officers with more than one job title may be intentionally listed here more than once.

Lisa Grow, CEO
Steven Keen, CFO
Richard Dahl, Chairman of the Board
Kenneth Petersen, Chief Accounting Officer
Adam Richins, COO, Subsidiary
Brian Buckham, General Counsel
James Hanchey, Other Executive Officer
Jeffrey Malmen, Senior VP, Divisional
Sarah Griffin, Vice President, Divisional
Mitchel Colburn, Vice President, Subsidiary
Ryan Adelman, Vice President, Subsidiary

FINANCIAL DATA:
Note: Data for latest year may not have been available at press time.

In U.S. $	2021	2020	2019	2018	2017	2016
Revenue	1,458,084,000	1,350,729,000	1,346,383,000	1,370,752,000	1,349,486,000	1,262,020,000
R&D Expense						
Operating Income	314,402,000	297,656,000	287,350,000	281,141,000	304,351,000	271,776,000
Operating Margin %	.22%	.22%	.21%	.21%	.23%	.22%
SGA Expense	15,249,000	11,865,000	10,976,000	15,781,000	11,194,000	11,806,000
Net Income	245,550,000	237,417,000	232,854,000	226,801,000	212,419,000	198,288,000
Operating Cash Flow	363,264,000	388,131,000	366,625,000	491,626,000	435,161,000	344,195,000
Capital Expenditure	299,999,000	310,938,000	278,705,000	277,853,000	285,488,000	296,950,000
EBITDA	548,926,000	530,035,000	518,110,000	499,977,000	511,527,000	463,846,000
Return on Assets %	.03%	.03%	.04%	.04%	.03%	.03%
Return on Equity %	.09%	.09%	.10%	.10%	.10%	.09%
Debt to Equity	.75%	0.781	0.705	0.774	0.776	0.81

CONTACT INFORMATION:
Phone: 208 388-2200   Fax: 208 388-6916
Toll-Free:
Address: 1221 W. Idaho St., Boise, ID 83702-5627 United States

STOCK TICKER/OTHER:
Stock Ticker: IDA
Employees: 1,999
Parent Company:

Exchange: NYS
Fiscal Year Ends: 12/31

SALARIES/BONUSES:
Top Exec. Salary: $775,000   Bonus: $
Second Exec. Salary: $497,000   Bonus: $

OTHER THOUGHTS:
Estimated Female Officers or Directors: 1
Hot Spot for Advancement for Women/Minorities: Y

IFF Nutrition & Biosciences

www.dupontnutritionandbiosciences.com

NAIC Code: 325414

TYPES OF BUSINESS:
Biological Manufacturing
Biotech Research & Discovery
Biotechnology
Food Product Innovation
Flavorings
Food Enzymes
Extracts and Flavorants
Gels and Gums

BRANDS/DIVISIONS/AFFILIATES:
DuPont de Nemours Inc
International Flavors & Fragrances Inc
IFF
Dupont Nutrition & Biosciences

GROWTH PLANS/SPECIAL FEATURES:
IFF Nutrition & Biosciences is the largest specialty ingredients producer globally. The company sells ingredients for the food, beverage, health, household goods, personal care, and pharmaceutical industries. The company makes proprietary formulations, partnering with customers to deliver custom solutions. The nourish segment, which generates roughly half of revenue, is a leading flavor producer and also sell texturants, plant-based proteins, and other ingredients. The health and biosciences business, which generates around one fourth of revenue, is a global leader in probiotics and enzymes. IFF is also one of the leading fragrance producers in the world. The firm also sells pharmaceutical ingredients such as excipients and time-release polymers.

CONTACTS:
Note: Officers with more than one job title may be intentionally listed here more than once.

Simon Herriott, Pres.
Wendy B. Rosen, Contact-Media Rel.

FINANCIAL DATA:
Note: Data for latest year may not have been available at press time.

In U.S. $	2021	2020	2019	2018	2017	2016
Revenue	11,656,000,000	5,084,000,000	5,140,000,000			
R&D Expense	629,000,000	357,000,000	346,000,000			
Operating Income	625,000,000	587,000,000	698,000,000			
Operating Margin %	.05%	.12%	.14%			
SGA Expense	1,749,000,000	949,000,000	876,000,000			
Net Income	268,000,000	365,000,000	454,000,000			
Operating Cash Flow	1,437,000,000	714,000,000	699,000,000			
Capital Expenditure	397,000,000	192,000,000	242,000,000			
EBITDA	1,799,000,000	898,000,000	1,018,000,000			
Return on Assets %	.01%	.03%	.03%			
Return on Equity %	.02%	.06%	.07%			
Debt to Equity	.54%	0.641	0.643			

CONTACT INFORMATION:
Phone: 319-363-9601 Fax:
Toll-Free:
Address: 1000 41st Ave. Dr. SW, Cedar Rapids, IA 52404 United States

STOCK TICKER/OTHER:
Stock Ticker: IFF Exchange: NYS
Employees: 24,000 Fiscal Year Ends: 12/31
Parent Company: DuPont de Nemours Inc

SALARIES/BONUSES:
Top Exec. Salary: $1,300,000 Bonus: $
Second Exec. Salary: $662,870 Bonus: $

OTHER THOUGHTS:
Estimated Female Officers or Directors: 1
Hot Spot for Advancement for Women/Minorities:

Sales, profits and employees may be estimates. Financial information, benefits and other data can change quickly and may vary from those stated here.

Imperial Western Products Inc

www.imperialwesternproducts.com

NAIC Code: 325199

TYPES OF BUSINESS:
- Biodiesel
- Biodiesel
- Industrial Chemicals
- Janitorial Supplies
- Concrete & Asphalt
- Waste Pickup, Transportation & Packaging

BRANDS/DIVISIONS/AFFILIATES:
- Biotane Fuels
- Biotane Pumping
- Enforce Products
- Organic Solutions
- Bakery Solutions
- IWP Fabrication
- Denalie Water Solutions LLC

CONTACTS:
Note: Officers with more than one job title may be intentionally listed here more than once.

- Andy McNeill, CEO-Denali
- Bill Trawick, Pres.
- Curtis Wright, Mgr.-Methyl Ester & Glycerin Prod.
- Joseph Boyd, Lab Mgr.-Biotane

GROWTH PLANS/SPECIAL FEATURES:

Imperial Western Products, Inc. (IWP) provides diversified products and services, including the recycling of byproducts. The firm is involved in procurement, processing, services, manufacturing, transporting, warehousing, distribution and merchandising throughout the U.S., Canada, Mexico and Asia. The company is organized into six divisions, which are subsidiaries and brand names: Biotane Fuels, Biotane Pumping, Enforce Products, Organic Solutions, Bakery Solutions and IWP Fabrication. Biotane Fuels offers renewable and alternative fuels. This division manufactures biodiesel fuel from animal fats and vegetable oils; and will take customer's vegetable oil wastes in order to recycle it into an alternative fuel. Its California plant is BQ9000 certified as a producer and marketer of biodiesel. Biotane Pumping offers services for the collection of waste cooking oil, grease trap solutions and hydro jetting 24-hours-a-day, 7 days a week. Enforce Products manufactures tire products, pipe joint lubricants and release agents for the concrete and asphalt industries. All of these products are manufactured from recycled materials and are environmentally friendly. Organic Solutions helps companies complete their sustainability loop by providing the best re-use for all their organic-related waste. These materials include de-packaged fruit, vegetables, plate waste and grocery goods, including cooked food waste. Bakery Solutions specializes in the recycling of bakery-related food waste, as well as semi-cardboard, plastics, paper and metal recycling services and solutions. Last, IWP Fabrication manufactures high quality and durable metal containers in a variety of sizes and designs, mostly used by restaurants to store their waste cooking oil. This division also has the capability of manufacturing containers for food waste as well as custom-built compactors. IWP can customize a containment or container program to suit the needs of any restaurant business, regardless of size. During 2022, Denali Water Solutions, LLC acquired IWP.

FINANCIAL DATA:
Note: Data for latest year may not have been available at press time.

In U.S. $	2021	2020	2019	2018	2017	2016
Revenue						
R&D Expense						
Operating Income						
Operating Margin %						
SGA Expense						
Net Income						
Operating Cash Flow						
Capital Expenditure						
EBITDA						
Return on Assets %						
Return on Equity %						
Debt to Equity						

CONTACT INFORMATION:
Phone: 760-398-0815 Fax: 760-398-3476
Toll-Free: 800-975-6677
Address: 86-600 Ave. 54, Coachella, CA 92236 United States

SALARIES/BONUSES:
Top Exec. Salary: $ Bonus: $
Second Exec. Salary: $ Bonus: $

STOCK TICKER/OTHER:
Stock Ticker: Private Exchange:
Employees: 300 Fiscal Year Ends:
Parent Company: Denali Water Solutions LLC

OTHER THOUGHTS:
Estimated Female Officers or Directors:
Hot Spot for Advancement for Women/Minorities:

Sales, profits and employees may be estimates. Financial information, benefits and other data can change quickly and may vary from those stated here.

Invenergy

NAIC Code: 221115

invenergy.com

TYPES OF BUSINESS:
Wind Electric Power Generation
Solar Electric Power Generation
Wind Power Generation
Energy Solutions Development
Energy Solutions Operator
Natural Gas
Clean Water
Renewable Energy Storage

BRANDS/DIVISIONS/AFFILIATES:

GROWTH PLANS/SPECIAL FEATURES:
Invenergy is a privately-owned global developer and operator of sustainable energy solutions, having developed nearly 200 projects across four continents, totaling more than 29,000 megawatts (MW). The company's developments and solutions include wind, solar, natural gas, clean water and storage. Headquartered in Illinois, Invenergy has regional offices in Colorado, New York and Oregon, and international offices in Mexico, Canada, Colombia, Israel, Japan, Poland and Scotland. In January 2022, Invenergy and Lafayette Square, an impact investment platform, announced the launch of their joint venture Reactivate, a solar energy platform supporting renewable energy development in local communities.

CONTACTS:
Note: Officers with more than one job title may be intentionally listed here more than once.

Michael Polsky, CEO

FINANCIAL DATA:
Note: Data for latest year may not have been available at press time.

In U.S. $	2021	2020	2019	2018	2017	2016
Revenue						
R&D Expense						
Operating Income						
Operating Margin %						
SGA Expense						
Net Income						
Operating Cash Flow						
Capital Expenditure						
EBITDA						
Return on Assets %						
Return on Equity %						
Debt to Equity						

CONTACT INFORMATION:
Phone: 312 224 1400
Fax: 312 224 1444
Toll-Free:
Address: One S. Wacker Dr., Ste. 1800, Chicago, IL 60606 United States

STOCK TICKER/OTHER:
Stock Ticker: Private
Employees:
Parent Company:

Exchange:
Fiscal Year Ends:

SALARIES/BONUSES:
Top Exec. Salary: $
Bonus: $
Second Exec. Salary: $
Bonus: $

OTHER THOUGHTS:
Estimated Female Officers or Directors:
Hot Spot for Advancement for Women/Minorities:

Sales, profits and employees may be estimates. Financial information, benefits and other data can change quickly and may vary from those stated here.

Iogen Corporation

NAIC Code: 325193

www.iogen.ca

TYPES OF BUSINESS:
Bioethanol Production
Biofuel Production
Renewable Energy Technology
Renewable Natural Gas
Renewable Hydrogen
Fuel Production

BRANDS/DIVISIONS/AFFILIATES:

CONTACTS: Note: Officers with more than one job title may be intentionally listed here more than once.
Brian Foody, CEO
Patrick J. Foody, Chief Development Officer
Claire Dumville, VP-Finance
Patrick Foody, Exec. VP-Projects & Commercial Dev.
Claire Dumville, VP-Finance
Ziyad Rahme, Sr. VP

GROWTH PLANS/SPECIAL FEATURES:
Iogen Corporation, based in Ottawa, Canada, develops and implements processes for making cellulosic biofuels. Cellulosic biofuels technology incorporates the following process: feedstock handling, pre-treatment, enzymatic hydrolysis, lignin separation and processing, ethanol fermentation and distillation and process integration. The company is a leader in developing technology to make clean-burning, renewable cellulosic biofuels from agricultural residues and other organic wastes. Biofuel has the capability of replacing more than 30% of U.S. petroleum consumption, as well as reducing greenhouse gas emissions by up to 90% when compared to gasoline. Iogen has over 300 issued and pending patents, and claims to be the world's first company to successfully use modern enzymatic hydrolysis technology to produce commercial quantities of cellulosic ethanol for field demonstrations. The company continues to develop new ways to use biogas as a transportation fuel. For example, Iogen has created a low-cost way to use existing refineries to make drop-in renewable fuels. The process converts renewable natural gas (RNG) into renewable hydrogen and inserts the renewable hydrogen energy into gasoline, diesel and jet fuel. Partners, customers and suppliers of Iogen include Valero, Chevron, BP, Shell, Waste Management Company and Montauk Energy.

Iogen offers its employees an employee assistance program; relocation assistance; and medical, life, disability, dental and vision insurance.

FINANCIAL DATA: Note: Data for latest year may not have been available at press time.

In U.S. $	2021	2020	2019	2018	2017	2016
Revenue						
R&D Expense						
Operating Income						
Operating Margin %						
SGA Expense						
Net Income						
Operating Cash Flow						
Capital Expenditure						
EBITDA						
Return on Assets %						
Return on Equity %						
Debt to Equity						

CONTACT INFORMATION:
Phone: 613-733-9830   Fax: 613-733-0781
Toll-Free:
Address: 310 Hunt Club Rd. E., Ste. 101, Ottawa, ON K1V 1C1 Canada

STOCK TICKER/OTHER:
Stock Ticker: Private   Exchange:
Employees: Fiscal Year Ends:
Parent Company:

SALARIES/BONUSES:
Top Exec. Salary: $ Bonus: $
Second Exec. Salary: $ Bonus: $

OTHER THOUGHTS:
Estimated Female Officers or Directors: 1
Hot Spot for Advancement for Women/Minorities:

Sales, profits and employees may be estimates. Financial information, benefits and other data can change quickly and may vary from those stated here.

Ion Storage Systems Inc

ionstoragesystems.com

NAIC Code: 335912

TYPES OF BUSINESS:
Primary Battery Manufacturing
Solid-State Lithium Metal Batteries
Battery Technology
Battery Manufacture

BRANDS/DIVISIONS/AFFILIATES:
ION

CONTACTS:
Note: Officers with more than one job title may be intentionally listed here more than once.

Ricky Hanna, CEO
Ben Chiu, CFO
Elizabeth Santori, VP-R&D
Neil Ovadia, VP-Supply Chain
Gret Hitz, CTO
Eric Wachsman, Chmn.

GROWTH PLANS/SPECIAL FEATURES:
Ion Storage Systems, Inc. designs and manufactures solid-state lithium metal batteries using non-flammable and low-cost materials. The dense ceramic electrolyte assembly allows for the use as a sponge-like separator, blocking dendrite growth and self-discharge mechanisms. The ION-branded battery technology achieves ARPA-E and DOE VTO fast-charge goals for Li-cycling current density at room temperature. No compression nor fire barriers are required and there is no need for swelling allowance. The lithium metal anode enables maximum energy density and is compatible with multiple cathode technologies. The ION battery performs well at low, ambient and high temperatures with no cooling system required. It can be reused or recycled at end-of-life. All of these features contribute to reduced system overhead and cost. Applications for ION battery use span defense and aerospace, consumer electronics, electric vehicles and grid storage. During 2022, Ion Storage Systems announced the closing of its Series A funding round, exceeding $30 million, with investments from Toyota Ventures, Tenaska, Bangchak Corporation and others.

FINANCIAL DATA:
Note: Data for latest year may not have been available at press time.

In U.S. $	2021	2020	2019	2018	2017	2016
Revenue						
R&D Expense						
Operating Income						
Operating Margin %						
SGA Expense						
Net Income						
Operating Cash Flow						
Capital Expenditure						
EBITDA						
Return on Assets %						
Return on Equity %						
Debt to Equity						

CONTACT INFORMATION:
Phone: 240 384-6020   Fax:
Toll-Free:
Address: 12500 Baltimore Ave., Unit D, Beltsville, MD 20705 United States

STOCK TICKER/OTHER:
Stock Ticker: Private   Exchange:
Employees: Fiscal Year Ends:
Parent Company:

SALARIES/BONUSES:
Top Exec. Salary: $ Bonus: $
Second Exec. Salary: $ Bonus: $

OTHER THOUGHTS:
Estimated Female Officers or Directors:
Hot Spot for Advancement for Women/Minorities:

IronClad Energy Partners LLC

NAIC Code: 221117

ironclad-energy.com

TYPES OF BUSINESS:
Waste Heat-to-Energy Electric Generation
Energy Generation Investments
Energy Generation Facility Operations
Energy Business Acquisition and Development
Power Supply
Wastewater Treatment Services
Water Services
Compressed Air and Nitrogen Services

BRANDS/DIVISIONS/AFFILIATES:
Stonepeak Infrastructure Partners

CONTACTS: Note: Officers with more than one job title may be intentionally listed here more than once.
John Prunkl, CEO
Christopher Fanella, Pres.
Myra Karegianes, General Counsel
John Whitehouse, VP-Oper.
Eric Gottung, Sr. VP-Bus. Dev.
Dick Munson, Sr. VP-Public Affairs
Scott Kerrigan, Controller
Craig Bennett, VP
Leif Bergquist, VP-Bus. Dev.

GROWTH PLANS/SPECIAL FEATURES:
IronClad Energy Partners, LLC acquires, develops, owns and operates energy generation facilities. The firm serves industrial and commercial customers, and also provides and purchases grid power. IronClad's systems and facilities supply power, steam, hot or chilled water, compressed air, nitrogen, wastewater treatment or a combination of these services. The company acquires power and co-generation facilities or district energy systems and improves the operations technically, commercially, operationally and/or financially. IronClad also provides the capital to expand and upgrade major utility systems after acquisition, including major fuel switching projects. Current projects include: RED-Rochester, LLC, of which IronClad manages the utility infrastructure in the Eastman Business Park in Rochester and Greece, New York, and provides utility services to all the companies located in the business park; and a New England power generation portfolio of thermal generation facilities on behalf of parent Stonepeak, which includes Canal Generating LLC and Bucksport Generation LLC firms. IronClad Energy Partners is privately-owned by Stonepeak Infrastructure Partners.

FINANCIAL DATA: Note: Data for latest year may not have been available at press time.

In U.S. $	2021	2020	2019	2018	2017	2016
Revenue						
R&D Expense						
Operating Income						
Operating Margin %						
SGA Expense						
Net Income						
Operating Cash Flow						
Capital Expenditure						
EBITDA						
Return on Assets %						
Return on Equity %						
Debt to Equity						

CONTACT INFORMATION:
Phone: 630-590-6044
Fax: 630-590-6037
Toll-Free:
Address: 500 Waters Edge, Ste. 320, Lombard, IL 60148 United States

STOCK TICKER/OTHER:
Stock Ticker: Private
Employees: 23
Parent Company: Stonepeak Infrastructure Partners
Exchange:
Fiscal Year Ends:

SALARIES/BONUSES:
Top Exec. Salary: $
Second Exec. Salary: $
Bonus: $
Bonus: $

OTHER THOUGHTS:
Estimated Female Officers or Directors: 1
Hot Spot for Advancement for Women/Minorities:

Sales, profits and employees may be estimates. Financial information, benefits and other data can change quickly and may vary from those stated here.

Itaipu Binacional

NAIC Code: 221111

www.itaipu.gov.br

TYPES OF BUSINESS:
Hydroelectric Electricity
Hydropower Plant
Facility Construction and Operation
Power Generation
Electricity Production
Water Supply
Agriculture Services
Fish Production

BRANDS/DIVISIONS/AFFILIATES:

GROWTH PLANS/SPECIAL FEATURES:
Itaipu Binacional began in 1974 as a result of a partnership between the governments of Brazil and Paraguay, with the mission to build and operate the Itaipu hydropower plant located at the Parana River, which borders the two countries. The Itaipu hydropower plant has generated more than 2.8 billion megawatts-hour since its operation in 1984. Itaipu Binacional continues to follow sustainable development principles via integrated environmental, social and economic initiatives. The hydropower plant belongs equally to Brazil and Paraguay, each owning half of the electricity produced. It provides approximately 90% of the electricity consumed in Paraguay and 10% in Brazil. Itaipu's artificial lake is a reservoir that extends 105.6 miles (170km) along the river and serves multiple uses besides energy generation, including water supply, agriculture, fish production, tourism and wildlife conservation.

CONTACTS:
Note: Officers with more than one job title may be intentionally listed here more than once.

Joao Francisco Ferreira, Gen. Dir.-Brazil
Manuel Maria Caceres Cardozo, Gen. Dir.-Paraguay
Carlos Jorge Paris Ferraro, Exec. Dir.-Admin.
Benigno Maria Lopez Benitez, Exec. Dir.-Legal
Pedro Domaniczky Lanik, Exec. Dir.-Coordination

FINANCIAL DATA:
Note: Data for latest year may not have been available at press time.

In U.S. $	2021	2020	2019	2018	2017	2016
Revenue	3,700,000,000	3,558,945,000	3,584,195,000	3,743,936,000	3,740,514,000	3,811,499,000
R&D Expense						
Operating Income						
Operating Margin %						
SGA Expense						
Net Income		1,834,053,000	1,523,133,000	1,190,366,000	1,179,990,000	1,170,030,000
Operating Cash Flow						
Capital Expenditure						
EBITDA						
Return on Assets %						
Return on Equity %						
Debt to Equity						

CONTACT INFORMATION:
Phone: 55 45-3520-5252 Fax:
Toll-Free:
Address: Av. Tancredo Neves, 6731- Porto Belo, Foz do Iguac, Parana, 85865-970 Brazil

STOCK TICKER/OTHER:
Stock Ticker: Government-Owned
Employees: 2,900
Parent Company:

Exchange:
Fiscal Year Ends: 12/31

SALARIES/BONUSES:
Top Exec. Salary: $ Bonus: $
Second Exec. Salary: $ Bonus: $

OTHER THOUGHTS:
Estimated Female Officers or Directors: 6
Hot Spot for Advancement for Women/Minorities: Y

Sales, profits and employees may be estimates. Financial information, benefits and other data can change quickly and may vary from those stated here.

JA Solar Technology Co Ltd
NAIC Code: 334413A

www.jasolar.com

TYPES OF BUSINESS:
Photovoltaic Cell Manufacturing
Solar Module Manufacturing
Photovoltaic Energy Project Development
Solar Cells
Silicon Wafers
PV Power Stations

BRANDS/DIVISIONS/AFFILIATES:
JASO Holdings Limited

GROWTH PLANS/SPECIAL FEATURES:
JA Solar Technology Co., Ltd. is a China-based manufacturer of high-performance solar cells and solar power products. The company's business ranges from silicon wafers, cells and modules to photovoltaic (PV) power stations. JA Solar's PV products include Bifacial mono PERC double glass, half-cell, standard and multi-busbar (MBB) half-cell modules. The firm's products are sold in 135 countries and regions, including North America, Latin America, Europe, Asia, Oceania and Africa. Global projects by JA Solar include a 100-megawatt (MW) ground-mounted power plant in the Shanxi province of China, a 49-MW ground power station in the U.K., an 80-MW ground-mounted power plant in the U.S., a 10.1-MW ground-mounted power plant in Egypt, a 255-MW ground-mounted power plant in Brazil, and a 5.44-MW rooftop distributed power plant in Brazil, among others. JA Solar is privately-owned by JASO Holdings Limited.

CONTACTS: Note: Officers with more than one job title may be intentionally listed here more than once.

Baofang Jin, CEO

FINANCIAL DATA:
Note: Data for latest year may not have been available at press time.

In U.S. $	2021	2020	2019	2018	2017	2016
Revenue	5,679,944,000	3,959,810,000	3,027,410,000	2,856,710,000	2,960,092,160	2,369,476,096
R&D Expense						
Operating Income						
Operating Margin %						
SGA Expense						
Net Income	281,361,610	237,213,000	183,759,000	149,686,000	45,189,340	102,943,464
Operating Cash Flow						
Capital Expenditure						
EBITDA						
Return on Assets %						
Return on Equity %						
Debt to Equity						

CONTACT INFORMATION:
Phone: 86-21-6095-5888   Fax: 86-21-6095-5858
Toll-Free:
Address: Bldg. 8, Noble Center, Automobile Museum East Rd.,, Beijing, 10070 China

STOCK TICKER/OTHER:
Stock Ticker: 2459
Employees: 25,183
Parent Company: JASO Holdings Limited
Exchange: Shenzhen
Fiscal Year Ends: 12/31

SALARIES/BONUSES:
Top Exec. Salary: $ Bonus: $
Second Exec. Salary: $ Bonus: $

OTHER THOUGHTS:
Estimated Female Officers or Directors:
Hot Spot for Advancement for Women/Minorities:

Plunkett Research, Ltd.   261

JinkoSolar Holding Co Ltd
NAIC Code: 334413A   www.jinkosolar.com

TYPES OF BUSINESS:
Photovoltaic Cell Manufacturing
Solar Module Manufacturing

GROWTH PLANS/SPECIAL FEATURES:
JinkoSolar Holding Co Ltd is engaged in the photovoltaic industry. The firm has built a vertically integrated solar power product value chain, manufacturing from silicon wafers to solar modules. It sells solar modules under the JinkoSolar brand. The company's product includes Swan, Tiger, Cheetah, and others. Its geographical segments are China (including Hong Kong and Taiwan), North America, Europe, Asia Pacific (except China, which includes Hong Kong and Taiwan), and the Rest of the world.

BRANDS/DIVISIONS/AFFILIATES:
JinkoSolar

CONTACTS: *Note: Officers with more than one job title may be intentionally listed here more than once.*
Xiande Li, CEO
Hairyun (Charlie) Cao, CFO
Zhiqun Xu, VP-Production Dept.
Xianhua Li, VP
Musen Yu, VP
Xiande Li, Chmn.

FINANCIAL DATA: *Note: Data for latest year may not have been available at press time.*

In U.S. $	2021	2020	2019	2018	2017	2016
Revenue	5,738,092,000	4,937,380,000	4,180,785,000	3,519,693,000	3,720,723,000	3,007,820,000
R&D Expense	64,875,610	54,700,220	45,598,670	51,521,660	41,335,600	25,454,130
Operating Income	258,876,100	293,899,600	261,546,800	100,021,300	66,504,430	230,959,100
Operating Margin %	.05%	.06%	.06%	.03%	.02%	.08%
SGA Expense	677,445,800	545,798,100	465,124,700	349,640,700	333,408,800	311,005,700
Net Income	101,337,700	32,380,130	126,305,300	57,129,820	19,916,470	256,740,700
Operating Cash Flow	60,526,530	83,132,300	198,263,200	86,373,260	-24,890,050	-253,403,800
Capital Expenditure	1,220,818,000	582,709,300	522,396,700	364,476,800	365,832,800	591,463,000
EBITDA	494,167,800	368,998,800	392,435,100	225,264,400	150,209,900	342,462,100
Return on Assets %	.01%	.00%	.02%	.01%	.01%	.07%
Return on Equity %	.07%	.02%	.10%	.06%	.02%	.34%
Debt to Equity	1.05%	0.79	0.342	0.331	0.182	0.076

CONTACT INFORMATION:
Phone: 86 7938469699   Fax: 86 7938461152
Toll-Free:
Address: 1 Jingke Rd., Shangrao Economic Development Zone, Shangrao, 334100 China

STOCK TICKER/OTHER:
Stock Ticker: JKS
Employees: 24,361
Parent Company:

Exchange: NYS
Fiscal Year Ends: 12/31

SALARIES/BONUSES:
Top Exec. Salary: $ Bonus: $
Second Exec. Salary: $ Bonus: $

OTHER THOUGHTS:
Estimated Female Officers or Directors:
Hot Spot for Advancement for Women/Minorities:

Sales, profits and employees may be estimates. Financial information, benefits and other data can change quickly and may vary from those stated here.

Kyocera Corporation
NAIC Code: 333316

global.kyocera.com

TYPES OF BUSINESS:
Photographic and Photocopying Equipment Manufacturing
Cell Phone Manufacturing
Semiconductor Components
Optoelectronic Products
Consumer Electronics

GROWTH PLANS/SPECIAL FEATURES:
Kyocera is a Japanese conglomerate whose original business consisted of manufacturing fine ceramic components; the firm has since expanded into manufacturing handsets, printers, solar cells, and industrial tools. As a result of reorganization, the firm now consists of three major business segments, which are the core components business (28% of 2020 revenue), electronic components business (18% of revenue), and solutions business (55% of revenue).

BRANDS/DIVISIONS/AFFILIATES:

CONTACTS:
Note: Officers with more than one job title may be intentionally listed here more than once.
Hideo Tanimoto, Pres.
Tatsumi Maeda, Vice Chmn.
Goro Yamaguchi, Chmn.

FINANCIAL DATA:
Note: Data for latest year may not have been available at press time.

In U.S. $	2021	2020	2019	2018	2017	2016
Revenue	10,543,700,000	11,041,960,000	11,212,230,000	10,889,950,000	9,824,564,000	
R&D Expense						
Operating Income	487,819,000	691,864,200	654,782,700	626,305,100	721,895,400	
Operating Margin %	.05%	.06%	.06%	.06%	.07%	
SGA Expense	2,322,278,000	2,354,581,000	2,549,442,000	1,948,190,000	1,855,734,000	
Net Income	622,956,000	743,847,400	712,697,500	546,465,900	717,068,500	
Operating Cash Flow	1,524,838,000	1,482,088,000	1,519,342,000	1,097,289,000	1,134,067,000	
Capital Expenditure	912,371,600	833,706,200	818,659,600	631,069,800	502,092,300	
EBITDA	1,580,012,000	1,678,868,000	1,420,699,000	1,477,199,000	1,492,894,000	
Return on Assets %	.03%	.03%	.03%	.03%	.03%	
Return on Equity %	.04%	.05%	.04%	.03%	.05%	
Debt to Equity	.04%	0.032	0.002	0.003	0.002	

CONTACT INFORMATION:
Phone: 81 75-604-3500   Fax: 81-75-604-3501
Toll-Free:
Address: 6, Takeda Tobadono-cho, Fushimi-ku,, Kyoto, 612-8501 Japan

STOCK TICKER/OTHER:
Stock Ticker: KYOCY
Employees: 70,153
Parent Company:

Exchange: PINX
Fiscal Year Ends: 03/31

SALARIES/BONUSES:
Top Exec. Salary: $428,130   Bonus: $345,266
Second Exec. Salary: $386,698   Bonus: $310,739

OTHER THOUGHTS:
Estimated Female Officers or Directors:
Hot Spot for Advancement for Women/Minorities:

Sales, profits and employees may be estimates. Financial information, benefits and other data can change quickly and may vary from those stated here.

LG Energy Solution Ltd

NAIC Code: 335910

www.lgensol.com/en/index

TYPES OF BUSINESS:
Battery Manufacturing
Advanced Automotive Batteries
Cell, Module and Battery Pack Development
Product Manufacture
Advanced Technologies
Ultra-Slim Mobility and IT Batteries
Energy Storage Systems
Energy Management Solutions

BRANDS/DIVISIONS/AFFILIATES:

CONTACTS: *Note: Officers with more than one job title may be intentionally listed here more than once.*
Young Soo Kwon, CEO

GROWTH PLANS/SPECIAL FEATURES:
LG Energy Solution, Ltd. was established in 2020, and is a developer of advanced automotive battery, mobility, information technology (IT) battery and ESS (energy storage system) battery enterprises, for the purpose of green energy transition. LG Energy's advanced automotive battery division develops and manufactures cells, modules, battery management system (BMS) and battery pack products for electric vehicle batteries, utilizing advanced technology. The mobility and IT battery division develops and manufactures high-capacity, high-power and ultra-slim batteries for a wide variety of applications, including light electric vehicles, electric bicycles, power tools, wireless earphones and IT devices such as smartphones and laptops. Last, the ESS battery division leverages technology and mass production capabilities to serve the ESS market with a range of products for power grid, uninterruptible power supply (UPS) and commercial and residential uses. This segment develops high-energy and high-output products that store and manage energy, with applications spanning power plants, power transmission and distribution facilities, homes, factories and businesses. LG Energy is headquartered in South Korea, with research and development campuses throughout the country, as well as businesses in Germany, Poland, Australia, the U.S., China and Taiwan.

FINANCIAL DATA: *Note: Data for latest year may not have been available at press time.*

In U.S. $	2021	2020	2019	2018	2017	2016
Revenue						
R&D Expense						
Operating Income						
Operating Margin %						
SGA Expense						
Net Income						
Operating Cash Flow						
Capital Expenditure						
EBITDA						
Return on Assets %						
Return on Equity %						
Debt to Equity						

CONTACT INFORMATION:
Phone: 82-2-3777-1114 Fax:
Toll-Free:
Address: 108 Yeoui-daero, Yeongdeungpo-gu, Seoul, 07335 South Korea

STOCK TICKER/OTHER:
Stock Ticker: 373220 Exchange: Seoul
Employees: Fiscal Year Ends:
Parent Company:

SALARIES/BONUSES:
Top Exec. Salary: $ Bonus: $
Second Exec. Salary: $ Bonus: $

OTHER THOUGHTS:
Estimated Female Officers or Directors:
Hot Spot for Advancement for Women/Minorities:

Sales, profits and employees may be estimates. Financial information, benefits and other data can change quickly and may vary from those stated here.

Lightsource BP

NAIC Code: 221114

www.lightsourcebp.com

TYPES OF BUSINESS:
Solar Electric Power Generation
Solar Power Structure Construction
Solar Power Energy Solutions
Solar Power Management and Operation
Solar Asset Acquisition and Divesting
Solar and Green Assets
Investment Management
Renewable Energy Research and Development

BRANDS/DIVISIONS/AFFILIATES:
Lightsource
BP plc

CONTACTS: Note: Officers with more than one job title may be intentionally listed here more than once.
Nick Boyle, CEO
Ann Davies, COO
Bernardo Goarmon, CFO
Heather Hayes, Dir.-Global HR
Paul McCartie, CIO
Mike Roney, Chmn.

GROWTH PLANS/SPECIAL FEATURES:
Lightsource BP develops, manages and operates utility-scale renewable solar energy solutions, and acquires, owns and divests related assets. The company operates through three divisions: development and building, managing and operating, and owning and divesting. The development and building division develops and co-develops late-stage solar energy and green assets. It engages in power purchase agreements, environmental planning, grid and interconnections, commercial engineering, and construction and project management. The managing and operating division manages energy facilities and other energy assets, and engages in the operation and maintenance of them. The owning and divesting division monitors operational asset performance, and provides structured finance and modeling, investment management and asset divestment services. Lightsource BP is a 50/50 joint venture between Lightsource and BP plc. Currently, Lightsource BP is exploring how the pairing of solar and wind generation with energy storage can maximize the grid capacity available, and how these renewable hubs can speed deployment, bring more projects to fruition and generate consistent flows of clean power.

FINANCIAL DATA: Note: Data for latest year may not have been available at press time.

In U.S. $	2021	2020	2019	2018	2017	2016
Revenue						
R&D Expense						
Operating Income						
Operating Margin %						
SGA Expense						
Net Income						
Operating Cash Flow						
Capital Expenditure						
EBITDA						
Return on Assets %						
Return on Equity %						
Debt to Equity						

CONTACT INFORMATION:
Phone: 44 333 200 0755   Fax:
Toll-Free:
Address: 33 Holborn, London, EC1N 2HU United Kingdom

STOCK TICKER/OTHER:
Stock Ticker: Joint Venture   Exchange:
Employees: Fiscal Year Ends:
Parent Company: BP plc

SALARIES/BONUSES:
Top Exec. Salary: $ Bonus: $
Second Exec. Salary: $ Bonus: $

OTHER THOUGHTS:
Estimated Female Officers or Directors:
Hot Spot for Advancement for Women/Minorities:

Sales, profits and employees may be estimates. Financial information, benefits and other data can change quickly and may vary from those stated here.

Lithium Werks BV

lithiumwerks.com

NAIC Code: 335912

TYPES OF BUSINESS:
Lithium Batteries, Primary, Manufacturing
Lithium Battery Technology
Lithium Battery Manufacture
Nanophosphate Powder
Production Facilities

BRANDS/DIVISIONS/AFFILIATES:
Nanophosphate

GROWTH PLANS/SPECIAL FEATURES:
Lithium Werks BV was incorporated in 2017, and is a cobalt-free lithium battery technology and manufacturing firm, with operations in China and the U.S. Lithium Werks' batters are used in industrial, medical, marine, energy storage, commercial transportation and other applications. The company's proprietary Nanophosphate powder delivers unique power, safety and cycle life performance in addition to being environmental/social/governance (ESG) friendly. During 2022, Reliance Industries Ltd. agreed to acquire substantially all the assets of Lithium Werks BV for a total transaction of $61 million (USD), including funding for future growth. The definitive agreements occurred through Reliance subsidiary Reliance New Energy Limited, and include the entire patent portfolio of Lithium Werks, manufacturing facilities in China, key business contracts and more.

CONTACTS:
Note: Officers with more than one job title may be intentionally listed here more than once.

Joseph Fisher, CEO

FINANCIAL DATA:
Note: Data for latest year may not have been available at press time.

In U.S. $	2021	2020	2019	2018	2017	2016
Revenue						
R&D Expense						
Operating Income						
Operating Margin %						
SGA Expense						
Net Income						
Operating Cash Flow						
Capital Expenditure						
EBITDA						
Return on Assets %						
Return on Equity %						
Debt to Equity						

CONTACT INFORMATION:
Phone: 31-857431400 Fax:
Toll-Free:
Address: Colosseum 65, Enschede, 7521 PP Netherlands

STOCK TICKER/OTHER:
Stock Ticker: Private Exchange:
Employees: 550 Fiscal Year Ends:
Parent Company:

SALARIES/BONUSES:
Top Exec. Salary: $ Bonus: $
Second Exec. Salary: $ Bonus: $

OTHER THOUGHTS:
Estimated Female Officers or Directors:
Hot Spot for Advancement for Women/Minorities:

Sales, profits and employees may be estimates. Financial information, benefits and other data can change quickly and may vary from those stated here.

Lordstown Motors Corp

lordstownmotors.com

NAIC Code: 336112

TYPES OF BUSINESS:
Light Truck and Utility Vehicle Manufacturing
Electric Truck Manufacturing

GROWTH PLANS/SPECIAL FEATURES:
Lordstown Motors Corp is an electric vehicle innovator developing high-quality light duty commercial fleet vehicles, with the Endurance all electric pick-up truck as its first vehicle being launched in the Lordstown, Ohio facility. The Company is in its final design and testing phase related to their production of the Endurance and has yet to bring a completed product to market.

BRANDS/DIVISIONS/AFFILIATES:
Endurance
DiamondPeak Holdings Corp

CONTACTS:
Note: Officers with more than one job title may be intentionally listed here more than once.

Daniel Ninivaggi, CEO
Rebecca Roof, CFO
Jane Ritson-Parsons, Executive VP
Thomas Canepa, General Counsel
Shane Brown, Other Executive Officer
Edward Hightower, President
Shea Burns, Senior VP, Divisional
Carter Driscoll, Vice President, Divisional
Chuan Vo, Vice President, Divisional
Darren Post, Vice President, Divisional

FINANCIAL DATA:
Note: Data for latest year may not have been available at press time.

In U.S. $	2021	2020	2019	2018	2017	2016
Revenue						
R&D Expense	284,016,000	70,967,000	5,865,000			
Operating Income	-400,489,000	-102,283,000	-10,391,000			
Operating Margin %						
SGA Expense	105,362,000	31,316,000	4,526,000			
Net Income	-410,368,000	-124,050,000	-10,391,000			
Operating Cash Flow	-387,990,000	-99,596,000	-5,202,000			
Capital Expenditure	285,514,000	52,645,000	133,000			
EBITDA	-389,378,000	-102,283,000	-10,391,000			
Return on Assets %	-.56%	-.31%	-.31%			
Return on Equity %	-.70%	-.39%	-1.21%			
Debt to Equity		0.002				

CONTACT INFORMATION:
Phone: 234-285-4001 Fax:
Toll-Free:
Address: 2300 Hallock Young Rd., Lordstown, OH 44481 United States

STOCK TICKER/OTHER:
Stock Ticker: RIDE Exchange: NAS
Employees: 632 Fiscal Year Ends:
Parent Company:

SALARIES/BONUSES:
Top Exec. Salary: $500,000 Bonus: $
Second Exec. Salary: $397,885 Bonus: $

OTHER THOUGHTS:
Estimated Female Officers or Directors:
Hot Spot for Advancement for Women/Minorities:

Plunkett Research, Ltd.

Luna Innovations Incorporated
www.lunainnovations.com

NAIC Code: 541712

TYPES OF BUSINESS:
Nanomedicine Technologies
Optical Test & Measurement Technology
Communications Test and Control Products
Distributed Fiber Optic Sensing Products
Stress and Temperature Measurement
Research Services

BRANDS/DIVISIONS/AFFILIATES:

GROWTH PLANS/SPECIAL FEATURES:
Luna Innovations Inc is active in advanced optical technology business. It provides high-performance fiber optic test, measurement and control products for the telecommunications and photonics industries; and distributed fiber optic sensing solutions that measure and monitor materials and structures for applications in aerospace, automotive, energy, oil and gas, security and infrastructure. The company's Lightwave segment develops, manufactures and markets distributed fiber optic sensing products and fiber optic communications test and control products. Geographically, the group has a business presence in the U.S., Asia, Europe and Canada, Central and South America, of which key revenue is derived from the U.S.
Luna offers its employees life, AD&D, disability, health and dental insurance; an employee assistance plan; a 401(k); and flexible spending accounts.

CONTACTS:
Note: Officers with more than one job title may be intentionally listed here more than once.

Scott Graeff, CEO
Eugene Nestro, CFO
Richard Roedel, Chairman of the Board
Brian Soller, COO

FINANCIAL DATA:
Note: Data for latest year may not have been available at press time.

In U.S. $	2021	2020	2019	2018	2017	2016
Revenue	87,513,000	59,115,000	70,516,000	42,917,240	33,081,860	41,867,770
R&D Expense	10,190,000	6,714,000	7,496,000	3,766,160	2,653,337	3,540,227
Operating Income	-2,590,000	813,000	4,343,000	877,535	-2,208,148	-2,499,236
Operating Margin %	-.03%	.01%	.06%	.02%	-.07%	-.06%
SGA Expense	43,956,000	28,353,000	23,344,000	14,794,210	12,923,840	14,763,710
Net Income	1,382,000	3,291,000	5,343,000	11,004,240	14,614,910	-2,369,492
Operating Cash Flow	4,483,000	2,856,000	4,798,000	-3,308,826	915,042	-399,837
Capital Expenditure	1,768,000	1,060,000	811,000	761,656	1,848,128	2,000,184
EBITDA	1,997,000	3,922,000	6,202,000	2,612,223	328,911	1,211,406
Return on Assets %	.01%	.03%	.06%	.15%	.24%	-.04%
Return on Equity %	.02%	.05%	.08%	.19%	.34%	-.07%
Debt to Equity	.19%	0.28	0.03	0.001	0.014	0.072

CONTACT INFORMATION:
Phone: 540 769-8400   Fax: 540 951-0760
Toll-Free: 866 586-2682
Address: 301 First St. SW, Ste. 200, Roanoke, VA 24011 United States

SALARIES/BONUSES:
Top Exec. Salary: $410,000   Bonus: $
Second Exec. Salary: $290,000   Bonus: $

STOCK TICKER/OTHER:
Stock Ticker: LUNA
Employees: 392
Parent Company:

Exchange: NAS
Fiscal Year Ends: 12/31

OTHER THOUGHTS:
Estimated Female Officers or Directors:
Hot Spot for Advancement for Women/Minorities:

Sales, profits and employees may be estimates. Financial information, benefits and other data can change quickly and may vary from those stated here.

Manitoba Hydro-Electric

NAIC Code: 221111

www.hydro.mb.ca

TYPES OF BUSINESS:
Electric Utility-Hydroelectric
Utility Services
Pipelines
Electricity Trading
Hydro Power
Wind Power
Natural Gas

BRANDS/DIVISIONS/AFFILIATES:

CONTACTS: Note: Officers with more than one job title may be intentionally listed here more than once.
Jay Grewal, CEO
Shane Mailey, VP-Oper.
Aurel Tess, CFO
Jeffrey W. Betker, VP-Communications
Jamie Hanly, VP-Human Resources
Ian Fish, VP-Digital & Transformation
Ken M. Tennenhouse, General Counsel
Darren Rainkie, Sr. VP-Finance & Regulatory
Ken R. F. Adams, Sr. VP-Power Supply
Ruth Kristjanson, VP-Corp. Rel.
Shane Mailey, VP-Transmission
Edward Kennedy, Chmn.
G. Brent Reed, VP-Dist. & Customer Service

GROWTH PLANS/SPECIAL FEATURES:

Manitoba Hydro-Electric is the Canadian province's major energy utility. The firm serves approximately 601,000 electric customers and 290,500 natural gas customers throughout southern Manitoba. The company also trades electricity within four wholesale markets in the midwestern U.S. and Canada. Manitoba Hydro-Electric generates nearly all its electricity (96%) from self-renewing water power using 15 hydroelectric generating stations, primarily on the Winnipeg, Saskatchewan, Burntwood, Laurie and Nelson rivers. The province's remaining electricity needs are fulfilled by one thermal generating station, four remote diesel generation stations and wind power purchases from independent wind farms in Manitoba. Manitoba Hydro-Electric delivers electricity across 6,863 miles (11,045 km) of transmission lines and 46,800 miles (75,320 km) of distribution lines on average every year. As for natural gas, Manitoba Hydro-Electric delivers natural gas across 6,632 miles (10,673 km) to 132 communities within Manitoba every year. Most of the natural gas is brought in from western Canada by a gas transportation pipeline owned by TransCanada Pipelines Limited (TCPL). Natural gas is transferred into Manitoba Hydro-Electric's system at several points along the TCPL pipeline, and when it is distributed to homes and businesses on the firm's systems, the pressure is first lowered at a regulating station.

Manitoba offers its employees health and retirement benefits, disability and life insurance, employee development support and more.

FINANCIAL DATA: Note: Data for latest year may not have been available at press time.

In U.S. $	2021	2020	2019	2018	2017	2016
Revenue	2,236,587,535	1,862,470,000	1,929,000,000	1,707,830,000	1,746,180,000	1,803,539,160
R&D Expense						
Operating Income						
Operating Margin %						
SGA Expense						
Net Income	92,761,695	70,135,000	88,362,400	21,256,200	44,273,700	31,150,588
Operating Cash Flow						
Capital Expenditure						
EBITDA						
Return on Assets %						
Return on Equity %						
Debt to Equity						

CONTACT INFORMATION:
Phone: 204-480-5900   Fax: 204-360-6155
Toll-Free: 888-624-9376
Address: 360 Portage Ave., Winnipeg, MB R3C 0G8 Canada

SALARIES/BONUSES:
Top Exec. Salary: $ Bonus: $
Second Exec. Salary: $ Bonus: $

STOCK TICKER/OTHER:
Stock Ticker: Government-Owned   Exchange:
Employees: 4,900   Fiscal Year Ends: 03/31
Parent Company:

OTHER THOUGHTS:
Estimated Female Officers or Directors: 3
Hot Spot for Advancement for Women/Minorities: Y

McDermott International Ltd

NAIC Code: 541330

www.mcdermott.com

TYPES OF BUSINESS:
Engineering Services
Energy Engineering Services
Energy Construction Services
Energy Transformation Services
Consulting Services
Procurement and Supply Chain Management
Commissioning Services
Operations Services

BRANDS/DIVISIONS/AFFILIATES:

GROWTH PLANS/SPECIAL FEATURES:

McDermott International Ltd. is a fully integrated provider of engineering and construction solutions to the energy industry. The firm designs and builds infrastructure solutions so that its customers can transport and transform global energy resources into products. McDermott offers technology, engineering and fabrication services, onshore construction, marine construction vessels, procurement and supply chain management, startup/commissioning and related operations, and consulting services. Markets served by McDermott are categorized into upstream, refining, chemicals and petrochemicals, liquefied natural gas (LNG), power, industrial storage, water and wastewater. McDermott operates in over 50 countries, and its globally-integrated resources include a diversified fleet of specialty marine construction vessels and fabrication facilities.

CONTACTS:
Note: Officers with more than one job title may be intentionally listed here more than once.

Michael McKelvy, CEO
Vaseem Khan, Sr. VP-Global Oper.
Gary Luquette, Chairman of the Board
Travis Brantley, CFO
Gentry Brann, Chief People Officer
David Dickson, Director
Daniel McCarthy, Executive VP, Divisional
Samik Mukherjee, Executive VP
John Freeman, Executive VP
Brian McLaughlin, Other Executive Officer
Stephen Allen, Other Executive Officer
Scott Munro, Other Executive Officer
Neil Gunnion, Senior VP, Divisional
Mark Coscio, Senior VP, Geographical
Linh Austin, Senior VP, Geographical
Ian Prescott, Senior VP, Geographical

FINANCIAL DATA:
Note: Data for latest year may not have been available at press time.

In U.S. $	2021	2020	2019	2018	2017	2016
Revenue	6,507,280,000	6,257,000,000	7,847,000,000	6,322,000,000	2,984,768,000	2,635,983,104
R&D Expense						
Operating Income						
Operating Margin %						
SGA Expense						
Net Income		463,000,000	-2,884,000,000	-2,687,000,064	178,546,000	34,117,000
Operating Cash Flow						
Capital Expenditure						
EBITDA						
Return on Assets %						
Return on Equity %						
Debt to Equity						

CONTACT INFORMATION:
Phone: 281 58806600 Fax:
Toll-Free:
Address: 915 N. Eldridge Pkwy., Houston, TX 77079 United States

STOCK TICKER/OTHER:
Stock Ticker: Private Exchange:
Employees: 40,000 Fiscal Year Ends: 12/31
Parent Company:

SALARIES/BONUSES:
Top Exec. Salary: $ Bonus: $
Second Exec. Salary: $ Bonus: $

OTHER THOUGHTS:
Estimated Female Officers or Directors: 4
Hot Spot for Advancement for Women/Minorities: Y

Methanex Corporation

NAIC Code: 325194

www.methanex.com

TYPES OF BUSINESS:
Methyl Alcohol (methanol), Natural, Manufacturing
Methanol Tankers

BRANDS/DIVISIONS/AFFILIATES:
Waterfront Shipping Company Limited

GROWTH PLANS/SPECIAL FEATURES:
Methanex Corp manufactures and sells methanol. Methanex's customers use methanol as a feedstock to produce end-products including adhesives, foams, solvents, and windshield washer fluids. The firm also sells its products to the oil refining industry, where the methanol is blended with gasoline to produce a high-octane fuel or blended as a component of biodiesel. Methanex distributes its products through a global supply chain that includes the operation of port terminals, tankers, barges, rail cars, trucks, and pipelines. China generates the most revenue of any geographical segment.

CONTACTS:
Note: Officers with more than one job title may be intentionally listed here more than once.

John Floren, CEO
Ian Cameron, CFO
Douglas Arnell, Chairman of the Board
Michael Herz, Senior VP, Divisional
Vanessa James, Senior VP, Divisional
Kevin Henderson, Senior VP, Divisional

FINANCIAL DATA:
Note: Data for latest year may not have been available at press time.

In U.S. $	2021	2020	2019	2018	2017	2016
Revenue	4,414,559,000	2,649,963,000	3,283,514,000	4,482,702,000	3,060,642,000	1,998,429,000
R&D Expense						
Operating Income	711,965,000	-62,289,000	139,450,000	829,624,000	476,468,000	-4,054,000
Operating Margin %	.16%	-.02%	.04%	.19%	.16%	.00%
SGA Expense	210,849,000	246,779,000	184,171,000	182,519,000	243,707,000	204,762,000
Net Income	482,358,000	-156,678,000	87,767,000	568,982,000	316,135,000	-12,545,000
Operating Cash Flow	993,926,000	461,082,000	515,431,000	980,206,000	780,220,000	226,667,000
Capital Expenditure	245,437,000	341,816,000	323,860,000	244,476,000	103,170,000	99,947,000
EBITDA	1,173,828,000	334,534,000	589,393,000	1,151,194,000	798,065,000	280,610,000
Return on Assets %	.08%	-.03%	.02%	.12%	.07%	.00%
Return on Equity %	.34%	-.13%	.06%	.38%	.20%	-.01%
Debt to Equity	1.64%	2.566	1.772	0.837	0.964	0.941

CONTACT INFORMATION:
Phone: 604 661-2600 Fax: 604 661-2676
Toll-Free: 800-661-8851
Address: 1800 Waterfront Centre, 200 Burrard St.,, Vancouver, BC V6C 3M1 Canada

SALARIES/BONUSES:
Top Exec. Salary: $1,287,000   Bonus: $
Second Exec. Salary: $648,900   Bonus: $

STOCK TICKER/OTHER:
Stock Ticker: MEOH
Employees: 1,300
Parent Company:

Exchange: NAS
Fiscal Year Ends: 12/31

OTHER THOUGHTS:
Estimated Female Officers or Directors: 2
Hot Spot for Advancement for Women/Minorities: Y

Sales, profits and employees may be estimates. Financial information, benefits and other data can change quickly and may vary from those stated here.

MiaSole Hi-Tech Corp

NAIC Code: 334413A

www.miasole.com

TYPES OF BUSINESS:
Photovoltaic Cell Manufacturing
Solar Panels
Copper Indium Gallium Selenide (CIGS)
Solar Technologies
Photovoltaic Solar Products
Flexible Solar Cells
Custom Solar Modules
Consumer Chargers

BRANDS/DIVISIONS/AFFILIATES:
Hanergy Holdings Group Co Ltd
SolarRide
FLEX

GROWTH PLANS/SPECIAL FEATURES:
MiaSole Hi-Tech Corp. develops and produces copper indium gallium selenide (CIGS) thin-film photovoltaic (PV) solar products. The firm's SolarRide transportation solution is comprised of solar modules and a charge controller, with auxiliary power that reduces fuel consumption, maintenance costs and emission, and provides stand-by power as well as power to truck de-icing systems. SolarRide's target applications span lift-gates, auxiliary power unit (APU) charging and refrigeration. Other products include flexible solar cells, custom modules and consumer chargers. Modules are branded under the FLEX name, and include the N, M and W series. MiaSole solutions include commercial and residential roofs, transportation, marine, carports, non-roofs, consumer charging and more. Consulting and spare part services are provided. In addition, MiaSole builds and sells turnkey production lines for the manufacturing of CIGS thin-film solar cells and modules, including test equipment to ensure the quality of the modules. MiaSole operates as a subsidiary of Hanergy Holdings Group Co. Ltd.

CONTACTS:
Note: Officers with more than one job title may be intentionally listed here more than once.

Jie Zhang, CEO
Mike Ma, VP-Global Bus. Dev.

FINANCIAL DATA:
Note: Data for latest year may not have been available at press time.

In U.S. $	2021	2020	2019	2018	2017	2016
Revenue						
R&D Expense						
Operating Income						
Operating Margin %						
SGA Expense						
Net Income						
Operating Cash Flow						
Capital Expenditure						
EBITDA						
Return on Assets %						
Return on Equity %						
Debt to Equity						

CONTACT INFORMATION:
Phone: 408-919-5700
Fax: 408-919-5701
Toll-Free:
Address: 2590 Walsh Ave., Santa Clara, CA 95051 United States

STOCK TICKER/OTHER:
Stock Ticker: Subsidiary
Exchange:
Employees: 227
Fiscal Year Ends:
Parent Company: Hanergy Holdings Group Co Ltd

SALARIES/BONUSES:
Top Exec. Salary: $
Bonus: $
Second Exec. Salary: $
Bonus: $

OTHER THOUGHTS:
Estimated Female Officers or Directors: 2
Hot Spot for Advancement for Women/Minorities:

Sales, profits and employees may be estimates. Financial information, benefits and other data can change quickly and may vary from those stated here.

Mitsubishi Corporation

NAIC Code: 333000

www.mitsubishicorp.com

TYPES OF BUSINESS:
Machinery Manufacturing
Automobile Manufacturing
Metals Mining & Production
Chemicals
Food Products & Commodities
Petroleum Exploration & Production
IT Services & Equipment
Machinery Manufacturing

GROWTH PLANS/SPECIAL FEATURES:
Mitsubishi Corp is a conglomerate that operates businesses in various industries. Its operating segments include Natural Gas, Industrial materials, Petroleum & chemicals, Mineral resource, Industrial Infrastructure, Automotive, Food & Consumer Industry, Power Solution, and Urban Development.

BRANDS/DIVISIONS/AFFILIATES:

CONTACTS:
Note: Officers with more than one job title may be intentionally listed here more than once.

Takehiko Kakiuchi, CEO
Hideyuki Nabeshima, Sr. Exec. VP-Admin.
Hideyuki Nabeshima, Sr. Exec. VP-Legal
Hideto Nakahara, Sr. Exec. VP-Global Strategy & Bus. Dev.
Hideyuki Nabeshima, Sr. Exec. VP-Corporate Communications
Jun Yanai, Sr. Exec. VP
Jun Kinukawa, Sr. Exec. VP
Takahisa Miyauchi, Sr. Exec. VP
Nobuaki Kojima, Exec. VP
Ken Kobayashi, Chmn.

FINANCIAL DATA:
Note: Data for latest year may not have been available at press time.

In U.S. $	2021	2020	2019	2018	2017	2016
Revenue	88,971,670,000	102,058,700,000	111,201,600,000	52,255,240,000	44,371,900,000	
R&D Expense						
Operating Income	1,432,155,000	2,471,405,000	4,036,080,000	3,448,335,000	2,734,719,000	
Operating Margin %	.02%	.02%	.04%	.07%	.06%	
SGA Expense	9,651,607,000	9,883,107,000	9,690,379,000	2,226,702,000	6,439,944,000	
Net Income	1,191,512,000	3,696,781,000	4,079,225,000	3,868,171,000	3,040,362,000	
Operating Cash Flow	7,026,503,000	5,867,639,000	4,506,968,000	5,127,072,000	4,025,826,000	
Capital Expenditure	2,686,036,000	2,251,229,000	2,178,723,000	1,915,921,000	1,105,230,000	
EBITDA	5,687,610,000	8,060,678,000	8,089,369,000	7,727,178,000	5,883,977,000	
Return on Assets %	.01%	.03%	.04%	.04%	.03%	
Return on Equity %	.03%	.10%	.11%	.11%	.09%	
Debt to Equity	1.01%	1.068	0.667	0.691	0.841	

CONTACT INFORMATION:
Phone: 81 332102121   Fax:
Toll-Free:
Address: 3-1 Marunouchi 2-chome, Chiyoda-ku, Tokyo, 100-8086 Japan

STOCK TICKER/OTHER:
Stock Ticker: MSBHF
Employees: 104,168
Parent Company:

Exchange: PINX
Fiscal Year Ends: 03/31

SALARIES/BONUSES:
Top Exec. Salary: $ Bonus: $
Second Exec. Salary: $ Bonus: $

OTHER THOUGHTS:
Estimated Female Officers or Directors: 1
Hot Spot for Advancement for Women/Minorities:

Sales, profits and employees may be estimates. Financial information, benefits and other data can change quickly and may vary from those stated here.

Mitsubishi Electric Corporation

NAIC Code: 335311

www.mitsubishielectric.com

TYPES OF BUSINESS:
Electrical and Electronic Equipment Manufacturer
Power Plant Manufacturing, Nuclear & Fossil
Wind & Solar Generation Systems
Consumer Electronics
Telecommunications & Computer Equipment
Industrial Automation Systems
Chips & Memory Devices
Semiconductors

BRANDS/DIVISIONS/AFFILIATES:
Mitsubishi Corporation

GROWTH PLANS/SPECIAL FEATURES:
Mitsubishi Electric is a general electric diversified industrials company that develops, manufactures, distributes, and sells electrical equipment worldwide. The company's core segments include: industrial automation systems, energy and electric systems, electric devices, information and communication systems, and home appliances (which includes commercial air conditioning). Mitsubishi Electric was founded in 1921 and is headquartered in Tokyo.

CONTACTS:
Note: Officers with more than one job title may be intentionally listed here more than once.

Kei Uruma, CEO
Tadashi Kawagoishi, CFO
Kuniaki Masuda, General Affairs and Human Resources
Kazuhiko Tsutsumi, Exec. Officer-R&D
Eiichiro Mitani, CIO
Masaharu Moriyaso, Exec. Officer-Total Productivity Mgmt.
Tsuyoshi Nakamura, Exec. Officer-Legal Affairs & Compliance
Noritomo Hashimoto, Sr. VP-Corp. Strategic Planning & Oper.
Takayuki Sueki, Exec. Officer-Global Strategic Planning & Mktg.
Masayuki Ichige, Exec. Officer-Govt & External & Public Rel.
Masayuki Ichige, Exec. Officer-Auditing
Yoshiaki Nakatani, Exec. Officer-Energy & Industrial Systems
Takashi Sasakawa, Exec. Officer-Electronic Systems
Mitsuo Muneyuki, Exec. VP-Export Control & Building Systems
Masaki Sakuyama, Exec. VP-Semiconductors & Device
Mitoji Yabunaka, Chmn.

FINANCIAL DATA:
Note: Data for latest year may not have been available at press time.

In U.S. $	2021	2020	2019	2018	2017	2016
Revenue	28,943,160,000	30,815,030,000	31,211,470,000	30,690,150,000	29,269,320,000	
R&D Expense					1,277,235,000	
Operating Income	1,589,569,000	1,793,041,000	2,005,835,000	2,261,104,000	1,888,935,000	
Operating Margin %	.05%	.06%	.06%	.07%	.06%	
SGA Expense	6,584,922,000	7,023,223,000	7,204,273,000	7,052,819,000	5,727,440,000	
Net Income	1,333,637,000	1,531,834,000	1,565,076,000	1,766,069,000	1,453,520,000	
Operating Cash Flow	3,743,502,000	2,733,358,000	1,656,012,000	1,835,212,000	2,527,000,000	
Capital Expenditure	1,300,678,000	1,499,814,000	1,505,545,000	1,444,536,000	1,154,327,000	
EBITDA	3,279,348,000	3,450,447,000	3,429,090,000	3,710,046,000	3,045,644,000	
Return on Assets %	.04%	.05%	.05%	.06%	.05%	
Return on Equity %	.07%	.09%	.10%	.12%	.11%	
Debt to Equity	.08%	0.10	0.081	0.082	0.11	

CONTACT INFORMATION:
Phone: 81 332182111 Fax: 81 332182431
Toll-Free:
Address: Tokyo Bldg. 2-7-3 Marunouchi, Chiyoda-ku, Tokyo, 100-8310 Japan

STOCK TICKER/OTHER:
Stock Ticker: MIELY Exchange: PINX
Employees: 146,518 Fiscal Year Ends: 03/31
Parent Company: Mitsubishi Corporation

SALARIES/BONUSES:
Top Exec. Salary: $ Bonus: $
Second Exec. Salary: $ Bonus: $

OTHER THOUGHTS:
Estimated Female Officers or Directors:
Hot Spot for Advancement for Women/Minorities:

Modine Manufacturing Company

NAIC Code: 336300

www.modine.com

TYPES OF BUSINESS:
Automobile Parts Manufacturer
Heat Exchangers & Systems
Oil Cores
Electronics Cooling
Heating & Air Conditioning Products
Radiator Cores
Fuel Cells

BRANDS/DIVISIONS/AFFILIATES:

GROWTH PLANS/SPECIAL FEATURES:

Modine Manufacturing Co provides thermal management solutions to diversified markets and customers. The company provides engineered heat transfer systems and heat transfer components for use in on- and off-highway original equipment manufacturer (OEM) vehicular applications primarily in the United States. It offers powertrain cooling products, such as engine cooling assemblies, radiators, condensers, and charge air coolers; auxiliary cooling products, including power steering and transmission oil coolers.

Modine offers employees medical benefits, educational assistance, retirement plans, life insurance and flexible spending accounts.

CONTACTS:
Note: Officers with more than one job title may be intentionally listed here more than once.

Neil Brinker, CEO
Michael Lucareli, CFO
Marsha Williams, Chairman of the Board
Sylvia Stein, Chief Compliance Officer
Matt Powell, General Manager, Divisional
Scott Miller, Vice President, Divisional
Brian Agen, Vice President, Divisional
Matthew McBurney, Vice President, Divisional

FINANCIAL DATA:
Note: Data for latest year may not have been available at press time.

In U.S. $	2021	2020	2019	2018	2017	2016
Revenue	1,808,400,000	1,975,500,000	2,212,700,000	2,103,100,000	1,503,000,000	
R&D Expense						
Operating Income	82,500,000	57,900,000	121,400,000	110,700,000	51,200,000	
Operating Margin %	.05%	.03%	.05%	.05%	.03%	
SGA Expense	210,900,000	249,600,000	244,100,000	245,800,000	203,200,000	
Net Income	-210,700,000	-2,200,000	84,800,000	22,200,000	14,200,000	
Operating Cash Flow	149,800,000	57,900,000	103,300,000	124,200,000	41,700,000	
Capital Expenditure	32,700,000	71,300,000	73,900,000	71,000,000	64,400,000	
EBITDA	-31,300,000	110,200,000	182,500,000	165,600,000	96,300,000	
Return on Assets %	-.15%	.00%	.05%	.01%	.01%	
Return on Equity %	-.50%	.00%	.16%	.05%	.04%	
Debt to Equity	.89%	0.926	0.716	0.788	0.98	

CONTACT INFORMATION:
Phone: 262 636-1200 Fax: 262 636-1424
Toll-Free:
Address: 1500 DeKoven Ave., Racine, WI 53403 United States

STOCK TICKER/OTHER:
Stock Ticker: MOD Exchange: NYS
Employees: 11,100 Fiscal Year Ends: 02/28
Parent Company:

SALARIES/BONUSES:
Top Exec. Salary: $825,846 Bonus: $
Second Exec. Salary: $510,615 Bonus: $

OTHER THOUGHTS:
Estimated Female Officers or Directors: 4
Hot Spot for Advancement for Women/Minorities: Y

Sales, profits and employees may be estimates. Financial information, benefits and other data can change quickly and may vary from those stated here.

Motech Industries Inc

NAIC Code: 334413

www.motechsolar.com

TYPES OF BUSINESS:
Solar Cells
Solar Product Development and Manufacture
Solar Power Supply Systems
Photovoltaic Cells
PV Modules
PV Power Systems

BRANDS/DIVISIONS/AFFILIATES:
Motech Solar
Motech Power
I-Cells

CONTACTS:
Note: Officers with more than one job title may be intentionally listed here more than once.

Fred Yeh, Pres.
Ting Wang, CFOVP
Steve Tseng, Chmn.

GROWTH PLANS/SPECIAL FEATURES:
Motech Industries, Inc., headquartered in Taiwan, researches, develops, manufactures and sells solar products and services. These products include photovoltaic (PV) cells, PV modules and PV systems. The company operates through two business divisions: Motech Solar and Motech Power. Motech Solar was one of the first companies in Taiwan to manufacture solar cells, which it currently supplies to solar module manufacturers worldwide. This division specializes in producing mono-crystalline silicon and multi-crystalline silicon solar cells, including its I-Cells, which are isotopically acid-etched cells with higher output than other, alkaline-etched cell designs. Motech Power builds and installs photovoltaic power systems in Taiwan, and manufactures and sells portable systems and components outside of Taiwan. This division also develops PV inverters, a key component for PV systems. These solar inverters convert the variable direct current (DC) output of a PV solar panel into a utility frequency alternating current (AC) that can be fed into a commercial electrical grid or used by a local, off-grid electrical network. Motech has international locations in China and Japan.

FINANCIAL DATA:
Note: Data for latest year may not have been available at press time.

In U.S. $	2021	2020	2019	2018	2017	2016
Revenue	184,470,930	130,822,000	176,144,000	463,309,000	780,398,000	912,482,000
R&D Expense						
Operating Income						
Operating Margin %						
SGA Expense						
Net Income	3,360,870	3,981,220	-44,790,300	-224,550,000	-102,272,000	-28,621,800
Operating Cash Flow						
Capital Expenditure						
EBITDA						
Return on Assets %						
Return on Equity %						
Debt to Equity						

CONTACT INFORMATION:
Phone: 886-6-505-0789   Fax:
Toll-Free:
Address: Da-Shun 9th Rd., No. 2, Hsin-Shi, Tainan, 74145 Taiwan

STOCK TICKER/OTHER:
Stock Ticker: 6244   Exchange: TWSE
Employees: 3,500   Fiscal Year Ends: 12/31
Parent Company:

SALARIES/BONUSES:
Top Exec. Salary: $ Bonus: $
Second Exec. Salary: $ Bonus: $

OTHER THOUGHTS:
Estimated Female Officers or Directors:
Hot Spot for Advancement for Women/Minorities:

Sales, profits and employees may be estimates. Financial information, benefits and other data can change quickly and may vary from those stated here.

Nanosys Inc

NAIC Code: 335912

www.nanosysinc.com

TYPES OF BUSINESS:
Batteries and Nanostructure Fabrication Processes
Quantum Dot Technology
Display Technology
micro LED Technology
Quantum Dot Sheets

BRANDS/DIVISIONS/AFFILIATES:
microLED

CONTACTS: Note: Officers with more than one job title may be intentionally listed here more than once.
Jason Hartlove, CEO
Jian Chen, VP-R&D
Andrew Filler, VP-Intellectual Property

GROWTH PLANS/SPECIAL FEATURES:

Nanosys, Inc. develops and produces quantum dot technology for displays. The firm has partnered with leading display makers since its 2001 founding, for the creation of standout tablets, TVs and smartphones. Quantum dot technology makes displays thinner, lighter, brighter and more colorful and lifelike. Quantum dots are tiny man-made crystals so small they cannot be seen with a typical microscope. They are 10,000 times narrower than a human hair; yet, these dots can convert incoming energy and therefore can control the color of light emitted by each quantum dot. They have the capability of projecting color purity, recreating the full palette of colors that the human eyes see in nature. During the early 2020's, Nanosys began combining quantum dot with microLED (light-emitting diode) to create visual experiences that are bolder, brighter and more immersive than before. The company has more than 900 patents in its portfolio. The firm's slide-in quantum dot sheet makes it easy for manufacturers to integrate it into any display stack without having to invest in expensive equipment. With microLED and quantum dot technologies, manufacturers can create devices with limitless variations of size, shapes, use cases and applications. Creators who produce visual and immersive experiences utilizing Nanosys' display technology, can provide a hyperreal color pallet that gives viewers an experience beyond what can be seen in nature. In mid-2022, Nanosys announced that it raised more than $50 million in Series B equity and debt financing, with investors funds managed by affiliates of Fortress Investment Group, Centerbridge Partners and Kilonova Capital. The Series B financing supports the rapid expansion of QDEF and xQDEF quantum dot technologies for liquid crystal displays (LCDs), and drives the commercialization of Nanosys' microLED technology platform as well as the development of next-generation nano LEDs.

FINANCIAL DATA: Note: Data for latest year may not have been available at press time.

In U.S. $	2021	2020	2019	2018	2017	2016
Revenue						
R&D Expense						
Operating Income						
Operating Margin %						
SGA Expense						
Net Income						
Operating Cash Flow						
Capital Expenditure						
EBITDA						
Return on Assets %						
Return on Equity %						
Debt to Equity						

CONTACT INFORMATION:
Phone: 408-240-6700   Fax:
Toll-Free:
Address: 233 South Hillview Dr., Milpitas, CA 95035 United States

STOCK TICKER/OTHER:
Stock Ticker: Private   Exchange:
Employees: 120   Fiscal Year Ends: 12/31
Parent Company: Lux Capital

SALARIES/BONUSES:
Top Exec. Salary: $ Bonus: $
Second Exec. Salary: $ Bonus: $

OTHER THOUGHTS:
Estimated Female Officers or Directors:
Hot Spot for Advancement for Women/Minorities:

Sales, profits and employees may be estimates. Financial information, benefits and other data can change quickly and may vary from those stated here.

New York Power Authority

NAIC Code: 221111

www.nypa.gov

TYPES OF BUSINESS:
Hydroelectric Energy Generation
Energy-Efficiency Services
Energy Research and Development
Hydroelectric Plants
Renewable Hydropower
Electric Transmission Lines
Electricity Sales
Advisory and Energy Management Solutions

BRANDS/DIVISIONS/AFFILIATES:
Power Authority of the State of New York (The)

CONTACTS: *Note: Officers with more than one job title may be intentionally listed here more than once.*
Justin E. Driscol, CEO
Joseph Kessler, COO
Adam Barsky, CFO
Sarah Orban Salati, CCO
Kristine Pizzo, Chief Human Resources Officer
Robert Piascik, CIO
Judith C. McCarthy, General Counsel
Robert F. Lurie, Sr. VP-Strategic Planning
Michael Saltzman, Dir.-Media Rel.
Joan Tursi, Sr. VP-Corp. Support Svcs.
Joseph Leary, VP-Community & Gov't Rel.
John R. Koelmel, Chmn.

GROWTH PLANS/SPECIAL FEATURES:
New York Power Authority (NYPA), officially The Power Authority of the State of New York, is a leading state-owned power organization in the U.S. NYPA is a nonprofit, public-benefit energy corporation that does not use any tax revenues or state credit, but finances its operations through the sale of bonds and revenues earned in large part through sales of electricity. More than 80% of the electricity NYPA produces is clean renewable hydropower. The organization operates 16 electricity-generating facilities which provide roughly a quarter of New York's electricity, and over 1,400 miles of transmission line. Its generating facilities include three major hydroelectric facilities: the St. Lawrence-Franklin D. Roosevelt Power Project, the Niagara Power Project and the Blenheim-Gilboa Pumped Storage Power Project. NYPA sells power to government agencies, co-ops, private enterprises, neighboring states and private utilities, which are required to pass this electricity along without markup. The organization also provides advisory services, energy efficiency solutions, energy management solutions, smart street lighting solutions, electric vehicle infrastructure solutions, solar and storage solutions, community solar solutions, blended power solutions and more. NYPA continually engages in digital utility innovation and renewable power research and development and smart energy solutions.

NYPA offers employees comprehensive plans and benefits.

FINANCIAL DATA: *Note: Data for latest year may not have been available at press time.*

In U.S. $	2021	2020	2019	2018	2017	2016
Revenue	2,741,000,000	2,265,000,000	2,370,000,000	2,689,000,000	2,573,000,000	2,421,000,000
R&D Expense						
Operating Income						
Operating Margin %						
SGA Expense						
Net Income	13,900,000	-17,000,000	26,000,000	102,000,000	119,000,000	22,000,000
Operating Cash Flow						
Capital Expenditure						
EBITDA						
Return on Assets %						
Return on Equity %						
Debt to Equity						

CONTACT INFORMATION:
Phone: 914-681-6200 Fax:
Toll-Free:
Address: 123 Main St, Mail Stop 10-B, White Plains, NY 10601-3170 United States

STOCK TICKER/OTHER:
Stock Ticker: Government-Owned
Employees: 2,400
Parent Company:

Exchange:
Fiscal Year Ends: 12/31

SALARIES/BONUSES:
Top Exec. Salary: $ Bonus: $
Second Exec. Salary: $ Bonus: $

OTHER THOUGHTS:
Estimated Female Officers or Directors:
Hot Spot for Advancement for Women/Minorities: Y

Sales, profits and employees may be estimates. Financial information, benefits and other data can change quickly and may vary from those stated here.

Newfoundland and Labrador Hydro

NAIC Code: 221111

nlhydro.com

TYPES OF BUSINESS:
Electric Utility
Hydroelectric Plants
Electricity Generation and Distribution
Oil-Fired Plant
Gas Turbines
Diesel Generating and Distribution Systems
Electric Terminal Stations
Wind Energy

BRANDS/DIVISIONS/AFFILIATES:
Nalcor Energy

GROWTH PLANS/SPECIAL FEATURES:
Newfoundland and Labrador Hydro is a government-owned corporation and subsidiary of Nalcor Energy, which generates, transmits and distributes electrical power and energy to customers throughout the Canadian province of Newfoundland and Labrador. The company has both regulated and unregulated operations across the province, with power generation assets in Churchill Falls, Muskrat Falls, Bay d'Espoir and Holyrood. Regulated assets include nine hydroelectric generation stations, one oil-fired plant, four gas turbines and 25 isolated diesel generating and distribution systems. Hydro also maintains more than 50 high-voltage terminal stations, 25 lower-voltage interconnected distribution stations and nearly 4,000 miles (6,400 km) of transmission and distribution lines. As part of Hydro's strategy to leverage wind as a renewable energy source, the company has purchase agreements for 54 MW of wind energy on the island with NeWind Group Inc. and with Elemental Energy. Hydro sells electricity to three primary customer groups: Newfoundland Power, industrial customers and residential/commercial customers.

CONTACTS: Note: Officers with more than one job title may be intentionally listed here more than once.

Jennifer Williams, CEO
Scott Crosbie, VP-Hydro Oper.
Lisa Hutchens, CFO
Gail Collins, VP-People
John MacIsaac, VP-Eng. Svcs., Asset Mgmt. & Project Execution
Derrick Sturge, VP-Finance
Rob Henderson, VP
Paul Humphries, VP-System Oper. & Planning.
John Green, Chmn.

FINANCIAL DATA: Note: Data for latest year may not have been available at press time.

In U.S. $	2021	2020	2019	2018	2017	2016
Revenue	752,334,840	549,161,000	572,399,000	506,484,000	529,734,000	501,500,000
R&D Expense						
Operating Income						
Operating Margin %						
SGA Expense						
Net Income	53,472,960	46,936,900	19,896,200	10,994,600	54,964,900	41,939,500
Operating Cash Flow						
Capital Expenditure						
EBITDA						
Return on Assets %						
Return on Equity %						
Debt to Equity						

CONTACT INFORMATION:
Phone: 709-737-1400   Fax: 709-737-1800
Toll-Free:
Address: 500 Columbus Dr., St. John's, NL A1B 4K7 Canada

STOCK TICKER/OTHER:
Stock Ticker: Government-Owned   Exchange:
Employees: 900   Fiscal Year Ends: 12/31
Parent Company: Nalcor Energy

SALARIES/BONUSES:
Top Exec. Salary: $ Bonus: $
Second Exec. Salary: $ Bonus: $

OTHER THOUGHTS:
Estimated Female Officers or Directors: 1
Hot Spot for Advancement for Women/Minorities:

Sales, profits and employees may be estimates. Financial information, benefits and other data can change quickly and may vary from those stated here.

NextEra Energy Inc

NAIC Code: 221115

www.nexteraenergy.com

TYPES OF BUSINESS:
Wind Electric Power Generation
Fiber-Optic Services
Financial Services
Nuclear Power
Energy Trading & Marketing
Electric Power
Solar Power
Electricity Distribution

BRANDS/DIVISIONS/AFFILIATES:
Florida Power & Light Company
NextEra Energy Resources LLC
NextEra Energy Capital Holdings Inc
GridLiance Holdco LP
GridLiance GP LLC

GROWTH PLANS/SPECIAL FEATURES:
NextEra Energy's regulated utility, Florida Power & Light, distributes power to more than 5 million customers in Florida. FP&L contributes more than 60% of the group's operating earnings. The renewable energy segment generates and sells power throughout the United States and Canada. Consolidated generation capacity totals more than 50 gigawatts and includes natural gas, nuclear, wind, and solar assets.

NextEra Energy offers employees medical, dental and vision benefits; flexible spending plans; life insurance and dependent life insurance; vacation time; and education and adoption assistance.

CONTACTS:
Note: Officers with more than one job title may be intentionally listed here more than once.

Paul Cutler, Assistant Secretary
Eric Silagy, CEO, Subsidiary
John Ketchum, CEO, Subsidiary
James Robo, CEO
Rebecca Kujawa, CFO
Keith Ferguson, Chief Accounting Officer, Subsidiary
James May, Chief Accounting Officer
Deborah Caplan, Executive VP, Divisional
Miguel Arechabala, Executive VP, Divisional
Donald Moul, Executive VP, Divisional
Ronald Reagan, Executive VP, Divisional
Charles Sieving, Executive VP

FINANCIAL DATA:
Note: Data for latest year may not have been available at press time.

In U.S. $	2021	2020	2019	2018	2017	2016
Revenue	17,069,000,000	17,997,000,000	19,204,000,000	16,727,000,000	17,173,000,000	16,138,000,000
R&D Expense						
Operating Income	2,864,000,000	4,946,000,000	5,181,000,000	4,203,000,000	5,832,000,000	4,154,000,000
Operating Margin %	.17%	.27%	.27%	.25%	.34%	.26%
SGA Expense						
Net Income	3,573,000,000	2,919,000,000	3,769,000,000	6,638,000,000	5,380,000,000	2,906,000,000
Operating Cash Flow	7,553,000,000	7,983,000,000	8,155,000,000	6,593,000,000	6,458,000,000	6,369,000,000
Capital Expenditure	7,830,000,000	7,759,000,000	11,077,000,000	5,959,000,000	5,405,000,000	4,240,000,000
EBITDA	8,659,000,000	8,678,000,000	10,563,000,000	12,997,000,000	8,859,000,000	8,903,999,000
Return on Assets %	.03%	.02%	.03%	.07%	.06%	.03%
Return on Equity %	.10%	.08%	.11%	.21%	.20%	.12%
Debt to Equity	1.37%	1.149	1.015	0.784	1.112	1.143

CONTACT INFORMATION:
Phone: 561 694-4000 Fax: 561 694-4620
Toll-Free: 888-218-4392
Address: 700 Universe Blvd., Juno Beach, FL 33408 United States

STOCK TICKER/OTHER:
Stock Ticker: NEE
Employees: 9,700
Parent Company:

Exchange: NYS
Fiscal Year Ends: 12/31

SALARIES/BONUSES:
Top Exec. Salary: $1,560,000 Bonus: $
Second Exec. Salary: $1,400,000 Bonus: $

OTHER THOUGHTS:
Estimated Female Officers or Directors: 5
Hot Spot for Advancement for Women/Minorities: Y

Sales, profits and employees may be estimates. Financial information, benefits and other data can change quickly and may vary from those stated here.

NextEra Energy Resources LLC

www.nexteraenergyresources.com

NAIC Code: 221115

TYPES OF BUSINESS:
Wind Electric Power Generation
Clean Energy Generation
Power Plant Construction, Operation & Management
Electricity & Natural Gas Marketing
Construction Management Services
Wind and Solar Power Facilities
Nuclear and Natural Gas Facilities
Battery Management System

BRANDS/DIVISIONS/AFFILIATES:
NextEra Energy Inc

CONTACTS: Note: Officers with more than one job title may be intentionally listed here more than once.
Rebecca J. Kujawa, CEO
John Ketchum, General Counsel
Michael O'Sullivan, Sr. VP-Dev.
Mark R. Sorensen, Sr. VP-Finance
Mark Maisto, Pres., Commodities & Retail Markets
Mark Ianni, Pres., Gexa Energy GP, LLC

GROWTH PLANS/SPECIAL FEATURES:
NextEra Energy Resources, LLC owns, develops, constructs, manages and operates diversified energy power plants. The company operates 28,000 megawatts (MW) of generating capacity with a presence in the U.S. and Canada. NextEra Energy owns and operates 119 wind facilities, and operates more than 2,000 MW of universal-scale solar energy. The firm's nuclear portfolio includes the Point Beach plant in Wisconsin (1,200 MW) and the Seabrook Station plant (1,250+ MW). NextEra's natural gas portfolio consists of facilities with a total generating capacity of more than 1,600 MW. These electric-generating facilities are powered by gas-fired plants using combined-cycle technology, as well as oil-fired and dual-fired plants. NextEra has universal energy storage sites in operation and development throughout the U.S. and in Canada. Its battery management system monitors connected equipment to ensure the safe and reliable transfer of energy; a computerized monitoring system evaluates factors such as weather forecasts and power prices to determine when to use the energy storage system; and inverters convert alternating current (AC) to direct current (DC) and charge the batteries, and when the energy is needed the inverters convert the DC from the batteries back into AC. This energy is stepped up in voltage and ultimately delivered to the power system and distributed to consumers. NextEra's marketing division provides a wide range of electricity and gas commodity products and marketing/trading services to electric and gas utilities, municipalities, cooperatives and other load-serving entities, as well as to owners of electric generation facilities. In addition, NextEra participates in pipeline infrastructure development, construction, management and operations via wholly owned subsidiaries and joint ventures; and engages in the transition to sustainable electric transportation, from feasibility stage to operations and maintenance and electric charging infrastructure for commercial vehicles. The company operates as a subsidiary of NextEra Energy, Inc.

FINANCIAL DATA: Note: Data for latest year may not have been available at press time.

In U.S. $	2021	2020	2019	2018	2017	2016
Revenue	3,053,000,000	5,046,000,000	5,639,000,000	4,984,000,000	5,186,000,000	4,893,000,000
R&D Expense						
Operating Income						
Operating Margin %						
SGA Expense						
Net Income	-147,000,000	-19,000,000	1,426,000,000	3,842,000,000	2,905,000,000	1,218,000,000
Operating Cash Flow						
Capital Expenditure						
EBITDA						
Return on Assets %						
Return on Equity %						
Debt to Equity						

CONTACT INFORMATION:
Phone: 561-694-4000 Fax:
Toll-Free: 877-715-4360
Address: PO Box 14000, Juno Beach, FL 33408-0420 United States

STOCK TICKER/OTHER:
Stock Ticker: Subsidiary
Employees: 5,300
Parent Company: NextEra Energy Inc
Exchange:
Fiscal Year Ends: 12/31

SALARIES/BONUSES:
Top Exec. Salary: $ Bonus: $
Second Exec. Salary: $ Bonus: $

OTHER THOUGHTS:
Estimated Female Officers or Directors:
Hot Spot for Advancement for Women/Minorities:

Sales, profits and employees may be estimates. Financial information, benefits and other data can change quickly and may vary from those stated here.

Nordex SE

NAIC Code: 333611

www.nordex-online.com

TYPES OF BUSINESS:
Wind Turbine Manufacturing

GROWTH PLANS/SPECIAL FEATURES:
Nordex SE is a German company that develops, manufactures, services, and markets wind power systems. Besides developing and manufacturing, the company also provides preliminary project-development services, including data analysis and processing, noise emission and shade projections, project engineering, and others. The company generates most of its revenue from the European market.

BRANDS/DIVISIONS/AFFILIATES:
Nordex Energy GmbH
Delta

CONTACTS:
Note: Officers with more than one job title may be intentionally listed here more than once.

Jose Juis Blanco Dieguez, CEO
Ilya Hartmann, CFO
Patxi Landa, Chief Sales Officer
Wolfgang Ziebart, Chmn.

FINANCIAL DATA:
Note: Data for latest year may not have been available at press time.

In U.S. $	2021	2020	2019	2018	2017	2016
Revenue	5,331,091,000	4,554,325,000	3,216,480,000	2,408,144,000	3,013,982,000	3,324,650,000
R&D Expense						
Operating Income	-107,465,000	-392,914,000	11,366,370	-37,108,410	60,104,580	172,609,800
Operating Margin %	-.02%	-.09%	.00%	-.02%	.02%	.05%
SGA Expense	53,758,920	54,634,390	46,023,680	26,432,420	52,315,480	70,083,340
Net Income	-225,384,600	-127,016,100	-71,065,540	-82,114,630	322,179	93,376,220
Operating Cash Flow	124,917,500	-344,895,600	37,195,570	122,337,100	89,510,070	141,404,500
Capital Expenditure	166,137,900	160,463,000	169,917,800	111,326,200	147,964,600	102,852,600
EBITDA	57,781,760	102,214,100	129,280,100	104,612,400	201,715,700	287,404,600
Return on Assets %	-.05%	-.03%	-.02%	-.03%	.00%	.04%
Return on Equity %	-.25%	-.17%	-.10%	-.10%	.00%	.14%
Debt to Equity	.42%	0.533	0.857	0.807	0.672	0.67

CONTACT INFORMATION:
Phone: 49 4030030-1000 Fax: 49 4030030-1101
Toll-Free:
Address: Langenhorner Chaussee 600, Hamburg, 22419 Germany

STOCK TICKER/OTHER:
Stock Ticker: NRXXY   Exchange: PINX
Employees: 8,658   Fiscal Year Ends: 12/31
Parent Company:

SALARIES/BONUSES:
Top Exec. Salary: $ Bonus: $
Second Exec. Salary: $ Bonus: $

OTHER THOUGHTS:
Estimated Female Officers or Directors: 1
Hot Spot for Advancement for Women/Minorities:

Sales, profits and employees may be estimates. Financial information, benefits and other data can change quickly and may vary from those stated here.

Northvolt AB

NAIC Code: 335912

northvolt.com

TYPES OF BUSINESS:
Lithium Batteries, Primary, Manufacturing
Lithium-Ion Battery Production
Battery Recycling
Next-Generation Battery Cells
Energy Storage Packs and Systems
Research and Development
Manufacturing Facilities

BRANDS/DIVISIONS/AFFILIATES:
Lingonberry NMC
Voltblocks
Voltpacks
Voltracks
Hydrovolt
Northvolt Ett
Northvolt Dwa
Northvolt Labs

CONTACTS: Note: Officers with more than one job title may be intentionally listed here more than once.
Peter Carlsson, CEO
Paolo Cerruti, COO
Alexander Hartman, CFO
Yasuo Anno, Chief Development Officer
Cecilia Lundin, Chief People Officer
Mikael Soderberg, Chief Digital Officer
Carl-Erik Lagercrantz, Chmn.

GROWTH PLANS/SPECIAL FEATURES:

Northvolt AB is a European manufacturer and supplier of sustainable, high-quality battery cells and systems. Founded in 2016, Northvolt's mission is to deliver the world's greenest lithium-ion battery with a minimal CO2 footprint. The firm's products include battery cells in cylindrical 21/70 and prismatic PHEV2 (plug-in hybrid electric vehicle) formats; and energy storage systems such as battery modules and systems, including blocks, packs and mobile packs. Northvolt's products serve the automotive, construction, eMobility, energy storage, grid, industrial, micromobility and portable markets. Brands of the company include Lingonberry NMC, Voltblocks, Voltpacks and Voltracks. Northvolt facilities include Northvolt Ett, a battery Gigafactory in northern Sweden and is Northvolt's primary site for manufacturing active materials, cell assembly and recycling; Northvolt Dwa, a battery system assembly plant in Gdansk, Poland; Northvolt Labs, a research and development facility in Vasteras, Sweden, and engaged in the design, development and production of batteries; Volthouse, where the company's batteries are designed, software is developed and factories are planned. Northvolt batteries are approximately 95% recyclable, recovering used batteries and recycling them into raw materials for new batteries. During the first half of 2022, Northvolt began commercial recycling operations at Hydrovolt in Norway, a joint venture company with Hydro, and is a leading vehicle battery recycling plant in Europe; and Northvolt announced the signing of a $1.1 billion convertible note to finance its expansion of battery cell and cathode material production in Europe to support the demand for batteries.

FINANCIAL DATA: Note: Data for latest year may not have been available at press time.

In U.S. $	2021	2020	2019	2018	2017	2016
Revenue						
R&D Expense						
Operating Income						
Operating Margin %						
SGA Expense						
Net Income						
Operating Cash Flow						
Capital Expenditure						
EBITDA						
Return on Assets %						
Return on Equity %						
Debt to Equity						

CONTACT INFORMATION:
Phone: 46 761309427 Fax:
Toll-Free:
Address: Alstromergatan 20, Stockholm, SE-112 47 Sweden

SALARIES/BONUSES:
Top Exec. Salary: $ Bonus: $
Second Exec. Salary: $ Bonus: $

STOCK TICKER/OTHER:
Stock Ticker: Private   Exchange:
Employees: 1,500   Fiscal Year Ends:
Parent Company:

OTHER THOUGHTS:
Estimated Female Officers or Directors:
Hot Spot for Advancement for Women/Minorities:

Sales, profits and employees may be estimates. Financial information, benefits and other data can change quickly and may vary from those stated here.

Novozymes A/S

NAIC Code: 325414

www.novozymes.com

TYPES OF BUSINESS:
Industrial Enzyme & Microorganism Production
Biopharmaceuticals
Enzymes
Microbiology

GROWTH PLANS/SPECIAL FEATURES:
Novozymes is the world leader in industrial enzymes. In recent years, the company has expanded into micro-organisms, primarily for agricultural markets. The firm supplies five major industry groups: household care, food and beverages, bioenergy, agriculture and feed, and technical and pharma. Its biological solutions create value for its customers by improving yield efficiency and performance, while saving energy and generating less waste. The company is headquartered in Denmark.

BRANDS/DIVISIONS/AFFILIATES:
PrecisionBiotics Group Limited
Microbiome Labs

CONTACTS:
Note: Officers with more than one job title may be intentionally listed here more than once.

Ester Baiget, CEO
Graziela Malucelli, COO
Lars Green, CFO
Per Falholt, Exec. VP-R&D
Thomas Videbaek, Exec. VP-Bus. Dev
Andrew Fordyce, Exec. VP-Bus. Oper.
Jorgen Buhl Rasmussen, Chmn.
Thomas Nagy, Exec. VP-Supply Chain Oper.

FINANCIAL DATA:
Note: Data for latest year may not have been available at press time.

In U.S. $	2021	2020	2019	2018	2017	2016
Revenue	1,968,921,000	1,845,262,000	1,892,935,000	1,895,042,000	1,913,610,000	1,862,382,000
R&D Expense	264,568,400	255,086,600	258,905,600	245,604,800	251,926,000	245,604,800
Operating Income	511,621,800	475,406,600	466,846,600	535,984,700	541,647,400	519,654,900
Operating Margin %	.26%	.26%	.25%	.28%	.28%	.28%
SGA Expense	368,078,000	305,524,400	325,146,500	311,187,200	322,644,400	320,273,900
Net Income	414,301,700	372,028,700	415,355,200	424,837,000	410,746,000	401,659,300
Operating Cash Flow	534,931,200	573,516,800	420,886,300	484,493,300	535,062,900	505,695,600
Capital Expenditure	163,297,600	123,790,100	131,296,500	183,314,700	222,822,100	160,137,000
EBITDA	716,665,500	638,704,100	667,281,200	663,330,500	650,951,500	643,445,100
Return on Assets %	.14%	.14%	.16%	.17%	.17%	.17%
Return on Equity %	.27%	.25%	.28%	.28%	.27%	.26%
Debt to Equity	.03%	0.034	0.281	0.129	0.116	0.146

CONTACT INFORMATION:
Phone: 45 44460000 Fax: 45 44469999
Toll-Free:
Address: Krogshoejvej 36, Bagsvaerd, 2880 Denmark

STOCK TICKER/OTHER:
Stock Ticker: NVZMY Exchange: PINX
Employees: 6,527 Fiscal Year Ends: 12/31
Parent Company:

SALARIES/BONUSES:
Top Exec. Salary: $ Bonus: $
Second Exec. Salary: $ Bonus: $

OTHER THOUGHTS:
Estimated Female Officers or Directors: 3
Hot Spot for Advancement for Women/Minorities: Y

Sales, profits and employees may be estimates. Financial information, benefits and other data can change quickly and may vary from those stated here.

Nuvera Fuel Cells LLC

NAIC Code: 335999A

www.nuvera.com

TYPES OF BUSINESS:
Fuel Cell Manufacturing
Fuel Cell Engines
Mid- and Heavy-Duty Vehicle Engines
Compressor and Coolant Pump
Open Flow Stack Architecture
Shock-Resistant Metal Plates
Innovative Engine Controls
Design and Manufacture

BRANDS/DIVISIONS/AFFILIATES:
Hyster-Yale Group Inc
NACCO Materials Handling Group Inc
E-Series
E-40
E-60

CONTACTS:
Note: Officers with more than one job title may be intentionally listed here more than once.

Lucien Robroek, CEO
Neil Gillen, COO
Darwin Scussel, Chief Finance and Administration Officer
Kedar Murthy, CCO
John Gartner, VP-Prod. Dev. & Supplier Dev.
Francesco Fragasso, VP-Oper.
Francesco Fragasso, VP-Finance
Sandy Pipitone Davis, VP-Organizational Effectiveness
Prabhu K. Rao, Chief Commercial Officer

GROWTH PLANS/SPECIAL FEATURES:
Nuvera Fuel Cells, LLC manufactures heavy-duty, zero-emission engines for mobility applications. The company has operations in the U.S., Europe and Asia, offering products designed to meet the needs of industrial vehicles and other transportation markets. Nuvera's E-Series fuel cell engines provide performance for motive platforms in outputs ranging from five to 120 kilowatts (kW) and higher. The Nuvera E-45 and E-60 fuel cell engines can power mid- and heavy-duty vehicles such as buses, trucks, port equipment, delivery vans and more. For high-power applications, multiple engines can be combined. The E-Series fuel cell engines comprise an integrated compact compressor and coolant pump, an open flow field stack architecture for increased efficiency and power density, uncoated metal plates to resist shock and vibration, and patented controls to optimize operation and manage engine performance. Nuvera Fuel Cells operates as a subsidiary of NACCO Materials Handling Group, Inc., which itself is a subsidiary of Hyster-Yale Group, Inc.

FINANCIAL DATA:
Note: Data for latest year may not have been available at press time.

In U.S. $	2021	2020	2019	2018	2017	2016
Revenue	-320,000	3,900,000	10,100,000	17,000,000	3,700,000	2,500,000
R&D Expense						
Operating Income						
Operating Margin %						
SGA Expense						
Net Income		-12,200,000	-11,200,000	-6,000,000	-2,100,000	-2,700,000
Operating Cash Flow						
Capital Expenditure						
EBITDA						
Return on Assets %						
Return on Equity %						
Debt to Equity						

CONTACT INFORMATION:
Phone: 617-245-7500   Fax: 617-245-7511
Toll-Free:
Address: 129 Concord Rd., Bldg. 1, Billerica, MA 01821 United States

STOCK TICKER/OTHER:
Stock Ticker: Subsidiary   Exchange:
Employees: 200   Fiscal Year Ends: 12/31
Parent Company: Hyster-Yale Group Inc

SALARIES/BONUSES:
Top Exec. Salary: $ Bonus: $
Second Exec. Salary: $ Bonus: $

OTHER THOUGHTS:
Estimated Female Officers or Directors: 1
Hot Spot for Advancement for Women/Minorities:

Ontario Power Generation Inc

NAIC Code: 221112

www.opg.com

TYPES OF BUSINESS:
Electric Utility
Electricity Generation
Hydroelectric Stations
Nuclear Stations
Solar Facility
Biomass Facility
Oil and Gas Generation Facility
Combined-cycle Gas Turbine Station

BRANDS/DIVISIONS/AFFILIATES:
Eagle Creek Renewable Energy
Atura Power

GROWTH PLANS/SPECIAL FEATURES:
Ontario Power Generation, Inc. (OPG) is principally engaged in the generation and sale of electricity to customers in Ontario, Canada and the U.S. OPG's generation portfolio includes 66 hydroelectric stations, two nuclear stations, a solar facility, a biomass station, a dual oil/gas station and four combined-cycle gas turbine stations. In addition, OPG wholly or jointly owns and operates 85 hydroelectric generating stations and holds minority interests in 14 hydroelectric and two solar facilities in the U.S. through U.S.-based wholly-owned subsidiary Eagle Creek Renewable Energy; operates four combined cycle gas turbine generating stations in Ontario through subsidiary Atura Power; and owns two other nuclear generating stations in Ontario that are leased to Bruce Power LP.

CONTACTS: Note: Officers with more than one job title may be intentionally listed here more than once.
Ken Hartwick, CEO
Nicolle Butcher, COO
Aida Cipolla, CFO
Scott Martin, Sr. VP-Admin. & Bus. Svcs.
Christopher F. Ginther, General Counsel
Carlo Crozzoli, Exec. VP-Corp. Bus. Dev.
John Lee, Treas.
Carlo Crozzoli, Chief Risk Officer
John Murphy, Exec. VP-Strategic Initiatives
Mike Martelli, Sr. VP-Hydro-Thermal Oper.
Wayne Robbins, Chief Nuclear Officer
Wendy Kei, Chmn.

FINANCIAL DATA: Note: Data for latest year may not have been available at press time.

In U.S. $	2021	2020	2019	2018	2017	2016
Revenue	6,877,000,000	5,663,710,000	4,608,270,000	4,058,470,000	4,108,820,000	4,514,889,715
R&D Expense						
Operating Income						
Operating Margin %						
SGA Expense						
Net Income	1,344,000,000	1,076,420,000	861,660,000	889,096,000	701,798,000	361,831,595
Operating Cash Flow						
Capital Expenditure						
EBITDA						
Return on Assets %						
Return on Equity %						
Debt to Equity						

CONTACT INFORMATION:
Phone: 416-592-2555 Fax:
Toll-Free: 877-592-2555
Address: 700 University Ave., Toronto, ON M5G 1X6 Canada

STOCK TICKER/OTHER:
Stock Ticker: Government-Owned
Employees: 9,325
Parent Company:

Exchange:
Fiscal Year Ends: 12/31

SALARIES/BONUSES:
Top Exec. Salary: $ Bonus: $
Second Exec. Salary: $ Bonus: $

OTHER THOUGHTS:
Estimated Female Officers or Directors: 4
Hot Spot for Advancement for Women/Minorities: Y

Sales, profits and employees may be estimates. Financial information, benefits and other data can change quickly and may vary from those stated here.

Orano SA

NAIC Code: 332410

www.orano.group

TYPES OF BUSINESS:
Nuclear Power Generation Equipment
Nuclear Power Plant Design, Construction & Maintenance
Electrical Transmission & Distribution Products
Electrical & Electronic Interconnect Systems
Uranium Mining & Processing
Forged Steel Equipment
Solar Thermal Technology (CSP)

BRANDS/DIVISIONS/AFFILIATES:
Orano Med
Societe de Transports Speciaux Industriels
Orano Projects
INEVO

CONTACTS: Note: Officers with more than one job title may be intentionally listed here more than once.

Philippe Knoche, CEO
Luc Oursel, Pres.
Olivier Wantz, Sr. VP-Mining
Claude Imauven, Chmn.

GROWTH PLANS/SPECIAL FEATURES:
Orano SA processes nuclear materials, allowing them to contribute to the fields of energy, medical radiological research and more. The firm offers high value-added products and services for the entire nuclear fuel cycle, from raw materials to waste processing. Its activities range from mining to dismantling, conversion, enrichment, recycling, logistics and engineering. Orano also provides nuclear facility supervision and management, whether during the operational stage, for maintenance or at the end-of-life cycle. It offers operational assistance services and implements site assistance, specialized maintenance and handling operations on all equipment. Orano draws ore where the uranium content is high, including mines in Canada, Kazakhstan and Niger. The company's uranium conversion and enrichment facilities include the Tricastin and Malvesi plants and the Comurhex II and Georges Besse II plants. Malvesi is responsible for the first phase of conversion, purifying the natural uranium ore from the mines into uranium tetrafluoride (UF4). The group also has facilities that are global benchmarks, such as the used-fuel recycling sites of La Hague and Melox. Subsidiary Orano Med specializes in nuclear medicine, with laboratories located in France and the U.S. Orano Med develops new therapies based on the use of radioactive elements to destroy cancer cells. In May 2022, subsidiary Orano Projects acquired INEVO, an engineering firm specializing in process engineering and the optimization of industrial performance.

FINANCIAL DATA: Note: Data for latest year may not have been available at press time.

In U.S. $	2021	2020	2019	2018	2017	2016
Revenue	4,819,400,192	3,756,806,912	3,861,842,432	4,090,483,200	4,242,692,864	11,803,449
R&D Expense						
Operating Income						
Operating Margin %						
SGA Expense						
Net Income	691,399,296	-72,403,176	416,063,296	-614,363,008	-272,397,088	-784,929,408
Operating Cash Flow						
Capital Expenditure						
EBITDA						
Return on Assets %						
Return on Equity %						
Debt to Equity						

CONTACT INFORMATION:
Phone: 33-1-34-96-00-00   Fax: 33-1-34-96-00-01
Toll-Free:
Address: 111 quai du President Roosevelt, Issy-les-Moulineaux, 92130 France

STOCK TICKER/OTHER:
Stock Ticker: ARVCF
Employees: 19,102
Parent Company:

Exchange: PINX
Fiscal Year Ends: 12/31

SALARIES/BONUSES:
Top Exec. Salary: $ Bonus: $
Second Exec. Salary: $ Bonus: $

OTHER THOUGHTS:
Estimated Female Officers or Directors: 3
Hot Spot for Advancement for Women/Minorities: Y

Sales, profits and employees may be estimates. Financial information, benefits and other data can change quickly and may vary from those stated here.

Ormat Technologies Inc

NAIC Code: 221116

www.ormat.com

TYPES OF BUSINESS:
Geothermal Electric Power Generation
Geothermal Plant Design & Construction
Small Electric Generators
Procurement Services
Maintenance Services
Construction Services
Engineering Services
Recovered Energy, Biomass & Solar Plants

GROWTH PLANS/SPECIAL FEATURES:
Ormat Technologies derives approximately 80% of its revenue from building and operating geothermal plants and the rest from manufacturing geothermal and recovered energy equipment. Nearly two thirds of its capacity is in the United States, with the balance in Africa and Central America. Nearly all the plants have long-term contracts with local utilities.

BRANDS/DIVISIONS/AFFILIATES:
Viridity Energy Solutions Inc
Ormat Energy Converter

CONTACTS:
Note: Officers with more than one job title may be intentionally listed here more than once.

Doron Blachar, CEO
Assaf Ginzburg, CFO
Isaac Angel, Chairman of the Board
Hezi Kattan, Chief Compliance Officer
Ofer Benyosef, Executive VP, Divisional
Shimon Hatzir, Executive VP, Divisional
Jessica Woelfel, General Counsel
Shlomi Argas, Other Corporate Officer

FINANCIAL DATA:
Note: Data for latest year may not have been available at press time.

In U.S. $	2021	2020	2019	2018	2017	2016
Revenue	663,084,000	705,342,000	746,044,000	719,267,000	692,812,000	662,591,000
R&D Expense	4,129,000	5,395,000	4,647,000	4,183,000	3,157,000	2,762,000
Operating Income	169,109,000	193,270,000	193,796,000	198,700,000	206,814,000	204,899,000
Operating Margin %	.26%	.27%	.26%	.28%	.30%	.31%
SGA Expense	91,100,000	77,610,000	70,880,000	67,552,000	58,481,000	63,134,000
Net Income	62,092,000	85,456,000	88,095,000	97,966,000	132,414,000	88,708,000
Operating Cash Flow	258,822,000	265,005,000	236,493,000	145,822,000	245,575,000	159,285,000
Capital Expenditure	419,272,000	320,738,000	279,986,000	258,521,000	260,102,000	151,930,000
EBITDA	369,181,000	403,282,000	366,448,000	340,338,000	340,018,000	314,454,000
Return on Assets %	.01%	.02%	.03%	.03%	.05%	.04%
Return on Equity %	.03%	.05%	.06%	.08%	.12%	.09%
Debt to Equity	.83%	0.775	0.745	0.789	0.664	0.811

CONTACT INFORMATION:
Phone: 775 356-9029   Fax: 775 356-9039
Toll-Free:
Address: 6140 Plumas St., Reno, NV 89519-6075 United States

STOCK TICKER/OTHER:
Stock Ticker: ORA
Employees: 1,385
Parent Company:

Exchange: NYS
Fiscal Year Ends: 12/31

SALARIES/BONUSES:
Top Exec. Salary: $506,886   Bonus: $70,000
Second Exec. Salary: $355,759   Bonus: $29,000

OTHER THOUGHTS:
Estimated Female Officers or Directors: 2
Hot Spot for Advancement for Women/Minorities:

Sales, profits and employees may be estimates. Financial information, benefits and other data can change quickly and may vary from those stated here.

Orsted A/S

NAIC Code: 221115

orsted.com/en

TYPES OF BUSINESS:
Wind Electric Power Generation
Offshore Wind Farms
Onshore Wind Farms
Solar Farms
Renewable Hydrogen
Biomass Conversion
Energy Marketing Services
Corporate Power Purchase Agreements

BRANDS/DIVISIONS/AFFILIATES:

GROWTH PLANS/SPECIAL FEATURES:
Danish company Orsted was named Dong Energy until the sale of all its oil and gas fields to Ineos in 2017, soon after the May 2016 initial public offering. Orsted is now focused on renewable assets, especially offshore wind farms. It operated 7.6 GW of offshore wind farms at the end of 2020. The U.K. is the biggest country of operation, ahead of Germany and Denmark. The group intends to develop its footprint outside Europe with projects in Taiwan and in the U.S. Orsted is also involved in more traditional utilities business like conventional power plants and gas supply, but these activities are noncore. Orsted intends to phase out coal by 2023.

CONTACTS:
Note: Officers with more than one job title may be intentionally listed here more than once.

Mads Nipper, CEO
Richard Hunter, COO
Marianne Wiinholt, CFO
Martin Neubert, CCO
Henriette Fenger Ellekrog, Chief Human Resources Officer
Thomas Thune Andersen, Chmn.

FINANCIAL DATA:
Note: Data for latest year may not have been available at press time.

In U.S. $	2021	2020	2019	2018	2017	2016
Revenue	9,105,023,000	4,885,889,000	7,814,314,000	9,040,099,000	7,863,173,000	7,558,175,000
R&D Expense						
Operating Income	1,091,987,000	1,005,465,000	1,464,015,000	1,279,252,000	734,048,800	1,151,248,000
Operating Margin %	.12%	.21%	.19%	.14%	.09%	.15%
SGA Expense	758,543,500	760,387,200	802,133,400	772,371,100	558,503,900	537,038,300
Net Income	1,443,603,000	2,054,125,000	945,677,200	2,403,503,000	2,559,426,000	1,059,590,000
Operating Cash Flow	1,599,789,000	2,168,433,000	1,722,394,000	1,362,086,000	134,720,500	1,484,427,000
Capital Expenditure	4,552,446,000	3,550,010,000	2,955,817,000	1,929,940,000	2,316,718,000	1,972,740,000
EBITDA	3,057,747,000	3,558,043,000	2,664,252,000	3,796,010,000	2,976,493,000	2,486,337,000
Return on Assets %	.04%	.08%	.04%	.11%	.13%	.05%
Return on Equity %	.12%	.17%	.08%	.24%	.31%	.15%
Debt to Equity	.47%	0.41	0.472	0.307	0.378	0.423

CONTACT INFORMATION:
Phone: 45-99-55-11-11   Fax: 45-99-55-00-11
Toll-Free:
Address: Kraftvaerksvej 53, Fredericia, DK-7000 Denmark

SALARIES/BONUSES:
Top Exec. Salary: $ Bonus: $
Second Exec. Salary: $ Bonus: $

STOCK TICKER/OTHER:
Stock Ticker: DNNGY   Exchange: PINX
Employees: 6,836   Fiscal Year Ends: 12/31
Parent Company:

OTHER THOUGHTS:
Estimated Female Officers or Directors:
Hot Spot for Advancement for Women/Minorities:

Sales, profits and employees may be estimates. Financial information, benefits and other data can change quickly and may vary from those stated here.

PacifiCorp

www.pacificorp.com

NAIC Code: 221112

TYPES OF BUSINESS:
Electric Utility
Electric Generation and Distribution
Thermal Generation
Mining Activities
Coal and Natural Gas Facilities
Hydroelectric and Geothermal Facilities
Wind and Solar Facilities
Distribution and Transmission Lines

BRANDS/DIVISIONS/AFFILIATES:
Berkshire Hathaway Inc
Pacific Power
Rocky Mountain Power

GROWTH PLANS/SPECIAL FEATURES:
PacifiCorp is a regulated electric utility company. It is principally engaged in the business of generating, transmitting, distributing and selling electricity. The company serves retail electric customers in portions of Utah, Oregon, Wyoming, Washington, Idaho, and California. It aids various industries including agriculture, manufacturing, forest products, food processing, technology, government and primary metals. In addition, the company buys and sells electricity on the wholesale market with other utilities, energy marketing companies, financial institutions, and other market participants. The company earns its revenue through the sale of electricity and natural gas and other services.

PacifiCorp offers employee benefits including medical, dental, vision, life and accident insurance; disability coverage; flexible spending accounts; and an employee assistance program.

CONTACTS:
Note: Officers with more than one job title may be intentionally listed here more than once.

Stefan Bird, CEO
Gary Hoogeveen, CEO

FINANCIAL DATA:
Note: Data for latest year may not have been available at press time.

In U.S. $	2021	2020	2019	2018	2017	2016
Revenue	5,296,000,000	5,341,000,000	5,068,000,000	5,026,000,000	5,237,000,000	5,201,000,000
R&D Expense						
Operating Income	1,133,000,000	924,000,000	1,072,000,000	1,051,000,000	1,440,000,000	1,428,000,000
Operating Margin %	.21%	.17%	.21%	.21%	.27%	.27%
SGA Expense						
Net Income	888,000,000	739,000,000	771,000,000	738,000,000	768,000,000	763,000,000
Operating Cash Flow	1,804,000,000	1,583,000,000	1,547,000,000	1,811,000,000	1,602,000,000	1,594,000,000
Capital Expenditure	1,513,000,000	2,540,000,000	2,175,000,000	1,257,000,000	769,000,000	903,000,000
EBITDA	2,303,000,000	2,251,000,000	2,151,000,000	2,088,000,000	2,294,000,000	2,238,000,000
Return on Assets %	.03%	.03%	.03%	.03%	.03%	.03%
Return on Equity %	.09%	.08%	.09%	.10%	.10%	.10%
Debt to Equity	.87%	0.893	0.903	0.85	0.852	0.95

CONTACT INFORMATION:
Phone: 503-813-5608   Fax:
Toll-Free: 888-221-7070
Address: 825 NE Multnomah St., Portland, OR 97232 United States

SALARIES/BONUSES:
Top Exec. Salary: $ Bonus: $
Second Exec. Salary: $ Bonus: $

STOCK TICKER/OTHER:
Stock Ticker: PPWLO   Exchange: PINX
Employees: 5,200   Fiscal Year Ends: 12/31
Parent Company: Berkshire Hathaway Inc

OTHER THOUGHTS:
Estimated Female Officers or Directors:
Hot Spot for Advancement for Women/Minorities:

Sales, profits and employees may be estimates. Financial information, benefits and other data can change quickly and may vary from those stated here.

Panasonic Corporation

NAIC Code: 334310

www.panasonic.com/global/home.html

TYPES OF BUSINESS:
Audio & Video Equipment, Manufacturing
Appliances
Automotive Systems
Digital Cameras
Housing Construction Systems
Industrial Connected Systems
Batteries
Business-to-Business Solutions

BRANDS/DIVISIONS/AFFILIATES:
Blue Yonder

GROWTH PLANS/SPECIAL FEATURES:
Panasonic Holdings Corp is a conglomerate that has diversified from its consumer electronics roots. It has five main business units: appliances (air conditioners, refrigerators, laundry machines, and TVs); life solutions (LED lighting, housing systems, and solar panels; connected solutions (PCs, factory automations, and in-flight entertainment systems); automotive (infotainment systems and rechargeable batteries); and industrial solutions (electronic devices). After the crisis in 2012, former president Kazuhiro Tsuga has focused on shifting the business portfolio to increase the proportion of B2B businesses to mitigate the tough competition in consumer electronics products.

CONTACTS: Note: Officers with more than one job title may be intentionally listed here more than once.

Yuki Kusumi, CEO
Kazuhiro Tsuga, Chmn.

FINANCIAL DATA: Note: Data for latest year may not have been available at press time.

In U.S. $	2021	2020	2019	2018	2017	2016
Revenue	46,257,280,000	51,724,960,000	55,261,390,000	55,119,360,000	50,710,610,000	
R&D Expense						
Operating Income	1,929,020,000	1,991,859,000	2,766,580,000	2,558,178,000	1,853,428,000	
Operating Margin %	.04%	.04%	.05%	.05%	.04%	
SGA Expense	11,515,970,000	12,874,140,000	13,392,630,000	13,382,570,000	12,726,000,000	
Net Income	1,139,909,000	1,558,578,000	1,962,138,000	1,629,930,000	1,031,378,000	
Operating Cash Flow	3,480,541,000	2,971,377,000	1,406,454,000	2,922,205,000	2,661,377,000	
Capital Expenditure	2,046,922,000	2,384,322,000	2,754,275,000	3,284,188,000	2,360,333,000	
EBITDA	4,122,597,000	4,820,504,000	5,062,576,000	4,772,021,000	3,931,769,000	
Return on Assets %	.03%	.04%	.05%	.04%	.03%	
Return on Equity %	.07%	.12%	.16%	.14%	.10%	
Debt to Equity	.42%	0.579	0.318	0.506	0.602	

CONTACT INFORMATION:
Phone: 81 669081121   Fax:
Toll-Free:
Address: 1006 Oaza Kadoma, Kadoma City, Osaka, 571-8501 Japan

STOCK TICKER/OTHER:
Stock Ticker: PCRFF
Employees: 271,869
Parent Company:

Exchange: PINX
Fiscal Year Ends: 03/31

SALARIES/BONUSES:
Top Exec. Salary: $ Bonus: $
Second Exec. Salary: $ Bonus: $

OTHER THOUGHTS:
Estimated Female Officers or Directors:
Hot Spot for Advancement for Women/Minorities:

Sales, profits and employees may be estimates. Financial information, benefits and other data can change quickly and may vary from those stated here.

Peter Cremer North America LP

www.petercremerna.com

NAIC Code: 311200

TYPES OF BUSINESS:
Oleochemicals
Oleochemical Production
Oleochemical Marketing
Glycerin
Esters
Waxes
Gels
Vegetable Oils

BRANDS/DIVISIONS/AFFILIATES:
Peter Cremer Holding GmbH & Co KG

CONTACTS:
Note: Officers with more than one job title may be intentionally listed here more than once.
Ivan Van Handel, CEO
Stefan Cremer, Co-Managing Dir.-Peter Cremer Holding
Ullrich Wegner, Co-Managing Dir.-Peter Cremer Holding

GROWTH PLANS/SPECIAL FEATURES:

Peter Cremer North America, LP (PCNA) is a manufacturer, marketer and supplier of a full line of oleochemicals, which are designed for commercial use as base materials, additives and process aids. The company is part of the German group Peter Cremer Holding GmbH & Co. KG, which operates an international network involved in oleochemical products, shipping and commodity trading/processing. PCNA's products include glycerin; cremer care products such as triglycerides, emollients, esters, waxes, gels, vegetable oils and soap bases; oleic acid; distilled fatty acids, including light cuts; vegetable stearic and palmitic acid; fractionated and hydrogenated fatty acids; fatty alcohol; broad, mid, light and heavy cuts of methyl ester; and Rheolease mandrel lubricants. Products PCNA supports include foods, pharmaceuticals, personal care, cosmetics, soaps, detergents, paints/coatings, textiles, plastics, agricultural, mining and oil field. PCNA can flake, drum, blend, package and store a range of these chemicals, with facility space for over 4.7 million gallons of bulk product. The firm can also package 25,000 gallons per line per day in its two toting and drumming lines. PCNA maintains its own packing and shipping operations and provides contract manufacturing as well as analytical services. PCNA has earned certification in the American Chemical Council's Responsible Care Management System and ISO 14001.

FINANCIAL DATA:
Note: Data for latest year may not have been available at press time.

In U.S. $	2021	2020	2019	2018	2017	2016
Revenue						
R&D Expense						
Operating Income						
Operating Margin %						
SGA Expense						
Net Income						
Operating Cash Flow						
Capital Expenditure						
EBITDA						
Return on Assets %						
Return on Equity %						
Debt to Equity						

CONTACT INFORMATION:
Phone: 513-471-7200   Fax: 513-244-7775
Toll-Free: 877-901-7262
Address: 3117 Southside Ave., Cincinnati, OH 45204 United States

SALARIES/BONUSES:
Top Exec. Salary: $ Bonus: $
Second Exec. Salary: $ Bonus: $

STOCK TICKER/OTHER:
Stock Ticker: Subsidiary   Exchange:
Employees: 1,900   Fiscal Year Ends: 12/31
Parent Company: Peter Cremer Holding GmbH & Co KG

OTHER THOUGHTS:
Estimated Female Officers or Directors:
Hot Spot for Advancement for Women/Minorities:

Sales, profits and employees may be estimates. Financial information, benefits and other data can change quickly and may vary from those stated here.

PG&E Corporation

NAIC Code: 221111

www.pgecorp.com

TYPES OF BUSINESS:
Hydroelectric Power Generation
Electric and Gas Utility
Transmission
Distribution

BRANDS/DIVISIONS/AFFILIATES:
Pacific Gas and Electric Company

GROWTH PLANS/SPECIAL FEATURES:
PG&E is a holding company whose main subsidiary is Pacific Gas and Electric, a regulated utility operating in Central and Northern California that serves 5.3 million electricity customers and 4.6 million gas customers in 47 of the state's 58 counties. PG&E operated under bankruptcy court supervision between January 2019 and June 2020. In 2004, PG&E sold its unregulated assets as part of an earlier post bankruptcy reorganization.

CONTACTS:
Note: Officers with more than one job title may be intentionally listed here more than once.

Jason Glickman, CEO, Subsidiary
Marlene Santos, CEO, Subsidiary
David Thomason, CFO, Subsidiary
Chris Foster, CFO
Dean Seavers, Chairman of the Board, Subsidiary
Robert Flexon, Chairman of the Board
John Simon, Chief Compliance Officer
Sumeet Singh, Chief Risk Officer
Adam Wright, Co-CEO
Patricia Poppe, Co-CEO
Julius Cox, Executive VP, Divisional
Michael Lewis, President, Subsidiary

FINANCIAL DATA:
Note: Data for latest year may not have been available at press time.

In U.S. $	2021	2020	2019	2018	2017	2016
Revenue	20,642,000,000	18,469,000,000	17,129,000,000	16,759,000,000	17,135,000,000	17,666,000,000
R&D Expense						
Operating Income	2,141,000,000	2,006,000,000	1,341,000,000	2,071,000,000	2,905,000,000	2,205,000,000
Operating Margin %	.10%	.11%	.08%	.12%	.17%	.12%
SGA Expense						
Net Income	-88,000,000	-1,304,000,000	-7,642,000,000	-6,837,000,000	1,660,000,000	1,407,000,000
Operating Cash Flow	2,448,000,000	-19,047,000,000	4,810,000,000	4,704,000,000	5,977,000,000	4,409,000,000
Capital Expenditure	7,689,000,000	7,690,000,000	6,313,000,000	6,514,000,000	5,641,000,000	5,709,000,000
EBITDA	5,752,000,000	3,787,000,000	-6,874,000,000	-6,164,000,000	5,913,000,000	5,046,000,000
Return on Assets %	.00%	-.01%	-.09%	-.09%	.02%	.02%
Return on Equity %	.00%	-.09%	-.86%	-.43%	.09%	.08%
Debt to Equity	1.36%	1.343	0.337		0.924	0.904

CONTACT INFORMATION:
Phone: 415 973-8200   Fax: 415 973-8719
Toll-Free: 800-719-9056
Address: 77 Beale Street, 24/F, San Francisco, CA 94177 United States

STOCK TICKER/OTHER:
Stock Ticker: PCG
Employees: 26,000
Parent Company:

Exchange: NYS
Fiscal Year Ends: 12/31

SALARIES/BONUSES:
Top Exec. Salary: $1,344,643   Bonus: $6,600,000
Second Exec. Salary: $657,609   Bonus: $900,000

OTHER THOUGHTS:
Estimated Female Officers or Directors: 15
Hot Spot for Advancement for Women/Minorities: Y

Sales, profits and employees may be estimates. Financial information, benefits and other data can change quickly and may vary from those stated here.

Photowatt International SAS

www.photowatt.com/en

NAIC Code: 334413A

TYPES OF BUSINESS:
Photovoltaic Cell Manufacturing
Solar Panels
Photovoltaic Cells
Photovoltaic Modules
Photovoltaic Bricks
Photovoltaic Wafers
PV Manufacture
Crystalline Silicon Technology

BRANDS/DIVISIONS/AFFILIATES:
EDF Energies Nouvelles Reparties SAS
SOREN

GROWTH PLANS/SPECIAL FEATURES:
Photowatt International SAS, a subsidiary of EDF Energies Nouvelles Reparties SAS, is a producer of photovoltaic products. Based in France, the company manufactures photovoltaic cells, wafers and modules using 100% French technology. These solar products are based on crystalline silicon technology, useful for various types of applications, including residential equipment and ground-based solar power plants. Photowatt is a co-founder of SOREN, a solar panel that is 96% recyclable. The firm melts silicon in ingots and becomes crystallized, and then the ingots are cut into bricks before being polished. The bricks are cut into slices to produce low-carbon wafers, which are texturized and become available as cells and modules ready for assembly by solar partners. Photowatt has an annual production capacity of 200 megawatts-peak (MWp), and a 600 MWp total installed capacity equipped with Photowatt modules.

CONTACTS:
Note: Officers with more than one job title may be intentionally listed here more than once.

Henri Proglio, CEO-EDF Group
Bruno Bensasson, Chmn.-EDF

FINANCIAL DATA:
Note: Data for latest year may not have been available at press time.

In U.S. $	2021	2020	2019	2018	2017	2016
Revenue						
R&D Expense						
Operating Income						
Operating Margin %						
SGA Expense						
Net Income						
Operating Cash Flow						
Capital Expenditure						
EBITDA						
Return on Assets %						
Return on Equity %						
Debt to Equity						

CONTACT INFORMATION:
Phone: 33-4-74-93-80-20 Fax: 33-4-74-93-80-40
Toll-Free:
Address: 33 Rue Saint-Honore, Bourgoin-Jallieu, 38300 France

STOCK TICKER/OTHER:
Stock Ticker: Subsidiary Exchange:
Employees: 200 Fiscal Year Ends: 03/31
Parent Company: EDF Energies Nouvelles Reparties SAS

SALARIES/BONUSES:
Top Exec. Salary: $ Bonus: $
Second Exec. Salary: $ Bonus: $

OTHER THOUGHTS:
Estimated Female Officers or Directors:
Hot Spot for Advancement for Women/Minorities:

Sales, profits and employees may be estimates. Financial information, benefits and other data can change quickly and may vary from those stated here.

Plug Power Inc

NAIC Code: 335999A

www.plugpower.com

TYPES OF BUSINESS:
Fuel Cell Manufacturing
Onsite Generation Systems
Proton Exchange Membrane Technology
Back-Up Power Systems

BRANDS/DIVISIONS/AFFILIATES:
GenDrive
GenCare
GenFuel
GenKey
GenSure
GenSure HP
ProGen
Applied Cryo Technologies Inc

CONTACTS:
Note: Officers with more than one job title may be intentionally listed here more than once.

Andrew Marsh, CEO
Paul Middleton, CFO
George Mcnamee, Chairman of the Board
Martin Hull, Chief Accounting Officer
Sanjay Shrestha, Chief Strategy Officer
Keith Schmid, COO
Gerard Conway, General Counsel
Jose Crespo, Vice President, Divisional

GROWTH PLANS/SPECIAL FEATURES:
Plug Power is building an end-to-end green hydrogen ecosystem, from production, storage and delivery to energy generation. The company plans to build and operate green hydrogen highways across North America and Europe. Plug will deliver its green hydrogen solutions directly to its customers and through joint venture partners into multiple end markets, including material handling, e-mobility, power generation, and industrial applications.

Plug Power offers its employees comprehensive health benefits and retirement plans.

FINANCIAL DATA:
Note: Data for latest year may not have been available at press time.

In U.S. $	2021	2020	2019	2018	2017	2016
Revenue	502,342,000	-93,237,000	229,975,000	174,215,000	100,153,000	82,819,000
R&D Expense	64,762,000	27,848,000	15,059,000	12,750,000	28,693,000	21,177,000
Operating Income	-415,924,000	-576,612,000	-47,613,000	-76,439,000	-101,792,000	-51,519,000
Operating Margin %	-.83%		-.21%	-.44%	-1.02%	-.62%
SGA Expense	179,852,000	79,348,000	43,202,000	37,685,000	45,010,000	34,288,000
Net Income	-459,965,000	-596,155,000	-83,743,000	-85,608,000	-127,080,000	-57,487,000
Operating Cash Flow	-358,176,000	-155,476,000	-53,324,000	-58,350,000	-60,182,000	-29,636,000
Capital Expenditure	193,266,000	50,221,000	14,619,000	19,572,000	44,363,000	58,075,000
EBITDA	-409,568,000	-550,947,000	-35,416,000	-59,628,000	-107,197,000	-41,935,000
Return on Assets %	-.13%	-.53%	-.13%	-.26%	-.51%	-.26%
Return on Equity %	-.18%	-1.45%	-.72%	-2.24%	-1.64%	-.55%
Debt to Equity	.16%	0.756	1.864	66.884	0.685	0.595

CONTACT INFORMATION:
Phone: 518 782-7700 Fax: 518 782-9060
Toll-Free:
Address: 968 Albany Shaker Rd., Latham, NY 12110 United States

SALARIES/BONUSES:
Top Exec. Salary: $750,000 Bonus: $
Second Exec. Salary: $386,616 Bonus: $100,000

STOCK TICKER/OTHER:
Stock Ticker: PLUG Exchange: NAS
Employees: 2,449 Fiscal Year Ends: 12/31
Parent Company:

OTHER THOUGHTS:
Estimated Female Officers or Directors:
Hot Spot for Advancement for Women/Minorities:

Sales, profits and employees may be estimates. Financial information, benefits and other data can change quickly and may vary from those stated here.

PNM Resources Inc

www.pnmresources.com

NAIC Code: 221112

TYPES OF BUSINESS:
Electric Utility
Energy & Technology Services
Electric Utilities
Electric Transmission and Distribution
Electric Generation

BRANDS/DIVISIONS/AFFILIATES:
Public Service Company of New Mexico
Texas-New Mexico Power Company

GROWTH PLANS/SPECIAL FEATURES:

PNM Resources Inc, or PNMR, is a holding company that owns regulated utilities companies providing electricity and electric services. PNMR segments its operations by its two subsidiaries, PNM and TNMP. PNM provides electric generation, transmission, and distribution services mainly to areas of New Mexico. While PNM uses a variety of fuel sources across its power plant portfolio, its coal and gas-fueled sites produce most of the energy. TNMP owns and operates transmission and distribution services primarily in small to medium-sized communities in Texas. Both subsidiaries generate revenue for PNMR through the sale of electricity and transmission service fees fairly evenly split between residential and commercial customers. PNM generates the vast majority of PNMR's total revenue.

PNM offers its employees medical, dental and vision insurance; an employee assistance plan; flexible spending accounts; life insurance; disability coverage; credit union membership; educational assistance; a 401(k) plan; and stock options.

CONTACTS:
Note: Officers with more than one job title may be intentionally listed here more than once.

Patricia Collawn, CEO
Joseph Tarry, CFO
Henry Monroy, Chief Accounting Officer
Charles Eldred, Executive VP, Divisional
Patrick Apodaca, General Counsel
Ronald Darnell, Senior VP, Divisional
Chris Olson, Senior VP, Divisional

FINANCIAL DATA:
Note: Data for latest year may not have been available at press time.

In U.S. $	2021	2020	2019	2018	2017	2016
Revenue	1,779,873,000	1,523,012,000	1,457,603,000	1,436,613,000	1,445,003,000	1,362,951,000
R&D Expense						
Operating Income	309,347,000	286,379,000	295,295,000	301,645,000	342,075,000	299,736,000
Operating Margin %	.17%	.19%	.20%	.21%	.24%	.22%
SGA Expense	311,627,000	294,277,000	259,089,000	264,904,000	249,367,000	251,001,000
Net Income	196,357,000	173,303,000	77,890,000	86,170,000	80,402,000	117,377,000
Operating Cash Flow	547,873,000	485,700,000	503,163,000	428,226,000	523,462,000	408,283,000
Capital Expenditure	935,016,000	679,028,000	616,273,000	501,213,000	500,461,000	600,076,000
EBITDA	661,516,000	637,012,000	488,933,000	511,942,000	621,578,000	565,840,000
Return on Assets %	.02%	.02%	.01%	.01%	.01%	.02%
Return on Equity %	.09%	.09%	.05%	.05%	.05%	.07%
Debt to Equity	1.65%	1.367	1.562	1.581	1.286	1.265

CONTACT INFORMATION:
Phone: 505 241-2700   Fax: 505 241-2359
Toll-Free:
Address: 414 Silver Ave. SW, Albuquerque, NM 87102-3289 United States

STOCK TICKER/OTHER:
Stock Ticker: PNM   Exchange: NYS
Employees: 1,646   Fiscal Year Ends: 12/31
Parent Company:

SALARIES/BONUSES:
Top Exec. Salary: $957,981   Bonus: $740,000
Second Exec. Salary: $522,690   Bonus: $260,000

OTHER THOUGHTS:
Estimated Female Officers or Directors: 2
Hot Spot for Advancement for Women/Minorities: Y

Sales, profits and employees may be estimates. Financial information, benefits and other data can change quickly and may vary from those stated here.

Portland General Electric Company

NAIC Code: 221111

www.portlandgeneral.com

TYPES OF BUSINESS:
Hydroelectric Power Generation
Energy Marketing
Natural Gas Pipeline
Electric Utility
Wind Power Generation
Fossil Fuels
Wholesale Distribution

BRANDS/DIVISIONS/AFFILIATES:

GROWTH PLANS/SPECIAL FEATURES:
Portland General Electric is a regulated electric utility providing generation, transmission, and distribution services to 917,000 customers representing about half of all Oregon residents. The company owns (wholly or through joint ventures) a total of 3.3 gigawatts of gas, coal, wind, and hydro generation.
PGE offers employees benefits including medical insurance, training and development programs, a savings plan, education assistance programs and gym access.

CONTACTS:
Note: Officers with more than one job title may be intentionally listed here more than once.

Maria Pope, CEO
William Robertson, VP, Divisional
James Ajello, CFO
Jack Davis, Chairman of the Board
John Kochavatr, Chief Information Officer
Lisa Kaner, General Counsel
John McFarland, Other Executive Officer
Brett Sims, Vice President, Divisional
Larry Bekkedahl, Vice President, Divisional
Anne Mersereau, Vice President, Divisional
Bradley Jenkins, Vice President, Divisional
Kristin Stathis, Vice President, Divisional

FINANCIAL DATA:
Note: Data for latest year may not have been available at press time.

In U.S. $	2021	2020	2019	2018	2017	2016
Revenue	2,396,000,000	2,145,000,000	2,123,000,000	1,991,000,000	2,009,000,000	1,923,000,000
R&D Expense						
Operating Income	378,000,000	269,000,000	353,000,000	346,000,000	380,000,000	340,000,000
Operating Margin %	.16%	.13%	.17%	.17%	.19%	.18%
SGA Expense	646,000,000	576,000,000	613,000,000	563,000,000	569,000,000	526,000,000
Net Income	244,000,000	155,000,000	214,000,000	212,000,000	187,000,000	193,000,000
Operating Cash Flow	532,000,000	567,000,000	546,000,000	630,000,000	597,000,000	562,000,000
Capital Expenditure	636,000,000	784,000,000	606,000,000	595,000,000	514,000,000	584,000,000
EBITDA	808,000,000	745,000,000	778,000,000	735,000,000	738,000,000	676,000,000
Return on Assets %	.03%	.02%	.03%	.03%	.02%	.03%
Return on Equity %	.09%	.06%	.08%	.09%	.08%	.08%
Debt to Equity	1.31%	1.154	1.054	0.869	1.004	0.939

CONTACT INFORMATION:
Phone: 503 464-8000 Fax: 503 464-2236
Toll-Free: 800-542-8818
Address: 121 SW Salmon St., Portland, OR 97204 United States

STOCK TICKER/OTHER:
Stock Ticker: POR
Employees: 2,839
Parent Company:

Exchange: NYS
Fiscal Year Ends: 12/31

SALARIES/BONUSES:
Top Exec. Salary: $1,025,692 Bonus: $
Second Exec. Salary: $542,445 Bonus: $

OTHER THOUGHTS:
Estimated Female Officers or Directors: 4
Hot Spot for Advancement for Women/Minorities: Y

Porvair plc

NAIC Code: 333413

www.porvair.com

TYPES OF BUSINESS:
Filtration Systems
Fuel Cell Components
Molten Metal Filtration Systems
Clean Coal Filtration Equipment
Nuclear Generation Equipment

BRANDS/DIVISIONS/AFFILIATES:
Porvair Filtration Group Ltd
Seal Analytical
Porvair Sciences
Rohasys BV
JG Finneran
Selee Corporation

GROWTH PLANS/SPECIAL FEATURES:
Porvair PLC is an environmental treatment control company. It develops filtration solutions to be used by various types of industries. The company caters to its clients through three divisions, Aerospace and Industrial, Laboratory and Metal Melt Quality. Aerospace and Industrial Division is a key revenue generator, designs and manufactures specialist filtration equipment for application in aerospace, energy, bioscience, water and industrial applications. Laboratory Division designs and manufactures instruments and consumables for use in environmental and bioscience laboratories. Metal Melt Quality Division designs and manufactures porous ceramic filters for the filtration of molten metals. The company generates most of its revenue from sales in the United States.

CONTACTS:
Note: Officers with more than one job title may be intentionally listed here more than once.

Ben Stocks, CEO
Jasi Halai, COO
James Mills, Group Dir.-Finance
John Nicholas, Chmn.

FINANCIAL DATA:
Note: Data for latest year may not have been available at press time.

In U.S. $	2021	2020	2019	2018	2017	2016
Revenue	162,997,700	150,410,000	161,462,500	143,516,200	129,701,900	121,836,600
R&D Expense						
Operating Income	17,648,890	13,989,220	16,473,560	14,335,690	13,746,350	11,885,880
Operating Margin %	.11%	.09%	.10%	.10%	.11%	.10%
SGA Expense	34,663,890	34,519,060	36,362,830	35,105,060	28,957,690	28,234,670
Net Income	13,306,300	9,405,985	11,996,170	11,190,700	9,871,661	8,618,346
Operating Cash Flow	17,938,550	11,499,300	14,659,880	14,004,810	10,356,280	12,370,490
Capital Expenditure	3,597,291	4,037,343	4,797,130	4,959,783	6,043,760	5,039,995
EBITDA	24,112,650	20,408,410	20,651,280	18,360,780	17,346,980	14,740,090
Return on Assets %	.07%	.05%	.07%	.07%	.07%	.07%
Return on Equity %	.12%	.09%	.12%	.12%	.12%	.12%
Debt to Equity	.14%	0.213	0.093	0.054	0.12%	0.036

CONTACT INFORMATION:
Phone: 44 1553765500   Fax: 44 1553765599
Toll-Free:
Address: 7 Regis Place, Bergen Way, King's Lynn, Norfolk, PE30 2JN United Kingdom

STOCK TICKER/OTHER:
Stock Ticker: PVARF
Employees: 850
Parent Company:

Exchange: PINX
Fiscal Year Ends: 11/30

SALARIES/BONUSES:
Top Exec. Salary: $358,726   Bonus: $323,077
Second Exec. Salary: $139,257   Bonus: $122,546

OTHER THOUGHTS:
Estimated Female Officers or Directors:
Hot Spot for Advancement for Women/Minorities:

Sales, profits and employees may be estimates. Financial information, benefits and other data can change quickly and may vary from those stated here.

PowerFilm Solar Inc

NAIC Code: 334413A

www.powerfilmsolar.com

TYPES OF BUSINESS:
Photovoltaic Cell Manufacturing
Thin-Film Products
Semi-Flexible
Photovoltaic
Solar
Product Design and Manufacture
Silicon Solar Panels
Power Charge Controllers

BRANDS/DIVISIONS/AFFILIATES:
PowerFilm
Soltronix
PowerBoost

GROWTH PLANS/SPECIAL FEATURES:
PowerFilm Solar, Inc. designs, engineers, manufactures and assembles custom solar solutions. The company delivers innovative remote, portable power solutions to meet its clients' needs, with markets including government, Department of Defense, Internet of Things (IoT), transportation, marine and golf. PowerFilm's proprietary manufacturing provides custom amorphous silicon panels that work in any light environment, including the indoor, industrial lighting of many IoT sensor applications. The Soltronix brand offers semi-flexible crystalline silicon solutions for applications, including panels, encapsulation, semi-flexible substrates, proprietary PowerBoost charge controllers, etc. Additional products by PowerFilm include related wireless components, development kits, foldable solar panels, rollable solar panels, light savers, solar panels for electric vehicles such as golf cars, accessories and face shields. Powerfilm works with multiple photovoltaic (PV) technologies, including thin-film, semi-flexible and ultra-high efficiency.

CONTACTS: Note: Officers with more than one job title may be intentionally listed here more than once.

Daniel Stieler, Pres.
Frank Jeffrey, Chmn.

FINANCIAL DATA: Note: Data for latest year may not have been available at press time.

In U.S. $	2021	2020	2019	2018	2017	2016
Revenue	12,500,000	10,887,000	9,550,000	9,450,000	9,000,000	8,100,000
R&D Expense						
Operating Income						
Operating Margin %						
SGA Expense						
Net Income						
Operating Cash Flow						
Capital Expenditure						
EBITDA						
Return on Assets %						
Return on Equity %						
Debt to Equity						

CONTACT INFORMATION:
Phone: 515-292-7606   Fax: 515-292-1922
Toll-Free: 888-354-7773
Address: 1287 XE Pl., Ames, IA 50014 United States

STOCK TICKER/OTHER:
Stock Ticker: Private   Exchange:
Employees: 72   Fiscal Year Ends: 12/31
Parent Company:

SALARIES/BONUSES:
Top Exec. Salary: $ Bonus: $
Second Exec. Salary: $ Bonus: $

OTHER THOUGHTS:
Estimated Female Officers or Directors:
Hot Spot for Advancement for Women/Minorities:

Sales, profits and employees may be estimates. Financial information, benefits and other data can change quickly and may vary from those stated here.

Plunkett Research, Ltd. 299

Primearth EV Energy Co Ltd
NAIC Code: 335911

www.peve.jp

TYPES OF BUSINESS:
Battery Manufacturing-Hybrid Cars
Battery Management Systems
Battery Development
Battery Manufacture
Nickel Metal-Hydride Batteries
Hybrid and Electric Vehicle Batteries

BRANDS/DIVISIONS/AFFILIATES:
Toyota Motor Corporation
Panasonic Holdings Corporation
NP2.5
NP2
Corun Peve Automotive Battery Co Ltd
Sinogy Toyota Automotive Energy System Co Ltd

CONTACTS:
Note: Officers with more than one job title may be intentionally listed here more than once.

Masamichi Okada, Pres.

GROWTH PLANS/SPECIAL FEATURES:
Primearth EV Energy Co., Ltd. develops, manufactures and sells nickel metal-hydride batteries, primarily for hybrid and plug-in electric vehicles (HEVs/PEVs). Founded in 1996, Primearth is majority-owned by Toyota Motor Corporation (TMC), with the rest being held by Panasonic Holdings Corporation. The battery system for the company's EVs consists of a battery module, an electronic control unit (ECU), a cooling system and a switch for connecting with the vehicle. Primearth produces two battery modules, the NP2.5 and the NP2. NP2.5 utilizes a metal case, achieves enhanced cooling performance and is flexible for adopting to various types of cars. It has an output density of 1,800 W/kg and an energy density of 41Wh/kg. NP2 utilizes a resin case, has an output density of 1,300 W/kg and an energy density of 46 Wh/kg. Primearth offers battery systems according to customers' requirements and include features such as sensors for measuring battery condition and wire harnesses for combining devices which are designed to provide vibration resistance, impact resistance, weather resistance and more. The firm's three production sites are located in Shizuoka and Miyagi, Japan. Affiliated companies of Primearth include: Corun Peve Automotive Battery Co., Ltd. and Sinogy Toyota Automotive Energy System Co., Ltd., each based in China.

FINANCIAL DATA:
Note: Data for latest year may not have been available at press time.

In U.S. $	2021	2020	2019	2018	2017	2016
Revenue	1,640,481,430	1,577,385,991	1,643,110,408	1,562,001,000	1,487,620,000	1,401,600,000
R&D Expense						
Operating Income						
Operating Margin %						
SGA Expense						
Net Income						
Operating Cash Flow						
Capital Expenditure						
EBITDA						
Return on Assets %						
Return on Equity %						
Debt to Equity						

CONTACT INFORMATION:
Phone: 81-53-577-3111 Fax:
Toll-Free: 800-211-7262
Address: 20 Okasaki, Kosai-shi, Shizuoka-ken, 431-0422 Japan

STOCK TICKER/OTHER:
Stock Ticker: Joint Venture   Exchange:
Employees: 4,462   Fiscal Year Ends: 03/31
Parent Company: Toyota Motor Corporation

SALARIES/BONUSES:
Top Exec. Salary: $ Bonus: $
Second Exec. Salary: $ Bonus: $

OTHER THOUGHTS:
Estimated Female Officers or Directors:
Hot Spot for Advancement for Women/Minorities:

Sales, profits and employees may be estimates. Financial information, benefits and other data can change quickly and may vary from those stated here.

Puget Energy Inc

NAIC Code: 221111

www.pugetenergy.com

TYPES OF BUSINESS:
Hydroelectric Power Generation
Electric Utility
Natural Gas Utility
Regulated Utilities

GROWTH PLANS/SPECIAL FEATURES:
Puget Energy, Inc. is an energy services holding company whose operations are conducted through Puget Sound Energy (PSE). PSE is a regulated utility that provides electric and natural gas service to western Washington. Puget Energy's focus is on retail electric and natural gas utility service within a regulated environment. PSE has a 6,000-square-mile service area across 10 Washington counties, primarily in the Puget Sound region. PSE serves 1.1 million electric customers and 790,000 natural gas customers. Puget Energy, Inc. itself is an indirect, wholly owned subsidiary of Puget Holdings, LLC.

BRANDS/DIVISIONS/AFFILIATES:
Puget Holdings LLC
Puget Sound Energy Inc

CONTACTS:
Note: Officers with more than one job title may be intentionally listed here more than once.

Mary E. Kipp, CEO
William Ayers, Chmn.-Puget Sound Energy, Inc.
Susan McLain, Sr. VP-Delivery Oper., Puget Sound Energy, Inc.
Donald E. Gaines, VP-Finance
Scott Armstrong, Chmn.

FINANCIAL DATA:
Note: Data for latest year may not have been available at press time.

In U.S. $	2021	2020	2019	2018	2017	2016
Revenue	3,805,661,000	3,326,450,000	3,401,130,000	3,346,496,000	3,460,276,000	3,164,301,000
R&D Expense						
Operating Income						
Operating Margin %						
SGA Expense						
Net Income	260,849,000	182,717,000	292,924,000	235,622,000	175,194,000	312,889,000
Operating Cash Flow						
Capital Expenditure						
EBITDA						
Return on Assets %						
Return on Equity %						
Debt to Equity						

CONTACT INFORMATION:
Phone: 425-454-6363 Fax:
Toll-Free:
Address: 10885 NE 4th St., Ste. 1200, Bellevue, WA 98004 United States

STOCK TICKER/OTHER:
Stock Ticker: Subsidiary
Employees: 3,185
Parent Company: Puget Holdings LLC

Exchange:
Fiscal Year Ends: 12/31

SALARIES/BONUSES:
Top Exec. Salary: $ Bonus: $
Second Exec. Salary: $ Bonus: $

OTHER THOUGHTS:
Estimated Female Officers or Directors: 3
Hot Spot for Advancement for Women/Minorities: Y

Quantum Fuel Systems LLC

NAIC Code: 336300

www.qtww.com

TYPES OF BUSINESS:
Fuel Storage Systems
Design & Testing Services
Fuel Delivery & Control Systems
Hydrogen Refueling Products
Fuel-Cell Vehicle Infrastructure
Lithium Ion & Advanced Battery Control Systems
Systems Integration
Hydrogen Fuel Systems

BRANDS/DIVISIONS/AFFILIATES:
Douglas Acquisitions LLC
Q-Lite
Q-Rail
Q-Cab
Q-VP

CONTACTS:
Note: Officers with more than one job title may be intentionally listed here more than once.
Mark Arold, Pres.
David Mazaika, Other Corporate Officer

GROWTH PLANS/SPECIAL FEATURES:
Quantum Fuel Systems, LLC designs, develops and manufactures advanced and lightweight compressed natural gas (CNG) storage tanks and cylinders. The company is an industry leader in clean vehicle technology, building tanks and systems for light-, medium- and heavy-duty trucks across a full range of industries, as well as for CNG infrastructure through its virtual pipeline (VP) trailers. The firm's VP trailers for CNG have gas transportation capabilities that include biogas, hydrogen and flare gas. In addition, Quantum Fuel develops and integrates powertrain systems and embedded control components. The firm's medium-duty CNG rail-mounted system is a first in the industry; the Q-Lite uses a cross-linked polyethylene liner with a carbon fiber overwrap to achieve its fuel density for light- medium and heavy-duty truck applications; its Q-Rail, a grid-friendly hook-and-hang frame-rail that mounts Quantum's CNG fuel systems in medium- and heavy-duty trucks, and available in 41.2 and 46.5 diesel gas equivalent (DGE) sizes; the Q-Cab, a 3-tank CNG fuel module is a behind-the-cab or medium- and heavy-duty trucks; the Q-VP virtual pipeline CNG trailer with lightweight storage tanks packed into a 45-foot, 40-foot or 20-foot or High-Cube shipping container; and the Q-VP virtual pipeline trailer, equipped with Type IV Q-Lite tanks in a 10-foot-long standard ISO shipping container towable by a 1-ton pickup truck. In addition, Quantum's hydrogen fuel systems and infrastructure consist of tanks for hydrogen, in-tank regulators, refueling systems, compressors, powertrain integration solutions and more. Quantum Fuel Systems is a subsidiary of Douglas Acquisitions LLC.

FINANCIAL DATA:
Note: Data for latest year may not have been available at press time.

In U.S. $	2021	2020	2019	2018	2017	2016
Revenue	40,273,000	39,100,000	39,000,000	38,587,500	36,750,000	35,000,000
R&D Expense						
Operating Income						
Operating Margin %						
SGA Expense						
Net Income						
Operating Cash Flow						
Capital Expenditure						
EBITDA						
Return on Assets %						
Return on Equity %						
Debt to Equity						

CONTACT INFORMATION:
Phone: 949 930-3400   Fax:
Toll-Free:
Address: 25372 Commercentre Dr., Lake Forest, CA 92630 United States

STOCK TICKER/OTHER:
Stock Ticker: Private   Exchange:
Employees: 147   Fiscal Year Ends: 04/30
Parent Company: Douglas Acquisitions LLC

SALARIES/BONUSES:
Top Exec. Salary: $ Bonus: $
Second Exec. Salary: $ Bonus: $

OTHER THOUGHTS:
Estimated Female Officers or Directors:
Hot Spot for Advancement for Women/Minorities:

Sales, profits and employees may be estimates. Financial information, benefits and other data can change quickly and may vary from those stated here.

QuantumScape Corporation

NAIC Code: 335912

www.quantumscape.com

TYPES OF BUSINESS:
Primary Battery Manufacturing
Lithium-Metal Solid-State Batteries
Technologies

GROWTH PLANS/SPECIAL FEATURES:
QuantumScape Corp is engaged in the development of next-generation solid-state lithium-metal batteries for use in electric vehicles. It developed anode-less cell design, which delivers high energy density while lowering material costs and simplifying manufacturing.

BRANDS/DIVISIONS/AFFILIATES:
QS-1

CONTACTS:
Note: Officers with more than one job title may be intentionally listed here more than once.

Jagdeep Singh, CEO
Kevin Hettrich, CFO
Michael McCarthy, Chief Legal Officer
Timothy Holme, Chief Technology Officer
Mohit Singh, Other Executive Officer
Celina Mikolajczak, Vice President, Subsidiary

FINANCIAL DATA:
Note: Data for latest year may not have been available at press time.

In U.S. $	2021	2020	2019	2018	2017	2016
Revenue						
R&D Expense	151,496,000	65,103,000	45,944,000			
Operating Income	-215,266,000	-81,021,000	-55,818,000			
Operating Margin %						
SGA Expense	63,770,000	15,918,000	9,874,000			
Net Income	-45,966,000	-1,681,777,000	-51,283,000			
Operating Cash Flow	-127,909,000	-61,263,000	-41,731,000			
Capital Expenditure	127,178,000	24,093,000	9,846,000			
EBITDA	-29,859,000	-1,652,938,000	-45,306,000			
Return on Assets %	-.03%	-2.71%	-.30%			
Return on Equity %	-.05%	-6.72%	-.34%			
Debt to Equity	.05%	0.032	0.084			

CONTACT INFORMATION:
Phone: 408 452-2000   Fax:
Toll-Free:
Address: 1730 Technology Dr., San Jose, CA 95110 United States

SALARIES/BONUSES:
Top Exec. Salary: $382,096   Bonus: $
Second Exec. Salary: $373,716   Bonus: $

STOCK TICKER/OTHER:
Stock Ticker: QS   Exchange: NYS
Employees: 570   Fiscal Year Ends:
Parent Company:

OTHER THOUGHTS:
Estimated Female Officers or Directors:
Hot Spot for Advancement for Women/Minorities:

Sales, profits and employees may be estimates. Financial information, benefits and other data can change quickly and may vary from those stated here.

Raytheon Technologies Corporation

NAIC Code: 336412

www.rtx.com

TYPES OF BUSINESS:
Aircraft Engine and Engine Parts Manufacturing
Advanced Aerospace Products
Defense Products
Aftermarket Aircraft Solutions
Avionic Systems
Aircraft Engines
Sensors
Communication Systems

BRANDS/DIVISIONS/AFFILIATES:
Collins Aerospace Systems
Pratt & Whitney
Raytheon Intelligence & Space
Raytheon Missiles & Defense

GROWTH PLANS/SPECIAL FEATURES:
Raytheon Technologies is a diversified aerospace and defense industrial company formed from the merger of United Technologies and Raytheon, with roughly equal exposure as a supplier to the commercial aerospace manufactures and to the defense market as a prime and subprime contractor. The company operates in four segments: Pratt & Whitney, an engine manufacturer; Collins Aerospace, a diversified aerospace supplier; intelligence, space and airborne systems, a mix between a sensors business and a government IT contractor; and integrated defense and missile systems, a defense prime contractor focusing on missiles and missile defense hardware.

CONTACTS:
Note: Officers with more than one job title may be intentionally listed here more than once.

Gregory Hayes, CEO
Wesley Kremer, Pres., Divisional
Neil Mitchill, CFO
Thomas Kennedy, Chairman of the Board
Amy Johnson, Chief Accounting Officer
Steven Forrest, Controller
Frank Jimenez, Executive VP
Michael Dumais, Executive VP
Dantaya Williams, Executive VP
Stephen Timm, President, Divisional
Roy Azevedo, President, Divisional
Christopher Calio, President, Subsidiary
Kevin DaSilva, Treasurer

FINANCIAL DATA:
Note: Data for latest year may not have been available at press time.

In U.S. $	2021	2020	2019	2018	2017	2016
Revenue	64,388,000,000	56,587,000,000	45,349,000,000	34,701,000,000	59,837,000,000	57,244,000,000
R&D Expense	2,732,000,000	2,582,000,000	2,452,000,000	1,878,000,000	2,427,000,000	2,376,000,000
Operating Income	4,958,000,000	1,294,000,000	4,914,000,000	2,877,000,000	8,138,000,000	8,221,000,000
Operating Margin %	.08%	.02%	.11%	.08%	.14%	.14%
SGA Expense	5,224,000,000	5,540,000,000	3,711,000,000	2,864,000,000	6,429,000,000	5,958,000,000
Net Income	3,864,000,000	-3,519,000,000	5,537,000,000	5,269,000,000	4,552,000,000	5,055,000,000
Operating Cash Flow	7,071,000,000	3,606,000,000	8,883,000,000	6,322,000,000	5,631,000,000	3,880,000,000
Capital Expenditure	2,322,000,000	1,967,000,000	2,219,000,000	1,867,000,000	2,394,000,000	2,087,000,000
EBITDA	10,846,000,000	3,211,000,000	8,571,000,000	5,582,000,000	10,920,000,000	10,256,000,000
Return on Assets %	.02%	-.02%	.04%	.05%	.05%	.06%
Return on Equity %	.05%	-.06%	.14%	.15%	.16%	.18%
Debt to Equity	.45%	0.451	0.929	1.071	0.844	0.787

CONTACT INFORMATION:
Phone: 781-522-3000   Fax:
Toll-Free:
Address: 870 Winter St., Waltham, MA 02451 United States

STOCK TICKER/OTHER:
Stock Ticker: RTX   Exchange: NYS
Employees: 174,000   Fiscal Year Ends: 12/31
Parent Company:

SALARIES/BONUSES:
Top Exec. Salary: $1,600,000   Bonus: $4,992,000
Second Exec. Salary: $254,449   Bonus: $3,238,924

OTHER THOUGHTS:
Estimated Female Officers or Directors: 2
Hot Spot for Advancement for Women/Minorities: Y

Sales, profits and employees may be estimates. Financial information, benefits and other data can change quickly and may vary from those stated here.

Reliance Power Limited

NAIC Code: 221112

www.reliancepower.co.in

TYPES OF BUSINESS:
Electric Power Generation
Hydroelectric Power Generation
Coal-fired Power Generation
Gas-Fired Projects
Power Generation Development
Power Generation Construction
Power Generation Operation

BRANDS/DIVISIONS/AFFILIATES:
Reliance Anil Dhirubhai Ambani Group

CONTACTS: Note: Officers with more than one job title may be intentionally listed here more than once.
Anil Dhirubhai Ambani, Chmn.

GROWTH PLANS/SPECIAL FEATURES:
Reliance Power Limited is a member of Reliance Anil Dhirubhai Ambani Group, and focuses on the development, construction and operation of power generation projects in India and internationally. The company, on its own and through its subsidiaries has a large portfolio of power generation capacity, both in operation as well as under development. Reliance Power has approximately 6,000 megawatts (MW) of operational power generation assets. Projects under development include coal-fired projects to be fueled by reserves from captive mines and supplies from India and elsewhere; gas-fired projects; and 12 hydroelectric projects, six of which are in Arunachal Pradesh, five in Himachal Pradesh and one in Uttarakhand. Reliance Power's project portfolio includes the 3,960 MW Sasan ultra-mega power project in Madhya Pradesh. Ultra-mega power plants (UMPPs) are a significant part of the Indian government's initiative to collaborate with power generation companies to set up 4,000 MW projects for the purpose of easing the country's power deficit. Reliance Power also has registered projects with the Clean Development Mechanism executive board for issuance of Certified Emission Reduction certificates.

FINANCIAL DATA: Note: Data for latest year may not have been available at press time.

In U.S. $	2021	2020	2019	2018	2017	2016
Revenue	1,143,307,460	1,090,206,920	1,633,957,500	1,556,150,000	1,678,130,000	1,319,100,000
R&D Expense						
Operating Income						
Operating Margin %						
SGA Expense						
Net Income	31,160,669	-541,831,807	167,030,850	159,077,000	170,123,000	130,648,000
Operating Cash Flow						
Capital Expenditure						
EBITDA						
Return on Assets %						
Return on Equity %						
Debt to Equity						

CONTACT INFORMATION:
Phone: 91-22-4303-1000   Fax: 91-22-4303 3166
Toll-Free:
Address: Reliance Centre, Ground Fl, 19, Walchand Hirachand Marg, Ballard Estate, Mumbai, 400 001 India

STOCK TICKER/OTHER:
Stock Ticker: 532939   Exchange: Bombay
Employees: 8,191   Fiscal Year Ends: 03/31
Parent Company: Anil Dhirubhai Ambani Group

SALARIES/BONUSES:
Top Exec. Salary: $ Bonus: $
Second Exec. Salary: $ Bonus: $

OTHER THOUGHTS:
Estimated Female Officers or Directors:
Hot Spot for Advancement for Women/Minorities:

Sales, profits and employees may be estimates. Financial information, benefits and other data can change quickly and may vary from those stated here.

Renewable Energy Group Inc

NAIC Code: 325199

www.regi.com

TYPES OF BUSINESS:
Biodiesel
Sustainable Fuels
Fuel Production and Distribution
Biorefinery Facilities
Renewable Fuel Conversion Products
Heating Oils
Fuel Blends
Renewable Propane

BRANDS/DIVISIONS/AFFILIATES:
Chevron Corporation
EnDura Fuels
InfiniD
PuriD
UltralCleanBlenD
VelociD
BeyonD

CONTACTS:
Note: Officers with more than one job title may be intentionally listed here more than once.

Natalie Merrill, Sr. VP-Bus. Dev.
Craig Bealmear, CFO
Bob Kenyon, Sr. VP-Mktg. & Sales
Trisha Conley, Sr. VP-People Development
Jeffrey Stroburg, Director
Randolph Howard, Director
Eric Bowen, General Counsel
Todd Robinson, Other Executive Officer
Brad Albin, Senior VP, Divisional

GROWTH PLANS/SPECIAL FEATURES:

Renewable Energy Group, Inc. is an international producer of sustainable fuels, utilizing an integrated procurement, distribution and logistics network of 11 biorefineries in the U.S. and Europe. The firm offers products, services and solutions to a range of industries for converting renewable resources into sustainable fuels. The company itself Renewable Energy's line of EnDura Fuels include: InfiniD, a clean-burning biodiesel solution that provides engine performance and emissions benefits to fleets; PuriD, a next-generation renewable fuel produced by using advanced refining processes and testing for seamless blending with renewable diesel; UltraCleanBlenD, a renewable fuel combination that allows for decarbonization in any diesel application; VelociD, which can serve as a replacement to petroleum diesel for engine performance and reduce emissions across the fleet; and BeyonD, a low-carbon sustainable aviation fuel. Heating products include traditional heating oil used for heating buildings, and Bioheat biodiesel blended fuel for heating homes and businesses. Other products by Renewable Energy include bio-residual oil for BTU performance, blended fuel, diesel fuel, gasoline and ethanol blends, glycerin, methyl esters, renewable naphtha and renewable propane. Industries served by the company include agriculture, aviation, construction, heating, power generation, mining, marine, railroad and trucking. During 2021, Renewable Energy Group produced 480 million gallons of sustainable fuels. In June 2022, Renewable Energy Group was acquired by Chevron Corporation.

Renewable Energy offers its employees comprehensive health benefits, spending and savings accounts, life/accident/disability coverage, retirement plans, tuition reimbursement and more.

FINANCIAL DATA:
Note: Data for latest year may not have been available at press time.

In U.S. $	2021	2020	2019	2018	2017	2016
Revenue	3,200,000,000	2,137,148,032	2,641,392,896	2,382,987,008	2,158,243,072	2,041,232,000
R&D Expense						
Operating Income						
Operating Margin %						
SGA Expense						
Net Income		122,813,000	380,064,000	292,316,000	-79,079,000	44,327,000
Operating Cash Flow						
Capital Expenditure						
EBITDA						
Return on Assets %						
Return on Equity %						
Debt to Equity						

CONTACT INFORMATION:
Phone: 515 239-8000   Fax: 515 239-8009
Toll-Free:
Address: 416 South Bell Ave., PO Box 888, Ames, IA 50010 United States

STOCK TICKER/OTHER:
Stock Ticker: Subsidiary   Exchange:
Employees: 1,200   Fiscal Year Ends: 12/31
Parent Company: Chevron Corporation

SALARIES/BONUSES:
Top Exec. Salary: $ Bonus: $
Second Exec. Salary: $ Bonus: $

OTHER THOUGHTS:
Estimated Female Officers or Directors:
Hot Spot for Advancement for Women/Minorities:

Sales, profits and employees may be estimates. Financial information, benefits and other data can change quickly and may vary from those stated here.

Renewable Energy Systems Ltd

www.res-group.com

NAIC Code: 221115

TYPES OF BUSINESS:
Wind Electric Power Generation
Sustainability Consultancy
Renewable Energy Projects
Energy Project Development
Energy Project Management
Wind Generation

BRANDS/DIVISIONS/AFFILIATES:

CONTACTS: Note: Officers with more than one job title may be intentionally listed here more than once.
Eduardo Medina, CEO
Stephen Balint, Dir.-Strategy & Comm.
Anna Stanford, Head-Corp. Comm.
Susan Reilly, CEO-RES Americas

GROWTH PLANS/SPECIAL FEATURES:

Renewable Energy Systems Ltd. (RES) is a U.K.-based developer and operator of renewable energy projects, with a primary focus on wind generation. The firm's solutions include wind, solar, energy storage and/or transmission and distribution projects, with expertise and capabilities in project development, build-own-transfer, engineering, procurement, financing, construction, balance of plant/systems, asset management, operations/maintenance, power purchase agreements and equipment leasing. RES' solutions provide controllable competitive and predictable power located on customer sites, including solar, energy storage and micro-grid technologies. The company has constructed miles of transmission lines, miles of underground and overhead distribution lines, as well as related substations. It operates in both the centralized energy market and the evolving distributed energy market worldwide. RES has delivered more than 32 GW of renewable energy projects across the globe and supports an operational asset portfolio exceeding 10 GW worldwide for a large client base. The firm has secured 1.5 GW of power purchase agreements, enabling access to energy at low costs. RES is a global company, with offices in Australia, Canada, France, Germany, Ireland, the Nordics, Turkey, the U.K. and the United States.

FINANCIAL DATA: Note: Data for latest year may not have been available at press time.

In U.S. $	2021	2020	2019	2018	2017	2016
Revenue	83,208,112	80,007,800	79,767,500	109,867,000	153,928,000	297,895,000
R&D Expense						
Operating Income						
Operating Margin %						
SGA Expense						
Net Income		61,864,300	-139,504,000	24,493,200	48,292,000	27,000,400
Operating Cash Flow						
Capital Expenditure						
EBITDA						
Return on Assets %						
Return on Equity %						
Debt to Equity						

CONTACT INFORMATION:
Phone: 44-1923-299-200   Fax: 44-1923-299-299
Toll-Free:
Address: Beaufort Court, Egg Farm Lane, Kings Langley, Hertfordshire, WD4 8LR United Kingdom

SALARIES/BONUSES:
Top Exec. Salary: $ Bonus: $
Second Exec. Salary: $ Bonus: $

STOCK TICKER/OTHER:
Stock Ticker: Private   Exchange:
Employees: 2,000   Fiscal Year Ends: 10/31
Parent Company:

OTHER THOUGHTS:
Estimated Female Officers or Directors: 2
Hot Spot for Advancement for Women/Minorities:

Sales, profits and employees may be estimates. Financial information, benefits and other data can change quickly and may vary from those stated here.

ReNu Energy Limited

NAIC Code: 221330

renuenergy.com.au

TYPES OF BUSINESS:
Geothermal Energy Technology
Clean Energy Investment
Renewable Energy Projects
Business Support Services
Business Acquisitions and Divestitures

BRANDS/DIVISIONS/AFFILIATES:
Uniflow Power Limited
Cobber
Enosi Australia Pty Ltd
Powertracer
Countrywide Renewable Hydrogen

GROWTH PLANS/SPECIAL FEATURES:
Renu Energy Ltd is an independent power producer which delivers clean energy products and services. It builds, owns, operates, and maintains renewable energy assets so its customers can access renewable energy, at a lower price, with no upfront cost. The company operates in three segments namely geothermal energy exploration and evaluation, biogas energy, and solar energy. The company generates maximum revenue from the biogas energy segment.

CONTACTS:
Note: Officers with more than one job title may be intentionally listed here more than once.

Amy Hodson, Mgr.-Well Eng.
Kevin Coates, Mgr.-Oper.
Meredith Bird, Mgr.-Corp. Affairs
Kevin Coates, Mgr.-Safety
Robert Hogarth, Mgr.-Reservoir Dev.
Boyd White, Chmn.

FINANCIAL DATA:
Note: Data for latest year may not have been available at press time.

In U.S. $	2021	2020	2019	2018	2017	2016
Revenue		97,084	782,073			
R&D Expense			-16,052			
Operating Income	-919,676	-1,979,328	-2,206,241			
Operating Margin %		-20.39%	-2.82%			
SGA Expense	840,624	1,619,416	2,033,517			
Net Income	-736,713	-2,894,305	-2,240,914			
Operating Cash Flow						
Capital Expenditure		13,168	1,064,595			
EBITDA	-698,891	-2,560,848	-2,249,904			
Return on Assets %	-.30%	-.59%	-.27%			
Return on Equity %	-.45%	-.96%	-.44%			
Debt to Equity			0.161			

CONTACT INFORMATION:
Phone: 61 737217500 Fax: 61 737217599
Toll-Free:
Address: Level 2, 52 McDougall St., Kings Row 1, Milton, QLD 4064 Australia

STOCK TICKER/OTHER:
Stock Ticker: GDYMF
Employees: 14
Parent Company:

Exchange: PINX
Fiscal Year Ends: 06/30

SALARIES/BONUSES:
Top Exec. Salary: $ Bonus: $
Second Exec. Salary: $ Bonus: $

OTHER THOUGHTS:
Estimated Female Officers or Directors: 2
Hot Spot for Advancement for Women/Minorities: Y

Sales, profits and employees may be estimates. Financial information, benefits and other data can change quickly and may vary from those stated here.

REX American Resources Corporation

www.rexamerican.com/corp/page1.aspx

NAIC Code: 325193

TYPES OF BUSINESS:
Ethanol Production
Ethanol Production
Ethanol Sales
Distillers Grain
Corn Oil

GROWTH PLANS/SPECIAL FEATURES:
REX American Resources Corp operates as a holding company, which engages in investment in alternative energy and ethanol production entities. Its operating segments include Ethanol and By-Products. Its products include dried distillers grains, modified distillers grains, and non-food grade corn oil.

BRANDS/DIVISIONS/AFFILIATES:
NuGen Energy LLC
One Earth Energy LLC
Big River Resources LLC
Big River Resources West Burlington LLC
Big River Resources Galva LLC
Big River United Energy LLC
Big River Resources Boyceville LLC

CONTACTS:
Note: Officers with more than one job title may be intentionally listed here more than once.

Zafar Rizvi, CEO
Douglas Bruggeman, CFO
Stuart Rose, Chairman of the Board
Edward Kress, Director

FINANCIAL DATA:
Note: Data for latest year may not have been available at press time.

In U.S. $	2021	2020	2019	2018	2017	2016
Revenue	372,664,000	417,700,000	486,671,000	452,586,000	453,799,000	
R&D Expense						
Operating Income	1,894,000	870,000	9,664,000	20,792,000	49,651,000	
Operating Margin %	.01%	.00%	.02%	.05%	.11%	
SGA Expense	17,639,000	19,532,000	20,551,000	24,060,000	21,388,000	
Net Income	3,001,000	7,427,000	31,645,000	39,706,000	32,333,000	
Operating Cash Flow	8,623,000	10,343,000	47,931,000	40,969,000	69,109,000	
Capital Expenditure	10,412,000	3,776,000	10,775,000	24,017,000	14,208,000	
EBITDA	25,368,000	27,391,000	34,492,000	42,254,000	69,170,000	
Return on Assets %	.01%	.02%	.07%	.09%	.07%	
Return on Equity %	.01%	.02%	.08%	.11%	.10%	
Debt to Equity	.02%	0.027				

CONTACT INFORMATION:
Phone: 937 276-3931   Fax: 937 276-8643
Toll-Free:
Address: 7720 Paragon Rd., Dayton, OH 45459 United States

STOCK TICKER/OTHER:
Stock Ticker: REX   Exchange: NYS
Employees: 124   Fiscal Year Ends: 01/31
Parent Company:

SALARIES/BONUSES:
Top Exec. Salary: $275,700   Bonus: $
Second Exec. Salary: $225,000   Bonus: $

OTHER THOUGHTS:
Estimated Female Officers or Directors:
Hot Spot for Advancement for Women/Minorities:

Sales, profits and employees may be estimates. Financial information, benefits and other data can change quickly and may vary from those stated here.

RWE AG

NAIC Code: 221112

www.rwe.com

TYPES OF BUSINESS:
Utilities-Electricity, Natural Gas & Water
Wind Energy Generation
Photovoltaic Systems
Battery Storage Systems
Power Plants
Hydropower
Biomass
Lignite

BRANDS/DIVISIONS/AFFILIATES:
RWE Renewables
RWE Generation
RWE Power AG
RWE Supply & Trading

GROWTH PLANS/SPECIAL FEATURES:
Since the deal with E.On, RWE is refocused on power generation, mostly in Europe. It owns 38 gigawatts of power generation capacity: 25% from lignite and hard coal plants, 37% from gas plants, 29% from renewables, 4% from nuclear (which will be shut down by 2022), and 5% from pumped storage and batteries. Besides Germany, RWE's power plants are chiefly located in the United Kingdom, the Netherlands, Turkey, and the United States for many onshore wind farms.

CONTACTS:
Note: Officers with more than one job title may be intentionally listed here more than once.

Markus Krebber, CEO
Michael Mueller, CFO
Rolf Martin Schmitz, Deputy CEO
Werner Brandt, Chmn.

FINANCIAL DATA:
Note: Data for latest year may not have been available at press time.

In U.S. $	2021	2020	2019	2018	2017	2016
Revenue	24,017,550,000	13,404,230,000	12,852,900,000	13,128,080,000	13,535,450,000	42,686,330,000
R&D Expense						
Operating Income	1,700,011,000	-1,984,978,000	-1,485,551,000	140,035,400	1,366,080,000	-4,224,566,000
Operating Margin %	.07%	-.15%	-.12%	.01%	.10%	-.10%
SGA Expense	444,588,100	425,002,700	390,728,300	275,174,600	252,651,400	823,565,100
Net Income	706,052,900	1,029,212,000	8,336,516,000	385,831,900	1,901,740,000	-5,533,848,000
Operating Cash Flow	7,123,202,000	4,088,447,000	-1,491,427,000	6,510,179,000	-1,717,638,000	2,303,240,000
Capital Expenditure	3,612,523,000	2,237,629,000	1,734,285,000	1,028,232,000	670,799,200	1,984,978,000
EBITDA	4,299,970,000	4,873,821,000	3,479,342,000	1,420,919,000	3,828,941,000	3,000,480,000
Return on Assets %	.01%	.02%	.12%	.00%	.03%	-.07%
Return on Equity %	.04%	.06%	.64%	.04%	.33%	-1.09%
Debt to Equity	.38%	0.19	0.187	0.188	1.739	4.073

CONTACT INFORMATION:
Phone: 49 2011200 Fax:
Toll-Free:
Address: RWE Platz 1, Essen, NW 45141 Germany

STOCK TICKER/OTHER:
Stock Ticker: RWEOY
Employees: 19,498
Parent Company:

Exchange: PINX
Fiscal Year Ends: 12/31

SALARIES/BONUSES:
Top Exec. Salary: $ Bonus: $
Second Exec. Salary: $ Bonus: $

OTHER THOUGHTS:
Estimated Female Officers or Directors: 2
Hot Spot for Advancement for Women/Minorities:

Sales, profits and employees may be estimates. Financial information, benefits and other data can change quickly and may vary from those stated here.

Sacramento Municipal Utility District

NAIC Code: 221111

www.smud.org

TYPES OF BUSINESS:
Hydroelectric Power Generation
Hydroelectric Generation
Solar Generation
Wind Generation
Electric Utility
Electric Distribution Lines
Hydroelectric Projects

BRANDS/DIVISIONS/AFFILIATES:

CONTACTS: Note: Officers with more than one job title may be intentionally listed here more than once.
Paul Lau, CEO
Frankie McDermott, COO
Jennifer Davidson, CFO
Farres Everly, Dir.-Mktg. & Communications
Suresh Kotha, CIO
Gary King, CTO
Arlen Orchard, General Counsel
Paul Lau, Assistant Gen. Mgr.-Power Supply & Grid Oper.
Elisabeth Brinton, Chief Customer Officer
Michael Gianunzio, Chief Legislative & Regulatory Officer
Scott Martin, Chief Strategy Officer

GROWTH PLANS/SPECIAL FEATURES:

Sacramento Municipal Utility District (SMUD) is one of the largest electric utilities in the U.S. that is owned by a local government. The company serves a 900-square-mile area in the counties of Sacramento and Placer, California. It serves over 1.5 million residential and business customers. SMUD owns 10,500 circuit miles of distribution lines. The firm uses hydroelectric and cogeneration power plants to generate more than half of its electricity and purchases the remainder from alternative energy generation plants. SMUD has one of the largest solar energy distribution systems in the U.S. SMUD's renewable supply is comprised of biomass and biowaste materials, wind, biomethane, solar, biogas, geothermal and eligible hydro, of which 50% of its power comes from these resources. The company has increased generation capacity and created its own transmission control area in order to decrease dependence on third-party energy generators and compete in California's deregulated power market. The Federal Energy Regulatory Commission issued SMUD a license for the Upper American River Project (UARP), assuring a sustainable supply of hydroelectricity for the next 50 years (to 2064). The UARP is a system of 11 reservoirs and eight powerhouses in surrounding El Dorado County which provides up to 20% of SMUD's power in a normal water year.

SMUD offers its employees health benefits, retirement options and employee assistance programs.

FINANCIAL DATA: Note: Data for latest year may not have been available at press time.

In U.S. $	2021	2020	2019	2018	2017	2016
Revenue	1,791,000,000	1,587,905,000	1,559,224,000	1,595,455,000	1,559,336,000	1,494,833,000
R&D Expense						
Operating Income						
Operating Margin %						
SGA Expense						
Net Income	341,000,000	153,235,000	78,915,000	209,138,000	177,893,000	195,258,000
Operating Cash Flow						
Capital Expenditure						
EBITDA						
Return on Assets %						
Return on Equity %						
Debt to Equity						

CONTACT INFORMATION:
Phone: 916-452-3211   Fax: 916-732-5835
Toll-Free:
Address: 6301 S St., Sacramento, CA 95817 United States

STOCK TICKER/OTHER:
Stock Ticker: Government-Owned   Exchange:
Employees: 2,192   Fiscal Year Ends: 12/31
Parent Company:

SALARIES/BONUSES:
Top Exec. Salary: $ Bonus: $
Second Exec. Salary: $ Bonus: $

OTHER THOUGHTS:
Estimated Female Officers or Directors: 1
Hot Spot for Advancement for Women/Minorities:

Sales, profits and employees may be estimates. Financial information, benefits and other data can change quickly and may vary from those stated here.

Plunkett Research, Ltd.   311

Samsung Electronics Co Ltd
NAIC Code: 334310   www.samsung.com

TYPES OF BUSINESS:
Consumer Electronics
Semiconductors and Memory Products
Smartphones
Computers & Accessories
Digital Cameras
Fuel-Cell Technology
LCD Displays
Solar Energy Panels

BRANDS/DIVISIONS/AFFILIATES:
Samsung Group

GROWTH PLANS/SPECIAL FEATURES:
Samsung Electronics is a diversified electronics conglomerate that manufactures and sells a wide range of products, including smartphones, semiconductor chips, printers, home appliances, medical equipment, and telecom network equipment. About half of its profit is generated from semiconductor business, and a further 30%-35% is generated from its mobile handset business, although these percentages vary with the fortunes of each of these businesses. It is the largest smartphone and television manufacturer in the world, which helps provide a base demand for its component businesses, such as memory chips and displays, and is also the largest manufacturer of these globally.

CONTACTS: Note: Officers with more than one job title may be intentionally listed here more than once.
Ki Nam Kim, CEO
Oh-Hyun Kwon, Vice Chmn.

FINANCIAL DATA: Note: Data for latest year may not have been available at press time.

In U.S. $	2021	2020	2019	2018	2017	2016
Revenue	194,273,900,000	164,537,300,000	160,086,200,000	169,376,300,000	166,460,800,000	140,260,200,000
R&D Expense	15,565,080,000	14,668,600,000	13,831,870,000	12,752,710,000	11,364,140,000	9,804,813,000
Operating Income	35,876,030,000	25,009,120,000	19,294,010,000	40,915,400,000	37,273,430,000	20,316,890,000
Operating Margin %	.18%	.15%	.12%	.24%	.22%	.14%
SGA Expense	20,516,540,000	18,124,130,000	18,775,440,000	18,230,010,000	22,338,530,000	21,719,180,000
Net Income	27,267,210,000	18,128,340,000	14,942,060,000	30,496,090,000	28,726,870,000	15,574,760,000
Operating Cash Flow	45,236,310,000	45,362,460,000	31,532,780,000	46,574,810,000	43,191,180,000	32,924,300,000
Capital Expenditure	34,622,000,000	27,981,500,000	19,884,010,000	21,245,340,000	30,416,250,000	17,502,860,000
EBITDA	61,165,160,000	46,735,930,000	42,186,580,000	61,363,800,000	54,868,760,000	36,140,470,000
Return on Assets %	.10%	.07%	.06%	.14%	.15%	.09%
Return on Equity %	.14%	.10%	.09%	.20%	.21%	.12%
Debt to Equity	.01%	0.011	0.012	0.004	0.013	0.007

CONTACT INFORMATION:
Phone: 82 31-200-1114   Fax: 82-31-200-7538
Toll-Free:
Address: 129, Samsung-ro, Suwon-si, 443-742 South Korea

STOCK TICKER/OTHER:
Stock Ticker: SSNHZ
Employees: 95,798
Parent Company: Samsung Group

Exchange: PINX
Fiscal Year Ends: 12/31

SALARIES/BONUSES:
Top Exec. Salary: $ Bonus: $
Second Exec. Salary: $ Bonus: $

OTHER THOUGHTS:
Estimated Female Officers or Directors:
Hot Spot for Advancement for Women/Minorities:

Sales, profits and employees may be estimates. Financial information, benefits and other data can change quickly and may vary from those stated here.

Scottish and Southern Energy plc (SSE)

NAIC Code: 221112

www.sse.com

TYPES OF BUSINESS:
Electric Utilities
Regulated Electricity Networks
Renewable Power Generation
Power Distribution
Power Transmission
Thermal Generation
Infrastructure Services
Natural Gas

BRANDS/DIVISIONS/AFFILIATES:
SSE Renewables
SSEN Distribution
SSEN Transmission
SSE Thermal
SSE Energy Solutions
SSE Enterprise
SSE Airtricity
Energy Portfolio Management

GROWTH PLANS/SPECIAL FEATURES:
SSE is an energy holding company based in the United Kingdom. The bulk of SSE's profit comes from the company's 11.1 GW of power generation and its regulated networks business, which includes electric and gas distribution and transmission systems. The firm is also involved in smaller related businesses such as gas storage, home energy services, contracting, and oil and gas production.

CONTACTS:
Note: Officers with more than one job title may be intentionally listed here more than once.

Alistair Phillips-Davies, CEO
Gregor Alexander, Dir.-Finance
Rob McDonald, Managing Dir.-Strategy & Regulation
Alan Young, Managing Dir.-Corp. Affairs
Gregor Alexander, Dir.-Finance
John Manzoni, Chmn.

FINANCIAL DATA: Note: Data for latest year may not have been available at press time.

In U.S. $	2021	2020	2019	2018	2017	2016
Revenue	7,605,000,000	7,576,258,000	8,134,288,000	30,358,500,000	32,349,880,000	
R&D Expense					134,021,100	
Operating Income	1,963,637,000	1,138,121,000	527,951,700	1,300,773,000	1,863,372,000	
Operating Margin %	.26%	.15%	.06%	.04%	.06%	
SGA Expense				1,278,046,000	1,902,030,000	
Net Income	2,535,817,000	-65,729,370	1,569,818,000	915,309,400	1,781,934,000	
Operating Cash Flow	2,024,465,000	1,448,497,000	1,310,911,000	1,924,422,000	2,375,170,000	
Capital Expenditure	1,311,580,000	1,349,012,000	1,680,889,000	1,736,035,000	1,968,985,000	
EBITDA	3,818,988,000	2,126,958,000	2,678,193,000	2,514,204,000	3,589,269,000	
Return on Assets %	.11%	.00%	.07%	.04%	.07%	
Return on Equity %	.39%	-.01%	.26%	.14%	.28%	
Debt to Equity	1.27%	1.611	1.218	1.549	1.266	

CONTACT INFORMATION:
Phone: 44 1738456000 Fax: 44 1738457005
Toll-Free:
Address: 200 Dunkeld Rd., Inveralmond House, Perth, PH1 3AQ United Kingdom

STOCK TICKER/OTHER:
Stock Ticker: SSEZY
Employees: 19,182
Parent Company:

Exchange: PINX
Fiscal Year Ends: 03/31

SALARIES/BONUSES:
Top Exec. Salary: $1,029,389 Bonus: $
Second Exec. Salary: $795,437 Bonus: $

OTHER THOUGHTS:
Estimated Female Officers or Directors: 2
Hot Spot for Advancement for Women/Minorities:

Sales, profits and employees may be estimates. Financial information, benefits and other data can change quickly and may vary from those stated here.

SeQuential

NAIC Code: 325199

choosesq.com

TYPES OF BUSINESS:
Biofuels Marketing
Biodiesel Production
Re-used Cooking Oil
Grease Trap Cleaning Services

BRANDS/DIVISIONS/AFFILIATES:
Crimson Renewable Energy LLC

GROWTH PLANS/SPECIAL FEATURES:
SeQuential is a commercial biodiesel producer based in the Pacific Northwest. The company collects used cooking oil from all over the region and transforms it into biodiesel, which is a cleaner, non-toxic diesel fuel that offers a 50% reduction in harmful particulate matter and hydrocarbon emissions. The collected oil in Oregon is taken to SeQuential's production facility in Salem, Oregon, and the collected oil in California is taken to its plant in Bakersfield. The firm also offers grease trap cleaning services, allowing a single vendor for grease management needs. SeQuential is owned by Crimson Renewable Energy LLC, a leading biodiesel producer in California. In partnership with Crimson, SeQuential collects used cooking oil, refines it into biodiesel for the refueling of vehicles, fleets, fuel stations and local communities.

CONTACTS:
Note: Officers with more than one job title may be intentionally listed here more than once.

Harry Simpson, CEO
Tyson Keever, COO
Tyson Keever, Gen. Mgr.-SeQuential Pacific Biodiesel LLC

FINANCIAL DATA:
Note: Data for latest year may not have been available at press time.

In U.S. $	2021	2020	2019	2018	2017	2016
Revenue						
R&D Expense						
Operating Income						
Operating Margin %						
SGA Expense						
Net Income						
Operating Cash Flow						
Capital Expenditure						
EBITDA						
Return on Assets %						
Return on Equity %						
Debt to Equity						

CONTACT INFORMATION:
Phone: 503-954-2154 Fax:
Toll-Free:
Address: 3333 NW 35th Ave., Bldg. C, Portland, OR 97210 United States

STOCK TICKER/OTHER:
Stock Ticker: Subsidiary Exchange:
Employees: Fiscal Year Ends:
Parent Company: Crimson Renewable Energy LLC

SALARIES/BONUSES:
Top Exec. Salary: $ Bonus: $
Second Exec. Salary: $ Bonus: $

OTHER THOUGHTS:
Estimated Female Officers or Directors:
Hot Spot for Advancement for Women/Minorities:

Sales, profits and employees may be estimates. Financial information, benefits and other data can change quickly and may vary from those stated here.

SFC Energy AG

NAIC Code: 335999A

www.sfc.com

TYPES OF BUSINESS:
Fuel Cell Manufacturing

BRANDS/DIVISIONS/AFFILIATES:
EFOY
EFOY Hydrogen
SFC EMILY
SFC JENNY
SFC Power Manager 3G

GROWTH PLANS/SPECIAL FEATURES:
SFC Energy AG is engaged in the development, production, and distribution of power generation systems and their components for off-grid and on on-grid applications based on fuel cell and other technologies, as well as investment in the equipment and facilities required for these activities and transaction of all other related business. The company's product portfolio comprises of accessories and spare parts, fuel cartridges, combining fuel cell products with other power sources, power storage units, and electrical devices. The group serves the core segments namely Clean Energy and Mobility, Oil and Gas, Defense and Security and Industry. North American market constitutes the majority of the total income followed by Europe excluding Germany.

CONTACTS:
Note: Officers with more than one job title may be intentionally listed here more than once.

Peter Podesser, CEO
Hans Pol, COO
Daniel Saxena, CFO
Hubertus Krossa, Chmn.

FINANCIAL DATA:
Note: Data for latest year may not have been available at press time.

In U.S. $	2021	2020	2019	2018	2017	2016
Revenue	62,986,870	52,119,400	57,324,580	60,425,040	53,166,290	43,128,350
R&D Expense	3,189,707	2,783,925	3,039,260	3,451,954	3,811,327	4,062,299
Operating Income	-5,358,717	-4,051,443	-1,358,490	1,785,598	-754,842	-4,819,382
Operating Margin %	-.09%	-.08%	-.02%	.03%	-.01%	-.11%
SGA Expense	5,333,954	5,054,131	5,460,536	5,307,756	4,686,113	5,218,372
Net Income	-5,708,607	-5,076,583	-1,887,163	-506	-2,029,263	-4,889,226
Operating Cash Flow	1,055,980	-583,034	-1,234,636	1,963,905	1,668,792	-5,122,942
Capital Expenditure	3,704,681	4,190,081	3,614,691	2,324,032	1,313,507	901,165
EBITDA	-780,307	-965,344	1,999,697	2,426,512	868,245	-2,248,473
Return on Assets %	-.07%	-.07%	-.03%	.00%	-.06%	-.14%
Return on Equity %	-.11%	-.11%	-.07%	.00%	-.15%	-.33%
Debt to Equity	.10%	0.123	0.172	0.097	0.002	0.366

CONTACT INFORMATION:
Phone: 49 89673592368   Fax: 49 89673592169
Toll-Free:
Address: Eugen-Saenger-Ring 7, Brunnthal, 85649 Germany

STOCK TICKER/OTHER:
Stock Ticker: SSMFF   Exchange: PINX
Employees: 288   Fiscal Year Ends: 12/31
Parent Company:

SALARIES/BONUSES:
Top Exec. Salary: $ Bonus: $
Second Exec. Salary: $ Bonus: $

OTHER THOUGHTS:
Estimated Female Officers or Directors:
Hot Spot for Advancement for Women/Minorities:

Sales, profits and employees may be estimates. Financial information, benefits and other data can change quickly and may vary from those stated here.

Sharp Corporation

NAIC Code: 334310

global.sharp

TYPES OF BUSINESS:
Audiovisual & Communications Equipment
Electronic Components
Solar Cells & Advanced Batteries
Home Appliances
Consumer Electronics
Manufacturing
Product Distribution
Communication Equipment

BRANDS/DIVISIONS/AFFILIATES:
Foxconn Technology Co Ltd
Smart Appliances & Solutions BU
Smart Business Solutions BU
Digital Imaging Solutions BU
Mobile Communication BU

GROWTH PLANS/SPECIAL FEATURES:
Sharp Corp is a Japan-based company that is principally engaged in producing and selling a broad range of consumer and industrial electronic products. The company's business segments consist of the consumer electronics segment, the energy solutions segment, the business solutions segment, the electronic components and devices segment, and the display devices segment. The company generates over half of its revenue from the consumer electronics segment and the display devices segment. It has a global business presence, with China, Japan, the Americas, and Europe its four largest markets.

CONTACTS:
Note: Officers with more than one job title may be intentionally listed here more than once.

Jeng-Wu Tai, CEO
Katsuaki Nomura, Pres.
Mototaka Taneya, Exec. Gen. Mgr.-Corp. R&D Group
Toshihiko Fujimoto, Exec. Gen. Mgr.-Bus. Dev. Group
Shogo Fukahori, Chief Officer-In-House Comm.
Shinichi Niihara, Exec. Officer
Fujikazu Nakayama, Sr. Exec. Managing Officer-Products Bus. Group
Akihiko Imaya, Exec. Group Gen. Mgr.-Display Device Business
Masahiro Okitsu, Exec. Group Gen. Mgr.-Health & Environment
Paul Molyneux, Exec. Gen. Mgr.-Sales & Mktg., Europe

FINANCIAL DATA:
Note: Data for latest year may not have been available at press time.

In U.S. $	2021	2020	2019	2018	2017	2016
Revenue	16,751,670,000	15,621,780,000	16,573,250,000	16,761,070,000	14,160,310,000	
R&D Expense						
Operating Income	573,914,500	355,382,000	581,020,000	622,348,400	431,264,500	
Operating Margin %	.03%	.02%	.04%	.04%	.03%	
SGA Expense						
Net Income	367,797,800	94,782,340	512,553,900	484,925,700	-171,783,500	
Operating Cash Flow	1,413,117,000	472,689,500	545,816,800	726,922,500	878,570,000	
Capital Expenditure	354,808,900	649,831,600	986,410,400	805,353,000	534,450,600	
EBITDA	993,640,300	757,223,000	1,096,647,000	1,176,203,000	511,283,300	
Return on Assets %	.03%	.01%	.04%	.04%	-.01%	
Return on Equity %	.18%	.05%	.20%	.21%	-.20%	
Debt to Equity	1.60%	2.10	1.534	1.419	1.803	

CONTACT INFORMATION:
Phone: 81 666211221 Fax:
Toll-Free:
Address: 1 Takumi-cho. Sakai-Ku, Sakai City, Osaka, 590-8522 Japan

STOCK TICKER/OTHER:
Stock Ticker: SHCAF
Employees: 54,156
Parent Company: Foxconn Technology Co Ltd

Exchange: PINX
Fiscal Year Ends: 03/31

SALARIES/BONUSES:
Top Exec. Salary: $ Bonus: $
Second Exec. Salary: $ Bonus: $

OTHER THOUGHTS:
Estimated Female Officers or Directors:
Hot Spot for Advancement for Women/Minorities:

Sales, profits and employees may be estimates. Financial information, benefits and other data can change quickly and may vary from those stated here.

Shell Oil Company

NAIC Code: 211111

www.shell.us

TYPES OF BUSINESS:
Oil & Gas Exploration & Production
Chemicals
Power Generation
Nanocomposites
Nanocatalysts
Refineries
Pipelines & Shipping
Hydrogen Storage Technology

BRANDS/DIVISIONS/AFFILIATES:
Royal Dutch Shell plc
MSTS Payments LLC
TreviPay
Savion LLC

CONTACTS:
Note: Officers with more than one job title may be intentionally listed here more than once.

Ben van Beurden, CEO
Marvin E. Odum, Dir.-Upstream Americas-Royal Dutch Shell plc
Ben van Beurden, CEO-Royal Dutch Shell plc

GROWTH PLANS/SPECIAL FEATURES:

Shell Oil Company, a subsidiary of Royal Dutch Shell plc, is a natural gas, chemical and oil producer in the U.S. and internationally, with employees in more than 70 countries. Shell Oil's operations are divided into four businesses. The upstream business explores for new liquids and natural gas reserves, and develops major new projects where the company's technology and expertise adds value for resource holders. Within the integrated gas and new energies business, integrated gas focuses on LNG and converting gas to liquids so that it can be safely stores and shipped to markets worldwide; and new energies explores and invests in new low-carbon opportunities. The downstream business turns crude oil into a range of refined products, which are moved and marketed for domestic, industrial and transport use worldwide. It also produces and sells petrochemicals for industrial use; and oil sands North American mining activities are included this segment. Last, the projects and technology business is responsible for delivering new development projects, as well as the research and development that leads to innovative and low-cost investments for future use. Shell Oil's products and services include motor oils, lubricants, preventative maintenance services, chemicals, gasoline, diesel, heating oils and more. The firm also operates pipelines; trades natural gas, electrical power, crude oil, refined products, chemical feedstocks and environmental products; operates gasoline stations; provides commercial cards; and operates ecommerce sites for a range of Shell-branded items, including wearables, collectables and memorabilia. In late-2021, Shell Oil acquired MSTS Payments LLC and its multi-service fuel card business from Multi Service Technology Solutions Inc. (dba TreviPay); and acquired Savion LLC, a large utility-scale solar and energy storage developer in the U.S.

Shell Oil offers its employees comprehensive health benefits, and pension and savings plans.

FINANCIAL DATA:
Note: Data for latest year may not have been available at press time.

In U.S. $	2021	2020	2019	2018	2017	2016
Revenue	6,871,700,000	6,247,000,000	10,424,000,000	9,881,000,000	6,199,000,000	4,603,000,000
R&D Expense						
Operating Income						
Operating Margin %						
SGA Expense						
Net Income						
Operating Cash Flow						
Capital Expenditure						
EBITDA						
Return on Assets %						
Return on Equity %						
Debt to Equity						

CONTACT INFORMATION:
Phone: 713-241-6161 Fax: 713-241-4044
Toll-Free:
Address: 910 Louisiana St., Houston, TX 77002 United States

STOCK TICKER/OTHER:
Stock Ticker: Subsidiary
Employees: 35,000
Parent Company: Royal Dutch Shell plc

Exchange:
Fiscal Year Ends: 12/31

SALARIES/BONUSES:
Top Exec. Salary: $ Bonus: $
Second Exec. Salary: $ Bonus: $

OTHER THOUGHTS:
Estimated Female Officers or Directors:
Hot Spot for Advancement for Women/Minorities:

Sales, profits and employees may be estimates. Financial information, benefits and other data can change quickly and may vary from those stated here.

Shell plc

NAIC Code: 211111

www.shell.com

TYPES OF BUSINESS:
Oil & Gas-Exploration & Production
Gas Stations
Refineries
Solar & Wind Power
Chemicals
Consulting & Technology Services
Hydrogen & Fuel Cell Technology

BRANDS/DIVISIONS/AFFILIATES:
Royal Dutch Shell plc

GROWTH PLANS/SPECIAL FEATURES:
Shell is an integrated oil and gas company that explores for, produces, and refines oil around the world. In 2021, it produced 1.7 million barrels of liquids and 8.7 billion cubic feet of natural gas per day. At year-end 2021, reserves stood at 9.2 billion barrels of oil equivalent, 50% of which consisted of liquids. Its production and reserves are in Europe, Asia, Oceania, Africa, and North and South America. The company operates refineries with capacity of 1.8 mmb/d located in the Americas, Asia, Africa, and Europe and sells 15 mtpa of chemicals. Its largest chemical plants, often integrated with its local refineries, are in Central Europe, China, Singapore, and North America.

CONTACTS:
Note: Officers with more than one job title may be intentionally listed here more than once.

Ben van Beurden, CEO
Jessica Uhl, CFO
Peter Rees, Dir.-Legal
Marvin Odum, Dir.-Upstream Americas
John Abbot, Dir.-Downstream
Andrew Brown, Dir.-Upstream Intl
Charles O. Holliday, Chmn.

FINANCIAL DATA:
Note: Data for latest year may not have been available at press time.

In U.S. $	2021	2020	2019	2018	2017	2016
Revenue	261,504,000,000	180,543,000,000	344,877,000,000	388,379,000,000	305,179,000,000	233,591,000,000
R&D Expense	815,000,000	907,000,000	962,000,000	986,000,000	922,000,000	1,014,000,000
Operating Income	22,283,000,000	-25,530,000,000	22,946,000,000	31,189,000,000	15,481,000,000	2,367,000,000
Operating Margin %	.09%	-.14%	.07%	.08%	.05%	.01%
SGA Expense	11,328,000,000	9,881,000,000	10,493,000,000	11,360,000,000	10,509,000,000	12,101,000,000
Net Income	20,101,000,000	-21,680,000,000	15,842,000,000	23,352,000,000	12,977,000,000	4,575,000,000
Operating Cash Flow	45,104,000,000	34,105,000,000	42,178,000,000	53,085,000,000	35,650,000,000	20,615,000,000
Capital Expenditure	19,000,000,000	16,585,000,000	22,971,000,000	23,011,000,000	20,845,000,000	22,116,000,000
EBITDA	60,356,000,000	29,534,000,000	58,744,000,000	61,332,000,000	48,281,000,000	34,100,000,000
Return on Assets %	.05%	-.06%			.03%	
Return on Equity %	.12%	-.14%			.07%	
Debt to Equity	.47%	0.587	0.436	0.336	0.38	0.445

CONTACT INFORMATION:
Phone: 31 703779111 Fax: 31 703773953
Toll-Free:
Address: Carel van Bylandtlaan 16, The Hague, 2596 HR Netherlands

STOCK TICKER/OTHER:
Stock Ticker: SHEL Exchange: NYS
Employees: 87,000 Fiscal Year Ends: 12/31
Parent Company:

SALARIES/BONUSES:
Top Exec. Salary: $1,555,079 Bonus: $2,506,928
Second Exec. Salary: $1,013,543 Bonus: $1,566,830

OTHER THOUGHTS:
Estimated Female Officers or Directors: 1
Hot Spot for Advancement for Women/Minorities: Y

Sales, profits and employees may be estimates. Financial information, benefits and other data can change quickly and may vary from those stated here.

Shell WindEnergy Inc

www.shell.us/energy-and-innovation/shell-windenergy.html

NAIC Code: 221115

TYPES OF BUSINESS:
Wind Electric Power Generation
Onshore Wind Farms
Wind Power
Electric Generation
Electric Trading
Electric Supply
Offshore Wind Projects

BRANDS/DIVISIONS/AFFILIATES:
Shell plc

GROWTH PLANS/SPECIAL FEATURES:
Shell WindEnergy, Inc. operates within Shell plc's USA division, and is engaged in the business of integrated and lower-carbon power, from generating, buying and selling electricity to storing and supplying it directly to customers to power residences, businesses and vehicles. Shell WindEnergy has an installed capacity of 263 megawatts (MW) from three onshore wind farms that provide power in California and Texas. As of mid-2022, the company had two offshore wind leases in development with a capacity to generate 4.5 GW of wind energy off coasts of New Jersey and New York; and one lease to generate 2 GW of offshore wind energy off the coast of Massachusetts, enough to power 1 million homes.

CONTACTS:
Note: Officers with more than one job title may be intentionally listed here more than once.

Charles O. Holliday, Chmn.

FINANCIAL DATA:
Note: Data for latest year may not have been available at press time.

In U.S. $	2021	2020	2019	2018	2017	2016
Revenue						
R&D Expense						
Operating Income						
Operating Margin %						
SGA Expense						
Net Income						
Operating Cash Flow						
Capital Expenditure						
EBITDA						
Return on Assets %						
Return on Equity %						
Debt to Equity						

CONTACT INFORMATION:
Phone: 31-70-377-9111   Fax: 31-70-377-3113
Toll-Free:
Address: 150 N. Dairy Ashford Rd., Houston, TX 77079 United States

STOCK TICKER/OTHER:
Stock Ticker: Subsidiary
Employees:
Parent Company: Shell plc

Exchange:
Fiscal Year Ends:

SALARIES/BONUSES:
Top Exec. Salary: $ Bonus: $
Second Exec. Salary: $ Bonus: $

OTHER THOUGHTS:
Estimated Female Officers or Directors:
Hot Spot for Advancement for Women/Minorities:

Sales, profits and employees may be estimates. Financial information, benefits and other data can change quickly and may vary from those stated here.

Siemens AG

NAIC Code: 334513

www.siemens.com

TYPES OF BUSINESS:
Industrial Control Manufacturing
Digitalization
Smart Infrastructure
Mobility
Advanced Technologies
Artificial Intelligence
Internet of Things
Robotics

GROWTH PLANS/SPECIAL FEATURES:
Siemens AG is an industrial conglomerate, with businesses selling components and equipment for factory automation, railway equipment, electrical distribution equipment, and medical equipment. Its separately listed business units include Siemens Healthineers, Siemens Energy, and Siemens Gamesa, which supply medical imaging equipment, power generation, and wind turbines, respectively.

BRANDS/DIVISIONS/AFFILIATES:
Siemens Advanta
Siemens Healthineers AG
Siemens Financial Services
Siemens Real Estate
Next47

CONTACTS: Note: Officers with more than one job title may be intentionally listed here more than once.
Joe Kaeser, CEO
Ralf P. Thomas, CFO
Peter Y. Solmssen, Head-Corp. Legal & Compliance
Joe Kaeser, Head-Controlling
Roland Busch, CEO-Infrastructure & Cities Sector
Hermann Requardt, CEO-Health Care Sector
Michael Suess, CEO-Energy Sector
Siegfried Russwurm, CEO-Industry Sector
Jim Hagemenn Snabe, Chmn.
Barbara Kux, Chief Sustainability Officer

FINANCIAL DATA: Note: Data for latest year may not have been available at press time.

In U.S. $	2021	2020	2019	2018	2017	2016
Revenue	60,974,170,000	54,108,520,000	57,270,580,000	81,322,400,000	81,145,150,000	77,992,890,000
R&D Expense	4,758,267,000	4,474,279,000	4,572,207,000	5,442,777,000	5,056,945,000	4,633,901,000
Operating Income	6,288,865,000	4,295,073,000	5,977,457,000	5,789,437,000	7,073,259,000	6,991,980,000
Operating Margin %	.10%	.08%	.10%	.07%	.09%	.09%
SGA Expense	10,957,040,000	10,460,550,000	10,466,430,000	12,672,720,000	12,103,760,000	11,427,090,000
Net Income	6,033,275,000	3,946,454,000	5,066,737,000	5,686,614,000	5,837,422,000	5,337,015,000
Operating Cash Flow	9,788,771,000	8,678,280,000	8,280,697,000	8,250,340,000	7,027,233,000	7,453,215,000
Capital Expenditure	1,694,135,000	1,466,945,000	1,743,098,000	2,548,057,000	2,356,121,000	2,090,739,000
EBITDA	10,982,500,000	9,218,836,000	9,966,999,000	12,297,660,000	12,192,880,000	10,925,700,000
Return on Assets %	.05%	.03%	.04%	.04%	.05%	.04%
Return on Equity %	.15%	.10%	.11%	.13%	.15%	.16%
Debt to Equity	.92%	1.044	0.632	0.596	0.62	0.72

CONTACT INFORMATION:
Phone: 49 8963633032   Fax: 49 8932825
Toll-Free:
Address: Werner-von-Siemens-Strabe 1, Munich, BY 80333 Germany

STOCK TICKER/OTHER:
Stock Ticker: SMAWF   Exchange: PINX
Employees: 293,000   Fiscal Year Ends: 09/30
Parent Company:

SALARIES/BONUSES:
Top Exec. Salary: $1,958,538   Bonus: $1,331,708
Second Exec. Salary: $1,331,766   Bonus: $539,342

OTHER THOUGHTS:
Estimated Female Officers or Directors: 5
Hot Spot for Advancement for Women/Minorities: Y

Sales, profits and employees may be estimates. Financial information, benefits and other data can change quickly and may vary from those stated here.

Siemens Gamesa Renewable Energy SA

www.siemensgamesa.com/en-int
NAIC Code: 333611

TYPES OF BUSINESS:
Wind Turbine Manufacturing
Wind Farms
Turbines
Product Development
Technology
Diagnostic Services
Hybrid Power Solutions
Energy Storage Solutions

BRANDS/DIVISIONS/AFFILIATES:
Siemens AG
Digital Ventures Lab

GROWTH PLANS/SPECIAL FEATURES:
Siemens Gamesa is a leading manufacturer of onshore and offshore wind turbines. The company is the product of the merger between Siemens Wind Power and Gamesa in 2017. The firm operates in two business segments: wind turbines and services. Siemens Gamesa retained its position as the leading installer of offshore turbines in 2020. Siemens Energy (a recent spinoff from Siemens AG) owns 67% of Siemens Gamesa's shares.

CONTACTS:
Note: Officers with more than one job title may be intentionally listed here more than once.
Andreas Nauen, CEO
Christoph Wollny, COO
Beatriz Puente, CFO
Javier Fernandez-Combarro, Dir.-Human Resources
Ricardo Chocarro, Manager-Oper.
Xabier Etxeberria, CEO-Business

FINANCIAL DATA:
Note: Data for latest year may not have been available at press time.

In U.S. $	2021	2020	2019	2018	2017	2016
Revenue	9,986,405,000	9,286,611,000	10,014,860,000	8,933,157,000	6,402,654,000	6,036,111,000
R&D Expense	286,329,400	226,605,800	203,625,200	162,161,000	138,034,800	194,275,200
Operating Income	-511,499,600	-937,724,400	247,424,000	206,497,400	-2,938	497,620,400
Operating Margin %	-.05%	-.10%	.02%	.02%		.08%
SGA Expense	481,996,100	611,430,000	485,961,200	555,730,200	405,611,200	283,849,900
Net Income	-613,649,000	-899,143,100	137,099,600	68,541,970	-14,891,740	433,721,100
Operating Cash Flow	784,570,600	650,230,700	767,434,400	713,635,300	-341,758,000	845,292,200
Capital Expenditure	662,725,100	588,819,600	487,446,800	406,471,000	403,326,600	384,405,200
EBITDA	249,263,100	-104,699,500	898,759,200	838,645,800	459,878,400	660,136,900
Return on Assets %	-.04%	-.06%	.01%	.00%		.09%
Return on Equity %	-.13%	-.16%	.02%	.01%		.42%
Debt to Equity	.40%	0.251		0.082	0.139	0.003

CONTACT INFORMATION:
Phone: 34-9144-037352 Fax:
Toll-Free:
Address: Parque Tecnologico de Bizkaia, Edificio 222, Zamudio, 48170 Spain

STOCK TICKER/OTHER:
Stock Ticker: GCTAY
Employees: 25,458
Parent Company: Siemens AG

Exchange: PINX
Fiscal Year Ends: 12/31

SALARIES/BONUSES:
Top Exec. Salary: $ Bonus: $
Second Exec. Salary: $ Bonus: $

OTHER THOUGHTS:
Estimated Female Officers or Directors:
Hot Spot for Advancement for Women/Minorities: Y

Sales, profits and employees may be estimates. Financial information, benefits and other data can change quickly and may vary from those stated here.

Silicon Ranch Corporation

NAIC Code: 221114

www.siliconranch.com

TYPES OF BUSINESS:
Solar Electric Power Generation
Solar Power Production
Battery Storage Solutions
Solar Power Project Operation
Solar Power Assets
Solar Power Plant Design and Construction
Solar Project Investments

BRANDS/DIVISIONS/AFFILIATES:
Shell plc
Regenerative Energy
Clearloop

GROWTH PLANS/SPECIAL FEATURES:
Silicon Ranch Corporation operates Silicon Ranch, an independent solar power producer in the U.S. The company is a fully-integrated provider of customized renewable energy, carbon and battery storage solutions for a range of industry partners across North America. Silicon Ranch's portfolio includes more than 5 gigawatts (GW) of solar and battery storage systems that are contracted, under construction, or operating across the U.S. and Canada. Silicon Ranch owns and operates every project in its portfolio and has successfully commissioned them. The firm has trademarked Regenerative Energy for its solar power plant design, construction and operations that normalizes regenerative agriculture practices on solar farm sites; and acquired Clearloop in 2021, which helps businesses of all sizes to make direct investments in building new solar projects while expanding access to clean energy. Shell plc holds an approximate 43.8% interest in Silicon Ranch Corporation.

CONTACTS:
Note: Officers with more than one job title may be intentionally listed here more than once.

Reagan Farr, CEO
Michael Payne, CFO
Matt Kisber, Chmn.

FINANCIAL DATA:
Note: Data for latest year may not have been available at press time.

In U.S. $	2021	2020	2019	2018	2017	2016
Revenue						
R&D Expense						
Operating Income						
Operating Margin %						
SGA Expense						
Net Income						
Operating Cash Flow						
Capital Expenditure						
EBITDA						
Return on Assets %						
Return on Equity %						
Debt to Equity						

CONTACT INFORMATION:
Phone: 615 577-4786 Fax:
Toll-Free:
Address: 222 2nd Ave. S., Ste. 1900, Nashville, TN 37201 United States

STOCK TICKER/OTHER:
Stock Ticker: Private   Exchange:
Employees: Fiscal Year Ends:
Parent Company:

SALARIES/BONUSES:
Top Exec. Salary: $ Bonus: $
Second Exec. Salary: $ Bonus: $

OTHER THOUGHTS:
Estimated Female Officers or Directors:
Hot Spot for Advancement for Women/Minorities:

Sales, profits and employees may be estimates. Financial information, benefits and other data can change quickly and may vary from those stated here.

Sinovel Wind Group Co Ltd

NAIC Code: 333611

www.sinovel.com

TYPES OF BUSINESS:
Wind Turbine Manufacturing
Wind Power Equipment R&D
Wind Project Consulting
Wind Power Turbines
Turbine Engineering
Turbine Manufacturing

BRANDS/DIVISIONS/AFFILIATES:

GROWTH PLANS/SPECIAL FEATURES:
Sinovel Wind Group Co., Ltd. is a China-based company that researches, develops, manufactures and sells large-scale onshore, offshore and intertidal wind turbines. Sinovel's primary products include the SL 1500, SL 2000, SL 3000 and the SL 6000 wind turbines, of which each number represents kilowatts (KW) of power per unit. The firm's cumulative installed generating capacity of Sinovel wind turbines has reached a total of more than 17,085 MW.

CONTACTS: Note: Officers with more than one job title may be intentionally listed here more than once.
Ma Zhong, Pres.
Gang Tao, Sr. VP
Deng Yan, VP
Lecheng Li, VP

FINANCIAL DATA: Note: Data for latest year may not have been available at press time.

In U.S. $	2021	2020	2019	2018	2017	2016
Revenue	94,000,000	91,350,614	87,000,585	82,857,700	18,272,100	138,974,105
R&D Expense						
Operating Income						
Operating Margin %						
SGA Expense						
Net Income						
Operating Cash Flow						
Capital Expenditure						
EBITDA						
Return on Assets %						
Return on Equity %						
Debt to Equity						

CONTACT INFORMATION:
Phone: 86-10-6251-5566 Fax: 86-10-8250-0072
Toll-Free:
Address: 59 Zhongguancun St., Culture Bldg., Beijing, 100872 China

STOCK TICKER/OTHER:
Stock Ticker: Private
Employees: 1,181
Parent Company:

Exchange:
Fiscal Year Ends: 12/31

SALARIES/BONUSES:
Top Exec. Salary: $ Bonus: $
Second Exec. Salary: $ Bonus: $

OTHER THOUGHTS:
Estimated Female Officers or Directors:
Hot Spot for Advancement for Women/Minorities:

Sales, profits and employees may be estimates. Financial information, benefits and other data can change quickly and may vary from those stated here.

SkyPower Limited

NAIC Code: 221114

www.skypower.com

TYPES OF BUSINESS:
Solar Electric Power Generation
Solar Energy Project Development
Solar Energy Project Construction
Solar Energy Project Operation
Solar Power Facilities

BRANDS/DIVISIONS/AFFILIATES:
CIM Group Inc

GROWTH PLANS/SPECIAL FEATURES:
SkyPower Limited is majority-owned by CIM Group, Inc. and is a Canadian developer of solar energy projects, active in the construction and operation of solar power facilities. SkyPower has built, assembled and acquired a pipeline of 25+ gigawatts (GW) worldwide, some of which were built in the Middle East, Africa and South Asia. The firm contains consultants and advisors in offices located globally, supporting development activities worldwide. More than 30 solar parks have been developed by SkyPower.

CONTACTS:
Note: Officers with more than one job title may be intentionally listed here more than once.

Kerry Adler, CEO
Charles Cohen, CCO
Ava Wojcik, Sr. Dir.-Admin.
James Pagonis, Sr. VP-Oper.
Li Koo, Sr. Dir.-Comm.
Brian Moncik, Sr. VP-Finance
Benoit Fortin, VP-Dev.- Africa & India
Robert Carillo, VP
Lorraine Chen, Controller
Charmaine Thompson, VP-Ontario Projects
Li Koo, Sr. Dir.-Int'l Affairs

FINANCIAL DATA:
Note: Data for latest year may not have been available at press time.

In U.S. $	2021	2020	2019	2018	2017	2016
Revenue						
R&D Expense						
Operating Income						
Operating Margin %						
SGA Expense						
Net Income						
Operating Cash Flow						
Capital Expenditure						
EBITDA						
Return on Assets %						
Return on Equity %						
Debt to Equity						

CONTACT INFORMATION:
Phone: 416-979-4625 Fax: 416-981-8686
Toll-Free:
Address: Commerce Ct., Fl. 44, 199 Bay St., Toronto, ON M5L 1E9 Canada

STOCK TICKER/OTHER:
Stock Ticker: Subsidiary
Employees:
Parent Company: CIM Group Inc

Exchange:
Fiscal Year Ends:

SALARIES/BONUSES:
Top Exec. Salary: $ Bonus: $
Second Exec. Salary: $ Bonus: $

OTHER THOUGHTS:
Estimated Female Officers or Directors: 3
Hot Spot for Advancement for Women/Minorities: Y

Soluna Holdings Inc

NAIC Code: 335999A

www.solunacomputing.com

TYPES OF BUSINESS:
Fuel Cell Manufacturing
Data Centers
Renewable Energy
Cryptocurrency Mining
Vibration Measurement Systems
Balancing Systems
Precision Linear Displacement Systems
Wafer Inspection Tools

BRANDS/DIVISIONS/AFFILIATES:
EcoChain Inc
MTI Instruments Inc
Mechanical Technology Incorporated

GROWTH PLANS/SPECIAL FEATURES:
Soluna Holdings Inc, is a U.S based company which conducts operations through its subsidiary. It supplies precision linear displacement solutions, vibration measurement and system balancing solutions, and wafer inspection tools. Its product offerings include Accumeasure Series, Microtrak 4, Microtrak PRO-2D, MTI-2100 Fotonic Sensor Series, Accumeasure D Series and Microtrak TGS. The company operates in the United States, Association of southeast Asian Nations, Europe, the Middle East and Africa, North America and South America.

CONTACTS:
Note: Officers with more than one job title may be intentionally listed here more than once.

Michael Toporek, CEO
Jessica Thomas, CFO
David Michaels, Chairman of the Board
Moshe Binyamin, President, Subsidiary

FINANCIAL DATA:
Note: Data for latest year may not have been available at press time.

In U.S. $	2021	2020	2019	2018	2017	2016
Revenue	14,345,000	595,000	6,571,000		7,061,000	7,056,000
R&D Expense			1,381,000		1,149,000	1,243,000
Operating Income	-4,476,000	-1,642,000	259,000		588,000	-361,000
Operating Margin %	-.31%	-2.76%	.04%		.08%	-.05%
SGA Expense	10,751,000	1,832,000	2,726,000		3,090,000	3,452,000
Net Income	-5,261,000	1,946,000	323,000		582,000	-359,000
Operating Cash Flow	5,552,000	1,901,000	289,000		363,000	522,000
Capital Expenditure	57,268,000	1,084,000	83,000		107,000	136,000
EBITDA	-593,000	-1,375,000	346,000		669,000	-276,000
Return on Assets %	-.09%	.27%	.06%		.10%	-.09%
Return on Equity %	-.12%	.40%	.08%		.13%	-.13%
Debt to Equity	.00%		0.05	0.202		

CONTACT INFORMATION:
Phone: 518 218-2550 Fax:
Toll-Free:
Address: 325 Washington Ave. Extension, Albany, NY 12205 United States

STOCK TICKER/OTHER:
Stock Ticker: SLNH
Employees: 62
Parent Company:

Exchange: NAS
Fiscal Year Ends: 12/31

SALARIES/BONUSES:
Top Exec. Salary: $180,247 Bonus: $115,000
Second Exec. Salary: $240,423 Bonus: $

OTHER THOUGHTS:
Estimated Female Officers or Directors:
Hot Spot for Advancement for Women/Minorities:

Southern California Edison Company

www.sce.com

NAIC Code: 221112

TYPES OF BUSINESS:
Electric Utility
Electric Utilities
Electric Power Generation
Electric Power Distribution
Transmission Line Maintenance
Distribution Line Maintenance
Distribution Transformers
Substation Transformers

BRANDS/DIVISIONS/AFFILIATES:
Edison International

GROWTH PLANS/SPECIAL FEATURES:
Southern California Edison Company (SCE) is one of the largest electric utilities in the U.S. The firm is the largest subsidiary of Edison International, an electric power generator and distributor as well as an investor in infrastructure and renewable energy projects. SCE serves around 15 million individuals, as well as businesses (small and large), across a 50,000-square-mile service area within central, coastal and southern California, excluding Los Angeles. SCE monitors and maintains 12,635 miles of transmission lines, 91,375 miles of distribution lines, more than 1.43 million electric poles, 720,800 distribution transformers and nearly 3,000 substation transformers.

SCE offers its employees AD&D, disability, life, medical, dental and vision insurance; a 401(k) plan with company match; an employee assistance program; a retirement pension plan; wellness programs; and educational reimbursements.

CONTACTS:
Note: Officers with more than one job title may be intentionally listed here more than once.

Steven D. Powell, CEO
Jill C. Anderson, Exec. VP-Oper.
Aaron D. Moss, CFO
Beth M. Foley, VP-Communications
Natalie Schilling, Chief Human Resources Officer
Peter T. Dietrich, Chief Nuclear Officer
Todd L. Inlander, CIO
Kevin M. Payne, VP-Eng.
Russell C. Swartz, General Counsel
Chris Dominski, VP-Planning & Performance Reporting
Janet Clayton, Sr. VP-Corp. Comm.
Chris C. Dominski, Controller
Lynda L. Ziegler, Exec. VP-Power Delivery Svcs.
Barbara E. Mathews, Chief Governance Officer
Gaddi H. Vasquez, Sr. VP-Govt Affairs
Stephen E. Pickett, Exec. VP-External Rel.
Albert Ma, VP-IT
Douglas R. Bauder, Chief Procurement Officer

FINANCIAL DATA:
Note: Data for latest year may not have been available at press time.

In U.S. $	2021	2020	2019	2018	2017	2016
Revenue	14,905,000,000	13,546,000,000	12,306,000,000	12,611,000,000	12,254,000,000	11,830,000,000
R&D Expense						
Operating Income						
Operating Margin %						
SGA Expense						
Net Income	925,000,000	942,000,000	1,530,000,000	-189,000,000	668,000,000	1,499,000,000
Operating Cash Flow						
Capital Expenditure						
EBITDA						
Return on Assets %						
Return on Equity %						
Debt to Equity						

CONTACT INFORMATION:
Phone: 626 302-1212 Fax:
Toll-Free: 800-655-4555
Address: 2244 Walnut Grove Ave., Rosemead, CA 91770 United States

STOCK TICKER/OTHER:
Stock Ticker: Subsidiary
Employees: 13,003
Parent Company: Edison International
Exchange:
Fiscal Year Ends: 12/31

SALARIES/BONUSES:
Top Exec. Salary: $ Bonus: $
Second Exec. Salary: $ Bonus: $

OTHER THOUGHTS:
Estimated Female Officers or Directors: 10
Hot Spot for Advancement for Women/Minorities: Y

Sales, profits and employees may be estimates. Financial information, benefits and other data can change quickly and may vary from those stated here.

Southern Company

NAIC Code: 221112

www.southerncompany.com

TYPES OF BUSINESS:
Electric Utility
Wireless Communications Services
Fiber Optic Solutions
Nuclear Power Operating Services
Consulting Services
Power Generation Construction
Biomass

BRANDS/DIVISIONS/AFFILIATES:
Alabama Power Company
Georgia Power Company
Mississippi Power Company
Southern Power Company
Southern Company Gas
Cloverly

GROWTH PLANS/SPECIAL FEATURES:
Southern Co. is one of the largest utilities in the U.S. The company distributes electricity and natural gas to approximately 9 million customers in nine states. It owns 50 gigawatts of rate-regulated generating capacity, primarily for serving customers in Georgia, Alabama, and Mississippi. Subsidiary Southern Power Co. owns 12 gigawatts of mostly non-rate-regulated renewable energy capacity and sells the electricity primarily under long-term power sales agreements. The solar and wind farms are located in Southern's regulated jurisdictions but also in Texas, California, and other states.

CONTACTS:
Note: Officers with more than one job title may be intentionally listed here more than once.

W. Bowers, CEO, Subsidiary
Kimberly Greene, CEO, Subsidiary
Mark Lantrip, CEO, Subsidiary
Stephen Kuczynski, CEO, Subsidiary
Anthony Wilson, CEO, Subsidiary
Mark Crosswhite, CEO, Subsidiary
Christopher Cummiskey, CEO, Subsidiary
Thomas Fanning, CEO
Philip Raymond, CFO, Subsidiary
David Poroch, CFO, Subsidiary
Daniel Tucker, CFO, Subsidiary
Moses Feagin, CFO, Subsidiary
Elliott Spencer, CFO, Subsidiary
Andrew Evans, CFO
Matthew Grice, Chief Accounting Officer, Subsidiary
Jelena Andrin, Chief Accounting Officer, Subsidiary
Grace Kolvereid, Chief Accounting Officer, Subsidiary
Anita Allcorn-Walker, Chief Accounting Officer, Subsidiary
Sarah Adams, Chief Accounting Officer, Subsidiary
Ann Daiss, Chief Accounting Officer
James Kerr, Chief Compliance Officer

FINANCIAL DATA:
Note: Data for latest year may not have been available at press time.

In U.S. $	2021	2020	2019	2018	2017	2016
Revenue	23,113,000,000	20,375,000,000	21,419,000,000	23,495,000,000	23,031,000,000	19,896,000,000
R&D Expense						
Operating Income	3,514,000,000	4,820,000,000	5,335,000,000	4,110,000,000	2,293,000,000	4,487,000,000
Operating Margin %	.15%	.24%	.25%	.17%	.10%	.23%
SGA Expense						
Net Income	2,408,000,000	3,134,000,000	4,754,000,000	2,242,000,000	880,000,000	2,493,000,000
Operating Cash Flow	6,169,000,000	6,696,000,000	5,781,000,000	6,945,000,000	6,394,000,000	4,894,000,000
Capital Expenditure	7,240,000,000	7,441,000,000	7,555,000,000	8,001,000,000	7,423,000,000	7,310,000,000
EBITDA	8,386,000,000	9,222,000,000	11,609,000,000	8,140,000,000	6,219,000,000	7,720,000,000
Return on Assets %	.02%	.03%	.04%	.02%	.01%	.03%
Return on Equity %	.09%	.11%	.18%	.09%	.03%	.11%
Debt to Equity	1.85%	1.669	1.578	1.648	1.84	1.722

CONTACT INFORMATION:
Phone: 404 506-5000 Fax: 404 506-0344
Toll-Free:
Address: 30 Ivan Allen Jr. Blvd., NW, Atlanta, GA 30308 United States

STOCK TICKER/OTHER:
Stock Ticker: SO
Employees: 27,300
Parent Company:

Exchange: NYS
Fiscal Year Ends: 12/31

SALARIES/BONUSES:
Top Exec. Salary: $1,582,692 Bonus: $
Second Exec. Salary: $880,351 Bonus: $

OTHER THOUGHTS:
Estimated Female Officers or Directors: 3
Hot Spot for Advancement for Women/Minorities: Y

Sales, profits and employees may be estimates. Financial information, benefits and other data can change quickly and may vary from those stated here.

Spectrolab Inc

NAIC Code: 334413A

www.spectrolab.com

TYPES OF BUSINESS:
Photovoltaic Cell Manufacturing
Aerospace Components-Solar Cells
Optoelectronic Products
Solar Simulators
Searchlight Systems

BRANDS/DIVISIONS/AFFILIATES:
Boeing Company (The)
Nightsun
SX
SpectroLink

CONTACTS:
Note: Officers with more than one job title may be intentionally listed here more than once.

Tony Mueller, Pres.

GROWTH PLANS/SPECIAL FEATURES:

Spectrolab, Inc., a wholly owned subsidiary of The Boeing Company, is a leading global manufacturer and supplier of multi-junction solar cells and panels for use in spacecraft power systems. The company has several products lines, including photovoltaics, searchlights and sensors. The firm's solar cells have been used in space since 1958, powering Pioneer 1, NASA's first launched spacecraft; Explorer 6, the satellite that provided the first photograph of the Earth from space; the Apollo 11 mission, which placed the first solar cell panel on the moon; and the Spirit and Opportunity Mars rovers. Spectrolab's photovoltaic products include a range of GaInP/GaAs/Ge multi-junction solar cells; solar cells assembly kits, which include interconnects and space-qualified cover glass for protection against cosmic radiation; space solar panels; solar panels for commercial, science and military program solar arrays that integrate onto spacecraft by satellite contractors; and concentrator cells, with performance optimized to concentrations above 1,000 suns available, and sold either as bare cells or binned discrete cells in waffle trays. Searchlights include illumination and sensor products marketed under the following labels: Nightsun, SX and SpectroLink. Sensors include products for power conversion and detection, including laser power converters and InGaAs PiN photodetectors. Photodetectors, sensors, searchlights and simulators are primarily used for military, maritime and search and rescue operations.

Spectrolab offers its employees medical, dental and vision insurance; flexible spending accounts; a savings plan; retirement benefits; AD&D; short- and long-term disability; and education opportunities.

FINANCIAL DATA:
Note: Data for latest year may not have been available at press time.

In U.S. $	2021	2020	2019	2018	2017	2016
Revenue						
R&D Expense						
Operating Income						
Operating Margin %						
SGA Expense						
Net Income						
Operating Cash Flow						
Capital Expenditure						
EBITDA						
Return on Assets %						
Return on Equity %						
Debt to Equity						

CONTACT INFORMATION:
Phone: 818-365-4611 Fax: 818-361-5102
Toll-Free:
Address: 12500 Gladstone Ave., Sylmar, CA 91342 United States

STOCK TICKER/OTHER:
Stock Ticker: Subsidiary Exchange:
Employees: Fiscal Year Ends: 12/31
Parent Company: Boeing Company (The)

SALARIES/BONUSES:
Top Exec. Salary: $ Bonus: $
Second Exec. Salary: $ Bonus: $

OTHER THOUGHTS:
Estimated Female Officers or Directors:
Hot Spot for Advancement for Women/Minorities:

Sales, profits and employees may be estimates. Financial information, benefits and other data can change quickly and may vary from those stated here.

Spruce Power Holdings Corp

investors.sprucepower.com/overview/default.aspx

NAIC Code: 336999

TYPES OF BUSINESS:
ATV, Snowmobile, Golf Cart, Go-cart and Race Car Equipment Manufacturing
Solar Power as a Service

BRANDS/DIVISIONS/AFFILIATES:

GROWTH PLANS/SPECIAL FEATURES:
Spruce Power Holdings Corp. is a leading owner and operator of distributed solar energy assets across the United States. It provides subscription-based services that make it easy for homeowners and small businesses to own and maintain rooftop solar and battery storage. Its as-a-service model allows consumers to access new technology without making a significant upfront investment or incurring maintenance costs. The company has more than 51,000 subscribers across the United States.

CONTACTS:
Note: Officers with more than one job title may be intentionally listed here more than once.

Eric Tech, CEO
Don Klein, CFO
Sandra Ponichtera, VP-People
Deb Frodl, Chmn.

FINANCIAL DATA:
Note: Data for latest year may not have been available at press time.

In U.S. $	2021	2020	2019	2018	2017	2016
Revenue	15,600,000	20,338,000	7,215,000			
R&D Expense						
Operating Income						
Operating Margin %						
SGA Expense						
Net Income	28,790,000	-60,606,000	-14,901,000			
Operating Cash Flow						
Capital Expenditure						
EBITDA						
Return on Assets %						
Return on Equity %						
Debt to Equity						

CONTACT INFORMATION:
Phone: 617 718-0329 Fax:
Toll-Free:
Address: 145 Newton Street, Boston, TX 2135 United States

STOCK TICKER/OTHER:
Stock Ticker: SPRU Exchange: NYS
Employees: Fiscal Year Ends: 12/31
Parent Company:

SALARIES/BONUSES:
Top Exec. Salary: $ Bonus: $
Second Exec. Salary: $ Bonus: $

OTHER THOUGHTS:
Estimated Female Officers or Directors:
Hot Spot for Advancement for Women/Minorities:

Sales, profits and employees may be estimates. Financial information, benefits and other data can change quickly and may vary from those stated here.

SSE Airtricity Limited

NAIC Code: 221115

www.sseairtricity.com/ie/home

TYPES OF BUSINESS:
Wind Electric Power Generation
Retail Electricity Sales
Hydropower Purchase & Resale
Electricity & Gas Duel Fuel Plans
Electricity Plans
Gas Plans
Onshore Wind Farms
Offshore Wind Farms

BRANDS/DIVISIONS/AFFILIATES:
SSE plc
SSE Airtricity Community Fund

GROWTH PLANS/SPECIAL FEATURES:
SSE Airtricity Limited provides 100% green electricity, natural gas and related services to homes and businesses throughout Ireland. The company's 28 onshore wind farms have a combined generation capacity of 720 megawatts (MW), including the country's largest onshore wind farm, the 169MW Galway Wind Park, which was jointly developed with Coillte. SSE Airtricity serves approximately 800,000 customers. Its SSE Airtricity Community Fund has supported more than 2,500 community projects. SSE Airtricity itself is a subsidiary of the SSE plc, a generator of renewable energy in the U.K. and Ireland.

CONTACTS:
Note: Officers with more than one job title may be intentionally listed here more than once.

Klair Neenan, Managing Dir.

FINANCIAL DATA:
Note: Data for latest year may not have been available at press time.

In U.S. $	2021	2020	2019	2018	2017	2016
Revenue	1,746,981,600	1,679,790,000	1,381,380,000	1,315,600,000	1,279,510,000	1,181,080,000
R&D Expense						
Operating Income						
Operating Margin %						
SGA Expense						
Net Income						
Operating Cash Flow						
Capital Expenditure						
EBITDA						
Return on Assets %						
Return on Equity %						
Debt to Equity						

CONTACT INFORMATION:
Phone: 353-1-655 6400　　Fax: 353-1-655 6444
Toll-Free:
Address: Red Oak South, South County Bus. Pk, Leopardstown, Dublin, D18 2688 Ireland

STOCK TICKER/OTHER:
Stock Ticker: Subsidiary　　Exchange:
Employees: 1,100　　Fiscal Year Ends: 03/31
Parent Company: SSE plc

SALARIES/BONUSES:
Top Exec. Salary: $　　Bonus: $
Second Exec. Salary: $　　Bonus: $

OTHER THOUGHTS:
Estimated Female Officers or Directors:
Hot Spot for Advancement for Women/Minorities:

Sales, profits and employees may be estimates. Financial information, benefits and other data can change quickly and may vary from those stated here.

Stryten Energy LLC

NAIC Code: 335911

www.stryten.com

TYPES OF BUSINESS:
Battery Manufacturing
Energy Storage Technologies
Lead and Lithium Batteries
Polypropylene Components
Application Software
Manufacturing and Design
Essential Power Backup Solutions
Battery Chargers

BRANDS/DIVISIONS/AFFILIATES:
Atlas Holdings LLC

CONTACTS:
Note: Officers with more than one job title may be intentionally listed here more than once.

Tim Vargo, CEO
Mike Judd, Pres.
Lou Martinez, CFO
Melissa Floyd, VP-Communications & Digital Mktg.
Wendy Henderson, CHRO
Brian Woodworth, CIO
Rodger Meyer, Sr. VP-Oper.

GROWTH PLANS/SPECIAL FEATURES:

Stryten Energy LLC is an innovative stored energy solutions provider to the transportation, motive and essential power industries. The company invests in and develops energy storage technologies. Stryten's transportation solutions span advanced lead and lithium batteries, intelligent chargers and cloud-based software in order to help companies make smart fleet design decisions. The transportation division offers a comprehensive product portfolio across vehicles, from Standard Flooded batteries to advanced technologies such as Enhanced Flooded Batteries (EFB) and Absorbed Glass Mat (AGM) for automotive, truck, SUV, heavy duty, agriculture, marine, recreational vehicle and lawn and garden applications. Stryten's motive power division offers a comprehensive portfolio of motive power batteries, performance management tools and chargers for material handling, mining, railway, military and other applications, including tailored solutions for specific battery procurement needs. Stryten's essential power division offers a suite of advanced lead battery technologies and services, including chargers and racking systems, used for backup power in the telecommunications, uninterruptible power supply (UPS), railway, utility and renewable industries. Stryten also provides batteries to the U.S. military and government, including advanced lead and lithium battery solutions for critical applications and demanding environments; and provides power and/or backup power for combat vehicles, submarines, military communication systems, data centers, material handling, microgrids, ground logistics and more. Stryten's engineered components division utilizes plastic injection molding methodology to produce critical automotive, motive and essential power battery components. Components include SLI plastic battery containers, covers, vents, terminals, polypropylene for injection molding battery components, and related handles and terminal protectors. company's facilities are ISO 9001:2015 certified. Stryten operates manufacturing plants throughout the U.S., and is a subsidiary of Atlas Holdings, LLC.

FINANCIAL DATA:
Note: Data for latest year may not have been available at press time.

In U.S. $	2021	2020	2019	2018	2017	2016
Revenue						
R&D Expense						
Operating Income						
Operating Margin %						
SGA Expense						
Net Income						
Operating Cash Flow						
Capital Expenditure						
EBITDA						
Return on Assets %						
Return on Equity %						
Debt to Equity						

CONTACT INFORMATION:
Phone: 678-566-9000 Fax:
Toll-Free:
Address: 3700 Mansell Rd., Ste. 400, Alpharetta, GA 30022 United States

STOCK TICKER/OTHER:
Stock Ticker: Subsidiary Exchange:
Employees: 2,000 Fiscal Year Ends:
Parent Company: Atlas Holdings LLC

SALARIES/BONUSES:
Top Exec. Salary: $ Bonus: $
Second Exec. Salary: $ Bonus: $

OTHER THOUGHTS:
Estimated Female Officers or Directors:
Hot Spot for Advancement for Women/Minorities:

Sulzer AG

NAIC Code: 325510

www.sulzer.com

TYPES OF BUSINESS:
Machinery & Services
Flow Control
Applicators
Manufacturing
Engineering
Pump Solutions
Rotating Equipment

BRANDS/DIVISIONS/AFFILIATES:
medmix AG

GROWTH PLANS/SPECIAL FEATURES:
Sulzer AG specializes in pumping solutions, rotating equipment maintenance, and mixing technology. It serves customers operating in the oil and gas, power, and water markets. Pumping solutions focus on transporting and processing oil and derivatives, treating water, and renewable power generation. In addition, the company offers solutions for turbines, compressors, motors, and other rotating components and has technicians to provide maintenance. Sulzer's business segments include Flow Equipment, Services, Chemtech, and Others which primarily serve across the globe. While most of its revenues are generated from its Flow equipment and Services segment.

CONTACTS:
Note: Officers with more than one job title may be intentionally listed here more than once.

Greg Poux-Guillaume, CEO
Jill Lee, CFO
Armand Sohet, Chief Human Resources Officer
Scot Smith, Pres., Sulzer Pumps
Cesar Montenegro, Pres., Sulzer Metco
Urs Fankhauser, Pres., Sulzer Chemtech
Peter Alexander, Pres., Sulzer Turbo Svcs.
Peter Loscher, Chmn.

FINANCIAL DATA:
Note: Data for latest year may not have been available at press time.

In U.S. $	2021	2020	2019	2018	2017	2016
Revenue	3,201,238,000	3,011,008,000	3,782,783,000	3,413,889,000	3,093,390,000	2,918,582,000
R&D Expense	65,337,590	64,728,860	86,846,240	87,657,890	82,179,270	72,439,500
Operating Income	234,768,900	195,302,600	275,351,300	197,636,100	174,504,100	193,172,000
Operating Margin %	.07%	.06%	.07%	.06%	.06%	.07%
SGA Expense	688,784,000	655,709,400	794,501,100	749,556,100	710,089,800	643,027,500
Net Income	1,437,326,000	84,817,130	156,242,100	115,355,400	84,411,300	59,858,980
Operating Cash Flow	320,499,200	374,067,900	324,253,000	264,597,000	186,374,500	267,031,900
Capital Expenditure	87,353,520	107,036,000	116,572,800	97,600,570	82,382,180	75,990,460
EBITDA	402,374,100	317,455,500	415,157,500	335,819,000	285,598,300	251,407,700
Return on Assets %	.27%	.02%	.03%	.03%	.02%	.01%
Return on Equity %	1.06%	.06%	.10%	.07%	.05%	.03%
Debt to Equity	.96%	1.126	0.811	0.808	0.273	0.29

CONTACT INFORMATION:
Phone: 41 52 262 20 22 Fax:
Toll-Free:
Address: Zurcherstrasse 12, Winterthur, 8401 Switzerland

STOCK TICKER/OTHER:
Stock Ticker: SULZF
Employees: 16,506
Parent Company:

Exchange: PINX
Fiscal Year Ends: 12/31

SALARIES/BONUSES:
Top Exec. Salary: $ Bonus: $
Second Exec. Salary: $ Bonus: $

OTHER THOUGHTS:
Estimated Female Officers or Directors:
Hot Spot for Advancement for Women/Minorities:

Sales, profits and employees may be estimates. Financial information, benefits and other data can change quickly and may vary from those stated here.

Suncor Energy Inc

NAIC Code: 211111

www.suncor.com

TYPES OF BUSINESS:
Oil & Gas Exploration & Production
Wind Power
Oil Sands Production
Oil Refining & Transportation
Energy Marketing
Ethanol Production
Solar Power Projects

BRANDS/DIVISIONS/AFFILIATES:

GROWTH PLANS/SPECIAL FEATURES:
Suncor Energy Inc is an integrated energy company. The company's operations include oil sands development, production and upgrading, offshore oil and gas, petroleum refining in Canada and the U.S. and the company's PetroCanada retail and wholesale distribution networks. The company is developing petroleum resources while advancing the transition to a low-emissions future through investment in power, renewable fuels and hydrogen. It also conducts energy trading activities focused principally on the marketing and trading of crude oil, natural gas, byproducts, refined products and power.

Suncor offers comprehensive employee benefits.

CONTACTS:
Note: Officers with more than one job title may be intentionally listed here more than once.

Mark Little, CEO
Alister Cowan, CFO
Michael Wilson, Chairman of the Board
Arlene Strom, Chief Legal Officer
Kris Smith, Executive VP, Divisional
Mike MacSween, Executive VP, Divisional
Paul Gardner, Other Executive Officer
Bruno Francoeur, Other Executive Officer
Martha Findlay, Other Executive Officer
Joe Vetrone, Senior VP, Divisional

FINANCIAL DATA:
Note: Data for latest year may not have been available at press time.

In U.S. $	2021	2020	2019	2018	2017	2016
Revenue	29,833,980,000	18,060,100,000	27,811,100,000	27,954,710,000	23,176,400,000	19,443,250,000
R&D Expense						
Operating Income	4,779,036,000	-4,012,388,000	1,639,915,000	4,853,742,000	3,545,292,000	268,362,900
Operating Margin %	.16%	-.22%	.06%	.17%	.15%	.01%
SGA Expense	3,551,094,000	2,585,713,000	3,529,335,000	3,017,995,000	2,763,412,000	2,965,047,000
Net Income	2,987,532,000	-3,132,593,000	2,102,660,000	2,388,430,000	3,233,410,000	314,782,400
Operating Cash Flow	8,532,490,000	1,940,191,000	7,558,405,000	7,673,728,000	6,503,086,000	4,119,733,000
Capital Expenditure	3,303,765,000	2,847,548,000	4,031,246,000	3,921,000,000	4,751,474,000	4,773,959,000
EBITDA	9,200,496,000	3,440,122,000	10,418,280,000	8,587,613,000	8,734,850,000	5,037,969,000
Return on Assets %	.05%	-.05%	.03%	.04%	.05%	.01%
Return on Equity %	.11%	-.11%	.07%	.07%	.10%	.01%
Debt to Equity	.45	0.46	0.369	0.316	0.295	0.361

CONTACT INFORMATION:
Phone: 403 296-8000 Fax: 403 296-3030
Toll-Free:
Address: 150-6th Avenue SW, Calgary, AB T2P 3E3 Canada

STOCK TICKER/OTHER:
Stock Ticker: SU Exchange: NYS
Employees: 12,591 Fiscal Year Ends: 12/31
Parent Company:

SALARIES/BONUSES:
Top Exec. Salary: $1,145,769 Bonus: $
Second Exec. Salary: $771,538 Bonus: $

OTHER THOUGHTS:
Estimated Female Officers or Directors: 3
Hot Spot for Advancement for Women/Minorities: Y

Sales, profits and employees may be estimates. Financial information, benefits and other data can change quickly and may vary from those stated here.

SunPower Corporation

us.sunpower.com

NAIC Code: 334413A

TYPES OF BUSINESS:
Photovoltaic Solar Cells
Solar Panels & Modules
Power Plant Operations

BRANDS/DIVISIONS/AFFILIATES:
Equinox
InvisiMount
Helix
Blue Ravin Solar

GROWTH PLANS/SPECIAL FEATURES:
SunPower is a leading solar technology and energy services provider that offers fully integrated solar, storage, and home energy solutions to customers primarily in the United States and Canada through an array of hardware, software, and financing options and smart energy solutions. The company's sales channels include a network of both installing and non-installing dealers and resellers that operate in residential and commercial markets as well as a group of in-house sales teams in each segment engaged in direct sales to end customers. SunPower is a majority-owned subsidiary of TotalEnergies Solar.

The firm offers U.S. employees health and wellness programs, a 401(k) and employee assistance programs.

CONTACTS:
Note: Officers with more than one job title may be intentionally listed here more than once.

Peter Faricy, CEO
Manavendra Sial, CFO
Vichheka Heang, Chief Accounting Officer
Kenneth Mahaffey, Chief Compliance Officer
Regan MacPherson, Chief Legal Officer
Douglas Richards, Executive VP, Divisional

FINANCIAL DATA:
Note: Data for latest year may not have been available at press time.

In U.S. $	2021	2020	2019	2018	2017	2016
Revenue	1,323,493,000	1,124,829,000	1,092,226,000	1,202,311,000	1,794,047,000	2,552,637,000
R&D Expense	17,070,000	22,381,000	34,217,000	49,240,000	82,247,000	116,889,000
Operating Income	-23,461,000	-13,697,000	-42,848,000	-100,812,000	-379,537,000	-227,827,000
Operating Margin %	-.02%	-.01%	-.04%	-.08%	-.21%	-.09%
SGA Expense	232,253,000	164,703,000	172,109,000	200,069,000	278,645,000	332,757,000
Net Income	-37,358,000	475,048,000	22,159,000	-811,091,000	-929,121,000	-448,635,000
Operating Cash Flow	-44,476,000	-187,391,000	-270,413,000	-543,389,000	-267,412,000	-312,283,000
Capital Expenditure	14,178,000	21,105,000	111,602,000	183,330,000	282,878,000	310,650,000
EBITDA	7,762,000	736,026,000	320,051,000	-131,074,000	-925,179,000	-296,582,000
Return on Assets %	-.02%	.25%	.01%	-.25%	-.22%	-.10%
Return on Equity %	-.09%	2.29%		-4.27%	-1.16%	-.37%
Debt to Equity	1.19%	1.293	95.371		2.935	1.785

CONTACT INFORMATION:
Phone: 408 240-5500   Fax: 408 739-7713
Toll-Free: 800-786-7693
Address: 77 Rio Robles, San Jose, CA 95134 United States

STOCK TICKER/OTHER:
Stock Ticker: SPWR
Employees: 8,902
Parent Company:

Exchange: NAS
Fiscal Year Ends: 12/31

SALARIES/BONUSES:
Top Exec. Salary: $496,154   Bonus: $
Second Exec. Salary: $456,923   Bonus: $

OTHER THOUGHTS:
Estimated Female Officers or Directors: 1
Hot Spot for Advancement for Women/Minorities: Y

Sales, profits and employees may be estimates. Financial information, benefits and other data can change quickly and may vary from those stated here.

Sunrun Inc

NAIC Code: 221114

www.sunrunhome.com

TYPES OF BUSINESS:
Solar Electric Power Generation

BRANDS/DIVISIONS/AFFILIATES:
BrightBox
Vivint Solar Inc

GROWTH PLANS/SPECIAL FEATURES:
Sunrun is engaged in the design, development, installation, sale, ownership, and maintenance of residential solar energy systems in the United States. The company acquires customers directly and through relationships with various solar and strategic partners. The solar systems are constructed either by Sunrun or by Sunrun's partners and are owned by the company. Sunrun's customers typically enter into 20- to 25-year agreements to utilize its solar energy system. The company also sells solar energy systems and products, such as panels and racking, and solar leads generated to customers.

CONTACTS:
Note: Officers with more than one job title may be intentionally listed here more than once.

Lynn Jurich, CEO
Tom vonReichbauer, CFO
Edward Fenster, Chairman of the Board
Michelle Philpot, Chief Accounting Officer
Christopher Dawson, COO
Jeanna Steele, General Counsel

FINANCIAL DATA:
Note: Data for latest year may not have been available at press time.

In U.S. $	2021	2020	2019	2018	2017	2016
Revenue	1,609,954,000	922,191,000	858,578,000	759,981,000	532,542,000	477,107,000
R&D Expense	23,165,000	19,548,000	23,563,000	18,844,000	15,079,000	10,199,000
Operating Income	-666,187,000	-465,108,000	-215,740,000	-121,881,000	-181,133,000	-192,076,000
Operating Margin %	-.41%	-.50%	-.25%	-.16%	-.34%	-.40%
SGA Expense	882,134,000	619,045,000	400,171,000	323,891,000	253,826,000	261,153,000
Net Income	-79,423,000	-173,394,000	26,335,000	26,657,000	125,489,000	75,129,000
Operating Cash Flow	-817,186,000	-317,972,000	-204,487,000	-62,461,000	-96,103,000	-200,141,000
Capital Expenditure	1,686,185,000	969,675,000	840,533,000	811,316,000	777,319,000	690,802,000
EBITDA	-255,463,000	-213,978,000	-37,831,000	36,914,000	-54,320,000	-92,743,000
Return on Assets %	-.01%	-.02%	.00%	.01%	.03%	.02%
Return on Equity %	-.01%	-.05%	.03%	.03%	.16%	.12%
Debt to Equity	1.06%	0.812	2.654	2.172	1.602	1.538

CONTACT INFORMATION:
Phone: 415-982-9000 Fax: 415-982-9021
Toll-Free: 855-478-6786
Address: 595 Market St., 29/Fl, San Francisco, CA 94105 United States

STOCK TICKER/OTHER:
Stock Ticker: RUN
Employees: 11,383
Parent Company:

Exchange: NAS
Fiscal Year Ends: 12/31

SALARIES/BONUSES:
Top Exec. Salary: $313,846   Bonus: $1,500,000
Second Exec. Salary: $606,154   Bonus: $

OTHER THOUGHTS:
Estimated Female Officers or Directors: 4
Hot Spot for Advancement for Women/Minorities: Y

Sales, profits and employees may be estimates. Financial information, benefits and other data can change quickly and may vary from those stated here.

Suzlon Energy Limited

NAIC Code: 333611

www.suzlon.com

TYPES OF BUSINESS:
Wind Turbine Generator Manufacturing
Wind Turbine Generators
Wind Turbines
Product Design and Manufacture
Manufacturing Facilities
Rotor Blades and Nacelles
Wind Energy Control Panels
Wind Energy Towers

BRANDS/DIVISIONS/AFFILIATES:
S111
S120
S128
S133
S88
S82
S66
S52

CONTACTS:
Note: Officers with more than one job title may be intentionally listed here more than once.

Ashwani Kumar, CEO
Vinod Tanti, COO
Himanshu Mody, CFO
JP Chalasani, Strategic Advisor - Project Mgmt..
Bernhard Telgmann, Pres.-Technology
Tulsi R. Tanti, Chmn.

GROWTH PLANS/SPECIAL FEATURES:

Suzlon Energy Limited is an Indian firm engaged in the manufacture, design, development and marketing of wind energy systems, specializing in wind turbine generators. Suzlon's product portfolio includes: the S111 wind turbine generator with a rotor diameter of 111.8 meters, and is designed for higher energy generation; the S120 wind turbine generator, built on a 2.1-megawatt (MW) platform; the S128 wind turbine generator, built on a 2.6 MW platform; and the S133 wind turbine generator, built on a 2.6 to 3.0 MW platform. Suzlon's classic fleet of turbines include the S97-2.1 MW series, the S88-2.1MW series; the S82-1.5MW series; the S66-1.25MW series; and the S52-600 kilowatt (KW) series. Suzlon's products are onshore, all of which help in reducing carbon emission by more than 39 million tons annually. The firm operates and maintains its products, managing each asset throughout the entire life cycle. The company, which operates in 17 countries, has an installed capacity of over 19,440 MW of wind energy. Suzlon maintains 14 manufacturing facilities spread across India and China (through a joint venture) that produce a range of rotor blades, nacelles and nacelle covers, control panels, tubular towers and generators. Its key research and development centers are located in Germany (Hamburg, Rostock, Berlin and Bochum), India (Pune, Vadodara and Chennai), Denmark (Aarhus) and the Netherlands (Hengelo).

FINANCIAL DATA:
Note: Data for latest year may not have been available at press time.

In U.S. $	2021	2020	2019	2018	2017	2016
Revenue	458,708,000	398,795,000	729,408,000	1,293,290,000	1,972,640,000	1,383,590,000
R&D Expense						
Operating Income						
Operating Margin %						
SGA Expense						
Net Income	14,118,600	-357,781,000	-220,922,000	-59,030,600	131,216,000	131,320,000
Operating Cash Flow						
Capital Expenditure						
EBITDA						
Return on Assets %						
Return on Equity %						
Debt to Equity						

CONTACT INFORMATION:
Phone: 91-20-4012-2000   Fax: 91-20-4012-2100
Toll-Free:
Address: One Earth, Magarpatta City, Hadapsar, Pune, 411028 India

STOCK TICKER/OTHER:
Stock Ticker: 532667
Employees: 7,500
Parent Company:

Exchange: Bombay
Fiscal Year Ends: 03/31

SALARIES/BONUSES:
Top Exec. Salary: $ Bonus: $
Second Exec. Salary: $ Bonus: $

OTHER THOUGHTS:
Estimated Female Officers or Directors: 2
Hot Spot for Advancement for Women/Minorities:

Sales, profits and employees may be estimates. Financial information, benefits and other data can change quickly and may vary from those stated here.

Swell Energy Inc

NAIC Code: 221114

www.swellenergy.com

TYPES OF BUSINESS:
Solar Electric Power Generation (Solar Energy)
Home Energy Battery
Energy Management Solutions
Smart Grid Solutions
Virtual Power Plant Programs
Smart Lithium-Ion Batteries

BRANDS/DIVISIONS/AFFILIATES:

CONTACTS:
Note: Officers with more than one job title may be intentionally listed here more than once.

Suleman Khan, CEO

GROWTH PLANS/SPECIAL FEATURES:

Swell Energy, Inc. is an energy management and smart grid solutions provider. The company's products and solutions help accelerate the adoption of distributed clean energy technologies by enabling customers to take control of their energy use and cost, achieve energy security and participate in the transactive grid. Swell Energy provides homeowners and businesses with financing and virtual power plant programs, and partners with local solar and solar storage companies for seamless installations. Swell's home battery product acts like a barrier between the home and the power grid. It plugs into current electrical systems to optimize daily energy use and to provide backup power through the home's solar panels during a grid failure. Swell specializes in next-generation smart, lithium-ion home batteries. Swell's virtual power plant programs provide a variety of grid service capabilities through projects in utility territories across Hawaii, California and New York, aiding utilities in their mandate to deliver cleaner energy to customers and reduce the grid's dependence on fossil fuel peak-demand plants. In November 2022, Swell Energy announced that it raised $120 million to further its virtual power plant programs. The round was led by SoftBank Vision Fund 2 and Greenbacker Development Opportunities Fund I LP, with participation from an Ares Infrastructure Opportunities fund and Ontario Power Generation Pension Fund.

FINANCIAL DATA:
Note: Data for latest year may not have been available at press time.

In U.S. $	2021	2020	2019	2018	2017	2016
Revenue						
R&D Expense						
Operating Income						
Operating Margin %						
SGA Expense						
Net Income						
Operating Cash Flow						
Capital Expenditure						
EBITDA						
Return on Assets %						
Return on Equity %						
Debt to Equity						

CONTACT INFORMATION:
Phone: 678 464-7266 Fax:
Toll-Free: 888 465-1784
Address: 1515 7th St., Ste. 049, Santa Monica, CA 90401 United States

STOCK TICKER/OTHER:
Stock Ticker: Private
Employees:
Parent Company:

Exchange:
Fiscal Year Ends:

SALARIES/BONUSES:
Top Exec. Salary: $ Bonus: $
Second Exec. Salary: $ Bonus: $

OTHER THOUGHTS:
Estimated Female Officers or Directors:
Hot Spot for Advancement for Women/Minorities:

Sales, profits and employees may be estimates. Financial information, benefits and other data can change quickly and may vary from those stated here.

Syncrude Canada Ltd

NAIC Code: 211111

www.syncrude.ca

TYPES OF BUSINESS:
Oil Sands Production
Crude Oil Production & Refining
Bitumen Refining & Treatment
Synthetic Crude Oil
Oil Sands Mining
Fluid Coking
Hydroprocessing
Re-blending

BRANDS/DIVISIONS/AFFILIATES:
Suncor Energy Inc
Imperial Oil Resources Limited
Sinopec Oil Sands Partnership
CNOOC Oil Sands Canada
Suncor Energy (Syncrude) Operating Inc
Syncrude Project

CONTACTS:
Note: Officers with more than one job title may be intentionally listed here more than once.

Mark Little, CEO
Andrew Rosser, Sr. VP-Oper.
Christian Matte, VP-Technical & Engineering Svcs.
Brian Schleckser, VP-Tech.
Ray Hansen, General Counsel
John McCall, VP-Technical & Oper. Support
Peter Read, VP-Strategic Planning
Kara Flynn, VP-Gov't & Public Affairs
Murray Jamieson, VP-Maintenance
Greg Fuhr, VP-Production-Mining
Jim Glenen, VP-Production-Extraction & Upgrading
Murray Jamieson, VP-Maintenance
Jerry McPherson, VP-Project Dev. & Execution

GROWTH PLANS/SPECIAL FEATURES:
Syncrude Canada Ltd. is a producer of crude oil from oil sands. The Syncrude Project produces low sulfur crude oil, a leading source of oil in Canada with cumulative production exceeding 3 billion barrels. Syncrude's production process incorporates oil sands surface mining, followed by water-based extraction of the raw oil, bitumen, from the sad, and then upgrading that bitumen into a high-quality, light, sweet crude oil through fluid coking, hydroprocessing, hydrotreating and re-blending. The company's crude oil is sent by pipeline to Edmonton area refineries and to pipeline terminals which ship it to refineries in Canada and the U.S. Once that product leaves Syncrude's plant site, transportation and marketing become the responsibilities of its joint venture participants. Syncrude has invested in research and development since its inception, with more than half of expenditures focused on environmental priorities such as reclamation research programs and collaborative efforts through Canada's Oil Sands Innovation Alliance. More than 5,600 hectares of land disturbed by Syncrude oil sands mining operations is permanently reclaimed or ready for re-vegetation. Syncrude Canada is a joint venture among Suncor Energy Inc., Imperial Oil Resources Limited, Sinopec Oil Sands Partnership, and CNOOC Oil Sands Canada. Suncore Energy owns the project, and Suncor Energy (Syncrude) Operating Inc. is the project operator.

FINANCIAL DATA:
Note: Data for latest year may not have been available at press time.

In U.S. $	2021	2020	2019	2018	2017	2016
Revenue	4,200,000,000	3,955,990,000	6,100,490,000	4,715,210,000	4,907,810,000	4,199,830,000
R&D Expense						
Operating Income						
Operating Margin %						
SGA Expense						
Net Income						
Operating Cash Flow						
Capital Expenditure						
EBITDA						
Return on Assets %						
Return on Equity %						
Debt to Equity						

CONTACT INFORMATION:
Phone: 780-790-5911   Fax: 780-790-6270
Toll-Free: 800-667-9494
Address: 150-6 Avenue SW, Calgary, AB T2P 3E3 Canada

STOCK TICKER/OTHER:
Stock Ticker: Joint Venture   Exchange:
Employees: 4,900   Fiscal Year Ends: 12/31
Parent Company:

SALARIES/BONUSES:
Top Exec. Salary: $ Bonus: $
Second Exec. Salary: $ Bonus: $

OTHER THOUGHTS:
Estimated Female Officers or Directors: 1
Hot Spot for Advancement for Women/Minorities:

Sales, profits and employees may be estimates. Financial information, benefits and other data can change quickly and may vary from those stated here.

Talbott's Biomass Energy Systems Ltd

NAIC Code: 332410

www.talbotts.co.uk

TYPES OF BUSINESS:
Boiler & Heater Manufacturing
Biomass-Fueled Heaters and Boilers
Biomass-Fueled Electrical Generators
Biofuels Technology
Biomass-to-Electricity Conversion
Product Design and Manufacture
Manufacturing Facilities
Wood Shredders and Dust Extraction Systems

BRANDS/DIVISIONS/AFFILIATES:
Talbott
UNTHA
Air Plants Dust Extraction
COMPTE.R

CONTACTS:
Note: Officers with more than one job title may be intentionally listed here more than once.

Mick Johnson, Managing Dir.

GROWTH PLANS/SPECIAL FEATURES:

Talbott's Biomass Energy Systems Ltd. is one of the U.K.'s leading manufacturers of biomass heaters and boilers for the conversion of biomass to electricity, as well as a leading biofuel specialist. Biomass is a renewable energy source, a biological material from living, or recently living organisms, including wood chips, pellets and wood waste. Biomass is defined by any product which is more than 90% organic matter. The company's Talbott brand of heating systems come fully automated or hand fired, producing either hot air or hot water. Biomass heating boilers save carbon emissions, proven to reduce CO2 emissions by up to 90%, compared with non-renewable sources such as oil or gas. Talbott's services include the manufacture, design, supply, installation and after sales servicing of its boiler products. In addition, Talbott's distributes the UNTHA brand of wood shredders, which are designed, produced and mounted to meet very high-quality requirements. The wood shredders are sturdy and comprise a powerful cutting system. Talbott's also offers a full range of engineered dust extraction systems manufactured by Air Plants Dust Extraction in the UK; and industrial biomass systems manufactured by COMPTE.R, which can be specified for use with food waste, agricultural residues and landfill waste as a fuel, with systems ranging in size up to 10 megawatts.

FINANCIAL DATA:
Note: Data for latest year may not have been available at press time.

In U.S. $	2021	2020	2019	2018	2017	2016
Revenue	7,082,500	5,114,990	5,146,290	3,826,740	4,682,870	4,445,950
R&D Expense						
Operating Income						
Operating Margin %						
SGA Expense						
Net Income	426,354	102,987	-23,721	255,140	309,649	-241,348
Operating Cash Flow						
Capital Expenditure						
EBITDA						
Return on Assets %						
Return on Equity %						
Debt to Equity						

CONTACT INFORMATION:
Phone: 44-01785-813772 Fax: 44-01785-256418
Toll-Free:
Address: Unit 13, Walton Industrial Estate, Beacon Rd., Stone, ST15 0NN United Kingdom

STOCK TICKER/OTHER:
Stock Ticker: Private
Employees: 37
Parent Company:

Exchange:
Fiscal Year Ends: 09/30

SALARIES/BONUSES:
Top Exec. Salary: $ Bonus: $
Second Exec. Salary: $ Bonus: $

OTHER THOUGHTS:
Estimated Female Officers or Directors: 1
Hot Spot for Advancement for Women/Minorities:

Tata Power Co Ltd

NAIC Code: 221112

www.tatapower.com

TYPES OF BUSINESS:
Electric Utility
Electricity Transmission & Distribution
Solar Modules
Solar Pumps
Microgrids
Electric Vehicle Solutions
Home Automation Solutions
Renewable Energy Generation

BRANDS/DIVISIONS/AFFILIATES:
Tata Group

GROWTH PLANS/SPECIAL FEATURES:
Tata Power Co Ltd is an Indian electric utility company within the Tata Group multinational conglomerate that builds, operates, and maintains power generation and distribution facilities. With the help of its seven key subsidiaries and numerous joint-venture companies, Tata Power generates Most of its revenue through the generation, transmission, distribution, and trading of electricity throughout India. Most of this energy is produced from thermal fuel sources, such as coal, oil, and gas. Additionally, Tata Power engages in the production of energy from hydroelectric and renewable sources, including multiple hydroelectric and wind power projects located throughout Africa. Its segment comprises Generation; Renewables; Transmission and Distribution; and Others.

CONTACTS:
Note: Officers with more than one job title may be intentionally listed here more than once.

Praveer Sinha, CEO
Ramesh Subramanyam, CFO
H.M. Mistry, Corp. Sec.
Sankaranarayanan Padmanabhan, Exec. Dir.-Oper.
Sowmyan Ramakrishnan, Exec. Dir.-Finance
Natarajan Chandrasekaran, Chmn.

FINANCIAL DATA:
Note: Data for latest year may not have been available at press time.

In U.S. $	2021	2020	2019	2018	2017	2016
Revenue	3,948,983,000	3,502,470,000	3,568,498,000	3,292,397,000	3,384,108,000	
R&D Expense						
Operating Income	521,815,700	639,402,200	516,798,700	496,385,600	512,408,400	
Operating Margin %	.13%	.18%	.14%	.15%	.15%	
SGA Expense	27,578,070	25,048,670	22,989,080	28,845,220	26,708,360	
Net Income	138,292,700	124,799,300	289,027,500	295,419,700	109,977,400	
Operating Cash Flow	1,023,674,000	904,710,800	561,054,600	780,636,500	860,410,700	
Capital Expenditure	409,192,400	273,034,200	438,685,300	436,741,100	407,534,000	
EBITDA	1,045,425,000	1,143,593,000	1,231,257,000	1,053,579,000	805,241,100	
Return on Assets %	.01%	.01%	.03%	.03%	.01%	
Return on Equity %	.05%	.04%	.13%	.15%	.06%	
Debt to Equity	1.49%	1.834	1.701	1.365	1.726	

CONTACT INFORMATION:
Phone: 91 2266658282 Fax: 91 2266658282
Toll-Free:
Address: 24 Homi Mody St., Bombay House, Mumbai, Maharashtra 400 001 India

STOCK TICKER/OTHER:
Stock Ticker: TAATF   Exchange: PINX
Employees: 3,156   Fiscal Year Ends: 03/31
Parent Company: Tata Group

SALARIES/BONUSES:
Top Exec. Salary: $206,265   Bonus: $
Second Exec. Salary: $ Bonus: $

OTHER THOUGHTS:
Estimated Female Officers or Directors:
Hot Spot for Advancement for Women/Minorities:

Sales, profits and employees may be estimates. Financial information, benefits and other data can change quickly and may vary from those stated here.

Teledyne Technologies Inc

NAIC Code: 334511

www.teledyne.com

TYPES OF BUSINESS:
Defense Electronics and Instrumentation
Systems Engineering Solutions
Aerospace Engines & Components
Energy Systems

BRANDS/DIVISIONS/AFFILIATES:
Teledyne Scientific Company
Teledyne Optech Inc
Teledyne Brown Engineering Inc
FLIR Systems Inc

GROWTH PLANS/SPECIAL FEATURES:
Teledyne Technologies Inc sells technologies for industrial markets. Roughly a fourth of Teledyne's revenue comes from contracts with the United States government. The firm operates in four segments: instrumentation, digital imaging, aerospace and defense electronics, and engineered systems. The instrumentation segment contributes the largest proportion of revenue and provides monitoring instruments primarily for marine and environmental applications. The digital imaging segment includes image sensors and cameras for industrial, government, and medical customers. The aerospace and defense electronics segment provides electronic components and communication products for aircraft. The engineered systems segment provides solutions for defense, space, environmental, and energy applications.

CONTACTS:
Note: Officers with more than one job title may be intentionally listed here more than once.

Aldo Pichelli, CEO
Susan Main, CFO
Robert Mehrabian, Chairman of the Board
Cynthia Belak, Chief Accounting Officer
Melanie Cibik, Chief Compliance Officer
Jason VanWees, Executive VP
Edwin Roks, Executive VP, Subsidiary
George Bobb, President, Divisional
Stephen Blackwood, Senior VP

FINANCIAL DATA:
Note: Data for latest year may not have been available at press time.

In U.S. $	2021	2020	2019	2018	2017	2016
Revenue	4,614,300,000	3,086,200,000	3,163,600,000	2,901,800,000	2,603,800,000	2,149,900,000
R&D Expense						
Operating Income	624,300,000	480,100,000	491,700,000	416,600,000	321,700,000	240,500,000
Operating Margin %	.14%	.16%	.16%	.14%	.12%	.11%
SGA Expense	1,067,800,000	662,000,000	715,100,000	694,200,000	658,100,000	579,900,000
Net Income	445,300,000	401,900,000	402,300,000	333,800,000	227,200,000	190,900,000
Operating Cash Flow	824,600,000	618,900,000	482,100,000	446,900,000	374,700,000	317,000,000
Capital Expenditure	101,600,000	71,400,000	88,400,000	86,800,000	58,500,000	87,600,000
EBITDA	1,009,800,000	601,200,000	606,600,000	532,400,000	433,100,000	351,800,000
Return on Assets %	.05%	.08%	.10%	.09%	.07%	.07%
Return on Equity %	.08%	.14%	.16%	.16%	.13%	.13%
Debt to Equity	.54%	0.211	0.276	0.274	0.549	0.332

CONTACT INFORMATION:
Phone: 805 373-4545   Fax: 310 893-1669
Toll-Free:
Address: 1049 Camino Dos Rios, Thousand Oaks, CA 91360 United States

STOCK TICKER/OTHER:
Stock Ticker: TDY
Employees: 10,670
Parent Company:

Exchange: NYS
Fiscal Year Ends: 12/31

SALARIES/BONUSES:
Top Exec. Salary: $943,077   Bonus: $
Second Exec. Salary: $817,308   Bonus: $

OTHER THOUGHTS:
Estimated Female Officers or Directors: 6
Hot Spot for Advancement for Women/Minorities: Y

Sales, profits and employees may be estimates. Financial information, benefits and other data can change quickly and may vary from those stated here.

Tennessee Valley Authority (TVA)

NAIC Code: 221112

www.tva.gov

TYPES OF BUSINESS:
Electric Utility
Power Generation
Electric Generation and Distribution
Hydroelectric Facilities
Nuclear Facilities
Gas Facilities
Wind and Solar Facilities
Coal Facilities

BRANDS/DIVISIONS/AFFILIATES:

CONTACTS: *Note: Officers with more than one job title may be intentionally listed here more than once.*
Jeffrey J. Lyash, CEO
Don Moul, COO
John M. Thomas, III, CFO
Sue Collins, Chief People Officer
Anda A. Ray, Environment & Sustainability Officer
Janet C. Herrin, Chief Admin. Officer
Ralph Rodgers, General Counsel
Kathy Black, Sr. VP-Comm.
John Hoskins, Treas.
Robin E. Manning, Chief External Relations Officer
William Kilbride, Chmn.

GROWTH PLANS/SPECIAL FEATURES:

Tennessee Valley Authority (TVA) is a government-owned corporation and the largest public power company in the U.S., providing electricity for more than 150 local power companies which serve 10 million people. TVA is active in almost all of Tennessee and parts of Mississippi, Kentucky, Alabama, Georgia, North Carolina and Virginia, as well as directly to 57 large industrial customers and federal installations. TVA's generating assets include: 29 conventional hydroelectric sites, one pumped-storage hydroelectric site, five coal-fired sites, three nuclear sites, nine combustion turbine gas sites, eight combined cycle gas sites, one co-generation unit and 14 solar energy sites. TVA's generation portfolio consists of 41% nuclear, 28% gas, 16% coal-fired, 12% hydro and 3% wind and solar power. The company's transmission system is comprised of 16,400 miles of high-voltage lines and 69 interconnections with neighboring electric systems.

TVA offers its employees medical, dental, disability, life, AD&D, long-term care and critical illness insurance; onsite fitness centers; flexible spending accounts; transportation assistance; an employee assistance program; pension; a 401(k); and tuition

FINANCIAL DATA: *Note: Data for latest year may not have been available at press time.*

In U.S. $	2021	2020	2019	2018	2017	2016
Revenue	10,503,000,000	10,249,000,000	11,318,000,000	11,233,000,000	10,739,000,000	10,616,000,000
R&D Expense						
Operating Income						
Operating Margin %						
SGA Expense						
Net Income	1,512,000,000	1,352,000,000	1,417,000,000	1,119,000,000	685,000,000	1,233,000,000
Operating Cash Flow						
Capital Expenditure						
EBITDA						
Return on Assets %						
Return on Equity %						
Debt to Equity						

CONTACT INFORMATION:
Phone: 865-632-2101   Fax: 865-633-0372
Toll-Free: 888-882-4967
Address: 400 W. Summit Hill Dr., Knoxville, TN 37902 United States

STOCK TICKER/OTHER:
Stock Ticker: Government-Owned
Employees: 6,000
Parent Company:

Exchange:
Fiscal Year Ends: 09/30

SALARIES/BONUSES:
Top Exec. Salary: $ Bonus: $
Second Exec. Salary: $ Bonus: $

OTHER THOUGHTS:
Estimated Female Officers or Directors: 3
Hot Spot for Advancement for Women/Minorities: Y

Sales, profits and employees may be estimates. Financial information, benefits and other data can change quickly and may vary from those stated here.

TerraForm Power Operating LLC

NAIC Code: 221114

www.terraform.com

TYPES OF BUSINESS:
Solar Electric Power Generation
Wind Electric Power Generation
Solar Power Generation
Renewable Power Operations

BRANDS/DIVISIONS/AFFILIATES:
Brookfield Asset Management Inc
Brookfield Renewable Partners LP

GROWTH PLANS/SPECIAL FEATURES:
TerraForm Power Operating, LLC acquires, owns and operates solar and wind assets in North America and Western Europe. The company owns and operates more than 4,200 megawatts (MWs) of high-quality solar and wind assets underpinned by long-term contracts. TerraForm Power is controlled by Brookfield Renewable Partners LP, the flagship listed renewable power company of Brookfield Asset Management, Inc.

CONTACTS:
Note: Officers with more than one job title may be intentionally listed here more than once.

John Stinebaugh, CEO
Kimiball Osmars, COO
Michael Tebbutt, CFO
William Fyfe, General Counsel

FINANCIAL DATA:
Note: Data for latest year may not have been available at press time.

In U.S. $	2021	2020	2019	2018	2017	2016
Revenue	1,280,000,000	1,118,857,000	941,240,000	766,569,984	610,470,976	654,556,032
R&D Expense						
Operating Income						
Operating Margin %						
SGA Expense						
Net Income		-64,679,000	-198,573,000	12,380,000	-170,918,000	-129,847,000
Operating Cash Flow						
Capital Expenditure						
EBITDA						
Return on Assets %						
Return on Equity %						
Debt to Equity						

CONTACT INFORMATION:
Phone: 646-992-2400 Fax:
Toll-Free:
Address: 200 Liberty St., Fl. 14, New York, NY 10281 United States

STOCK TICKER/OTHER:
Stock Ticker: Subsidiary Exchange:
Employees: 174 Fiscal Year Ends: 12/31
Parent Company: Brookfield Asset Management Inc

SALARIES/BONUSES:
Top Exec. Salary: $ Bonus: $
Second Exec. Salary: $ Bonus: $

OTHER THOUGHTS:
Estimated Female Officers or Directors:
Hot Spot for Advancement for Women/Minorities:

Sales, profits and employees may be estimates. Financial information, benefits and other data can change quickly and may vary from those stated here.

Plunkett Research, Ltd. 343

Tesla Inc
NAIC Code: 336111

www.teslamotors.com

TYPES OF BUSINESS:
Automobile Manufacturing, All-Electric
Battery Manufacturing
Lithium Ion Battery Storage Technologies
Energy Storage Systems
Automobile Manufacturing
Electric Vehicles

GROWTH PLANS/SPECIAL FEATURES:
Founded in 2003 and based in Palo Alto, California, Tesla is a vertically integrated sustainable energy company that also aims to transition the world to electric mobility by making electric vehicles. The company sells solar panels and solar roofs for energy generation plus batteries for stationary storage for residential and commercial properties including utilities. Tesla has multiple vehicles in its fleet, which include luxury and midsize sedans and crossover SUVs. The company also plans to begin selling more affordable sedans and small SUVs, a light truck, a semi truck, and a sports car. Global deliveries in 2021 were a little over 936,000 units.

BRANDS/DIVISIONS/AFFILIATES:
Model S
Model X
Model 3
Model Y
Roadster
Tesla Semi
Tesla Cybertruck
Gigafactory

CONTACTS:
Note: Officers with more than one job title may be intentionally listed here more than once.

Elon Musk, CEO
Zachary Kirkhorn, CFO
Robyn Denholm, Chairman of the Board
Vaibhav Taneja, Chief Accounting Officer
Andrew Baglino, Senior VP, Divisional

FINANCIAL DATA:
Note: Data for latest year may not have been available at press time.

In U.S. $	2021	2020	2019	2018	2017	2016
Revenue	53,823,000,000	31,536,000,000	24,578,000,000	21,461,000,000	11,759,000,000	7,000,132,000
R&D Expense	2,593,000,000	1,491,000,000	1,343,000,000	1,460,000,000	1,378,000,000	834,408,000
Operating Income	6,496,000,000	1,994,000,000	80,000,000	-253,000,000	-1,632,000,000	-667,340,000
Operating Margin %	.12%	.06%	.00%	-.01%	-.14%	-.10%
SGA Expense	4,517,000,000	3,145,000,000	2,646,000,000	2,835,000,000	2,477,000,000	1,432,189,000
Net Income	5,519,000,000	721,000,000	-862,000,000	-976,000,000	-1,962,000,000	-674,914,000
Operating Cash Flow	11,497,000,000	5,943,000,000	2,405,000,000	2,098,000,000	-61,000,000	-123,829,000
Capital Expenditure	8,014,000,000	3,242,000,000	1,437,000,000	2,319,000,000	4,081,000,000	1,440,471,000
EBITDA	9,625,000,000	4,224,000,000	2,174,000,000	1,559,000,000	-102,000,000	399,561,000
Return on Assets %	.10%	.02%	-.03%	-.03%	-.08%	-.04%
Return on Equity %	.21%	.05%	-.15%	-.21%	-.44%	-.23%
Debt to Equity	.23%	0.489	1.902	2.258	2.632	1.554

CONTACT INFORMATION:
Phone: 650 681-5000   Fax:
Toll-Free:
Address: 3500 Deer Creek Rd., Palo Alto, CA 94304 United States

STOCK TICKER/OTHER:
Stock Ticker: TSLA
Employees: 99,290
Parent Company:

Exchange: NAS
Fiscal Year Ends: 12/31

SALARIES/BONUSES:
Top Exec. Salary: $301,154   Bonus: $
Second Exec. Salary: $301,154   Bonus: $

OTHER THOUGHTS:
Estimated Female Officers or Directors: 1
Hot Spot for Advancement for Women/Minorities:

Sales, profits and employees may be estimates. Financial information, benefits and other data can change quickly and may vary from those stated here.

Toshiba Corporation

NAIC Code: 334413

www.toshiba.co.jp

TYPES OF BUSINESS:
Memory Chip Manufacturing
Infrastructure Systems
Digital Products
Electronic Devices
Power Systems
Retail
Identification
Semiconductor

BRANDS/DIVISIONS/AFFILIATES:

GROWTH PLANS/SPECIAL FEATURES:
Founded in 1875, Toshiba is Japan's largest semiconductor manufacturer and its second-largest diversified industrial conglomerate. After the accounting scandal in 2015, Toshiba reorganized into six major segments: energy systems and solutions; infrastructure systems and solutions; building solutions; retail and printing solutions; storage and electronic devices solutions; and digital solutions. Toshiba is the second-largest manufacturer of NAND flash memory with a market share of 16.5% in 2017, and it concentrates business resources in this area.

CONTACTS:
Note: Officers with more than one job title may be intentionally listed here more than once.

Nobuaki Kurumatani, CEO
Norio Sasaki, Vice Chmn.
Hidejiro Shimomitsu, Sr. Exec. VP
Hideo Kitamura, Sr. Exec. VP
Makoto Kubo, Sr. Exec. VP
Satoshi Tsunakawa, Chmn.

FINANCIAL DATA:
Note: Data for latest year may not have been available at press time.

In U.S. $	2021	2020	2019	2018	2017	2016
Revenue	21,091,420,000	23,408,130,000	25,505,050,000	27,259,390,000	27,923,270,000	
R&D Expense						
Operating Income	720,928,600	900,867,300	312,707,200	595,127,600	683,135,900	
Operating Margin %	.03%	.04%	.01%	.02%	.02%	
SGA Expense	4,966,005,000	5,437,307,000	5,970,956,000	6,065,442,000	6,419,256,000	
Net Income	787,074,600	-791,576,900	6,996,852,000	5,551,949,000	-6,668,207,000	
Operating Cash Flow	1,002,272,000	-981,576,600	862,163,100	258,030,900	926,437,700	
Capital Expenditure	960,895,200	933,377,500	954,570,000	1,380,428,000	1,248,032,000	
EBITDA	1,679,704,000	258,845,700	690,462,400	1,586,924,000	1,563,771,000	
Return on Assets %	.03%	-.03%	.23%	.18%	-.20%	
Return on Equity %	.11%	-.10%	.90%	6.99%		
Debt to Equity	.40%	0.306	0.053	0.499		

CONTACT INFORMATION:
Phone: 81 334572096   Fax: 81 354449202
Toll-Free:
Address: 1-1, Shibaura 1-chome, Minato-ku, Tokyo, 105-8001 Japan

STOCK TICKER/OTHER:
Stock Ticker: TOSBF
Employees: 128,697
Parent Company:

Exchange: PINX
Fiscal Year Ends: 03/31

SALARIES/BONUSES:
Top Exec. Salary: $ Bonus: $
Second Exec. Salary: $ Bonus: $

OTHER THOUGHTS:
Estimated Female Officers or Directors:
Hot Spot for Advancement for Women/Minorities:

Sales, profits and employees may be estimates. Financial information, benefits and other data can change quickly and may vary from those stated here.

TotalEnergies SE

NAIC Code: 211111

www.totalenergies.com

TYPES OF BUSINESS:
Oil & Gas Exploration & Production
Oil and Gas
Renewable Energy
Bioenergy
Exploration and Production
Electricity
Petrochemicals
Trading

BRANDS/DIVISIONS/AFFILIATES:
Hutchinson
Total SE

GROWTH PLANS/SPECIAL FEATURES:
TotalEnergies is an integrated oil and gas company that explores for, produces, and refines oil around the world. In 2021, it produced 1.5 million barrels of liquids and 7.2 billion cubic feet of natural gas per day. At year-end 2020, reserves stood at 12.1 billion barrels of oil equivalent, 45% of which are liquids. During 2021, it had LNG sales of 42 Mt. The company owns interests in refineries with capacity of nearly 1.8 million barrels a day, primarily in Europe, distributes refined products in 65 countries, and manufactures commodity and specialty chemicals. It also holds a 19% interest in Russian oil company Novatek. At year-end, its gross installed renewable power generation capacity was 10.3 GW.

CONTACTS:
Note: Officers with more than one job title may be intentionally listed here more than once.

Patrick Pouyanne, CEO
Yves-Louis Darricarrere, Pres., Exploration & Prod.
Jean-Jacques Guilbaud, Chief Admin. Officer
Patrick Pouyanne, Pres., Refining Chemicals

FINANCIAL DATA:
Note: Data for latest year may not have been available at press time.

In U.S. $	2021	2020	2019	2018	2017	2016
Revenue	184,634,000,000	119,704,000,000	176,249,000,000	184,106,000,000	149,099,000,000	127,925,000,000
R&D Expense						
Operating Income	23,925,000,000	-7,265,000,000	15,352,000,000	15,262,000,000	7,019,000,000	4,592,000,000
Operating Margin %	.13%	-.06%	.09%	.08%	.05%	.04%
SGA Expense						
Net Income	16,032,000,000	-7,242,000,000	11,267,000,000	11,446,000,000	8,631,000,000	6,196,000,000
Operating Cash Flow	30,410,000,000	14,803,000,000	24,685,000,000	24,703,000,000	22,319,000,000	16,521,000,000
Capital Expenditure	12,343,000,000	10,764,000,000	11,810,000,000	17,080,000,000	13,767,000,000	18,106,000,000
EBITDA	42,200,000,000	17,990,000,000	36,063,000,000	34,771,000,000	29,335,000,000	22,707,000,000
Return on Assets %	.06%	-.03%	.04%	.05%	.04%	.03%
Return on Equity %	.15%	-.07%	.10%	.10%	.08%	.06%
Debt to Equity	.44%	0.581	0.409	0.347	0.371	0.436

CONTACT INFORMATION:
Phone: 33 147444546 Fax: 33 147444944
Toll-Free:
Address: 2 Place Jean Millier, Courbevoie, 92400 France

STOCK TICKER/OTHER:
Stock Ticker: TTE
Employees: 101,309
Parent Company:

Exchange: NYS
Fiscal Year Ends: 12/31

SALARIES/BONUSES:
Top Exec. Salary: $ Bonus: $
Second Exec. Salary: $ Bonus: $

OTHER THOUGHTS:
Estimated Female Officers or Directors: 4
Hot Spot for Advancement for Women/Minorities: Y

Sales, profits and employees may be estimates. Financial information, benefits and other data can change quickly and may vary from those stated here.

Trane Technologies plc

NAIC Code: 333400

www.tranetechnologies.com/en

TYPES OF BUSINESS:
Refrigeration Systems & Controls
Heating Systems
Cooling Systems
Building Climate Controls
Energy Solutions
Transport Refrigeration Systems

GROWTH PLANS/SPECIAL FEATURES:
Trane Technologies manufactures and services commercial and residential HVAC systems and transportation refrigeration solutions under its prominent Trane, American Standard, and Thermo King brands. The $14 billion company generates approximately 70% of sales from equipment and 30% from parts and services. While the firm is domiciled in Ireland, North America accounts for over 70% of its revenue.

BRANDS/DIVISIONS/AFFILIATES:
Trane
Thermo King
Ingersoll Rand plc

CONTACTS:
Note: Officers with more than one job title may be intentionally listed here more than once.

Dave Regnery, CEO
Chris Kuehn, CFO
Paul Camuti, CTO
Marcia J. Avedon, Sr. VP-Human Resources
Steve Hagood, CIO
Robert L. Katz, General Counsel
Todd Wyman, Sr. VP-Global Oper.
Marcia J. Avedon, Sr. VP-Comm.
Didier Teirlinck, Sr. VP
Robert G. Zafari, Pres., Industrial Tech. Sector
John W. Conover, IV, Sr. VP
Gary Michel, Sr. VP
Michael W. Lamach, Chmn.
Venky Valluri, Chmn.
Todd Wyman, Sr. VP-Integrated Supply Chain

FINANCIAL DATA:
Note: Data for latest year may not have been available at press time.

In U.S. $	2021	2020	2019	2018	2017	2016
Revenue	14,136,400,000	12,454,700,000	13,075,900,000	12,343,800,000	14,197,600,000	13,508,900,000
R&D Expense						
Operating Income	2,023,300,000	1,532,800,000	1,670,100,000	1,512,100,000	1,665,300,000	1,603,200,000
Operating Margin %	.14%	.12%	.13%	.12%	.12%	.12%
SGA Expense	2,446,300,000	2,270,600,000	2,320,300,000	2,249,200,000	2,720,700,000	2,597,800,000
Net Income	1,423,400,000	854,900,000	1,410,900,000	1,337,600,000	1,302,600,000	1,476,200,000
Operating Cash Flow	1,588,300,000	1,435,000,000	1,919,500,000	1,407,800,000	1,523,500,000	1,521,900,000
Capital Expenditure	223,000,000	146,200,000	205,400,000	284,700,000	221,300,000	182,700,000
EBITDA	2,323,800,000	1,831,200,000	1,930,500,000	1,761,100,000	1,987,000,000	2,315,000,000
Return on Assets %	.08%	.04%	.07%	.07%	.07%	.09%
Return on Equity %	.22%	.13%	.20%	.19%	.19%	.24%
Debt to Equity	.72%	0.702	0.677	0.533	0.414	0.558

CONTACT INFORMATION:
Phone: 353 18707400
Fax:
Toll-Free:
Address: 170/175 Lakeview Dr., Airside Business Park, Dublin, 2 Ireland

STOCK TICKER/OTHER:
Stock Ticker: TT
Employees: 37,000
Parent Company:

Exchange: NYS
Fiscal Year Ends: 12/31

SALARIES/BONUSES:
Top Exec. Salary: $1,410,000   Bonus: $
Second Exec. Salary: $1,307,500   Bonus: $

OTHER THOUGHTS:
Estimated Female Officers or Directors: 3
Hot Spot for Advancement for Women/Minorities: Y

Tri Global Energy LLC

NAIC Code: 221115

www.triglobalenergy.com

TYPES OF BUSINESS:
Wind Electric Power Generation
Renewable Energy
Project Development
Renewable Energy Financing
Renewable Energy Project Construction
Renewable Energy Operations
Wind and Solar Energy
Energy Storage

BRANDS/DIVISIONS/AFFILIATES:

GROWTH PLANS/SPECIAL FEATURES:
Tri Global Energy, LLC was founded in 2009 and is a leader in the development of renewable energy sources. Tri Global comprises more than 8,700 megawatts (MW) of development projects in financing, construction or operations. The firm currently develops and owns utility-scale wind, solar and energy storage projects in Texas, Nebraska, Illinois, Indiana, Virginia, Pennsylvania and Wyoming. Tri Global has initiated renewable energy projects located on approximately one million acres of land with thousands of participating landowners and community investors. The firm's mission is to improve communities through local economic development generated by developing and commercializing renewable energy projects. Headquartered in Dallas, Texas, Tri Global has regional development offices in Lubbock, Texas; El Paso and Forreston, Illinois; and Reynolds and Hartford City, Indiana.

CONTACTS:
Note: Officers with more than one job title may be intentionally listed here more than once.

John B. Billingsley, Jr., CEO
Tom Carbone, Pres.
Henry Schopfer, CFO
Susie Lomelino, CMO
Ryan Nayar, Chief Legal Officer
Mike Kelly, Sr. VP
John B. Billingsley, Jr., Chmn.

FINANCIAL DATA:
Note: Data for latest year may not have been available at press time.

In U.S. $	2021	2020	2019	2018	2017	2016
Revenue						
R&D Expense						
Operating Income						
Operating Margin %						
SGA Expense						
Net Income						
Operating Cash Flow						
Capital Expenditure						
EBITDA						
Return on Assets %						
Return on Equity %						
Debt to Equity						

CONTACT INFORMATION:
Phone: 972 290-0825 Fax:
Toll-Free:
Address: 17300 North Dallas Pkwy, Ste. 2020, Dallas, TX 75248 United States

STOCK TICKER/OTHER:
Stock Ticker: Private Exchange:
Employees: Fiscal Year Ends:
Parent Company:

SALARIES/BONUSES:
Top Exec. Salary: $ Bonus: $
Second Exec. Salary: $ Bonus: $

OTHER THOUGHTS:
Estimated Female Officers or Directors:
Hot Spot for Advancement for Women/Minorities:

Sales, profits and employees may be estimates. Financial information, benefits and other data can change quickly and may vary from those stated here.

Trina Solar Co Ltd

NAIC Code: 334413A

www.trinasolar.com

TYPES OF BUSINESS:
Photovoltaic Cell Manufacturing
Smart Solar Solutions
Photovoltaic (PV) Solar Products
Solar Power Innovation
Solar Modules
Solar PV Project Development and Construction
Solar PV Operations and Management
Sales and Marketing

BRANDS/DIVISIONS/AFFILIATES:
Fortune Solar Holdings Limited

CONTACTS: Note: Officers with more than one job title may be intentionally listed here more than once.
Jifan Gao, CEO
Thomas Young, VP-Investor Rel.
Zhiguo Zhu, Sr. VP
Qi Lin, Pres., China Region
Jim Wang, Pres., European & American PV Systems
Mark Mendenhall, Pres., Trina Solar Americas

GROWTH PLANS/SPECIAL FEATURES:
Trina Solar Limited was founded in 1997, and is an integrated smart solar solutions provider in China, delivering photovoltaic (PV) products, applications and services. Through continuous innovation, the firm creates greater grid parity of PV power and renewable energy. Trina Solar has delivered more than 80 gigawatts (GW) of solar modules worldwide. In addition, the firm's downstream business includes solar PV project development, financing, design, construction, operations and management, and one-stop system integration solutions for customers. Trina Solar has connected over 5.5GW of solar power plants to the grid worldwide, and its cumulative shipments of PV modules exceeded 100GW in April 2022. Trina Solar markets its products to distributors, wholesalers and PV (photovoltaic) system integrators worldwide. The company's manufacturing capabilities are concentrated in Changzhou, China, but has production bases in Vietnam and Thailand. Trina Solar has regional headquarters in Singapore, Japan, Switzerland, United Arab Emirates and the USA; and global sales and office centers in Spain, Mexico, Chile, Italy, Germany, Australia, UAE, France, Colombia, Brazil and India, selling products in more than 100 countries. Trina Solar has an energy Internet of Things (IoT) industrial innovation center at its headquarters which partners with leading companies and research institutes to research new energy IoT and establish innovative systems such as new energy power generation and management, storage technology, smart terminals technology, and energy cloud. Fortune Solar Holdings Limited holds a controlling stake in Trina Solar.

FINANCIAL DATA: Note: Data for latest year may not have been available at press time.

In U.S. $	2021	2020	2019	2018	2017	2016
Revenue	7,030,000,000	4,506,970,000	3,337,410,000	3,800,000,000	3,675,000,000	3,500,000,000
R&D Expense						
Operating Income						
Operating Margin %						
SGA Expense						
Net Income	297,000,000	188,923,000	100,493,000			
Operating Cash Flow						
Capital Expenditure						
EBITDA						
Return on Assets %						
Return on Equity %						
Debt to Equity						

CONTACT INFORMATION:
Phone: 86 51985482008 Fax: 86 51985176023
Toll-Free:
Address: No. 2 Tian He Rd., Electronics Park, Changzhou, Changzhou, Jiangsu 213031 China

STOCK TICKER/OTHER:
Stock Ticker: 688599 Exchange: Shanghai
Employees: 14,130 Fiscal Year Ends: 12/31
Parent Company: Fortune Solar Holdings Limited

SALARIES/BONUSES:
Top Exec. Salary: $ Bonus: $
Second Exec. Salary: $ Bonus: $

OTHER THOUGHTS:
Estimated Female Officers or Directors: 1
Hot Spot for Advancement for Women/Minorities:

Sales, profits and employees may be estimates. Financial information, benefits and other data can change quickly and may vary from those stated here.

Trinity Solar Inc

NAIC Code: 221114

www.trinity-solar.com

TYPES OF BUSINESS:
Solar Electric Power Generation
Solar Panel Installation
Solar Electric Systems
Solar Financing
Solar System Monitoring and Maintenance
Solar System Sales

BRANDS/DIVISIONS/AFFILIATES:

GROWTH PLANS/SPECIAL FEATURES:
Trinity Solar, Inc. is a designer and integrator of solar electric systems primarily in the northeastern portion of the U.S. As of late-2022, the company has installed more than 77,000 systems. Trinity Solar provides turn-key solar power solutions, beginning with site evaluation and financial modeling. This first step outlines the customer's energy needs and gives an estimate of the cost of installation. Next, the company designs, installs and commissions the panels, taking on the responsibility of processing paperwork related to rebates, permits and utility interconnection. Special financing options are then arranged with the client as well as brokering services for Solar Renewable Energy Credits (SRECs). After installation, Trinity Solar monitors and maintains the systems under its five-year warranty. Trinity is headquartered in New Jersey, and serves the states of Connecticut, Delaware, Florida, Maryland, Massachusetts, New Jersey, New York, Pennsylvania and Rhode Island.

CONTACTS:
Note: Officers with more than one job title may be intentionally listed here more than once.

Tom Pollock, CEO
Tom Pollock, Pres.

FINANCIAL DATA:
Note: Data for latest year may not have been available at press time.

In U.S. $	2021	2020	2019	2018	2017	2016
Revenue	310,000,000	300,000,000	289,170,000	275,400,000	250,000,000	221,200,000
R&D Expense						
Operating Income						
Operating Margin %						
SGA Expense						
Net Income						
Operating Cash Flow						
Capital Expenditure						
EBITDA						
Return on Assets %						
Return on Equity %						
Debt to Equity						

CONTACT INFORMATION:
Phone: 732-780-3779 Fax:
Toll-Free: 877-786-7283
Address: 2211 Allenwood Rd., Wall, NJ 07719 United States

STOCK TICKER/OTHER:
Stock Ticker: Private
Employees: 1,600
Parent Company:

Exchange:
Fiscal Year Ends: 12/31

SALARIES/BONUSES:
Top Exec. Salary: $ Bonus: $
Second Exec. Salary: $ Bonus: $

OTHER THOUGHTS:
Estimated Female Officers or Directors:
Hot Spot for Advancement for Women/Minorities:

Sales, profits and employees may be estimates. Financial information, benefits and other data can change quickly and may vary from those stated here.

Ultralife Corporation

NAIC Code: 335911

www.ultralifecorporation.com

TYPES OF BUSINESS:
Batteries
Lithium Ion Batteries
Rechargers & Accessories
Standby Power Systems
Integrated Communications Systems

BRANDS/DIVISIONS/AFFILIATES:
Ultralife Batteries (UK) Ltd
Ultralife Batteries India Private Limited
ABLE New Energy Co
Ultralife Batteries
ABLE
Lithium Power
McDowell Research
AMTI

GROWTH PLANS/SPECIAL FEATURES:

Ultralife Corp provides products and services ranging from power solutions to communications and electronics systems to customers across the globe in the government and defense, medical, safety and security, energy, and industrial sectors. The company design, manufacture, install and maintain power and communications systems including rechargeable and non-rechargeable batteries, charging systems, communications and electronics systems and accessories, and custom-engineered systems. The company's segments include Battery and Energy Products, and Communications Systems. It generates maximum revenue from Battery and Energy Products segment.

Ultralife offers comprehensive benefits and retirement options.

CONTACTS: Note: Officers with more than one job title may be intentionally listed here more than once.

Michael Popielec, CEO
Philip Fain, CFO
Bradford Whitmore, Chairman of the Board

FINANCIAL DATA: Note: Data for latest year may not have been available at press time.

In U.S. $	2021	2020	2019	2018	2017	2016
Revenue	98,267,000	107,712,000	106,795,000	87,190,000	85,531,000	82,460,000
R&D Expense	6,826,000	5,947,000	6,805,000	4,508,000	4,737,000	5,946,000
Operating Income	35,000	5,701,000	7,368,000	6,555,000	6,476,000	3,763,000
Operating Margin %	.00%	.05%	.07%	.08%	.08%	.05%
SGA Expense	17,781,000	17,511,000	16,992,000	14,520,000	15,019,000	15,399,000
Net Income	-234,000	5,232,000	5,205,000	24,930,000	7,648,000	3,509,000
Operating Cash Flow	4,325,000	21,720,000	-2,970,000	10,886,000	7,270,000	7,653,000
Capital Expenditure	2,814,000	3,101,000	6,281,000	4,185,000	1,392,000	1,219,000
EBITDA	3,630,000	10,394,000	10,055,000	9,045,000	8,905,000	6,569,000
Return on Assets %	.00%	.04%	.04%	.23%	.08%	.04%
Return on Equity %	.00%	.05%	.05%	.27%	.10%	.05%
Debt to Equity	.16%		0.144			

CONTACT INFORMATION:
Phone: 315 332-7100   Fax: 315 331-7800
Toll-Free: 800-332-5000
Address: 2000 Technology Pkwy., Newark, NY 14513 United States

STOCK TICKER/OTHER:
Stock Ticker: ULBI   Exchange: NAS
Employees: 560   Fiscal Year Ends: 12/31
Parent Company:

SALARIES/BONUSES:
Top Exec. Salary: $531,761   Bonus: $
Second Exec. Salary: $338,713   Bonus: $

OTHER THOUGHTS:
Estimated Female Officers or Directors: 1
Hot Spot for Advancement for Women/Minorities:

Umicore SA

NAIC Code: 333517

www.umicore.com

TYPES OF BUSINESS:
Precious Metals Products & Services
Zinc Smelting & Mining
Thin-Film Products
Battery Materials & Recycling
Electro-Optic Materials
Emissions Control Catalysts

BRANDS/DIVISIONS/AFFILIATES:

GROWTH PLANS/SPECIAL FEATURES:
Umicore SA offers solutions to treat pollutants, metals, and other industrial materials. It generates the majority of revenue from cleaning technologies, including emission control devices, components for rechargeable batteries, and recycling solutions. The company provides automotive emission systems for light and heavy-duty vehicles and transforms pollutants into harmless gases. Umicore has three business segments: catalysis, recycling, and energy & surface technologies. Recycling solutions apply to battery components, metals, platinum engineered materials, and other applications. Approximately half of the total sales derive from Europe, but the company has a worldwide presence and capabilities to reach many different regions.

CONTACTS:
Note: Officers with more than one job title may be intentionally listed here more than once.

Mathias Miedreich, CEO
Filip Platteeuw, CFO
Wilfried Muller, Sr. VP-R&D
Geraldine Nolens, Sr. VP-Legal
Guy Beke, Sr. VP-Zinc Chemicals
Michel Cauwe, Sr. VP-Thin Film Products
Luc Gellens, Sr. VP-Umicore Japan
Ralf Drieselmann, Sr. VP-Precious Metals Management
Thomas Leysen, Chmn.
Bernhard Fuchs, Sr. VP-Umicor Greater China

FINANCIAL DATA:
Note: Data for latest year may not have been available at press time.

In U.S. $	2021	2020	2019	2018	2017	2016
Revenue	23,555,760,000	20,280,770,000	17,122,590,000	13,432,370,000	11,699,580,000	10,227,040,000
R&D Expense						
Operating Income	888,748,200	384,402,200	438,756,500	474,963,000	316,259,800	271,005,800
Operating Margin %	.04%	.02%	.03%	.04%	.03%	.03%
SGA Expense	56,621,320	40,743,460	40,489,830	33,107,120	35,576,840	27,733,870
Net Income	606,127,200	127,824,000	281,824,800	310,412,500	207,549,200	128,013,900
Operating Cash Flow	1,232,488,000	517,367,300	469,248,000	-26,733,060	150,134,600	376,747,300
Capital Expenditure	407,793,000	426,505,900	575,662,200	487,428,100	368,868,000	281,815,000
EBITDA	1,129,122,000	516,861,100	677,183,000	666,019,300	516,999,100	430,808,800
Return on Assets %	.07%	.02%	.04%	.06%	.05%	.03%
Return on Equity %	.22%	.05%	.11%	.14%	.12%	.07%
Debt to Equity	.56%	0.669	0.446	0.273	0.387	0.016

CONTACT INFORMATION:
Phone: 32 22277111 Fax: 32 22277900
Toll-Free:
Address: Rue du Marais 31, Brussels, B-1000 Belgium

STOCK TICKER/OTHER:
Stock Ticker: UMICY   Exchange: PINX
Employees: 13,139   Fiscal Year Ends: 12/31
Parent Company:

SALARIES/BONUSES:
Top Exec. Salary: $ Bonus: $
Second Exec. Salary: $ Bonus: $

OTHER THOUGHTS:
Estimated Female Officers or Directors: 3
Hot Spot for Advancement for Women/Minorities: Y

Uniper SE
NAIC Code: 221112

www.uniper.energy

TYPES OF BUSINESS:
Fossil Fuel Electric Power Generation
Power Generation
Energy Sales
Trading
Energy Storage

BRANDS/DIVISIONS/AFFILIATES:
Uniper Energy DMCC

GROWTH PLANS/SPECIAL FEATURES:
Uniper SE is a Germany-based energy generation and energy trading company. The firm operates through three segments: European Generation, Global Commodities, and Russian Power Generation. The European Generation segment generates power and owns coal, gas, oil and combined gas and steam power plants, hydroelectric power plants, nuclear power stations in Sweden, a biomass plant in France, as well as solar and wind power facilities; the Global Commodities segment bundles the energy trading activities, and the Russian Power Generation segment comprises power generation business of Uniper Group in Russia. The Global Commodities segment is responsible for a large majority of revenue.

CONTACTS: Note: Officers with more than one job title may be intentionally listed here more than once.
Andreas Schierenbeck, CEO
David Bryson, COO
Sascha Bibert, CFO

FINANCIAL DATA: Note: Data for latest year may not have been available at press time.

In U.S. $	2021	2020	2019	2018	2017	2016
Revenue	160,578,600,000	49,910,390,000	64,439,810,000	89,909,620,000	70,740,420,000	65,890,100,000
R&D Expense						
Operating Income	3,958,205,000	-203,687,900	-520,971,000	-195,853,800	346,661,200	-3,348,120,000
Operating Margin %	.02%	.00%	-.01%	.00%	.00%	-.05%
SGA Expense						
Net Income	-4,082,572,000	388,769,700	597,354,000	-392,686,800	-642,400,400	-3,150,308,000
Operating Cash Flow	3,545,933,000	1,215,273,000	912,678,600	1,215,273,000	1,356,287,000	2,138,723,000
Capital Expenditure	693,322,400	709,969,900	641,421,100	624,773,500	807,896,800	698,218,700
EBITDA	-3,107,220,000	1,926,222,000	2,883,947,000	1,380,769,000	1,165,330,000	334,910,000
Return on Assets %	-.05%	.01%	.01%	-.01%	-.01%	-.06%
Return on Equity %	-.49%	.04%	.05%	-.03%	-.05%	-.24%
Debt to Equity						0.194

CONTACT INFORMATION:
Phone: 49-211-4579-4400   Fax: 49-211-4579-2082
Toll-Free:
Address: Holzstrasse 6, Dusseldorf, 40221 Germany

STOCK TICKER/OTHER:
Stock Ticker: UNPRF   Exchange: PINX
Employees: 11,494   Fiscal Year Ends: 12/31
Parent Company:

SALARIES/BONUSES:
Top Exec. Salary: $ Bonus: $
Second Exec. Salary: $ Bonus: $

OTHER THOUGHTS:
Estimated Female Officers or Directors:
Hot Spot for Advancement for Women/Minorities:

Sales, profits and employees may be estimates. Financial information, benefits and other data can change quickly and may vary from those stated here.

Plunkett Research, Ltd. 353

United Renewable Energy LLC

NAIC Code: 334413A

u-renew.com

TYPES OF BUSINESS:
Photovoltaic Cell Manufacturing
Solar Modules
Solar Cells
Solar Panels
Energy Storage Systems
Product Design and Production
Product Installation and Maintenance
Community Solar Farm Projects

BRANDS/DIVISIONS/AFFILIATES:
URE

GROWTH PLANS/SPECIAL FEATURES:
United Renewable Energy, LLC develops, designs, builds and maintains solar photovoltaic (PV) and energy storage systems for utilities, industrial and commercial companies, as well as independent power producers and electrical membership cooperatives. United Renewable's operations span project development, engineering, procurement, construction, operations and maintenance. The company's innovative battery solutions are marketed under the URE brand, with applications including load shifting, peak shaving, frequency regulation, microgrid application, renewable smoothing and more. United Renewable's community solar offerings enable homeowners, renters and businesses to obtain power from a clean, renewable energy source without the long-term commitment of installing solar panels. Solar energy generated through URE community solar farms appears as a line item on the member's electric bill, as if the solar panels were installed on their own roof. To date, URE community solar farms are located in New York and Georgia, with additional community solar projects under development (as of September 2022).

CONTACTS:
Note: Officers with more than one job title may be intentionally listed here more than once.

William Silva, CEO
Wen-Whe Pan, Pres.
Guiwu Huang, Asst. Gen. Mgr.-R&D
J. M. Lee, VP-Eng. Div.
David W.S. Liu, VP-Admin.
Sam Yang, Dir.-Mfg. Department
Stone Liu, VP-Production Div.
Jason Juang, VP-Intl. Bus. Div.
David W.S. Liu, VP-Purchasing

FINANCIAL DATA:
Note: Data for latest year may not have been available at press time.

In U.S. $	2021	2020	2019	2018	2017	2016
Revenue	449,225,820	444,955,000	586,839,528	424,017,000	344,886,000	511,308,000
R&D Expense						
Operating Income						
Operating Margin %						
SGA Expense						
Net Income	-40,456,080	-219,162,000	-13,928,892	-15,140,100	-152,225,000	-208,863,000
Operating Cash Flow						
Capital Expenditure						
EBITDA						
Return on Assets %						
Return on Equity %						
Debt to Equity						

CONTACT INFORMATION:
Phone: 678-881-0014   Fax:
Toll-Free:
Address: 1230 Samples Industrial Dr., Ste. 100, Cumming, GA 30041 United States

STOCK TICKER/OTHER:
Stock Ticker: 3576
Employees: 3,127
Parent Company:

Exchange: TWSE
Fiscal Year Ends: 12/31

SALARIES/BONUSES:
Top Exec. Salary: $ Bonus: $
Second Exec. Salary: $ Bonus: $

OTHER THOUGHTS:
Estimated Female Officers or Directors: 1
Hot Spot for Advancement for Women/Minorities:

Sales, profits and employees may be estimates. Financial information, benefits and other data can change quickly and may vary from those stated here.

UNS Energy Corporation

NAIC Code: 221112

www.uns.com

TYPES OF BUSINESS:
Utilities-Electricity & Natural Gas
Utilities
Electric Power
Natural Gas

BRANDS/DIVISIONS/AFFILIATES:
Fortis Inc
Tucson Electric Power Company
UniSource Energy Services Inc

GROWTH PLANS/SPECIAL FEATURES:
UNS Energy Corporation is a public utility holding company with operations in Arizona. The firm is the parent company to two energy providing subsidiaries: Tucson Electric Power Company (TEP) and UniSource Energy Services, Inc. (UES). TEP serves approximately 432,000 customers with energy in southern Arizona, while UES provides natural gas and electric service for approximately 256,000 customers in northern and southern Arizona. UNS Energy is a wholly-owned subsidiary of Fortis, Inc., which is the largest investor-owned electric and gas distribution utility in Canada.

CONTACTS: Note: Officers with more than one job title may be intentionally listed here more than once.
Susan Gray, CEO
Todd C. Hixon, Sr. VP
Frank P. Marino, CFO
Erik Bakken, VP-System Oper. & Energy Resources
Gail Zody-Serbia, VP-Human Resources
Cynthia Garcia, CIO
Todd C. Hixon, General Counsel
Kentton C. Grant, VP-Finance & Rates
Philip J. Dion, VP-Public Policy
Mark Mansfield, VP-Generation
Herlinda H. Kennedy, Corp. Sec.
Karen G. Kissinger, Chief Compliance Officer
Louise Francesconi, Chmn.

FINANCIAL DATA: Note: Data for latest year may not have been available at press time.

In U.S. $	2021	2020	2019	2018	2017	2016
Revenue	2,334,000,000	1,767,950,000	1,692,710,000	1,614,010,000	1,656,910,000	1,486,310,000
R&D Expense						
Operating Income						
Operating Margin %						
SGA Expense						
Net Income						
Operating Cash Flow						
Capital Expenditure						
EBITDA						
Return on Assets %						
Return on Equity %						
Debt to Equity						

CONTACT INFORMATION:
Phone: 520-571-4000 Fax: 520-884-3602
Toll-Free:
Address: 88 E. Broadway, Tucson, AZ 85702 United States

STOCK TICKER/OTHER:
Stock Ticker: Subsidiary
Employees: 2,028
Parent Company: Fortis Inc

Exchange:
Fiscal Year Ends: 12/31

SALARIES/BONUSES:
Top Exec. Salary: $ Bonus: $
Second Exec. Salary: $ Bonus: $

OTHER THOUGHTS:
Estimated Female Officers or Directors: 5
Hot Spot for Advancement for Women/Minorities: Y

Sales, profits and employees may be estimates. Financial information, benefits and other data can change quickly and may vary from those stated here.

Vattenfall AB

NAIC Code: 221112

group.vattenfall.com

TYPES OF BUSINESS:
Utilities-Electricity & Natural Gas
Electricity Supplier
Natural Gas
Power Production and Distribution
Energy Sales
Hydro Power
Nuclear Power
Coal Power

BRANDS/DIVISIONS/AFFILIATES:

CONTACTS: *Note: Officers with more than one job title may be intentionally listed here more than once.*
Anna Borg, CEO
Kerstin Ahlfont, CFO
Christian Barthelemy, Sr. VP-Human Resources
Tuomo Hatakka, Head-Prod.
Anne Gynnerstedt, Head-Legal Affairs
Torbjorn Wahlborg, Head-Nuclear Power
Peter Smink, Head-Sustainable Energy Projects
Stefan Dohler, Sr. VP-Asset Optimization & Trading
Mats Granryd, Chmn.
Anders Dahle, Sr. VP-Dist. & Sales

GROWTH PLANS/SPECIAL FEATURES:
Vattenfall AB generates, distributes, trades and sells electricity and gas used for powering residential and commercial areas. Most of the firm's electricity sales are made to industrial customers and energy companies, with primary markets occurring in Sweden, Germany, Netherlands, Denmark and the U.K. Vattenfall operates through five business divisions: power production, electricity distribution, sales of electricity and heat and gas, district heating, and energy services and decentralized generation. The power production division produces electricity from many types of energy sources, including hydro, nuclear, coal, natural gas, wind, solar, biomass and waste. The electricity distribution division conducts electricity grid operations in Sweden and the U.K., and its networks enable customers to feed self-generated electricity into the grid. The sales of electricity, heat and gas division sells these products to consumer and business customers. The district heating division produces and distributes district heating, supplying households and industries in metropolitan areas. In partnership with cities and regions, this division is engaged in the transformation of fossil-free heating solutions, such as by integrating surplus or waste heat from third parties in its district heating networks. Last, the energy services and decentralized generation division offers energy services, including battery storage, network services, charging solutions for electric vehicles, solar panels, heat pumps and smart meters. Vattenfall's fossil-free research and development, innovations and engagement spans fossil-free steel, aviation fuel, plastic, hydrogen, electric driving, home energy solutions, wind energy and heat. In mid-2022, Vattenfall and St1 formed a partnership to develop a fossil-free value chain for the production of synthetic electro fuel via offshore wind.

FINANCIAL DATA: *Note: Data for latest year may not have been available at press time.*

In U.S. $	2021	2020	2019	2018	2017	2016
Revenue	16,745,930,000	19,391,900,000	17,828,700,000	17,450,300,000	16,463,000,000	17,479,861,119
R&D Expense						
Operating Income						
Operating Margin %						
SGA Expense						
Net Income	704,630,700	941,962,000	2,689,410,000	1,336,060,000	1,164,620,000	-272,587,573
Operating Cash Flow						
Capital Expenditure						
EBITDA						
Return on Assets %						
Return on Equity %						
Debt to Equity						

CONTACT INFORMATION:
Phone: 46-8-739-5000 Fax: 46-8-17-8506
Toll-Free:
Address: Evenemangsgatan 13C, Solna, SE-169 79 Sweden

STOCK TICKER/OTHER:
Stock Ticker: Government-Owned
Employees: 19,000
Parent Company:

Exchange:
Fiscal Year Ends: 12/31

SALARIES/BONUSES:
Top Exec. Salary: $ Bonus: $
Second Exec. Salary: $ Bonus: $

OTHER THOUGHTS:
Estimated Female Officers or Directors: 2
Hot Spot for Advancement for Women/Minorities: Y

Sales, profits and employees may be estimates. Financial information, benefits and other data can change quickly and may vary from those stated here.

Veolia Environnement SA

NAIC Code: 221310

www.veolia.com

TYPES OF BUSINESS:
Water & Sewage Treatment
Water Treatment Plant Engineering & Construction
HVAC Installations Management
Energy Services
Public Transportation Services
Waste Management & Recycling

BRANDS/DIVISIONS/AFFILIATES:
Waste2Glass

GROWTH PLANS/SPECIAL FEATURES:
Veolia is the largest water company globally and a leading player in France. It is also involved in waste management with a significant exposure to France, the United Kingdom, Germany, the United States, and Australia. The third pillar of the group is energy services, giving the group significant exposure to Central Europe. Veolia started to refocus its activities in 2011, leading to the exit of almost half of its countries and of its transport activity, which should be completed within the next few years.

CONTACTS: Note: Officers with more than one job title may be intentionally listed here more than once.
Antoine Frerot, CEO
Estelle Brachlianoff, COO
Claude Laruelle, CFO
Jean-Marie Lambert, Sr. Exec. VP-Human Resources
Helman le Pas de Secheval, General Counsel
Franck Lacroix, Sr. Exec. VP-Energy Svcs. Div.
Estelle Brachlianoff, Dir.-Northern Europe
Regis Calmels, Dir.-Asia Zone
Philippe Guitard, Dir.-Central & Eastern Zone
Antoine Frerot, Chmn.
Jean-Michel Herrewyn, Dir.-Global Enterprises

FINANCIAL DATA: Note: Data for latest year may not have been available at press time.

In U.S. $	2021	2020	2019	2018	2017	2016
Revenue	27,917,090,000	25,470,680,000	26,625,050,000	25,413,300,000	24,303,880,000	23,685,580,000
R&D Expense						
Operating Income	1,396,437,000	968,692,700	1,444,911,000	1,444,422,000	1,307,716,000	1,330,141,000
Operating Margin %	.05%	.04%	.05%	.06%	.05%	.06%
SGA Expense	2,832,633,000	2,649,999,000	2,710,616,000	2,703,076,000	2,758,894,000	2,772,506,000
Net Income	395,918,400	86,959,070	611,945,100	431,465,900	389,455,200	375,157,900
Operating Cash Flow	3,081,955,000	2,668,508,000	3,023,786,000	2,781,417,000	2,401,363,000	2,502,913,000
Capital Expenditure						
EBITDA	3,365,257,000	2,845,853,000	3,624,862,000	3,093,510,000	2,616,606,000	2,657,246,000
Return on Assets %	.01%	.00%	.02%	.01%	.01%	.01%
Return on Equity %	.04%	.01%	.10%	.06%	.04%	.05%
Debt to Equity	.96%	1.589	1.727	0.265	1.189	0.994

CONTACT INFORMATION:
Phone: 33 171750000 Fax: 33 171751045
Toll-Free:
Address: 30, rue Madeleine Vionnet, Aubervilliers, 93300 France

SALARIES/BONUSES:
Top Exec. Salary: $881,342 Bonus: $665,211
Second Exec. Salary: $ Bonus: $

STOCK TICKER/OTHER:
Stock Ticker: VEOEF Exchange: PINX
Employees: 171,495 Fiscal Year Ends: 12/31
Parent Company:

OTHER THOUGHTS:
Estimated Female Officers or Directors: 1
Hot Spot for Advancement for Women/Minorities:

Sales, profits and employees may be estimates. Financial information, benefits and other data can change quickly and may vary from those stated here.

Vestas Wind Systems A/S

NAIC Code: 333611

www.vestas.com

TYPES OF BUSINESS:
Wind Turbine Manufacturing
Turbine Installation, Repair & Maintenance Services
Online Turbine Operating Systems
Turbine Technology
Plant Solutions and Services
Plant Design
Plant Integration
Performance Options

BRANDS/DIVISIONS/AFFILIATES:
EnVentus

GROWTH PLANS/SPECIAL FEATURES:
Vestas is a leading manufacturer of wind turbines with the highest installed capacity under service in the world. The firm operates two business segments: power solutions and services. The power solutions segment designs, manufactures, and installs onshore and offshore wind turbines. The services segment performs operating and maintenance service work on wind turbines. The U.S. accounted for approximately 19% of revenue in 2021.

CONTACTS:
Note: Officers with more than one job title may be intentionally listed here more than once.

Henrik Andersen, CEO
Tommy Rahbek Nielsen, COO
Markia Fredriksson, CFO
Christian Venderby, Chief Sales Officer
Anders Vedel, Chief Turbines Officer
Anders Vedel, CTO
Bert Nordberg, Chmn.

FINANCIAL DATA:
Note: Data for latest year may not have been available at press time.

In U.S. $	2021	2020	2019	2018	2017	2016
Revenue	15,263,860,000	14,511,780,000	11,895,180,000	9,923,910,000	9,746,663,000	10,024,770,000
R&D Expense	356,453,900	259,506,200	262,444,000	224,252,600	230,128,200	222,294,000
Operating Income	391,707,600	731,513,900	983,185,900	939,118,800	1,204,501,000	1,391,541,000
Operating Margin %	.03%	.05%	.08%	.09%	.12%	.14%
SGA Expense	719,762,600	512,157,600	478,862,500	433,816,100	487,675,900	468,090,500
Net Income	163,537,900	749,140,700	689,405,200	669,819,900	875,466,400	944,994,400
Operating Cash Flow	975,351,700	727,596,700	805,938,200	999,833,500	1,591,312,000	2,135,785,000
Capital Expenditure	857,839,600	673,737,000	759,912,600	594,416,200	480,821,000	478,862,500
EBITDA	1,271,091,000	1,623,628,000	1,470,862,000	1,361,184,000	1,594,250,000	1,682,384,000
Return on Assets %	.01%	.05%	.05%	.06%	.09%	.10%
Return on Equity %	.04%	.19%	.22%	.22%	.28%	.32%
Debt to Equity	.15%	0.186	0.201	0.161	0.16	0.155

CONTACT INFORMATION:
Phone: 45 97300000 Fax: 45 97300001
Toll-Free:
Address: Hedeager 42, Aarhus, 8200 Denmark

STOCK TICKER/OTHER:
Stock Ticker: VWSYF
Employees: 29,427
Parent Company:

Exchange: PINX
Fiscal Year Ends: 12/31

SALARIES/BONUSES:
Top Exec. Salary: $ Bonus: $
Second Exec. Salary: $ Bonus: $

OTHER THOUGHTS:
Estimated Female Officers or Directors: 3
Hot Spot for Advancement for Women/Minorities: Y

Sales, profits and employees may be estimates. Financial information, benefits and other data can change quickly and may vary from those stated here.

VINCI SA

NAIC Code: 237310

www.vinci.com

TYPES OF BUSINESS:
Highway, Street, and Bridge Construction
Infrastructure Management
Information & Energy Technologies
Commercial Construction
Engineering Services
Highway Construction
Airport Management & Support Services
Power Transmission Services

BRANDS/DIVISIONS/AFFILIATES:
VINCI Concessions SA
VINCI Contracting LLC
VINCI Autoroutes
VINCI Airports
VINCI Energies
Eurovia
VINCI Construction

GROWTH PLANS/SPECIAL FEATURES:
Vinci is one of the world's largest investors in transport infrastructure. Significant concession assets include 4,400 kilometers of toll roads in France and 45 airports across 12 countries, making Vinci the world's second-largest airport operator in terms of managed passenger numbers. The concession's business contributes less than one fifth of group revenue but the majority of operating profit. Vinci's contracting business is made up of three divisions, offering a broad variety of engineering and construction services.

CONTACTS:
Note: Officers with more than one job title may be intentionally listed here more than once.

Xavier Huillard, CEO
Christian Labeyrie, CFO
Jocelyne Vassoille, VP-Human Resources

FINANCIAL DATA:
Note: Data for latest year may not have been available at press time.

In U.S. $	2021	2020	2019	2018	2017	2016
Revenue	49,188,680,000	43,203,380,000	47,935,210,000	43,434,490,000	40,225,420,000	37,876,160,000
R&D Expense						
Operating Income	4,298,011,000	2,552,954,000	5,316,451,000	4,652,506,000	4,264,716,000	4,012,065,000
Operating Margin %	.09%	.06%	.11%	.11%	.11%	.11%
SGA Expense	5,418,295,000	4,628,025,000	5,272,383,000	5,388,917,000	5,231,255,000	4,885,573,000
Net Income	2,543,161,000	1,216,252,000	3,192,417,000	2,921,159,000	2,690,052,000	2,453,068,000
Operating Cash Flow	7,644,173,000	6,536,620,000	6,943,016,000	5,035,401,000	4,191,271,000	4,255,902,000
Capital Expenditure	2,020,232,000	2,115,221,000	2,346,328,000	2,037,858,000	1,880,196,000	1,498,281,000
EBITDA	7,601,085,000	5,661,153,000	8,459,903,000	7,142,787,000	6,663,925,000	6,069,509,000
Return on Assets %	.03%	.01%	.04%	.04%	.04%	.04%
Return on Equity %	.12%	.06%	.16%	.16%	.16%	.16%
Debt to Equity	1.16%	1.337	1.357	1.022	0.934	0.988

CONTACT INFORMATION:
Phone: 33 157986100 Fax:
Toll-Free:
Address: 1973 bd de la Defense, CS 10268, Nanterre Cedex, 92757 France

STOCK TICKER/OTHER:
Stock Ticker: VCISF
Employees: 217,731
Parent Company:

Exchange: PINX
Fiscal Year Ends: 12/31

SALARIES/BONUSES:
Top Exec. Salary: $ Bonus: $
Second Exec. Salary: $ Bonus: $

OTHER THOUGHTS:
Estimated Female Officers or Directors: 2
Hot Spot for Advancement for Women/Minorities:

Sales, profits and employees may be estimates. Financial information, benefits and other data can change quickly and may vary from those stated here.

Plunkett Research, Ltd.

Viridos Inc

www.viridos.com

NAIC Code: 325199

TYPES OF BUSINESS:
Biofuels
Genomics-Based Technologies
Biotechnology
Climate Change Mitigation
Micro-Algae Products and Solutions

BRANDS/DIVISIONS/AFFILIATES:

CONTACTS: *Note: Officers with more than one job title may be intentionally listed here more than once.*
Oliver Fetzer, CEO
Michele Rubino, Head-Bus. Dev.
Doug Miller, CFO
Brittney Maxey, Head-HR
Hamilton O. Smith, Co-Chief Scientific Officer
Kelly T. Clark, Head-IT & Security
Fernanda Gandara, Sr. VP-Bus. Dev.
J. Craig Venter, Co-Chief Scientific Officer
Toby Richardson, VP-Bioinformatics

GROWTH PLANS/SPECIAL FEATURES:
Viridos, Inc is a biotechnology company utilizing the power of photosynthesis to create transformative solutions to mitigate climate change. Founded in 2005, Viridos engages in genomic innovation and the development of advanced bioengineering tools to create new products and processes that will support a sustainable bioeconomy, including industry sectors such as pharmaceuticals, energy, agriculture, life sciences and heavy transportation (aviation, commercial trucking, rail and marine shipping). The firm aims to design technologies, products and deployment systems that enable businesses and governments to implement sustainable solutions to mitigate climate change, primarily by reducing greenhouse gas emissions. Regarding gasoline, Viridos is utilizing genome-sequenced microalgae to convert CO2 and sunlight into biomass by adapting microalgae to function as cell factories producing energy-dense oils that can be refined into renewable diesel and jet fuel. This process can ultimately reduce greenhouse gas emissions by 70%. The company grows algae for oil, and farms in saltwater on marginal land to avoid competing with resources required for food production. Beyond algae biofuels, Viridos' genomic and algal optimization expertise, intellectual property and ability to translate innovation from the lab to production settings has enabled opportunities to arise that complement its core algae biofuels. Potential examples include, but are not limited to: the use of residual carbohydrate and protein-rich biomass after algae oil extraction as low carbon fuel, feedstock or animal feed; growing algae oils instead of using fish oils; replacing seafood protein with microalgae protein; and creating bio-polymers from microalgae.

FINANCIAL DATA: *Note: Data for latest year may not have been available at press time.*

In U.S. $	2021	2020	2019	2018	2017	2016
Revenue						
R&D Expense						
Operating Income						
Operating Margin %						
SGA Expense						
Net Income						
Operating Cash Flow						
Capital Expenditure						
EBITDA						
Return on Assets %						
Return on Equity %						
Debt to Equity						

CONTACT INFORMATION:
Phone: 858-754-2900　　Fax: 858-724-3905
Toll-Free:
Address: 11149 N. Torrey Pines Rd., La Jolla, CA 92037 United States

STOCK TICKER/OTHER:
Stock Ticker: Private　　　　Exchange:
Employees: 400　　　　　　Fiscal Year Ends:
Parent Company:

SALARIES/BONUSES:
Top Exec. Salary: $　　Bonus: $
Second Exec. Salary: $　　Bonus: $

OTHER THOUGHTS:
Estimated Female Officers or Directors:
Hot Spot for Advancement for Women/Minorities: Y

Sales, profits and employees may be estimates. Financial information, benefits and other data can change quickly and may vary from those stated here.

Waste Management Inc

NAIC Code: 562000

www.wm.com

TYPES OF BUSINESS:
Waste Disposal
Recycling Services
Landfill Operation
Hazardous Waste Management
Transfer Stations
Recycled Commodity Trading
Waste Methane Generation

BRANDS/DIVISIONS/AFFILIATES:
Think Green

GROWTH PLANS/SPECIAL FEATURES:
Waste Management ranks as the largest integrated provider of traditional solid waste services in the United States, operating approximately 260 active landfills and about 340 transfer stations. The company serves residential, commercial, and industrial end markets and is also a leading recycler in North America.

Waste Management offers comprehensive benefits, retirement and savings options, and employee assistance programs.

CONTACTS: Note: Officers with more than one job title may be intentionally listed here more than once.
James Fish, CEO
Devina Rankin, CFO
Thomas Weidemeyer, Chairman of the Board
Charles Boettcher, Chief Legal Officer
John Morris, COO
Nikolaj Sjoqvist, Other Executive Officer
Michael Watson, Other Executive Officer
Tamla Oates-Forney, Other Executive Officer
Steven Batchelor, Senior VP, Divisional
Tara Hemmer, Senior VP, Divisional
Leslie Nagy, Vice President

FINANCIAL DATA: Note: Data for latest year may not have been available at press time.

In U.S. $	2021	2020	2019	2018	2017	2016
Revenue	17,931,000,000	15,218,000,000	15,455,000,000	14,914,000,000	14,485,000,000	13,609,000,000
R&D Expense						
Operating Income	2,957,000,000	2,478,000,000	2,754,000,000	2,735,000,000	2,620,000,000	2,412,000,000
Operating Margin %	.16%	.16%	.18%	.18%	.18%	.18%
SGA Expense	1,827,000,000	1,674,000,000	1,593,000,000	1,400,000,000	1,426,000,000	1,370,000,000
Net Income	1,816,000,000	1,496,000,000	1,670,000,000	1,925,000,000	1,949,000,000	1,182,000,000
Operating Cash Flow	4,338,000,000	3,403,000,000	3,874,000,000	3,570,000,000	3,180,000,000	3,003,000,000
Capital Expenditure	1,904,000,000	1,632,000,000	1,818,000,000	1,694,000,000	1,509,000,000	1,339,000,000
EBITDA	4,713,000,000	3,989,000,000	4,090,000,000	4,227,000,000	3,930,000,000	3,499,000,000
Return on Assets %	.06%	.05%	.07%	.09%	.09%	.06%
Return on Equity %	.25%	.21%	.25%	.31%	.34%	.22%
Debt to Equity	1.78%	1.779	1.879	1.529	1.454	1.679

CONTACT INFORMATION:
Phone: 713 512-6200   Fax:
Toll-Free:
Address: 1001 Fannin St., Ste. 4000, Houston, TX 77002 United States

SALARIES/BONUSES:
Top Exec. Salary: $1,294,231   Bonus: $
Second Exec. Salary: $728,138   Bonus: $

STOCK TICKER/OTHER:
Stock Ticker: WM   Exchange: NYS
Employees: 48,500   Fiscal Year Ends: 12/31
Parent Company:

OTHER THOUGHTS:
Estimated Female Officers or Directors: 1
Hot Spot for Advancement for Women/Minorities: Y

Plunkett Research, Ltd.   361

Webuild SpA
NAIC Code: 237000

www.webuildgroup.com

TYPES OF BUSINESS:
Heavy Construction
Civil Engineering
Construction
Railways
Roads
Bridges
Tunnels
Hydroelectric Plants

GROWTH PLANS/SPECIAL FEATURES:
WeBuild SpA is a global construction company specialized in building large works and complex infrastructure for the sustainable mobility, hydroelectric energy, water, green buildings and the tunnelling sectors. It works in partnerships with other architects and designers to provide innovative solutions. Operating segments are reported by geographical regions: Italy and abroad.

BRANDS/DIVISIONS/AFFILIATES:
Salini Impregilo SpA
Astaldi SpA

CONTACTS:
Note: Officers with more than one job title may be intentionally listed here more than once.

Pietro Salini, CEO
Massimo Ferrari, CFO
Donato Iacovone, Chmn.

FINANCIAL DATA:
Note: Data for latest year may not have been available at press time.

In U.S. $	2021	2020	2019	2018	2017	2016
Revenue	5,853,894,000	4,159,118,000	4,671,733,000	4,763,302,000	5,177,232,000	5,640,939,000
R&D Expense						
Operating Income	-279,330,600	-78,566,740	149,387,500	73,240,500	176,347,700	291,104,300
Operating Margin %	-.05%	-.02%	.03%	.02%	.03%	.05%
SGA Expense						
Net Income	-298,627,000	135,525,900	-21,669,260	53,073,430	-114,802,600	58,678,770
Operating Cash Flow	1,188,609,000	191,965,100	84,996,620	-305,748,300	244,817	250,817,200
Capital Expenditure	210,630,000	179,957,300	96,818,350	118,023,400	167,739,000	254,662,800
EBITDA	314,740,900	451,957,100	323,132,300	203,271,700	202,920,200	559,627,600
Return on Assets %	-.03%	.01%	.00%	.01%	-.01%	.01%
Return on Equity %	-.20%	.10%	-.02%	.07%	-.12%	.05%
Debt to Equity	1.20%	1.517	1.392	2.108	1.993	1.539

CONTACT INFORMATION:
Phone: 39 244422111 Fax: 39 244422293
Toll-Free:
Address: Via Adige, 19, Milan, 20135 Italy

STOCK TICKER/OTHER:
Stock Ticker: IMPJY   Exchange: PINX
Employees: 24,526   Fiscal Year Ends: 12/31
Parent Company: Salini Costruttori SpA

SALARIES/BONUSES:
Top Exec. Salary: $ Bonus: $
Second Exec. Salary: $ Bonus: $

OTHER THOUGHTS:
Estimated Female Officers or Directors: 1
Hot Spot for Advancement for Women/Minorities:

Sales, profits and employees may be estimates. Financial information, benefits and other data can change quickly and may vary from those stated here.

WEC Energy Group Inc

NAIC Code: 221112

www.wecenergygroup.com

TYPES OF BUSINESS:
Electric Power Generation
Non-utility Energy
Real Estate Development

GROWTH PLANS/SPECIAL FEATURES:
WEC Energy Group's electric and gas utility businesses serve electric and gas customers in its Illinois, Michigan, Minnesota, and Wisconsin service territories. The company also owns a 60% stake in American Transmission Co. WEC's asset mix is approximately 47% electric generation and distribution, 36% gas distribution, 12% electric transmission, and 5% unregulated renewable generation.

BRANDS/DIVISIONS/AFFILIATES:
WE Energies
Wisconsin Public Service
Peoples Gas
North Shore Gas
Minnesota Energy Resources
Michigan Gas Utilities
Upper Michigan Energy Resources
Bluewater Gas Storage

CONTACTS:
Note: Officers with more than one job title may be intentionally listed here more than once.

Charles Matthews, CEO, Subsidiary
Joseph Fletcher, CEO
Xia Liu, CFO
Gale Klappa, Chairman of the Board
William Guc, Chief Accounting Officer
Scott Lauber, COO
Robert Garvin, Executive VP, Divisional
Daniel Krueger, Executive VP, Subsidiary
Margaret Kelsey, Executive VP, Subsidiary
Tom Metcalfe, President, Subsidiary
Mary Straka, Senior VP, Divisional
Anthony Reese, Treasurer

FINANCIAL DATA:
Note: Data for latest year may not have been available at press time.

In U.S. $	2021	2020	2019	2018	2017	2016
Revenue	8,316,000,000	7,241,700,000	7,523,100,000	7,679,500,000	7,648,500,000	7,472,300,000
R&D Expense						
Operating Income	1,714,900,000	1,706,100,000	1,531,400,000	1,468,400,000	1,776,100,000	1,696,300,000
Operating Margin %	.21%	.24%	.20%	.19%	.23%	.23%
SGA Expense						
Net Income	1,301,500,000	1,201,100,000	1,135,200,000	1,060,500,000	1,204,900,000	940,200,000
Operating Cash Flow	2,032,700,000	2,196,000,000	2,345,500,000	2,445,500,000	2,078,600,000	2,103,800,000
Capital Expenditure	2,252,800,000	2,238,800,000	2,260,800,000	2,115,700,000	1,959,500,000	1,423,700,000
EBITDA	3,044,200,000	2,898,900,000	2,687,500,000	2,521,200,000	2,802,700,000	2,672,000,000
Return on Assets %	.03%	.03%	.03%	.03%	.04%	.03%
Return on Equity %	.12%	.12%	.11%	.11%	.13%	.11%
Debt to Equity	1.24%	1.12	1.109	1.021	0.924	1.026

CONTACT INFORMATION:
Phone: 414 221-2345 Fax:
Toll-Free:
Address: 231 W. Michigan St., Milwaukee, WI 53203 United States

STOCK TICKER/OTHER:
Stock Ticker: WEC
Employees: 6,938
Parent Company:

Exchange: NYS
Fiscal Year Ends: 12/31

SALARIES/BONUSES:
Top Exec. Salary: $1,102,727 Bonus: $
Second Exec. Salary: $1,098,334 Bonus: $

OTHER THOUGHTS:
Estimated Female Officers or Directors: 2
Hot Spot for Advancement for Women/Minorities: Y

Western Area Power Administration

www.wapa.gov/Pages/western.aspx
NAIC Code: 221111

TYPES OF BUSINESS:
Hydroelectric Power Supplier
Electricity Power Administration
Wholesale Electricity
Hydropower Plants
Transmission Lines

BRANDS/DIVISIONS/AFFILIATES:

GROWTH PLANS/SPECIAL FEATURES:
Western Area Power Administration (WAPA) is a power marketing administration within the U.S. Department of Energy organized to market and transmit wholesale electricity from multi-use water projects. WAPA's service area is comprised of a 15-state region within the central and western portion of the country where more than 17,000 miles of transmission lines carry electricity from 57 hydropower plants operated by the Bureau of Reclamation, U.S. Army Corps of Engineers and the International Boundary and Water Commission. Together, these plants have an installed capacity of 10,504 megawatts (MW). WAPA sells its power to customers such as federal and state agencies, cities and towns, rural electric cooperatives, public utility districts, irrigation districts and Native American tribes. They, in turn, provide retail electric service to missions of consumers in the western area of the U.S. Headquartered in Colorado, WAPA has regional offices in Montana, Colorado, Arizona and California. WAPA also has a Colorado River Storage Project Management Center in Montrose, Colorado.

CONTACTS: Note: Officers with more than one job title may be intentionally listed here more than once.
Tracey LeBeau, CEO
Tina Ko, COO
Michael Peterson, CFO
Michael Montoya, CIO
John Bremer, General Counsel
Theresa Williams, Chief Strategy Officer
Tom Boyko, Regional Mgr.-Sierra Nevada
Darrick Moe, Regional Mgr.-Desert Southwest
Brad Warren, Regional Mgr.-Rocky Mountain
Bob Harris, Regional Mgr.-Upper Great Plains
Chief Risk Officer, Matt Miller

FINANCIAL DATA: Note: Data for latest year may not have been available at press time.

In U.S. $	2021	2020	2019	2018	2017	2016
Revenue	1,444,898,840	1,331,704,000	1,442,697,000	1,376,420,000	1,407,361,000	1,320,940,000
R&D Expense						
Operating Income						
Operating Margin %						
SGA Expense						
Net Income		150,456,000	256,848,000	143,210,000	242,693,000	262,551,000
Operating Cash Flow						
Capital Expenditure						
EBITDA						
Return on Assets %						
Return on Equity %						
Debt to Equity						

CONTACT INFORMATION:
Phone: 720-962-7000   Fax: 720-962-7200
Toll-Free:
Address: PO Box 281213, Lakewood, CO 80228-8213 United States

STOCK TICKER/OTHER:
Stock Ticker: Government-Owned   Exchange:
Employees: 1,900   Fiscal Year Ends: 09/30
Parent Company:

SALARIES/BONUSES:
Top Exec. Salary: $ Bonus: $
Second Exec. Salary: $ Bonus: $

OTHER THOUGHTS:
Estimated Female Officers or Directors: 2
Hot Spot for Advancement for Women/Minorities: Y

Sales, profits and employees may be estimates. Financial information, benefits and other data can change quickly and may vary from those stated here.

Westinghouse Electric Company LLC   www.westinghousenuclear.com
NAIC Code: 332410

TYPES OF BUSINESS:
Nuclear Power Plant Equipment
Nuclear Power Plant Repair Services
Nuclear Fuel
Nuclear Power Plant Design & Engineering
Micro-Reactor Development

BRANDS/DIVISIONS/AFFILIATES:
Brookfield Business Partners LP
AP1000 PWR
eVinci

CONTACTS: Note: Officers with more than one job title may be intentionally listed here more than once.
Patrick Fragman, CEO
Pavan Pattada, Exec. VP-Global Oper. Svcs.
Dan Sumner, CFO
Robert Massey, Exec. VP-People & Culture
Melissa Cummings, Exec. VP-Digital & Innovation
Yves Brachet, Pres., EMEA
Jack Allen, Pres., Asia

GROWTH PLANS/SPECIAL FEATURES:
Westinghouse Electric Company, LLC provides plant design, services, fuel, technology and equipment to utility, government and industrial clients in the international commercial nuclear electric power market. The company operates in four segments: nuclear services, nuclear automation, nuclear fuel and nuclear power plants. The nuclear services division provides field services, such as outage support, component services and training; engineering services that improve plant reliability, including plant analyses and management programs; and installation and modification services, including plant engineering, welding and machining, site installation and decommissioning and dismantling services. Westinghouse's nuclear automation segment offers instrumentation and control solutions and related services for new nuclear power plant designs and the operation of existing plants. The nuclear fuel division offers fuel products, materials and components, services and technology for pressurized water reactors (PWRs), boiling water reactors (BWRs) and advanced gas-cooled reactors (AGRs). The nuclear power plants division supplies plant design expertise, equipment and component manufacturing for nuclear power plants. The firm states that its AP1000 PWR nuclear power plant is the safest and most economical within the global commercial marketplace. Westinghouse is currently developing the eVinci micro-reactor, a next-generation, very small modular reactor for decentralized remote applications. Westinghouse's regional operations are categorized into the Americas, Asia and EMEA (Europe, the Middle East and Africa). The firm operates as a subsidiary of Brookfield Business Partners LP. In April 2022, Westinghouse Electric Company agreed to acquire BHI Energy, which would expand Westinghouse's global capabilities and expertise in nuclear plant maintenance and modification services, industrial, power delivery and complimentary renewables including solar, wind and hydro power.

FINANCIAL DATA: Note: Data for latest year may not have been available at press time.

In U.S. $	2021	2020	2019	2018	2017	2016
Revenue	4,334,575,000	3,995,000,000	4,250,000,000	4,200,000,000	4,150,000,000	4,000,000,000
R&D Expense						
Operating Income						
Operating Margin %						
SGA Expense						
Net Income						
Operating Cash Flow						
Capital Expenditure						
EBITDA						
Return on Assets %						
Return on Equity %						
Debt to Equity						

CONTACT INFORMATION:
Phone: 412-374-4111   Fax: 412-374-3272
Toll-Free: 888-943-8442
Address: 1000 Westinghouse Dr., Ste. 572A, Cranberry Township, PA 16066 United States

STOCK TICKER/OTHER:
Stock Ticker: Subsidiary   Exchange:
Employees: 9,000   Fiscal Year Ends: 03/31
Parent Company: Brookfield Business Partners LP

SALARIES/BONUSES:
Top Exec. Salary: $ Bonus: $
Second Exec. Salary: $ Bonus: $

OTHER THOUGHTS:
Estimated Female Officers or Directors:
Hot Spot for Advancement for Women/Minorities:

World Energy LLC

www.worldenergy.net

NAIC Code: 325199

TYPES OF BUSINESS:
Biodiesel Production
Biofuel Production
Biofuel Distribution
Biomass-Based Diesel Fuels
Fuel Blends
Biodiesel Innovation
Glycerin
Fatty Acids

BRANDS/DIVISIONS/AFFILIATES:
Thornvale Holdings Limited
CFFI Ventures Inc

CONTACTS: *Note: Officers with more than one job title may be intentionally listed here more than once.*
Gene Gebolys, CEO
John Zeidler, COO
Kevin Golding, Chairman of the Board
Eric D. Batchelder, CFO
Scott Lewis, Executive VP, Divisional
Nakyun Paik, Vice President, Divisional

GROWTH PLANS/SPECIAL FEATURES:
World Energy, LLC is a Boston-based producer and distributor of biofuel. The company's supplies a wide range of biomass-based diesel fuels and blends to meet varying customer specifications, all of which meet the highest standards for quality assurance and control. Biodiesel is delivered by truck, rail or barge, and all products sourced through World Energy are renewable identification number (RIN) verified making the suitable for advanced biofuels and renewable fuel. The firm engages in process improvements and innovation in regards to production supply and management, routinely producing biodiesel at below .2% monoglycerides while reducing catalyst utilizing and improving throughput. World Energy also provides tailored engineering and process design services. The company's co-products are key ingredients in customer formulations, and including glycerin (up to 95% pure) and fatty acids (up to 50% pure). World Energy's renewable smart fuel is delivered as a drop-in solution that can be used in all modern diesel engines; and its sustainable aviation fuel is a drop-in fuel solution that requires no changes in aircraft or engine fuel systems, distribution infrastructure or storage facilities. World Energy is headquartered in Massachusetts, with additional locations and subsidiaries in Georgia, Pennsylvania, Mississippi, Texas, California, and in Ontario, Canada. World Energy LLC operates as a subsidiary of CFFI Ventures, Inc., which is itself a subsidiary of Thornvale Holdings Limited.

FINANCIAL DATA: *Note: Data for latest year may not have been available at press time.*

In U.S. $	2021	2020	2019	2018	2017	2016
Revenue	110,000,000	105,302,723	106,366,387	99,407,839	94,674,132	90,165,840
R&D Expense						
Operating Income						
Operating Margin %						
SGA Expense						
Net Income						
Operating Cash Flow						
Capital Expenditure						
EBITDA						
Return on Assets %						
Return on Equity %						
Debt to Equity						

CONTACT INFORMATION:
Phone: 617-889-7300　　　Fax: 617-887-2411
Toll-Free:
Address: 225 Franklin St., Ste 2330, Boston, MA 02110 United States

STOCK TICKER/OTHER:
Stock Ticker: Subsidiary　　　Exchange:
Employees: 50　　　Fiscal Year Ends: 12/31
Parent Company: Thornvale Holdings Limited

SALARIES/BONUSES:
Top Exec. Salary: $　　　Bonus: $
Second Exec. Salary: $　　　Bonus: $

OTHER THOUGHTS:
Estimated Female Officers or Directors:
Hot Spot for Advancement for Women/Minorities:

Sales, profits and employees may be estimates. Financial information, benefits and other data can change quickly and may vary from those stated here.

Wurth Elektronik GmbH & Co KG

NAIC Code: 334418

www.we-online.com

TYPES OF BUSINESS:
Printed Circuit Assembly (Electronic Assembly) Manufacturing
Electronic Components
ElectroMechanical Components
Printed Circuit Boards
Intelligent Power Systems
Power Control Systems
Product Design and Manufacture
Manufacturing Facilities

BRANDS/DIVISIONS/AFFILIATES:
Wurth Group
Wurth Electronics Midcom
Wurth Elektronik iBE
Wurth Elektronik Stelvio Kontek
Wurth Elektronik eiSos
Wurth Elektronik CBT

CONTACTS: Note: Officers with more than one job title may be intentionally listed here more than once.
Thomas Wild, CEO
Jorg Murawski, Co-Managing Dir.

GROWTH PLANS/SPECIAL FEATURES:
Wurth Elektronik GmbH & Co. KG is a leading printed circuit board (PCB) manufacturer in Europe, with more than 20 production locations worldwide. The company's products are grouped into three categories: electronic and electro-mechanical components, PCBs, and intelligent power and control systems. Electronic and electro-mechanical component products include passive components, optoelectronics, thermal management, power modules, electromechanical components, automotive electronic components, wireless connectivity products and sensors, and custom magnets, along with related service and support. This division operates through Wurth Electronics Midcom, Wurth Elektronik iBE, Wurth Elektronik Stelvio Kontek and Wurth Elektronik eiSos. PCB products include flexible, rigid, multi-layer, slim-flexible, stretchable electronics, high density interconnection (with Microvia technology), embedding technology, thermal management, wire bonding and more. This division operates through Wurth Elektronik CBT. Last, intelligent power products and control systems span power management, controllers, high voltage solutions, human machine interface, connection solutions, connection and mounting elements, lead-free power elements, direct plug-in technology solutions and more. This division partners with many commercial vehicle manufacturers, and its project management team accompanies business partners from idea to series production. Wurth Elektronik GmbH & Co. KG operates as a subsidiary of Wurth Group.

FINANCIAL DATA: Note: Data for latest year may not have been available at press time.

In U.S. $	2021	2020	2019	2018	2017	2016
Revenue	1,004,420,000	1,010,841,520	1,222,944,000	1,019,120,000	1,109,220,000	915,663,000
R&D Expense						
Operating Income						
Operating Margin %						
SGA Expense						
Net Income						
Operating Cash Flow						
Capital Expenditure						
EBITDA						
Return on Assets %						
Return on Equity %						
Debt to Equity						

CONTACT INFORMATION:
Phone: 49-79-40-946-0 Fax:
Toll-Free:
Address: Salzstrasse 21, Niedernhall, D-74676 Germany

STOCK TICKER/OTHER:
Stock Ticker: Subsidiary
Employees: 7,300
Parent Company: Wurth Group

Exchange:
Fiscal Year Ends: 12/31

SALARIES/BONUSES:
Top Exec. Salary: $ Bonus: $
Second Exec. Salary: $ Bonus: $

OTHER THOUGHTS:
Estimated Female Officers or Directors:
Hot Spot for Advancement for Women/Minorities:

Sales, profits and employees may be estimates. Financial information, benefits and other data can change quickly and may vary from those stated here.

Wuxi Suntech Power Co Ltd

NAIC Code: 334413A

www.suntech-power.com

TYPES OF BUSINESS:
Photovoltaic Cell Manufacturing
Silicon Solar Cells and Wafers
Photovoltaic Modules
Solar Systems
Product Design and Manufacture
Solar and Manufacturing Technologies
Manufacturing Facilities
Research and Development

BRANDS/DIVISIONS/AFFILIATES:
Shunfeng International Clean Energy Limited
Ultra X
Ultra V
Ultra V Pro

CONTACTS:
Note: Officers with more than one job title may be intentionally listed here more than once.

Zhengrong Shi, Chief Strategy Officer
Mick McDaniel, Managing Dir.-Suntech America
Thilo Kinkel, Head-Sales, Suntech Europe
Yutaka Yamamoto, Pres., Suntech Japan
Fubo Zhang, Chmn.
Xin Luo, Sr. VP-Global Supply Chain

GROWTH PLANS/SPECIAL FEATURES:

Wuxi Suntech Power Co., Ltd. designs, develops, manufactures and markets crystalline silicon solar cells, modules and systems. The company's products have been installed in more than 100 countries worldwide, with a cumulative shipment of photovoltaic (PV) modules exceeding 30 gigawatts (GW). Suntech is devoted to the research and development of new technologies in order to improve product and manufacturing techniques. The firm's products include the Ultra X series of 210 mm large format silicon wafers and PERC monocrystalline cells, with module efficiency up to 21.6%; the Ultra V series of 182 mm large format silicon wafers with module efficiency up to 21.5%; and the Ultra V Pro series which use 182 mm large N-type silicon wafers with cell efficiency over 24.5%, and also has near zero-LID performance, which enhances module power. Suntech's products are used by residential, commercial and industrial customers. The company's module factory can work for various advanced production requirements, including intelligent manufacturing. Suntech's SAP (system application processing) and ERP (enterprise resource planning) business platforms can achieve real-time interaction, planning, execution, reporting and analysis. Suntech invests in the improvement of its production technology and research and development technology to ensure the reliability and quality of its processes, products and solutions. Headquartered in Wuxi, China, Suntech has international offices in Germany, Japan, South Africa and Australia. The company is a subsidiary of Shunfeng International Clean Energy Limited.

FINANCIAL DATA:
Note: Data for latest year may not have been available at press time.

In U.S. $	2021	2020	2019	2018	2017	2016
Revenue	1,601,374,000	1,272,375,000	1,131,000,000	1,083,000,000	940,000,000	690,000,000
R&D Expense						
Operating Income						
Operating Margin %						
SGA Expense						
Net Income						
Operating Cash Flow						
Capital Expenditure						
EBITDA						
Return on Assets %						
Return on Equity %						
Debt to Equity						

CONTACT INFORMATION:
Phone: 86-510-8531-8888   Fax: 86-510-8534-0006
Toll-Free:
Address: 9 Xinhua Rd., Xinwu Dist., Wuxi, Jiangsu 214028 China

STOCK TICKER/OTHER:
Stock Ticker: Subsidiary   Exchange:
Employees: 20,231   Fiscal Year Ends: 12/31
Parent Company: Shunfeng International Clean Energy Limited

SALARIES/BONUSES:
Top Exec. Salary: $ Bonus: $
Second Exec. Salary: $ Bonus: $

OTHER THOUGHTS:
Estimated Female Officers or Directors: 1
Hot Spot for Advancement for Women/Minorities:

Sales, profits and employees may be estimates. Financial information, benefits and other data can change quickly and may vary from those stated here.

Xinjiang Goldwind Science & Technology Co Ltd

www.goldwindglobal.com
NAIC Code: 333611

TYPES OF BUSINESS:
Wind Turbine Manufacturing
Wind Farm Development
Site Selection & Design
Spare Parts
Equipment Maintenance

BRANDS/DIVISIONS/AFFILIATES:
iGO (intelligent Goldwind Offshore Platform)

GROWTH PLANS/SPECIAL FEATURES:
Xinjiang Goldwind Science & Technology Co Ltd manufactures and markets wind turbines and other wind power solutions. It has the experience and capability to construct wind farms, and offers support and service through the lifecycle of products and projects. This includes research and development, manufacturing, sales, and aftermarket service and maintenance to help products last several years. In addition, the company offers wind-power-related consultancy, and its completed winds farms in operation are managed by specialized and experienced service personnel. The company has three primary business segments: Wind, turbine, and generator manufacturing; Wind power services; and Wind farm investment and Development. The majority of the company's customers are in China.

CONTACTS:
Note: Officers with more than one job title may be intentionally listed here more than once.

Cao Zhigang, Pres.
Wang Hongyan, CFO
Liu He, Chief Eng.
Ma Jinru, Corp. Sec.
Cao Zhigang, Exec. VP
Wang Xiangming, VP
Yang Hua, VP
Wu Kai, VP
Wu Gang, Chmn.

FINANCIAL DATA:
Note: Data for latest year may not have been available at press time.

In U.S. $	2021	2020	2019	2018	2017	2016
Revenue	7,107,621,000	7,907,956,000	5,375,201,000	4,038,033,000	3,531,898,000	3,709,885,000
R&D Expense	222,560,700	207,744,600	132,980,300	149,265,700	281,449,800	105,546,400
Operating Income	719,736,100	431,330,900	312,527,300	455,094,900	472,154,200	508,414,100
Operating Margin %	.10%	.05%	.06%	.11%	.13%	.14%
SGA Expense	511,187,500	571,693,400	423,261,900	300,081,400	201,262,000	331,985,600
Net Income	485,868,200	416,516,400	310,590,800	452,087,700	429,326,400	422,063,500
Operating Cash Flow	686,789,700	755,790,000	833,279,400	439,262,800	433,033,600	436,056,600
Capital Expenditure	1,502,253,000	1,076,697,000	1,586,610,000	846,926,500	689,439,900	794,463,500
EBITDA	1,098,702,000	859,152,400	742,665,300	857,651,800	763,117,300	725,257,300
Return on Assets %	.03%	.03%	.02%	.04%	.04%	.05%
Return on Equity %	.10%	.09%	.08%	.14%	.14%	.16%
Debt to Equity	.74%	0.584	0.523	0.772	0.706	0.772

CONTACT INFORMATION:
Phone: 86 9913767402   Fax: 86 9913761781
Toll-Free:
Address: No. 107 Shanghai Road, Urumqi, 830026 China

STOCK TICKER/OTHER:
Stock Ticker: XJNGF
Employees: 10,781
Parent Company:

Exchange: PINX
Fiscal Year Ends: 12/31

SALARIES/BONUSES:
Top Exec. Salary: $ Bonus: $
Second Exec. Salary: $ Bonus: $

OTHER THOUGHTS:
Estimated Female Officers or Directors: 2
Hot Spot for Advancement for Women/Minorities:

Plunkett Research, Ltd. 369

Yingli Energy (China) Co Ltd

NAIC Code: 334413A

www.yinglisolar.com/en

TYPES OF BUSINESS:
Photovoltaic Cell Manufacturing
Solar Modules
Photovoltaic System Installation
Polysilicon Production

BRANDS/DIVISIONS/AFFILIATES:
Baoding Tianwei Yingli New Energy Resources Co Ltd
Yingli Energy (China) Co Ltd
Yingli Green Energy Chile SpA
Yingli Green Energy Americas Inc
Yingli Green Energy Capital Holding (Hong Kong)
Yingli Green Energy Singapore Company Pte Ltd
Yingli Energy (Beijing) Co Ltd
Yingli Green Energy Mexico

CONTACTS:
Note: Officers with more than one job title may be intentionally listed here more than once.

Liansheng Miao, CEO
Xiaoqiang Zheng, COO
Yiyu Wang, CFO
Cindy Zhiyan Hu, Chief Commercial Officer
Dengyuan Song, Chief Technology Officer
Yiyu Wang, Chief Strategy Officer
Qing Miao, VP-Corp. Comm.
Jingfeng Xiong, VP
Zhiheng Zhao, Sr. VP
Xiangdong Wang, VP
Robert Petrina, Managing Dir.-Yingli Green Energy Americas
Liansheng Miao, Chmn.
Darren Thompson, Managing Dir.-Yingli Green Energy Europe

GROWTH PLANS/SPECIAL FEATURES:
Yingli Energy (China) Co., Ltd. designs, manufactures, markets and installs photovoltaic (PV) products and systems. Through subsidiary Baoding Tianwei Yingli New Energy Resources Co., Ltd., Yingli designs, manufactures and sells PV modules and also designs, assembles, sells and installs PV systems that are connected to electricity transmission grids or that operate on a stand-alone basis. The firm has installed more than 90 million Yingli solar panels, representing over 24 gigawatts (GW) of solar power worldwide. Other subsidiaries of the firm include Yingli Energy (China) Co. Ltd., engaged in the research, manufacturing, sale and installation of renewable energy products; Yingli Green Energy Chile SpA, engaged in the sale and marketing of PV products in Chile; Yingli Green Energy Americas, Inc., engaged in the production, sale and marketing of PV products; Yingli Green Energy Capital Holding (Hong Kong) Co. Ltd., engaged in import and export trading and investments; Yingli Green Energy Singapore Company Pte. Ltd., engaged in the research and experimental development of electronics; and Yingli Energy (Beijing) Co. Ltd. and Yingli Green Energy Mexico, each of which are engaged in the sale and manufacture of PV modules and PV systems in their respective regions.

FINANCIAL DATA:
Note: Data for latest year may not have been available at press time.

In U.S. $	2021	2020	2019	2018	2017	2016
Revenue			636,620,000	659,818,368	1,178,321,152	1,240,223,744
R&D Expense						
Operating Income						
Operating Margin %						
SGA Expense						
Net Income			-230,480,000	-238,873,680	-467,459,584	-310,593,344
Operating Cash Flow						
Capital Expenditure						
EBITDA						
Return on Assets %						
Return on Equity %						
Debt to Equity						

CONTACT INFORMATION:
Phone: 86 3128929700   Fax: 86 3128929800
Toll-Free:
Address: 3399 North Chaoyang Ave., Baoding, 071051 China

STOCK TICKER/OTHER:
Stock Ticker: Private   Exchange:
Employees: 10,625   Fiscal Year Ends: 12/31
Parent Company:

SALARIES/BONUSES:
Top Exec. Salary: $ Bonus: $
Second Exec. Salary: $ Bonus: $

OTHER THOUGHTS:
Estimated Female Officers or Directors: 3
Hot Spot for Advancement for Women/Minorities: Y

Sales, profits and employees may be estimates. Financial information, benefits and other data can change quickly and may vary from those stated here.

Zorlu Enerji Elektrik Uretim AS
NAIC Code: 221121

www.zorluenerji.com.tr

TYPES OF BUSINESS:
Electricity Generation
Natural Gas Distribution
Turnkey Projects
Electricity Generation
Renewable Energy Sources
Hydroelectric Plants
Wind Power
Geothermal Power

BRANDS/DIVISIONS/AFFILIATES:
Zorlu Group
Zorlu Osmangazi Enerji Sanayi ve Ticaret AS
Zorlu Enerji Dagtim AS

CONTACTS: Note: Officers with more than one job title may be intentionally listed here more than once.
Ibrahim Sinan Ak, CEO
Elif Yener, Gen, Mgr.-Finance
Serpil Kosker, Gen, Mgr.-Human Resources
Huseyin Morkoyun, Dir.-Financial Affairs
Ali Kindap, Assistant Gen. Mgr.
Zeki Zorlu, Chmn.

GROWTH PLANS/SPECIAL FEATURES:
Zorlu Enerji Elektrik Uretim AS, based in Turkey, operates in the energy sector. Founded in 1993, the company is part of the Zorlu Group, a holding company with activities in the textile, electronics, energy and property markets. Zorlu Enerji has a total installed electricity generation capacity of 990 megawatts (MW), 643 MW of which is installed in Turkey. Of Zorlu Enerji's activities in Turkey 87% of its total installed capacity is based on renewable sources. Globally, 62% of its total installed capacity is based on renewable sources. The firm's electric generation portfolio consists of hydroelectric, geothermal, wind and natural gas power plants in Turkey; wind power plants in Pakistan; and natural gas power plants in Israel. Zorlu's electricity distribution and retail sales division distributes electricity and provides retail sales through subsidiary Zorlu Osmangazi Enerji Sanayi ve Ticaret AS. Zorlu's natural gas distribution division is operated through Zorlu Enerji Dagtim AS, which provides natural gas services to subscribers in the Gaziantep and Kilis provinces, as well as to subscribers in the Thrace region (Kirklareli, Edirne and Tekirdag provinces).

FINANCIAL DATA: Note: Data for latest year may not have been available at press time.

In U.S. $	2021	2020	2019	2018	2017	2016
Revenue	625,603,626	1,163,070,000	1,378,810,000	1,168,570,000	1,022,220,000	320,640,000
R&D Expense						
Operating Income						
Operating Margin %						
SGA Expense						
Net Income	148,941,825	-4,394,100	-35,024,400	14,294,000	13,711,200	-1,168,900
Operating Cash Flow						
Capital Expenditure						
EBITDA						
Return on Assets %						
Return on Equity %						
Debt to Equity						

CONTACT INFORMATION:
Phone: 90-212-456-2300 Fax: 90-212-422-0099
Toll-Free:
Address: Levent 199, Buyukdere Caddesi No. 199, Istanbul, 34394 Turkey

STOCK TICKER/OTHER:
Stock Ticker: ZOREN
Employees: 2,160
Parent Company: Zorlu Group

Exchange: Istanbul
Fiscal Year Ends: 12/31

SALARIES/BONUSES:
Top Exec. Salary: $ Bonus: $
Second Exec. Salary: $ Bonus: $

OTHER THOUGHTS:
Estimated Female Officers or Directors:
Hot Spot for Advancement for Women/Minorities:

Sales, profits and employees may be estimates. Financial information, benefits and other data can change quickly and may vary from those stated here.

ADDITIONAL INDEXES

CONTENTS:

Index of Firms Noted as "Hot Spots for Advancement" for Women/Minorities	**372**
Index by Subsidiaries, Brand Names and Selected Affiliations	**373**

INDEX OF FIRMS NOTED AS HOT SPOTS FOR ADVANCEMENT FOR WOMEN & MINORITIES

3M Company
ABB Ltd
Abengoa SA
Active Power Inc
AES Corporation (The)
Air Products and Chemicals Inc
Alliander NV
Alstom SA
Ameresco Inc
Amyris Inc
Applied Materials Inc
Archer-Daniels-Midland Company (ADM)
Arizona Public Service Company
Atomic Energy of Canada Limited (AECL)
ATS Automation Tooling Systems Inc
Avista Corporation
Babcock & Wilcox Enterprises Inc
Badger Meter Inc
BASF SE
Bechtel Group Inc
BIOS-BIOENERGYSYSTEME GmbH
Black & Veatch Holding Company
Bonneville Power Administration
BP plc
BrightSource Energy Inc
British Columbia Hydro and Power Authority
Brookfield Asset Management Inc
Cabot Corporation
Calpine Corporation
Cameco Corporation
Cargill Incorporated
Caterpillar Inc
Centrus Energy Corp
Chevron Corporation
CK Infrastructure Holdings Limited
CSUN Solar Tech Co Ltd
Cummins Inc
Dominion Energy Inc
Dow Inc
Electricite de France SA (EDF)
Enel Green Power SpA
Energy Recovery Inc
ENGlobal Corporation
Eni SpA
Entergy Corporation
Equinor ASA
Exelon Corporation
Exide Technologies LLC
Exxon Mobil Corporation (ExxonMobil)
Falck Renewables SpA
First Solar Inc
FirstEnergy Corporation
Flowserve Corporation
Fluor Corporation
Fomento de Construcciones y Contratas SA (FCC)
General Electric Company (GE)
Green Mountain Power Corporation
GRID Alternatives
Halliburton Company
Hydro-Quebec
Iberdrola SA
IDACORP Inc
Itaipu Binacional
Manitoba Hydro-Electric
McDermott International Ltd
Methanex Corporation
Modine Manufacturing Company
New York Power Authority
NextEra Energy Inc
Novozymes A/S
Ontario Power Generation Inc
Orano SA
PG&E Corporation
PNM Resources Inc
Portland General Electric Company
Puget Energy Inc
Raytheon Technologies Corporation
ReNu Energy Limited
Shell plc
Siemens AG
Siemens Gamesa Renewable Energy SA
SkyPower Limited
Southern California Edison Company
Southern Company
Suncor Energy Inc
SunPower Corporation
Sunrun Inc
Teledyne Technologies Inc
Tennessee Valley Authority (TVA)
TotalEnergies SE
Trane Technologies plc
Umicore SA
UNS Energy Corporation
Vattenfall AB
Vestas Wind Systems A/S
Viridos Inc
Waste Management Inc
WEC Energy Group Inc
Western Area Power Administration
Yingli Energy (China) Co Ltd

INDEX OF SUBSIDIARIES, BRAND NAMES AND AFFILIATIONS

Abdul Latif Jameel Energy and Environmental Srvcs; **Fotowatio Renewable Ventures SLU**
Abertis; **HOCHTIEF AG**
ABLE; **Ultralife Corporation**
ABLE New Energy Co; **Ultralife Corporation**
Accel Energy Limited; **AGL Energy Limited**
Ace; **3M Company**
Adani Hybrid Energy Jaisalmer One Ltd; **Adani Green Energy Limited**
AES Tiete SA; **AES Corporation (The)**
AGL Australia Limited; **AGL Energy Limited**
Air Liquide Advanced Technologies US LLC; **Air Liquide US LLC**
Air Liquide Electronics US; **Air Liquide US LLC**
Air Liquide Global E&C Solutions US Inc; **Air Liquide US LLC**
Air Liquide USA; **Air Liquide US LLC**
Air Plants Dust Extraction; **Talbott's Biomass Energy Systems Ltd**
Airgas; **Air Liquide US LLC**
Alabama Power Company; **Southern Company**
Alaska Electric Light and Power Company; **Avista Corporation**
Alaska Energy and Resources Company; **Avista Corporation**
Aldetec Incorporated; **Arotech Corporation**
Alizent; **Air Liquide US LLC**
Alliander Telecom; **Alliander NV**
Almidones Mexicanos SA; **Archer-Daniels-Midland Company (ADM)**
Ameresco Canada Inc; **Ameresco Inc**
AminoPlus; **AG Processing Inc**
AMPCO Marketing LLC; **Atlantic Methanol Production Company LLC**
AMPCO Services LLC; **Atlantic Methanol Production Company LLC**
Amperium; **American Superconductor Corporation**
AMTI; **Ultralife Corporation**
AP1000 PWR; **Westinghouse Electric Company LLC**
Applied Cryo Technologies Inc; **Plug Power Inc**
APS Solar Communities; **Arizona Public Service Company**
AquaBold; **Energy Recovery Inc**
ARC; **Commonwealth Fusion Systems LLC**
Arcola Energy; **Ballard Power Systems Inc**
Astaldi SpA; **Webuild SpA**
Atlantic Methanol Services BV; **Atlantic Methanol Production Company LLC**
Atlas Holdings LLC; **Stryten Energy LLC**
Atonix Digital; **Black & Veatch Holding Company**
Atura Power; **Ontario Power Generation Inc**
Avangrid Renewables; **Iberdrola SA**
Bakery Solutions; **Imperial Western Products Inc**
Baltimore Gas and Electric Company; **Exelon Corporation**
Baoding Tianwei Yingli New Energy Resources Co Ltd; **Yingli Energy (China) Co Ltd**
Baroid; **Halliburton Company**
BEACON; **Badger Meter Inc**
Berkshire Hathaway Inc; **Berkshire Hathaway Energy Company**
Berkshire Hathaway Inc; **PacifiCorp**
Bestinver Gestion; **Acciona SA**
Bestinver Securities; **Acciona SA**
BeyonD; **Renewable Energy Group Inc**
BHE Renewables; **Berkshire Hathaway Energy Company**
Big River Resources Boyceville LLC; **REX American Resources Corporation**
Big River Resources Galva LLC; **REX American Resources Corporation**
Big River Resources LLC; **REX American Resources Corporation**
Big River Resources West Burlington LLC; **REX American Resources Corporation**
Big River United Energy LLC; **REX American Resources Corporation**
BIOBIL 2020; **BIOS-BIOENERGYSYSTEME GmbH**
Biologic Environmental Services and Waste; **Covanta Holding Corporation**
Biotane Fuels; **Imperial Western Products Inc**
Biotane Pumping; **Imperial Western Products Inc**
Birdseye; **Dominion Energy Inc**
Black & Veatch Construction Inc; **Black & Veatch Holding Company**
Blind River; **Cameco Corporation**
Bloom Energy Server; **Bloom Energy Corporation**
Blue Ravin Solar; **SunPower Corporation**
Blue Yonder; **Panasonic Corporation**
Bluewater Gas Storage; **WEC Energy Group Inc**
Boeing Company (The); **Spectrolab Inc**
Bombardier Transportation; **Alstom SA**
BP plc; **Lightsource BP**
BrightBox; **Sunrun Inc**
Broadband Wireless Technologies; **Arotech Corporation**
Brookfield Asset Management Inc; **TerraForm Power Operating LLC**
Brookfield Business Partners LP; **Westinghouse Electric Company LLC**
Brookfield Business Partners LP; **Brookfield Asset Management Inc**
Brookfield Infrastructure Partners LP; **Brookfield Asset Management Inc**
Brookfield Property Partners LP; **Brookfield Asset Management Inc**
Brookfield Renewable Energy Partners LP; **Brookfield Asset Management Inc**
Brookfield Renewable Partners LP; **TerraForm Power Operating LLC**
Calpine Energy Solutions; **Calpine Corporation**
Caltex; **Chevron Corporation**
Cameco Fuel Manufacturing; **Cameco Corporation**
Canadian Solar; **Canadian Solar Inc**

INDEX OF SUBSIDIARIES, BRAND NAMES AND AFFILIATIONS, CONT.

Capstone Turbine Corporation; **Capstone Green Energy Corporation**
Cat; **Caterpillar Inc**
Caterpillar Financial Services Corporation; **Caterpillar Inc**
Caterpillar Insurance Holdings Inc; **Caterpillar Inc**
CATL Xiamen Institute of New Energy; **Contemporary Amperex Technology Co Limited (CATL)**
CDMA Utilities; **Alliander NV**
Cementos Portland Valderrivas; **Fomento de Construcciones y Contratas SA (FCC)**
Cemig Distribuicao SA; **Companhia Energetica de Minas Gerais SA (CEMIG)**
CFFI Ventures Inc; **World Energy LLC**
Champion Energy Services; **Calpine Corporation**
Chevron; **Chevron Corporation**
Chevron Corporation; **Chevron Technology Ventures LLC**
Chevron Corporation; **Renewable Energy Group Inc**
Chevron Corporation; **Atlantic Methanol Production Company LLC**
Chevron Phillips Chemical Company LLC; **Chevron Corporation**
Chevron Venture Capital; **Chevron Technology Ventures LLC**
China Datang Corporation; **Guangxi Guiguan Electric Power Co Ltd**
China Electric Equipment Group Co Ltd (CEEG); **CSUN Solar Tech Co Ltd**
China Guodian Corporation; **China Longyuan Power Group Corporation Limited**
China National Building Materials Group Co Ltd; **AVANCIS GmbH**
CIM Group Inc; **SkyPower Limited**
CIMIC Group; **HOCHTIEF AG**
Clean Energy Cryogenics; **Clean Energy Fuels Corp**
Clean Energy Renewables; **Clean Energy Fuels Corp**
CleanSource; **Active Power Inc**
ClearGen II; **Ballard Power Systems Inc**
Clearloop; **Silicon Ranch Corporation**
Cloverly; **Southern Company**
CNOOC Oil Sands Canada; **Syncrude Canada Ltd**
Cobber; **ReNu Energy Limited**
Collins Aerospace Systems; **Raytheon Technologies Corporation**
Command; **3M Company**
Commonwealth Edison Company; **Exelon Corporation**
Companhia de Gas de Sao Paulo (Comgas); **Cosan SA**
COMPTE.R; **Talbott's Biomass Energy Systems Ltd**
Constellation; **Exelon Corporation**
Contemporary Amperex Technology (USA) Inc; **Contemporary Amperex Technology Co Limited (CATL)**
Contemporary Amperex Technology Canada Limited; **Contemporary Amperex Technology Co Limited (CATL)**
Contemporary Amperex Technology France; **Contemporary Amperex Technology Co Limited (CATL)**
Contemporary Amperex Technology GmbH; **Contemporary Amperex Technology Co Limited (CATL)**
Control Empresarial de Capitales SA de CV; **Fomento de Construcciones y Contratas SA (FCC)**
Copel Comercializacao SA; **Companhia Paranaense de Energia - Copel**
Copel Distribuicao SA; **Companhia Paranaense de Energia - Copel**
Copel Geracao y Transmissao SA; **Companhia Paranaense de Energia - Copel**
Copel Renovaveis SA; **Companhia Paranaense de Energia - Copel**
Copel Telecomunicacoes SA; **Companhia Paranaense de Energia - Copel**
Corun Peve Automotive Battery Co Ltd; **Primearth EV Energy Co Ltd**
Cory Environmental Holdings Ltd; **Cory Group (Cory Topco Limited)**
Cory Environmental Ltd; **Cory Group (Cory Topco Limited)**
Cory Riverside (Holdings) Ltd; **Cory Group (Cory Topco Limited)**
Cory Ship Repair Services Ltd; **Cory Group (Cory Topco Limited)**
Cosan Logistica SA; **Cosan SA**
Cosan SA; **Cosan SA**
Countrywide Renewable Hydrogen; **ReNu Energy Limited**
CPB Contractors; **HOCHTIEF AG**
CPN Management LP; **Calpine Corporation**
CPN Pipeline; **Calpine Corporation**
Crimson Renewable Energy LLC; **SeQuential**
DAC-E1/BPAC-E1; **Central Electronics Limited**
DACF-710P; **Central Electronics Limited**
DACF-720P; **Central Electronics Limited**
DACF-730P; **Central Electronics Limited**
DAC-RS232; **Central Electronics Limited**
DATEVAL1.0; **BIOS-BIOENERGYSYSTEME GmbH**
Delmarva Power & Light; **Exelon Corporation**
Delo; **Chevron Corporation**
Delta; **Nordex SE**
Denalie Water Solutions LLC; **Imperial Western Products Inc**
DiamondPeak Holdings Corp; **Lordstown Motors Corp**
Digital Imaging Solutions BU; **Sharp Corporation**
Digital Ventures Lab; **Siemens Gamesa Renewable Energy SA**
Diode Ventures; **Black & Veatch Holding Company**
Direct Wafer; **CubicPV**
Douglas Acquisitions LLC; **Quantum Fuel Systems LLC**
Dryolysis; **Group14 Technologies Inc**

INDEX OF SUBSIDIARIES, BRAND NAMES AND AFFILIATIONS, CONT.

Duke Energy Commercial Enterprises Inc; **Duke Energy Sustainable Solutions**
Duke Energy Corporation; **Duke Energy Sustainable Solutions**
Duke Energy One Inc; **Duke Energy Sustainable Solutions**
Duke Energy Renewables Inc; **Duke Energy Sustainable Solutions**
Duke Energy Renewables Storage LLC; **Duke Energy Sustainable Solutions**
Duke Energy Renewables Wind LLC; **Duke Energy Sustainable Solutions**
DuPont de Nemours Inc; **IFF Nutrition & Biosciences**
Dupont Nutrition & Biosciences; **IFF Nutrition & Biosciences**
E.ON SE; **Essent NV**
E-40; **Nuvera Fuel Cells LLC**
E-60; **Nuvera Fuel Cells LLC**
Eagle Creek Renewable Energy; **Ontario Power Generation Inc**
EcoChain Inc; **Soluna Holdings Inc**
EDF Energies Nouvelles Reparties SAS; **Photowatt International SAS**
Edison International; **Southern California Edison Company**
EFOY; **SFC Energy AG**
EFOY Hydrogen; **SFC Energy AG**
Electricite de France SA (EDF); **EDF Energy Nuclear Generation Group Limited**
EnDura Fuels; **Renewable Energy Group Inc**
Endurance; **Lordstown Motors Corp**
Enel Green Power; **Enel SpA**
Enel SpA; **Enel Green Power SpA**
Enel SpA; **Enel X North America Inc**
Enel X; **Enel SpA**
ENERCON SCADA Metro; **ENERCON GmbH**
Energiedirect.nl; **Essent NV**
Energir Inc; **Green Mountain Power Corporation**
Energy Capital Partners; **Calpine Corporation**
Energy Portfolio Management; **Scottish and Southern Energy plc (SSE)**
Energy Vault SA; **Energy Vault Holdings Inc**
Enforce Products; **Imperial Western Products Inc**
ENGIE; **ENGIE Global Energy Management & Sales**
enjoy; **Eni SpA**
Enosi Australia Pty Ltd; **ReNu Energy Limited**
Entergy Arkansas LLC; **Entergy Corporation**
Entergy Louisiana LLC; **Entergy Corporation**
Entergy Mississippi LLC; **Entergy Corporation**
Entergy New Orleans LLC; **Entergy Corporation**
Entergy Texas Inc; **Entergy Corporation**
EnVentus; **Vestas Wind Systems A/S**
Envision Group; **Envision AESC SDI Co Ltd**
Epsilor; **Arotech Corporation**
EQT AB Group; **Covanta Holding Corporation**

EQT Infrastructure V Fund; **Covanta Holding Corporation**
Equinox; **SunPower Corporation**
ERI; **Energy Recovery Inc**
E-Series; **Nuvera Fuel Cells LLC**
Esso; **Exxon Mobil Corporation (ExxonMobil)**
Eurovia; **VINCI SA**
eVinci; **Westinghouse Electric Company LLC**
Evonik Nutrition & Care GmbH; **Evonik Industries AG**
Evonik Performance Materials GmbH; **Evonik Industries AG**
Evonik Resource Efficiency GmbH; **Evonik Industries AG**
Evonik Technology & Infrastructure GmbH; **Evonik Industries AG**
Exelon Generation Company LLC; **Exelon Corporation**
Exxon; **Exxon Mobil Corporation (ExxonMobil)**
ExxonMobil; **Exxon Mobil Corporation (ExxonMobil)**
FAAC Incorporated; **Arotech Corporation**
FACC Industrial; **Fomento de Construcciones y Contratas SA (FCC)**
FCC Aqualia; **Fomento de Construcciones y Contratas SA (FCC)**
FCC Concessiones; **Fomento de Construcciones y Contratas SA (FCC)**
FCC Construction; **Fomento de Construcciones y Contratas SA (FCC)**
FCgen; **Ballard Power Systems Inc**
FCgen-H2PM; **Ballard Power Systems Inc**
FCmove; **Ballard Power Systems Inc**
FCvelocity; **Ballard Power Systems Inc**
FCwave; **Ballard Power Systems Inc**
Filtrete; **3M Company**
Flatiron; **HOCHTIEF AG**
Flertex; **Alstom SA**
FLEX; **MiaSole Hi-Tech Corp**
FLIR Systems Inc; **Teledyne Technologies Inc**
Florida Chemical Company; **Archer-Daniels-Midland Company (ADM)**
Florida Power & Light Company; **NextEra Energy Inc**
Fortis Inc; **UNS Energy Corporation**
Fortune Solar Holdings Limited; **Trina Solar Co Ltd**
Fosler Construction Company Inc; **Babcock & Wilcox Enterprises Inc**
Foxconn Technology Co Ltd; **Sharp Corporation**
Fuel Cell Extended Run; **APC by Schneider Electric**
Future Energy Fund; **Chevron Technology Ventures LLC**
Future Energy Fund II; **Chevron Technology Ventures LLC**
Futuro; **3M Company**
Gasmig; **Companhia Energetica de Minas Gerais SA (CEMIG)**
GE Energy Consulting; **GE Power**
GE Gas Power; **GE Power**
GE Hitachi Nuclear Energy; **GE Power**

INDEX OF SUBSIDIARIES, BRAND NAMES AND AFFILIATIONS, CONT.

GE Power Conversion; **GE Power**
GE Steam Power; **GE Power**
GE Vernova; **GE Renewable Energy**
GenCare; **Plug Power Inc**
GenDrive; **Plug Power Inc**
Generacion Espana; **Iberdrola SA**
General Electric Co. (GE); **GE Renewable Energy**
General Electric Company; **GE Global Research**
General Electric Company; **GE Vernova**
General Electric Company (GE); **GE Power**
GenFuel; **Plug Power Inc**
GenKey; **Plug Power Inc**
GenSure; **Plug Power Inc**
GenSure HP; **Plug Power Inc**
Georgia Power Company; **Southern Company**
Gigafactory; **Tesla Inc**
Gleadell Agriculture Ltd; **Archer-Daniels-Midland Company (ADM)**
Green Bidco SpA; **Falck Renewables SpA**
Green Island Cement; **CK Infrastructure Holdings Limited**
GridLiance GP LLC; **NextEra Energy Inc**
GridLiance Holdco LP; **NextEra Energy Inc**
Gridtec Solutions; **American Superconductor Corporation**
Groupe Aecon Quebec Ltee; **Aecon Group Inc**
Guangdong Brunp Recycling Technology Limited; **Contemporary Amperex Technology Co Limited (CATL)**
Halliburton Labs; **Halliburton Company**
Hanergy Holding Group Limited; **Global Solar Energy Inc**
Hanergy Holdings Group Co Ltd; **MiaSole Hi-Tech Corp**
Hanwha Q Cells; **Hanwha Solutions Corporation**
Hanwha Solutions Corporation; **Hanwha Q Cells**
Havoline; **Chevron Corporation**
Helion Hydrogen Power; **Alstom SA**
Helix; **SunPower Corporation**
Hitachi Astemo Ltd; **Hitachi Limited**
Hitachi GE Nuclear Ltd; **Hitachi Limited**
Hitachi High-tech Amata Smart Services Co Ltd; **Hitachi Limited**
Hitachi Industry & Control Solutions Ltd; **Hitachi Limited**
Hitachi Rail STS Mobilinx Hurontario GP Inc; **Hitachi Limited**
Hitachi Solutions Technology Ltd; **Hitachi Limited**
HOCHTIEF Infrastructure; **HOCHTIEF AG**
HOCHTIEF PPP; **HOCHTIEF AG**
Hungrana Ltd; **Archer-Daniels-Midland Company (ADM)**
Hutchinson; **TotalEnergies SE**
Hydro-Quebec TransEnergie; **Hydro-Quebec**
Hydrovolt; **Northvolt AB**
Hyster-Yale Group Inc; **Nuvera Fuel Cells LLC**
Iberdrola Distribucion Electrica; **Iberdrola SA**

Iberdrola Generacion Mexico; **Iberdrola SA**
Iberdrola Renovables Energia; **Iberdrola SA**
I-Cells; **Motech Industries Inc**
IDACORP Financial Services Inc; **IDACORP Inc**
Idaho Power Company; **IDACORP Inc**
Ida-West Energy Company; **IDACORP Inc**
IFF; **IFF Nutrition & Biosciences**
iGO (intelligent Goldwind Offshore Platform); **Xinjiang Goldwind Science & Technology Co Ltd**
Illuminating Company (The); **FirstEnergy Corporation**
Imperial Oil Resources Limited; **Syncrude Canada Ltd**
INEVO; **Orano SA**
InfiniD; **Renewable Energy Group Inc**
InfraStruXure; **APC by Schneider Electric**
Ingersoll Rand plc; **Trane Technologies plc**
Innovation Campus Delaware; **Air Liquide US LLC**
Integer Holdings Corporation; **Electrochem**
Inter-Coastal Electronics; **Arotech Corporation**
International Flavors & Fragrances Inc; **IFF Nutrition & Biosciences**
InvisiMount; **SunPower Corporation**
ION; **Ion Storage Systems Inc**
IsoBoost; **Energy Recovery Inc**
IsoGen; **Energy Recovery Inc**
IWP Fabrication; **Imperial Western Products Inc**
JASO Holdings Limited; **JA Solar Technology Co Ltd**
Jersey Central Power & Light; **FirstEnergy Corporation**
JG Finneran; **Porvair plc**
JinkoSolar; **JinkoSolar Holding Co Ltd**
Kenter; **Alliander NV**
Kern River Gas Transmission Company; **Berkshire Hathaway Energy Company**
Landmark; **Halliburton Company**
Langley Holdings PLC; **Active Power Inc**
Leighton Asia; **HOCHTIEF AG**
Liander; **Alliander NV**
Liberty; **Clipper Windpower LLC**
Lightsource; **Lightsource BP**
Lingonberry NMC; **Northvolt AB**
Lithium Power; **Ultralife Corporation**
Littmann; **3M Company**
LM Wind Power; **GE Renewable Energy**
Macquarie Group Limited; **Blueleaf Energy**
Marathon Oil Corporation; **Atlantic Methanol Production Company LLC**
Marinetec Solutions; **American Superconductor Corporation**
McDowell Research; **Ultralife Corporation**
Mechanical Technology Incorporated; **Soluna Holdings Inc**
medmix AG; **Sulzer AG**
Met-Ed; **FirstEnergy Corporation**
Michigan Gas Utilities; **WEC Energy Group Inc**
Microbiome Labs; **Novozymes A/S**
microLED; **Nanosys Inc**

INDEX OF SUBSIDIARIES, BRAND NAMES AND AFFILIATIONS, CONT.

MidAmerican Energy Company; **Berkshire Hathaway Energy Company**
Miller Environmental Transfer; **Covanta Holding Corporation**
MILO; **Arotech Corporation**
Minnesota Energy Resources; **WEC Energy Group Inc**
Mississippi Power Company; **Southern Company**
Mitsubishi Corporation; **Mitsubishi Electric Corporation**
Mobil; **Exxon Mobil Corporation (ExxonMobil)**
Mobile Communication BU; **Sharp Corporation**
Model 3; **Tesla Inc**
Model S; **Tesla Inc**
Model X; **Tesla Inc**
Model Y; **Tesla Inc**
Mon Power; **FirstEnergy Corporation**
Moove; **Cosan SA**
Motech Power; **Motech Industries Inc**
Motech Solar; **Motech Industries Inc**
MOXIE+; **EnerDel Inc**
MSTS Payments LLC; **Shell Oil Company**
MTI Instruments Inc; **Soluna Holdings Inc**
NACCO Materials Handling Group Inc; **Nuvera Fuel Cells LLC**
Nalcor Energy; **Newfoundland and Labrador Hydro**
Nanophosphate; **Lithium Werks BV**
Neovia SAS; **Archer-Daniels-Midland Company (ADM)**
Nexcare; **3M Company**
Next47; **Siemens AG**
NextEra Energy Capital Holdings Inc; **NextEra Energy Inc**
NextEra Energy Inc; **NextEra Energy Resources LLC**
NextEra Energy Resources LLC; **NextEra Energy Inc**
NG Advantage LLC; **Clean Energy Fuels Corp**
Nightsun; **Spectrolab Inc**
No Compromise; **Amyris Inc**
Nordex Energy GmbH; **Nordex SE**
North Shore Gas; **WEC Energy Group Inc**
Northeast Power Systems Inc; **American Superconductor Corporation**
Northern Natural Gas Company; **Berkshire Hathaway Energy Company**
Northern Powergrid; **Berkshire Hathaway Energy Company**
Northumbrian Water; **CK Infrastructure Holdings Limited**
Northvolt Dwa; **Northvolt AB**
Northvolt Ett; **Northvolt AB**
Northvolt Labs; **Northvolt AB**
Nothern New Englang Energy Corporation; **Green Mountain Power Corporation**
NP2; **Primearth EV Energy Co Ltd**
NP2.5; **Primearth EV Energy Co Ltd**
NuGen Energy LLC; **REX American Resources Corporation**
NV Energy Inc; **Berkshire Hathaway Energy Company**
Oaktree Capital Management LLC; **Brookfield Asset Management Inc**
Ohio Edison; **FirstEnergy Corporation**
OMERS Infrastructure Management Inc; **Fotowatio Renewable Ventures SLU**
One Earth Energy LLC; **REX American Resources Corporation**
Orano Med; **Orano SA**
Orano Projects; **Orano SA**
Organic Solutions; **Imperial Western Products Inc**
ORION; **Badger Meter Inc**
Ormat Energy Converter; **Ormat Technologies Inc**
Overland Contracting; **Black & Veatch Holding Company**
Pacific Ethanol Inc; **Alto Ingredients Inc**
Pacific Gas and Electric Company; **PG&E Corporation**
Pacific Power; **PacifiCorp**
Pacificor; **Archer-Daniels-Midland Company (ADM)**
PacifiCorp; **Berkshire Hathaway Energy Company**
Panasonic Holdings Corporation; **Primearth EV Energy Co Ltd**
PECO Energy Company; **Exelon Corporation**
Penelec; **FirstEnergy Corporation**
Peoples Gas; **WEC Energy Group Inc**
Pepco Holdings LLC; **Exelon Corporation**
PeroxyChem; **Evonik Industries AG**
Peter Cremer Holding GmbH & Co KG; **Peter Cremer North America LP**
Piller Group GmbH; **Active Power Inc**
Piller Power Systems Inc; **Active Power Inc**
Pinnacle West Capital Corporation; **Arizona Public Service Company**
Platinum Equity LLC; **Clipper Windpower LLC**
PLH Energy LLC; **EnerDel Inc**
Porocel Group; **Evonik Industries AG**
Port Hope Conversion Facility; **Cameco Corporation**
Porvair Filtration Group Ltd; **Porvair plc**
Porvair Sciences; **Porvair plc**
Post-it; **3M Company**
Potomac Edison; **FirstEnergy Corporation**
Potomac Electric Power Company; **Exelon Corporation**
PoweFLEX+; **Global Solar Energy Inc**
Power Authority of the State of New York (The); **New York Power Authority**
PowerBoost; **PowerFilm Solar Inc**
Powercor; **CK Infrastructure Holdings Limited**
Powerex Corporation; **British Columbia Hydro and Power Authority**
PowerFilm; **PowerFilm Solar Inc**
PowerFLEX; **Global Solar Energy Inc**
PowerFLEX + FG-M1; **Global Solar Energy Inc**
Powerhouse; **Essent NV**
PowerHouse; **Active Power Inc**
PowerModule; **American Superconductor Corporation**
Powertech Labs Inc; **British Columbia Hydro and Power Authority**

INDEX OF SUBSIDIARIES, BRAND NAMES AND AFFILIATIONS, CONT.

Powertracer; **ReNu Energy Limited**
Pratt & Whitney; **Raytheon Technologies Corporation**
PrecisionBiotics Group Limited; **Novozymes A/S**
Pressure Exchanger; **Energy Recovery Inc**
ProGen; **Plug Power Inc**
Project 24; **Green Plains Inc**
Public Service Company of New Mexico; **PNM Resources Inc**
Puget Holdings LLC; **Puget Energy Inc**
Puget Sound Energy Inc; **Puget Energy Inc**
Pump Engineering; **Energy Recovery Inc**
PURECANE; **Amyris Inc**
PuriD; **Renewable Energy Group Inc**
PX; **Energy Recovery Inc**
Q.ANTUM; **Hanwha Q Cells**
Q-Cab; **Quantum Fuel Systems LLC**
Q-Lite; **Quantum Fuel Systems LLC**
Q-Rail; **Quantum Fuel Systems LLC**
QS-1; **QuantumScape Corporation**
Q-VP; **Quantum Fuel Systems LLC**
RAG Foundation; **Evonik Industries AG**
Raizen Combustiveis SA; **Cosan SA**
Raizen Energia SA; **Cosan SA**
Raytheon Intelligence & Space; **Raytheon Technologies Corporation**
Raytheon Missiles & Defense; **Raytheon Technologies Corporation**
Realtime Technologies; **Arotech Corporation**
REC Solar Commercial Corporation; **Duke Energy Sustainable Solutions**
Recurrent Energy LLC; **Canadian Solar Inc**
Redeem; **Clean Energy Fuels Corp**
Regenerative Energy; **Silicon Ranch Corporation**
Reliance Anil Dhirubhai Ambani Group; **Reliance Power Limited**
Reliance Home Comfort; **CK Infrastructure Holdings Limited**
RGA Investments LLC; **Beacon Power LLC**
Riverside (Thames) Ltd; **Cory Group (Cory Topco Limited)**
Riverside Energy Park Ltd; **Cory Group (Cory Topco Limited)**
Riverside Resource Recovery Ltd; **Cory Group (Cory Topco Limited)**
Roadster; **Tesla Inc**
Rocky Mountain Power; **PacifiCorp**
Rohasys BV; **Porvair plc**
Royal Dutch Shell plc; **Shell Oil Company**
Royal Dutch Shell plc; **Shell plc**
Rumo SA; **Cosan SA**
RWE Generation; **RWE AG**
RWE Power AG; **RWE AG**
RWE Renewables; **RWE AG**
RWE Supply & Trading; **RWE AG**
S111; **Suzlon Energy Limited**

S120; **Suzlon Energy Limited**
S128; **Suzlon Energy Limited**
S133; **Suzlon Energy Limited**
S52; **Suzlon Energy Limited**
S66; **Suzlon Energy Limited**
S82; **Suzlon Energy Limited**
S88; **Suzlon Energy Limited**
SA Power Networks; **CK Infrastructure Holdings Limited**
Salini Impregilo SpA; **Webuild SpA**
Samsung Group; **Samsung Electronics Co Ltd**
Savion LLC; **Shell Oil Company**
SB Energy Holdings Ltd; **Adani Green Energy Limited**
SB Energy India; **Adani Green Energy Limited**
SCADA Remote; **ENERCON GmbH**
SCANA Server; **ENERCON GmbH**
SCC55; **Group14 Technologies Inc**
Schneider Electric SE; **APC by Schneider Electric**
Scotch; **3M Company**
ScottishPower Energy Networks; **Iberdrola SA**
ScottishPower Generation Holdings; **Iberdrola SA**
ScottishPower Renewable Energy; **Iberdrola SA**
Seal Analytical; **Porvair plc**
Selee Corporation; **Porvair plc**
SEPPIC Inc; **Air Liquide US LLC**
SFC EMILY; **SFC Energy AG**
SFC JENNY; **SFC Energy AG**
SFC Power Manager 3G; **SFC Energy AG**
Shell plc; **Shell WindEnergy Inc**
Shell plc; **Silicon Ranch Corporation**
Shenhua Baoshen Railway Group Co Ltd; **China Shenhua Energy Company Limited**
Shenhua Baotou Energy Co Ltd; **China Shenhua Energy Company Limited**
Shenhua Information Technology Co Ltd; **China Shenhua Energy Company Limited**
Shenhua Logistics Group Co Ltd; **China Shenhua Energy Company Limited**
Shenhua Sales Group Co Ltd; **China Shenhua Energy Company Limited**
Shenhua Shendong Coal Group Co Ltd; **China Shenhua Energy Company Limited**
Shen-Shan Highway; **CK Infrastructure Holdings Limited**
Shunfeng International Clean Energy Limited; **Wuxi Suntech Power Co Ltd**
Shunter; **Alstom SA**
Siemens Advanta; **Siemens AG**
Siemens AG; **Siemens Gamesa Renewable Energy SA**
Siemens Financial Services; **Siemens AG**
Siemens Healthineers AG; **Siemens AG**
Siemens Real Estate; **Siemens AG**
Siligenesis; **Group14 Technologies Inc**
Sinogy Toyota Automotive Energy System Co Ltd; **Primearth EV Energy Co Ltd**

INDEX OF SUBSIDIARIES, BRAND NAMES AND AFFILIATIONS, CONT.

Sinopec Oil Sands Partnership; **Syncrude Canada Ltd**
Smart Appliances & Solutions BU; **Sharp Corporation**
Smart Business Solutions BU; **Sharp Corporation**
Societe de Transports Speciaux Industriels; **Orano SA**
SolarRide; **MiaSole Hi-Tech Corp**
Soltronix; **PowerFilm Solar Inc**
SONAGAS GE; **Atlantic Methanol Production Company LLC**
SOREN; **Photowatt International SAS**
Southern Company Gas; **Southern Company**
Southern Power Company; **Southern Company**
SPARC; **Commonwealth Fusion Systems LLC**
SpectroLink; **Spectrolab Inc**
Sperry; **Halliburton Company**
SSE Airtricity; **Scottish and Southern Energy plc (SSE)**
SSE Airtricity Community Fund; **SSE Airtricity Limited**
SSE Energy Solutions; **Scottish and Southern Energy plc (SSE)**
SSE Enterprise; **Scottish and Southern Energy plc (SSE)**
SSE plc; **SSE Airtricity Limited**
SSE Renewables; **Scottish and Southern Energy plc (SSE)**
SSE Thermal; **Scottish and Southern Energy plc (SSE)**
SSEN Distribution; **Scottish and Southern Energy plc (SSE)**
SSEN Transmission; **Scottish and Southern Energy plc (SSE)**
Stam Heerhugowaard Holding; **Alliander NV**
Stonepeak Infrastructure Partners; **IronClad Energy Partners LLC**
StreetHub; **Carmanah Technologies Corporation**
Suncor Energy (Syncrude) Operating Inc; **Syncrude Canada Ltd**
Suncor Energy Inc; **Syncrude Canada Ltd**
SX; **Spectrolab Inc**
Syncrude Project; **Syncrude Canada Ltd**
System Energy Resources Inc; **Entergy Corporation**
Talbott; **Talbott's Biomass Energy Systems Ltd**
Taro; **Chevron Corporation**
Tata Group; **Tata Power Co Ltd**
Teledyne Brown Engineering Inc; **Teledyne Technologies Inc**
Teledyne Optech Inc; **Teledyne Technologies Inc**
Teledyne Scientific Company; **Teledyne Technologies Inc**
Terasana; **Amyris Inc**
Tesla Cybertruck; **Tesla Inc**
Tesla Semi; **Tesla Inc**
Texaco; **Chevron Corporation**
Texas-New Mexico Power Company; **PNM Resources Inc**
Thermo King; **Trane Technologies plc**
Think Green; **Waste Management Inc**
Thornvale Holdings Limited; **World Energy LLC**
Total SE; **TotalEnergies SE**
Toyota Motor Corporation; **Primearth EV Energy Co Ltd**
Trane; **Trane Technologies plc**

TreviPay; **Shell Oil Company**
Tucson Electric Power Company; **UNS Energy Corporation**
Turner; **HOCHTIEF AG**
UEC Electronics LLC; **Arotech Corporation**
UK Power Networks; **CK Infrastructure Holdings Limited**
Ultra V; **Wuxi Suntech Power Co Ltd**
Ultra V Pro; **Wuxi Suntech Power Co Ltd**
Ultra X; **Wuxi Suntech Power Co Ltd**
UltralCleanBlenD; **Renewable Energy Group Inc**
Ultralife Batteries; **Ultralife Corporation**
Ultralife Batteries (UK) Ltd; **Ultralife Corporation**
Ultralife Batteries India Private Limited; **Ultralife Corporation**
Ultraphosphate; **A123 Systems LLC**
Uniflow Power Limited; **ReNu Energy Limited**
Uniper Energy DMCC; **Uniper SE**
UniSource Energy Services Inc; **UNS Energy Corporation**
United Auto Battery Co; **Contemporary Amperex Technology Co Limited (CATL)**
UNTHA; **Talbott's Biomass Energy Systems Ltd**
Upper Michigan Energy Resources; **WEC Energy Group Inc**
URE; **United Renewable Energy LLC**
Ursa; **Chevron Corporation**
Vance Street Capital LLC; **Carmanah Technologies Corporation**
Vandebron; **Essent NV**
VelociD; **Renewable Energy Group Inc**
VIGOR+; **EnerDel Inc**
VINCI Airports; **VINCI SA**
VINCI Autoroutes; **VINCI SA**
VINCI Concessions SA; **VINCI SA**
VINCI Construction; **VINCI SA**
VINCI Contracting LLC; **VINCI SA**
VINCI Energies; **VINCI SA**
Viridity Energy Solutions Inc; **Ormat Technologies Inc**
Vivint Solar Inc; **Sunrun Inc**
VODA A/S; **Babcock & Wilcox Enterprises Inc**
Voltblocks; **Northvolt AB**
Voltpacks; **Northvolt AB**
Voltracks; **Northvolt AB**
VorTeq; **Energy Recovery Inc**
Wanxiang Group Corporation; **A123 Systems LLC**
Waste2Glass; **Veolia Environnement SA**
Waterfront Shipping Company Limited; **Methanex Corporation**
WE Energies; **WEC Energy Group Inc**
Wellington Electricity; **CK Infrastructure Holdings Limited**
West Penn Power; **FirstEnergy Corporation**
Wilmar International Limited; **Archer-Daniels-Midland Company (ADM)**

INDEX OF SUBSIDIARIES, BRAND NAMES AND AFFILIATIONS, CONT.

Windtec Solutions; **American Superconductor Corporation**
Wisconsin Public Service; **WEC Energy Group Inc**
Wurth Electronics Midcom; **Wurth Elektronik GmbH & Co KG**
Wurth Elektronik CBT; **Wurth Elektronik GmbH & Co KG**
Wurth Elektronik eiSos; **Wurth Elektronik GmbH & Co KG**
Wurth Elektronik iBE; **Wurth Elektronik GmbH & Co KG**
Wurth Elektronik Stelvio Kontek; **Wurth Elektronik GmbH & Co KG**
Wurth Group; **Wurth Elektronik GmbH & Co KG**
XTO; **Exxon Mobil Corporation (ExxonMobil)**
Yingli Energy (Beijing) Co Ltd; **Yingli Energy (China) Co Ltd**
Yingli Energy (China) Co Ltd; **Yingli Energy (China) Co Ltd**
Yingli Green Energy Americas Inc; **Yingli Energy (China) Co Ltd**
Yingli Green Energy Capital Holding (Hong Kong); **Yingli Energy (China) Co Ltd**
Yingli Green Energy Chile SpA; **Yingli Energy (China) Co Ltd**
Yingli Green Energy Mexico; **Yingli Energy (China) Co Ltd**
Yingli Green Energy Singapore Company Pte Ltd; **Yingli Energy (China) Co Ltd**
Ziegler Group (The); **Archer-Daniels-Midland Company (ADM)**
Zorlu Enerji Dagtim AS; **Zorlu Enerji Elektrik Uretim AS**
Zorlu Group; **Zorlu Enerji Elektrik Uretim AS**
Zorlu Osmangazi Enerji Sanayi ve Ticaret AS; **Zorlu Enerji Elektrik Uretim AS**

A Short Solar Power, Wind Power and Renewable Energy Industry Glossary

Alcohol: The family name of a group of organic chemical compounds composed of carbon, hydrogen and oxygen. The series of molecules vary in chain length and are composed of a hydrocarbon plus a hydroxyl group. Alcohols include methanol and ethanol. Alcohol is frequently used in fuel, organic solvents, anti-freeze and beverages. Also see "Ethanol."

Alternating Current (AC): An electric current that reverses its direction at regularly recurring intervals, usually 50 or 60 times per second.

Alternative Fuel: Includes methanol, denatured ethanol and other alcohols, separately or in mixtures of 85% by volume or more with gasoline or other fuels, CNG, LNG, LPG, hydrogen, coal derived liquid fuels, fuels other than alcohols derived from biological materials, electricity, neat biodiesel, or any other fuel determined to be substantially not petroleum and yielding substantial energy security benefits and substantial environmental benefits. It is defined pursuant to the EPACT (Energy Policy Act of 1992), alternative fuels.

Alternative Fuels Data Center (AFDC): A program sponsored by the Department of Energy to collect emissions, operational and maintenance data on all types of alternative fuel vehicles across the country.

Alternative Fuels Utilization Program (AFUP): A program managed by Department of Energy with the goals of improving national energy security by displacing imported oil: improving air quality through the development and widespread use of alternative fuels for transportation and increasing the production of alternative fuel vehicles.

Alternative Motor Fuels Act of 1988 (AMFA): Public Law 100-494. Encourages the development, production and demonstration of alternative motor fuels and alternative fuel vehicles.

Alternative-Fuel Provider: A fuel provider (or any affiliate or business unit under its control) is an alternative-fuel provider if its principal business is producing, storing, refining, processing, transporting, distributing, importing or selling (at wholesale or retail) any alternative fuel (other than electricity): or generating, transmitting, importing or selling (at wholesale or retail) electricity: or if that fuel provider produces, imports, or produces and imports (in combination) an average of 50,000 barrels per day of petroleum, and 30% (a substantial portion) or more of its gross annual revenues are derived from producing alternative fuels.

Amorphous Silicon: An alloy of silica and hydrogen, with a disordered, noncrystalline internal atomic arrangement, that can be deposited in thin layers (a few micrometers in thickness) by a number of deposition methods to produce thin-film photovoltaic cells on glass, metal or plastic substrates.

Analytics: Generally refers to the deep examination of massive amounts of data, often on a continual or real-time basis. The goal is to discover deeper insights, make recommendations or generate predictions. Advanced analytics includes such techniques as big data, predictive analytics, text analytics, data mining, forecasting, optimization and simulation.

Anhydrous: Describes a compound that does not contain any water. Ethanol produced for fuel use is often referred to as anhydrous ethanol, as it has had almost all water removed.

APAC: Asia Pacific Advisory Committee. A multi-country committee representing the Asia and Pacific region.

Applied Research: The application of compounds, processes, materials or other items discovered during basic research to practical uses. The goal is to move discoveries along to the final development phase.

Barrel (Petroleum): A unit of volume equal to 42 U.S. gallons.

Barrels of Oil Equivalent (BOE): A measure of the energy of non-oil fuels. For example, a BOE of natural gas is roughly 6,000 cubic feet. The measure is derived by assessing the amount of a fuel required to generate the same heat content as a typical barrel of oil.

Basic Research: Attempts to discover compounds, materials, processes or other items that may be largely or entirely new and/or unique. Basic research may start with a theoretical concept that has yet to be proven. The goal is to create discoveries that can be moved along to applied research. Basic research is sometimes referred to as "blue sky" research.

Bbl: See "Barrel (Petroleum)."

Bcf: One billion cubic feet.

Bcfe: One billion cubic feet of natural gas equivalent.

Bi-Fuel Vehicle: A vehicle with two separate fuel systems designed to run either on an alternative fuel, or on gasoline or diesel, using only one fuel at a time. Bi-fuel vehicles are referred to as "dual-fuel" vehicles in the CAA and EPACT.

Binary Cycle Generation: A method of geothermal electricity generation where lower-temperature geothermal sources are tapped. The geothermal steam source is used to heat another liquid that has a lower boiling point, which then drives the turbine. Also see "Flash Steam Generation."

Biochemical Conversion: The use of enzymes and catalysts to change biological substances chemically to produce energy products. The digestion of organic wastes or sewage by microorganisms to produce methane is an example of biochemical conversion.

Biodiesel: A fuel derived when glycerin is separated from vegetable oils or animal fats. The resulting byproducts are methyl esters (the chemical name for biodiesel) and glycerin which can be used in soaps and cleaning products. It has lower emissions than petroleum diesel and is currently used as an additive to that fuel since it helps with lubricity.

Bioenergy: Useful, renewable energy produced from organic matter, which may either be used directly as a fuel or processed into liquids and gases. See "Biomass."

Bioethanol: A fuel produced by the fermentation of plant matter such as corn. Fermentation is enhanced through the use of enzymes that are created through biotechnology. Also, see "Ethanol."

Biomass: Organic, non-fossil material of biological origin constituting a renewable energy source. The biomass can be burnt as fuel in a system that creates steam to turn a turbine, generating electricity. For example, biomass can include wood chips and agricultural crops.

Biorefinery: A refinery that produces fuels from biomass. These fuels may include bioethanol (produced from corn or other plant matter) or biodiesel (produced from plant or animal matter).

Bitumen: A naturally occurring viscous mixture, mainly of hydrocarbons heavier than pentane, that may contain sulfur compounds. Also, see "Tar Sands (Oil Sands)."

Boiling Water Reactor: A type of nuclear power reactor that uses ordinary water for both the coolant and the neutron moderator. The steam is used to directly produce electricity through generators.

Breeder Reactor: A breeder reactor is a nuclear plant that produces more fissile material (such as U-235 or plutonium) that it actually consumes. A Fast Breeder Reactor (FBR), once initially started, can utilize depleted uranium from traditional reactors as fuel, thus helping to alleviate the problem of storing spent nuclear fuel rods. This method is used in many nations, but not in the U.S. America does not use FBRs because they create as a byproduct weapons-grade plutonium. A Thermal Breeder Reactor (TBR), once started with enriched uranium or other fissile material, can then be kept running with thorium (a chemical element that is radioactive and found in abundance in nature). Some researchers consider a TBR to be the ultimate, safest, most efficient type of nuclear reactor, due to its use of low-cost thorium as fuel.

British Thermal Unit (Btu): The quantity of heat needed to raise the temperature of 1 pound of water by 1 degree Fahrenheit at or near 39.2 degrees Fahrenheit.

Butane: A normally gaseous straight-chain or branch-chain hydrocarbon (C4H10), extracted from natural gas or refinery gas streams. It includes isobutane and normal butane.

Butanol (Biobutanol): Butyl alcohol, sometimes used as a solvent. In the form of biobutanol, it is an ethanol substitute, generally derived from sugar beets to be used as a fuel additive.

Butyl Alcohol: Alcohol derived from butane that is used in organic synthesis and as a solvent.

CAES: Compressed Air Energy Storage.

CAFTA-DR: See "Central American-Dominican Republic Free Trade Agreement (CAFTA-DR)."

California Air Resources Board (CARB): The state agency that regulates the air quality in California. Air quality regulations established by CARB are often stricter than those set by the federal government.

California Low-Emission Vehicle Program: A state requirement for automakers to produce vehicles with fewer emissions than current EPA standards. The five categories of California Low-Emission Vehicle Program standards, from least to most stringent, are TLEV, LEV, ULEV, SULEV and ZEV.

CANDU Reactor: A pressurized heavy-water, natural-uranium power reactor designed by a consortium of Canadian government and private industry participants. CANDU utilizes natural, unenriched uranium oxide as fuel. Because unenriched uranium is cheaper, this kind of reactor is attractive to developing countries. The fuel is contained in hundreds of tubes that are pressure resistant. This means that a tube can be refueled while the reactor is operating. CANDU is a registered trademark of the CANDU consortium.

Cap and Trade: A system in which governments attempt to reduce carbon emissions by major industry. First, an overall "cap" is placed, by government regulation, on total carbon emissions for particular companies and/or their industries. The "trade" part of cap and trade allows companies that operate efficiently on a carbon basis, and thereby emit a lower amount of carbon than law allows, to sell or trade the unused part of their carbon allowances to firms that are less efficient.

Capacity Factor: The ratio of the electrical energy produced by a generating unit for a certain period of time to the electrical energy that could have been produced at continuous full-power operation during the same period.

Capex: Capital expenditures.

Captive Offshoring: Used to describe a company-owned offshore operation. For example, Microsoft owns and operates significant captive offshore research and development centers in China and elsewhere that are offshore from Microsoft's U.S. home base. Also see "Offshoring."

Carbon Capture and Storage: See "Carbon Sequestration."

Carbon Dioxide (CO2): A product of combustion that has become an environmental concern in recent years. CO2 does not directly impair human health but is a "greenhouse gas" that traps the earth's heat and contributes to the potential for global warming.

Carbon Intensity: The amount of carbon dioxide that a nation emits, on average, in order to create a unit of GDP (gross domestic product, a measure of economic output).

Carbon Monoxide (CO): A colorless, odorless gas produced by the incomplete combustion of fuels with a limited oxygen supply, as in automobile engines.

Carbon Sequestration: The absorption and storage of CO2 from the atmosphere by the roots and leaves of plants: the carbon builds up as organic matter in the soil. In the energy industry, carbon sequestration refers to the process of isolating and storing carbon dioxide (a so-called greenhouse gas). One use is to avoid releasing carbon dioxide into the air when burning coal at a coal-fired power plant. Instead, the carbon dioxide is stored in the ground or otherwise stored in a permanent or semi-permanent fashion. Other uses include the return to the ground of carbon dioxide that is produced at natural gas wells, and the introduction of carbon dioxide into oil wells in order to increase internal pressure and production. This process is also known as carbon capture and storage (CCS).

Cast Silicon: Crystalline silicon obtained by pouring pure molten silicon into a vertical mold and adjusting the temperature gradient along the mold volume during cooling to obtain slow, vertically advancing crystallization of the silicon. The polycrystalline ingot thus formed is composed of large, relatively parallel, interlocking crystals. The cast ingots are sawed into wafers for further fabrication into photovoltaic cells. Cast-silicon wafers and ribbon-silicon sheets fabricated into cells are usually referred to as polycrystalline photovoltaic cells.

CCS: See "Carbon Sequestration."

Cellulosic Ethanol: See "Ethanol."

Central American-Dominican Republic Free Trade Agreement (CAFTA-DR): A trade agreement signed into law in 2005 that aimed to open up the Central American and Dominican Republic markets to American goods. Member nations include Guatemala, Nicaragua, Costa Rica, El Salvador, Honduras and the Dominican Republic. Before the law was signed, products from those countries could enter the U.S. almost tariff-free, while American goods heading into those countries faced stiff tariffs. The goal of this agreement was to create U.S. jobs while at the same time offering the non-U.S. member citizens a chance for a better quality of life through access to U.S.-made goods.

Cetane: Ignition performance rating of diesel fuel: the diesel equivalent to gasoline octane.

CHP: See "Combined Cycle."

Clean Air Act (CAA): A law setting emissions standards for stationary sources (e.g., factories and power plants). The original Clean Air Act was signed in 1963, and has been amended several times, most recently in 1990 (P.L. 101-549). The amendments of 1970 introduced motor vehicle emission standards (e.g., automobiles and trucks). Criteria pollutants included lead, ozone, CO, SO2, NOx and PM, as well as air toxics. In 1990, reformulated gasoline (RFG) and oxygenated gasoline provisions were added. The RFG provision requires use of RFG all year in certain areas. The oxygenated gasoline provision requires the use of oxygenated gasoline during certain months, when CO and ozone pollution are most serious. The regulations also require certain fleet operators to use clean fuel vehicles in 22 cities.

Clean Fuel Vehicle (CFV): Any vehicle certified by the Environmental Protection Agency as meeting certain federal emissions standards. The three categories of federal CFV standards, from least to most stringent, are LEV, ULEV and ZEV. The ILEV standard is voluntary and does not need to be adopted by states as part of the Clean-Fuel Fleet Program. CFVs are eligible for two federal programs, the California Pilot Program and the Clean-Fuel Fleet Program. CFV exhaust emissions standards for light-duty vehicles and light-duty trucks are numerically similar to those of CARB's California Low-Emission Vehicle Program.

Climate Change (Greenhouse Effect): A theory that assumes an increasing mean global surface temperature of the Earth caused by gases (sometimes referred to as greenhouse gases) in the atmosphere (including carbon dioxide, methane, nitrous oxide, ozone and chlorofluorocarbons). The greenhouse effect allows solar radiation to penetrate the Earth's atmosphere but absorbs the infrared radiation returning to space.

CNG: Compressed Natural Gas.

Coalbed Methane (CBM): A natural gas that is found in coal seams, while traditional natural gas deposits are trapped in porous rock formations. CBM is produced commercially in many areas, including the Rocky Mountains and other coal-rich areas throughout the U.S., in Australia and in other nations.

Cogeneration: See "Combined Heat and Power (CHP) Plant."

Combined Cycle: An electric generating technology in which electricity is produced from waste heat that would otherwise be lost when exiting from one or more gas (combustion) turbines. The exiting heat is routed to a conventional boiler or to a heat recovery steam generator for utilization by a steam turbine in the production of electricity. Such designs increase the efficiency of the electric generating unit. This process is also known as cogeneration or "combined heat and power" (CHP). One novel approach, know as ISCC or integrated solar combined cycle, adds the use of concentrated solar power (CSP) from mirrors, focused on a tower in order to generate additional steam, which is fed into the system. (See "Concentrating Solar Power (CSP).")

Combined Heat and Power (CHP) Plant: A facility that generates power via combined cycle technology. See "Combined Cycle."

Compact Fluorescent Lamp (CFL): A type of light bulb that provides considerable energy savings over traditional incandescent light bulbs.

Compressed Air Energy Storage (CAES): A storage system that directs surplus electricity to a compressor, which pumps air deep into layers of porous sandstone underneath dense, almost impermeable shale. The sandstone expands, trapping the air, which is later released. As the air rushes upward, it fires a turbine on the surface, thereby producing energy.

Compressed Natural Gas (CNG): Natural gas that has been compressed under high pressures, typically between 2000 and 3600 psi, held in a container. The gas expands when released for use as a fuel.

Compressor: A device to increase gas pressure capable of causing the flow of gas.

Concentrating Photovoltaic Power (CPV): An enhanced solar energy generating plant that relies on photovoltaic technology, but uses an advanced optical system such as mirrors to focus a large area of sunlight onto each cell for maximum efficiency. CPV panels are mounted on trackers (heliostats) to keep the focal point on the cell as the sun moves across the sky.

Concentrating Solar Power (CSP): The use of solar thermal collectors to absorb solar heat and then heat water, oil or other substances with that energy. CSP technologies include the use of large numbers of mirrors that reflect and concentrate sunlight upon "solar towers." As heat accumulates in the solar towers, it produces steam that is used to drive turbines and generate electricity. In the latest systems, CSP utilizes heliostats, or motor-driven mirrors, to track the sun through the sky during the day. (See "Heliostat.")

Conventional Thermal Electricity Generation: Electricity generated by an electric power plant using coal, petroleum or gas as its source of energy.

CPV: See "Concentrating Photovoltaic Power (CPV)."

CSP: See "Concentrating Solar Power (CSP)."

Denatured Alcohol: Ethanol that contains a small amount of a toxic substance, such as methanol or gasoline, which cannot be removed easily by chemical or physical means. Alcohols intended for industrial use must be denatured to avoid federal alcoholic beverage tax.

Dendrimer: A type of molecule that can be used with small molecules to give them certain desirable characteristics. Dendrimers are utilized in technologies for electronic displays. See "Organic LED (OLED)."

Direct Current (DC): An electric current that flows in a constant direction. The magnitude of the current does not vary or has a slight variation.

Direct Methanol Fuel Cell (DMFC): A new energy concept for mobile electronic devices such as laptops and cell phones. Toshiba, the pioneer in this field, has exhibited tiny DMFCs capable of delivering up to 300 milliwatts for up to 35 hours of operation. A fuel cartridge can be replaced on an as-needed basis.

Distributed Power Generation: A method of generating electricity at or near the site where it will be consumed, such as the use of small, local generators, solar cells or fuel cells to power individual buildings, homes or neighborhoods. Such a system may also include storage batteries. Distributed power is thought by many analysts to offer distinct advantages. For example, electricity generated in this manner is not reliant upon the grid for distribution to the end user.

Distribution System: The portion of an electric system that is dedicated to delivering electric energy to an end user.

E10 (Gasohol): Ethanol/gasoline mixture containing 10% denatured ethanol and 90% gasoline, by volume.

E85: Ethanol/gasoline mixture containing 85% denatured ethanol and 15% gasoline, by volume.

E93: Ethanol mixture containing 93% ethanol, 5% methanol and 2% kerosene, by volume.

E95: Ethanol/gasoline mixture containing 95% denatured ethanol and 5% gasoline, by volume.

Electric Power Industry: The privately, publicly, federally and cooperatively owned electric utilities of the United States taken as a whole. Does not include special-purpose electric facilities.

Electric Power System: An individual electric power entity.

Electric Utility: A corporation, person, agency, authority or other legal entity or instrumentality that owns and/or operates facilities within the United States for the generation, transmission, distribution or sale of electric energy primarily for use by the public.

EMEA: The region comprised of Europe, the Middle East and Africa.

Emission: The release or discharge of a substance into the environment. Generally refers to the release of gases or particulates into the air.

Energy: The capacity for doing work as measured by the capability of doing work (potential energy) or the conversion of this capability to motion (kinetic energy). Most of the world's convertible energy comes from fossil fuels that are burned to produce heat that is then used as a transfer medium to mechanical or other means in order to accomplish tasks.

Energy Information Administration (EIA): An independent agency within the U.S. Department of Energy, the Energy Information Administration (EIA) develops surveys, collects energy data and does analytical and modeling analyses of energy issues.

Energy Intensity: The amount of energy needed for a nation to produce a unit of GDP (gross domestic product, a measure of economic output).

Energy Policy Act of 1992 (EPACT): (P.L. 102-486) A broad-ranging act signed into law on October 24, 1992. Titles III, IV, V, XV and XIX of EPACT deal with alternative transportation fuels. EPACT accelerates the purchase requirements for alternative fuel vehicles (AFVs) by the federal fleet, proposes eliminating the cap on CAFE credits that manufacturers can earn by producing dual- and flexible-fuel vehicles and requires fleets in large urban areas to purchase AFVs. EPACT also establishes tax incentives for purchasing AFVs, converting conventional gasoline vehicles to operate on alternative fuels and installing refueling or recharging facilities by the private sector.

Energy Service Company (ESCO): A company that provides energy-efficiency-related and other value-added services and for which performance contracting is a core part of its energy-efficiency services business. In a performance contract, the ESCO guarantees energy and/or dollar savings for the project and the ESCO's compensation is therefore linked in some fashion to the performance of the project.

ESCO: See "Energy Service Company (ESCO)."

Ethanol: A clear, colorless, flammable, oxygenated hydrocarbon, also called ethyl alcohol. In the U.S., it is used as a gasoline octane enhancer and oxygenate in a 10% blend called E10. Ethanol can be used in higher concentrations (such as an 85% blend called E85) in vehicles designed for its use. It is typically produced chemically from ethylene or biologically from fermentation of various sugars from carbohydrates found in agricultural crops and cellulose residues from crops or wood. Grain ethanol production is typically based on corn or sugarcane. Cellulosic ethanol production is based on agricultural waste, such as wheat stalks, that has been treated with enzymes to break the waste down into component sugars.

Ethyl Ester: A fatty ester formed when organically derived oils are combined with ethanol in the presence of a catalyst. After water washing, vacuum drying and filtration, the resulting ethyl ester has characteristics similar to petroleum-based diesel motor fuels.

Ethyl Tertiary Butyl Ether (ETBE): An aliphatic ether similar to MTBE (Methyl Tertiary Butyl Ether). This fuel oxygenate is manufactured by reacting isobutylene with ethanol. Having high octane and low volatility characteristics, ETBE can be added to gasoline up to a level of approximately 17% by volume. ETBE is not yet commercially available.

EU: See "European Union (EU)."

EU Competence: The jurisdiction in which the European Union (EU) can take legal action.

European Union (EU): A consolidation of European countries (member states) functioning as one body to facilitate trade. Previously known as the European Community (EC). The EU has a unified currency, the Euro. See europa.eu.int.

Exempt Wholesale Generator (EWG): A non-utility electricity generator that is not a qualifying facility under the Public Utility Regulatory Policies Act of 1978.

FASB: See "Financial Accounting Standards Board (FASB)."

Fast Breeder Reactor: See "Breeder Reactor."

Fast Neutron Reactor (FNR): A fast reactor is a type of nuclear plant that uses uranium-238 as a fuel, in addition to the U-235 isotope used in traditional reactors. Variances in design determine the actual designation of a reactor. Reactors that produce more "fissile material" (plutonium, U-235, etc.) than they consume are referred to as Breeder Reactors, or Fast

Breeder Reactors (FBR). On the other hand if they are net consumers of fissile material, they are Fast Neutron Reactors (FNR). (Also, see "Breeder Reactor.")

Fast Reactor: An advanced technology nuclear reactor that uses a fast fission process utilizing fast neutrons that would split some of the U-258 atoms as well as transuranic isotopes. The goal is to use nuclear material more efficiently and safely in the production of nuclear energy.

Federal Energy Regulatory Commission (FERC): A quasi-independent regulatory agency within the Department of Energy having jurisdiction over interstate electricity sales, wholesale electricity rates, hydro-electric licensing, natural gas pricing, oil pipeline rates and gas pipeline certification.

Federal Power Act: Regulates licensing of non-federal hydroelectric projects, as well as the interstate transmission of electrical energy and rates for its sale at wholesale in interstate commerce. It was enacted in 1920 and amended in 1935.

Federal Power Commission: The predecessor agency of the FERC, abolished when the Department of Energy was created.

Feed-in Tariff (FIT): Guaranteed prices for output from electric generation, typically offered in long-term contracts to firms that operate renewable electric generating plants based on solar, wind or wave technology. The prices are typically much higher than those paid for electricity from conventional power plants, because most renewable sources operate at lower efficiency and higher cost per KWH. The intent is to encourage investment in renewable plants by guaranteeing a price for output that will create a positive return on investment.

Feedstock: Any material converted to another form of fuel or energy product. For example, corn starch can be used as a feedstock for ethanol production.

FERC: See "Federal Energy Regulatory Commission (FERC)."

Financial Accounting Standards Board (FASB): An independent organization that establishes the Generally Accepted Accounting Principles (GAAP).

Fissile Material: Generally, fissile material is material than can be used as nuclear fuel in a reactor, such as Uranium-233, Uranium-235, Plutonium-239 and Plutonium-241.

Flash Steam Generation: The most common type of hydroelectric power generation technique. Flash steam describes a system where a high temperature geothermal steam source can be used to directly drive a turbine. Also see "Binary Cycle Generation."

Flexible-Fuel Vehicles (FFVs): Vehicles with a common fuel tank designed to run on varying blends of unleaded gasoline with either ethanol or methanol.

Flow Battery: A massive electricity storage device (sometimes referred to as a flow cell battery). A flow battery consists of tanks that contain liquid electrolytes. The electrolytes flow through modules, known as cells or half-cells, within the battery, mix with energy-storing materials such as iron, zinc or vanadium, and react with the electrodes in order to generate electricity. Researchers are continuously experimenting with various types of energy-storing materials in order to reduce costs and boost efficiency. An organic molecule, known as quinone, is showing promise in this regard, which may lead to much lower costs. The greatest potential of flow batteries is in storing excess electricity generated by renewable methods such as wind or solar. The power could then be drawn down when needed during times when the solar or wind sources are not productive.

Flywheel: In energy storage, the use of a rotor, or flywheel, in which energy is first used to rotate the flywheel at a very high speed, thus storing the energy in the system as rotational energy. The energy is converted back by to use by slowing down the flywheel. The flywheel system itself is a kinetic, or mechanical battery, spinning at very high speeds to store energy that is instantly available when needed.

Fossil Fuel: Any naturally occurring organic fuel, such as petroleum, coal or natural gas.

Fuel Cell: An environmentally friendly electrochemical engine that generates electricity using hydrogen and oxygen as fuel, emitting only heat and water as byproducts.

Fusion: See "Nuclear Fusion."

GAAP: See "Generally Accepted Accounting Principles (GAAP)."

Gas Hydrates: Gas hydrates are solid particles of methane (which is normally found in gas form) and water molecules in a crystalline form. They are widely found in many parts of the world, including the U.S., South Korea, India and China, often offshore. Gas hydrates have immense potential as a source of energy and may possibly exist in much larger quantities than all other known forms of fossil fuels. Unfortunately, they are not stable except under high pressure. Gas hydrate reserves could be very expensive and difficult to develop as a commercial source of energy. Nonetheless, today's very high prices for oil and gas may eventually make them a viable energy source.

Gas Turbine: Typically consists of an axial-flow air compressor and one or more combustion chambers where liquid or gaseous fuel is burned. The hot gases are passed to the turbine, in which they expand to drive the generator and are then used to run the compressor.

Gas Turbine Plant: A plant in which the prime mover is a gas turbine.

Gasification: Any chemical or heat process used to convert a feedstock to a gaseous fuel.

Gasohol: A blend of finished motor gasoline containing alcohol (generally ethanol but sometimes methanol) at a concentration of 10% or less by volume. Data on gasohol that has at least 2.7% oxygen, by weight, and is intended for sale inside carbon monoxide non-attainment areas are included in data on oxygenated gasoline.

Gas-to-Liquids (GTL): A process that converts natural gas into fuels, which may include gasoline, diesel or jet fuel.

GDP: See "Gross Domestic Product (GDP)."

Generally Accepted Accounting Principles (GAAP): A set of accounting standards administered by the Financial Accounting Standards Board (FASB) and enforced by the U.S. Security and Exchange Commission (SEC). GAAP is primarily used in the U.S.

Generating Unit: Any combination of physically connected generators, reactors, boilers, combustion turbines or other prime movers operated together to produce electric power.

Generation (Electricity): The process of producing electric energy: also, the amount of electric energy produced, expressed in watt-hours (Wh).

Geoengineering: The attempt to modify the Earth's environment through artificial means in order to counteract undesirable changes in weather, water or other natural systems.

Geothermal Electric Power Generation: An electric generation plant which is typically powered by a steam turbine. In order to generate steam, long shafts are drilled below the Earth's surface in order to reach hot spots. Water is piped down the shafts where it is heated to a relatively high temperature. The hot water is returned to the surface where it is used to generate steam that turns a turbine. California is a leading producer of geothermal energy. Also see "Flash Steam Generation," "Binary Cycle Generation" and "Hot Dry Rock Geothermal Energy Technology (HDR)."

GHG: See "Greenhouse Gas (GHG)."

Gigawatt: Equal to one billion watts of power. It is also equal to one million kilowatts or 1,000 megawatts.

Global Warming: An increase in the near-surface temperature of the Earth. Global warming has occurred in the distant past as the result of natural influences, but the term is most often used to refer to a theory that warming occurs as a result of increased use of hydrocarbon fuels by man. See "Climate Change (Greenhouse Effect)."

Grain Ethanol: See "Ethanol."

Green Building: A building that has energy conservation and renewable energy features designed to reduce energy consumption.

Green Hydrogen: Hydrogen produced by splitting water into hydrogen and oxygen using renewable electricity

Green Pricing: In the case of renewable electricity, green pricing represents a market solution to the various problems associated with regulatory valuation of the non-market benefits of renewables. Green pricing programs allow electricity customers to express their willingness to pay for renewable energy development through direct payments on their monthly utility bills.

Greenhouse Gas (GHG): See "Climate Change (Greenhouse Effect)."

Grid (The): In the U.S., the networks of local electric lines that businesses and consumers depend on every day are connected with and interdependent upon a national series of major lines collectively called "the grid." The grid is divided into three major regions: the East, West and Texas regions. The regions are also known as "interconnects." In total, the grid consists of about 200,000 miles of high-voltage backbone lines and millions of miles of smaller local lines.

Gross Domestic Product (GDP): The total value of a nation's output, income and expenditures produced with a nation's physical borders.

Gross National Product (GNP): A country's total output of goods and services from all forms of economic activity measured at market prices for one calendar year. It differs from Gross Domestic Product (GDP) in that GNP includes income from investments made in foreign nations.

Heat Pump: A year-round heating and air-conditioning system employing a refrigeration cycle.

Heliostat: A motor-driven mirror which is used in concentrating solar power and in concentrating photovoltaic power. The mirror is engineered so that it tracks the sun's movement through the sky during the day, thus capturing the maximum amount of solar output. (See "Concentrating Solar Power (CSP)" and "Concentrating Photovoltaic Power (CPV).")

High-Temperature Collector: A solar thermal collector designed to operate at a temperature of 180 degrees Fahrenheit or higher.

Hot Dry Rock Geothermal Energy Technology (HDR): A technique that drills holes into the ground until rock of a suitably high temperature is reached. Pipes are then installed in a closed loop. Water is pumped down one pipe, where it is heated to extraordinarily high temperatures, and then is pumped up the other pipes as steam. The resulting steam shoots up to the surface, which drives a turbine to power an electric generating plant. As the steam cools, it returns to a liquid state which is then is pumped back into the ground. The technology was developed by the Los Alamos National labs in New Mexico.

HTS: High Temperature Superconductor wire. See "Superconductivity."

Hybrid-Electric Vehicle (HEV): A vehicle that is powered by two or more energy sources, one of which is electricity. HEVs may combine the engine and fuel system of a conventional vehicle with the batteries and electric motor of an electric vehicle in a single drive train.

Hydrocarbons: Organic compounds of hydrogen and carbon. Mixtures including various hydrocarbons include crude oil, natural gas, natural gas condensate and methane.

Hydroelectric Energy: The production of electricity from kinetic energy in flowing water.

Hydroelectric Plant: An electric generating plant in which the turbine generators are driven by falling water, typically located at a dam or major waterfall.

Hydroelectric Power Generation: Electricity generated by an electric power plant whose turbines are driven by falling water. It includes electric utility and industrial generation of hydroelectricity, unless otherwise specified. Generation is reported on a net basis, i.e., on the amount of electric energy generated after deducting the energy consumed by station auxiliaries and the losses in the transformers that are considered integral parts of the station.

IEEE: See "Institute of Electrical and Electronic Engineers (IEEE)."

IFRS: See "International Financials Reporting Standards (IFRS)."

Independent Power Producer: A corporation, person, agency, authority or other legal entity or instrumentality that owns electric generating capacity and is a wholesale electric producer without a designated franchised service area.

Independent System Operator (ISO): One of many independent, nonprofit organizations created by many states in the U.S. during the deregulation of the electricity industry. Its function is to ensure that electric generating companies have equal access to the power grid. It may be replaced by larger Regional

Transmission Organizations (RTOs), which would each cover a major area of the U.S.

Industrial Biotechnology: The application of biotechnology to serve industrial needs. This is a rapidly growing field on a global basis. The current focus on industrial biotechnology is primarily on enzymes and other substances for renewable energy such as biofuels: chemicals such as pharmaceuticals, food additives, solvents and colorants: and bioplastics. Industrial biotech attempts to create synergies between biochemistry, genetics and microbiology in order to develop exciting new substances.

Industry Code: A descriptive code assigned to any company in order to group it with firms that operate in similar businesses. Common industry codes include the NAICS (North American Industrial Classification System) and the SIC (Standard Industrial Classification), both of which are standards widely used in America, as well as the International Standard Industrial Classification of all Economic Activities (ISIC), the Standard International Trade Classification established by the United Nations (SITC) and the General Industrial Classification of Economic Activities within the European Communities (NACE).

Initial Public Offering (IPO): A company's first effort to sell its stock to investors (the public). Investors in an up-trending market eagerly seek stocks offered in many IPOs because the stocks of newly public companies that seem to have great promise may appreciate very rapidly in price, reaping great profits for those who were able to get the stock at the first offering. In the United States, IPOs are regulated by the SEC (U.S. Securities Exchange Commission) and by the state-level regulatory agencies of the states in which the IPO shares are offered.

Institute of Electrical and Electronic Engineers (IEEE): An organization that sets global technical standards and acts as an authority in technical areas including computer engineering, biomedical technology, telecommunications, electric power, aerospace and consumer electronics, among others. www.ieee.org.

Integrated Solar Combined Cycle (ISCC): See "Combined Cycle."

Intellectual Property (IP): The exclusive ownership of original concepts, ideas, designs, engineering plans or other assets that are protected by law. Examples include items covered by trademarks, copyrights and patents. Items such as software, engineering plans, fashion designs and architectural designs, as well as games, books, songs and other entertainment items are among the many things that may be considered to be intellectual property. (Also, see "Patent.")

International Financials Reporting Standards (IFRS): A set of accounting standards established by the International Accounting Standards Board (IASB) for the preparation of public financial statements. IFRS has been adopted by much of the world, including the European Union, Russia and Singapore.

Investor-Owned Electric Utility: A class of utility that is investor-owned and organized as a tax-paying business.

IP: See "Intellectual Property (IP)."

ISO 9000, 9001, 9002, 9003: Standards set by the International Organization for Standardization. ISO 9000, 9001, 9002 and 9003 are the highest quality certifications awarded to organizations that meet exacting standards in their operating practices and procedures.

Joule: The meter-kilogram-second unit of work or energy, equal to the work done by a force of one Newton when its point of application moves through a distance of one meter in the direction of the force: equivalent to 107 ergs and one watt-second.

Just-in-Time (JIT) Delivery: Refers to a supply chain practice whereby manufacturers receive components on or just before the time that they are needed on the assembly line, rather than bearing the cost of maintaining several days' or weeks' supply in a warehouse. This adds greatly to the cost-effectiveness of a manufacturing plant and puts the burden of warehousing and timely delivery on the supplier of the components.

Kerogen: See "Oil Shale."

Kilowatt (kW): One thousand watts.

Kilowatthour (kWh): One thousand watt-hours.

Knowledge Process Outsourcing (KPO): The use of outsourced and/or offshore workers to perform business tasks that require judgment and analysis.

Examples include such professional tasks as patent research, legal research, architecture, design, engineering, market research, scientific research, accounting and tax return preparation. Also, see "Business Process Outsourcing (BPO)."

LAC: An acronym for Latin America and the Caribbean.

LDCs: See "Least Developed Countries (LDCs)."

Least Developed Countries (LDCs): Nations determined by the U.N. Economic and Social Council to be the poorest and weakest members of the international community. There are currently 50 LDCs, of which 34 are in Africa, 15 are in Asia Pacific and the remaining one (Haiti) is in Latin America. The top 10 on the LDC list, in descending order from top to 10th, are Afghanistan, Angola, Bangladesh, Benin, Bhutan, Burkina Faso, Burundi, Cambodia, Cape Verde and the Central African Republic. Sixteen of the LDCs are also Landlocked Least Developed Countries (LLDCs) which present them with additional difficulties often due to the high cost of transporting trade goods. Eleven of the LDCs are Small Island Developing States (SIDS), which are often at risk of extreme weather phenomenon (hurricanes, typhoons, Tsunami): have fragile ecosystems: are often dependent on foreign energy sources: can have high disease rates for HIV/AIDS and malaria: and can have poor market access and trade terms.

Liquefied Natural Gas (LNG): Natural gas that is liquefied by reducing its temperature to -260 degrees Fahrenheit (-162 degrees Celsius) at atmospheric pressure. The volume of the LNG is 1/600 that of the gas in its vapor state. LNG requires special processing and transportation. First, the natural gas must be chilled in order for it to change into a liquid state. Next, the LNG is put on specially designed ships where extensive insulation and refrigeration maintain the cold temperature. Finally, it is offloaded at special receiving facilities where it is converted, via regasification, into a state suitable for distribution via pipelines.

Liquid Collector: A medium-temperature solar thermal collector, employed predominantly in water heating, which uses pumped liquid as the heat-transfer medium.

Load (Electric): The amount of electric power delivered or required at any specific point or points on a system. The requirement originates at the energy-consuming equipment of the consumers.

LOHAS: Lifestyles of Health and Sustainability. A marketing term that refers to consumers who choose to purchase and/or live with items that are natural, organic, less polluting, etc. Such consumers may also prefer products powered by alternative energy, such as hybrid cars.

Low-E: A coating for windows that can prevent warmth from escaping from the inside of a building during the winter, while preventing solar heat from entering the building during the summer. Significant savings in energy usage can result.

Low-Emission Vehicle (LEV): Describes a vehicle meeting either the EPA's CFV LEV standards or CARB's California Low-Emission Vehicle Program LEV standards.

Low-Temperature Collectors: Metallic or nonmetallic solar thermal collectors that generally operate at temperatures below 110 degrees Fahrenheit and use pumped liquid or air as the heat-transfer medium. They usually contain no glazing and no insulation, and they are often made of plastic or rubber, although some are made of metal.

M85: 85% methanol and 15% unleaded gasoline by volume.

Magnetic Confinement Fusion (MCF): A fusion process in which strong magnetic fields confine plasma at extremely high pressures and temperatures. This technology relies on ultrapowerful, high-temperature superconducting magnets to cause the atomic nuclei to fuse.

Marginal Cost: The change in cost associated with a unit change in quantity supplied or produced.

Mbbl: One thousand barrels.

MCF: See "Magnetic Confinement Fusion (MCF)."

Mcf (measurement): One thousand cubic feet.

Mcfe: One thousand cubic feet of natural gas equivalent, using the ratio of six Mcf of natural gas to one Bbl of crude oil, condensate and natural gas liquids.

Medium-Temperature Collectors: Solar thermal collectors designed to operate in the temperature range of 140 degrees to 180 degrees Fahrenheit, but that can also operate at a temperature as low as 110 degrees Fahrenheit. The collector typically consists of a metal frame, metal absorption panels with integral flow channels (attached tubing for liquid collectors or integral ducting for air collectors) and glazing and insulation on the sides and back.

Megawatt (MW): One million watts.

Megawatthour (MWh): One million watt-hours.

Methane: A colorless, odorless, flammable hydrocarbon gas (CH_4): the major component of natural gas. It is also an important source of hydrogen in various industrial processes. Also, see "Coalbed Methane (CBN)."

Methane Hydrate: Natural gas (methane) which is trapped in a lattice of ice. Underground or seabed gas can migrate towards the surface, but become trapped under high pressure and combine with water, at low temperature, to form methane hydrate. It has the potential to be a massive source of energy, but producing it commercially is not yet feasible.

Methanol: A light, volatile alcohol (CH_3OH) eligible for motor gasoline blending. It is also used as a feedstock for synthetic textiles, plastics, paints, adhesives, foam, medicines and more.

Methyl Ester: A fatty ester formed when organically derived oils are combined with methanol in the presence of a catalyst. Methyl ester has characteristics similar to petroleum-based diesel motor fuels.

Methyl Tertiary Butyl Ether (MTBE): An ether manufactured by reacting methanol and isobutylene. The resulting ether has high octane and low volatility. MTBE is a fuel oxygenate and is permitted in unleaded gasoline up to a level of 15% by volume.

Microgrid: See "Distributed Power Generation."

Microturbine: A small, scaled-down turbine engine that may be fueled by natural gas, methane or other types of gas.

Mmbtu: One million British thermal units.

Mmcf: One million cubic feet.

Mmcfe: One million cubic feet of natural gas equivalent.

MOX Fuel (Mixed Oxide Fuel): A method of reprocessing spent nuclear material. Surplus plutonium is mixed with uranium to fabricate MOX fuel for use in a commercial nuclear power plant. Traditionally, fuel for commercial nuclear power plants is made of low-enriched uranium. MOX fuel contains 5 percent plutonium. European countries such as the United Kingdom, Germany, Belgium and France have been fabricating MOX fuel for many years. Commercial MOX-fueled light water reactors are used in France, the United Kingdom, Germany, Switzerland, and Belgium. In the U.S., MOX fuel was fabricated and used in several commercial reactors in the 1970's as part of a development program.

NAICS: North American Industrial Classification System. See "Industry Code."

Nanotechnology: The science of designing, building or utilizing unique structures that are smaller than 100 nanometers (a nanometer is one billionth of a meter). This involves microscopic structures that are no larger than the width of some cell membranes.

Net Generation: Gross generation minus plant use from all electric utility-owned plants. The energy required for pumping at a pumped-storage plant is regarded as plant use and must be deducted from the gross generation.

Net Metering: A system in which customers who generate their own electricity from solar, wind, hydroelectric or other renewable power feed electricity they do not use into the electric grid for general use. In return, the customers receive a credit on their electric bill. That is, their electric meter may run backwards while they are exporting electricity.

Net Summer Capability: The steady hourly output that generating equipment is expected to supply to system load exclusive of auxiliary power, as demonstrated by tests at the time of summer peak demand.

Net Zero: See "Zero Energy Building."

NGV: See "Natural Gas Vehicle (NGV)."

Nonutility Power Producer: A corporation, person, agency, authority or other legal entity or instrumentality that owns electric generating capacity and is not an electric utility.

Nuclear Electric Power Generation: Electricity generated by nuclear reactors of various types, such as heavy water, light water and boiling water. Generation is reported on a net basis and excludes energy that is used by the electric power plant for its own operating purposes and not for commercial use.

Nuclear Fuel: Fissionable materials that have been enriched to such a composition that, when placed in a nuclear reactor, they will support a self-sustaining fission chain reaction, producing heat in a controlled manner for process use.

Nuclear Fusion: An atomic energy-releasing process in which light weight atomic nuclei, which might be hydrogen or deuterium, combine to form heavier nuclei, such as helium. The result is the release of a tremendous amount of energy in the form of heat. This is potentially an endless supply of energy for mankind, somewhat similar to the power of the Sun. Fusion is undergoing significant research efforts, including a multinational research consortium named ITER. In one approach, magnetic fusion, plasma heated to 100 million-degrees Celsius creates multiple fusion bursts controlled by powerful magnets. Under a different research approach, massive lasers bombard a frozen pellet of fuel creating a brief, intense fusion.

Nuclear Power Plant: A facility in which heat produced in a reactor by the fission of nuclear fuel is used to drive a steam turbine, which in turn powers electric generation equipment. This method is sometimes described as "atomic power." There are several different types of nuclear power plants. The newest models incorporate advanced safety and disaster recovery features that are vastly superior to early models.

Nuclear Reactor: An apparatus in which the nuclear fission chain can be initiated, maintained and controlled so that energy is released at a specific rate.

NYMEX: New York Mercantile Exchange, Inc. (NYMEX Exchange). The company is a major provider of financial services to the energy and metals industries including the trading of energy futures and options contracts. It is owned by the CME Group.

Octane Rating: A number used to indicate motor gasoline's antiknock performance in motor vehicle engines. The two recognized laboratory engine test methods for determining the antiknock rating, or octane rating, of gasoline are the research method and the motor method. To provide a single number as guidance to the customer, the antiknock index (R + M)/2, which is the average of the research and motor octane numbers, was developed.

OECD: See "Organisation for Economic Co-operation and Development (OECD)."

Offshoring: The rapidly growing tendency among U.S., Japanese and Western European firms to send knowledge-based and manufacturing work overseas. The intent is to take advantage of lower wages and operating costs in such nations as China, India, Hungary and Russia. The choice of a nation for offshore work may be influenced by such factors as language and education of the local workforce, transportation systems or natural resources. For example, China and India are graduating high numbers of skilled engineers and scientists from their universities. Also, some nations are noted for large numbers of workers skilled in the English language, such as the Philippines and India. Also see "Captive Offshoring" and "Outsourcing."

Ohm: The unit of measurement of electrical resistance: the resistance of a circuit in which a potential difference of one volt produces a current of one ampere.

Oil Shale: Sedimentary rock that contains kerogen, a solid, waxy mixture of hydrocarbon compounds. Heating the rock to very high temperatures will convert the kerogen to a vapor, which can then be condensed to form a slow flowing heavy oil that can later be refined or used for commercial purposes. The United States contains vast amounts of oil shale deposits, but so far it has been considered not economically feasible to produce from them on a large scale. (Not to be confused with crude oil that is produced from shale formulations.)

OLED: See "Organic LED (OLED)."

Onshoring: The opposite of "offshoring." Providing or maintaining manufacturing or services within or nearby a company's domestic location. Sometimes referred to as reshoring.

Organic LED (OLED): A type of electronic display based on the use of organic materials that produce light when stimulated by electricity. Also see "Polymer," "Polymer Light Emitting Diode (PLED)," "Small Molecule Organic Light Emitting Diode (SMOLED)" and "Dendrimer."

Organic Polymer: See "Polymer."

Organisation for Economic Co-operation and Development (OECD): A group of more than 30 nations that are strongly committed to the market economy and democracy. Some of the OECD members include Japan, the U.S., Spain, Germany, Australia, Korea, the U.K., Canada and Mexico. Although not members, Estonia, Israel and Russia are invited to member talks: and Brazil, China, India, Indonesia and South Africa have enhanced engagement policies with the OECD. The Organisation provides statistics, as well as social and economic data: and researches social changes, including patterns in evolving fiscal policy, agriculture, technology, trade, the environment and other areas. It publishes over 250 titles annually: publishes a corporate magazine, the OECD Observer: has radio and TV studios: and has centers in Tokyo, Washington, D.C., Berlin and Mexico City that distributed the Organisation's work and organizes events.

Outsourcing: The hiring of an outside company to perform a task otherwise performed internally by the company, generally with the goal of lowering costs and/or streamlining work flow. Outsourcing contracts are generally several years in length. Companies that hire outsourced services providers often prefer to focus on their core strengths while sending more routine tasks outside for others to perform. Typical outsourced services include the running of human resources departments, telephone call centers and computer departments. When outsourcing is performed overseas, it may be referred to as offshoring. Also see "Offshoring."

Ozone: A molecule made up of three atoms of oxygen. It occurs naturally in the stratosphere and provides a protective layer shielding the Earth from harmful ultraviolet radiation. In the troposphere, it is a chemical oxidant, a greenhouse gas and a major component of photochemical smog.

Ozone-Depleting Substances: Gases containing chlorine that are being controlled because they deplete ozone. They are thought to have some indeterminate impact on greenhouse gases.

Passive Solar: A system in which solar energy (heat from sunlight) alone is used for the transfer of thermal energy. Heat transfer devices that depend on energy other than solar are not used. A good example is a passive solar water heater on the roof of a building.

Patent: An intellectual property right granted by a national government to an inventor to exclude others from making, using, offering for sale, or selling the invention throughout that nation or importing the invention into the nation for a limited time in exchange for public disclosure of the invention when the patent is granted. In addition to national patenting agencies, such as the United States Patent and Trademark Office, and regional organizations such as the European Patent Office, there is a cooperative international patent organization, the World Intellectual Property Organization, or WIPO, established by the United Nations.

Peak Watt: A manufacturer's unit indicating the amount of power a photovoltaic cell or module will produce at standard test conditions (normally 1,000 watts per square meter and 25 degrees Celsius).

Pebble-Bed Modular Reactor (PBMR): A nuclear reactor technology that utilizes tiny silicon carbide-coated uranium oxide granules sealed in "pebbles" about the size of oranges, made of graphite. Helium is used as the coolant and energy transfer medium. This containment of the radioactive material in small quantities has the potential to achieve an unprecedented level of safety. This technology may become popular in the development of new nuclear power plants.

Photovoltaic (PV) Cell: An electronic device consisting of layers of semiconductor materials fabricated to form a junction (adjacent layers of materials with different electronic characteristics) and electrical contacts, capable of converting incident light directly into electricity (direct current). Photovoltaic technology works by harnessing the movement of electrons between the layers of a solar cell when the sun strikes the material.

Photovoltaic (PV) Module: An integrated assembly of interconnected photovoltaic cells designed to deliver a selected level of working voltage and current at its output terminals, packaged for protection against environment degradation and suited for incorporation in photovoltaic power systems.

Plasma Containment: Refers to technology that contains plasma in an extreme environment (such as high heat or a magnetic field) that are necessary for nuclear fusion.

PLED: See "Polymer Light Emitting Diode (PLED)."

Plug-in Hybrid Electric Vehicles (PHEV): A PHEV is an automobile that features an extra high-capacity battery bank that gives the vehicle a longer electric-only range than standard hybrids. These cars are designed so that they can be plugged into a standard electric outlet for recharging. The intent is to minimize or eliminate the need to use the car's gasoline engine and rely on the electric engine instead.

Polymer: An organic or inorganic substance of many parts. Most common polymers, such as polyethylene and polypropylene, are organic. Organic polymers consist of molecules from organic sources (carbon compounds). Polymer means many parts. Generally, a polymer is constructed of many structural units (smaller, simpler molecules) that are joined together by a chemical bond. Some polymers are natural. For example, rubber is a natural polymer. Scientists have developed ways to manufacture synthetic polymers from organic materials. Plastic is a synthetic polymer.

Polymer Light Emitting Diode (PLED): An advanced technology that utilizes plastics (polymers) for the creation of electronic displays (screens). It is based on the use of organic polymers which emit light when stimulated with electricity. They are solution processable, which means they can be applied to substrates via ink jet printing. Also referred to as P-OLEDs.

Power (Electrical): The rate at which energy is transferred. A volt ampere, an electric measurement unit of power, is equal to the product of one volt and one ampere. This is equivalent to one watt for a direct current system. A unit of apparent power is separated into real and reactive power. Real power is the work-producing part of apparent power that measures the rate of supply of energy and is denoted in kilowatts.

Predictive Analytics: See "Analytics."

Pressurized Water Reactor (PWR): A type of nuclear power reactor that uses ordinary water as both the coolant and the neutron moderator. The heat produced is transferred to a secondary coolant which is subsequently boiled to produce steam for power generation.

Primary Energy Consumption: The consumption of unprocessed, unrefined fuels including coal, natural gas and crude oil. Since uranium is a raw fuel, it may also be included. Analysis of primary energy consumption may sometimes include renewable power sources, such as hydroelectric, geothermal or even solar and wind. Primary energy analysis is focused on raw fuels, prior to their use in generating electricity and other purposes. Also, see "Secondary Energy Consumption."

Propane: A normally gaseous straight-chain hydrocarbon (C_3H_8). Propane is a colorless paraffinic gas that boils at a temperature of –43.67 degrees Fahrenheit. It is extracted from natural gas or refinery gas streams.

Public Utility: An enterprise providing essential public services, such as electric, gas, telephone, water and sewer services, under legally established monopoly conditions.

Public Utility District (PUD): A municipal corporation organized to provide electric service to both incorporated cities and towns and unincorporated rural areas. Public utility districts operate in six states.

Public Utility Regulatory Policies Act of 1978 (PURPA): A part of the National Energy Act. PURPA contains measures designed to encourage the conservation of energy, more efficient use of resources and equitable rates. Principal among these were suggested retail rate reforms and new incentives for production of electricity by cogenerators and users of renewable resources.

Publicly Owned Electric Utility: A class of ownership found in the electric power industry. This group includes those utilities operated by municipalities and state and federal power agencies.

Pumped-Storage Hydroelectric Plant: A method of energy storage. Stored water is used to generate electric energy during peak load periods by using water previously pumped into an elevated reservoir during off-peak periods, when excess generating capacity is available to do so. When additional generating capacity is needed, the water can be released from the reservoir through a conduit to turn turbine generators located in a power plant at a lower level.

PV: See "Photovoltaic (PV) Cell."

Qualifying Facility (QF): A cogeneration or small power production facility that meets certain ownership, operating and efficiency criteria established by the Federal Energy Regulatory Commission (FERC) pursuant to the Public Utility Regulatory Policies Act of 1978 (PURPA).

R&D: Research and development. Also see "Applied Research" and "Basic Research."

Rate Base: The value of property upon which a utility is permitted to earn a specified rate of return as established by a regulatory authority. The rate base generally represents the value of property used by the utility in providing service.

Ratemaking Authority: A utility commission's legal authority to fix, modify, approve or disapprove rates, as determined by the powers given to the commission by a state or federal legislature.

REC: See "Renewable Energy Certificate (REC)."

Reformulated Gasoline (RFG): Gasoline that has its composition and/or characteristics altered to reduce vehicular emissions of pollutants, particularly pursuant to EPA regulations under the CAA.

Refuse-Derived Fuel (RDF): Fuel processed from municipal solid waste that can be in shredded, fluff or dense pellet forms.

Regional Transmission Organization (RTO): See "Independent System Operator (ISO)."

Regulated Business (Utility Companies): The business of providing natural gas or electric service to customers under regulations and at prices set by government regulatory agencies. Generally, utilities have been required to operate at set prices and profit ratios because they have been granted monopoly or near-monopoly status to serve a given geographic market. Under deregulation, utility companies are being granted greater flexibility to set prices and to enter new geographic markets. At the same time, consumers gain the right to choose among several different utilities providers.

Renewable Energy Certificate (REC): A market-based instrument that represents the property rights to the environmental, social, and other non-power attributes of renewable electricity generation. RECs are issued when one megawatt-hour (MWh) of electricity is generated and delivered to the electricity grid from a renewable energy resource. RECs can be sold and traded among energy users.

Renewable Energy Resources: Energy resources that are naturally replenishing but flow-limited. They are virtually inexhaustible in duration but limited in the amount of energy that is available per unit of time. Renewable energy resources include biomass, hydro, geothermal, solar, wind, ocean thermal, wave action and tidal action.

Reseller: A firm (other than a refiner) that carries on the trade or business of purchasing refined petroleum products and reselling them to purchasers other than ultimate consumers.

Resistivity (R): Measures a material's characteristic resistance to the flow of electrical current. Resistivity is the reciprocal of conductivity. It is denoted by the symbol R.

Rural Electrification Administration (REA): A lending agency of the U.S. Department of Agriculture. It makes self-liquidation loans to qualified borrowers to finance electric and telephone service to rural areas. The REA also finances the construction and operation of generating plants, electric transmission and distribution lines, or systems for the furnishing of initial and continued adequate electric services to persons in rural areas not receiving central station service.

R-Value (R Value): A method of measuring the effectiveness of building materials such as insulation. Technically, it is the resistance that a material has to heat flow. The higher the R-Value, the better the insulation provided. It is the inverse of U-Value. See "U-Value (U Value)."

SaaS: See "Software as a Service (SaaS)."

Secondary Energy Consumption: The consumption of electricity, petroleum, and other refined, processed or generated energy supplies. Also, see "Primary Energy Consumption."

Semiconductor: A generic term for a device that controls electrical signals. It specifically refers to a material (such as silicon, germanium or gallium arsenide) that can be altered either to conduct electrical current or to block its passage. Carbon nanotubes may eventually be used as semiconductors. Semiconductors are partly responsible for the miniaturization of modern electronic devices, as they are vital components in computer memory and processor chips. The manufacture of semiconductors is carried out by small firms, and by industry giants such as Intel and Advanced Micro Devices.

SIC: Standard Industrial Classification. See "Industry Code."

Silicon: A semiconductor material made from silica, purified for photovoltaic applications.

Single-Crystal Silicon (Czochralski): An extremely pure form of crystalline silicon produced by the Czochralski method of dipping a single crystal seed into a pool of molten silicon under high-vacuum conditions and slowly withdrawing a solidifying single-crystal boule rod of silicon. The boule is sawed into thin wafers and fabricated into single-crystal photovoltaic cells.

Small Molecule Organic Light Emitting Diode (SMOLED): A type of organic LED that relies on expensive manufacturing methods. Newer technologies are more promising. See "Polymer" and "Polymer Light Emitting Diode (PLED)."

Small Power Producer: A producer that generates electricity by using renewable energy (wood, waste, conventional hydroelectric, wind, solar or geothermal) as a primary energy source. Fossil fuels can be used, but renewable resources must provide at least 75% of the total energy input. It is part of the Public Utility Regulatory Policies Act, a small power producer.

Smart Buildings: Buildings or homes that have been designed with interconnected electronic sensors and electrical systems which can be controlled by computers. Advantages include the ability to turn appliances and systems on or off remotely or on a set schedule, leading to greatly enhanced energy efficiency.

Smart Grid: The use of computers to monitor and improve the efficiency of distribution systems for electricity. Components may include remote sensors, automated controls and integrated communications between various parties on the grid. The intent is to eliminate brown outs and better anticipate and deliver power.

Smart Meter: High-tech electric meters that relay information to electricity providers on a continual basis, showing the amount of power being used by a consumer or business. The intent is to better inform consumers about their usage, while enabling electricity providers to charge higher fees during times of the day when usage is higher across its entire distribution network. The theory is that higher fees during peak times and better informed consumers will lead to lower peak loads.

SMOLED: See "Small Molecule Organic Light Emitting Diode (SMOLED)."

Software as a Service (SaaS): Refers to the practice of providing users with software applications that are hosted on remote servers and accessed via the Internet. Excellent examples include the CRM (Customer Relationship Management) software provided in SaaS format by Salesforce. An earlier technology that operated in a similar, but less sophisticated, manner was called ASP or Application Service Provider.

Solar Energy: Energy produced from the sun's radiation for the purposes of heating or electric generation. Also, see "Photovoltaic (PV) Cell," "Concentrating Solar Power (CSP)" and "Passive Solar."

Solar Thermal Collector: A device designed to receive solar radiation and convert it into thermal energy. Normally, a solar thermal collector includes a frame, glazing and an absorber, together with the appropriate insulation. The heat collected by the solar thermal collector may be used immediately or stored for later use. Typical use is in solar hot water heating systems. Also, see "Passive Solar" and "Concentrating Solar Power (CSP)."

Solar Tower: See "Concentrating Solar Power (CSP)."

Solar Updraft Tower: A renewable energy power plant that heats air in a large greenhouse, thereby creating convection that causes air to rise and escape through a tall, specially designed tower. The upward moving air drives electricity-producing turbines.

Spot Price: The price for a one-time market transaction for immediate delivery to the specific location where the commodity is purchased "on the spot," at current market rates.

Standard Cubic Foot (SCF): A regulated measure of natural gas volumes, based on a standardized surface temperature of 60 degrees Fahrenheit and surface pressure of 14.65 psi.

Steam-Electric Plant (Conventional): A plant in which the prime mover is a steam turbine. The steam used to drive the turbine is produced in a boiler where fossil fuels are burned.

Structural Map: A contour map detailing elevations of sub-surface rock layers, calibrated either in linear measure of feet or meters, or in time measure based on seismic surveys.

Subsidiary, Wholly-Owned: A company that is wholly controlled by another company through stock ownership.

Substation: Facility equipment that switches, changes or regulates electric voltage.

Superconductivity: The ability of a material to act as a conductor for electricity without the gradual loss of electricity over distance (due to resistance) that is normally associated with electric transmission. There are two types of superconductivity. "Low-temperature" superconductivity (LTS) requires that transmission cable be cooled to -418 degrees Fahrenheit. Newer technologies are creating a so-called "high-temperature" superconductivity (HTS) that requires cooling to a much warmer -351 degrees Fahrenheit.

Supply Chain: The complete set of suppliers of goods and services required for a company to operate its business. For example, a manufacturer's supply chain may include providers of raw materials, components, custom-made parts and packaging materials.

Sustainable Development: Development that ensures that the use of resources and the environment today does not impair their availability to be used by future generations.

Switching Station: Facility equipment used to tie together two or more electric circuits through switches. The switches are selectively arranged to permit a circuit to be disconnected, or to change the electric connection between the circuits.

Syngas: The synthetic creation of gas to be used as a fuel, typically from coal. See "Gasification."

System (Electric): See "Transmission System (Electric)."

Tar Sands: Sands that contain bitumen, which is a tar-like oil substance that can be processed and refined into a synthetic light oil. Typically, tar sands are mined from vast open pits where deposits are softened with blasts of steam. They are produced by injecting steam in the wells and then pumping out melted bitumen. The Athabasca sands in Alberta, Canada and the Orinoco sands in Venezuela contain vast amounts of tar sands. The Athabasca sands are now producing commercially in high volume. Also known as oil sands.

Thermal Breeder Reactor (TBR): See "Breeder Reactor."

Thorium: See "Breeder Reactor."

Tidal Energy: A source of power derived from the movement of waves. Tidal energy traditionally involves erecting a dam across the opening to a tidal basin. The dam includes a sluice that is opened to allow the tide to flow into the basin: the sluice is then closed, and as the sea level drops, traditional hydropower technologies can be used to generate electricity from the elevated water in the basin.

Time to Depth Conversion: A translation process to recalibrate seismic records from time measures in millisecond units to linear measures of depth in feet or meters.

Tokamak: A reactor used in nuclear fusion in which a spiral magnetic field inside doughnut-shaped tube is used to confine high temperature plasma produced during fusion. See "Nuclear Fusion."

Toluene: A basic aromatic compound derived from petroleum. It is the most common hydrocarbon purchased for use in increasing octane. Toluene is also used to produce phenol and TNT.

Transformer: An electrical device for changing the voltage of an alternating current.

Transmission (Electricity): The movement or transfer of electric energy over an interconnected group of lines and associated equipment between points of supply and points at which it is transformed for delivery to consumers or delivered to other electric systems. Transmission is considered to end when the energy is transformed for distribution to the consumer.

Transmission System (Electric): An interconnected group of electric transmission lines and associated equipment for moving or transferring electric energy in bulk between points of supply and points at which it is transformed for delivery to consumers or delivered to other electric systems.

Turbine: A machine for generating rotary mechanical power from the energy of a stream of fluid (such as water, steam or hot gas). Turbines convert the kinetic energy of fluids to mechanical energy through the principles of impulse and reaction or a mixture of the two.

Unfinished Oils: All oils that require further processing, except those requiring only mechanical blending.

Uranium: A heavy, naturally radioactive, metallic element (atomic number 92). Its two principally occurring isotopes are uranium-235 and uranium-238. Uranium-235 is indispensable to the nuclear industry, because it is the only isotope existing in nature to any appreciable extent that is fissionable by thermal neutrons. Uranium-238 is also important, because it absorbs neutrons to produce a radioactive isotope that subsequently decays to plutonium-239, another isotope that is fissionable by thermal neutrons.

U-Value (U Value): A measure of the amount of heat that is transferred into or out of a building. The lower the U-Value, the higher the insulating value of a window or other building material being rated. It is the reciprocal of an R-Value. See "R-Value (R Value)."

Value Added Tax (VAT): A tax that imposes a levy on businesses at every stage of manufacturing based on the value it adds to a product. Each business in the supply chain pays its own VAT and is subsequently repaid by the next link down the chain: hence, a VAT is ultimately paid by the consumer, being the last link in the supply chain, making it comparable to a sales tax. Generally, VAT only applies to goods bought for consumption within a given country: export goods are exempt from VAT, and purchasers from other countries taking goods back home may apply for a VAT refund.

Vertical Integration: A business model in which one company owns many (or all) of the means of production of the many goods that comprise its product line. For example, founder Henry Ford designed Ford Motor Company's early River Rogue plant so that coal, iron ore and other needed raw materials arrived at one end of the plant and were processed into steel, which was then converted on-site into finished components. At the final stage of the plant, completed automobiles were assembled.

VSC: Voltage Source Converters.

Waste Energy (Waste-to-Energy): The use of garbage, biogases, industrial steam, sewerage gas or industrial, agricultural and urban refuse ("biomass") as a fuel or power source used in turning turbines to generate electricity or as a method of providing heat.

Watt (Electric): The electrical unit of power equal to the power dissipated by a current of one ampere flowing across a resistance of one ohm.

Watt (Thermal): A unit of power in the metric system, expressed in terms of energy per second, equal to the work done at a rate of one joule per second.

Watthour (Wh): An electrical energy unit equal to one watt of power supplied to, or taken from, an electric circuit steadily for one hour.

Wind Energy: Energy present in wind motion that can be converted to mechanical energy for driving pumps, mills and electric power generators. Wind pushes against sails, vanes or blades radiating from a central rotating shaft.

Wind Turbine: A system in which blades (windmills) collect wind power to propel a turbine that generates electricity.

World Trade Organization (WTO): One of the only globally active international organizations dealing with the trade rules between nations. Its goal is to assist the free flow of trade goods, ensuring a smooth, predictable supply of goods to help raise the quality of life of member citizens. Members form consensus decisions that are then ratified by their respective parliaments. The WTO's conflict resolution process generally emphasizes interpreting existing commitments and agreements, and discovers how to ensure trade policies to conform to those agreements, with the ultimate aim of avoiding military or political conflict.

WTO: See "World Trade Organization (WTO)."

Zero Energy Building: A building that has zero net energy consumption from the traditional electric grid. Sometimes referred to as net zero, it may accomplish this through the generation of its own energy via solar, wind or other means. It may use energy storage devices on-site, or it may draw power from the grid at some times, while selling power back to the grid when it generates more than it requires. Typically, such projects are also designed to create zero net carbon emissions. Some subdivisions have been established with the goal of having all dwellings in the neighborhood be net zero. Also, some commercial buildings are net zero in design

Zero-Emission Vehicle (ZEV): Describes a vehicle meeting either the EPA's CFV ZEV standards or CARB's California Low-Emission Vehicle Program ZEV standards. ZEV standards, usually met with electric vehicles, require zero vehicle emissions.

ZigBee: A wireless control system for home and office lighting and entertainment systems. The ZigBee Alliance is an association of companies working together to enable reliable, cost-effective, low-power, wirelessly networked monitoring and control products based on an open global standard, 802.15.4 entertainment systems.